Integrated Accounting

for Windows

6th edition

Dale H. Klooster, Ed.D.

Warren W. Allen, M.A.

SOUTH-WESTERN
CENGAGE Learning

Australia • Canada • Mexico • Singapore • Spain • United Kingdom • United States

SOUTH-WESTERN
CENGAGE Learning

Integrated Accounting for Windows, 6th Edition
Dale H. Klooster and Warren W. Allen

Vice President of Editorial, Business: Jack W. Calhoun

Publisher: Rob Dewey

Sr. Acquisitions Editor: Sharon Oblinger

Developmental Editor: Ted Knight

Marketing Manager: Steven Joos

Marketing Coordinator: Gretchen Wildauer

Content Project Manager: D. Jean Buttrom

Manager of Technology, Editorial: John Barans

Media Editor: Scott Hamilton

Website Project Manager: Brian Courter

Frontlist Buyer, Manufacturing: Doug Wilke

Production Service: Integra Software Services

Copyeditor: Graphic World, Inc.

Compositor: Integra Software Services

Art Director: Stacy Jenkins Shirley

Internal Designers: Patti Hudepohl/Chris Miller

Cover Designer: Chris Miller

Cover Image: Getty Images/Photodisc

For product information and technology assistance, contact us at
Cengage Learning Customer & Sales Support, 1-800-354-9706
For permission to use material from this text or product, submit all requests online at **www.cengage.com/permissions**
Further permissions questions can be emailed to
permissionrequest@cengage.com

Library of Congress Control Number: 2008930439
Student Edition ISBN 13: 978-0-324-66486-7
Student Edition ISBN 10: 0-324-66486-9
Student Edition with CD ISBN 13: 978-0-324-66485-0
Student Edition with CD ISBN 10: 0-324-66485-0

South-Western Cengage Learning
5191 Natorp Boulevard
Mason, OH 45040
USA

Cengage Learning products are represented in Canada by Nelson Education, Ltd.

For your course and learning solutions, visit
academic.cengage.com

Purchase any of our products at your local college store or at our preferred online store **www.ichapters.com**

Printed in the United States of America
1 2 3 4 5 6 7 12 11 10 09 08

We live in an era in which powerful, low-cost personal computers are meeting a wide variety of business recordkeeping and accounting needs. During the past few decades we have seen an expansion of capability that will continue in the future. Today's PCs use powerful graphical user interface operating systems such as Microsoft® Windows®[1] and OS/2 from IBM®.[2] The Windows version of *Integrated Accounting* 6e software that accompanies this text-workbook enables students to learn how today's computer systems are used for accounting applications.

Major Features

The major features of *Integrated Accounting* 6e are its seamless integration within the *Integrated Accounting* 6e software applications of general ledger, accounts payable, accounts receivable, bank reconciliation, budgeting, purchase order processing and inventory, sales order processing and inventory, fixed assets, and payroll. For example, when a sales invoice is processed, the system automatically generates a sales invoice form and updates inventory, the sales journal, the customer's account, and the general ledger accounts. In addition, menu options are available to generate periodic journal entries such as depreciation adjusting entries and both the employee and employer's payroll taxes. The *Integrated Accounting* 6e software also offers integration with other application software such as spreadsheets and word processors, via copy and paste capabilities.

Highlights of *Integrated Accounting* 6e

This version of *Integrated Accounting* 6e retains the features that made the previous versions successful, while taking full advantage of the Windows 95, 98, NT, Me, 2000, XP, and Vista environments. The design and development of the software follows the standard conventions of the graphic user interface operating system. This standardization has been extremely helpful to users. When you have learned to use one application, you have learned the essentials for using most other applications that run in the same environment. The authors have taken great care in the development of the software to follow the standard interface to ensure that operating procedures learned while running other applications are immediately transferable to and from *Integrated Accounting* 6e.

---

1. Microsoft and Windows are registered trademarks of Microsoft Corporation. Any reference to Microsoft or Windows refers to this footnote.

2. IBM is a registered trademark of International Business Machines Corporation. Any reference to IBM refers to this footnote.

Among the major features found in this version of *Integrated Accounting* 6e are the following:

- For distance learning or online users, the student completed problem solution files may be sent to their instructors as e-mail attachments. On receipt of the student's solution files, *Inspector* 6e software (provided to instructors) may be used to check the student's completed problem solution files, and generate detailed reports of the results. Capabilities have been added to the *Inspector* 6e software that enable the instructor to copy and paste the contents of the report into the student's original e-mail and then send it back as a reply.

- All of the frequently used options are accessible by clicking on newly updated toolbar buttons, which takes the user to windows containing multiple tabs. The tabs access various grid-based data entry screens that facilitate efficient entry of multiple transactions.

- In addition to the toolbar buttons, *Integrated Accounting* also provides the user with navigation buttons to facilitate fast, efficient, and intuitive movement throughout its systems. The navigation buttons are arranged in a vertical column along the left side of the display screen. Each of these buttons represents commonly used systems within the accounting application software (e.g., general ledger, purchases, sales, inventory, payroll, assets, etc.). When one of these buttons is selected, its associated menu items are displayed immediately to the right of the selected button. Because the menu items are grouped by system, they provide easy and fast access to the tasks associated with that system.

- Dynamic screen sizing capability has been added to the *Integrated Accounting* software that facilitates data entry screens to dynamically horizontally resize to take advantage of larger computer display screens. Therefore, the maximum number of columns can be displayed and thus avoid the necessity of horizontal scrolling.

- Smaller toolbar and navigation button icons displayed on the computer's screen have been replaced with larger, more modern icons, like those in Windows Vista.

- Commas have been added to numeric data fields of various reports to improve readability.

- A comprehensive setup accounting system capability permits customization to be centralized in one window with six tabs.

- A features selection is provided which allows the user to select which systems are active. The accounting system is always active. Fixed assets, payroll, inventory, and budgeting are optional. If a system is not selected, all traces of it disappear from the software. For example, if payroll is inactive, the employee maintenance and payroll transaction tabs disappear from the respective input windows, all menu options pertaining to payroll disappear, and all payroll reports disappear from the report selection options.

- The setup process is intuitive. For example, the software automatically classifies accounts to the most likely possibility so most often no keying is needed. The required accounts needed for system integration are also automatically determined by examining account titles based on the type of business and business organization.

- A journal wizard is provided which allows users to create their own special journals and to tailor journals to the many varieties of problems in this text-workbook and most other accounting texts and applications.

- Accounting review textual material with accompanying computer drills have been provided as a review of the basic accounting principles associated with (1) the accounting equation, (2) classifying accounts, and (3) analyzing transactions.

- An Explorer feature has been provided that enables the user to access data stored by the software to perform audit checks, check account activity, isolate errors, and perform other tasks that are helpful in managing account information.

- An Information/Web browser feature is available that uses the computer system's default browser to access the Internet to complete the optional Internet activities provided in the computer problems at the end of each chapter. Also, this feature may be used to access and display check figures (while offline) that are available for student reference during solution of all A computer problems.

- A student solution checker feature for all A designated problems is available that compares the student's work-in-process, currently stored in memory (and saved to their disk and folder), with the appropriate answer key file. A detailed report will be generated identifying any discrepancies between the answer key file and their work. For each incorrect item, the correct item is also shown.

- Bank reconciliation software has been provided that simplifies the reconciliation process by automatically bringing the Cash account balance forward, displaying all checks stored by the computer from which outstanding checks may be selected, and performing all bank reconciliation computations.

- A tax table allows the user to change federal and state tax tables and tax rates and limits for social security, Medicare, unemployment, and city tax rates.

- Five planning tools are provided for personal use and for problems in the textbook. The planning tools are the: (1) College Planner, (2) Savings Planner, (3) Retirement Planner, (4) Loan Planner, and (5) Notes & Interest Planner.

- The software automatically generates closing entries. Journal entries are retained after closing so that errors discovered after closing can be corrected easily.

- Powerful application integration permits all the accounting reports to be copied to the clipboard for pasting to spreadsheet or word processor application software.

- A check writing feature is available that will prepare checks when cash payment transactions involving a vendor are posted and/or when an employee's payroll information is entered.

- A menu option is provided to automatically generate the depreciation adjusting entries for plant assets.

- Menu options are available that automatically generate the current payroll journal entry and the employer's payroll taxes journal entry.

- An accounts payable: Purchase order processing and inventory control capability has been fully integrated to process purchase orders, purchases, and purchases returns. When a purchase order transaction is entered, the system automatically generates a purchase order form, updates inventory, and stores the information for later retrieval. When the merchandise is received and entered, the system automatically generates a voucher (or purchase invoice) form, and updates inventory, the vouchers (purchases) journal, the vendor account, and the general ledger accounts. Additional content has been added to the text-workbook to describe the detailed integration performed by the computer between the accounting and inventory systems via discussion and illustrated examples.

- An accounts receivable: Sales order processing and inventory control capability has been fully integrated to process sales and sales return transactions. As the invoice is processed, the system automatically generates a sales invoice form, and updates inventory, the sales journal, the customer account, and the general ledger accounts. Additional content has been added to the text-workbook to describe the detailed integration performed by the computer between the accounting and inventory systems via discussion and illustrated examples.

- The software is capable of handling both perpetual and periodic inventory systems. Three methods of inventory valuation are provided: average cost; last in, first out (LIFO); and first in, first out (FIFO). When using a perpetual inventory system, previous history transaction data is used to automatically create the cost of merchandise sold and merchandise inventory parts of the sales journal entry based on the valuation method used.

- A budgeting system has been provided for income statement accounts. A budget report can be generated that shows an income statement with account balances, budgets, and variances.

- The software allows users to specify font, font size, and so on to exploit the capabilities of their particular printers.

- A graphing feature automatically generates the following graphs: (1) income statement bar graph, (2) expense distribution pie graphs, (3) actual-versus-budgeted income statement bar graph, (4) balance sheet bar graph, (5) sales line graphs, (6) top five customers bar graph, (7) labor distribution by expense account graph, (8) depreciation comparison line graph comparing asset depreciation by several methods, (9) five most profitable inventory items graph, and (10) five least profitable inventory items graph.

- Run dates (which appear on all reports) are automatically determined by the software. When a report is selected, the default run date appears as editable text so it can be accepted or changed. All dates used by the computer can be changed by clicking on a calendar icon button and selecting the desired date, by striking the + and − keys, or by keying the desired date.

An extensive, comprehensive, context-sensitive help system has been provided that offers a quick way to find information about operating the software.

Required Hardware

The *Integrated Accounting* 6e package may be installed and executed on computers capable of running Microsoft Windows 95, 98, NT, Me, 2000, XP (SP2), and Vista. At least 15 megabytes (Mb) of available hard drive space and a CD drive are required for installation. Access to a printer is optional but recommended.

Organizational Features

The text-workbook consists of 12 chapters and three comprehensive problems. Each chapter begins with an introduction that describes the topics to be covered. The introduction is followed by textual instructional material with ample illustrations and notes that present the information required to process the accounting material presented. A chapter summary is followed by a computer sample problem that contains detailed step-by-step instructions for completing a problem that covers the material presented in the chapter. Following the sample problem is a student exercise and an A and B computer hands-on problem. Computer A problems have check figures available for student reference. Both computer A and B problems have associated audit questions designed to interpret the computer-generated output. In addition, each computer A problem in the text-workbook uses student solution checker software to permit students to check their work in process. Finally, each computer problem contains optional spreadsheet, word processing, and Internet activities. These optional activities are not required to complete the problems; however, if access to a spreadsheet, word processor, or the Internet is available, it is highly recommended that they be completed.

Learning Objectives

This courseware package is intended for students who want to learn about computerized accounting principles. Therefore, its three major objectives are (1) to present and integrate accounting principles in such a way that no prior knowledge of computers or computerized accounting is required, (2) to provide a hands-on approach to learning how modern computerized accounting systems function, and (3) to provide knowledge and hands-on experience in integrating accounting with other business applications such as spreadsheets, word processors, and the Internet. Each chapter identifies the learning objectives to be mastered for that chapter.

Additional flexibility has been designed into the computer software to permit use with most traditional accounting textbooks. The computer may be used to solve manual accounting problems in these textbooks.

Message to the Student

The *Integrated Accounting* 6e software is designed so that computer-generated output and the accounting procedures are similar to those currently used in business and industry. The significant difference between the software used in this package and a commercial accounting software system is the simplicity of computer operation.

When a business uses a commercial, computerized accounting system to control such valuable assets as cash, inventory, and accounts receivable, tight controls are maintained on security, data entry, and audit trail procedures. These controls often complicate the operation of a computerized system. Some of these restrictions have been intentionally omitted from this package to simplify the operations and provide a usable, relevant educational tool.

Message to the Instructor

This package has been designed so that the material and the computer problems presented in this text-workbook can be introduced gradually through the use of opening balance files that permit the processing of ongoing accounting systems. In this way, students can concentrate on learning accounting topics while they gain experience with the various features of the software.

Each chapter (except Chapter 9) contains a sample problem. Each chapter also contains a student exercise, two computer problems (with audit questions), and use of the student-solution checker feature to ensure that the students comprehend the material presented. This approach permits the students to work independently and at their own speed.

An instructor's manual is provided to assist you while using *Integrated Accounting* 6e. In addition, a solution-checker disk called *Inspector* 6e is available to check all your students' solutions electronically. The contents of these answer key files provided with the *Inspector* 6e software are the same answer keys provided in print form in the instructor's manual.

About the Authors

Dale Klooster   Dale Klooster is an author of educational courseware products. For 4 years, he was affiliated with a major publishing company. In addition, he spent 6 years working with various computer systems in business and industry, 13 years as an educator in the field of computer information processing, and the past 23 years as an author of computer-related products. He has also been a consultant to many businesses and educational institutions. He earned his B.S. and M.S. degrees from Minnesota State University and his Ed.D. from the University of Northern Colorado. Dr. Klooster has co-authored *Integrated Accounting; Automated Accounting; Advanced Automated Accounting; Enrichment Activities; Computerized Inventory Procedures; Computerized Payroll Procedures; Computerized Record-Keeping and Bookkeeping; Financial Information Processing; Computers and Information Processing; Technology for Productivity and Decision Making; Computerized Principles of Financial Accounting* (Internet based); *Accounting Foundations: A Complete Online Course;* several spreadsheet accounting textbooks; a word processing, spreadsheet, and database textbook; and several accounting simulations and other educational software packages.

Warren Allen Warren Allen is an author and developer of software for numerous educational courseware products. For 14 years he taught accounting and computer programming, and has spent the past 23 years as an author of computer-related products. He has designed, developed, and installed numerous computerized accounting systems for businesses and governmental organizations. He earned his B.S. from Southern State College and his M.A. from the University of South Dakota. Mr. Allen has co-authored *Integrated Accounting; Automated Accounting; Advanced Automated Accounting; Enrichment Activities; Computerized Inventory Procedures; Computerized Payroll Procedures; Computerized Record-Keeping and Bookkeeping; Financial Information Processing; Computers and Information Processing; Technology for Productivity and Decision Making; Computerized Principles of Financial Accounting* (Internet based); *Accounting Foundations: A Complete Online Course;* several spreadsheet accounting textbooks; a word processing, spreadsheet, and database textbook; and several accounting simulations and other educational software packages.

Acknowledgments

We would like to express our appreciation to all our fellow educators who have provided helpful comments and suggestions. Many useful comments from instructors and students have resulted in significant improvements in the text-workbook and software. Namely,

Marjorie Ashton
Truckee Meadows Community College
Linda A. Bolduc
Mount Wachusett Community College
Gary Bower
Community College Of Rhode Island
Jose L. Duenas
Texas State Technical College
Art Espinoza, MBA
Mount San Jacinto College
Stephan C. Itnyre
Northern Virginia Community College
David A. Lanning, E.A.
Tompkins Cortland
    Community College

Patti Lopez
Valencia Community College
Thomas E. Murphy, M.B.A.
Cleveland Community College
Joseph Malino Nicassio,
    CMA, CFM
Westmoreland County
    Community College
D. Pete Rector
Victor Valley College
Chuck Smith
Iowa Western Community College
John Teter
Saint Petersburg College

We would also like to acknowledge the excellent support received from the sales, editorial, and production staffs at South-Western, a part of Cengage Learning. Their expertise, professionalism, and commitment to quality have made our association with them a rewarding working experience.

Dale H. Klooster

Warren W. Allen

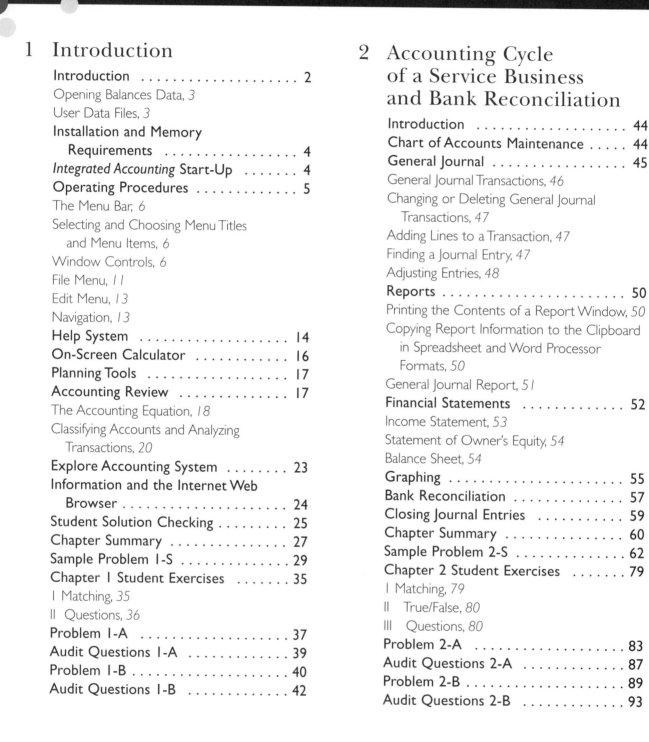

Contents

3 Accounting Cycle of a Merchandising Business

4 Voucher System and Budgeting

Comprehensive Problem 1

5 Accounts Payable: Purchase Order Processing and Inventory Control

6 Accounts Receivable Sales Order Processing and Inventory Control

7 Fixed Assets

8 Payroll

9 Partnerships and Corporations

Comprehensive Problem 2

10 Financial Statement Analysis

11 Departmentalized Accounting

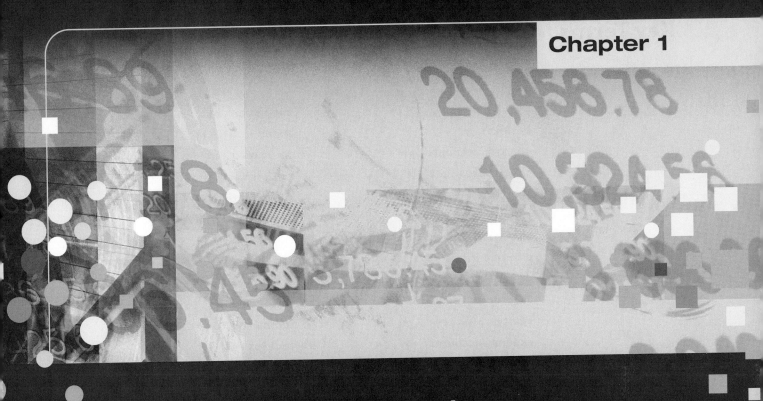

Introduction

Upon completion of this chapter, you will be able to:

- Identify and define the features of the *Integrated Accounting* software and text-workbook.

- Perform installation and start-up procedures.

- Make use of menus, toolbar, and navigation buttons.

- Use window controls.

- Perform file-handling tasks (e.g., loading data from disk and saving data to disk).

- Use planning tools.

- Access Help system information.

- Use the on-screen calculator.

- Apply basic principles of accounting concepts.

- Use the Explore Accounting System feature of the software.

- Use the Information and Internet Web Browser features of the software.

- Use the student solution checking feature of the software.

Key Terms

Introduction

All of us use accounting to some extent. For example, we use accounting when we purchase or sell goods and services, pay our bills, balance our checkbooks, budget our money, and prepare our tax returns. Businesses also use accounting to prepare reports for individuals, other businesses, and various government agencies regarding their financial activities. We can define **accounting** as an informational system that plans, analyzes, records, and reports financial information. An **accountant** is someone who summarizes detailed accounting information and then analyzes and interprets that information to assist owners and managers in making financial decisions. In many businesses, personnel called **bookkeepers** and **accounting clerks** assist the accountant and perform general accounting tasks, such as recording, reporting, and filing, that are required on a routine basis.

A **business** is an economic entity that endeavors to sell goods and services to customers at prices that will cover the costs of doing business and return a profit to the owners. To help achieve this goal, many businesses have turned to the computer as a tool for collecting, organizing, and reporting large amounts of information. The informational needs of today's business are stored and managed by what is called a **management information system (MIS)**. A typical MIS consists of several computer-integrated systems that provide all the informational needs of the business. The accounting system is one of the most important of these systems because it is used to manage the internal and external flow of the business's financial data. Business owners, managers, accountants, bookkeepers, and

2

accounting clerks need to know how to use modern MIS computerized accounting systems to perform accounting tasks efficiently. The objective of this text is to teach you about computerized accounting, accounting spreadsheet applications, and word processing applications using a hands-on approach. You will learn to operate the software by entering realistic accounting transactions for a variety of business applications and by generating financial statements, spreadsheet, and other management information reports.

The *Integrated Accounting* software uses a standard Windows **user interface** that includes drop-down menus, a toolbar, navigation buttons, movable overlapping windows, on-screen help, and other operational conventions. Because this software uses the standard Windows interface, the techniques and terminology you learn from this text and accompanying software can be applied to many other software application packages. This facilitates the learning process and greatly reduces the need to retrain for each new application you use in the future.

The *Integrated Accounting* software that accompanies this text-workbook is designed to handle general ledger, accounts payable, accounts receivable, financial statement analysis processing, bank reconciliation, budgeting, fixed assets, purchase order processing, sales order processing, inventory, and payroll. In addition, data from the *Integrated Accounting* software may be transferred to most spreadsheet programs (i.e., Excel) for further analysis. Report contents may be imported into most word processing programs (e.g., Word, WordPerfect, and Works) for use in formal reporting or presentations. You will learn several of these applications in the following chapters. You are not required to have access to spreadsheet or word processing software to use *Integrated Accounting*. Each of the end-of-chapter problems in this text-workbook contains optional steps for further spreadsheet and word processing analysis and reporting. It is recommended that you complete these optional applications if you have the software available.

Opening Balances Data

The installation disk includes files that contain opening balance data for each problem in this text-workbook. When *Integrated Accounting* is installed on your hard drive or network server, the opening balance files will automatically be included in the same folder as the software. Before a problem can be solved, the opening balances file must be loaded from this folder.

User Data Files

Integrated Accounting permits you to store data on a separate data disk, hard drive, or network file server. This feature enables you to save your work for completion at a later time. If you are using a floppy disk, flash memory drive, or something else to save your data, make sure that it is properly formatted before use. For information on formatting a disk, refer to your computer system's operations manual or Help system.

Installation and Memory Requirements

Integrated Accounting comes complete on a standard CD. To use the software you need a processor running in the Windows 95, 98, NT, 2000, Me, XP, or Vista environment. In addition, installation procedures require a hard drive with at least 15 megabytes (Mb) of available disk space and a CD drive. A printer is optional, but it is highly recommended.

The installation CD included in the software package contains compressed *Integrated Accounting* program files, opening balance files, student solution check files, and optional spreadsheet and word processing files required to complete all of the problems in this text-workbook. During the installation process, all of these compressed files are expanded into an executable format onto your computer's hard drive. The installation is a common procedure. Detailed step-by-step instructions are provided on the installation disk's label. Your instructor or computer center technician has probably already completed this one-time installation procedure.

 It is possible, in rare cases, when the colors chosen by the user within the computer's color control panel conflict with the colors used by *Integrated Accounting* in such a way that images or text may appear invisible. If you experience any problems with colors, go to the control panel that controls the colors and change colors. Choose the default colors provided by your user interface system software to prevent this conflict.

Also, in the rare case when the screen resolution settings are set too large to hold the display of the entire toolbar (see Figure 1.1), the software will leave off the "Drills" and "Check" toolbar buttons. In this instance, you may select these features from the menus provided, or adjust your screen resolution size in the computer's display control panel.

Integrated Accounting Start-Up

After installation is completed, you can begin working with *Integrated Accounting* by performing the following steps: (1) click the Windows Start button, (2) click or select Programs, (3) position the pointer on *Integrated Accounting Version 6*, and (4) click on *Integrated Accounting Version 6* when the submenu appears. To start the software in Windows NT Workstation, double-click the *Integrated Accounting's* icon in the Office program group.

Integrated Accounting contains several components that you will use to perform accounting tasks. Review Figure 1.1 to acquaint yourself with terminology and **toolbar buttons**, which are icons representing a shortcut method of accessing common menu items. Notice the information message dialog "End accounting system," which is called a Tooltip. **Tooltips** are brief informational messages that automatically appear when the pointer is positioned on a toolbar button. As shown in Figure 1.1, the "End accounting system" message appears when the pointer is positioned on the Exit toolbar button.

In the computer industry, the term *navigation* is used to describe the methods used to move from one task, link, or menu item to another. A computer application or Internet Web page with good navigation simplifies its operational requirements. *Integrated Accounting* provides the user with **navigation buttons** to facilitate fast, efficient, and intuitive movement throughout its systems. As shown in Figure 1.1, the navigation buttons are arranged in

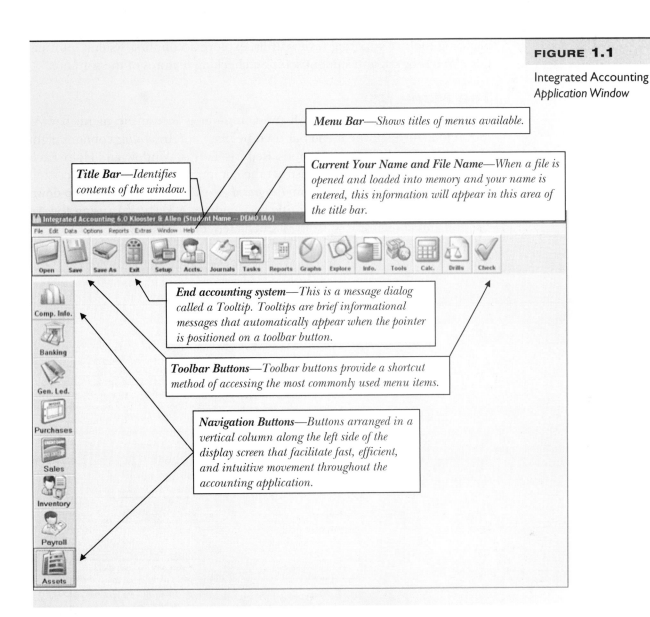

FIGURE 1.1

Integrated Accounting
Application Window

a vertical column along the left side of the display screen. Each of these buttons represents commonly used systems within the accounting application software (e.g., general ledger, purchases, sales, inventory, payroll, assets, etc.). When one of these buttons is selected, its associated menu items are displayed immediately to the right of the selected button. Because the menu items are grouped by system, they provide an easy and fast access to the tasks associated with that system. Only the navigation buttons that pertain to the accounting needs of a business are displayed. For example, if the business does not use payroll and fixed assets, the Payroll and Assets buttons do not appear. We will revisit navigation buttons in Chapter 2, where you will begin using them to complete problems at the end of each chapter in this text-workbook.

Operating Procedures

The following sections cover use of the menu bar, menu item selection, window controls, selecting text, and other special features that have been provided to make the operation of the software easy and efficient. Following the operating procedures, we will cover the Help system, on-screen calculator, planning tools, accounting review drills, explore accounting system, information/Web browser, and student solution checking features of the software.

The Menu Bar

One way of communicating with the computer is to use the menu bar. As shown in Figure 1.1, the **menu bar** used by *Integrated Accounting* contains eight menu titles: File, Edit, Data, Options, Reports, Extras, Window, and Help. Each title contains **menu items** that instruct the computer to perform its processing tasks. The type of menu used in *Integrated Accounting* is called a **drop-down menu** because selecting a menu title via a mouse or keyboard (using the Alt key and directional arrow keys), immediately displays a list of menu items below the menu title selected. Figure 1.2 illustrates the menu items of the *Integrated Accounting* File drop-down menu. As mentioned, you may use the mouse or the keyboard to select drop-down menus and choose menu items.

FIGURE 1.2

File Drop-Down Menu

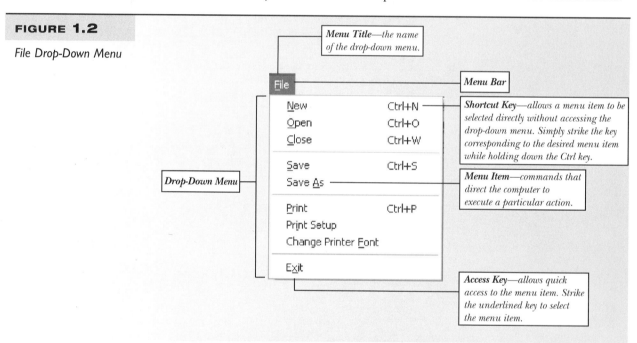

Selecting and Choosing Menu Titles and Menu Items

In this text-workbook, the terms **select** and **choose** have different meanings. When menu titles on the menu bar or menu items are selected, they are highlighted. When a highlighted (or selected) menu title or item is chosen, the software will take the appropriate action. **Dimmed items** are not available for selection. (You may need to select another item or perform a processing task before a dimmed item is activated.)

Window Controls

Users interact with the computer to perform *Integrated Accounting* procedures through windows. A **window** is a rectangular area of the screen in which the software is communicating with the user. Often the display screen contains only one window. Though two or more overlapping windows may appear on the screen at once, only one window is active at a time. *Integrated*

Accounting uses several different windows to perform its accounting activities. For example, some windows contain tabs consisting of text boxes and grid cells used to enter data from the keyboard; some contain lists and reports; and others may display dialog box messages and operational information. Regardless of the activity, the part of the window that will receive input is said to have the **focus**. For example, a data field that has the focus is identified by the **insertion point** (also referred to as the pipe character), which appears as a vertical bar (|). A dotted rectangular box indicates which decision or choice of several options has the focus.

Many of the windows that appear may be moved, resized, maximized, minimized, made inactive or active, and so on. For example, to move a window, point to the window's **title bar** (located at the top of the window) and drag the mouse. The pointer and an outline of the window will move as you drag. For specific information regarding moving a window, changing its size, minimizing or maximizing it, making it inactive or active, consult your computer's user interface operational manual.

It is important to understand how the operational controls contained in the windows enable you to enter and edit data, select items from lists, and navigate the grids and controls. The following paragraphs identify these controls and describe how to use them. You can refer to this section of the text as you encounter these controls later in this text-workbook.

Tabs   *Integrated Accounting* uses the visual image of windows to clarify and simplify operations. Several menu items (or toolbar selections) contain windows that include multiple tabs. These tabs provide for additional entry of data, options, and processing. For example, the Account Maintenance window that appears when the Maintain Accounts menu item is chosen from the Data menu (or the *Accts.* Toolbar button is clicked) is shown in Figure 1.3. Notice that the window contains six different tabs: Accounts, Vendors, Customers, Fixed Assets, Employees, and Inventory. The first tab (Accounts) appears as the active tab and is used to maintain accounts in the chart of accounts. To switch to another account maintenance function within the window, simply click on the desired tab. For example, to perform vendor maintenance, click on the tab labeled Vendors.

Text Boxes   Users can type information into what are known as **text boxes**, as shown in Figure 1.4. The user can accept the current text, edit it, or delete it. When a text box receives the focus, existing text is selected and the insertion point appears to the right of the last character of text. Selected text is highlighted (indicated with light text on a dark background). An example of selected text is shown in Figure 1.5. If the insertion point is moved, the text is deselected. If the user starts typing while text is selected, the selected text is replaced with the newly typed data.

Grid Cells   Most data that you enter into the *Integrated Accounting* software will be entered into windows that contain grid cells. **Grid cells** are arrangements of rows and columns that, like text boxes, are used to enter, edit, or delete data and text. When a grid cell receives the focus, any existing data or text within it is selected (highlighted) and the insertion point appears to the right of the last character within the cell. Figure 1.6 shows an example of data that has been entered into grid cells. Notice the amount $14,000.00, under the Julia Holland, Capital column has been selected. If the insertion point is

FIGURE 1.3

Tabs in the Account Maintenance Window

Active Tab

Inactive Tabs

Maximize button—Expands the size of the window horizontally for viewing of additional fields within the active tab.

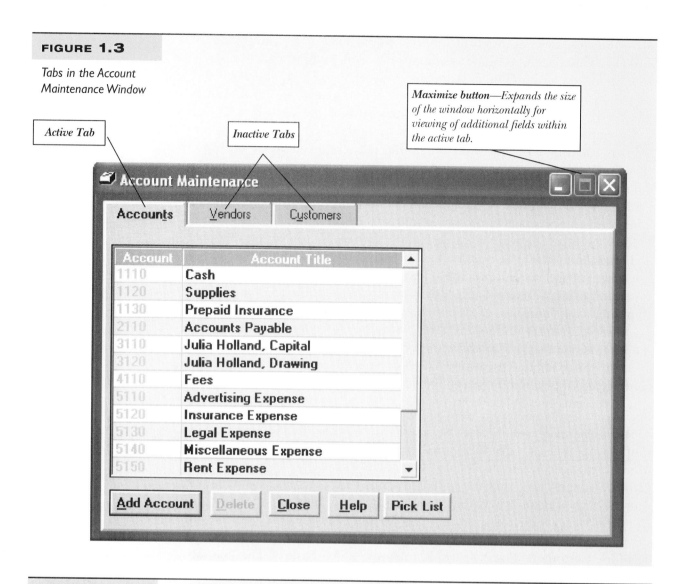

FIGURE 1.4

Text Boxes

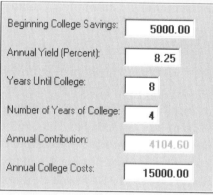

moved within the cell, the text is deselected and the contents may be edited. If the user types data while text is selected, the selected text within the cell is replaced with the newly entered data.

List Boxes   A **list box** is used to display choices for the user. A list box and a drop-down list are similar in that each allows the user to select a single entry from a list of items. Figure 1.7 shows a chart of accounts list box. A highlight bar (or underline) identifies the currently selected item. Both the mouse and

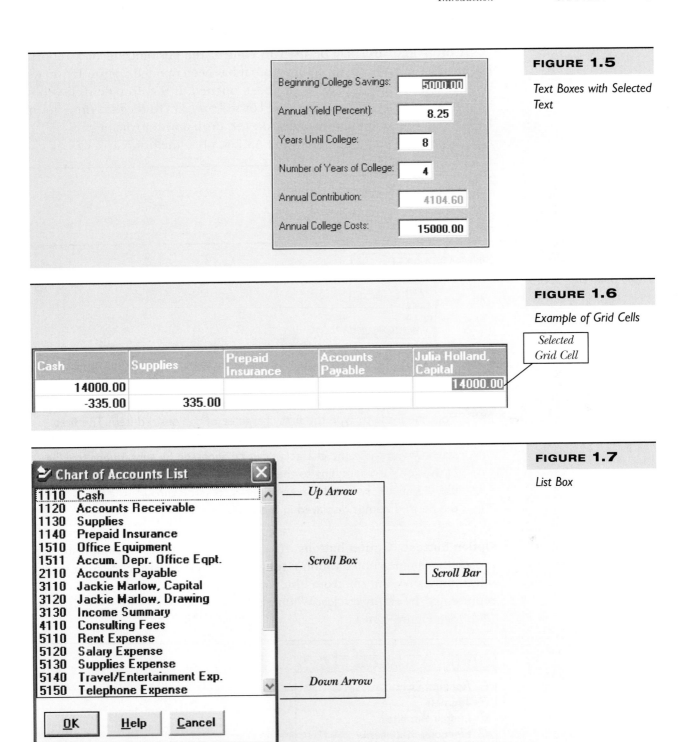

FIGURE 1.5

Text Boxes with Selected Text

FIGURE 1.6

Example of Grid Cells

FIGURE 1.7

List Box

keyboard can be used to scroll through the list and choose items from the list. To select an item from the list, simply click on the desired item and then click OK (or double-click on the desired item).

Drop-Down List   The **drop-down list** consists of a text box with a drop-down arrow button immediately to the right. The text must be selected from among the items in the drop-down list. The drop-down list does not allow the user to enter new data that is not in the existing list into the text box. However, the user may enter an item that *is* in the drop-down list into the text box. As the user types the first one or two characters, the computer starts searching the list and places the first occurrence of the matching item from the list in the text box.

A drop-down list may be used to control the customizing of a report. Figure 1.8 shows a drop-down list before it has been opened. Figure 1.9 shows the same drop-down list after it has been opened. If the drop-down list contains more items than will fit, a scroll bar will appear. To toggle a drop-down list between open and closed, click on the drop-down arrow or press Alt + down arrow (while holding down the Alt key, press the down arrow key).

FIGURE 1.8

Drop-Down List (Closed)

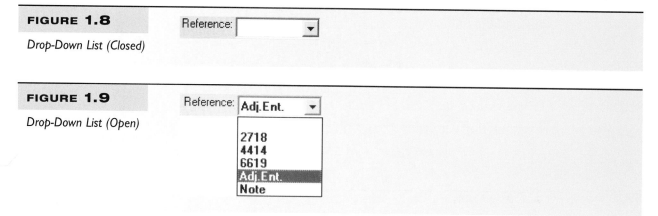

FIGURE 1.9

Drop-Down List (Open)

NOTE While the drop-down list has the focus, an easy way to select an item from the list is to type the first character of the desired item. The first occurrence will appear in the text box. Succeeding occurrences of items starting with the same character can be accessed by subsequent striking of the key corresponding to the first character. As an alternative, you may use the up arrow and down arrow keys to scroll through the items until the desired item is displayed in the text box.

Option Buttons. Option buttons (sometimes referred to as radio buttons) represent a single choice within a set of mutually exclusive choices. You can select only one button from the choices provided. Option buttons are represented by empty circles. When an option is selected, the circle is filled (⊙). (See Figure 1.10.)

FIGURE 1.10

Option Buttons within a Group Box

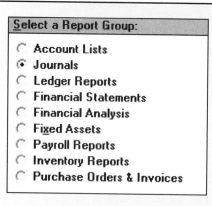

Check Boxes Check boxes are used to control the selection of individual choices. When a task requiring multiple choices is selected, a group section will appear containing check boxes (☐) to the left of each choice. The check boxes are turned on or off in any combination. When a check box is selected, a check mark (☑) appears inside it. Figure 1.11 shows the check boxes that allow the

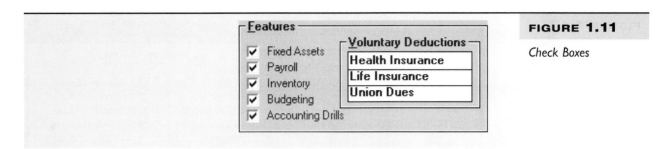

FIGURE 1.11

Check Boxes

user to select the Fixed Assets, Payroll, Inventory, Budgeting, and Accounting Drills features of the software.

Command Buttons   A **command button** is a rectangular shaped figure containing a label that specifies an immediate action or response that will be taken by the computer when it is chosen. When a command button has a dotted line or dark shadow around the button (see the OK button in Figure 1.12) it is said to be the default button. The default command button can be chosen from anywhere in the window by pressing the Enter key. Any command button may be chosen by striking the underlined key while holding down the Alt key.

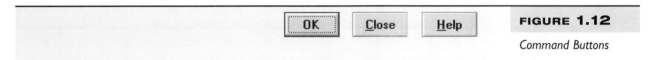

FIGURE 1.12

Command Buttons

File Menu

When the File menu is selected from the menu bar, the drop-down menu we saw in Figure 1.2 appears. We examine here several of the menu items you will need to complete the problems at the end of this chapter.

Open   The Open menu item is used to load a data file stored on disk into the computer's memory for processing. Figure 1.13 shows the Open dialog box. The highlighted file name identifies the currently selected file. Both the mouse and keyboard can be used to choose files from the list. To choose a file, simply click on the desired file name and then click on the Open button (or double-click on the desired item). To choose a file using the keyboard, press the Tab key until a file in the file list has the focus, strike the up and down arrow keys to highlight the desired file, then press the Enter key.

Close   Use the Close menu item in the File menu to close the current file displayed in the active window (removes the data from the computer's memory). When Close is chosen, the active window and all other windows containing data from the same file are closed. Close does *not* remove any data from disk.

Save   Use the Save menu item in the File menu to store your data to a disk so that you can continue a problem in a later session. The data will be saved to disk with the current path (disk drive and folder) with the file name displayed in the title bar located at the top of the *Integrated Accounting* application window. If you wish to save your data with a path (disk drive or folder) or file name different from the current path and file name, use Save As.

 You *cannot* save a file to disk with the same file name as an opening balance file.

FIGURE 1.13

Open Dialog Box

Selected
File

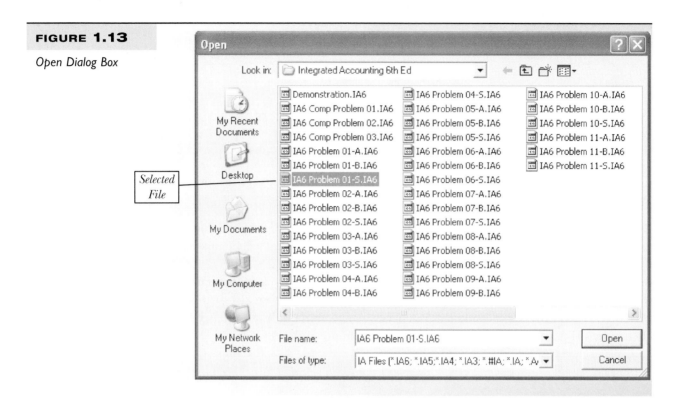

Save As   This menu item is the same as Save except that the data can be saved with a path or file name different from the current path and file name. Save As is useful for making a backup copy of a data file. For example, you may want to make a backup of your data file before entering adjusting entries or generating period-end closing entries. To make a backup copy, open the data file you wish to back up and use Save As to save it under a different name. Remember: If you just want to create a backup file, you must change the file name or you will overwrite the original file.

Print   The purpose of Print is to create a printed version of the contents currently displayed in a report or graphic window. The entire contents of the active report or graphics window will be printed when Print is chosen.

Print Setup   Clicking the Print button while a report is displayed or choosing the Print Setup menu item from the File menu, brings up a Print Setup dialog box. The Print Setup dialog box offers choices about the printer(s) connected to your computer, such as desired paper size and printing enhancements. You will not need to use Print Setup unless you are having trouble printing. Check with your instructor for the proper information before making changes to your print setup. *Integrated Accounting* uses the current printer information specified in your computer's user interface when processing a print command.

Change Printer Font   When reports are printed to an attached printer, *Integrated Accounting* uses the font, font style, and size specified in the printer's Font dialog box. You may want to change these options to make your reports more attractive or to reduce the type size if fields are overflowing or wrapping incorrectly. Also, changing the font to one that is native to the printer you are using (e.g., courier) will often increase the print speed.

Exit   This menu item is used to end *Integrated Accounting*. When Exit is chosen, the computer checks to see whether the current data in its memory have been saved. If not, a dialog box will appear asking if you wish to save your data to disk.

Edit Menu

The Edit menu (shown in Figure 1.14) contains several menu items that can be used to remove and copy data from one location within *Integrated Accounting* or from other application programs. Five menu items are available for your use. Each of these menu items will be discussed in detail because they are used throughout the text. The Cut, Copy, and Paste menu items are discussed next so that you may use them as desired at any time while working with the software.

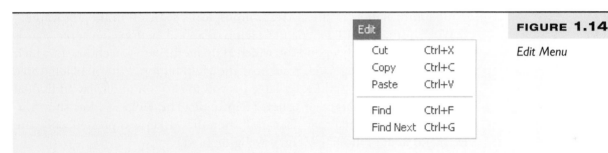

FIGURE 1.14

Edit Menu

Cut, Copy, and Paste   The Cut and Copy menu items in the Edit menu may be used to place copies of the current selection (data highlighted in text or grid cell boxes) to the **clipboard**, a temporary storage area, in preparation for being pasted elsewhere. Copy leaves the source intact, whereas Cut erases it. The Cut, Copy, and Paste menu items in *Integrated Accounting* work as in other Windows applications.

 NOTE   If the destination already contains data, you may overwrite it when you choose Paste. Be careful that you allow enough space for the complete source to be pasted.

Navigation

Grid cells, text boxes, option buttons, check boxes, and command buttons should be filled in or selected in the normal tab sequence. The **tab sequence** is the logical sequence in which the computer is expecting each grid cell, text box, button, or command to be accessed. The sequence is usually left to right and top to bottom.

As you have already learned, the focus identifies the location within a window, tab, list, or dialog box in which the computer will receive the next input. For example, when the Tab key is pressed, the focus moves to the next item in the tab sequence. Pressing Shift+Tab moves the focus to the previous item in the tab sequence. When a grid cell or text box has the focus, an insertion point character will appear to mark the current position where data will be entered or edited. When data is typed, the insertion point moves one character to the right for each character typed. Press the Enter key to choose the action or response of the default command button or command button that currently has the focus. Use the Esc key to choose Cancel or Close within the active window, tab, list, or dialog box.

Help System

Integrated Accounting's on-screen Help system offers a quick way to find information about operating the software. To access Help, you can (1) choose the Help Contents and Index menu item from the Help menu, (2) press the F1 function key at any time, or (3) choose the Help command button that appears at the bottom of various windows. The Help window shown in Figure 1.15 appears when the Help Contents and Index menu item is chosen from the Help menu. This initial display provides instructions for the basic operation of the Help system.

The Help window consists of two frames. The frame on the left contains tabs that display the contents, an index, or search option. This frame is used to select, or help find, a specific topic. The frame on the right displays the detailed information of the corresponding topic selected in the left frame.

When using the F1 key or the Help command button, the topic that is selected and displayed depends on which Help menu item you choose or which window you were using when you chose the Help button. Within a Help topic one or more "jumps" may be available for you to click on to display additional information about a term or a new Help topic. The Help window shown in Figure 1.16 was automatically displayed when the F1 key was pressed while the Save menu item in the File menu was highlighted.

FIGURE 1.15

Help Window (left contents frame and right topics frame)

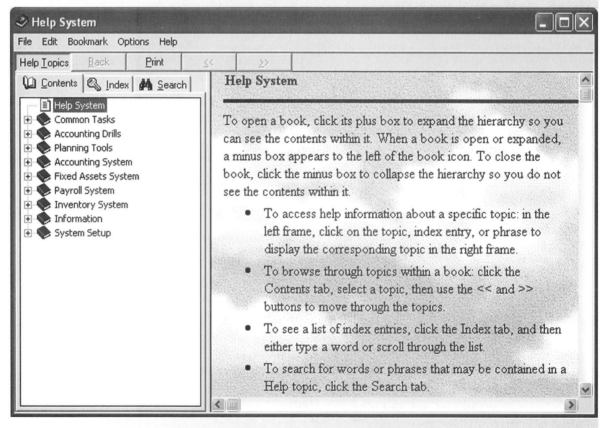

FIGURE 1.16

*Help Window
(saving a file)*

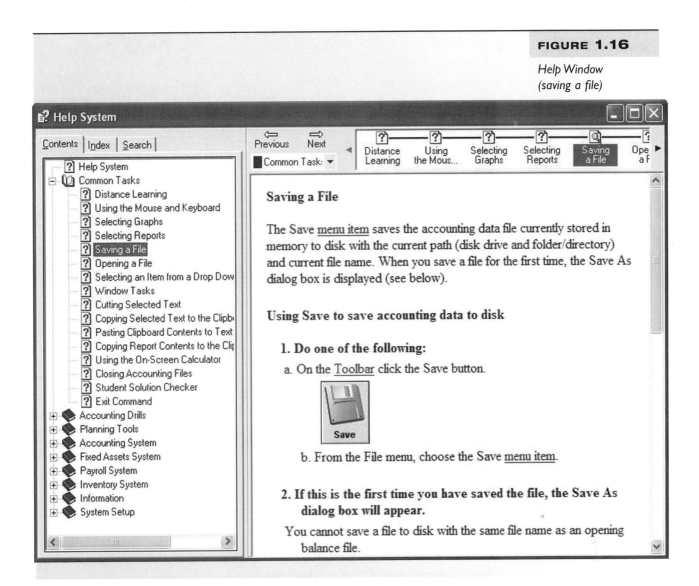

You can use the Index and Search tabs to find words or topics quickly. The Help window shown in Figure 1.17 appeared when *save* was keyed into the text box at the top of the Index tab. The Search tab can also be used to find information about save.

FIGURE 1.17

Help Window (using Index Tab)

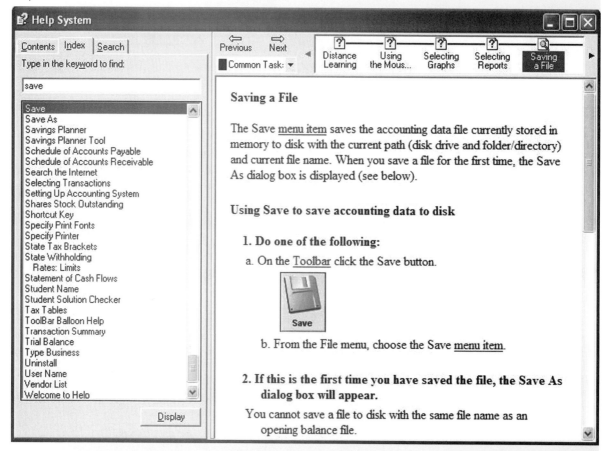

On-Screen Calculator

The on-screen calculator is operated like a handheld calculator. Your computer's standard calculator can perform all the calculations required in this text-workbook. The results can be copied and pasted into the text box that has the focus. Once the calculator appears (as shown in Figure 1.18), a Help menu is available to provide detailed explanation of the calculator operation.

FIGURE 1.18

Standard On-Screen Calculator

Planning Tools

Planning tools are convenient, fast, easy-to-use ways of producing results for commonly used applications. These applications may be for your personal use or business use. Five different planners are provided: College, Savings, Loan, Retirement, and Notes & Interest. Each planner contains options that direct the computer to calculate different information. Select the tab identifying the desired planner, enter the data required, and click on Report to have the computer calculate the desired result(s) and display a report.

 An accounting file does not have to be loaded into memory to use any of the planning tools.

The College Planner is illustrated in this chapter to show you how to select calculation options, enter data, and generate a report showing the results using any of the planning tools provided. The operational procedure of each of the planning tools is the same and will not be covered again in this text. The College Planner is used to calculate the annual contribution required to reach a particular savings amount and to calculate the amount saved for each year of college. A completed College Planner is illustrated in Figure 1.19. The figure shows the calculate option set to Annual Contribution and the data entered into the appropriate text boxes.

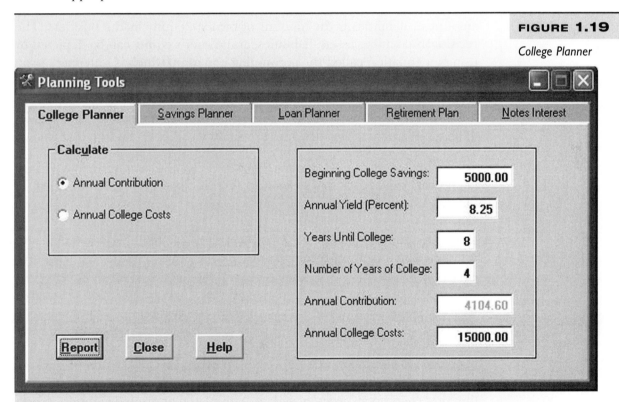

FIGURE 1.19

College Planner

Accounting Review

A **chart of accounts** lists all the accounts used by a business. Each account consists of an account number and account title. In a manual accounting system, each account is kept on a separate sheet of paper or on a legal-sized, cardboard-like card. Each of these sheets of paper, or cards, placed together in a book or file drawer is called a **general ledger**. Similarly, in modern computerized accounting systems, the data for each account is kept in a separate record that is stored on disk or tape. These records, stored together in a file, are referred to by accountants as the general ledger.

In the following material, you will review basic accounting principles and how the application of these principles affects the chart of accounts and general ledger. At the end of this chapter, you will use computer drill problems to reinforce your knowledge of these basic accounting principles.

 To access the accounting drills, you must open the applicable accounting file first, then select Accounting Drills from the Data menu or click on the Drills icon on the toolbar. To access the accounting equation, click on the Accounting Equation, tab found in the Accounting Drills window.

The Accounting Equation

Most all accounting systems, whether computerized or manual, use similar accounting practices and procedures regardless of the size of an organization, its type of business, or its complexity. All accounting systems have **assets**, **liabilities**, and **equity**. Examples of assets include cash, supplies, insurance, buildings, and land. Liabilities are the amounts owed by the business. The difference between the total amount of assets and the total amount of liabilities is the amount of owner's equity in the business. The relationship among assets, liabilities, and owner's equity can be depicted by using an equation called the **accounting equation**, which is stated as:

Assets = Liabilities + Owner's Equity

The accounting equation must always be equal. That is, the total of the amounts on the left side must equal the total of the amounts on the right side.

Transactions and the Accounting Equation   Transactions completed by an organization during a specific period of time may number from a few to thousands depending on the size and complexity of the organization and its accounting system. Each transaction causes increases or decreases in assets, liabilities, or owner's equity. Accountants must be careful to record transactions in a systematic manner so that the accounting equation is always in balance after each transaction is recorded. Increases and decreases that are caused by a transaction are recorded in specific accounts. Each account has an account balance and an account title. For example, the asset account titled Cash is used to record and store the amount of money available to the business. The computer stores each account title and balance used by the business.

As transactions are entered, the appropriate account balance is updated. After all transactions have been entered, the account information can be further processed (totals accumulated, etc.), displayed or printed in various report formats, and stored to disk for recall at a later time. To see how this process works, consider the following transactions:

Sept. 1 Received cash from owner as an investment, $14,000.00.

2 Paid cash for supplies, $335.00.

Paid cash for insurance, $750.00. (Note: Prepaid Insurance account is used.)

4 Bought supplies on account, $2,500.00.

6 Paid cash on account, $1,500.00.

The transactions entered into the accounting equation are shown in Figure 1.20. Notice that each transaction affects at least two accounts and has been entered on separate lines in the date order in which it occurred. Also notice how the equation at the bottom of the figure shows that the last transaction entered is in balance.

Click the maximize button to expand the size of the window horizontally to view additional data fields within the active tab.

FIGURE 1.20

Transactions Entered into Accounting Equation

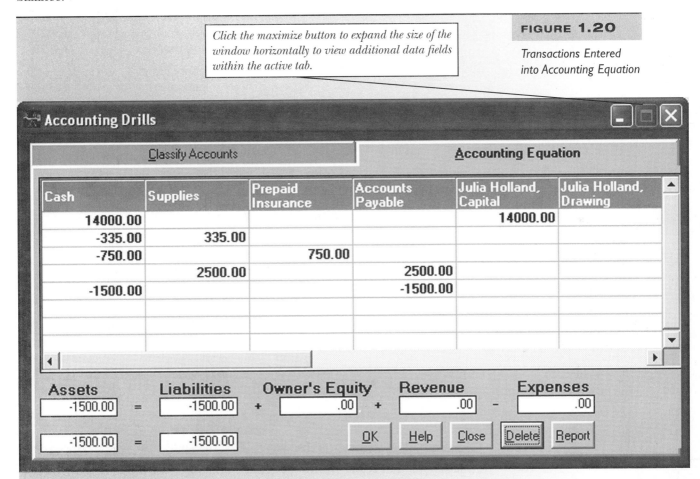

After all the transactions have been entered into the accounting equation and stored by the computer, an accounting equation report can be generated. Figure 1.21 shows the accounting equation report listing each account's beginning balance, transaction activity, and new balance. Notice that the accounts are grouped by assets, liabilities, and owner's equity just as they are in the accounting equation. At the end of the report, the computer prints the total of all the assets ($15,000.00) and the total of all liabilities plus the owner's equity account, and it balances ($15,000.00) proving that it is in balance. When the report appears, click the maximize button to expand the size of the Accounting Equation Report window.

FIGURE 1.21

Accounting Equation Report

**Holland Ad Agency
Accounting Equation Report
09/01/—**

Account	Classification	Description	Amount
Cash	Asset	Balance Forward	.00
		Transaction	14,000.00
		Transaction	−335.00
		Transaction	−750.00
		Transaction	−1,500.00
		New Balance	11,415.00
Supplies	Asset	Balance Forward	.00
		Transaction	335.00
		Transaction	2,500.00
		New Balance	2,835.00
Prepaid Insurance	Asset	Balance Forward	.00
		Transaction	750.00
		New Balance	750.00
Accounts Payable	Liability	Balance Forward	.00
		Transaction	2,500.00
		Transaction	−1,500.00
		New Balance	1,000.00
Julia Holland, Capital	Owner's Equity	Balance Forward	.00
		Transaction	14,000.00
		New Balance	14,000.00
Julia Holland, Drawing	Owner's Equity	Balance Forward	.00
		New Balance	.00
		Assets =	15,000.00
		Liabilities + Equity	15,000.00

Equation in Balance

Classifying Accounts and Analyzing Transactions

Transactions that result from a business's operation must be recorded in the accounting system. Before transactions can be recorded, however, they must be analyzed and assigned to their appropriate accounts. For example, a transaction for the cash purchase of supplies affects the assets of the company. In this case, the Cash and Supplies accounts (classified as asset accounts) are used to record this transaction in the accounting system.

All accounts that are used by a business and stored in the general ledger are grouped into their appropriate categories via an **account classification**. As shown in Figure 1.22, each account is assigned an account number that is used to identify the account and the category or group to which it belongs. Notice that the business assigns a four-digit account number to each account. The first digit of the account number is the account classification that identifies the general ledger category to which it belongs. The remaining three digits indicate the location of each account within the category and serve to further group the accounts. Holland Ad Agency assigns account numbers in increments of 10 so that new accounts can be added easily.

FIGURE 1.22

Chart of Accounts

**Holland Ad Agency
Chart of Accounts
09/01/—**

Assets

1110   Cash
1120   Supplies
1130   Prepaid Insurance

Liabilities

2110   Accounts Payable

Owner's Equity

3110   Julia Holland, Capital
3120   Julia Holland, Drawing

Revenue

4110   Fees

Expenses

5110   Advertising Expense
5120   Insurance Expense
5130   Legal Expense
5140   Miscellaneous Expense
5150   Rent Expense
5160   Supplies Expense
5170   Utilities Expense

In the chart of accounts in Figure 1.22, account numbers beginning with the digit 1 are classified as asset accounts. Account numbers that begin with the digit 2 are liabilities, and those that begin with the digit 3 are owner's equity accounts. Notice two additional account classifications have been added: revenue and expenses. Revenue accounts begin with the digit 4, and expense accounts begin with the digit 5. **Revenue accounts** are used to record the sale of goods or services, they have a normal credit balance, and they result in an increase in owner's equity. **Expense accounts** are used to record transactions for goods or services needed to operate the business, they have normal debit balances, and they result in a decrease in the asset account Cash (and, therefore, a decrease in owner's equity).

The Double-Entry Accounting System   The double-entry accounting system is based on recording debit and credit parts of a transaction so that the total dollar amount of debits and credits equal each other. The way the system is designed, each transaction affects at least two general ledger accounts. At least one debit or credit is recorded in each of these accounts in such a way that the entire system is always in balance. For example, a transaction in which $335.00 cash is paid for supplies affects the Cash and Supplies general ledger accounts. The Cash account is decreased by $335.00 and the Supplies account is increased by $335.00, which ensures that the accounting system remains in balance. To help analyze transactions and visualize their effect on accounts in the double-entry accounting system, we use a T account.

The T Account   Each account in the general ledger can be portrayed as consisting of three parts: (1) an account title, (2) a debit side, located on the left side, and (3) a credit side, located on the right side. This illustrative format of an account, shown in Figure 1.23, is called a *T* account because it resembles the letter T.

FIGURE 1.23

T Account

Account Title	
Debit Side (*Left Side*)	**Credit Side** (*Right Side*)

An entry made on the left side is called a debit (or debit entry), whereas an entry made on the right side is called a credit (or credit entry). Accounts are increased and decreased based on their normal account balance. To illustrate how this works, note how the accounting equation you worked with previously (which includes revenue and expense classifications) has been formatted into T accounts in Figure 1.24 with debit and credit sides for each account classification.

FIGURE 1.24

Accounting Equation (with T Accounts)

Assets		=	Liabilities		+	Owner's Equity	
Debit Side (*Left Side*) *for increases* **Normal Balance**	**Credit Side** (*Right Side*) *for decreases*		**Debit Side** (*Left Side*) *for decreases*	**Credit Side** (*Right Side*) *for increases* **Normal Balance**		**Debit Side** (*Left Side*) *for decreases*	**Credit Side** (*Right Side*) *for increases* **Normal Balance**

Revenue	
Debit Side (*Left Side*) *for decreases*	**Credit Side** (*Right Side*) *for increases* **Normal Balance**

Expenses	
Debit Side (*Left Side*) *for increases* **Normal Balance**	**Credit Side** (*Right Side*) *for decreases*

Notice that accounts classified as assets and expenses have a normal debit balance; accounts classified as liabilities, owner's equity, and revenue have normal credit balances. The basic rule that regulates increases and decreases in account balances states: *Account balances increase on the normal balance side of an account and decrease on the opposite side.* Therefore, a debit amount would increase an asset and expense account, whereas a credit would increase a liability, owner's equity, and revenue account. Similarly, a credit amount would decrease an asset and expense account, whereas a debit would decrease a liability, owner's equity, and revenue account. As stated another way: (1) Increases to accounts classified as assets and expenses are debited and decreases are credited, and (2)Increases to accounts classified as liabilities, owner's equity, and revenue are credited and decreases are debited.

Three Analytical Questions.   When recording a transaction, it is helpful to answer the following three questions in the order stated:

1. **What general ledger accounts are affected?** To obtain a list of the general ledger accounts refer to the chart of accounts.

2. **How is each of the affected accounts classified?** Holland Ad Agency classifies its accounts as assets, liabilities, owner's equity, revenue, and expenses.

3. **How is each amount entered in the affected accounts?** The amount is either debited or credited to increase or decrease the affected accounts' normal account balance.

Figure 1.25 illustrates the use of the previous three questions using the example in which $335.00 in cash is paid for supplies: (1) the Cash and Supplies general ledger accounts are affected, (2) both the Cash and Supplies accounts are classified as asset accounts, and (3) the Cash account is credited $335.00 (decreased because it has a normal debit balance) and the Supplies account is debited $325.00 (increased because it has a normal debit balance).

FIGURE 1.25
Transaction Analysis

Cash

Debit Side *(Normal Balance)*	*Credit Side*
	Decrease **$335.00**

Supplies

Debit Side Normal Balance	*Credit Side*
Increase **$335.00**	

Notice that the total amount of debits equals the total amount of credits. Therefore, the accounting system remains in balance after recording this transaction.

Explore Accounting System

When the Explore Accounting System menu item is chosen from the Reports menu, or the Explore toolbar button is clicked, the Explore Accounting System window will appear. The Explore Accounting System window is used to access data stored by the software to perform audit checks, check account activity, isolate errors, and other tasks helpful to managing account information. An example of the Explore Accounting System window showing all the Cash account data activity is shown in Figure 1.26.

Explore

To use the Explore Accounting System, select the plus box of the desired accounting system in the left frame and then click on the desired account.

FIGURE 1.26

*Explore Accounting
System Window*

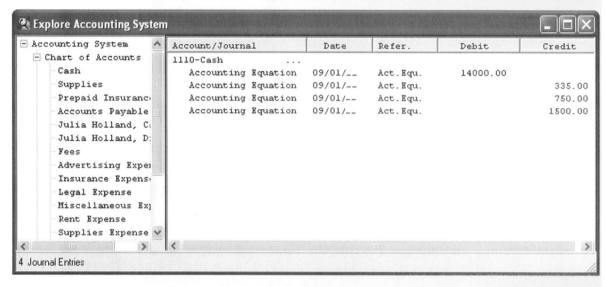

A detailed report will appear in the right frame showing the selected account's activity.

Information and the Internet Web Browser

When a file is loaded into the *Integrated Accounting* software, it is checked to determine if there is additional information helpful for problem solution. If such information exists, a dialog box is displayed indicating that this information may be displayed now (by clicking Yes) or later (by clicking No). At anytime during problem solution, click Info. on the toolbar to cause the computer to display the information provided for the current problem on your system's default Internet Web browser.

Three different types of information are provided by *Integrated Accounting*: (1) step-by-step problem instructions, (2) problem check figures, and (3) instructions for using your browser to access the Internet. Step-by-step problem instructions are used when the Demonstration. IA6 file is opened and loaded. These step-by-step instructions guide you through sample tasks designed to demonstrate many of features and capabilities of the software. Check figures are provided for the end-of-chapter A problems to assist you in problem solution. These check figures are especially helpful for those problems that require large amounts of data input. Finally, default instructions highlighting commonly used operating instructions for using your browser to complete the end-of-chapter optional Internet activities are provided.

If your computer has been set up on a local area network (LAN) or an Internet service provider's (ISP) program has been installed, then you are most likely ready to connect to the Internet. Figure 1.27 shows a browser window that appears when the Info. toolbar button is clicked or the Information menu item is chosen from the Reports menu. The browser

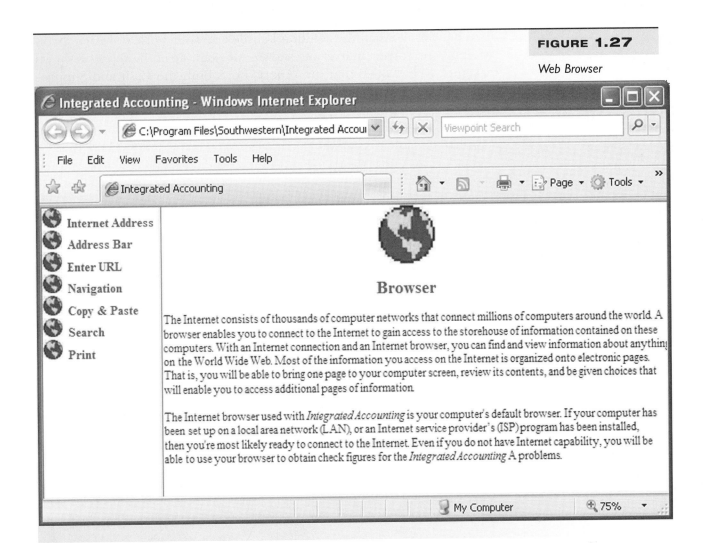

FIGURE 1.27

Web Browser

application window can be sized to fit within the *Integrated Accounting* window for ease of operation. An Internet Web Browser is *not* required to complete the problems in this text-workbook.

To learn how to use the basic operational features of your browser, click on the Info. toolbar button immediately after *Integrated Accounting* loads and before you open an accounting problem file. Then simply click on the desired Earth icon next to a topic in the left frame. Detailed instructional information about the selected topic will appear in the right frame.

Student Solution Checking

During installation of the *Integrated Accounting* software, the solution key files for end-of-chapter "Sample" and most "A" designated problems in this text-workbook were automatically included in the same folder as the software and opening balance data files. As you complete these problems, a Check feature may be used to assist you in checking your work. Once you have saved your work to disk, the Check toolbar button will become active. You may click on the Check toolbar button (see Figure 1.1) to initiate the student solution checking software. The student solution checking software will compare your work that is currently stored in memory with the appropriate solution key file. A detailed report will be generated identifying any discrepancies between the solution key file and your work. For each incorrect item, the correct item is also shown. An example of the report is shown in Figure 1.28. Notice that the report shows both the Cash and Supplies account balances to be incorrect. By going back to the Explore Accounting System feature and viewing the activity in the Cash and Supplies accounts, it can be observed that the cash amount paid for supplies (as shown in Figure 1.20) was entered incorrectly as $330.00 instead of $335.00; thereby causing the account balances in both the Cash and Supplies accounts to be incorrect by $5.00.

FIGURE 1.28

Student Solution Checker Report and Explorer Information

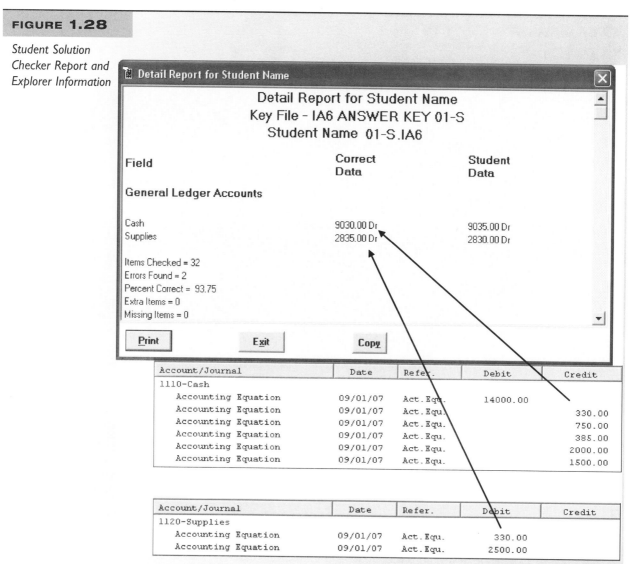

The student solution checking software checks the following items:

Accounting System: Business organization, type of business, departmental code, type of accounting system, required accounts, appropriation accounts, current account balances, previous year account balances, department numbers, vendor account balances, customer account balances, missing or extraneous accounts, missing or extraneous vendors, and missing or extraneous customers.

Fixed Assets: Missing and extraneous assets; and for each asset, purchase date, depreciation method, useful life, costs, salvage value, and general ledger account numbers.

Payroll: Missing and extraneous employees; and for each employee, social security number, number of pay periods, marital status, withholding allowances, general ledger account numbers, salary amount, hourly rate, piece rate, and commission. For each payroll transaction: transaction date, gross pay, federal income tax, state income tax, Social Security withheld, Medicare withheld, deduction one, deduction two, deduction three, regular hours worked, overtime hours worked, number of pieces produced, and commission sales.

Inventory: Missing or extraneous inventory items; and for each item, the units of measure, reorder point, quantity on hand, quantity on order, yearly quantity sold, yearly dollars sold, retail price, and last cost.

Chapter Summary

■ Accounting can be defined as an informational system that plans, analyzes, records, and reports financial information. An accountant summarizes detailed accounting information and then analyzes and interprets the information. In many cases, accountants are assisted by personnel called bookkeepers and accounting clerks.

■ A business is an economic entity that endeavors to sell goods and services to customers at prices that will cover the costs of doing business while returning a profit to the owners. The informational needs of today's businesses are stored and managed by what is called an MIS.

■ A user interface uses drop-down menus, toolbar, navigation buttons, movable overlapping windows, on-screen help, and other operational conventions.

■ *Integrated Accounting* contains integrated features designed to handle general ledger, accounts payable, accounts receivable, financial statement analysis, bank reconciliation, budgeting, fixed assets, purchase order processing, sales order processing, inventory, and payroll. In addition, data may be transferred to spreadsheet and word processing applications for a variety of other accounting-related uses.

■ Opening balance files must be opened and loaded before the end-of-chapter problems can be solved.

■ *Integrated Accounting* permits you to store data on a separate data disk, hard drive, or network file server for future reference or completion.

■ One way to communicate with the computer is through the menu bar. When a menu is chosen from the menu bar, a list of menu items that instruct the computer to perform its processing tasks display immediately below the menu title.

■ A window is a rectangular area of the screen in which the software communicates with the user. At times, two or more overlapping windows may appear on the screen. However, only one window is active at a time. *Integrated Accounting* uses several different windows to perform its accounting activities. Some windows contain tabs consisting of text boxes and grid cells used to enter data from the keyboard; some contain lists and reports; and others may display dialog box messages and operational information.

■ The File menu contains menu items used to handle files and print related input and output operations.

■ Navigation, or tab sequence, is the logical sequence in which the computer is expecting each grid cell, text box, button, and command to be accessed. The sequence is usually left to right and top to bottom. The focus identifies the location within a window in which the computer will receive the next piece of input.

■ The Help system provides a quick way to find information about operating the software. Information may be accessed by (1) choosing the Help Contents and Index menu item from the Help menu, (2) pressing the F1 key at any time, or (3) choosing the Help button that appears at the bottom of various windows.

■ The on-screen calculator can be accessed at any time and is operated like a handheld calculator. Results from the calculator can be copied and pasted into the text box that has the focus.

■ Planning tools are convenient, fast, easy-to-use ways of producing results for commonly used personal or business applications. The five planning tools provided in *Integrated Accounting* are: College, Savings, Loan, Retirement, and Notes & Interest.

■ The relationship among assets, liabilities, and owner's equity can be depicted by using the accounting equation: Assets = Liabilities + Owner's Equity.

■ Each account used by a business and stored in the general ledger is assigned an account number that identifies the account and the account classification to which it belongs.

■ The Explore Accounting System feature of the software accesses data stored by the computer to perform audit checks, check account activity, isolate errors, and complete other tasks helpful to managing account information.

■ The Information and Web Browser feature enables you to connect to the Internet and access check figure information for "A" problems in this text.

■ The purpose of the Check feature of the software is to assist you in checking your end-of-chapter "Sample" and "A" designed problems against solution key files as you complete these problems.

Sample Problem 1-S

Follow the step-by-step instructions in this problem to practice what you have learned in this chapter. Each step lists a task to be completed at the computer. More detailed information on how to complete the task is provided immediately following the step. If you need additional operating instructions to complete the task, refer back to the text material or access the *Integrated Accounting* Help system.

Before starting this problem, be sure you have a properly formatted data disk (or established a folder on a hard drive or network) for saving your data.

1 Start *Integrated Accounting* 6e.

2 Open the file named IA6 Problem 01-S.

Choose Open from the File menu or click on the Open toolbar button. When the Open file dialog box appears, choose file IA6 Problem 01-S from the list box. (If the opening balances files do not appear in the list, select the appropriate drive and folder containing the opening balances files, then choose file IA6 Problem 01-S.)

3 When the User Name dialog box appears, enter your name in the Your Name text box, and click OK.

Check carefully that you have entered your name correctly because you will not be able to change it for the duration of the problem.

4 Save the file to your disk or folder. Enter a file name of: 01-S followed by Your Name.

Choose *Save As* from the File menu or click on the *Save As* toolbar button and save the file to your disk and folder as: 01-S Your Name, where 01-S represents Chapter 1 Sample Problem.

5 Experiment with accessing the Help system.

Select the Help Contents and Index menu item from the Help menu or use the F1 function key to obtain information about accounting drills and planning tools.

6 Familiarize yourself with the use of the on-screen calculator by multiplying $245.00 by 5%.

Choose Calculator from the Extras menu or click on the Calc. toolbar button. When the calculator appears: type **245,** press the asterisk key (* for multiply), type **5,** and then press the % key. As an alternative, use the mouse to click on each of the appropriate keys to perform the calculation. The result should be **12.25.**

7 Calculate the annual contribution toward the cost of college using the College Planner.

Choose Planning Tools from the Extras menu or click Tools on the toolbar. When the Planning Tools window appears, click on the College Planner tab (if not already selected). Click on the *Annual Contribution* option in the Calculate section, and then enter the following information:

Beginning College Savings..........................$5,000.00
Annual Yield (Percent)...8.25
Years until College...8
Number of Years of College......................................4
Annual College Costs...............................$15,000.00

Press Tab after entering annual college costs and the calculated annual contribution will appear.

The College Savings Plan Schedules (Annual Contribution) is shown in Figure 1.29. Click Report to display the College Saving Plan, and then click the maximize button to expand the size of the display window.

The report consists of two schedules based on the data in the college planner. The first schedule shows the annual contribution, annual yield, and the total amount saved each year until college. The second schedule shows the effect of the $15,000.00 annual payments. Note that the amount of savings continues to generate interest. The calculated annual contribution is $4,104.60, which is the annual amount of savings required to provide $15,000.00 per year for 4 years of college expenses (given the other data provided). When finished, close the Report and Planning Tools windows.

FIGURE 1.29

College Savings Plan Schedules for Annual Contribution

College Savings Plan
09/01/—

Schedule of College Savings

Year	Annual Contribution	Annual Yield	College Savings
(Beginning Balance)			5,000.00
1	4,104.60	412.50	9,517.10
2	4,104.60	785.16	14,406.86
3	4,104.60	1,188.57	19,700.03
4	4,104.60	1,625.25	25,429.88
5	4,104.60	2,097.97	31,632.45
6	4,104.60	2,609.68	38,346.73
7	4,104.60	3,163.61	45,614.94
8	4,104.60	3,763.23	53,482.77

Schedule of College Payments

College Year	Annual Payments	Annual Yield	Savings Balance
(College Savings)			53,482.77
1	15,000.00	3,174.83	41,657.60
2	15,000.00	2,199.25	28,856.85
3	15,000.00	1,143.19	15,000.04
4	15,000.04		.00

8   Enter the following transactions into the accounting equation and display the accounting equation report.

Sept. I Received cash from owner as an investment, $14,000.00.

    2 Paid cash for supplies, $335.00.

    3 Paid cash for insurance, $750.00.

    4 Paid cash for legal expense, $385.00.

    5 Bought supplies on account, $2,500.00.

    6 Owner withdrew cash for personal use, $2,000.00.*

    7 Paid cash on account, $1,500.00.

a. Choose Accounting Drills by clicking on the Drills toolbar button.

b. Select the Accounting Equation tab.

c. Enter the accounting transactions (your entered transactions should match Figure 1.30). After entering the first line of transactions, press Enter or click OK to go to the next line.

FIGURE 1.30

Accounting Equation Tab

Cash	Supplies	Prepaid Insurance	Accounts Payable	Julia Holland, Capital	Julia Holland, Drawing	Fees	Advertising Expense	Insurance Expense	Legal Expense
14000.00				14000.00					
-335.00	335.00								
-750.00		750.00							
-385.00									385.00
	2500.00		2500.00						
-2000.00					2000.00				
-1500.00			-1500.00						

d. Click Report to obtain a display of your work, and then click the maximize button to expand the size of the Accounting Equation Report window (your report should match Figure 1.31). Click Close button.

* Julia Hollister, Drawing is a contra account. Contra accounts always reduce a related account. In this case, the owner's drawing account is a contra account (with a normal debit balance) to its related owner's capital account (with a normal credit balance).

Holland Ad Agency
Accounting Equation Report
09/01/—

Account	Classification	Description	Amount
Cash	Asset	Balance Forward	.00
		Transaction	14,000.00
		Transaction	−335.00
		Transaction	−750.00
		Transaction	−385.00
		Transaction	−2,000.00
		Transaction	−1,500.00
		New Balance	9,030.00
Supplies	Asset	Balance Forward	.00
		Transaction	335.00
		Transaction	2,500.00
		New Balance	2,835.00
Prepaid Insurance	Asset	Balance Forward	.00
		Transaction	750.00
		New Balance	750.00
Accounts Payable	Liability	Balance Forward	.00
		Transaction	2,500.00
		Transaction	−1,500.00
		New Balance	1,000.00
Julia Holland, Capital	Owner's Equity	Balance Forward	.00
		Transaction	14,000.00
		New Balance	14,000.00
Julia Holland, Drawing	Owner's Equity	Balance Forward	.00
		Transaction	2,000.00
		New Balance	2,000.00
Fees	Revenue	Balance Forward	.00
		New Balance	.00
Advertising Expense	Expense	Balance Forward	.00
		New Balance	.00
Insurance Expense	Expense	Balance Forward	.00
		New Balance	.00
Legal Expense	Expense	Balance Forward	.00
		Transaction	385.00
		New Balance	385.00
Miscellaneous Expense	Expense	Balance Forward	.00
		New Balance	.00
Rent Expense	Expense	Balance Forward	.00
		New Balance	.00
Supplies Expense	Expense	Balance Forward	.00
		New Balance	.00
Utilities Expense	Expense	Balance Forward	.00
		New Balance	.00
		Assets =	12,615.00
		Liabilities + Equity	12,615.00

Equation in Balance

9 **Identify account classifications, normal account balances, and debit or credit increases for each account in the general ledger.**

a. Choose Accounting Drills by clicking Drills on the toolbar, and then click on the Classify Accounts tab.

b. Select the desired account from the drop-down list by clicking on the drop-down arrow button and selecting one of the listed accounts. Click Next to proceed.

c. Select the account classification by clicking on the drop-down arrow button and selecting the appropriate account classification. Click Next to proceed.

d. Select the appropriate normal balance. Click Next to proceed.

e. Select whether the account is increased with a debit or credit. Click Finish.

f. Repeat steps (b) through (e) for each of the remaining accounts listed.

g. Click Report to obtain a display of your work (items that are incorrect are displayed in red). Click Close Report.

10 **Use the Explore Accounting System to display the Cash account's activity and current balance.**

Choose the Explore Accounting System by clicking on the Explore Accounting System menu item in the Reports menu or by clicking Explore on the toolbar.

Click on the plus sign (+) in front of Chart of Accounts in the left frame (a listing of all accounts will appear). Note that clicking on the Chart of Accounts title will cause the software to display a list of all the accounts in the chart of accounts.

Click on Cash in the left frame. The Cash account's activity will appear in the right frame.

Click on the Close box (X) in the upper right corner of the window to exit the Explore Accounting System.

11 **Check your work.**

Click Check on the toolbar to check your work against the solution key file. If errors appear, use the Explore Accounting System and editing features of the software to find and correct your errors.

12 **Access the Web Browser to learn how to find information on the World Wide Web.**

Choose the browser by clicking on the Information menu item in the Reports menu or by clicking Info. on the toolbar.

Click on the Earth icon in front of Search in the left frame. Read the corresponding information that appears in the right frame.

Click on the Close box (X) in the upper right corner of the window to exit the browser.

13 **Save the data file.**

Click Save on the toolbar. The file will be saved to disk with the current path and file name (note the file name in the title bar of the *Integrated Accounting* 6e application window).

INTERNET ACTIVITY

If you have access to the Internet, use the browser to find information about a national accounting association. *Hint:* Use a search argument of accounting organizations or national accounting associations to narrow your search. Select one of the associations and report your findings. Be sure to include the source and the URL (Web address) of your search.

14 **End the *Integrated Accounting 6e* session.**

Click on the Exit toolbar button.

Chapter 1 Student Exercises

NAME

I Matching

Directions *For each of the definitions, write the letter of the appropriate term in the space provided.*

a. Help system
b. option buttons
c. check boxes
d. command buttons
e. window
f. drop-down menu
g. list box
h. menu bar
i. toolbar
j. tab sequence
k. text boxes
l. insertion point
m. clipboard
n. focus
o. tooltips
p. grid cells
q. navigation buttons

1.____ The logical sequence in which the computer expects each text box, option button, or command to be traversed.

2.____ A bar displayed continuously on the top line of the screen, showing the menus available.

3.____ A list of items that appears immediately below the selected menu.

4.____ Fields in a window that are used to enter or change text.

5.____ A rectangular area of the screen in which the software communicates with the user.

6.____ A list of choices associated with a text box from which the user may choose.

7.____ Buttons representing options, where the selected option contains a filled circle icon and only one option may be selected.

8.____ A button that initiates an immediate action.

9.____ A box located to the left of each of several choices that contains either a blank or a ☑ and permits the user to select or deselect the choices.

10.____ A bar displayed on the top of the application window that contains icons representing common processing tasks that a user is most likely to perform.

11.____ An arrangement of rows and columns used to enter, edit, or delete data and text.

12.____ The location within a window in which the computer will receive the next piece of input as identified by a highlight bar, insertion point, or dotted box.

13.____ A character that appears when the mouse pointer is positioned over a text box to mark the current position where data will be entered or edited.

14.____ A provision within the software that offers a quick way to find information about key terms, what to enter into text boxes, the effect of option button settings, the steps required to perform a particular procedure, and shortcut keys the user may use to accomplish various tasks.

15.____ A brief informational message that automatically appears when the pointer is positioned on a toolbar button.

16.____ Buttons arranged in a vertical column along the left side of the display screen that facilitate fast, efficient, and intuitive movement throughout the accounting application.

17.____ A temporary storage area where data may be copied, then pasted elsewhere.

II Questions

Directions *Answer each of the following questions in the space provided.*

1. What is the definition of accounting? _____

2. What is the name of the occupation of a person who summarizes detailed accounting information, then analyzes, and interprets the information to assist owners and managers in making financial decisions? _____

3. What is a business? _____

4. What is an MIS? _____

5. State the accounting equation. _____

6. What is an account classification? _____

7. What is a double-entry accounting system? _____

8. What is the purpose of the Explore Accounting System? _____

9. What is the purpose of the Web browser? _____

10. Identify the five planning tools provided in *Integrated Accounting 6e.* _____

11. What is the purpose of the Check toolbar button? _____

Problem 1-A

The following problem provides practice of the applications described in this chapter. As you complete this problem, click Info. on the toolbar for helpful check figures to audit your work.

1   **Remove the Audit Test Questions 1-A at the end of this problem and fill in the answers as you work through the following steps.**

2   **Start *Integrated Accounting 6e.***

3   **Open and load file IA6 Problem 01-A.**

4   **Enter your name in the User Name dialog box.**

5   **Choose *Save As* and save the file to your disk or folder with a file name of 01-A Your Name.**

6   **Access the Help system to obtain information about using the Web browser to search the Internet.**

7   **Use the on-screen calculator to multiply $5225.50 by 2%.**

8   **Calculate the annual cost of college based on savings using the College Planner.**

With the Annual College Costs option set on, enter the following data, and then display the schedule of college savings and payments reports.

Beginning College Savings..........................$6,500.00
Annual Yield (Percent).............................7.75
Years until College...................................8
Number of Years of College....................4
Annual Contribution...............................$4,000.00

9   **Open the Accounting Drills window by clicking Drills on the toolbar; then select the Accounting Equation tab.**

Sept. 01   Received cash from owner as an investment, $10,000.00.

     02   Paid cash for supplies, $250.00.

     03   Paid cash for insurance, $395.00.

     04   Paid cash for advertising, $425.00.

     05   Bought supplies on account, $1,000.00.

     06   Owner withdrew cash for personal use, $1,500.00.

     06   Paid cash on account, $600.00.

10   **Display the accounting equation report.**

11   **Click Check on the toolbar to check your work.**

12 **Use the Classify Accounts tab in the Accounting Drills window to identify the account classification, normal account balance, and debit or credit increase for each of the following accounts:**

Cash
David Lorentz, Capital
Prepaid Insurance
Legal Expense
Miscellaneous Expense
Accounts Payable

13 **Display the classify accounts report.**

14 **Use the Explore Accounting System to display the Supplies account activity and current balance.**

15 **Save the data file.**

If you have access to the Internet, use the browser to find information about careers in the accounting field. *Hint:* Use a search string of accounting careers to narrow your search. Select one of the careers and report your findings. Be sure to include the source and the URL (Web address) of your search.

16 **End the *Integrated Accounting 6e* session.**

NOTE If you are using this product as a distance or online course, and your instructor has provided you his or her e-mail address, you may attach your solution files to your e-mail for electronic checking. Simply create an e-mail addressed to your instructor identifying yourself and this class, and attach your completed solution file (e.g., file 01-A Your Name). Your instructor will electronically check your work and then send you a report of the results. As an alternative, your instructor may ask you to use the Copy button of the checking software (software you used via the Check toolbar button) to copy and then paste the student solution checking report of your completed problems into your e-mail for his or her evaluation.

Audit Questions 1-A

NAME

Directions *Write the answers to the following questions in the space provided.*

1.　From the Help system, note the procedure for using the browser to search the Internet.

_____

_____

2.　What is the result of using the calculator to find 2% of $5,225.50?　_____

_____

3.　From the college planner, what is the calculated annual college payments?　_____

_____

4.　What is the total amount of assets shown on the accounting equation report?　_____

_____

5.　What account number is assigned to Fees?　_____

_____

6.　From the Explore Accounting System, note the transaction activity for the Supplies account.

_____

_____

Problem 1-B

The following problem provides practice of the applications described in this chapter.

1   **Remove the Audit Test Questions 1-B at the end of this problem and fill in the answers as you work through the following steps.**

2   **Start *Integrated Accounting 6e*.**

3   **Open and load file IA6 Problem 01-B.**

4   **Enter your name in the User Name dialog box.**

5   **Choose Save As and save the file to your disk or folder with a file name of 01-B Your Name.**

6   **Access the Help system to obtain information about copying *Integrated Accounting 6e* reports contents to the clipboard. (Hint: Enter copying as the search string in the search field of the Help system.)**

7   **Use the on-screen calculator to divide $50,820.00 by 12.**

8   **Calculate the annual cost of college based on savings using the College Planner.**

With the Annual College Costs option on, enter the following data, and then display the schedule of college savings and payments reports.

Beginning College Savings..........................$6,500.00
Annual Yield (Percent)..............................7.25
Years until College....................................12
Number of Years of College.........................4
Annual Contribution...............................$4,200.00

9   **Use the Accounting Equation tab in the Drills window to enter the following transactions.**

Sept. 01   Received cash from owner as an investment, $10,500.00.

       02   Paid cash for supplies, $375.00.

       02   Paid cash for insurance, $425.00.

       03   Bought supplies on account, $1,800.00.

       04   Paid cash for utility bills, $265.50.

       05   Owner withdrew cash for personal use, $2,500.00.

       06   Paid cash on account, $1,200.00.

10   **Display the accounting equation report.**

11   **Use the Classify Accounts tab in the Drills window to identify the account classification, normal account balance, and debit or credit increase for each of the following accounts:**

Supplies
Accounts Payable
Advertising Expense
Utilities Expense
David Lorentz, Drawing
Rent Expense

12   **Display the classify accounts report.**

13   **Use the Explore Accounting System to display the Accounts Payable account activity.**

14   **Save the data file.**

If you have access to the Internet, use the browser to find information about foreign currency exchange rates. *Hint:* Use a search string of world currency or foreign currency to narrow your search. Select one of the currency denominations and report your findings. Be sure to include the source and the URL (Web address) of your search.

INTERNET ACTIVITY

15   **End the *Integrated Accounting 6e* session.**

Audit Questions 1-B

NAME

Directions *Write the answers to the following questions in the space provided.*

1. From the Help system, note the procedure used to copy accounting data to the clipboard for pasting into word processor or spreadsheet applications. _____

   _____

2. What is the result of using the calculator to find the quotient of $50,820 divided by 12?

   _____

3. From the College Planner, what is the calculated annual college payments? _____

   _____

4. What is the total amount of assets shown on the accounting equation report? _____

   _____

5. What account number is assigned to Utilities Expense? _____

   _____

6. From the Explore Accounting System, note the transaction activity for Accounts Payable.

   _____

   _____

Accounting Cycle of a Service Business and Bank Reconciliation

Upon completion of this chapter, you will be able to:

- Enter additions, changes, and deletions to the chart of accounts.

- Enter and correct general journal transactions.

- Enter adjusting entries.

- Display account, journal, ledger, and financial statement reports.

- Generate graphs.

- Complete bank reconciliation.

- Generate and post closing entries.

Key Terms

accounting cycle *p44*	general journal report *p51*
adjusting entries *p48*	graph *p55*
balance sheet *p54*	income statement *p53*
bank reconciliation *p57*	journal *p45*
closing journal entries *p59*	maintaining accounts *p44*
component percentage *p53*	post-closing trial balance *p59*
copy and paste *p51*	posting *p45*
fiscal period *p44*	statement of owner's equity *p54*
general journal *p46*	

Introduction

Chapter 2 covers the ongoing process of accounting activities. You will see that the activities performed in computerized and manual accounting systems are quite similar. The major difference is that in a computerized accounting system, the computer does a good deal of the detail work (i.e., posting journal entries, analyzing and generating closing entries, and preparing financial reports and statements).

An **accounting cycle** includes all accounting activities, beginning with entering transactions and ending with closing. In both systems, the accounting cycle is usually completed each fiscal period. A **fiscal period**, also known as an accounting period, is defined as a regular interval of time for which a business analyzes its financial information. Most of the problems that accompany this text assume a fiscal period of a calendar year. Because the income statement provided by the accounting software provides monthly and yearly information, the adjusting entries are recorded at the end of each month. However, closing is not performed until the end of the year.

Later in this chapter, you will be taken through a typical computerized accounting cycle and monthly bank reconciliation for a service business. The chart of accounts will be updated and transactions will be recorded for the months of November and December for Morgan Consulting. All accounting activities through year-end closing will be covered.

Chart of Accounts Maintenance

A business's chart of accounts must be maintained. **Maintaining accounts** may involve adding new accounts to the chart of accounts, changing account numbers and titles, and deleting inactive accounts. The Accounts tab in the Account Maintenance window will be used to accomplish this task. When the Maintain Accounts menu item is chosen from the Data menu, the Accts. toolbar button is clicked on, or the Gen. Led. navigation button and its Maintain Accounts menu button is clicked, the Account Maintenance window will appear. Click on the Accounts tab to display the chart of accounts maintenance shown in Figure 2.1.

FIGURE 2.1

Account Maintenance

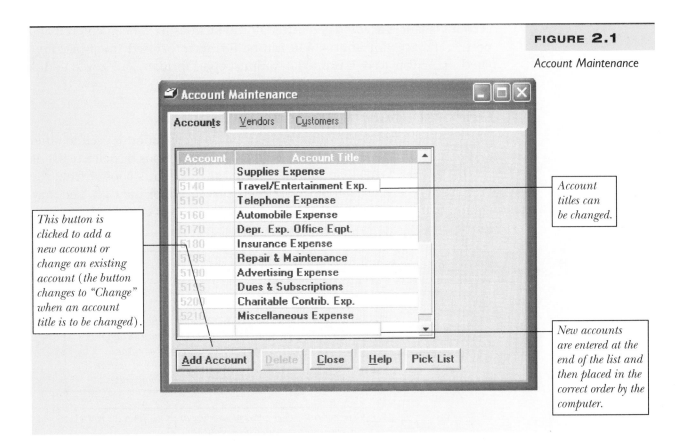

This button is clicked to add a new account or change an existing account (the button changes to "Change" when an account title is to be changed).

Account titles can be changed.

New accounts are entered at the end of the list and then placed in the correct order by the computer.

New accounts may be added by typing the account number and account title after the last item in the list and then clicking the Add Account button. The new account will be inserted into the chart of accounts in account number sequence. Existing account titles may be changed by selecting the account you wish to change, typing the correct account title, and then clicking on the Change Account button (the Add Account button changes to Change). An existing account may be deleted by simply selecting the account and clicking the Delete button.

 The account number cannot be changed. An account with an incorrect account number must be deleted then added back as a new account with the correct number. Also, general ledger accounts cannot be deleted unless the account being deleted has a zero balance.

When Pick List is clicked, a master chart of accounts list will appear. A later chapter will demonstrate how to use this account list to create a chart of accounts for a new business' computerized accounting system.

General Journal

A **journal** is a record of the debit and credit parts of each transaction recorded in date sequence. A journal does not show the current account balance of individual accounts. Therefore, the journal entry information must be transferred to a general ledger account. This process of updating the ledger account balances with all debits and credits is called **posting**.

Journals

The computer stores each account title and balance used by a business. As transactions are entered and posted to a journal, the appropriate ledger account balances are updated. After all transactions have been entered and posted, the account information can be further processed (totals accumulated, etc.), displayed or printed in various report formats, and stored to disk for recall at a later time.

General Journal Transactions

The **General Journal** tab within the Journal Entries window is used to enter and post general journal entries and to make corrections or delete existing journal entries. When the Journal Entries menu item is chosen from the Data menu, the Journal toolbar button is clicked on, or the Gen. Led. navigation button and its Journal Entries menu button is clicked, the Journal Entries window shown in Figure 2.2 will appear.

FIGURE 2.2

Journal Entries

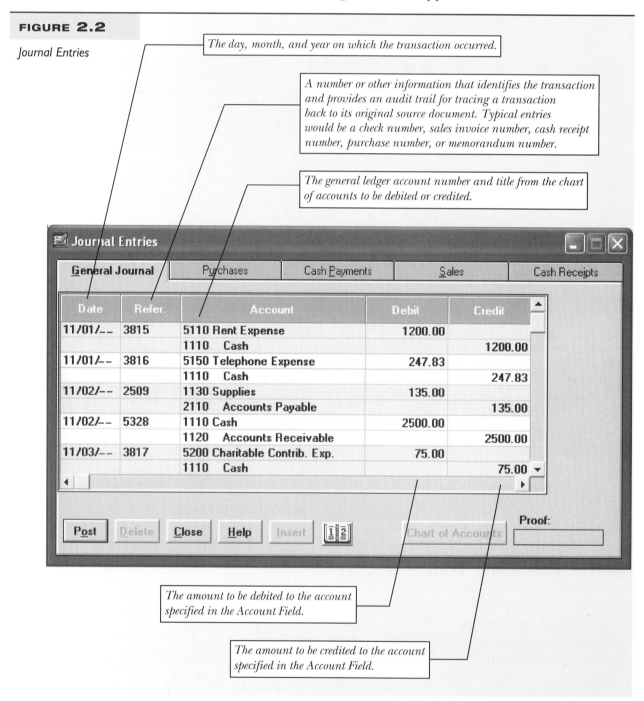

When the general journal first appears, the date column will contain the date of the last transaction that was entered (even if it was entered in a previous session). Press the (+) key to increase the date or the (−) key to decrease the date. Continue to press either key until the appropriate date appears. You could also key the day of the month. As another alternative, you may click on the calendar icon and select the desired date when the calendar appears.

The Refer. column will contain the next number in sequence after the last transaction that was entered. During the entering of journal entry transactions, the computer will attempt to intuitively anticipate the correct reference even if different, multiple references have been entered. If there are no transactions on file, the date column will contain a default date and the reference column will be blank.

Enter the account number, or first character of the account title, and then press the Tab key. The account number will be displayed along with its account title. As an alternative, and while the Account Grid Cell has the focus, click the Chart of Accounts button to display the chart of accounts selection list. Select an account and click OK.

Enter the debit or credit amount and then press the Tab key. Continue entering the account and debit or credit amounts for each part of the journal entry. When the journal entry is complete, click the Post button.

 NOTE A new general ledger account can be added, changed, or deleted while entering a journal entry. Choose the Maintain Accounts menu item from the Data menu or click on the Accts. toolbar button. When the Account Maintenance window appears, click on the Accounts tab to call up the Accounts window.

Changing or Deleting General Journal Transactions

Existing general journal transactions may be changed or deleted. Simply select the transaction that you wish to change, enter the corrections to the transaction, and click Post. If you wish to delete the transaction, click Delete.

Adding Lines to a Transaction

To add lines to an existing transaction, select the transaction and click on the Insert button. A blank line will be inserted at the end of the selected transaction on which you may enter the additional debit or credit part.

 NOTE To insert another blank line, press the Tab key. If you accidentally insert a blank line, leave it. It will be removed when the journal is posted.

Finding a Journal Entry

While a journal is displayed, you can use the Find menu item from the Edit menu to locate and display any previously entered transaction. The Find Journal Entry dialog box is shown in Figure 2.3.

FIGURE 2.3

Find Journal Entry Dialog Box

Find Journal Entry ☒

Find What: [   ]

[OK]   [Cancel]   [Help]

Enter the date, reference, amount, or any other data of the transaction you want to find in the Find What text box and click on the OK button. If a matching transaction is found, it will be displayed in the journal so that it may be changed or deleted. By choosing the Find Next item in the Edit menu you will locate the next occurrence of the search criteria.

Adjusting Entries

Changes entered into the computer to update general ledger accounts at the end of a fiscal period are called **adjusting entries**. Portions of assets such as supplies and prepaid insurance are consumed during the fiscal period and become expenses of the business. For example, the amount of supplies that have been consumed must be deducted from the Supplies asset account and entered in the Supplies Expense account. The amount of prepaid insurance that has expired must be deducted from the Prepaid Insurance asset account and entered in the Insurance Expense account.

Adjusting entries are not entered in the general journal until *after* all other transactions for the accounting period have been recorded, entered into the computer, and posted. The trial balance is then displayed or printed. This trial balance and the period-end adjustment data are the basis for the adjusting entries. The adjusting entries may now be entered into the computer and posted. Finally, a display of the journal entries in a journal entries report proves the equality of the debits and credits.

All the adjusting entries are for the same date and have the same information in the reference column (Adj.Ent.). A sample trial balance, before adjustments are made, is shown in Figure 2.4.

The adjustment data for Morgan Consulting follows. The adjusting entries have been entered into the general journal and are illustrated in Figure 2.5.

Insurance expired during November	$95.00
Inventory of supplies on November 30	$982.50
Depreciation on office equipment for November	$402.75

 NOTE The adjustment amount for Supplies is calculated as follows: Balance in Supplies from trial balance ($1,295.75) − current supplies inventory ($982.50) = supplies adjustment ($313.25).

Marlow Consulting
Trial Balance
11/30/—

FIGURE **2.4**

Trial Balance before Adjusting Entries

Acct. Number	Account Title	Debit	Credit
1110	Cash	9,042.17	
1120	Accounts Receivable	4,417.31	
1130	Supplies	1,295.75	
1140	Prepaid Insurance	530.00	
1510	Office Equipment	48,122.00	
1511	Accum. Depr. Office Eqpt.		14,833.00
2110	Accounts Payable		260.18
3110	Joyce Morgan, Capital		36,458.74
3120	Joyce Morgan, Drawing	33,500.00	
4110	Consulting Fees		109,907.73
5110	Rent Expense	16,200.00	
5120	Salary Expense	20,495.38	
5130	Supplies Expense	4,305.52	
5140	Travel/Entertainment Exp.	4,557.80	
5150	Telephone Expense	2,480.01	
5160	Automobile Expense	6,420.68	
5170	Depr. Exp. Office Eqpt.	4,027.88	
5180	Insurance Expense	692.25	
5185	Repair & Maintenance	400.00	
5190	Advertising Expense	3,175.00	
5195	Dues & Subscriptions	150.00	
5200	Charitable Contrib. Exp.	310.00	
5210	Miscellaneous Expense	1,337.90	
	Totals	161,459.65	161,459.65

Date	Refer.	Account	Debit	Credit
11/30/--	Adj.Ent.	5180 Insurance Expense	95.00	
		1140 Prepaid Insurance		95.00
11/30/--	Adj.Ent.	5130 Supplies Expense	313.25	
		1130 Supplies		313.25
11/30/--	Adj.Ent.	5170 Depr. Exp. Office Eqpt.	402.75	
		1511 Accum. Depr. Office Eqpt.		402.75

FIGURE **2.5**

General Journal (Adjusting Entries)

In a manual accounting system, a worksheet is used as a tool for analyzing the adjusting entries and preparing the financial statements. Because the computer generates the financial statements automatically from the general ledger data, a worksheet is not required for a computerized accounting system. Therefore, once the adjusting entries have been entered, posted, and verified, the financial statements may be displayed.

Reports

When the Reports Selection menu item is chosen from the Reports menu, Reports on the toolbar is selected, or the Gen. Led. navigation button and the desired reports menu button (journal, general ledger, financial statements, or financial statement analysis) is clicked, the Report Selection dialog box shown in Figure 2.6 will appear. The Run Date text box at the top right corner contains the date that will appear on the report. This date may be changed by entering a new date or by clicking on the calendar icon and using the calendar as discussed previously.

FIGURE 2.6

Report Selection Dialog Box

Based on the option button chosen in the Select a Report Group, a list of all reports within that chosen option will appear.

Report Selection

Select a Report Group:

- Account Lists
- Journals
- Ledger Reports
- Financial Statements
- Financial Analysis

Run Date: 11/30/— —

Choose a Report to Display:

General Journal
Purchases Journal
Cash Payments Journal
Sales Journal
Cash Receipts Journal
All Journals

OK   Close   Help

Option buttons are provided for various types of accounting system reports. Based on the option button chosen in the Select a Report Group, a list of all the reports within that chosen option will appear. Select the desired report and click OK. If insufficient data are available to generate a particular report, that report item will be dimmed to indicate that it is not active. The corresponding information displayed in the report window can be printed on an attached printer or copied for inclusion in another application (e.g., spreadsheet or word processor).

Printing the Contents of a Report Window

Any time a report is displayed in a report window, it can be printed by choosing the Print command button located at the bottom of the window. When the Print button is clicked, a Print Setup dialog box will appear that allows you to choose the printer, print orientation, and so on. The specific printer characteristics used by *Integrated Accounting* (resolution of print quality, paper size, paper source etc.) are those specified for the current default printer (as specified in the Print Setup menu item in the File menu). Click OK to proceed.

Copying Report Information to the Clipboard in Spreadsheet and Word Processor Formats

While a report is displayed in a report window, its entire contents can be copied to the clipboard, thereby replacing any previous contents. Once copied to the clipboard, the report may be pasted (or copied) to another application currently running in the computer. For example, a trial balance report displayed in a report window can be copied to the clipboard and then pasted into a spreadsheet or word processing document. This procedure is commonly referred to as **copy and paste**.

To copy and paste a report to the clipboard, click the Copy button located at the bottom of the report window. The dialog box shown in Figure 2.7 will appear. Select the desired option button for spreadsheet or word processor format and click OK. The entire report will be copied to the clipboard.

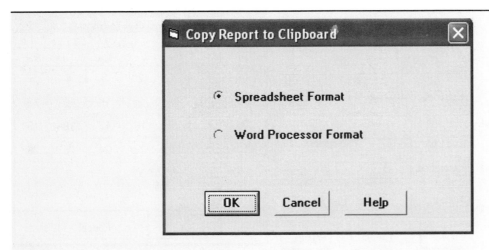

FIGURE 2.7

Copy Report to Clipboard

General Journal Report

The Journals option in the Report Selection list permits you to select journal reports and to specify which journal entries are to appear in the report. The **general journal report** is useful in detecting errors and verifying the equality of debits and credits. This report becomes a permanent accounting document, and it provides an audit trail so that transactions may be traced to their original source document.

To display a general journal report, choose the Report Selection menu item from the Reports menu, click Reports on the toolbar, or click on the Gen. Led. navigation button and its Journal Reports menu button. When the Report Selection window appears, choose the Journals option, select the General Journal report, and click OK. The Journal Report Selection dialog box shown in Figure 2.8 will appear, allowing you to display all the general journal entries or customize your general journal report.

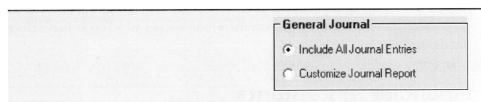

FIGURE 2.8

Journal Report Selection Dialog Box

Choose the Customize Journal Report option to control the data to be included on the report. If you want to include *all* journal transactions on the report, choose the Include All Journal Entries option. When the Customize Journal Report option is chosen, the dialog box shown in Figure 2.9 will appear. Notice the calendar appears on the right side of the dialog box because the calendar icon (located next to the start and end dates) was clicked. (An example of a general journal report for the month of November is shown in Figure 2.21 on page 66.)

FIGURE 2.9

*Customize Journal
Report Dialog Box*

Restricts the report to only those items within (and including) the start and end dates.

Restricts the report to only those items containing the specified reference.

Restricts the report to only those items containing the specified account number.

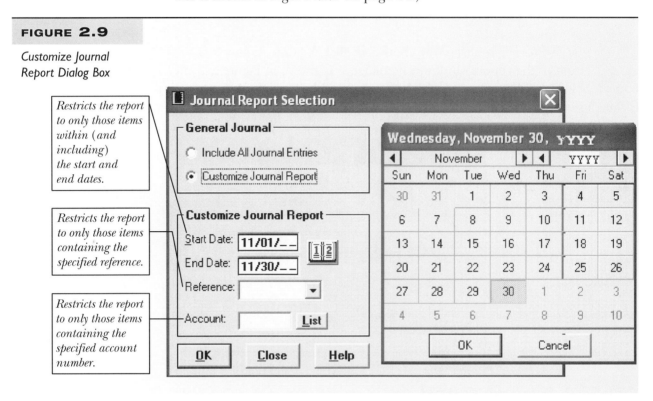

Enter the desired start and end dates. As an alternative, select the Start or End date text box, then click on the calendar icon. When the calendar appears, as shown in Figure 2.9, select the desired date (the selected date will be placed in the text box that has the focus).

Enter an identifying reference in the Reference text box if you wish to restrict the report to a particular reference by clicking on the drop-down arrow to obtain a list of all the references available. Use the up and down arrow keys to browse through the entries. For example, you might want to display only adjusting entries or only a certain invoice.

As an alternative, you may type the first character of the reference in the text box. The first entry that begins with that character will automatically be displayed in the text box.

Enter an account number in the Account Number text box if you wish to restrict the report to a particular account by clicking on the List button to obtain a chart of accounts selection list window from which you may select the desired account number.

Financial Statements

Any nondepartmentalized business that is organized as a sole proprietorship may have three types of financial statements: the income statement, statement of owner's equity, and balance sheet. To display financial statements select the Report Selection menu item from the Report menu, click on the Reports toolbar button or the click the Gen. Led. navigation button and its Financial statements menu button. Select the desired financial statement, and click OK.

Income Statement

The **income statement** provides information on a business' net income or net loss over a specific period of time. The up-to-date account balances stored by the computer are used to compute and display the revenue earned and the expenses incurred during a fiscal period. The difference between total revenue and total expenses is the net income (if this difference is negative, it is the net loss).

Integrated Accounting offers two formats of the income statement. Figure 2.10 illustrates the format used in this chapter. It shows the profitability of the business for the current month and for the year to date. The second format shows the business's profitability from the beginning of the fiscal period until the time when the income statement is displayed. Both formats calculate a **component percentage** that indicates each amount's percentage of total operating revenue.

FIGURE 2.10

Income Statement by Month and Year

> Click on any yearly account amount to cause the Show Detail button to appear.

**Morgan Consulting
Income Statement
For Period Ended 11/30/—**

	Monthly Amount	Monthly Percent	Yearly Amount	Yearly Percent
Operating Revenue				
Consulting Fees	9,525.00	100.00	109,907.73	100.00
Total Operating Revenue	9,525.00	100.00	109,907.73	100.00
Operating Expenses				
Rent Expense	1,200.00	12.60	16,200.00	14.74
Salary Expense	2,054.38	21.57	20,495.38	18.65
Supplies Expense	313.25	3.29	4,618.77	4.20
Travel/Entertainment Exp.	253.80	2.66	4,557.80	4.15
Telephone Expense	247.83	2.60	2,480.01	2.26
Automobile Expense	340.68	3.58	6,420.68	5.84
Depr. Exp. Office Eqpt.	402.75	4.23	4,430.63	4.03
Insurance Expense	95.00	1.00	787.25	0.72
Repair & Maintenance	400.00	4.20	400.00	0.36
Advertising Expense	425.00	4.46	3,175.00	2.89
Dues & Subscriptions	150.00	1.57	150.00	0.14
Charitable Contrib. Exp.	75.00	0.79	310.00	0.28
Miscellaneous Expense	50.00	0.52	1,337.90	1.22
Total Operating Expenses	6,007.69	63.07	65,363.42	59.47
Net Income	3,517.31	36.93	44,544.31	40.53

Income Statement Account Detail   The income statement contains a useful feature that aids in isolating errors or auditing account balances by allowing you to view and print the details of any account. While the income statement is displayed, click on any account balance. (A Show Detail command button will appear.) Click Show Detail to view the selected account's activity. Click Print to obtain a hard copy, or click Return to the Income Statement to return to the original Report Viewer Window. (An example of an income statement account detail report is shown in Figure 2.27 on page 72.)

Statement of Owner's Equity

The **statement of owner's equity** shows the changes to owner's equity that occurred during the fiscal period. The statement lists capital at the beginning of the period, shows any additions and subtractions to capital, and concludes with the capital at the end of the fiscal period. Business owners can review this report to determine whether their equity is increased or decreased and what might be causing the change. Changes to owner's equity are caused by additional investments, withdrawals, and net income or net loss. A sample owner's equity statement is shown in Figure 2.11.

FIGURE 2.11

Owner's Equity Statement

Morgan Consulting
Statement of Owner's Equity
For Period Ended 11/30/—

Joyce Morgan, Capital (Beg. of Period)	36,458.74
Joyce Morgan, Drawing	−33,500.00
Net Income	44,544.31
Joyce Morgan, Capital (End of Period)	47,503.05

Balance Sheet

The **balance sheet** provides information on the overall financial strength of a business as of a specific date (see Figure 2.12). Account balances stored by the computer are used to compute and display the business' assets, liabilities, and owner's equity at any time (because the computer's account balances are always up to date). Likewise, the balance sheet may be displayed at any time. A strong business must have adequate assets and few liabilities.

Balance Sheet Account Detail   Like the income statement, the balance sheet contains a feature that permits you to view and print the details of any account. While the balance sheet is displayed, click on any account balance. (A Show Detail command button will appear.) Click Show Detail to view the selected account's activity. Click Print to obtain a hard copy, or click Return to the Balance Sheet to return to the original Report Viewer Window. (An example of a balance sheet account detail report is shown in Figure 2.30 on page 74.)

FIGURE 2.12

Balance Sheet

Morgan Consulting
Balance Sheet
11/30/—

Assets		
Cash	9,042.17	
Accounts Receivable	4,417.31	
Supplies	982.50	
Prepaid Insurance	435.00	
Office Equipment	48,122.00	
Accum. Depr. Office Eqpt.	−15,235.75	
Total Assets		47,763.23
Liabilities		
Accounts Payable	260.18	
Total Liabilities		260.18
Owner's Equity		
Joyce Morgan, Capital	36,458.74	
Joyce Morgan, Drawing	−33,500.00	
Net Income	44,544.31	
Total Owner's Equity		47,503.05
Total Liabilities & Equity		47,763.23

Graphing

Graphs

Many accounting packages are capable of producing graphs of data contained within their files. **Graph** refers to a pictorial representation of data that can be depicted on a computer screen or printed. Computer-generated graphs are used to clarify the meaning of the words and numbers that appear. Graphs are commonly used to enhance presentations, track sales, monitor expenses, identify trends, and make forecasts. To generate graphs, simply choose the Graph Selection menu item from the Reports menu or click Graphs on the toolbar and the Graph Selection dialog box shown in Figure 2.13 will appear.

FIGURE 2.13

*Graph Selection
Dialog Box*

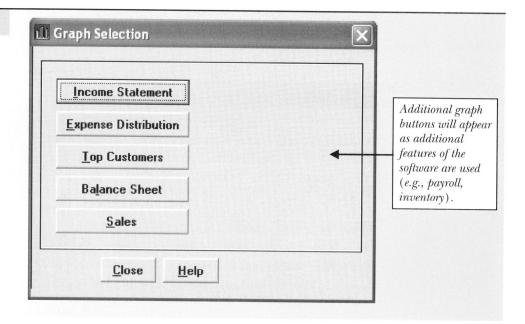

When the desired graph button is clicked, a three-dimensional graph illustrating the appropriate data will appear. Figure 2.14 shows an expense distribution graph generated by the *Integrated Accounting* software.

FIGURE 2.14

*Expense Distribution
Graph*

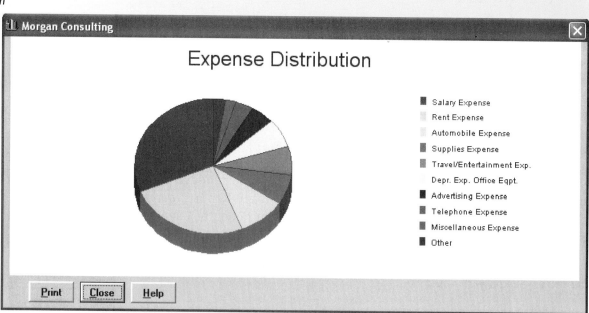

This pie chart illustrates the relative account balances in each of the expense accounts. In addition, it clearly shows that salary expense is the largest expense followed by rent expense.

Bank Reconciliation

The bank statement is reconciled to the checkbook balance every month. The **bank reconciliation** software is accessed either via the Other Tasks menu item in the Data menu, the Tasks Toolbar button, or the Banking navigation button and its Bank Reconciliation menu item. Information maintained by the computer, such as the checkbook balance and checks that were written during the period, will automatically be provided to make the reconciliation process simpler and more accurate.

To complete the bank reconciliation, choose the Other Tasks menu item from the Data menu, click on Tasks on the toolbar button, or click the Gen. Led. navigation button and its Bank Reconciliation menu button. When the Other Tasks window appears, click the Clear button, which will cause the computer to erase any previous reconciliation data. Enter the bank credit, bank charge, bank statement balance, and outstanding deposit amounts. Figure 2.15 shows a sample bank reconciliation.

 The Cash account balance automatically appears in the Checkbook Balance text box, and the checks written during the period are displayed in a list box. If necessary, you may key a different checkbook balance amount.

Select the outstanding checks by moving the pointer to the Checks from the Journal list, selecting the desired check (point and click to highlight), and then clicking the Select (or double-click on the desired check). The selected check will be moved to the Outstanding Checks list, and the Adjusted Bank Balance will be automatically updated. Repeat this procedure for each outstanding check.

 Click OK to record your data and to dismiss the bank reconciliation. Click Clear if you want to erase all the data entered or selected in the bank reconciliation.

FIGURE 2.15

Bank Reconciliation

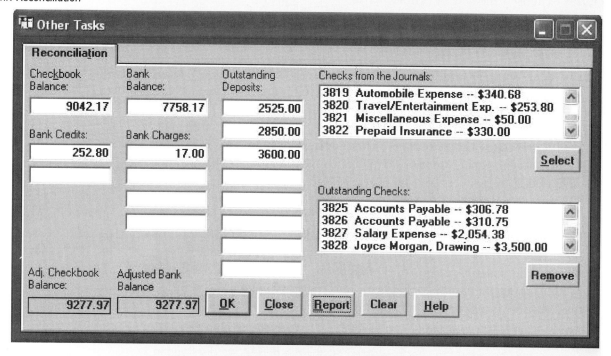

Click Report command button to display the bank reconciliation report. The completed and reconciled bank reconciliation report is shown in Figure 2.16. Notice that the adjusted checkbook balance is equal to the adjusted bank balance. Finally, after bank reconciliation has been completed, bank credit and bank charge amounts are entered into the general journal and posted to update Cash and other related account balances.

FIGURE 2.16

Bank Reconciliation Report

Morgan Consulting
Bank Reconciliation
11/30/—

Checkbook Balance		9042.17
Plus Bank Credits:		
	252.80	
		252.80
Less Bank Charges:		
	17.00	
		17.00
Adjusted Checkbook Balance		9277.97
Bank Statement Balance		7758.17

(continued)

FIGURE 2.16

(Concluded)

Plus Outstanding Deposits:			
		2525.00	
		2850.00	
		3600.00	
			8975.00
Less Outstanding Checks:			
	3823	487.63	
	3824	795.66	
	3825	306.78	
	3826	310.75	
	3827	2054.38	
	3828	3500.00	
			7455.20
Adjusted Bank Balance			9277.97

Closing Journal Entries

At the end of the fiscal period in a manual accounting system, closing entries are recorded in the journal and posted to the general ledger. In the computerized accounting system, the computer automatically generates and displays the **closing journal entries** to close all of the temporary income statement accounts to the income summary account, close the income summary account to the capital account, and close the drawing account to the capital account. When these closing entries are posted, the computer also copies the current account balances and stores them as the last fiscal period's account balances for use with financial statement analysis.

In the *Integrated Accounting* system, the closing journal entries remain stored by the computer after they are posted. Therefore, corrections can be made to the previous year's data if necessary.

After the period-end closing procedure is completed, a **post-closing trial balance** report verifies that debits equal credits in the general ledger accounts. In the *Integrated Accounting* system, the only difference between a regular trial balance and a post-closing trial balance is the time *when* each is displayed.

To generate the closing journal entries, choose the Generate Closing Journal Entries menu item from the Options menu, or click on the Gen. Led. navigation button and its Generate Closing Entries menu button. (The dialog box shown in Figure 2.17 will appear.)

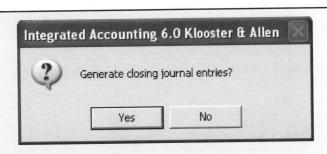

FIGURE 2.17

Generate Closing Journal Entries

Click Yes to proceed. A dialog box showing the closing entries automatically generated by the computer will appear. (Figure 2.18 shows the closing entries that were generated after all the December transactions and adjusting entries were entered and posted.)

FIGURE 2.18

Closing Entries

Closing Entries

Acct. #	Account Title	Debit	Credit
4110	Consulting Fees	119882.73	
3130	Income Summary		119882.73
3130	Income Summary	71654.85	
5110	Rent Expense		17400.00
5120	Salary Expense		22549.76
5130	Supplies Expense		4980.37
5140	Travel/Entertainment Exp.		4673.15
5150	Telephone Expense		2726.95
5160	Automobile Expense		6825.68
5170	Depr. Exp. Office Eqpt.		4835.79
5180	Insurance Expense		867.25
5185	Repair & Maintenance		685.00
5190	Advertising Expense		3925.00
5195	Dues & Subscriptions		450.00
5200	Charitable Contrib. Exp.		360.00
5210	Miscellaneous Expense		1375.90
3130	Income Summary	48227.88	
3110	Joyce Morgan, Capital		48227.88
3110	Joyce Morgan, Capital	36500.00	
3120	Joyce Morgan, Drawing		36500.00

Post   Cancel   Help

Click on Post button to instruct the computer to post the closing entries and store the last fiscal period's account balances for future use. The general journal will appear to show that the closing entries were posted with a reference of "Clo.Ent."

If an error is detected after closing, complete the following steps: (1) correct the erroneous journal entry, (2) delete the closing entries, and (3) again generate, display, and post the closing journal entries. If a closing entry is in error, correct the entry and post. Be sure to print another post-closing trial balance.

Journal entries may be purged (removed) from the system at any time or on reaching the maximum capacity of 600 journal entries. (This will not arise for any of the problems in this text-workbook.) Because the account balances are updated as journal entries are posted, all account balances will be correct after the journal entries are purged. Therefore, no information will be lost. The Purge Journal Entries menu item is located in the Options menu.

Chapter Summary

■ All accounting activities, beginning with entering transactions and ending with closing, make up an accounting cycle. The accounting cycle is usually completed during an interval of time known as a fiscal period.

- The Accounts tab within the Account Maintenance window is used to add new accounts to the chart of accounts, change account titles, and delete inactive accounts.

- A journal is used to record the debit and credit parts of each transaction in date sequence.

- Posting is the process of updating the ledger account balances with all debits and credits that affect each account.

- As transactions are entered and posted into the appropriate journal, the ledger account balances are automatically updated.

- The General Journal tab within the Journal Entries window is used to enter and post general journal entries and to make corrections to or delete existing journal entries.

- The Find menu item may be used to locate any previously entered journal entry.

- Adjusting entries are not entered into the general journal until all other transactions for the accounting period have been entered into the computer and posted. The trial balance is then displayed or printed. This trial balance and the period-end adjustment data are the basis for the adjusting entries.

- The general journal report is useful in detecting errors and verifying the equality of debits and credits.

- The income statement provides information on the net income or net loss of a business over a specific period of time. A component percentage is included for each amount on the income statement. This percentage indicates each amount's percentage of total operating revenue.

- The statement of owner's equity shows the changes to owner's equity that have occurred during the fiscal period.

- The balance sheet provides information on the overall financial strength of a business as of a specific date (usually at the end of a fiscal period).

- Graphs produced by the computer are used to clarify the meaning of the words and numbers, enhance presentations, track sales, monitor expenses, identify trends, and make forecasts.

- Information maintained by the computer, such as the checkbook balance and checks that were written during the period, are automatically included in the bank reconciliation to make the reconciliation process simpler and more accurate.

- The computer automatically generates, displays, and posts the closing journal entries. The process closes all temporary income statement accounts to the income summary account, closes the income summary account to the capital account, and closes the drawing account to the capital account. During posting, the computer also copies the current account balances and stores them as the last fiscal period's account balances for use in financial statement analysis.

Sample Problem 2-S

The operating procedures introduced in this chapter will be used in this computer problem. To complete the problem, follow the step-by-step instructions provided. Each step lists a task to be completed at the computer. More detailed information on how to complete the task is provided immediately following the step. Also, remember that the Help system is always available.

The transactions for Morgan Consulting occurred during the period of November 1 through November 30 of the current year. The general journal entries are illustrated within the step-by-step instructions (see Figure 2.19). Maintenance data for the chart of accounts are also provided.

1   Start *Integrated Accounting* 6e.

2   Load the opening balances problem file, IA6 Problem 02-S.

3   Enter your name in the Your Name text box and click on OK.

4   Save the file to your disk and folder with a file name of 02-S Your Name.

5   Enter the additions to the chart of accounts.

Click on the Gen. Led. navigation button (located along the left side of the screen). Click on Maintain Accounts menu button and enter the following maintenance data:

Add Repair & Maintenance to the chart of accounts. Assign account number 5185 for Repair & Maintenance so that it will be positioned immediately following Insurance Expense.

Add Dues & Subscriptions to the chart of accounts. Assign account number 5195 to Dues & Subscriptions so that it will be positioned immediately following Advertising Expense.

6   Enter the general journal transactions shown in Figure 2.19.

Click on the Gen. Led. navigation button and then the Journal Entries menu button. When the Journal Entries window appears, click on the General Journal tab (if not already the focus) and enter the following transactions. The reference numbers to be keyed into the journal are the check numbers and invoice numbers provided in the following transaction statements. When you are finished, your general journal should appear as shown in Figure 2.19.

General Journal Transactions

Nov. 01   Paid cash for month's rent, $1,200.00; Check No. 3815.

01   Paid cash for monthly telephone bill, $247.83; Check No. 3816.

02   Purchased supplies on account, $135.00; Invoice No. 2509.

02   Received cash on account, $2,500.00; Sales Invoice No. 5328.

03   Paid cash for charitable contribution, $75.00; Check No. 3817.

03   Paid cash on account, $95.40; Check No. 3818.

03   Purchased supplies on account, $310.75; Invoice No. 2510.

06   Paid cash for mileage reimbursement, $340.68; Check No. 3819. Charge to Automobile Expense.

06   Purchased computer repair services on account, $400.00; Invoice No. 2511.

07   Paid cash for travel expenses, $253.80; Check No. 3820.

07   Purchased office equipment on account, $225.00; Invoice No. 2512.

09   Billed client for services rendered, $2,525.00; Invoice No. 5432.

09   Received cash on account, $1,210.15; Sales Invoice No. 5430.

13   Billed client for services rendered, $3,250.00; Invoice No. 5433.

14   Purchased advertising on account, $425.00; Invoice No. 2513.

14   Paid cash for flowers, $50.00; Check No. 3821. Charge to Miscellaneous Expense.

17   Purchased a newsletter subscription on account, $150.00; Invoice No. 2514.

20   Billed client for services rendered, $3,750.00; Invoice No. 5434.

22   Paid cash for fire and theft insurance, $330.00; Check No. 3822.

27   Paid cash on account, $487.63; Check No. 3823.

27   Paid cash on account, $795.66; Check No. 3824.

28   Received cash on account, $2,525.00; Sales Invoice No. 5432.

28   Received cash on account, $2,850.00; Sales Invoice No. 5431.

30   Paid cash on account, $306.78; Check No. 3825.

30   Paid cash on account, $310.75; Check No. 3826.

30   Received cash on account, $3,500.00; Sales Invoice No. 5429.

30   Paid monthly salaries, $2,054.38; Check No. 3827.

30   Owner withdrew cash for personal use, $3,500.00; Check No. 3828.

FIGURE 2.19

Completed General Journal Window

Date	Refer.	Account	Debit	Credit
11/01/--	3815	5110 Rent Expense	1200.00	
		1110 Cash		1200.00
11/01/--	3816	5150 Telephone Expense	247.83	
		1110 Cash		247.83
11/02/--	2509	1130 Supplies	135.00	
		2110 Accounts Payable		135.00
11/02/--	5328	1110 Cash	2500.00	
		1120 Accounts Receivable		2500.00
11/03/--	3817	5200 Charitable Contrib. Exp.	75.00	
		1110 Cash		75.00
11/03/--	3818	2110 Accounts Payable	95.40	
		1110 Cash		95.40
11/03/--	2510	1130 Supplies	310.75	
		2110 Accounts Payable		310.75
11/06/--	3819	5160 Automobile Expense	340.68	
		1110 Cash		340.68
11/06/--	2511	5185 Repair & Maintenance	400.00	
		2110 Accounts Payable		400.00
11/07/--	3820	5140 Travel/Entertainment Exp.	253.80	
		1110 Cash		253.80
11/07/--	2512	1510 Office Equipment	225.00	
		2110 Accounts Payable		225.00
11/09/--	5432	1120 Accounts Receivable	2525.00	
		4110 Consulting Fees		2525.00
11/09/--	5430	1110 Cash	1210.15	
		1120 Accounts Receivable		1210.15
11/13/--	5433	1120 Accounts Receivable	3250.00	
		4110 Consulting Fees		3250.00
11/14/--	2513	5190 Advertising Expense	425.00	
		2110 Accounts Payable		425.00
11/14/--	3821	5210 Miscellaneous Expense	50.00	
		1110 Cash		50.00
11/17/--	2514	5195 Dues & Subscriptions	150.00	
		2110 Accounts Payable		150.00
11/20/--	5434	1120 Accounts Receivable	3750.00	
		4110 Consulting Fees		3750.00
11/22/--	3822	1140 Prepaid Insurance	330.00	
		1110 Cash		330.00
11/27/--	3823	2110 Accounts Payable	487.63	
		1110 Cash		487.63
11/27/--	3824	2110 Accounts Payable	795.66	
		1110 Cash		795.66
11/28/--	5432	1110 Cash	2525.00	
		1120 Accounts Receivable		2525.00
11/28/--	5431	1110 Cash	2850.00	
		1120 Accounts Receivable		2850.00
11/30/--	3825	2110 Accounts Payable	306.78	
		1110 Cash		306.78
11/30/--	3826	2110 Accounts Payable	310.75	
		1110 Cash		310.75
11/30/--	5429	1110 Cash	3500.00	
		1120 Accounts Receivable		3500.00
11/30/--	3827	5120 Salary Expense	2054.38	
		1110 Cash		2054.38
11/30/--	3828	3120 Joyce Morgan, Drawing	3500.00	
		1110 Cash		3500.00

7   Display the chart of accounts.

Click on the Gen. Led. navigation button, and then the Journal Reports menu button. When the Report Selection window appears, choose the Account Lists option from the Select a Report Group. Select the Chart of Accounts report from the Choose a Report to Display list (if not already highlighted), and click OK. Click the maximize button to expand the size of the display window. Examine the report in Figure 2.20, and verify that the accounts you entered in Step 5 are correct.

FIGURE 2.20

Chart of Accounts Report

Morgan Consulting
Chart of Accounts
11/30/—

Assets

1110	Cash
1120	Accounts Receivable
1130	Supplies
1140	Prepaid Insurance
1510	Office Equipment
1511	Accum. Depr. Office Eqpt.

Liabilities

2110	Accounts Payable

Owner's Equity

3110	Joyce Morgan, Capital
3120	Joyce Morgan, Drawing
3130	Income Summary

Revenue

4110	Consulting Fees

Expenses

5110	Rent Expense
5120	Salary Expense
5130	Supplies Expense
5140	Travel/Entertainment Exp.
5150	Telephone Expense
5160	Automobile Expense
5170	Depr. Exp. Office Eqpt.
5180	Insurance Expense
5185	Repair & Maintenance
5190	Advertising Expense
5195	Dues & Subscriptions
5200	Charitable Contrib. Exp.
5210	Miscellaneous Expense

8 Display the general journal report.

From the Report Selection window, choose the Journals option and the General Journal report, and then click OK. When the Journal Report Selection window appears, choose the Customize Journal Report option. Set the Start Date to 11/01/– and the End Date to 11/30/– (where – is the current year). Then click OK. Remember, click the maximize button to expand the size of the display window. *Note:* If the transactions were entered correctly, the start and end dates will be the default dates set automatically by the computer. The computer uses the first day of the month as the start date and the latest date of the general journal transactions that were entered as the end date. The general journal report is shown in Figure 2.21.

FIGURE 2.21

General Journal Entries Report

Morgan Consulting
General Journal
11/30/—

Date	Refer.	Acct.	Title	Debit	Credit
11/01	3815	5110	Rent Expense	1,200.00	
11/01	3815	1110	Cash		1,200.00
11/01	3816	5150	Telephone Expense	247.83	
11/01	3816	1110	Cash		247.83
11/02	2509	1130	Supplies	135.00	
11/02	2509	2110	Accounts Payable		135.00
11/02	5328	1110	Cash	2,500.00	
11/02	5328	1120	Accounts Receivable		2,500.00
11/03	3817	5200	Charitable Contrib. Exp.	75.00	
11/03	3817	1110	Cash		75.00
11/03	3818	2110	Accounts Payable	95.40	
11/03	3818	1110	Cash		95.40
11/03	2510	1130	Supplies	310.75	
11/03	2510	2110	Accounts Payable		310.75
11/06	3819	5160	Automobile Expense	340.68	
11/06	3819	1110	Cash		340.68
11/06	2511	5185	Repair & Maintenance	400.00	
11/06	2511	2110	Accounts Payable		400.00
11/07	3820	5140	Travel/Entertainment Exp.	253.80	
11/07	3820	1110	Cash		253.80
11/07	2512	1510	Office Equipment	225.00	
11/07	2512	2110	Accounts Payable		225.00
11/09	5432	1120	Accounts Receivable	2,525.00	
11/09	5432	4110	Consulting Fees		2,525.00
11/09	5430	1110	Cash	1,210.15	
11/09	5430	1120	Accounts Receivable		1,210.15

(continued)

11/13	5433	1120	Accounts Receivable	3,250.00	
11/13	5433	4110	Consulting Fees		3,250.00
11/14	2513	5190	Advertising Expense	425.00	
11/14	2513	2110	Accounts Payable		425.00
11/14	3821	5210	Miscellaneous Expense	50.00	
11/14	3821	1110	Cash		50.00
11/17	2514	5195	Dues & Subscriptions	150.00	
11/17	2514	2110	Accounts Payable		150.00
11/20	5434	1120	Accounts Receivable	3,750.00	
11/20	5434	4110	Consulting Fees		3,750.00
11/22	3822	1140	Prepaid Insurance	330.00	
11/22	3822	1110	Cash		330.00
11/27	3823	2110	Accounts Payable	487.63	
11/27	3823	1110	Cash		487.63
11/27	3824	2110	Accounts Payable	795.66	
11/27	3824	1110	Cash		795.66
11/28	5432	1110	Cash	2,525.00	
11/28	5432	1120	Accounts Receivable		2,525.00
11/28	5431	1110	Cash	2,850.00	
11/28	5431	1120	Accounts Receivable		2,850.00
11/30	3825	2110	Accounts Payable	306.78	
11/30	3825	1110	Cash		306.78
11/30	3826	2110	Accounts Payable	310.75	
11/30	3826	1110	Cash		310.75
11/30	5429	1110	Cash	3,500.00	
11/30	5429	1120	Accounts Receivable		3,500.00
11/30	3827	5120	Salary Expense	2,054.38	
11/30	3827	1110	Cash		2,054.38
11/30	3828	3120	Joyce Morgan, Drawing	3,500.00	
11/30	3828	1110	Cash		3,500.00
			Totals	33,803.81	33,803.81

FIGURE 2.21

(Concluded)

9 **Use the auditor and error correction features of the software to correct the following error:**

It was discovered that sales invoice number 5429, on November 30, was recorded as $100.00 less than the actual amount of cash received.

a. Click on the Explore toolbar button.

b. When the Explore Accounting System window appears, click on the Plus box preceding Chart of Accounts.

c. When the list of accounts appears in the left window pane, click on Accounts Receivable. Then, maximize the window.

d. In the right window pane, make a note of the amount of the incorrect credit to accounts receivable for sales invoice number 5429 on November 30, then exit the Explore window.

e. Click on the Gen. Led. navigation and the Journal Entries menu buttons to return to the general journal.

f. Find the incorrect journal entry, key the correct amount into both parts of the entry (the noted incorrect amount plus $100.00), and post the corrected journal entry.

10 **Display the corrected general journal report for the month of November.**

The corrected general journal report is shown in Figure 2.22.

FIGURE 2.22			**Morgan Consulting**		
			General Journal		
General Journal Entries Report			**11/30/—**		

Date	Refer.	Acct.	Title	Debit	Credit
11/01	3815	5110	Rent Expense	1,200.00	
11/01	3815	1110	Cash		1,200.00
11/01	3816	5150	Telephone Expense	247.83	
11/01	3816	1110	Cash		247.83
11/02	2509	1130	Supplies	135.00	
11/02	2509	2110	Accounts Payable		135.00
11/02	5328	1110	Cash	2,500.00	
11/02	5328	1120	Accounts Receivable		2,500.00
11/03	3817	5200	Charitable Contrib. Exp.	75.00	
11/03	3817	1110	Cash		75.00
11/03	3818	2110	Accounts Payable	95.40	
11/03	3818	1110	Cash		95.40
11/03	2510	1130	Supplies	310.75	
11/03	2510	2110	Accounts Payable		310.75
11/06	3819	5160	Automobile Expense	340.68	
11/06	3819	1110	Cash		340.68
11/06	2511	5185	Repair & Maintenance	400.00	
11/06	2511	2110	Accounts Payable		400.00
11/07	3820	5140	Travel/Entertainment Exp.	253.80	
11/07	3820	1110	Cash		253.80
11/07	2512	1510	Office Equipment	225.00	
11/07	2512	2110	Accounts Payable		225.00
11/09	5432	1120	Accounts Receivable	2,525.00	
11/09	5432	4110	Consulting Fees		2,525.00
11/09	5430	1110	Cash	1,210.15	
11/09	5430	1120	Accounts Receivable		1,210.15
11/13	5433	1120	Accounts Receivable	3,250.00	
11/13	5433	4110	Consulting Fees		3,250.00

(continued)

11/14	2513	5190	Advertising Expense	425.00	
11/14	2513	2110	Accounts Payable		425.00
11/14	3821	5210	Miscellaneous Expense	50.00	
11/14	3821	1110	Cash		50.00
11/17	2514	5195	Dues & Subscriptions	150.00	
11/17	2514	2110	Accounts Payable		150.00
11/20	5434	1120	Accounts Receivable	3,750.00	
11/20	5434	4110	Consulting Fees		3,750.00
11/22	3822	1140	Prepaid Insurance	330.00	
11/22	3822	1110	Cash		330.00
11/27	3823	2110	Accounts Payable	487.63	
11/27	3823	1110	Cash		487.63
11/27	3824	2110	Accounts Payable	795.66	
11/27	3824	1110	Cash		795.66
11/28	5432	1110	Cash	2,525.00	
11/28	5432	1120	Accounts Receivable		2,525.00
11/28	5431	1110	Cash	2,850.00	
11/28	5431	1120	Accounts Receivable		2,850.00
11/30	3825	2110	Accounts Payable	306.78	
11/30	3825	1110	Cash		306.78
11/30	3826	2110	Accounts Payable	310.75	
11/30	3826	1110	Cash		310.75
11/30	5429	1110	Cash	3,600.00	
11/30	5429	1120	Accounts Receivable		3,600.00
11/30	3827	5120	Salary Expense	2,054.38	
11/30	3827	1110	Cash		2,054.38
11/30	3828	3120	Joyce Morgan, Drawing	3,500.00	
11/30	3828	1110	Cash		3,500.00
			Totals	33,903.81	33,903.81

Corrected journal entry

FIGURE 2.22

(Concluded)

11   Display a trial balance.

Choose Ledger Reports in the Report Selection window, select Trial Balance, and click OK. A trial balance report will appear as shown in Figure 2.23.

Morgan Consulting
Trial Balance
11/30/—

Acct. Number	Account Title	Debit	Credit
1110	Cash	9,042.17	
1120	Accounts Receivable	4,417.31	
1130	Supplies	1,295.75	
1140	Prepaid Insurance	530.00	
1510	Office Equipment	48,122.00	

(continued)

FIGURE 2.23

Trial Balance Report

FIGURE 2.23

(Concluded)

1511	Accum. Depr. Office Eqpt.		14,833.00
2110	Accounts Payable		260.18
3110	Joyce Morgan, Capital		36,458.74
3120	Joyce Morgan, Drawing	33,500.00	
4110	Consulting Fees		109,907.73
5110	Rent Expense	16,200.00	
5120	Salary Expense	20,495.38	
5130	Supplies Expense	4,305.52	
5140	Travel/Entertainment Exp.	4,557.80	
5150	Telephone Expense	2,480.01	
5160	Automobile Expense	6,420.68	
5170	Depr. Exp. Office Eqpt.	4,027.88	
5180	Insurance Expense	692.25	
5185	Repair & Maintenance	400.00	
5190	Advertising Expense	3,175.00	
5195	Dues & Subscriptions	150.00	
5200	Charitable Contrib. Exp.	310.00	
5210	Miscellaneous Expense	1,337.90	
	Totals	161,459.65	161,459.65

12 Enter the adjustment data for the month of November for Morgan Consulting.

Click on the Gen. Led. navigation button, and then the Journal Entries menu button. When the Journal Entries window appears, click on the General Journal tab (if not already the focus) and enter the adjusting entries. The entered adjustment data are depicted in Figure 2.5 on page 49.

Insurance expired during November $95.00
Inventory of supplies on November 30 ....$982.50
Depreciation on office equipment for November.........................$402.75

13 Display the adjusting entries.

Click the Gen. Led. navigation button, and then the Journal Reports menu button. When the Reports Selection dialog box appears, choose the Journals option button, select the General Journal report, and click OK. When the Journal Report Selection dialog box appears (Figure 2.24), choose the Customize Journal Report option, and enter a reference restriction of Adj.Ent. so that only the adjusting entries are reported.

 NOTE When the A in Adj.Ent. is entered, the computer searches the drop-down list, finds the matching reference, and places it in the Reference text box. The report appears in Figure 2.25.

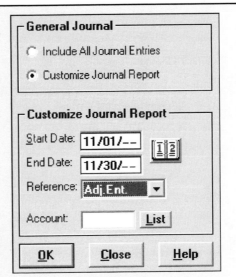

FIGURE **2.24**

Journal Report Selection Dialog Box

FIGURE **2.25**

General Journal Report (Adjusting Entries)

Morgan Consulting
General Journal
11/30/—

Date	Refer.	Acct.	Title	Debit	Credit
11/30	Adj.Ent.	5180	Insurance Expense	95.00	
11/30	Adj.Ent.	1140	Prepaid Insurance		95.00
11/30	Adj.Ent.	5130	Supplies Expense	313.25	
11/30	Adj.Ent.	1130	Supplies		313.25
11/30	Adj.Ent.	5170	Depr. Exp. Office Eqpt.	402.75	
11/30	Adj.Ent.	1511	Accum. Depr. Office Eqpt.		402.75
			Totals	811.00	811.00

14   Display the income statement.

Choose the Financial Statements option button from the Report Selection Dialog box, select the Income Statement report, and click OK. If desired, click the maximize button to expand the size of the display window. The income statement is shown in Figure 2.26.

FIGURE **2.26**

Income Statement

Morgan Consulting
Income Statement
For Period Ended 11/30/—

	Monthly Amount	Monthly Percent	Yearly Amount	Yearly Percent
Operating Revenue				
Consulting Fees	9,525.00	100.00	109,907.73	100.00
Total Operating Revenue	9,525.00	100.00	109,907.73	100.00
				(continued)

FIGURE 2.26

(Concluded)

Operating Expenses				
Rent Expense	1,200.00	12.60	16,200.00	14.74
Salary Expense	2,054.38	21.57	20,495.38	18.65
Supplies Expense	313.25	3.29	4,618.77	4.20
Travel/Entertainment Exp.	253.80	2.66	4,557.80	4.15
Telephone Expense	247.83	2.60	2,480.01	2.26
Automobile Expense	340.68	3.58	6,420.68	5.84
Depr. Exp. Office Eqpt.	402.75	4.23	4,430.63	4.03
Insurance Expense	95.00	1.00	787.25	0.72
Repair & Maintenance	400.00	4.20	400.00	0.36
Advertising Expense	425.00	4.46	3,175.00	2.89
Dues & Subscriptions	150.00	1.57	150.00	0.14
Charitable Contrib. Exp.	75.00	0.79	310.00	0.28
Miscellaneous Expense	50.00	0.52	1,337.90	1.22
Total Operating Expenses	6,007.69	63.07	65,363.42	59.47
Net Income	3,517.31	36.93	44,544.43	40.53

15 Display the yearly Consulting Fees account detail from the income statement.

Click on the yearly amount of Consulting Fees ($109,907.73), then click Show Detail. The account detail is shown in Figure 2.27. Note, in this sample problem, only detail data for the month of November exist.

FIGURE 2.27

*Yearly Consulting Fees
Account Detail*

Morgan Consulting
General Ledger
11/30/– –

Account	Journal	Date	Refer.	Debit	Credit	Balance
4110-Consulting Fees						
	Balance Forward					100,382.73 Cr
	General	11/09	5432		2,525.00	102,907.73 Cr
	General	11/13	5433		3,250.00	106,157.73 Cr
	General	11/20	5434		3,750.00	109,907.73 Cr

16 Display the statement of owner's equity.

Select the Statement of Owner's Equity report, then click OK. The report is shown in Figure 2.28.

FIGURE 2.28

Statement of Owner's Equity

Morgan Consulting
Statement of Owner's Equity
For Period Ended 11/30/—

Joyce Morgan, Capital (Beg. of Period)	36,458.74
Joyce Morgan, Drawing	−33,500.00
Net Income	44,544.31
Joyce Morgan, Capital (End of Period)	47,503.05

17   Display the balance sheet.

Select the Balance Sheet report, then click OK. The balance sheet is shown in Figure 2.29.

FIGURE 2.29

Balance Sheet

Morgan Consulting
Balance Sheet
11/30/—

Assets		
Cash	9,042.17	
Accounts Receivable	4,417.31	
Supplies	982.50	
Prepaid Insurance	435.00	
Office Equipment	48,122.00	
Accum. Depr. Office Eqpt.	−15,235.75	
Total Assets		47,763.23
Liabilities		
Accounts Payable	260.18	
Total Liabilities		260.18
Owner's Equity		
Jackie Marlow, Capital	36,458.74	
Jackie Marlow, Drawing	−33,500.00	
Net Income	44,544.31	
Total Owner's Equity		47,503.05
Total Liabilities & Equity		47,763.23

18   Display the Cash account detail from the balance sheet.

Click on the Cash amount ($9,042.17), then click Show Detail. The cash account detail is shown in Figure 2.30. Note, in this sample problem, only detail data for the month of November exist. Also, make sure that sales invoice number 5429, on November 30 (as per Step 9), appears corrected.

FIGURE 2.30

Cash Account Detail

Morgan Consulting
General Ledger
11/30/--

Account	Journal	Date	Refer.	Debit	Credit	Balance
1110-Cash						
	Balance Forward					6,404.93 Dr
	General	11/01	3815		1,200.00	5,204.93 Dr
	General	11/01	3816		247.83	4,957.10 Dr
	General	11/02	5328	2,500.00		7,457.10 Dr
	General	11/03	3817		75.00	7,382.10 Dr
	General	11/03	3818		95.40	7,286.70 Dr
	General	11/06	3819		340.68	6,946.02 Dr
	General	11/07	3820		253.80	6,692.22 Dr
	General	11/09	5430	1,210.15		7,902.37 Dr
	General	11/14	3821		50.00	7,852.37 Dr
	General	11/22	3822		330.00	7,522.37 Dr
	General	11/27	3823		487.63	7,034.74 Dr
	General	11/27	3824		795.66	6,239.08 Dr
	General	11/28	5432	2,525.00		8,764.08 Dr
	General	11/28	5431	2,850.00		11,614.08 Dr
	General	11/30	3825		306.78	11,307.30 Dr
	General	11/30	3826		310.75	10,996.55 Dr
	General	11/30	5429	3,600.00		14,596.55 Dr
	General	11/30	3827		2,054.38	12,542.17 Dr
	General	11/30	3828		3,500.00	9,042.17 Dr

19 **Generate a three-dimensional expense distribution graph.**

Click Graphs on the toolbar. When the Graph Selection dialog box appears, click Expense Distribution. The three-dimensional expense distribution pie chart that results is shown in Figure 2.31.

FIGURE 2.31

*Expense Distribution
Pie Chart*

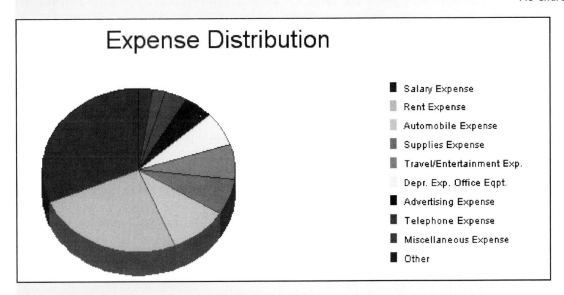

20 Process the bank reconciliation data.

Click on the Banking navigation button, and then click on the Bank Reconciliation menu button. When the Bank Reconciliation active tab appears, enter the bank credit, bank charge, balance shown on bank statement, and outstanding deposit amounts. (The checkbook balance will be provided by the computer.) To enter the outstanding checks, move the pointer to the Checks from the Journal list, select the desired check (point and click to highlight), and click Select. The selected check will appear in the Outstanding Checks list, and the Adjusted Bank Balance will automatically be updated. Repeat this procedure for each outstanding check.

Checkbook balance...$9,042.17
Bank credit $252.80
Bank charge $17.00
Balance shown on bank statement..........................$7,758.17
Outstanding deposits as follows:
$2,525.00
$2,850.00
$3,600.00
Outstanding checks as follows:

Check No.	Amount
3823	$487.63
3824	$795.66
3825	$306.78
3826	$310.75
3827	$2,054.38
3828	$3,500.00

21   **Display the bank reconciliation report.**

Click Report located at the bottom of Bank Reconciliation. The report is shown in Figure 2.16. Click Close, and when you are prompted to record changes, select No.

> **NOTE** Typically, after the bank reconciliation is complete, bank credit and bank charge amounts are entered into the general journal and posted to update Cash and other related account balances. However, these journal entries will not be entered in this problem (or the end-of-chapter A and B problems that follow) to keep the size of the chart of accounts minimal and to concentrate on the material discussed in this chapter.

22   **Check your work.**

Click Check on the toolbar. If errors appear, use the Explorer and other error correction features of the software to correct your errors.

23   **Save the data file.**

Click Save on the toolbar.

24   **Optional Spreadsheet Activity.**

Morgan Consulting has asked you to create a spreadsheet report showing only the amount of accounts receivable during the month of November from the accounting system data. To complete this task, follow the steps:

a. Display and copy the general journal report to the clipboard in spreadsheet format. Follow the procedure in Step 8 to display the general journal report. When the general journal report appears, click on the Copy button and select the option to copy the report to the clipboard in spreadsheet format.

b. Start your spreadsheet software.

c. Open and load spreadsheet template file: IA6 Spreadsheet 02-S. (The file will be found in the default folder where the *Integrated Accounting* software was installed.)

d. Select cell A1 as the current cell (if not already selected).

e. Paste the general journal report (copied to the clipboard in Step a) into the spreadsheet. Select the Paste item from the Edit menu.

f. Delete all rows of data that are not accounts receivable/consulting fees transactions.

g. Change the title of the report from General Journal to Accounts Receivable.

h. Replace the old totals with the sum of the debit and credit columns. Enter formulas in the appropriate format for your spreadsheet software.

i.   Format the spreadsheet to match the completed spreadsheet shown in Figure 2.32.

j.   Print the completed report.

k.   Save your spreadsheet file to your disk or folder with a file name of: 02-S Your Name.

l.   End your spreadsheet session and return to the *Integrated Accounting* application.

Student Name

Morgan Consulting
Accounts Receivable
As of 11/30/—

Date	Refer.	Acct.	Title	Debit	Credit
09-Nov	5432	1120	Accounts Receivable	$2,525.00	
09-Nov	5432	4110	Consulting Fees		$2,525.00
13-Nov	5433	1120	Accounts Receivable	$3,250.00	
13-Nov	5433	4110	Consulting Fees		$3,250.00
20-Nov	5434	1120	Accounts Receivable	$3,750.00	
20-Nov	5434	4110	Consulting Fees		$3,750.00
			Totals	$9,525.00	$9,525.00

FIGURE 2.32

Spreadsheet Cash Receipts Report (November)

If you have access to the Internet, use the browser to identify accounting professional organizations in other countries. For example, use Australia Accounting, Canada Accounting, South Africa Accounting, and so on, to narrow your search. Report your findings. Be sure to include the source and the URL (Web address) of your search.

INTERNET ACTIVITY

25   End the *Integrated Accounting* session.

Chapter 2 Student Exercises

NAME

I Matching

Directions *For each of the definitions, write the letter of the appropriate term in the space provided.*

a. accounting cycle
b. fiscal period
c. maintaining accounts
d. journal
e. posting
f. general journal
g. adjusting entries
h. general journal report

i. income statement
j. component percentage
k. balance sheet
l. statement of owner's equity
m. graph
n. closing journal entries
o. post-closing trial balance
p. bank reconciliation

1. _____ A pictorial representation of data that can be produced by the computer and depicted on the screen and printer.

2. _____ A tab used to enter and post general journal entries and to make corrections or delete existing journal entries.

3. _____ The process of updating the ledger accounts with all debits and credits affecting each account.

4. _____ A display or printout that is useful in detecting errors and verifying the equality of debits and credits.

5. _____ The process of adding new accounts, changing titles of existing accounts, and deleting inactive accounts from the chart of accounts.

6. _____ A financial statement used to show the changes that have occurred to the owner's equity during the fiscal period.

7. _____ A financial statement that provides information on the net income or net loss of a business over a period of time.

8. _____ A financial statement that provides information on the overall financial strength of a business.

9. _____ A value that represents a percent of total operating revenue.

10. _____ The process that involves all accounting activities, beginning with entering transactions and ending with closing.

11. _____ A regular interval of time for which a business analyzes its financial information.

12. _____ A record of the debit and credit parts of each transaction recorded in date sequence.

13. _____ Changes entered into the computer to update general ledger accounts at the end of a fiscal period.

14. _____ Journal entries automatically generated by the computer that close all temporary income statement accounts to the income summary account, close the income summary account to the capital account, and close the drawing account to the capital account.

15. _____ A report produced after the period-end closing procedure is completed to verify that debits equal credits in the general ledger accounts.

16. _____ A report that reconciles the bank statement balance with the checkbook balance.

II True/False

Directions *If the statement is true, write a T in the space provided.*
If the statement is false, write F in the space provided.

1.____ An entry to add a new account is entered in the General Journal window.

2.____ Only transactions that do not involve cash may be recorded in the General Journal window.

3.____ General ledger accounts cannot be deleted unless the account balance is zero.

4.____ The Find menu item in the Edit menu could be used to find a transaction that contained a specified debit or credit amount.

5.____ The Chart of Accounts button on the General Journal window generates a Chart of Accounts selection list.

6.____ A new general ledger account can be added (or changed) while entering a journal entry.

7.____ Instead of entering an account number in the general journal, you may select the account from a Chart of Accounts selection list window.

III Questions

Directions *Answer each of the following questions in the space provided.*

1. Describe the process for adding an account to the chart of accounts. _____

_____

_____

2. Describe the process for changing the title of an existing account in the chart of accounts.

_____

_____

3. Describe the process for deleting an account that has a zero balance from the chart of accounts.

_____

_____

4. What kind of transaction(s) may be entered in the general journal? _____

_____

_____

5. Describe the process for correcting a general journal entry. _____

_____

_____

6. Describe the process for deleting a general journal entry. _____

_____

_____

7.   Explain how the Chart of Accounts button can be used while entering general journal transactions.

_____

_____

8.   Complete the date range section of the following Journal Report Selection window to display all general journal entries from July 1 through July 31 of the current year.

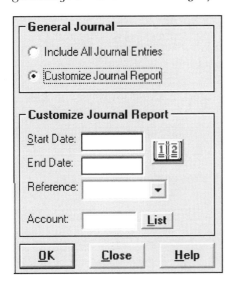

9.   Complete the following Journal Report Selection window to display all general journal entries from September 1 through September 10 of the current year with a reference of 5435.

General Journal

○ Include All Journal Entries

● Customize Journal Report

Customize Journal Report

Start Date: [   ]

End Date: [   ]

Reference: [▼]

Account: [   ]   **List**

OK   **Close**   **Help**

10.   If the balance in the Supplies account after all transactions for the fiscal period have been processed and before adjusting entries is $1,585.00 and the current supplies inventory is $1,250.00, what is the amount of the supplies adjusting entry?   _____

_____

_____

11. What financial statements are available for a nondepartmentalized business organized as a sole proprietorship? _____

_____

_____

12. What information is automatically provided by the computer to aid in the bank reconciliation process? _____

_____

_____

13. Briefly describe the closing entries automatically generated by the computer. _____

_____

_____

14. Describe the procedure to correct an error discovered after closing. _____

_____

_____

Problem 2-A

This problem is a continuation of Sample Problem 2-S. You will enter the general journal entries for the month of December of the current year and complete the end-of-fiscal period processing. Answer Audit Questions 2-A on pages 87–88 while you are working on this problem. As you complete this problem, click Info. on the toolbar for helpful check figures to audit your work.

General Journal Transactions

Dec. 01   Paid cash for month's rent, $1,200.00; Check No. 3829.

01   Paid cash for monthly telephone bill, $246.94; Check No. 3830.

02   Paid cash for delivery charges, $38.00; Check No. 3831. Charge to Miscellaneous Expense.

05   Purchased advertising on account, $250.00; Invoice No. 2515.

05   Billed client for services rendered, $3,200.00; Invoice No. 5435.

06   Purchased supplies on account, $128.65; Invoice No. 2516.

06   Paid cash for mileage reimbursement, $405.00; Check No. 3832. Charge to Automobile Expense.

07   Purchased repair services on account, $285.00; Invoice No. 2517.

07   Paid cash for travel expenses, $115.35; Check No. 3833.

09   Paid cash on account, $175.00; Check No. 3834.

09   Purchased supplies on account, $224.20; Invoice No. 2518.

09   Billed client for services rendered, $2,000.00; Invoice No. 5436.

12   Billed client for services rendered, $3,575.00; Invoice No. 5437.

13   Purchased advertising on account, $500.00; Invoice No. 2519.

14   Paid cash for dues for a professional organization, $300.00; Check No. 3835.

15   Received cash on account, $3,200.00; Invoice No. 5435.

16   Paid cash for charitable contribution, $50.00; Check No. 3836.

19   Received cash on account, $3,700.00; Invoice No. 5434.

20   Billed client for services rendered, $1,200.00; Invoice No. 5438.

21   Purchased supplies on account, $135.00; Invoice No. 2520.

23   Paid cash on account, $136.85; Check No. 3837.

27   Paid cash on account, $250.00; Check No. 3838.

29   Received cash on account, $3,250.00; Invoice No. 5433.

30   Paid cash on account, $311.86; Check No. 3839.

30   Received cash on account, $2,000.00; Invoice No. 5436.

30   Paid monthly salaries, $2,054.38; Check No. 3840.

30   The owner withdrew cash for personal use, $3,000.00; Check No. 3841.

1   Start *Integrated Accounting* 6e.

2   Open the opening balances file named IA6 Problem 02-A.

3   **Enter your name in the Your Name text box.**

4   **Save the file to your disk or folder with a file name of 02-ABC Your Name, where 02-A is the problem number, and BC stands for "Before Closing."**

5   **Enter the December general journal transactions.**

6   **Display the general journal report for the month of December.**

7   **Use the Explorer and other error correction features of the software to correct the following error:**

It was discovered that the cash received, invoice number 5434, on December 19, was recorded as $50.00 less than the actual amount of cash received. Use the Explore Accounting System window to find and make note of the amount of the transaction entered in error, then use the general journal to enter and post the correct amount of the journal entry in error.

8   **Display a corrected general journal report.**

9   **Display a trial balance.**

10 **Enter the December adjusting entries for the month of December for Morgan Consulting:**

Insurance expired during December.......................................$80.00
Inventory of supplies on December 31............................$1,108.75
Depreciation on office equipment for December.............$405.16

11 **Display the December adjusting entries.**

12 **Display the income statement.**

13 **Display the yearly Consulting Fees account detail from the income statement by clicking the Show Detail button on the income statement.**

14 **Display the statement of owner's equity.**

15 **Display the balance sheet.**

16 **Display the Supplies account detail from the balance sheet.**

17 **Generate an expense distribution graph.**

18 Process the following bank reconciliation data:

Checkbook balance $12,958.79
Bank credit $283.96
Bank charge $12.00
Balance shown on bank statement.......................$6,646.99
Outstanding deposits as follows:
$3,200.00
$3,750.00
$3,250.00
$2,000.00
Outstanding checks as follows:

Check No.	Amount
3838	$250.00
3839	$311.86
3840	$2,054.38
3841	$3,000.00

19 Display the bank reconciliation report.

20 Check your work.

Click Check on the toolbar button. If errors appear, use the Explorer and other error correction features of the software to correct your errors.

21 Save your data file (with a file name of 02-ABC Your Name).

22 Optional spreadsheet and word processing integration activity.

Joyce Morgan, owner, asked you to create a spreadsheet report showing only the cash receipt transactions entered into the accounting system for the month of December. Prepare an interoffice memorandum that contains this information. Use the following steps to complete this task:

a. Display and copy the general journal report to the clipboard in spreadsheet format.

b. Start your spreadsheet software and load spreadsheet template file IA6 Spreadsheet 02-S.

c. Select cell A1 as the current cell (if not already selected) and paste the general journal report into the spreadsheet.

d. Delete all rows of data that are not cash receipt transactions, change the title of the report from General Journal to Cash Receipts, and replace the old totals with the sum of the debit and credit columns. Format the spreadsheet similar to Figure 2.32.

e. Print the Cash Receipts report.

f. Save your spreadsheet file to your disk or folder with a file name of 02-A Your Name.

g. Select and copy the spreadsheet report to the clipboard.

h. End your spreadsheet application.

i. Start your word processing application software and load template file IA6 Wordprocessing 02-AB (load as a text file).

j. Replace FROM: Student Name with your name.

k. Position the insertion point one line after the last line in the document and paste the spreadsheet report. Format your document as necessary.

l. Print the completed document.

m. Save the document to your disk or folder with a file name of 02-A Your Name.

n. End your word processing application and return to the *Integrated Accounting* application.

23   Generate and post the closing journal entries.

Click on the Gen. Led. navigation button, and then click the Generate Closing Entries menu button. When the dialog box appears asking if you want to generate closing journal entries, click Yes. The closing journal entries automatically generated by the computer will appear in a dialog box. Click Post. When the general journal appears, showing that the closing entries have been posted, click Close.

24   Display the closing entries.

Click on the Gen. Led. navigation button, and then click the Journal Reports menu button. When the Report Selection window appears, choose the Journal option and the General Journal report (if not already selected) and click OK. When the Journal Report Selection dialog box appears, choose the Customize Journal Report option and enter a Reference restriction of Clo.Ent. so that only the closing entries are reported.

25   Display a trial balance (called the post-closing trial balance).

26   Save your data to disk with a file name of 02-AAC Your Name (where 02-A is the problem, and AC is "After Closing").

If you have access to the Internet, use the browser to find accounting services provided via the Internet. For example, use accounting services to narrow your search. Report what types of accounting services you find. Be sure to include the source and the URL (Web address) of your search.

27   Use the Check toolbar button to check your work.

28   End the *Integrated Accounting* 6e session.

Audit Questions 2-A

NAME

Directions   *Write the answers to the following questions in the space provided.*

1.   What is the amount of check number 3839 shown on the general journal report?

_____

2.   What are the total of the debit and credit columns of the general journal report (before the adjusting and closing entries)?   _____

_____

3.   What is the balance in the Rent Expense account?   _____

_____

4.   What is the balance in the Dues & Subscriptions Expense account you added to the chart of accounts?   _____

_____

5.   What are the debit and credit totals shown in the trial balance report (before adjusting entries)?

_____

6.   What are the total of the debit and credit columns of the adjusting entries shown on the general journal report for adjusting entries?   _____

_____

7.   What is the total operating revenue for the month?   _____

_____

8.   What are the total operating expenses for the year?   _____

_____

9.   What are the total operating expenses for the month as a percentage of total operating revenue?

_____

10.   What is the net income for the month?   _____

_____

11.   What is the net income for the year as a percentage of total operating revenue?   _____

_____

12.   What is the owner's equity at the end of the fiscal period?   _____

_____

13.   What are the total assets?   _____

_____

14.   What are the total liabilities?   _____

_____

15. From the Expense Distribution pie chart, what are the three highest expenses for the year?

    _____

16. From the bank reconciliation report, what is the amount of the adjusted checkbook and bank balances? _____

    _____

17. What are the totals of the debit and credit columns of the closing entries shown on the general journal report? _____

    _____

18. What are the debit and credit totals shown in the trial balance after closing? _____

    _____

Problem 2-B

This problem is a continuation of Sample Problem 2-S. You will enter the general journal entries for the month of December of the current year and complete the end-of-fiscal period processing. Answer Audit Questions 2-B on pages 93–94 as you complete this problem.

General Journal Transactions

Dec. 01   Paid cash for month's rent, $1,200.00; Check No. 3829.

01   Paid cash for monthly telephone bill, $335.17; Check No. 3830.

02   Paid cash for delivery charges, $25.00; Check No. 3831. Charge to Miscellaneous Expense.

05   Purchased advertising on account, $180.00; Invoice No. 2515.

05   Billed client for services rendered, $2,765.00; Invoice No. 5435.

06   Purchased supplies on account, $160.00; Invoice No. 2516.

06   Paid cash for mileage reimbursement, $358.60; Check No. 3832. Charge to Automobile Expense.

07   Purchased repair services on account, $325.00; Invoice No. 2517.

07   Paid cash for travel expenses, $100.00; Check No. 3833.

09   Paid cash on account, $137.42; Check No. 3834.

09   Purchased supplies on account, $239.95; Invoice No. 2518.

09   Billed client for services rendered, $1,500.00; Invoice No. 5436.

12   Billed client for services rendered, $4,000.00; Invoice No. 5437.

13   Purchased advertising on account, $635.00; Invoice No. 2519.

14   Paid cash for dues for a professional organization, $275.00; Check No. 3835.

15   Received cash on account, $2,765.00; Invoice No. 5435.

16   Paid cash for charitable contribution, $25.00; Check No. 3836.

19   Received cash on account, $3,750.00; Invoice No. 5434.

20   Billed client for services rendered, $1,000.00; Invoice No. 5438.

21   Purchased supplies on account, $105.00; Invoice No. 2520.

23   Paid cash on account, $145.00; Check No. 3837.

27   Paid cash on account, $215.00; Check No. 3838.

29   Received cash on account, $3,250.00; Invoice No. 5433.

30   Paid cash on account, $309.10; Check No. 3839.

30   Received cash on account, $1,000.00; Invoice No. 5436.

30   Paid monthly salaries, $2,054.38; Check No. 3840.

30   The owner withdrew cash for personal use, $3,200.00; Check No. 3841.

1   **Start *Integrated Accounting* 6e.**

2   **Open the opening balances file named IA6 Problem 02-B.**

3   **Enter your name in the Your Name text box.**

4   Save the file to your disk or folder with a file name of 02-BBC Your Name, where 02-B is the problem number, and BC stands for "Before Closing."

5   Enter the December general journal transactions.

6   Display the general journal report for the month of December.

7   Use the Explorer and other error correction features of the software to correct the following error:

It was discovered that the cash received, invoice number 5436, on December 30, was recorded as $500.00 less than the actual amount of cash received. Use the Explore Accounting System window to find and make note of the amount of the transaction entered in error, then use the general journal to enter and post the correct amount of the journal entry in error.

8   Display a corrected general journal report.

9   Display a trial balance.

10   Enter the December adjusting entries for the month of December for Morgan Consulting:

Insurance expired during December $82.00
Inventory of supplies on December 31 ....$1,218.10
Depreciation on office equipment for December....................$415.37

11   Display the December adjusting entries.

12   Display the income statement.

13   Display the yearly Consulting Fees account detail from the income statement.

14   Display the statement of owner's equity.

15   Display the balance sheet.

16   Display the Supplies account detail from the balance sheet.

17   Generate an expense distribution graph.

18 **Process the following bank reconciliation data:**

Checkbook balance $11,927.50
Bank credit...$219.62
Bank charge..$17.50
Balance shown on bank statement........................$6,788.10
Outstanding deposits as follows:
$2,765.00
$3,750.00
$3,250.00
$1,500.00
Outstanding checks as follows:

Check No.	Amount
3837	$145.00
3838	$215.00
3839	$309.10
3840	$2,054.38
3841	$3,200.00

19 **Display the bank reconciliation report.**

20 **Save your data file (with a file name of 02-BBC Your Name).**

21 **Optional spreadsheet and word processing integration activity.**

Joyce Morgan, owner, asked you to create a spreadsheet report showing only the cash receipt transactions entered into the accounting system for the month of December. Prepare an interoffice memorandum that contains this information. Use the following steps to complete this task:

a. Display and copy the general journal report to the clipboard in spreadsheet format.

b. Start your spreadsheet software and load spreadsheet template file IA6 Spreadsheet 02-S.

c. Select cell A1 as the current cell (if not already selected), and paste the general journal report into the spreadsheet.

d. Delete all rows of data that are not cash receipt transactions, change the title of the report from General Journal to Cash Receipts, and replace the old totals with the sum of the debit and credit columns. Format the spreadsheet similar to Figure 2.32.

e. Print the completed report.

f. Save your spreadsheet file to your disk or folder with a file name of 02-B Your Name.

g. Select and copy the spreadsheet report to the clipboard.

h. End your spreadsheet application.

i.   Start your word processing application software and load template file IA6 Wordprocessing 02-AB (load as a text file).

j.   Replace FROM: Student Name with your name.

k.   Position the insertion point one line after the last line in the document and paste the spreadsheet report. Format your document as necessary.

l.   Print the completed document.

m.   Save the document to your disk or folder with a file name of 02-B Your Name.

n.   End your word processing application and return to the *Integrated Accounting* application.

22   Generate and post the closing journal entries.

Click on the Gen. Led. navigation button, and then click the Generate Closing Entries menu button. When the dialog box appears asking if you want to generate closing journal entries, click Yes. The closing journal entries automatically generated by the computer will appear in a dialog box. Click Post. When the General Journal appears, showing that the closing entries have been posted, click Close.

23   Display the closing entries.

Click on the Gen. Led. navigation button, and then click the Journal Reports menu button. From the Reports menu, choose the Journal option and the General Journal report and click OK. When the Journal Report Selection dialog box appears, choose the Customize Journal Report option and enter a Reference restriction of Clo.Ent. so that only the closing entries are reported.

24   Display a trial balance (called the post-closing trial balance).

25   Save your data to disk with a file name of 02-BAC Your Name (where 02-B is the problem, and AC is "After Closing").

INTERNET ACTIVITY

If you have access to the Internet, use the browser to find accounting software services that are available via the Internet. For example, use Internet Accounting Software to narrow your search. Report on the services provided from one of the sites you find. Be sure to include the source and the URL (Web address) of your search.

26   End the *Integrated Accounting* 6e session.

Audit Questions 2-B

NAME

Directions   *Write the answers to the following questions in the space provided.*

1. What is the amount of check number 3838 shown on the general journal report?

   _____

2. What are the total of the debit and credit columns of the general journal reports (before the adjusting and closing entries)? _____

   _____

3. What is the balance in the Accounts Payable account? _____

   _____

4. What is the balance in the Advertising Expense account? _____

   _____

5. What are the debit and credit totals shown in the trial balance report (before adjusting entries)?

   _____

6. What are the totals of the debit and credit columns of the adjusting entries shown on the general journal report for adjusting entries? _____

   _____

7. What is the total operating revenue for the year? _____

   _____

8. What are the total operating expenses for the month?

   _____

9. What are the total operating expenses for the year as a percentage of total operating revenue?

   _____

10. What is the net income for the year? _____

    _____

11. What is the net income for the month as a percentage of total operating revenue?

    _____

12. What is the owner's equity at the end of the fiscal period? _____

    _____

13. What are the total assets? _____

    _____

14. What are the total liabilities? _____

    _____

15.   From the Expense Distribution pie chart, what are the two highest expenses?   _____

_____

16.   From the bank reconciliation report, what is the amount of the adjusted checkbook and bank balances?   _____

_____

17.   What are the totals of the debit and credit columns of the closing entries shown on the general journal report?   _____

_____

18.   What are the debit and credit totals shown in the trial balance after closing?   _____

_____

Accounting Cycle of a Merchandising Business

Upon completion of this chapter, you will be able to:

- Identify and describe the procedures to complete a computerized, merchandising-business accounting cycle.

- Enter vendor and customer maintenance.

- Enter debit and credit memorandums.

- Enter purchase transactions.

- Enter cash payment transactions.

- Enter sales transactions.

- Enter cash receipt transactions.

- Correct and delete journal transactions.

- Find journal transactions.

- Display and print ledger reports.

Key Terms

accounts payable *p98*

accounts payable ledger
    report *p102*

accounts receivable ledger
    report *p102*

cash payment *p99*

cash payments journal *p100*

cash receipt *p101*

cash receipt on account *p101*

cash receipts journal *p101*

cost of merchandise sold
    account *p96*

customer *p96*

direct receipt *p101*

merchandise *p96*

merchandise inventory *p96*

merchandising business *p96*

purchase on account *p98*

purchases journal *p98*

sales journal *p100*

sales transaction *p100*

schedule of accounts payable
    report *p102*

schedule of accounts receivable
    report *p102*

vendors *p96*

Introduction

In Chapter 2, you performed the accounting activities required to complete the accounting cycle for a service business. The chart of accounts was maintained, general journal transactions were entered into the computer, and various reports were generated. In this chapter, you will learn how to complete the accounting cycle for a merchandising business. A **merchandising business** purchases and resells goods. The goods purchased for resale are called **merchandise**.

The chart of accounts for a merchandising business includes a Merchandise Inventory account and Cost of Merchandise Sold accounts. **Merchandise inventory** is an asset account that shows the value of the merchandise on hand. The **cost of merchandise sold account** is a cost account that shows the cost or price of merchandise that has been sold to customers.

The examples used in this chapter are for a merchandising business called Reinke Wholesale Co., which is owned by Linda Reinke. The business uses a perpetual inventory system in which it purchases merchandise from manufacturers and sells it wholesale.

Vendor and Customer Maintenance

Businesses from which merchandise is purchased or supplies and other assets are bought are called **vendors**. A business or individual to whom merchandise or services are sold is called a **customer**. Vendors and customers may be added, changed, or deleted from the accounting system using a procedure similar to maintaining the chart of accounts.

When the Maintain Accounts menu item is chosen from the Data menu, the Accts. toolbar button is clicked, or the Gen. Led. navigation button and its Maintain Accounts menu button is clicked, the Account Maintenance window will appear. Choose the Vendors tab to display the vendors maintenance shown in Figure 3.1. Note that because the operational procedures for vendor and customer maintenance are identical, only the operational

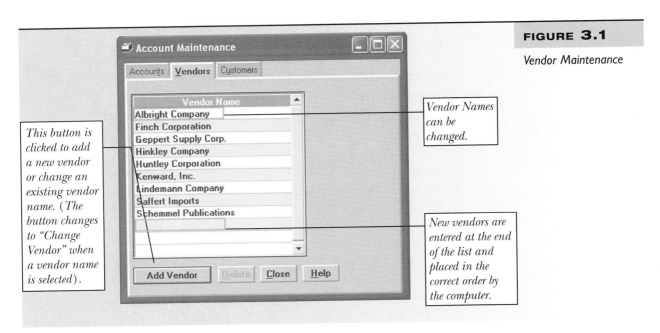

FIGURE 3.1

Vendor Maintenance

procedures for vendors will be shown. Also, note that as another alternative to selecting the Account Maintenance window, the Purchases and Sales navigation buttons may be chosen.

New vendors may be added by entering the vendor name after the last item in the list and pressing the Add Vendor button. The new vendor will be inserted into the vendor list in alphabetical order. Existing vendor names may be changed by selecting the vendor you wish to change, keying the correct vendor name, and clicking on the Change Vendor button. (The Add Vendor button changes to Change Vendor.) An existing vendor may be deleted by simply selecting the vendor that you wish to delete and clicking the Delete button.

 A vendor or customer cannot be deleted if it has a balance.

Journals

Because you learned how to enter general journal and adjusting entry transactions and generate financial statements in the previous chapter, that material will not be repeated here. In the following sections, you will discover how to enter debit memorandums, credit memorandums, purchases, purchases discounts, cash payments, sales, sales discounts, and cash receipts transactions.

As you work with the special journals in this chapter and throughout this text, you will find three useful window features of the software. First, the journals will dynamically resize themselves to fit a resized window; that is, if you enlarge or shrink a window (by positioning the pointer on a window's frame, then clicking and dragging the frame), the journal resizes itself within the window. Therefore, if a journal is wide, you can enlarge its window, thus causing more data field columns to appear in the window to make keying easier. Second, in the case of large journals with several columns, it can be advantageous to maximize the window (by clicking on the maximize button in the upper right corner of the Journal Entries window). Maximizing the window allows more data column grids to show for keying, thus minimizing horizontal scrolling. Finally, on windows with many data columns, the left most control columns will remain frozen while they are horizontally scrolled. On journals, these control columns are the date and reference columns.

General Journal—Debit and Credit Memorandums

In this accounting software, debit and credit memorandums are entered into the computer via the General Journal window. In Chapter 2, you learned how to enter and post general journal entries into the computer. The operational procedure to enter debit and credit memorandums is identical.

Figure 3.2 shows a general journal containing a debit memorandum and credit memorandum. The first transaction (reference number 5291) is an example of a credit memorandum. Account number 4111 (Sales Returns and Allowances) is debited, and account number 1120 (Accounts Receivable) and the customer account (Kimble Carpet Center) are credited $388.75. In addition, account number 1130 (Merchandise Inventory) is debited, and account number 5110 (Cost of Merchandise Sold) is credited $218.00. The second transaction (reference number 3507) is an example of a debit memorandum. Account number 2110 (Accounts Payable) and the vendor account (Lindemann Company) are debited, and account number 1130 (Merchandise Inventory) is credited $657.76.

FIGURE 3.2

Debit and Credit Memorandums

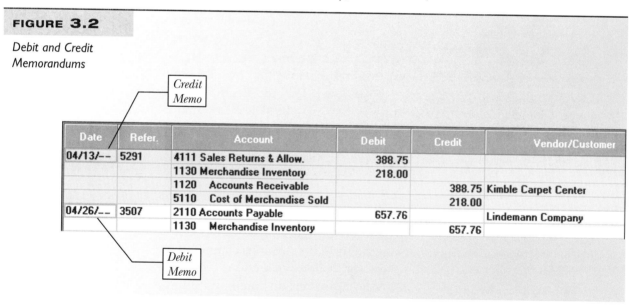

Purchases Journal

A transaction in which merchandise is purchased or goods or services is bought for payment at a later date is called a **purchase on account**. Businesses that purchase merchandise, goods, and services on account from many vendors maintain a separate vendor file to avoid creating a bulky general ledger. The detailed information regarding each vendor's activity is maintained by the computer in this file. The total owed to all vendors is summarized in a single general ledger liability account titled **accounts payable**.

The **purchases journal** is used for entering purchases on account transactions, for making corrections, and to delete existing purchases transactions. When the Purchases tab in the Journal Entries window is clicked, the Purchases Journal shown Figure 3.3 will appear. Two purchases transactions have already been entered as an example. The first transaction is an example of a purchase of merchandise on account, and the second transaction is an example of buying advertising on account.

> Apr. 01   Purchased merchandise on account from Albright Company, $4,200.00; Invoice No. 3526.
>
>   16   Purchased advertising on account from Schemmel Publications, $1,400.00; Invoice No. 3527.

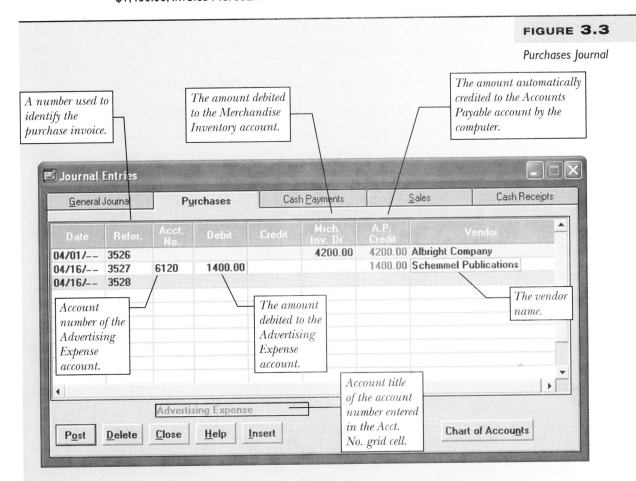

FIGURE 3.3

Purchases Journal

Transactions entered into the purchases journal (and the special journals described in the following sections) may be changed or deleted, and additional lines may be added using the same procedure you used in Chapter 2 for the general journal.

> **NOTE** You can click on the Chart of Accounts button and select an account from the chart of accounts list rather than entering the account number. You can choose a vendor name from the drop-down list by typing the first letter of the vendor's name. The first vendor in the list whose name begins with that letter will appear in the grid cell. Pressing the letter again will cause the next name beginning with that letter to appear.

Cash Payments Journal

Any type of transaction involving the payment (disbursement) of cash is called a **cash payment**. Cash payment transactions are entered into the computer for expenses, cash purchases, payments to vendors, and payments not

Journals

involving a check (such as a direct withdrawal from the bank for a service charge).

The **cash payments journal** is used to enter all cash payment transactions and to make corrections to or deletions from existing cash payment journal entries. It is not necessary to enter the credit to cash because it is automatically calculated and displayed by the computer. A cash payments journal is shown in Figure 3.4. Three cash payments transactions have already been entered as an example. The first two transactions are examples of cash disbursements that do *not* affect accounts payable, whereas the third transaction *does* affect accounts payable.

Apr. 02   Paid cash for month's rent, $850.00; Check No. 2228.

04   Paid cash for monthly telephone bill, $367.53; Check No. 2229.

04   Paid cash on account to Albright Company, covering an invoice amount of $1,544.06, less 2% discount, $30.88; Check No. 2230.

FIGURE 3.4

Cash Payments Journal

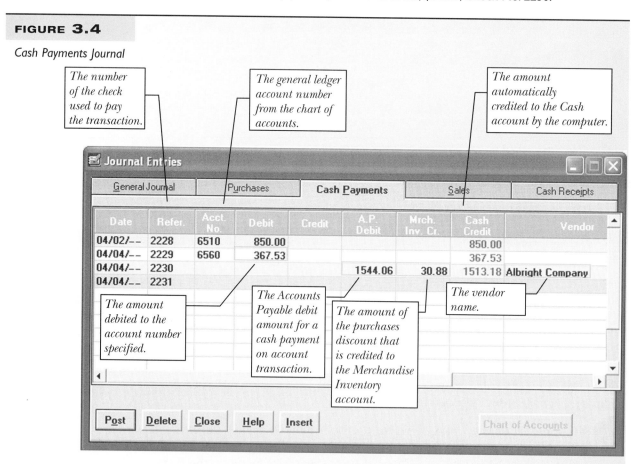

Sales Journal

A transaction in which merchandise is sold in exchange for another asset (usually money) is called a **sales transaction**. A sales transaction of merchandise may be for cash or on account.

The **sales journal** is used to enter sales on account transactions and to make corrections to or delete existing sales journal entries. Only sales on account transactions are entered into the sales journal. The computer automatically calculates and displays the accounts receivable debit amount. The following sample transaction has been entered and posted in the Sales Journal shown in Figure 3.5.

Apr. 08 Sold merchandise on account to Harris Market, $12,000.00; Sales Invoice No. 5356. The cost of the merchandise sold was $8,405.00.

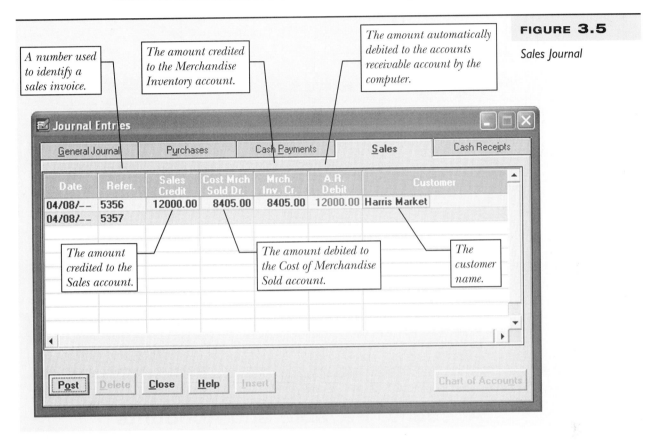

A number used to identify a sales invoice.

The amount credited to the Merchandise Inventory account.

The amount automatically debited to the accounts receivable account by the computer.

FIGURE 3.5

Sales Journal

The amount credited to the Sales account.

The amount debited to the Cost of Merchandise Sold account.

The customer name.

Cash Receipts Journal

Any type of transaction involving the receipt of cash is called a **cash receipt**. Cash receipt transactions must be entered and posted for cash that is received.

Journals

The **cash receipts journal** is used to enter all cash receipts transactions and to make corrections to or deletions from previously entered cash receipts transactions. Two cash receipts transactions have already been entered in the cash receipts journal shown in Figure 3.6. The first transaction is an example of a cash receipt on account, and the second transaction is a direct receipt. A **cash receipt on account** involves a receipt of cash from a customer on account and *does* affect accounts receivable. A **direct receipt** is a cash receipt that does *not* affect accounts receivable. Examples of direct receipts are cash sales, cash received from the sale of an asset, or cash received for money borrowed. As the data are entered, the computer automatically calculates and displays the debit to cash.

Apr. 05 Received cash on account from Campbell Interiors, covering Sales Invoice No. 5341 for $7,522.73, less 2% discount, $150.45.

16 Recorded cash sales for April 1 through April 15, $4,250.00, plus 6% sales tax, $255.00; total, $4,505.00. Cash Receipt No. 1201. The cost of the merchandise sold was $2,945.00.

FIGURE 3.6

Cash Receipts Journal

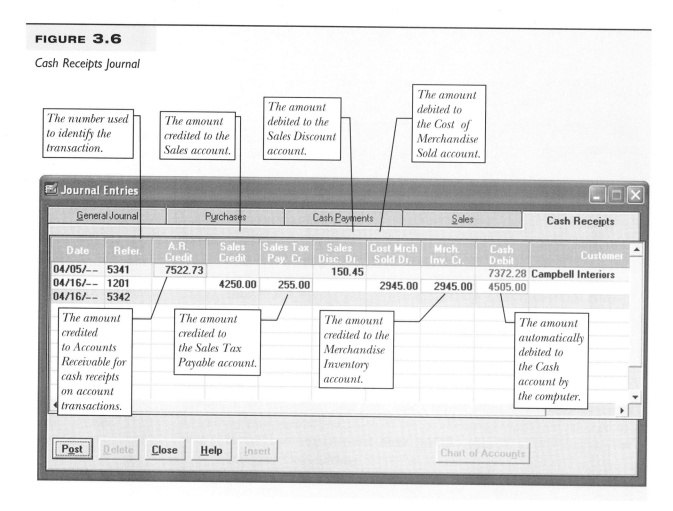

Accounts Payable and Accounts Receivable Ledger Reports

The Ledger Reports option in the Report Selection list permits you to select ledger reports and to specify which ledger entries are to appear in the report. The two reports pertaining to the accounts payable ledger are the **schedule of accounts payable report** and the **accounts payable ledger report**. The two reports pertaining to the accounts receivable ledger are the **schedule of accounts receivable report** and the **accounts receivable ledger report**. The schedules show the current balance for each vendor or customer. The ledger reports list all journal activity by vendor or customer, making them useful in locating errors in individual vendor or customer accounts.

Chapter Summary

■ A business that purchases and resells merchandise is called a merchandising business. A merchandising business's chart of accounts contains a merchandise inventory account used to show the value of the merchandise on hand.

■ An account that shows the cost or price of merchandise that has been sold to customers is called the cost of merchandise sold account.

- Businesses from which merchandise is purchased or supplies and other assets are bought are called vendors. Businesses or individuals to whom merchandise or supplies and other assets are sold are called customers.

- In this accounting software, debit and credit memorandums are entered into the general journal.

- A transaction in which merchandise is purchased for payment at a later date is called a purchase on account.

- The purchases journal is used for entering purchases on account transactions.

- Cash payment transactions are entered into the cash payments journal for expenses, cash purchases, payments to vendors, and payments not involving a check (such as a direct withdrawal from the bank for a service charge).

- Sales on account transactions are entered into the sales journal.

- Cash receipt transactions are entered into the cash receipts journal for cash received on account, cash sales, cash received from the sale of an asset, or cash received for money borrowed.

- Any journal entry previously entered and posted may by changed or deleted as necessary.

- The schedules of accounts payable and accounts receivable show the current balance for each vendor or customer. The accounts payable and accounts receivable ledger reports list all journal activity by vendor and customer.

Sample Problem 3-S

This sample problem illustrates the principles required to complete the accounting cycle for a merchandising business. It provides practice in working with a computerized accounting system to complete the accounting cycle using special journals.

The chart of accounts, vendor list, customer list, and opening balances for Reinke Wholesale Co., will be the basis for this sample problem. The following transactions for Reinke Wholesale Co., occurred during April of the current year. The transactions are illustrated within the step-by-step instructions. If you have a printer attached to your computer and you wish to print a displayed report, press the Print command button at the bottom of the report window.

1   **Start *Integrated Accounting* 6e.**

2   **Load the opening balances template file, IA6 Problem 03-S.**

3   **Enter your name in the Your Name text box and click OK.**

4   **Use Save As to save the data with a file name of 03-S Your Name.**

5   **Add three accounts to the chart of accounts: Delivery Expense, account number 6125; Telephone Expense, account number 6560; and Heating & Lighting Exp., account number 6570.**

Click on the Gen. Led. navigation button, and then the Maintain Accounts menu button. Enter the chart of accounts maintenance data.

6   **Delete Briggs & Associates from the customer list.**

Click on the Customers tab of the Account Maintenance window. Select Briggs & Associates from the customer list and click the Delete button.

7   **Change the name of the customer Mercy Clinic, Ltd., to Mercy Clinic, Assoc., and add a new customer, Mason Corporation, to the customer list.**

Use the Customers tab on the Account Maintenance window to enter the customer maintenance data.

8   **Enter the general journal transactions shown in Figure 3.7.**

Click on the Gen. Led. navigation button, and then the Journal Entries menu button. When the Journal Entries window appears, click the General Journal tab (if not already chosen) and enter the following journal entries as illustrated in Figure 3.7.

General Journal Transactions

Apr. 13   Received merchandise returned on account from Kimble Carpet Center, $388.75. The cost of the merchandise returned was $218.00. The credit memo applies to Sales Invoice No. 5291.

26   Returned merchandise purchased on account from Lindemann Company, $657.76. The debit memo applies to Invoice No. 3507.

FIGURE **3.7**

General Journal

Date	Refer.	Account	Debit	Credit	Vendor/Customer
04/13/--	5291	4111 Sales Returns & Allow.	388.75		
		1130 Merchandise Inventory	218.00		
		1120 Accounts Receivable		388.75	Kimble Carpet Center
		5110 Cost of Merchandise Sold		218.00	
04/26/--	3507	2110 Accounts Payable	657.76		Lindemann Company
		1130 Merchandise Inventory		657.76	

9 **Enter the following April purchases journal transaction data as illustrated in Figure 3.8.**

Click the Purchases tab and then enter the journal transactions. Each purchases journal entry includes a credit to accounts payable. In each case this entry will be made automatically by the computer.

Purchases Journal Transactions

Apr. 01 Purchased merchandise on account from Albright Company, $4,200.00; Invoice No. 3526.

16 Purchased advertising on account from Schemmel Publications, $1,400.00; Invoice No. 3527.

18 Purchased merchandise on account from Kenward, Inc., $8,500.00; Invoice 3528.

25 Purchased the following on account from Lindemann Company: supplies, $625.15; office equipment, $1,795.00; total, $2,420.15; Invoice No. 3529.

25 Purchased merchandise on account from Huntley Corporation, $9,950.00; Invoice No. 3530.

26 Purchased merchandise on account from Hinkley Company, $6,500.00; Invoice No. 3531.

27 Purchased merchandise on account from Geppert Supply Corp., $7,350.95; Invoice No. 3532.

FIGURE **3.8**

Purchases Journal

Date	Refer.	Acct. No.	Debit	Credit	Mrch. Inv. Dr.	A.P. Credit	Vendor
04/01/--	3526				4200.00	4200.00	Albright Company
04/16/--	3527	6120	1400.00			1400.00	Schemmel Publications
04/18/--	3528				8500.00	8500.00	Kenward, Inc.
04/25/--	3529	1150	625.15			2420.15	
		1520	1795.00				Lindemann Company
04/25/--	3530				9950.00	9950.00	Huntley Corporation
04/26/--	3531				6500.00	6500.00	Hinkley Company
04/27/--	3532				7350.95	7350.95	Geppert Supply Corp.

10 **Enter the following April cash payments journal transaction data as illustrated in Figure 3.9.**

Click the Cash Payments tab and then enter the cash payments journal transactions. Each cash payments journal entry includes a credit to cash. In each case this entry will be made automatically by the computer.

Cash Payments Journal Transactions

Apr. 02 Paid cash for month's rent, $850.00; Check No. 2228.

04 Paid cash for monthly telephone bill, $367.53; Check No. 2229.

04 Paid cash on account to Albright Company, covering an invoice amount of $1,544.06, less 2% discount, $30.88; Check No. 2230.

05 Paid $3000.00 on a note payable, plus interest of $207.96; total payment, $3,207.96; Check No. 2231.

10 Paid cash on account to Geppert Supply Corp., covering an invoice amount of $2,262.13, less 2% discount, $45.24; Check No 2232.

24 Paid cash on account to Finch Corporation, covering an invoice amount of $3,234.90, no discount; Check No. 2233.

26 Paid cash on account to Huntley Corporation, covering an invoice amount of $892.42, no discount; Check No. 2234.

28 Linda Reinke, owner, withdrew cash for personal use, $2,550.00; Check No. 2235.

28 Paid cash for insurance premium, $950.00; Check No. 2236.

29 Paid cash on account to Hinkley Company, covering an invoice amount of $2,040.50, no discount; Check No. 2237.

30 Paid cash for monthly salaries: sales salaries, $3,256.07; office salaries, $2,711.34; total, $5,967.41; Check No. 2238.

30 Paid cash for delivery charges, $80.00; Check No. 2239.

FIGURE 3.9

Cash Payments Journal

Date	Refer.	Acct. No.	Debit	Credit	A.P. Debit	Mrch. Inv. Cr.	Cash Credit	Vendor
04/02/--	2228	6510	850.00				850.00	
04/04/--	2229	6560	367.53				367.53	
04/04/--	2230				1544.06	30.88	1513.18	Albright Company
04/05/-	2231	2510	3000.00				3207.96	
		8110	207.96					
04/10/--	2232				2262.13	45.24	2216.89	Geppert Supply Corp.
04/24/--	2233				3234.90		3234.90	Finch Corporation
04/26/--	2234				892.42		892.42	Huntley Corporation
04/28/--	2235	3120	2550.00				2550.00	
04/28/--	2236	1140	950.00				950.00	
04/29/--	2237				2040.50		2040.50	Hinkley Company
04/30/--	2238	6110	3256.07				5967.41	
		6540	2711.34					
04/30/--	2239	6125	80.00				80.00	
04/30/--	2240	6570	670.45				670.45	
04/30/--	2241	2120	199.17				199.17	
04/30/--	2242				1182.05		1182.05	Kenward, Inc.

30   Paid cash for electric bill, $670.45; Check No. 2240.

30   Paid cash for sales tax liability, $199.17; Check No. 2241.

30   Paid cash on account to Kenward, Inc., covering an invoice amount of
$1,182.05; no discount; Check No. 2242.

11   **Enter the following April sales journal transaction data as illustrated in Figure 3.10.**

Click the Sales tab and then enter the sales journal transactions. Each sales journal entry includes a debit to accounts receivable. In each case this entry will be made automatically by the computer.

Sales Journal Transactions

Apr. 08   Sold merchandise on account to Harris Market, $12,000.00; Sales Invoice No. 5356. The cost of the merchandise sold was $8,405.00.

09   Sold merchandise on account to Baxter Legal Services, $795.00; Sales Invoice No. 5357. The cost of the merchandise sold was $557.00.

26   Sold merchandise on account to Stoffel Manufacturing, $4,300.00; Sales Invoice No. 5358. The cost of the merchandise sold was $3,010.00.

29   Sold merchandise on account to United Corporation, $4,895.95; Sales Invoice No. 5359. The cost of the merchandise sold was $3,425.00.

29   Sold merchandise on account to Mason Corporation, $1,200.00; Sales Invoice No. 5360. The cost of the merchandise sold was $835.00.

30   Sold merchandise on account to Campbell Interiors, $17,450.00; Sales Invoice No. 5361. The cost of the merchandise sold was $12,215.00.

30   Sold merchandise on account to Matson Boutique, $10,000.00; Sales Invoice No. 5362. The cost of the merchandise sold was $6,995.00.

Date	Refer.	Sales Credit	Cost Mrch Sold Dr.	Mrch. Inv. Cr.	A.R. Debit	Customer
04/08/--	5356	12000.00	8405.00	8405.00	12000.00	Harris Market
04/09/--	5357	795.00	557.00	557.00	795.00	Baxter Legal Services
04/26/--	5358	4300.00	3010.00	3010.00	4300.00	Stoffel Manufacturing
04/29/--	5359	4895.95	3425.00	3425.00	4895.95	United Corporation
04/29/--	5360	1200.00	835.00	835.00	1200.00	Mason Corporation
04/30/--	5361	17450.00	12215.00	12215.00	17450.00	Campbell Interiors
04/30/--	5362	10000.00	6995.00	6995.00	10000.00	Matson Boutique

FIGURE 3.10

Sales Journal

12   **Enter the April cash receipts journal transaction data as illustrated in Figure 3.11.**

Click the Cash Receipts tab and then enter the cash receipts journal transactions. Each cash receipts journal entry includes a debit to cash. In each case this entry will be made automatically by the computer.

Cash Receipts Journal Transactions

Apr. 05   Received cash on account from Campbell Interiors, covering Sales Invoice No. 5341 for $7,522.73, less 2% discount, $150.45.

09   Received cash on account from Mercy Clinic, Assoc., covering Sales Invoice No. 5336 for $8,135.00, less 2% discount, $162.70.

10   Received cash on account from Matson Boutique, covering Sales Invoice No. 5330 for $4,800.00; no discount.

11 Received cash on account from Telshaw Rental Agency, covering Sales Invoice No. 5338 for $1,019.44; no discount.

16 Recorded cash sales for April 1 through April 15, $4,250.00, plus 6% sales tax, $255.00; total, $4,505.00; Cash Receipt No. 1201. The cost of the merchandise sold was $2,945.00.

16 Received cash on account from Matson Boutique, covering Sales Invoice No. 5343 for $6,894.62; no discount.

17 Received cash on account from Baxter Legal Services, covering Sales Invoice No. 5328 for $8,688.77; no discount.

20 Received cash on account from Burgess Service Center, covering Sales Invoice No. 5321 for $200.00; no discount.

24 Received cash on account from Stoffel Manufacturing, covering Sales Invoice No. 5342 for $13,218.31; no discount.

29 Received cash on account from Burgess Service Center, covering Sales Invoice No. 5339 for $5,232.43; no discount.

30 Recorded cash sales for April 16 through April 30, $3,495.00, plus 6% sales tax, $209.70; total, $3,704.70; Cash Receipt No. 1202. The cost of the merchandise sold was $2,457.00.

FIGURE 3.11

Cash Receipts Journal

Date	Refer.	A.R. Credit	Sales Credit	Sales Tax Pay. Cr.	Sales Disc. Dr.	Cost Mrch Sold Dr.	Mrch. Inv. Cr.	Cash Debit	Customer
04/05/--	5341	7522.73			150.45			7372.28	Campbell Interiors
04/09/--	5336	8135.00			162.70			7972.30	Mercy Clinic, Assoc.
04/10/--	5330	4800.00						4800.00	Matson Boutique
04/11/--	5338	1019.44						1019.44	Telshaw Rental Agency
04/16/--	1201		4250.00	255.00		2945.00	2945.00	4505.00	
04/16/--	5343	6894.62						6894.62	Matson Boutique
04/17/--	5328	8688.77						8688.77	Baxter Legal Services
04/20/--	5321	200.00						200.00	Burgess Service Center
04/24/--	5342	13218.31						13218.31	Stoffel Manufacturing
04/29/--	5339	5232.43						5232.43	Burgess Service Center
04/30/--	1202		3495.00	209.70		2457.00	2457.00	3704.70	

13 **Display the chart of accounts.**

Click on the Gen. Led. navigation button, and then the Journal Reports menu button. When the Report Selection window appears, choose the Account Lists option from the Select a Report Group. Select the Chart of Accounts report from the Choose a Report to Display list (if not already highlighted), and click OK. The report is shown in Figure 3.12.

FIGURE 3.12

Chart of Accounts

Reinke Wholesale Co.
Chart of Accounts
04/30/—

Assets

1110	Cash
1120	Accounts Receivable
1130	Merchandise Inventory
1140	Prepaid Insurance
1150	Supplies
1510	Warehouse Equipment
1511	Accum. Depr. Wrhse. Eqpt.
1520	Office Equipment
1521	Accum. Depr. Office Eqpt.

Liabilities

2110	Accounts Payable
2120	Sales Tax Payable
2130	Salaries Payable
2510	Note Payable

Owner's Equity

3110	Linda Reinke, Capital
3120	Linda Reinke, Drawing
3130	Income Summary

Revenue

4110	Sales
4111	Sales Returns & Allow.
4112	Sales Discounts

Cost

5110	Cost of Merchandise Sold

Expenses

6110	Sales Salary Expense
6120	Advertising Expense
6125	Delivery Expense
6130	Depr. Exp. Wrhse. Eqpt.
6140	Supplies Expense
6150	Misc. Selling Expense
6510	Rent Expense
6520	Depr. Expense Off. Eqpt.
6530	Misc. General Expense
6540	Office Salary Expense
6550	Insurance Expense
6560	Telephone Expense
6570	Heating & Lighting Exp.

Other Revenue

7110	Interest Income

Other Expense

8110	Interest Expense

14 **Display the customer list.**

Select the Customer List and click OK. The report is shown in Figure 3.13.

FIGURE 3.13

Customer List

Reinke Wholesale Co.
Customer List
04/30/—

Customer Name

Baxter Legal Services
Burgess Service Center
Campbell Interiors
Harris Market
Kimble Carpet Center
Mason Corporation
Matson Boutique
Mercy Clinic, Assoc.
Stoffel Manufacturing
Telshaw Rental Agency
United Corporation

15 **Display the journal entries (general, purchases, cash payments, sales, and cash receipts journals).**

Choose Journals from the Select a Report Group list. Select the desired journal report from the Choose a Report to Display list, and then click OK. Click OK again to select Include All Journal Entries. The journal reports are shown in Figure 3.14(a) through 3.14(e), respectively.

FIGURE 3.14(A)

General Journal Report

Reinke Wholesale Co.
General Journal
04/30/—

Date	Refer.	Acct.	Title	Debit	Credit
04/13	5291	4111	Sales Returns & Allow.	388.75	
04/13	5291	1130	Merchandise Inventory	218.00	
04/13	5291	1120	AR/Kimble Carpet Center		388.75
04/13	5291	5110	Cost of Merchandise Sold		218.00
04/26	3507	2110	AP/Lindemann Company	657.76	
04/26	3507	1130	Merchandise Inventory		657.76
			Totals	1,264.51	1,264.51

Reinke Wholesale Co.
Purchases Journal
04/30/—

Date	Inv. No.	Acct.	Title	Debit	Credit
04/01	3526	1130	Merchandise Inventory	4,200.00	
04/01	3526	2110	AP/Albright Company		4,200.00
04/16	3527	6120	Advertising Expense	1,400.00	
04/16	3527	2110	AP/Schemmel Publications		1,400.00
04/18	3528	1130	Merchandise Inventory	8,500.00	
04/18	3528	2110	AP/Kenward, Inc.		8,500.00
04/25	3529	1150	Supplies	625.15	
04/25	3529	1520	Office Equipment	1,795.00	
04/25	3529	2110	AP/Lindemann Company		2,420.15
04/25	3530	1130	Merchandise Inventory	9,950.00	
04/25	3530	2110	AP/Huntley Corporation		9,950.00
04/26	3531	1130	Merchandise Inventory	6,500.00	
04/26	3531	2110	AP/Hinkley Company		6,500.00
04/27	3532	1130	Merchandise Inventory	7,350.95	
04/27	3532	2110	AP/Geppert Supply Corp.		7,350.95
			Totals	40,321.10	40,321.10

FIGURE 3.14(B)

Purchases Journal Report

Reinke Wholesale Co.
Cash Payments Journal
04/30/—

Date	Ck. No.	Acct.	Title	Debit	Credit
04/02	2228	6510	Rent Expense	850.00	
04/02	2228	1110	Cash		850.00
04/04	2229	6560	Telephone Expense	367.53	
04/04	2229	1110	Cash		367.53
04/04	2230	2110	AP/Albright Company	1,544.06	
04/04	2230	1110	Cash		1,513.18
04/04	2230	1130	Merchandise Inventory		30.88
04/05	2231	2510	Note Payable	3,000.00	
04/05	2231	8110	Interest Expense	207.96	
04/05	2231	1110	Cash		3,207.96
04/10	2232	2110	AP/Geppert Supply Corp.	2,262.13	
04/10	2232	1110	Cash		2,216.89
04/10	2232	1130	Merchandise Inventory		45.24
04/24	2233	2110	AP/Finch Corporation	3,234.90	
04/24	2233	1110	Cash		3,234.90
04/26	2234	2110	AP/Huntley Corporation	892.42	
04/26	2234	1110	Cash		892.42
04/28	2235	3120	Linda Reinke, Drawing	2,550.00	
04/28	2235	1110	Cash		2,550.00

(continued)

FIGURE 3.14(C)

Cash Payments Journal Report

FIGURE 3.14(c)	04/28	2236	1140	Prepaid Insurance	950.00	
	04/28	2236	1110	Cash		950.00
(Concluded)						
	04/29	2237	2110	AP/Hinkley Company	2,040.50	
	04/29	2237	1110	Cash		2,040.50
	04/30	2238	6110	Sales Salary Expense	3,256.07	
	04/30	2238	6540	Office Salary Expense	2,711.34	
	04/30	2238	1110	Cash		5,967.41
	04/30	2239	6125	Delivery Expense	80.00	
	04/30	2239	1110	Cash		80.00
	04/30	2240	6570	Heating & Lighting Exp.	670.45	
	04/30	2240	1110	Cash		670.45
	04/30	2241	2120	Sales Tax Payable	199.17	
	04/30	2241	1110	Cash		199.17
	04/30	2242	2110	AP/Kenward, Inc.	1,182.05	
	04/30	2242	1110	Cash		1,182.05
				Totals	25,998.58	25,998.58

FIGURE 3.14(d)

Sales Journal Report

Reinke Wholesale Co.
Sales Journal
04/30/—

Date	Inv. No.	Acct.	Title	Debit	Credit
04/08	5356	1120	AR/Harris Market	12,000.00	
04/08	5356	5110	Cost of Merchandise Sold	8,405.00	
04/08	5356	4110	Sales		12,000.00
04/08	5356	1130	Merchandise Inventory		8,405.00
04/09	5357	1120	AR/Baxter Legal Services	795.00	
04/09	5357	5110	Cost of Merchandise Sold	557.00	
04/09	5357	4110	Sales		795.00
04/09	5357	1130	Merchandise Inventory		557.00
04/26	5358	1120	AR/Stoffel Manufacturing	4,300.00	
04/26	5358	5110	Cost of Merchandise Sold	3,010.00	
04/26	5358	4110	Sales		4,300.00
04/26	5358	1130	Merchandise Inventory		3,010.00
04/29	5359	1120	AR/United Corporation	4,895.95	
04/29	5359	5110	Cost of Merchandise Sold	3,425.00	
04/29	5359	4110	Sales		4,895.95
04/29	5359	1130	Merchandise Inventory		3,425.00
04/29	5360	1120	AR/Mason Corporation	1,200.00	
04/29	5360	5110	Cost of Merchandise Sold	835.00	
04/29	5360	4110	Sales		1,200.00
04/29	5360	1130	Merchandise Inventory		835.00
04/30	5361	1120	AR/Campbell Interiors	17,450.00	
04/30	5361	5110	Cost of Merchandise Sold	12,215.00	
04/30	5361	4110	Sales		17,450.00
04/30	5361	1130	Merchandise Inventory		12,215.00

(continued)

04/30	5362	1120	AR/Matson Boutique	10,000.00	
04/30	5362	5110	Cost of Merchandise Sold	6,995.00	
04/30	5362	4110	Sales		10,000.00
04/30	5362	1130	Merchandise Inventory		6,995.00
			Totals	86,082.95	86,082.95

FIGURE 3.14(D)

(Concluded)

Reinke Wholesale Co.
Cash Receipts Journal
04/30/—

Date	Refer.	Acct.	Title	Debit	Credit
04/05	5341	1110	Cash	7,372.28	
04/05	5341	4112	Sales Discounts	150.45	
04/05	5341	1120	AR/Campbell Interiors		7,522.73
04/09	5336	1110	Cash	7,972.30	
04/09	5336	4112	Sales Discounts	162.70	
04/09	5336	1120	AR/Mercy Clinic, Assoc.		8,135.00
04/10	5330	1110	Cash	4,800.00	
04/10	5330	1120	AR/Matson Boutique		4,800.00
04/11	5338	1110	Cash	1,019.44	
04/11	5338	1120	AR/Telshaw Rental Agency		1,019.44
04/16	1201	1110	Cash	4,505.00	
04/16	1201	5110	Cost of Merchandise Sold	2,945.00	
04/16	1201	4110	Sales		4,250.00
04/16	1201	2120	Sales Tax Payable		255.00
04/16	1201	1130	Merchandise Inventory		2,945.00
04/16	5343	1110	Cash	6,894.62	
04/16	5343	1120	AR/Matson Boutique		6,894.62
04/17	5328	1110	Cash	8,688.77	
04/17	5328	1120	AR/Baxter Legal Services		8,688.77
04/20	5321	1110	Cash	200.00	
04/20	5321	1120	AR/Burgess Service Center		200.00
04/24	5342	1110	Cash	13,218.31	
04/24	5342	1120	AR/Stoffel Manufacturing		13,218.31
04/29	5339	1110	Cash	5,232.43	
04/29	5339	1120	AR/Burgess Service Center		5,232.43
04/30	1202	1110	Cash	3,704.70	
04/30	1202	5110	Cost of Merchandise Sold	2,457.00	
04/30	1202	4110	Sales		3,495.00
04/30	1202	2120	Sales Tax Payable		209.70
04/30	1202	1130	Merchandise Inventory		2,457.00
			Totals	69,323.00	69,323.00

FIGURE 3.14(E)

Cash Receipts Journal Report

16   Display a trial balance.

Choose Ledger Reports in the Report Selection window, select Trial Balance report, and then click OK. The trial balance dated April 30 of the current year is shown in Figure 3.15.

FIGURE 3.15

Trial Balance

Reinke Wholesale Co.
Trial Balance
04/30/—

Acct. Number	Account Title	Debit	Credit
1110	Cash	58,798.29	
1120	Accounts Receivable	82,157.90	
1130	Merchandise Inventory	132,902.57	
1140	Prepaid Insurance	4,000.00	
1150	Supplies	4,114.25	
1510	Warehouse Equipment	214,069.00	
1511	Accum. Depr. Wrhse. Eqpt.		97,725.00
1520	Office Equipment	74,081.10	
1521	Accum. Depr. Office Eqpt.		28,233.00
2110	Accounts Payable		41,326.88
2120	Sales Tax Payable		464.70
2510	Note Payable		33,980.00
3110	Linda Reinke, Capital		361,719.53
3120	Linda Reinke, Drawing	10,050.00	
4110	Sales		199,931.95
4111	Sales Returns & Allow.	4,128.75	
4112	Sales Discounts	2,806.15	
5110	Cost of Merchandise Sold	134,242.32	
6110	Sales Salary Expense	13,462.23	
6120	Advertising Expense	8,618.00	
6125	Delivery Expense	80.00	
6130	Depr. Exp. Wrhse. Eqpt.	1,944.20	
6140	Supplies Expense	736.30	
6150	Misc. Selling Expense	210.00	
6510	Rent Expense	3,400.00	
6520	Depr. Expense Off. Eqpt.	668.60	
6530	Misc. General Expense	312.88	
6540	Office Salary Expense	10,499.18	
6560	Telephone Expense	367.53	
6570	Heating & Lighting Exp.	670.45	
7110	Interest Income		104.50
8110	Interest Expense	1,165.86	
	Total	763,485.56	763,485.56

17 **Display the schedule of accounts payable and accounts payable ledger reports.**

Select the desired report then click OK (display all vendors in the accounts payable ledger report). The reports are shown in Figures 3.16(a) and (b), respectively.

Reinke Wholesale Co.
Schedule of Accounts Payable
04/30/—

Name	Balance
Albright Company	4,200.00
Geppert Supply Corp.	7,350.95
Hinkley Company	6,500.00
Huntley Corporation	9,950.00
Kenward, Inc.	8,500.00
Lindemann Company	2,420.15
Schemmel Publications	2,405.78
Total	41,326.88

FIGURE 3.16(A)

Schedule of Accounts Payable

Reinke Wholesale Co.
Accounts Payable Ledger
04/30/—

Account	Journal	Date	Refer.	Debit	Credit	Balance
Albright Company						
	Balance Forward					1,544.06Cr
	Purchases	04/01	3526		4,200.00	5,744.06Cr
	Cash Payments	04/04	2230	1,544.06		4,200.00Cr
Finch Corporation						
	Balance Forward					3,234.90Cr
	Cash Payments	04/24	2233	3,234.90		.00
Geppert Supply Corp.						
	Balance Forward					2,262.13Cr
	Cash Payments	04/10	2232	2,262.13		.00
	Purchases	04/27	3532		7,350.95	7,350.95Cr
Hinkley Company						
	Balance Forward					2,040.50Cr
	Purchases	04/26	3531		6,500.00	8,540.50Cr
	Cash Payments	04/29	2237	2,040.50		6,500.00Cr
Huntley Corporation						
	Balance Forward					892.42Cr
	Purchases	04/25	3530		9,950.00	10,842.42Cr
	Cash Payments	04/26	2234	892.42		9,950.00Cr

(continued)

FIGURE 3.16(B)

Accounts Payable Ledger

FIGURE 3.16(B)	Kenward, Inc.					
(Concluded)	Balance Forward					1,182.05Cr
	Purchases	04/18	3528		8,500.00	9,682.05Cr
	Cash Payments	04/30	2242	1,182.05		8,500.00Cr
	Lindemann Company					
	Balance Forward					657.76Cr
	Purchases	04/25	3529		2,420.15	3,077.91Cr
	General	04/26	3507	657.76		2,420.15Cr
	Saffert Imports					
	*** No Activity ***					.00
	Schemmel Publications					
	Balance Forward					1,005.78Cr
	Purchases	04/16	3527		1,400.00	2,405.78Cr

18   **Display the schedule of accounts receivable and accounts receivable ledger reports.**

Select the desired report then click OK (display all customers in the accounts receivable ledger report). The reports are shown in Figures 3.17(a) and (b), respectively.

FIGURE 3.17(A)		
Schedule of Accounts Receivable	**Reinke Wholesale Co.** **Schedule of Accounts Receivable** **04/30/—**	
	Name	Balance
	Baxter Legal Services	795.00
	Campbell Interiors	17,450.00
	Harris Market	12,000.00
	Kimble Carpet Center	16,787.75
	Mason Corporation	1,200.00
	Matson Boutique	10,000.00
	Stoffel Manufacturing	4,300.00
	United Corporation	19,625.15
	Total	82,157.90

FIGURE 3.17(B)

Accounts Receivable Ledger

Reinke Wholesale Co.
Accounts Receivable Ledger
04/30/—

Account Journal	Date	Refer.	Debit	Credit	Balance
Baxter Legal Services					
Balance Forward					8,688.77Dr
Sales	04/09	5357	795.00		9,483.77Dr
Cash Receipts	04/17	5328		8,688.77	795.00Dr
Burgess Service Center					
Balance Forward					5,432.43Dr
Cash Receipts	04/20	5321		200.00	5,232.43Dr
Cash Receipts	04/29	5339		5,232.43	.00
Campbell Interiors					
Balance Forward					7,522.73Dr
Cash Receipts	04/05	5341		7,522.73	.00
Sales	04/30	5361	17,450.00		17,450.00Dr
Harris Market					
Sales	04/08	5356	12,000.00		12,000.00Dr
Kimble Carpet Center					
Balance Forward					17,176.50Dr
General	04/13	5291		388.75	16,787.75Dr
Mason Corporation					
Sales	04/29	5360	1,200.00		1,200.00Dr
Matson Boutique					
Balance Forward					11,694.62Dr
Cash Receipts	04/10	5330		4,800.00	6,894.62Dr
Cash Receipts	04/16	5343		6,894.62	.00
Sales	04/30	5362	10,000.00		10,000.00Dr
Mercy Clinic, Assoc.					
Balance Forward					8,135.00Dr
Cash Receipts	04/09	5336		8,135.00	.00
Stoffel Manufacturing					
Balance Forward					13,218.31Dr
Cash Receipts	04/24	5342		13,218.31	.00
Sales	04/26	5358	4,300.00		4,300.00Dr
Telshaw Rental Agency					
Balance Forward					1,019.44Dr
Cash Receipts	04/11	5338		1,019.44	.00
United Corporation					
Balance Forward					14,729.20Dr
Sales	04/29	5359	4,895.95		19,625.15Dr

End-of-Month Activities

After the monthly transactions have been processed, the adjusting entries must be entered into the computer and printed. The financial statements may then be displayed. The adjustment data for the month of April for Reinke Wholesale Co., are listed here.

Insurance expired during April	$362.50
Inventory of supplies	$2,785.00
Depreciation for April:	
Warehouse equipment	$648.37
Office equipment	$232.00
Salaries Payable:	
Sales salaries	$430.00
Office salaries	$310.00

The completed adjusting entries are shown in Figure 3.18 as they would appear when entered and posted in the general journal.

FIGURE 3.18

*General Journal
(Adjusting Entries)*

Date	Refer.	Account	Debit	Credit	Vendor/Customer
04/30/--	Adj.Ent.	6550 Insurance Expense	362.50		
		1140 Prepaid Insurance		362.50	
04/30/--	Adj.Ent.	6140 Supplies Expense	1329.25		
		1150 Supplies		1329.25	
04/30/--	Adj.Ent.	6130 Depr. Exp. Wrhse. Eqpt.	648.37		
		1511 Accum. Depr. Wrhse. Eqpt.		648.37	
04/30/--	Adj.Ent.	6520 Depr. Expense Off. Eqpt.	232.00		
		1521 Accum. Depr. Office Eqpt.		232.00	
04/30/--	Adj.Ent.	6110 Sales Salary Expense	430.00		
		6540 Office Salary Expense	310.00		
		2130 Salaries Payable		740.00	

1   Enter the adjusting entries.

Click on the Gen. Led. navigation button, and then the Journal Entries menu button. Then click on the General Journal tab and enter the adjusting entries shown in Figure 3.18.

2   Display the adjusting entries.

Click on the Gen. Led. navigation button, and then the Journal Reports menu button. When the Reports Selection dialog box appears, choose the Journals option button, then select the General Journal report and click OK. When the Journal Report Selection dialog box appears, choose the Customize Journal Report option and enter a Reference restriction of Adj.Ent. so that only the adjusting entries are reported. Compare your journal entries report to the report shown in Figure 3.19. If the journal entries report is incorrect, make corrections.

FIGURE 3.19

*General Journal Report
(Adjusting Entries)*

Reinke Wholesale Co.
General Journal
04/30/—

Date	Refer.	Acct.	Title	Debit	Credit
04/30	Adj.Ent.	6550	Insurance Expense	362.50	
04/30	Adj.Ent.	1140	Prepaid Insurance		362.50
04/30	Adj.Ent.	6140	Supplies Expense	1,329.25	
04/30	Adj.Ent.	1150	Supplies		1,329.25
04/30	Adj.Ent.	6130	Depr. Exp. Wrhse. Eqpt.	648.37	
04/30	Adj.Ent.	1511	Accum. Depr. Wrhse. Eqpt.		648.37
04/30	Adj.Ent.	6520	Depr. Expense Off. Eqpt.	232.00	
04/30	Adj.Ent.	1521	Accum. Depr. Office Eqpt.		232.00
04/30	Adj.Ent.	6110	Sales Salary Expense	430.00	
04/30	Adj.Ent.	6540	Office Salary Expense	310.00	
04/30	Adj.Ent.	2130	Salaries Payable		740.00
			Totals	3,312.12	3,312.12

3 **Check your work.**

Click Check on the toolbar. If errors appear, use the Explorer and other error corrections features of the software to correct your errors.

4 **Display the income statement.**

Choose the Financial Statements option button from the Report Selection dialog box, select the Income Statement report, and then click OK. The income statement is shown in Figure 3.20.

FIGURE 3.20

Income Statement

Reinke Wholesale Co.
Income Statement
For Period Ended 04/30/—

	Monthly Amount	Monthly Percent	Yearly Amount	Yearly Percent
Operating Revenue				
Sales	58,385.95	101.22	199,931.95	103.59
Sales Returns & Allow.	−388.75	−0.67	−4,128.75	−2.14
Sales Discounts	−313.15	−0.54	−2,806.15	−1.45
Total Operating Revenue	57,684.05	100.00	192,997.05	100.00
Cost				
Cost of Merchandise Sold	40,626.00	70.43	134,242.32	69.56
Total Cost	40,626.00	70.43	134,242.32	69.56
Gross Profit	17,058.05	29.57	58,754.73	30.44
				(continued)

FIGURE 3.20

(Concluded)

Operating Expenses				
Sales Salary Expense	3,686.07	6.39	13,892.23	7.20
Advertising Expense	1,400.00	2.43	8,618.00	4.47
Delivery Expense	80.00	0.14	80.00	0.04
Depr. Exp. Wrhse. Eqpt.	648.37	1.12	2,592.57	1.34
Supplies Expense	1,329.25	2.30	2,065.55	1.07
Misc. Selling Expense			210.00	0.11
Total Selling Expenses	7,143.69	12.38	27,458.35	14.23
Rent Expense	850.00	1.47	3,400.00	1.76
Depr. Expense Off. Eqpt.	232.00	0.40	900.60	0.47
Misc. General Expense			312.88	0.16
Office Salary Expense	3,021.34	5.24	10,809.18	5.60
Insurance Expense	362.50	0.63	362.50	0.19
Telephone Expense	367.53	0.64	367.53	0.19
Heating & Lighting Exp.	670.45	1.16	670.45	0.35
Total Administrative Expenses	5,503.82	9.54	16,823.14	8.72
Total Operating Expenses	12,647.51	21.93	44,281.49	22.94
Net Income from Operations	4,410.54	7.65	14,473.24	7.50
Other Revenue				
Interest Income			104.50	0.05
Other Expense				
Interest Expense	207.96	0.36	1,165.86	0.60
Net Income	4,202.58	7.29	13,411.88	6.95

5   **Display the statement of owner's equity.**

Select the Statement of Owner's Equity report, then click OK. The statement of owner's equity is shown in Figure 3.21.

FIGURE 3.21

Statement of Owner's Equity

Reinke Wholesale Co.
Statement of Owner's Equity
For Period Ended 04/30/—

Linda Reinke, Capital (Beg. of Period)	361,719.53
Linda Reinke, Drawing	−10,050.00
Net Income	13,411.88
Linda Reinke, Capital (End of Period)	365,081.41

6   **Display the balance sheet.**

Select the Balance Sheet report, then click OK. The balance sheet is shown in Figure 3.22.

FIGURE 3.22

Balance Sheet

Reinke Wholesale Co.
Balance Sheet
04/30/—

Assets

Cash	58,798.29	
Accounts Receivable	82,157.90	
Merchandise Inventory	132,902.57	
Prepaid Insurance	3,637.50	
Supplies	2,785.00	
Total Current Assets	280,281.26	
Warehouse Equipment	214,069.00	
Accum. Depr. Wrhse. Eqpt.	−98,373.37	
Office Equipment	74,081.10	
Accum. Depr. Office Eqpt.	−28,465.00	
Total Plant Assets	161,311.73	
Total Assets		441,592.99
Liabilities		
Accounts Payable	41,326.88	
Sales Tax Payable	464.70	
Salaries Payable	740.00	
Total Current Liabilities	42,531.58	
Note Payable	33,980.00	
Total Long Term Liabilities	33,980.00	
Total Liabilities		76,511.58
Owner's Equity		
Linda Reinke, Capital	361,719.53	
Linda Reinke, Drawing	−10,050.00	
Net Income	13,411.88	
Total Owner's Equity		365,081.41
Total Liabilities & Equity		441,592.99

7   Generate a top customers and sales graph.

Click Graphs on the toolbar. Click on Top Customers to generate the customer sales bar graph shown in Figure 3.23(a). Click on Sales to generate the sales line graph shown in Figure 3.23(b).

FIGURE **3.23(A)**

*Customer Sales Bar
Graph*

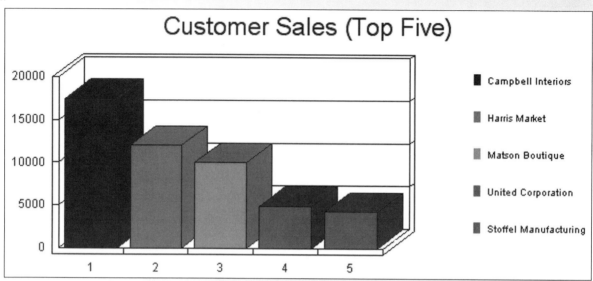

FIGURE **3.23(B)**

Sales Line Graph

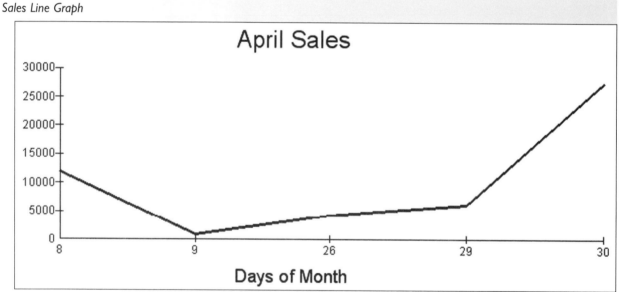

8   **Save the data file.**

Click Save on the toolbar.

9   **Optional spreadsheet integration activity.**

Use a spreadsheet to prepare a report and pie chart showing the component percent owed each vendor as of April 30. To complete this task, follow these steps:

a. Display and copy the schedule of accounts payable report to the clipboard in spreadsheet format.

b. Start your spreadsheet software and load template file IA6 Spreadsheet 03-S. (A blank, formatted worksheet will appear.)

c. Select cell A1 as the current cell (if not already selected).

d. Paste the schedule of accounts payable report (copied to the clipboard in step a) into the spreadsheet.

e. Enter Percent in cell C7.
Enter the formula to calculate the sum of the Balance column.
Enter the formula to calculate the component percent in cell C9.
Copy and paste the formula in cell C9 to cells C10–C15.

f. Format the amounts in currency format and the calculated percentages in percentage format if necessary.

g. Generate a pie chart.
Select the range of cells A9–B15, then choose the Chart or Graph menu item from the spreadsheet program you are using. If the computer asks for a graph name, enter Vendors in the graph name text box and click OK. Choose Pie Chart from the toolbar if the graph that appears is not a pie chart. Finally, if the spreadsheet you are using permits copying and pasting the graph into the worksheet, copy and paste the graph into cells A22–E40.

h. Print the spreadsheet and pie chart. The completed spreadsheet and pie chart are shown in Figure 3.24.

i. Save your spreadsheet data to your disk with a file name of 03-S Your Name.

j. What if Huntley Corporation's balance amount is changed to $8,750.00? Enter this change. Notice the affects of this change on the component percentages and pie chart.

k. End your spreadsheet session.

FIGURE 3.24

Spreadsheet Vendor Component Percentage Report and Pie Chart

Student Name
Reinke Wholesale Co.
Schedule of Accounts Payable
As Of 04/30/–

Name	Balance	Percent
Albright Company	$4,200.00	10.16%
Geppert Supply Corp.	$7,350.95	17.79%
Hinkley Company	$6,500.00	15.73%
Huntley Corporation	$9,950.00	24.08%
Kenward, Inc.	$8,500.00	20.57%
Lindemann Company	$2,420.15	5.86%
Schemmel Publications	$2,405.78	5.82%
Total	$41,326.88	

FIGURE 3.24

(Concluded)

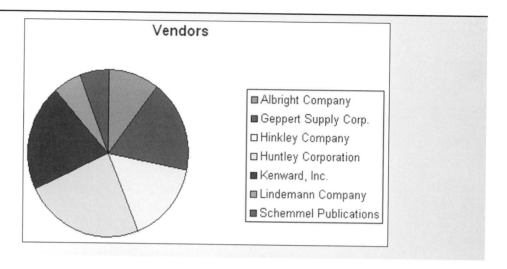

10 **Optional word processing integration activity.**

Reinke Wholesale Co., consults with Levine & Associates, a local accounting firm, for financial advice. As part of the information needed, Donald Levine, owner and CPA of the accounting firm, has asked you to fax him a list of the vendors and their account balances at the end of each month. Use the fax template of Reinke Wholesale Co., to prepare this document for the month ended April 30:

a. Display and copy the schedule of accounts payable report to the clipboard in word processing format.

b. Start your word processing application software and load template file IA6 Wordprocessing 03-S (load as a text file).

c. Enter your name in the FROM field and complete the remainder of the top portion of the facsimile as shown in Figure 3.25.

d. Position the insertion point one line after "Notes/Comments" and paste the report. Delete report headings, totals, and so on, and format the document to match Figure 3.25. Experiment with adding further enhancements to the appearance of the fax.

e. Print the completed document (to be faxed to the accounting firm). Note that many word processor software applications and computers now have the capability to fax documents electronically directly from the word processor.

f. Save the document to your disk with a file name of 03-S Your Name.

g. End your word processing session.

FIGURE 3.25

April 30 Facsimile

Reinke Wholesale Co.
3950 Maple Leaf Dr.
New Orleans, LA 70152–2530
(504) 555–9000
FACSIMILE

TO:	Donald Levine, CPA
COMPANY:	Levine & Associates
DATE:	(Today's Date)
PHONE NUMBER:	(504) 555–9000
FAX NUMBER:	(504) 555–9074
FROM:	(Your Name)
SUBJECT:	End of the Month Vendor Account Balances

Notes/Comments:

As per your request, our vendors and their account balances as of April 30 are as follows:

Albright Company	$4,200.00
Geppert Supply Corp.	7,350.95
Hinkley Company	6,500.00
Huntley Corporation	9,950.00
Kenward, Inc.	8,500.00
Lindemann Company	2,420.15
Schemmel Publications	2,405.78
Total	$41,326.88

If you have access to the Internet, use the browser to find the 12 U.S. Federal Reserve Banks. Use Federal Reserve Banks for your search. Identify the location of each of the 12 Federal Reserve Banks from your findings. Be sure to include the source and the URL (Web address) of your search.

INTERNET ACTIVITY

 11 **End your *Integrated Accounting* 6e session.**

Chapter 3 Student Exercises

NAME

I Matching

Directions   *For each of the definitions, write the letter of the appropriate term in the space provided.*

a. merchandise
b. merchandise inventory account
c. cost of merchandise sold account
d. vendors
e. customers
f. general journal
g. merchandising business
h. purchases on account

i. purchases journal
j. cash payments journal
k. sales journal
l. cash receipts journal
m. schedule of accounts payable and schedule of accounts receivable
n. accounts payable and accounts receivable ledger reports

1. _____ A business that purchases and resells goods.

2. _____ Transactions in which merchandise is purchased or goods or services are bought for payment at a later date.

3. _____ An account used to record the cost of the merchandise that has been sold to customers.

4. _____ An account that shows the value of the merchandise on hand.

5. _____ A term used to describe goods that are purchased for resale.

6. _____ Reports that list all journal activity by vendor or customer.

7. _____ Businesses from which merchandise is purchased or supplies and other assets are bought.

8. _____ Businesses or individuals to whom merchandise or services are sold.

9. _____ The journal used for entering purchases on account transactions.

10. _____ The journal used to enter all cash paid for expenses, cash purchases, payments to vendors, and payments not involving a check.

11. _____ The journal used to enter all sales on account transactions.

12. _____ The journal used to enter debit and credit memorandums.

13. _____ The journal used to enter all cash received on account, for cash sales, for sale of an asset, or for money borrowed.

14. _____ Reports that show the current balance for each vendor or customer.

II Questions

Directions   *Answer each of the following questions in the space provided.*

1. What account does the computer automatically calculate and display when a purchase transaction is entered? _____

_____

2. What account does the computer automatically calculate and display when a cash payment transaction is entered? _____

_____

3.   What account does the computer automatically calculate and display when a sales transaction is entered? _____

_____

4.   What account does the computer automatically calculate and display when a cash receipt is entered? _____

_____

Problem 3-A

Problem 3-A is a continuation of Sample Problem 3-S. Follow the step-by-step procedures provided to complete this problem for Reinke Wholesale Co., for the month of May of the current year. Answer audit questions 3-A on page 135 as you complete this problem. Display reports as necessary to answer the questions.

 As you complete this problem, click Info. on the toolbar for helpful check figures to audit your work.

1. Start *Integrated Accounting* 6e.

2. Open the file named IA6 Problem 03-A.

3. Enter your name in the Your Name text box.

4. Use Save As to save the data with a file name of 03-A Your Name.

5. Add Legal & Prof. Fees Exp. to the chart of accounts. Assign account number 6580 so that it will immediately follow Heating & Lighting Exp.

6. Delete Saffert Imports from the vendor list.

7. Change the name of the vendor Hinkley Company to Hinkley, Inc., and add a new vendor, Bresnan Mfg., Inc., to the vendor list.

8. Enter the general journal transactions.

General Journal Transactions

May 01   Reversing entries required by April adjustments. Using the adjustment data presented in sample Problem 3-S as the basis for your reversing entries, the only entry that requires reversing is for salaries payable.

Reversing Entries—Reversing entries are general journal entries made on the first day of a new accounting period that are the exact reverse of an adjusting entry made at the end of the previous period. In this reversing entry, $430.00 of sales salary and $310.00 of office salary (for a total of $740.00) from the previous accounting period applies to this accounting period.

Rev.Ent. 2130 Salaries Payable $740.00.

6110 Sales Salary Expense $430.00

6540 Office Salary Expense $310.00

26   Received merchandise returned on account from Stoffel Manufacturing, $950.00. The cost of the merchandise returned was $595.00. The credit memo applies to Sales Invoice No. 5358.

26   Returned merchandise purchased on account from Albright Company, $125.00; the debit memo applies to Invoice No. 3526.

9 **Enter the purchases journal transactions.**

Purchases Journal Transactions

May 03 Purchased merchandise on account from Albright Company, $2,950.00; Invoice No. 3533.

04 Purchased advertising on account from Schemmel Publications, $2,000.00; Invoice No. 3534.

05 Purchased merchandise on account from Kenward, Inc., $8,000.00; Invoice No. 3535.

05 Purchased the following on account from Lindemann Company: supplies, $925.00; office equipment, $895.00; total, $1,820.00; Invoice No. 3536.

10 Purchased merchandise on account from Huntley Corporation, $9,995.00; Invoice No. 3537.

12 Purchased merchandise on account from Hinkley, Inc., $8,200.00; Invoice No. 3538.

13 Purchased merchandise on account from Geppert Supply Corp., $10,048.14; Invoice No. 3539.

24 Purchased merchandise on account from Bresnan Mfg., Inc., $1,895.95; Invoice No. 3540.

10 **Enter the cash payments journal transactions.**

Cash Payments Journal Transactions

May 03 Paid cash for month's rent, $850.00; Check No. 2243.

04 Paid cash for monthly telephone bill, $479.63; Check No. 2244.

04 Paid cash on account to Schemmel Publications, covering an invoice amount of $2,405.78, no discount; Check No. 2245.

05 Paid $3,000.00 on a note payable, plus interest of $203.47; total payment, $3,203.47; Check No. 2246.

05 Paid cash on account to Huntley Corporation, covering an invoice amount of $9,950.00, less 2% discount, $199.00; Check No. 2247.

06 Paid cash on account to Lindemann Company, covering an invoice amount of $2,420.15, no discount; Check No. 2248.

07 Paid cash on account to Kenward, Inc., covering an invoice amount of $8,500.00, no discount; Check No. 2249.

17 Paid cash on account to Schemmel Publications, covering an invoice amount of $2,000.00, no discount; Check No. 2250.

18 Paid cash for delivery charges, $110.00; Check No. 2251.

19 Paid cash on account to Hinkley, Inc., covering an invoice amount of $6,500.00, no discount; Check No. 2252.

20 Paid cash for legal fees, $3,450.00; Check No. 2253.

21 Paid cash for printing business cards, $350.00; Check No. 2254. Charge Misc. Selling Expense.

27 Linda Reinke, owner, withdrew cash for personal use, $2,500.00; Check No. 2255.

27 Paid cash on account to Geppert Supply Corp., covering an invoice amount of $7,350.95, no discount; Check No. 2256.

30 Paid monthly salaries: sales salaries, $3,414.60; office salaries, $2,859.45; total, $6,274.05; Check No. 2257.

30 Paid cash for electric bill, $723.82; Check No. 2258.

30 Paid cash for sales tax liability, $464.70; Check No. 2259.

11 Enter the sales journal transactions.

Sales Journal Transactions

May 03 Sold merchandise on account to Harris Market, $15,000.00; Sales Invoice No. 5363. The cost of merchandise sold was $8,845.00.

04 Sold merchandise on account to Baxter Legal Services, $995.00; Sales Invoice No. 5364. The cost of merchandise sold was $570.00.

06 Sold merchandise on account to Stoffel Manufacturing, $3,520.00; Sales Invoice No. 5365. The cost of merchandise sold was $2,045.00.

10 Sold merchandise on account to United Corporation, $3,000.00; Sales Invoice No. 5366. The cost of merchandise sold was $1,798.00.

11 Sold merchandise on account to Mason Corporation, $1,250.00; Sales Invoice No. 5367. The cost of merchandise sold was $750.00.

14 Sold merchandise on account to Campbell Interiors, $12,000.00; Sales Invoice No. 5368. The cost of merchandise sold was $6,950.00.

18 Sold merchandise on account to Matson Boutique, $8,235.00; Sales Invoice No. 5369. The cost of merchandise sold was $4,940.00.

19 Sold merchandise on account to Mercy Clinic, Assoc., $5,000.00; Sales Invoice No. 5370. The cost of merchandise sold was $2,975.00.

21 Sold merchandise on account to Burgess Service Center, $1,785.99; Sales Invoice No. 5371. The cost of merchandise sold was $1,030.00.

24 Sold merchandise on account to Kimble Carpet Center, $11,650.00; Sales Invoice No. 5372. The cost of merchandise sold was $6,780.00.

12 Enter the cash receipts journal transactions.

Cash Receipts Journal Transactions

May 03 Received cash on account from Harris Market, covering Sales Invoice No. 5356 for $12,000.00, no discount.

07 Received cash on account from Matson Boutique, covering Sales Invoice No. 5362 for $10,000.00, less 2% discount, $200.00.

08 Received cash on account from Campbell Interiors, covering Sales Invoice No. 5361 for $17,450.00, less 2% discount, $349.00.

10 Received cash on account from Baxter Legal Services, covering Sales Invoice No. 5357 for $795.00, no discount.

11 Received cash on account from Kimble Carpet Center, covering Sales Invoice No. 5291 for $16,787.75, no discount.

13 Received cash on account from Mason Corporation, covering Sales Invoice No. 5360 for $1,200.00, no discount.

17 Sold merchandise for cash May 1 through May 15, $4,570.00, plus 6% sales tax, $274.20; total, $4,844.20. Cash Receipt No. 1203. The cost of the merchandise sold was $2,480.00.

17 Received cash on account from Baxter Legal Services, covering Sales Invoice No. 5364 for $995.00, no discount.

25 Received cash on account from United Corporation, covering Sales Invoice No. 5283 for $19,625.15, no discount.

31 Sold merchandise for cash May 16 through May 31, $4,118.00, plus 6% sales tax, $247.08; total, $4,365.08. Cash Receipt No. 1204. The cost of the merchandise sold was $2,470.00.

13 **Display the chart of accounts.**

14 **Display the vendor list.**

15 **Display the journal entries and make corrections, if necessary.**

16 **Display the trial balance.**

17 **Display the schedule of accounts payable and accounts payable ledger reports (for all vendors).**

18 **Display the schedule of accounts receivable and accounts receivable ledger reports (for all customers).**

End-of-Month Activities

After the monthly transactions have been processed, the adjusting entries must be entered into the computer and displayed. The financial statements may then be displayed. The adjustment data for the month of May for Reinke Wholesale Co., are listed next.

Insurance expired during May $397.00
Inventory of supplies $2,312.00
Depreciation for May:
    Warehouse equipment $646.54
    Office equipment $281.00
Salaries Payable:
    Sales salaries $455.00
    Office salaries $337.00

1 **Enter the adjusting entries in the general journal. Enter a reference of Adj.Ent. in the Reference text box.**

2 **Display the adjusting entries.**

3 **Use the Check toolbar button to check your work and made corrections if necessary.**

4 **Display the income statement.**

5 **Display the statement of owner's equity.**

6 **Display the balance sheet.**

7 **Display a balance sheet graph.**

8 **Click Save on the toolbar to save the data file.**

9 **Optional spreadsheet integration activity.**

Use a spreadsheet to prepare a report and pie chart showing the component percent owed by each customer as of May 31.

   a. Display and copy the schedule of accounts receivable report to the clipboard in spreadsheet format.

   b. Start your spreadsheet software and load template file IA6 Spreadsheet 03-S (a blank, formatted worksheet will appear).

   c. Select cell A1 as the current cell (if not already selected) and paste the schedule of accounts receivable report into the spreadsheet.

   d. Enter Percent in cell C7.
     Enter the formula to calculate the sum of the balance column.
     Enter the formula to calculate the component percent in cell C9.
     Copy and paste the formula in cell C9 to the appropriate cells.

   e. Format the amounts in currency format and the calculated percentages in percentage format if necessary.

   f. Generate a pie chart depicting the data in the report.

   g. Print the spreadsheet and pie chart.

   h. Save your spreadsheet data to your disk with a file name of 03-A Your Name.

   i. What if Campbell Interiors' balance is now $15,000.00 and Kimble Carpet Center's balance is now $10,000.00? Enter these changes. Notice the affects of these changes on the component percentages and pie chart.

   j. End your spreadsheet session.

10 **Optional word processing integration activity.**

Use the company's word processing fax template to prepare the customer account balance information for the accounting firm the month ended May 31:

   a. Display and copy the schedule of accounts receivable report to the clipboard in word processing format.

   b. Start your word processing application software and load template file IA6 Wordprocessing 03-S (load as a text file).

   c. Enter your name in the FROM field and complete the remainder of the top portion of the facsimile as shown in Figure 3.25 on page 125.

   d. Paste the report, delete report headings, totals, and so on, and format the document to match Figure 3.25.

e. Print the completed document.

f. Save the document to your disk with a file name of 03-A Your Name.

g. End your word processing session.

INTERNET ACTIVITY

If you have access to the Internet, use the browser to find the names of the members of the Federal Reserve Board of Governors. Report on your findings. Be sure to include the source and the URL (Web address) of your search.

11 **End the *Integrated Accounting* 6e session.**

Audit Questions 3-A

NAME

Directions   *Write the answers to the following questions in the space provided.*

1. What are the total debits and total credits shown on the purchases journal report for the month of May?

    Total debits: _____

    Total credits: _____

2. What are the total debits and total credits shown on the cash payments journal report for the month of May?

    Total debits: _____

    Total credits: _____

3. What are the total debits and total credits shown on the sales journal report for the month of May?

    Total debits: _____

    Total credits: _____

4. What are the total debits and total credits shown on the cash receipts journal report for the month of May?

    Total debits: _____

    Total credits: _____

5. As of May 31, what is the amount owed to Hinkley, Inc.?   _____

    _____

6. As of May 31, how much does Stoffel Manufacturing owe to Reinke Wholesale Co.?

    _____

7. From the income statement, what is the cost of merchandise sold for the month?

    _____

8. From the statement of owner's equity, what is Linda Reinke's capital at the end of the period?

    _____

9. From the balance sheet, what are the total assets?   _____

    _____

10. From the balance sheet, what are the total liabilities?   _____

    _____

Problem 3-B

Problem 3-B is a continuation of Sample Problem 3-S. Follow the step-by-step procedures provided to complete this problem for Reinke Wholesale Co., for the month of May of the current year. Answer audit questions 3-B on page 142 as you complete this problem. Display reports as necessary to answer the questions.

1   Start *Integrated Accounting* 6e.

2   Open the file named IA6 Problem 03-B.

3   Enter your name in the Your Name text box.

4   Use Save As to save the data with a file name of 03-B Your Name.

5   Add Legal & Prof. Fees Exp. to the chart of accounts. Assign account number 6580 so that it will immediately follow Heating & Lighting Exp.

6   Delete Saffert Imports from the vendor list.

7   Change the name of the vendor Hinkley Company to Hinkley, Inc., and add a new vendor, Bresnan Mfg., Inc., to the vendor list.

8   Enter the general journal transactions.

General Journal Transactions

May 01   Reversing entries required by April adjustments. Using the adjustment data presented in sample Problem 3-S as the basis for your reversing entries, the only entry that requires reversing is for salaries payable.

Rev. Ent. 2130 Salaries Payable $740.00.

6110 Sales Salary Expense $430.00

6540 Office Salary Expense $310.00

26   Received merchandise returned on account from Stoffel Manufacturing, $1,000.00. The cost of the merchandise returned was $605.00. The credit memo applies to Sales Invoice No. 5358.

26   Returned merchandise purchased on account from Albright Company, $95.00; the debit memo applies to Invoice No. 3526.

9   Enter the purchases journal transactions.

Purchases Journal Transactions

May 03   Purchased merchandise on account from Albright Company, $3,050.00; Invoice No. 3533.

04   Purchased advertising on account from Schemmel Publications, $1,850.00; Invoice No. 3534.

05   Purchased merchandise on account from Kenward, Inc., $8,495.00; Invoice No. 3535.

05   Purchased the following on account from Lindemann Company: supplies, $999.95; office equipment, $785.65; total, $1,785.60; Invoice No. 3536.

10   Purchased merchandise on account from Huntley Corporation, $10,200.00; Invoice No. 3537.

12   Purchased merchandise on account from Hinkley, Inc., $7,800.00; Invoice No. 3538.

13   Purchased merchandise on account from Geppert Supply Corp., $10,975.00; Invoice No. 3539.

24   Purchased merchandise on account from Bresnan Mfg., Inc., $1,625.00; Invoice No. 3540.

10   Enter the cash payments journal transactions.

Cash Payments Journal Transactions

May 03   Paid cash for month's rent, $850.00; Check No. 2243.

04   Paid cash for monthly telephone bill, $569.35; Check No. 2244.

04   Paid cash on account to Schemmel Publications, covering an invoice amount of $2,405.78, no discount; Check No. 2245.

05   Paid $3,000.00 on a note payable, plus interest of $203.47; total payment, $3,203.47; Check No. 2246.

05   Paid cash on account to Huntley Corporation, covering an invoice amount of $9,950.00, less 2% discount, $199.00; Check No. 2247.

06   Paid cash on account to Lindemann Company, covering an invoice amount of $2,420.15, no discount; Check No. 2248.

07   Paid cash on account to Kenward, Inc., covering an invoice amount of $8,500.00, no discount; Check No. 2249.

17   Paid cash on account to Schemmel Publications, covering an invoice amount of $1,850.00, no discount; Check No. 2250.

18   Paid cash for delivery charges, $100.00; Check No. 2251.

19   Paid cash on account to Hinkley, Inc., covering an invoice amount of $6,500.00, no discount; Check No. 2252.

20   Paid cash for legal fees, $3,000.00; Check No. 2253.

21   Paid cash for printing business cards, $335.00; Check No. 2254. Charge Misc. Selling Expense.

27   Linda Reinke, owner, withdrew cash for personal use, $2,800.00; Check No. 2255.

27   Paid cash on account to Geppert Supply Corp., covering an invoice amount of $7,350.95, no discount; Check No. 2256.

30   Paid monthly salaries: sales salaries, $3,569.70; office salaries, $2,910.30; total, $6,480.00; Check No. 2257.

30   Paid cash for electric bill, $689.48; Check No. 2258.

30   Paid cash for sales tax liability, $464.70; Check No. 2259.

11   **Enter the sales journal transactions.**

Sales Journal Transactions

May 03   Sold merchandise on account to Harris Market, $15,000.00; Sales Invoice No. 5363. The cost of the merchandise sold was $8,947.00.

04   Sold merchandise on account to Baxter Legal Services, $1,275.00; Sales Invoice No. 5364. The cost of the merchandise sold was $750.00.

06   Sold merchandise on account to Stoffel Manufacturing, $3,000.00; Sales Invoice No. 5365. The cost of the merchandise sold was $1,800.00.

10   Sold merchandise on account to United Corporation, $3,115.00; Sales Invoice No. 5366. The cost of the merchandise sold was $1,795.00.

11   Sold merchandise on account to Mason Corporation, $917.60; Sales Invoice No. 5367. The cost of the merchandise sold was $525.00.

14   Sold merchandise on account to Campbell Interiors, $13,725.50; Sales Invoice No. 5368. The cost of the merchandise sold was $8,135.30.

18   Sold merchandise on account to Matson Boutique, $8,075.00; Sales Invoice No. 5369. The cost of the merchandise sold was $4,685.00.

19   Sold merchandise on account to Mercy Clinic, Assoc., $5,410.35; Sales Invoice No. 5370. The cost of the merchandise sold was $3,137.45.

21   Sold merchandise on account to Burgess Service Center, $2,000.00; Sales Invoice No. 5371. The cost of the merchandise sold was $1,200.00.

24   Sold merchandise on account to Kimble Carpet Center, $11,500.00; Sales Invoice No. 5372. The cost of the merchandise sold was $6,650.00.

12   **Enter the cash receipts journal transactions.**

Cash Receipts Journal Transactions

May 03   Received cash on account from Harris Market, covering Sales Invoice No. 5356 for $12,000.00, no discount.

07   Received cash on account from Matson Boutique, covering Sales Invoice No. 5362 for $10,000.00, less 2% discount, $200.00.

08   Received cash on account from Campbell Interiors, covering Sales Invoice No. 5361 for $17,450.00, less 2% discount, $349.00.

10   Received cash on account from Baxter Legal Services, covering Sales Invoice No. 5357 for $795.00, no discount.

11   Received cash on account from Kimble Carpet Center, covering Sales Invoice No. 5291 for $16,787.75, no discount.

13   Received cash on account from Mason Corporation, covering Sales Invoice No. 5360 for $1,200.00, no discount.

17   Sold merchandise for cash May 1 through May 15, $4,518.64, plus 6% sales tax, $271.12; total, $4,789.76. Cash Receipt No. 1203. The cost of the merchandise sold was $2,710.00.

17   Received cash on account from Baxter Legal Services, covering Sales Invoice No. 5364 for $1,275.00, no discount.

25   Received cash on account from United Corporation, covering Sales Invoice No. 5283 for $19,625.15, no discount.

31   Sold merchandise for cash May 16 through May 31, $4,198.00, plus 6% sales tax, $251.88; total, $4,449.88. Cash Receipt No. 1204. The cost of the merchandise sold was $2,465.00.

(13)   **Display the chart of accounts.**

(14)   **Display the vendor list.**

(15)   **Display the journal entries and make corrections, if necessary.**

(16)   **Display the trial balance.**

(17)   **Display the schedule of accounts payable and accounts payable ledger reports (for all vendors).**

(18)   **Display the schedule of accounts receivable and accounts receivable ledger reports (for all customers).**

End-of-Month Activities

After the monthly transactions have been processed, the adjusting entries must be entered into the computer and displayed. The financial statements may then be displayed. The adjustment data for the month of May for Reinke Wholesale Co., are listed next.

Insurance expired during May	$420.00
Inventory of supplies	$2,218.00
Depreciation for May:	
Warehouse equipment	$654.34
Office equipment	$260.15
Salaries Payable:	
Sales salaries	$460.00
Office salaries	$335.00

(1)   **Enter the adjusting entries in the general journal. Enter a reference of Adj.Ent. in the Reference text box.**

(2)   **Display the adjusting entries.**

(3)   **Display the income statement.**

(4)   **Display the statement of owner's equity.**

(5)   **Display the balance sheet.**

(6)   **Display an income statement graph.**

(7)   **Click Save on the toolbar to save the data file.**

(8)   **Optional spreadsheet integration activity.**

Use a spreadsheet to prepare a report and pie chart showing the component percent owed by each customer as of May 31.

a. Display and copy the schedule of accounts receivable report to the clipboard in spreadsheet format.

b. Start your spreadsheet software and load template file IA6 Spreadsheet 03-S (a blank, formatted worksheet will appear).

c. Select cell A1 as the current cell (if not already selected) and paste the schedule of accounts receivable report into the spreadsheet.

d. Enter Percent in cell C7.
Enter the formula to calculate the sum of the balance column.
Enter the formula to calculate the component percent in cell C9.
Copy and paste the formula in cell C9 to the appropriate cells.

e. Format the amounts in currency format and the calculated percentages in percentage format if necessary.

f. Generate a pie chart depicting the data in the report.

g. Print the spreadsheet and pie chart.

h. Save your spreadsheet data to your disk with a file name of 03-B Your Name.

i. What if Burgess Service Center's balance is now $4,000.00 and Matson Boutique's balance is now $13,585.00? Enter these changes. Notice the affects of these changes on the component percentages and pie chart. Do not save these changes.

j. End your spreadsheet session.

9 **Optional word processing integration activity.**

Use the company's word processing fax template to prepare the customer account balance information for the accounting firm for the month ended May 31:

a. Display and copy the schedule of accounts receivable report to the clipboard in word processing format.

b. Start your word processing application software and load template file IA6 Wordprocessing 03-S (load as a text file).

c. Enter your name in the FROM field and complete the remainder of the top portion of the facsimile as shown in Figure 3.25 on page 125.

d. Paste the report, delete report headings, totals, and so on, and format the document to match Figure 3.25.

e. Print the completed document.

f. Save the document to your disk with a file name of 03-B Your Name.

g. End your word processing session.

If you have access to the Internet, use the browser to find the address and phone number of the U.S. Federal Reserve Bank nearest to where you live. Report on your findings. Be sure to include the source and the URL (Web address) of your search.

INTERNET ACTIVITY

10 **End the *Integrated Accounting* 6e session.**

Audit Questions 3-B

NAME

Directions   *Write the answers to the following questions in the space provided.*

1.   What are the total debits and total credits shown on the purchases journal report for the month of May?

Total debits: _____

Total credits: _____

2.   What are the total debits and total credits shown on the cash payments journal report for the month of May?

Total debits: _____

Total credits: _____

3.   What are the total debits and total credits shown on the sales journal report for the month of May?

Total debits: _____

Total credits: _____

4.   What are the total debits and total credits shown on the cash receipts journal report for the month of May?

Total debits: _____

Total credits: _____

5.   As of May 31, what is the amount owed to all vendors?

_____

6.   As of May 31, how much does Campbell Interiors owe to Reinke Wholesale Co.?

_____

7.   From the income statement, what is the cost of merchandise sold for the month?

_____

8.   From the statement of owner's equity, what is Linda Reinke's capital at the end of the period?

_____

9.   From the balance sheet, what are the total assets?

_____

10.   From the balance sheet, what are the total liabilities?

_____

Voucher System and Budgeting

Upon completion of this chapter, you will be able to:

- Identify the components and procedures used to process a computerized voucher system.

- Enter voucher transactions.

- Enter voucher cash payment transactions and generate checks.

- Display voucher and cash payments journals.

- Enter budgetary data and generate a budget report and graph.

Key Terms

Introduction

In the previous chapters, the businesses you worked with were treated as "standard accounting systems" by the computer software. In this chapter, you will use a voucher system to complete the monthly accounting cycle for Hubbell Building Supplies. A **voucher system** implements specific procedures for controlling a business's cash disbursements. For example, in a voucher system, all cash disbursements (with the possible exception of disbursements from a petty cash fund) are paid by check. Written authorization is required for each cash disbursement, usually in the form of a voucher. Consecutive numbers are assigned to each voucher to help control disbursements. Generally, a **vouchers payable account** is used in the general ledger rather than an accounts payable account.

When the standard accounting system used previously was in effect, it was unnecessary to enter vendors for direct cash payments. They were only entered for payments on account. When working with a voucher system, a vendor must exist for each cash disbursement.

During accounting system setup, the software determines whether a voucher system will be used based on the accounting system setting in the Customize Accounting System window (discussed in Chapter 12). This chapter discusses the differences between the standard accounting systems (with which you are already familiar) and a voucher system. Minor differences exist in entering journal entries and generating reports.

Vouchers Journal

One new journal is needed to complete the accounting cycle using a voucher system: the vouchers journal. A **vouchers journal** with the following three example transactions already entered and posted is shown in Figure 4.1. The first transaction involves the purchase of merchandise from Heritage Mfg. Co., Inc. The Merchandise Inventory account is debited and Vouchers Payable/Heritage Mfg. Co., Inc., is credited. The second transaction involves the recording of a voucher to pay the monthly rent to Ormsby Leasing Corporation. Account number 6130 (Rent Expense) and the amount of rent have been entered in the debit column. Vouchers Payable/Ormsby Leasing Corporation is credited. The third transaction involves the recording of a voucher for the monthly payment of a note payable to Harrington State Bank. Account number 2510 (Note Payable) is debited $585.64 and account number 8110 (Interest Expense) is debited $173.15. Vouchers Payable/Harrington State Bank is credited $758.79.

Apr. 02   Purchased merchandise on account from Heritage Mfg. Co., Inc., $1,200.00; Voucher No. 5703.

08   Record Voucher No. 5707 to Ormsby Leasing Corporation for monthly rent, $1,100.00.

25   Record Voucher No. 5711 to Harrington State Bank for a note payable, $758.79; principal, $585.64; interest, $173.15.

FIGURE 4.1

Vouchers Journal

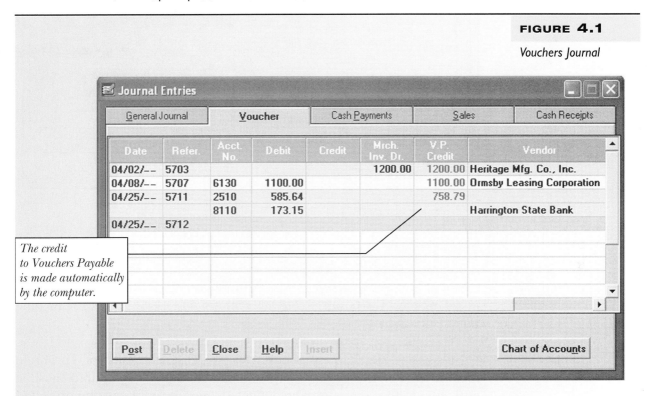

> The credit to Vouchers Payable is made automatically by the computer.

Enter the **voucher number** (a number used to identify a voucher) in the Refer. grid cell. If the voucher is for goods or services other than merchandise, enter the appropriate account number and debit amount. If more than one item is to be included (i.e., notes payable and interest expense) on the voucher, press the Tab key and continue entering the account numbers and debit amounts for the additional items on subsequent lines.

If the voucher is for merchandise, enter the amount in the merchandise inventory (Mrch. Inv. Dr.) grid cell.

Checks

Checks are generated for each vendor in payment of vouchers owed (if the Computer Checks check box is set to on, which will be covered later in Chapter 12). The checks will be automatically generated each time a cash payment transaction that involves a vendor is entered and posted in the cash payments journal. While the check appears on the display screen, it may be printed to an attached printer. A computer-generated check, similar to the example shown in Figure 4.2 will appear.

Click on Print to print the currently displayed check to an attached printer, or click on Close to dismiss the check and continue entering cash payment transactions.

FIGURE 4.2

Check

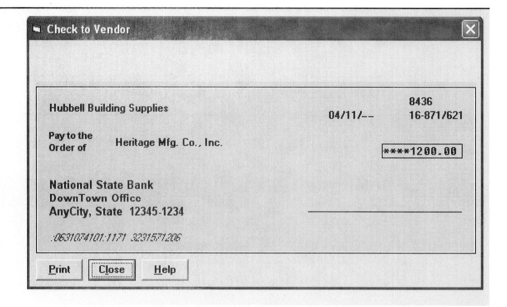

Budgets

A **budget** is a financial plan for the future that may be developed for a specific time, such as a month or year. Although budgets can be developed for many aspects of a business, *Integrated Accounting* uses budgets for income statement accounts only.

The budgeted amount of total revenue, cost of merchandise sold (if the business is a merchandising business), expense accounts, or corporate income tax accounts (if the business is organized as a corporation) must be entered into the computer. The budgeted amount represents the projected revenue, cost, or expense amount for a fiscal period. Once budget data are entered, a budget report may be generated that compares actual revenues and expenses with budgeted revenues and expenses. The software determines whether budgeting is in use based on the Budgeting check box in the Customize Accounting System window (discussed in Chapter 12) during accounting system setup. To enter data in the budgeting system, click Tasks on the toolbar, choose the Other Tasks menu item from the Data menu, or click the Comp. Info. navigation button and then the Enter Budgets menu button. When the Other Tasks window appears, click on the Budgets tab and enter the budgeted amounts. This task is usually performed at the beginning of a fiscal period (in this chapter, for illustrative purposes, it is completed in April in Sample Problem 4-S on page 149). A **budgeted amount** is the estimated balance for that particular account at the end of the fiscal period. The account titles and currently stored budget amounts (if any) are displayed in the window, as illustrated in Figure 4.3 for Hubbell Building Supplies, so that you may either enter new budget amounts or correct or change previously entered budgeted amounts.

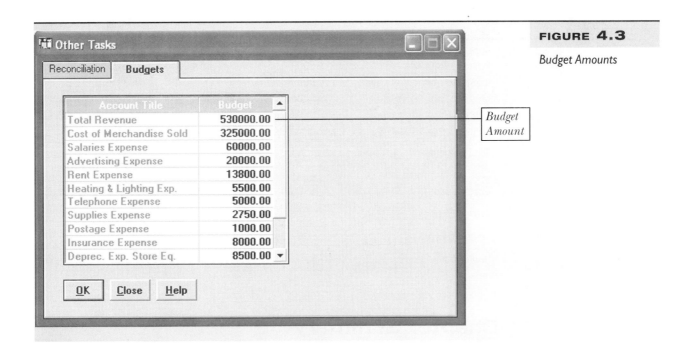

FIGURE 4.3

Budget Amounts

NOTE The accounts are scrollable. After you enter the amount for the last account shown in the window, the accounts will scroll up so that you can enter the next budget amount (assuming that the last account in the window is not the last income statement account in the chart of accounts).

Budget Report

The **budget report** compares actual revenues and expenses with budgeted revenues and expenses in income statement format. A budget report for Hubbell Building Supplies is shown in Figure 4.4.

Hubbell Building Supplies
Budget Report
For Period Ended 04/30/—

	Budget	Actual	Diff. From Budget	%
Operating Revenue				
Operating Revenue	530,000.00	184,260.60	−345,739.40	−65.23
Cost of Merchandise Sold	325,000.00	107,561.50	−217,438.50	−66.90
Gross Profit	205,000.00	76,699.10	−128,300.90	−62.59
Operating Expenses				
Salaries Expense	60,000.00	16,764.52	−43,235.48	−72.06
Advertising Expense	20,000.00	6,450.00	−13,550.00	−67.75
Rent Expense	13,800.00	4,400.00	−9,400.00	−68.12
Heating & Lighting Exp.	5,500.00	1,609.22	−3,890.78	−70.74
			(continued)	

FIGURE 4.4

Hubbell Building Supplies Budget Report

FIGURE 4.4

(Concluded)

Telephone Expense	5,000.00	1,455.43	−3,544.57	−70.89
Supplies Expense	2,750.00	271.85	−2,478.15	−90.11
Postage Expense	1,000.00	41.00	−959.00	−95.90
Insurance Expense	8,000.00	973.00	−7,027.00	−87.84
Deprec. Exp. Store Eq.	8,500.00	2,716.50	−5,783.50	−68.04
Deprec. Exp. Office Eq.	3,000.00	947.00	−2,053.00	−68.43
Miscellaneous Expense	1,000.00	285.00	−715.00	−71.50
Total Operating Expenses	128,550.00	35,913.52	−92,636.48	−72.06
Net Income from Operations	76,450.00	40,785.58	−35,664.42	−46.65
Other Expense				
Interest Expense	2,500.00	833.15	−1,666.85	−66.67
Net Income	73,950.00	39,952.43	−33,997.57	−45.97

Chapter Summary

■ A voucher system is a system in which specific procedures are implemented for the purpose of controlling a business's cash disbursements.

■ Consecutive numbers are assigned to each voucher entered into the system to help control disbursements.

■ Generally, a vouchers payable account is used in the general ledger rather than an accounts payable account.

■ When working with a voucher system, a vendor must exist for each cash disbursement.

■ A vouchers journal is used to enter all new vouchers.

■ A check will be generated each time a cash payment transaction involving a vendor is entered and posted.

■ A budget is a financial plan for the future. Budgets are developed for a specific time.

■ *Integrated Accounting* uses budgets for income statement accounts and generates a budget report that compares actual revenues and expenses with budgeted revenues and expenses in income statement format.

Sample Problem 4-S

This sample problem illustrates the use of a computerized voucher system. You need to process the transactions for the month of April of the current year, complete the monthly accounting cycle, and prepare a budget report and graph for Hubbell Building Supplies. The April transactions, budget amounts, and adjusting entries are illustrated within the step-by-step instructions that follow.

1   Start *Integrated Accounting* 6e.

2   Load the opening balance template file, IA6 Problem 04-S.

3   Enter your name in the Your Name text box and click OK.

4   Save the data with a file name of 04-S Your Name.

5   Add Postage Expense to the chart of accounts. Assign account number 6165 so that it will immediately follow Supplies Expense.

6   Add three vendors to the vendor list: Payroll Bank Account, Commissioner of Revenue, and Postmaster.

7   Change the name of the customer Schaefer Roofing Co., to Schaefer Roofing, Inc., and add a new customer, Lasker Window Co., to the customer list.

8   Enter the following budget data.

Click on the Comp. Info. navigation button, and then the Enter Budgets menu button. Click the Budgets tab (if not already chosen) and enter the following budget amounts. Be sure to scroll through the window to enter all the amounts.

Account Title	Budget
Total Revenue	$530,000.00
Cost of Merchandise Sold	$325,000.00
Salaries Expense	$60,000.00
Advertising Expense	$20,000.00
Rent Expense	$13,800.00
Heating & Lighting Expense	$5,500.00
Telephone Expense	$5,000.00
Supplies Expense	$2,750.00
Postage Expense	$1,000.00
Insurance Expense	$8,000.00
Deprec. Exp. Store Eq.	$8,500.00
Deprec. Exp. Office Eq.	$3,000.00
Miscellaneous Expense	$1,000.00
Interest Expense	$2,500.00

⑨ **Enter the general journal transactions shown in Figure 4.5.**

Click on the Gen. Led. navigation button and then the Journal Entries menu button. When the Journal Entries window appears, click on the General Journal tab (if not already chosen) and enter the journal entries listed here and illustrated in Figure 4.5.

General Journal Transactions

Apr. 11 Returned merchandise purchased on account from Byron, Inc., $200.00; the debit memo applies to Voucher No. 5679.

22 Received merchandise returned on account from Fuller Construction Co., $475.50. The cost of the merchandise returned was $285.30. The credit memo applies to Sales Invoice No. 7506.

FIGURE 4.5

General Journal

Date	Refer.	Account	Debit	Credit	Vendor/Customer
04/11/--	5679	2110 Vouchers Payable	200.00		Byron, Inc.
		1130 Merchandise Inventory		200.00	
04/22/--	7506	4120 Sales Returns & Allow.	475.50		
		1130 Merchandise Inventory	285.30		
		1120 Accounts Receivable		475.50	Fuller Construction Co.
		5110 Cost of Merchandise Sold		285.30	

⑩ **Enter the April vouchers journal transaction data shown here and illustrated in Figure 4.6.**

Click the Voucher tab and enter the journal transactions. Each voucher journal entry includes a credit to the Vouchers Payable account. In each case, this entry will be made automatically by the computer.

Vouchers Journal Transactions

Apr. 02 Purchased merchandise on account from Heritage Mfg. Co., Inc., $1,200.00; Voucher No. 5703.

02 Purchased merchandise on account from Schroeder Manufacturing, $995.00; Voucher No. 5704.

04 Purchased supplies on account from Meyer Office Supply Co., $146.85; no sales tax; Voucher No. 5705.

07 Purchased merchandise on account from Zimmerman, Inc., $7,600.00; Voucher No. 5706.

08 Record Voucher No. 5707 to Ormsby Leasing Corporation for monthly rent, $1,100.00.

15 Record Voucher No. 5708 to ACS Gas & Electric Co., for monthly electric bill, $402.38.

18 Purchased merchandise on account from Schroeder Manufacturing, $6,895.00; Voucher No. 5709.

19 Purchased merchandise on account from Robertson Mfg., Inc., $1,837.15; Voucher No. 5710.

25   Record Voucher No. 5711 to Harrington State Bank for a note payable, $758.79; principal, $585.64; interest, $173.15.

26   Record Voucher No. 5712 to Midwest Telephone Co., for monthly telephone bill, $357.43.

27   Record Voucher No. 5713 to reimburse the payroll bank account for monthly salaries expense, $4,103.42.

28   Purchased advertising on account from Sinclair Daily Newspaper, $575.00; Voucher No. 5714.

30   Record Voucher No. 5715 to Commissioner of Revenue for sales tax liability, $99.81.

30   Record Voucher No. 5716 to Postmaster for postage, $41.00.

30   Purchased merchandise on account from Heritage Mfg. Co., Inc., $9,025.00; Voucher No. 5717.

30   Record Voucher No. 5718 to William Hubbell for owner's use, $2,500.00.

FIGURE 4.6

Vouchers Journal

Date	Refer.	Acct. No.	Debit	Credit	Mrch. Inv. Dr.	V.P. Credit	Vendor
04/02/--	5703				1200.00	1200.00	Heritage Mfg. Co., Inc.
04/02/--	5704				995.00	995.00	Schroeder Manufacturing
04/04/--	5705	1150	146.85			146.85	Meyer Office Supply Co.
04/07/--	5706				7600.00	7600.00	Zimmerman, Inc.
04/08/--	5707	6130	1100.00			1100.00	Ormsby Leasing Corporation
04/15/--	5708	6140	402.38			402.38	ACS Gas & Electric Co.
04/18/--	5709				6895.00	6895.00	Schroeder Manufacturing
04/19/--	5710				1837.15	1837.15	Robertson Mfg., Inc.
04/25/--	5711	2510	585.64			758.79	
		8110	173.15				Harrington State Bank
04/26/--	5712	6150	357.43			357.43	Midwest Telephone Co.
04/27/--	5713	6110	4103.42			4103.42	Payroll Bank Account
04/28/--	5714	6120	575.00			575.00	Sinclair Daily Newspaper
04/30/--	5715	2120	99.81			99.81	Commissioner of Revenue
04/30/--	5716	6165	41.00			41.00	Postmaster
04/30/--	5717				9025.00	9025.00	Heritage Mfg. Co., Inc.
04/30/	5718	3120	2500.00			2500.00	William Hubbell

11   Enter the April cash payments journal transaction data listed here and illustrated in Figure 4.7.

Click the Cash Payments tab and enter the cash payments journal transactions.

Cash Payments Journal Transactions

Apr. 03   Paid Voucher No. 5669 to Heritage Mfg. Co., Inc., $3,624.46, no discount. Check No. 8431.

08   Paid Voucher No. 5671 to Schroeder Manufacturing, $4,743.26, no discount. Check No. 8432.

08   Paid Voucher No. 5707 to Ormsby Leasing Corporation, $1,100.00. Check No. 8433.

09   Paid Voucher No. 5673 to Robertson Mfg., Inc., $2,490.00, no discount. Check No. 8434.

11   Paid Voucher No. 5679 to Byron, Inc., $7,457.25, no discount. Check No. 8435.

11   Paid Voucher No. 5703 to Heritage Mfg. Co., Inc., $1,200.00, no discount. Check No. 8436.

12   Paid Voucher No. 5704 to Schroeder Manufacturing, $995.00, less 2% discount, $19.90. Check No. 8437.

15   Paid Voucher No. 5708 to ACS Gas & Electric Co., $402.38. Check No. 8438.

17   Paid Voucher No. 5684 to Zimmerman, Inc., $8,655.95, less 2% discount, $173.12. Check No. 8439.

25   Paid Voucher No. 5711 to Harrington State Bank, $758.79. Check No. 8440.

26   Paid Voucher No. 5712 to Midwest Telephone Co., $357.43. Check No. 8441.

27   Paid Voucher No. 5713 to Payroll Bank Account, $4,103.42. Check No. 8442.

30   Paid Voucher No. 5715 to Commissioner of Revenue, $99.81. Check No. 8443.

30   Paid Voucher No. 5716 to Postmaster, $41.00. Check No. 8444.

30   Paid Voucher No. 5718 to William Hubbell, $2,500.00. Check No. 8445.

FIGURE 4.7

Cash Payments Journal

Date	Refer.	V.P. Debit	Mrch. Inv. Cr.	Cash Credit	Vendor
04/03/--	8431	3624.46		3624.46	Heritage Mfg. Co., Inc.
04/08/--	8432	4743.26		4743.26	Schroeder Manufacturing
04/08/--	8433	1100.00		1100.00	Ormsby Leasing Corporation
04/09/--	8434	2490.00		2490.00	Robertson Mfg., Inc.
04/11/--	8435	7457.25		7457.25	Byron, Inc.
04/11/--	8436	1200.00		1200.00	Heritage Mfg. Co., Inc.
04/12/--	8437	995.00	19.90	975.10	Schroeder Manufacturing
04/15/--	8438	402.38		402.38	ACS Gas & Electric Co.
04/17/--	8439	8655.95	173.12	8482.83	Zimmerman, Inc.
04/25/--	8440	758.79		758.79	Harrington State Bank
04/26/--	8441	357.43		357.43	Midwest Telephone Co.
04/27/--	8442	4103.42		4103.42	Payroll Bank Account
04/30/--	8443	99.81		99.81	Commissioner of Revenue
04/30/--	8444	41.00		41.00	Postmaster
04/30/--	8445	2500.00		2500.00	William Hubbell

(12)   Enter the April sales journal transaction data listed here and illustrated in Figure 4.8.

Click the Sales tab and enter the sales journal transactions.

Sales Journal Transactions

Apr. 07   Sold merchandise on account to Osborn Company, $3,528.50, no sales tax. Sales Invoice No. 7591. The cost of the merchandise sold was $1,850.10.

16   Sold merchandise on account to Lasker Window Co., $4,550.00, plus 6% sales tax, $273.00; total, $4,823.00. Sales Invoice No. 7592. The cost of the merchandise sold was $2,670.00.

23   Sold merchandise on account to Alliance Construction, $8,975.00, no sales tax. Sales Invoice No. 7593. The cost of the merchandise sold was $5,245.50.

30   Sold merchandise on account to Designer Building Supply, $36,648.00, no sales tax. Sales Invoice No. 7594. The cost of the merchandise sold was $19,950.00.

30   Sold merchandise on account to Lewis Builders Supply, $24,760.00, no sales tax. Sales Invoice No. 7595. The cost of the merchandise sold was $14,458.00.

30   Sold merchandise on account to Elcor Contractors, $4,995.00, no sales tax. Sales Invoice No. 7596. The cost of the merchandise sold was $3,000.00.

FIGURE 4.8

Sales Journal

Date	Refer.	Sales Credit	Sales Tax Credit	Cost Mrch Sold Dr.	Mrch. Inv. Cr.	A.R. Debit	Customer
04/07/--	7591	3528.50		1850.10	1850.10	3528.50	Osborn Company
04/16/--	7592	4550.00	273.00	2670.00	2670.00	4823.00	Lasker Window Co.
04/23/--	7593	8975.00		5245.50	5245.50	8975.00	Alliance Construction
04/30/--	7594	36648.00		19950.00	19950.00	36648.00	Designer Building Supply
04/30/--	7595	24760.00		14458.00	14458.00	24760.00	Lewis Builders Supply
04/30/--	7596	4995.00		3000.00	3000.00	4995.00	Elcor Contractors

13   Enter the April cash receipts journal transaction data listed here and illustrated in Figure 4.9.

Click the Cash Receipts tab then enter the cash receipts journal transactions.

Cash Receipts Journal Transactions

Apr. 07   Received cash on account from Elcor Contractors, covering Sales Invoice No. 7486 for $2,498.38; no discount.

09   Received cash on account from Chatfield Building Company, covering Sales Invoice No. 7490 for $4,471.22, no discount.

17   Received cash on account from Schaefer Roofing, Inc., covering Sales Invoice No. 7580 for $14,520.00, less 2% discount, $290.40.

18   Sold merchandise for cash, $3,592.00, plus 6% sales tax, $215.52; total, $3,807.52. Cash Receipts No. 820. The cost of the merchandise sold was $2,029.20.

18   Received cash on account from Tierney Brothers Supply, covering Sales Invoice No. 7500 for $1,884.26, no discount.

27   Sold merchandise for cash, $4,256.00, plus 6% sales tax, $255.36; total, $4,511.36. Cash Receipts No. 821. The cost of the merchandise sold was $2,240.00.

30   Received cash on account from Fuller Construction Co., covering Sales Invoice No. 7506 for $5,813.74, no discount.

FIGURE 4.9

Cash Receipts Journal

Date	Refer.	A.R. Credit	Sales Credit	Sales Tax Pay. Cr.	Sales Disc. Dr.	Cost Mrch Sold Dr.	Mrch. Inv. Cr.	Cash Debit	Customer
04/07/--	7486	2498.38						2498.38	Elcor Contractors
04/09/--	7490	4471.22						4471.22	Chatfield Building Company
04/17/--	7580	14520.00			290.40			14229.60	Schaefer Roofing, Inc.
04/18/--	820		3592.00	215.52		2029.20	2029.20	3807.52	
04/18/--	7500	1884.26						1884.26	Tierney Brothers Supply
04/27/--	821		4256.00	255.36		2240.00	2240.00	4511.36	
04/30/--	7506	5813.74						5813.74	Fuller Construction Co.

14   **Display the chart of accounts.**

The report is shown in Figure 4.10.

FIGURE **4.10**

Chart of Accounts

Hubbell Building Supplies
Chart of Accounts
04/30/—

Assets
1110	Cash
1120	Accounts Receivable
1130	Merchandise Inventory
1140	Prepaid Insurance
1150	Supplies
1510	Store Equipment
1511	Accum. Deprec. Store Eq.
1520	Office Equipment
1521	Accum. Deprec. Office Eq.

Liabilities
2110	Vouchers Payable
2120	Sales Tax Payable
2140	Salaries Payable
2510	Note Payable

Owner's Equity
3110	William Hubbell, Capital
3120	William Hubbell, Drawing
3130	Income Summary

Revenue
4110	Sales
4120	Sales Returns & Allow.
4130	Sales Discounts

Cost
| 5110 | Cost of Merchandise Sold |

Expenses
6110	Salaries Expense
6120	Advertising Expense
6130	Rent Expense
6140	Heating & Lighting Exp.
6150	Telephone Expense
6160	Supplies Expense
6165	Postage Expense
6170	Insurance Expense
6180	Deprec. Exp. Store Eq.
6190	Deprec. Exp. Office Eq.
6200	Miscellaneous Expense

Other Expense
| 8110 | Interest Expense |

15 **Display the vendor list.**

The report is shown in Figure 4.11.

Hubbell Building Supplies
Vendor List
04/30/—

FIGURE 4.11

Vendor List

Vendor Name

ACS Gas & Electric Co.
Aurora Insurance Co.
Byron, Inc.
Commissioner of Revenue
Harrington State Bank
Heritage Mfg. Co., Inc.
Meyer Office Supply Co.
Midwest Telephone Co.
Ormsby Leasing Corporation
Payroll Bank Account
Postmaster
Robertson Mfg., Inc.
Schroeder Manufacturing
Sinclair Daily Newspaper
William Hubbell
Zimmerman, Inc.

16 **Display the customer list.**

The report is shown in Figure 4.12.

Hubbell Building Supplies
Customer List
04/30/—

FIGURE 4.12

Customer List

Customer Name

Alliance Construction
Chatfield Building Company
Designer Building Supply
Elcor Contractors
Fuller Construction Co.
Lasker Window Co.
Lewis Builders Supply
Osborn Company
Schaefer Roofing, Inc.
Slater & Son Construction
Tierney Brothers Supply

17 Display the journal entries (general, vouchers, cash payments, sales, and cash receipts Journals).

The journal reports are shown in Figure 4.13(a) through (e), respectively.

FIGURE 4.13(A)

General Journal Report

Hubbell Building Supplies
General Journal
04/30/—

Date	Refer.	Acct.	Title	Debit	Credit
04/11	5679	2110	VP/Byron, Inc.	200.00	
04/11	5679	1130	Merchandise Inventory		200.00
04/22	7506	4120	Sales Returns & Allow.	475.50	
04/22	7506	1130	Merchandise Inventory	285.30	
04/22	7506	1120	AR/Fuller Construction Co.		475.50
04/22	7506	5110	Cost of Merchandise Sold		285.30
			Totals	960.80	960.80

FIGURE 4.13(B)

Vouchers Journal Report

Hubbell Building Supplies
Vouchers Journal
04/30/—

Date	Inv. No.	Acct.	Title	Debit	Credit
04/02	5703	1130	Merchandise Inventory	1,200.00	
04/02	5703	2110	VP/Heritage Mfg. Co., Inc.		1,200.00
04/02	5704	1130	Merchandise Inventory	995.00	
04/02	5704	2110	VP/Schroeder Manufacturing		995.00
04/04	5705	1150	Supplies	146.85	
04/04	5705	2110	VP/Meyer Office Supply Co.		146.85
04/07	5706	1130	Merchandise Inventory	7,600.00	
04/07	5706	2110	VP/Zimmerman, Inc.		7,600.00
04/08	5707	6130	Rent Expense	1,100.00	
04/08	5707	2110	VP/Ormsby Leasing Corporatio		1,100.00
04/15	5708	6140	Heating & Lighting Exp.	402.38	
04/15	5708	2110	VP/ACS Gas & Electric Co.		402.38
04/18	5709	1130	Merchandise Inventory	6,895.00	
04/18	5709	2110	VP/Schroeder Manufacturing		6,895.00
04/19	5710	1130	Merchandise Inventory	1,837.15	
04/19	5710	2110	VP/Robertson Mfg., Inc.		1,837.15
04/25	5711	2510	Note Payable	585.64	
04/25	5711	8110	Interest Expense	173.15	
04/25	5711	2110	VP/Harrington State Bank		758.79
04/26	5712	6150	Telephone Expense	357.43	
04/26	5712	2110	VP/Midwest Telephone Co.		357.43
04/27	5713	6110	Salaries Expense	4,103.42	
04/27	5713	2110	VP/Payroll Bank Account		4,103.42

(continued)

04/28	5714	6120	Advertising Expense	575.00	
04/28	5714	2110	VP/Sinclair Daily Newspaper		575.00
04/30	5715	2120	Sales Tax Payable	99.81	
04/30	5715	2110	VP/Commissioner of Revenue		99.81
04/30	5716	6165	Postage Expense	41.00	
04/30	5716	2110	VP/Postmaster		41.00
04/30	5717	1130	Merchandise Inventory	9,025.00	
04/30	5717	2110	VP/Heritage Mfg. Co., Inc.		9,025.00
04/30	5718	3120	William Hubbell, Drawing	2,500.00	
04/30	5718	2110	VP/William Hubbell		2,500.00
			Totals	37,636.83	37,636.83

FIGURE 4.13(B)

(Concluded)

Hubbell Building Supplies
Cash Payments Journal
04/30/—

FIGURE 4.13(C)

Cash Payments Journal Report and First Check

Date	Ck. No.	Acct.	Title	Debit	Credit
04/03	8431	2110	VP/Heritage Mfg. Co., Inc.	3,624.46	
04/03	8431	1110	Cash		3,624.46
04/08	8432	2110	VP/Schroeder Manufacturing	4,743.26	
04/08	8432	1110	Cash		4,743.26
04/08	8433	2110	VP/Ormsby Leasing Corporation	1,100.00	
04/08	8433	1110	Cash		1,100.00
04/09	8434	2110	VP/Robertson Mfg., Inc.	2,490.00	
04/09	8434	1110	Cash		2,490.00
04/11	8435	2110	VP/Byron, Inc.	7,457.25	
04/11	8435	1110	Cash		7,457.25
04/11	8436	2110	VP/Heritage Mfg. Co., Inc.	1,200.00	
04/11	8436	1110	Cash		1,200.00
04/12	8437	2110	VP/Schroeder Manufacturing	995.00	
04/12	8437	1110	Cash		975.10
04/12	8437	1130	Merchandise Inventory		19.90
04/15	8438	2110	VP/ACS Gas & Electric Co.	402.38	
04/15	8438	1110	Cash		402.38
04/17	8439	2110	VP/Zimmerman, Inc.	8,655.95	
04/17	8439	1110	Cash		8,482.83
04/17	8439	1130	Merchandise Inventory		173.12
04/25	8440	2110	VP/Harrington State Bank	758.79	
04/25	8440	1110	Cash		758.79
04/26	8441	2110	VP/Midwest Telephone Co.	357.43	
04/26	8441	1110	Cash		357.43
04/27	8442	2110	VP/Payroll Bank Account	4,103.42	
04/27	8442	1110	Cash		4,103.42
04/30	8443	2110	VP/Commissioner of Revenue	99.81	
04/30	8443	1110	Cash		99.81

(continued)

FIGURE 4.13(c)

(Concluded)

04/30	8444	2110	VP/Postmaster	41.00	
04/30	8444	1110	Cash		41.00
04/30	8445	2110	VP/William Hubbell	2,500.00	
04/30	8445	1110	Cash		2,500.00
			Totals	38,528.75	38,528.75

Hubbell Building Supplies

04/03/–– 8431 16-871/621

Pay to the Order of   Heritage Mfg. Co., Inc.

****3624.46

National State Bank
DownTown Office
AnyCity, State 12345-1234

.06310741011171 323157 1206

FIGURE 4.13(D)

Sales Journal Report

**Hubbell Building Supplies
Sales Journal
04/30/—**

Date	Inv. No.	Acct.	Title	Debit	Credit
04/07	7591	1120	AR/Osborn Company	3,528.50	
04/07	7591	5110	Cost of Merchandise Sold	1,850.10	
04/07	7591	4110	Sales		3,528.50
04/07	7591	1130	Merchandise Inventory		1,850.10
04/16	7592	1120	AR/Lasker Window Co.	4,823.00	
04/16	7592	5110	Cost of Merchandise Sold	2,670.00	
04/16	7592	4110	Sales		4,550.00
04/16	7592	2120	Sales Tax Payable		273.00
04/16	7592	1130	Merchandise Inventory		2,670.00
04/23	7593	1120	AR/Alliance Construction	8,975.00	
04/23	7593	5110	Cost of Merchandise Sold	5,245.50	
04/23	7593	4110	Sales		8,975.00
04/23	7593	1130	Merchandise Inventory		5,245.50
04/30	7594	1120	AR/Designer Building Supply	36,648.00	
04/30	7594	5110	Cost of Merchandise Sold	19,950.00	
04/30	7594	4110	Sales		36,648.00
04/30	7594	1130	Merchandise Inventory		19,950.00
04/30	7595	1120	AR/Lewis Builders Supply	24,760.00	
04/30	7595	5110	Cost of Merchandise Sold	14,458.00	
04/30	7595	4110	Sales		24,760.00
04/30	7595	1130	Merchandise Inventory		14,458.00
04/30	7596	1120	AR/Elcor Contractors	4,995.00	
04/30	7596	5110	Cost of Merchandise Sold	3,000.00	
04/30	7596	4110	Sales		4,995.00
04/30	7596	1130	Merchandise Inventory		3,000.00
			Totals	130,903.10	130,903.10

Hubbell Building Supplies
Cash Receipts Journal
04/30/—

Date	Refer.	Acct.	Title	Debit	Credit
04/07	7486	1110	Cash	2,498.38	
04/07	7486	1120	AR/Elcor Contractors		2,498.38
04/09	7490	1110	Cash	4,471.22	
04/09	7490	1120	AR/Chatfield Building Company		4,471.22
04/17	7580	1110	Cash	14,229.60	
04/17	7580	4130	Sales Discounts	290.40	
04/17	7580	1120	AR/Schaefer Roofing, Inc.		14,520.00
04/18	820	1110	Cash	3,807.52	
04/18	820	5110	Cost of Merchandise Sold	2,029.20	
04/18	820	4110	Sales		3,592.00
04/18	820	2120	Sales Tax Payable		215.52
04/18	820	1130	Merchandise Inventory		2,029.20
04/18	7500	1110	Cash	1,884.26	
04/18	7500	1120	AR/Tierney Brothers Supply		1,884.26
04/27	821	1110	Cash	4,511.36	
04/27	821	5110	Cost of Merchandise Sold	2,240.00	
04/27	821	4110	Sales		4,256.00
04/27	821	2120	Sales Tax Payable		255.36
04/27	821	1130	Merchandise Inventory		2,240.00
04/30	7506	1110	Cash	5,813.74	
04/30	7506	1120	AR/Fuller Construction Co.		5,813.74
			Totals	41,775.68	41,775.68

FIGURE 4.13(E)

Cash Receipts Journal Report

18 Display the trial balance.

The trial balance dated April 30 of the current year is shown in Figure 4.14.

FIGURE 4.14

Trial Balance

Hubbell Building Supplies
Trial Balance
04/30/—

Acct. Number	Account Title	Debit	Credit
1110	Cash	7,390.43	
1120	Accounts Receivable	84,122.50	
1130	Merchandise Inventory	176,862.63	
1140	Prepaid Insurance	1,400.00	
1150	Supplies	1,296.85	
1510	Store Equipment	33,300.00	
1511	Accum. Deprec. Store Eq.		8,086.00
1520	Office Equipment	9,650.00	
1521	Accum. Deprec. Office Eq.		2,525.00
2110	Vouchers Payable		26,727.45
2120	Sales Tax Payable		743.88
2510	Note Payable		13,764.36
3110	William Hubbell, Capital		231,061.94
3120	William Hubbell, Drawing	10,000.00	
4110	Sales		187,246.50
4120	Sales Returns & Allow.	1,320.50	
4130	Sales Discounts	1,665.40	
5110	Cost of Merchandise Sold	107,561.50	
6110	Salaries Expense	16,529.52	
6120	Advertising Expense	6,450.00	
6130	Rent Expense	4,400.00	
6140	Heating & Lighting Exp.	1,609.22	
6150	Telephone Expense	1,455.43	
6165	Postage Expense	41.00	
6170	Insurance Expense	735.00	
6180	Deprec. Exp. Store Eq.	2,452.00	
6190	Deprec. Exp. Office Eq.	795.00	
6200	Miscellaneous Expense	285.00	
8110	Interest Expense	833.15	
	Totals	470,155.13	470,155.13

19 **Display the schedule of accounts payable and schedule of accounts receivable reports.**

Select desired report then click OK. The reports are shown in Figure 4.15 (a) and (b), respectively.

Hubbell Building Supplies Schedule of Accounts Payable 04/30/—	
Name	Balance
Heritage Mfg. Co., Inc.	9,025.00
Meyer Office Supply Co.	146.85
Robertson Mfg., Inc.	1,837.15
Schroeder Manufacturing	6,895.00
Sinclair Daily Newspaper	1,223.45
Zimmerman, Inc.	7,600.00
Total	26,727.45

FIGURE 4.15(A)

Schedule of Accounts Payable

Hubbell Building Supplies Schedule of Accounts Receivable 04/30/—	
Name	Balance
Alliance Construction	8,975.00
Designer Building Supply	36,648.00
Elcor Contractors	4,995.00
Lasker Window Co.	4,823.00
Lewis Builders Supply	24,760.00
Osborn Company	3,528.50
Slater & Son Construction	393.00
Total	84,122.50

FIGURE 4.15(B)

Schedule of Accounts Receivable

End-of-Month Activities

After the monthly transactions have been processed, the adjusting entries must be entered into the computer and printed. The adjustment data for the month of April for Hubbell Building Supplies are listed next.

Insurance expired during April $238.00
Inventory of supplies on April 30 . . . .$1,025.00
Depreciation for April:
   Store Equipment $264.50
   Office Equipment $152.00
   Salaries Payable $235.00

The completed adjusting entries are shown in Figure 4.16 as they would appear when entered and posted in the General Journal.

1 **Enter the adjusting entries.**

Click on the Gen. Led. navigation button and then the Journal Entries menu button. Click the General Journal tab, and enter the adjusting entries shown in Figure 4.16.

FIGURE 4.16

*General Journal
(Adjusting Entries)*

Date	Refer.	Account	Debit	Credit	Vendor/Customer
04/30/--	Adj.Ent.	6170 Insurance Expense	238.00		
		1140 Prepaid Insurance		238.00	
04/30/--	Adj.Ent.	6160 Supplies Expense	271.85		
		1150 Supplies		271.85	
04/30/--	Adj.Ent.	6180 Deprec. Exp. Store Eq.	264.50		
		1511 Accum. Deprec. Store Eq.		264.50	
04/30/--	Adj.Ent.	6190 Deprec. Exp. Office Eq.	152.00		
		1521 Accum. Deprec. Office Eq.		152.00	
04/30/--	Adj.Ent.	6110 Salaries Expense	235.00		
		2140 Salaries Payable		235.00	

2 **Display the adjusting entries.**

Click on the Gen. Leg. navigation button and then the Journal Reports menu button. When the Reports Selection dialog box appears, choose the Journals option, select the General Journal report, and click OK. When the Journal Report Selection dialog box appears, choose the Customize Journal Report option and enter a Reference restriction of Adj.Ent. so that only the adjusting entries are reported. Compare your journal entries report to the report shown in Figure 4.17. If the journal entries report is incorrect, make corrections.

FIGURE 4.17

*General Journal Report
(Adjusting Entries)*

**Hubbell Building Supplies
General Journal
04/30/—**

Date	Refer.	Acct.	Title	Debit	Credit
04/30	Adj.Ent.	6170	Insurance Expense	238.00	
04/30	Adj.Ent.	1140	Prepaid Insurance		238.00
04/30	Adj.Ent.	6160	Supplies Expense	271.85	
04/30	Adj.Ent.	1150	Supplies		271.85
04/30	Adj.Ent.	6180	Deprec. Exp. Store Eq.	264.50	
04/30	Adj.Ent.	1511	Accum. Deprec. Store Eq.		264.50
04/30	Adj.Ent.	6190	Deprec. Exp. Office Eq.	152.00	
04/30	Adj.Ent.	1521	Accum. Deprec. Office Eq.		152.00
04/30	Adj.Ent.	6110	Salaries Expense	235.00	
04/30	Adj.Ent.	2140	Salaries Payable		235.00
			Totals	1,161.35	1,161.35

3   **Check your work.**

Click Check on the toolbar. If errors appear, use the Explorer and other error corrections features of the software to correct your errors.

4   **Display the income statement.**

The income statement is shown in Figure 4.18.

Hubbell Building Supplies Income Statement For Period Ended 04/30/—	Monthly Amount	Monthly Percent	Yearly Amount	Yearly Percent
Operating Revenue				
Sales	91,304.50	100.85	187,246.50	101.62
Sales Returns & Allow.	−475.50	−0.53	−1,320.50	−0.72
Sales Discounts	−290.40	−0.32	−1,665.40	−0.90
Total Operating Revenue	90,538.60	100.00	184,260.60	100.00
Cost				
Cost of Merchandise Sold	51,157.50	56.50	107,561.50	58.37
Total Cost	51,157.50	56.50	107,561.50	58.37
Gross Profit	39,381.10	43.50	76,699.10	41.63
Operating Expenses				
Salaries Expense	4,338.42	4.79	16,764.52	9.10
Advertising Expense	575.00	0.64	6,450.00	3.50
Rent Expense	1,100.00	1.22	4,400.00	2.39
Heating & Lighting Exp.	402.38	0.44	1,609.22	0.87
Telephone Expense	357.43	0.39	1,455.43	0.79
Supplies Expense	271.85	0.30	271.85	0.15
Postage Expense	41.00	0.05	41.00	0.02
Insurance Expense	238.00	0.26	973.00	0.53
Deprec. Exp. Store Eq.	264.50	0.29	2,716.50	1.47
Deprec. Exp. Office Eq.	152.00	0.17	947.00	0.51
Miscellaneous Expense			285.00	0.15
Total Operating Expenses	7,740.58	8.55	35,913.52	19.49
Net Income from Operations	31,640.52	34.95	40,785.58	22.13
Other Expense				
Interest Expense	173.15	0.19	833.15	0.45
Net Income	31,467.37	34.76	39,952.43	21.68

FIGURE 4.18

Income Statement

5 **Display the statement of owner's equity.**

The statement of owner's equity is shown in Figure 4.19.

FIGURE 4.19	Hubbell Building Supplies Statement of Owner's Equity For Period Ended 04/30/—
Statement of Owner's Equity	

William Hubbell, Capital (Beg. of Period)	231,061.94
William Hubbell, Drawing	−10,000.00
Net Income	39,952.43
William Hubbell, Capital (End of Period)	261,014.37

6 **Display the balance sheet.**

The balance sheet is shown in Figure 4.20.

FIGURE 4.20	Hubbell Building Supplies Balance Sheet 04/30/—
Balance Sheet	

Assets		
Cash	7,390.43	
Accounts Receivable	84,122.50	
Merchandise Inventory	176,862.63	
Prepaid Insurance	1,162.00	
Supplies	1,025.00	
Total Current Assets	270,562.56	
Store Equipment	33,300.00	
Accum. Deprec. Store Eq.	−8,350.50	
Office Equipment	9,650.00	
Accum. Deprec. Office Eq.	−2,677.00	
Total Plant Assets	31,922.50	
Total Assets		302,485.06
Liabilities		
Vouchers Payable	26,727.45	
Sales Tax Payable	743.88	
Salaries Payable	235.00	
Total Current Liabilities	27,706.33	
Note Payable	13,764.36	
Total Long-Term Liabilities	13,764.36	
Total Liabilities		41,470.69
Owner's Equity		
William Hubbell, Capital	231,061.94	
William Hubbell, Drawing	−10,000.00	
Net Income	39,952.43	
Total Owner's Equity		261,014.37
Total Liabilities & Equity		302,485.06

7 **Display the budget report.**

Select the Bugdet Report, then click OK. The budget report is shown in Figure 4.21.

	Budget	Actual	Diff. From Budget	%
Hubbell Building Supplies Budget Report For Period Ended 04/30/—				
Operating Revenue				
Operating Revenue	530,000.00	184,260.60	−345,739.40	−65.23
Cost of Merchandise Sold	325,000.00	107,561.50	−217,438.50	−66.90
Gross Profit	205,000.00	76,699.10	−128,300.90	−62.59
Operating Expenses				
Salaries Expense	60,000.00	16,764.52	−43,235.48	−72.06
Advertising Expense	20,000.00	6,450.00	−13,550.00	−67.75
Rent Expense	13,800.00	4,400.00	−9,400.00	−68.12
Heating & Lighting Exp.	5,500.00	1,609.22	−3,890.78	−70.74
Telephone Expense	5,000.00	1,455.43	−3,544.57	−70.89
Supplies Expense	2,750.00	271.85	−2,478.15	−90.11
Postage Expense	1,000.00	41.00	−959.00	−95.90
Insurance Expense	8,000.00	973.00	−7,027.00	−87.84
Deprec. Exp. Store Eq.	8,500.00	2,716.50	−5,783.50	−68.04
Deprec. Exp. Office Eq.	3,000.00	947.00	−2,053.00	−68.43
Miscellaneous Expense	1,000.00	285.00	−715.00	−71.50
Total Operating Expenses	128,550.00	35,913.52	−92,636.48	−72.06
Net Income from Operations	76,450.00	40,785.58	−35,664.42	−46.65
Other Expense				
Interest Expense	2,500.00	833.15	−1,666.85	−66.67
Net Income	73,950.00	39,952.43	−33,997.57	−45.97

FIGURE 4.21

Budget Report

8   **Generate an actual versus budget graph.**

The actual versus budget graph is shown in Figure 4.22.

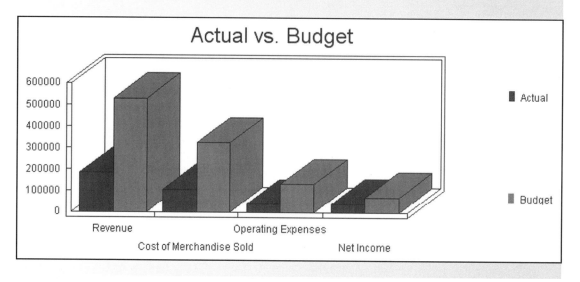

9   **Use the Save menu item to save your data file.**

10   **Calculate the annual retirement income using the Retirement Planner.**

Click Tools on the toolbar. When the Planning Tools window appears, click the Retirement Plan tab, and then click on the Annual Retirement Income option button. Enter the following retirement data and display the retirement schedule reports. The retirement schedule reports are shown in Figure 4.23.

Beginning Retirement Savings.................................$5,000.00
Annual Yield (Percent)..7.50
Current Age 25
Retirement Age 65
Withdraw Until Age...85
Annual Contribution..$3,600.00

Retirement Savings Plan
04/30/—

Schedule of Contributions

Age	Annual Contribution	Annual Yield	Retirement Savings
(Beginning Balance)			5,000.00
25	3,600.00	375.00	8,975.00
26	3,600.00	673.13	13,248.13
27	3,600.00	993.61	17,841.74

(continued)

28	3,600.00	1,338.13	22,779.87
29	3,600.00	1,708.49	28,088.36
30	3,600.00	2,106.63	33,794.99
31	3,600.00	2,534.62	39,929.61
32	3,600.00	2,994.72	46,524.33
/\			
60	3,600.00	46,361.26	668,111.38
61	3,600.00	50,108.35	721,819.73
62	3,600.00	54,136.48	779,556.21
63	3,600.00	58,466.72	841,622.93
64	3,600.00	63,121.72	908,344.65

FIGURE 4.23

(Concluded)

Schedule of Retirement Income

Age	Annual Income	Annual Yield	Savings Balance
(Retirement Savings)			908,344.65
65	82,885.13	61,909.46	887,368.98
66	82,885.13	60,336.29	864,820.14
67	82,885.13	58,645.13	840,580.14
68	82,885.13	56,827.13	814,522.14
69	82,885.13	54,872.78	786,509.79
70	82,885.13	52,771.85	756,396.51
/\			
81	82,885.13	16,165.88	231,710.90
82	82,885.13	11,161.93	159,987.70
83	82,885.13	5,782.69	82,885.26
84	82,885.26	.00	.00

11   Optional spreadsheet and word processing integration activity.

Use a spreadsheet to create a business summary report, then use a word processor to format and enhance the appearance of the report for management. The report should contain the cash balance, accounts receivable balance, vouchers payable balance, net sales (sales minus sales discounts and sales returns and allowances), and cost of merchandise sold from the current trial balance.

Spreadsheet:

a. Display and copy the trial balance to the clipboard in spreadsheet format.

b. Start your spreadsheet software and load template file IA6 Spreadsheet 04-S.

c. Select cell A1 as the current cell, and then paste the trial balance (copied to the clipboard in Step a) into the spreadsheet.

d. Enter the following labels and formulas in the cells indicated using the appropriate format for your spreadsheet program:

	B	C
50	copy cell B3	
51	Summary Report	
52	copy cell B5	
53		
54	copy cell B10	copy cell C10
55	copy cell B11	copy cell C11
56	copy cell B19	copy cell D19
57	Net Sales	cell D25 minus (cell C26 + cell C27)
58	copy cell B28	copy cell C28

e. Print the summary report (cells B50–C58). The completed summary report for April is shown in Figure 4.24.

f. Save the completed spreadsheet with a file name of 04-S Your Name.

 NOTE Subsequent trial balance reports for Hubbell Building Supplies that are saved to disk in spreadsheet format may be pasted into this template file whenever management requires an updated summary report.

Word Processing:

a. Start your word processing application software and create a new document. (Use a fixed font such as Courier.)

b. Copy and paste the spreadsheet summary report into the new document.

c. Format and enhance the report's appearance.

d. Print the report. The completed summary report is shown in Figure 4.24.

e. Save the document to disk with a file name of 04-S Your Name.

f. End your spreadsheet and word processing sessions.

FIGURE 4.24

Word Processed Business Summary Report

Hubbell Building Supplies
Summary Report
As of 04/30/—

Cash	$7,390.43
Accounts Receivable	$84,122.50
Vouchers Payable	$26,727.45
Net Sales	$184,260.60
Cost of Merchandise Sold	$107,561.50

INTERNET ACTIVITY

If you have access to the Internet, use the browser to locate your state's Web page or link, then find the link to your state's government. Identify the information provided. *Hint:* Enter a URL of "state-name US" (in Florida use www.Florida-US.com with the hyphen). Be sure to include the source and the URL (Web address) of your search.

12 End the *Integrated Accounting* 6e session

Chapter 4 Student Exercises

NAME

I Matching

Directions *For each of the definitions, write the letter of the appropriate term in the space provided.*

a.	voucher system	e.	vouchers payable account
b.	vouchers journal	f.	budget
c.	voucher number	g.	budgeted amount
d.	check	h.	budget report

1.____ Specific procedures that are implemented for the purpose of controlling a business's cash disbursements.

2.____ An input window used to enter voucher transactions.

3.____ The estimated balance for a particular account at the end of the fiscal period.

4.____ A computer-generated output given to each vendor in payment of vouchers owed.

5.____ A report that compares actual revenues and expenses with budgeted revenues and expenses.

6.____ An item used by the computer to identify each voucher.

7.____ The account used in the general ledger of a voucher system instead of accounts payable.

8.____ A financial plan for the future.

II Questions

Directions *Answer each of the following questions in the space provided.*

1. What is the major difference between a standard accounting system and a voucher system?

2. In the vouchers journal, what entry is automatically credited by the computer?

3. Why is a vendor required for each transaction when using a voucher system?

4. What information is contained on the computer-generated check?

5. What types of information are contained on the budget report?

Problem 4-A

Problem 4-A is a continuation of Sample Problem 4-S. Follow the step-by-step procedures provided to complete this problem for Hubbell Building Supplies for the month of May of the current year. Answer audit questions 4-A on page 177 as you complete this problem. Display reports as necessary to answer the questions. As you complete this problem, click Info. on the toolbar for helpful check figures to audit your work.

1. **Start *Integrated Accounting* 6e.**

2. **Open the file named IA6 Problem 04-A.**

3. **Enter your name in the Your Name text box.**

4. **Use Save As to save the data to your disk with a file name of 04-A Your Name.**

5. **Delete Byron, Inc., from the vendor list.**

6. **Change the name of the vendor Schroeder Manufacturing to Gramstad Company.**

7. **Add Clausen Building Co., to the vendor list.**

8. **Enter the following budget amount changes resulting from an anticipated increase in sales projected by management.**

Account Title	Budget
Total Revenue	$560,000.00
Cost of Merchandise Sold	$300,000.00
Salaries Expense	$65,000.00
Advertising Expense	$25,000.00

9. **Enter the general journal transactions.**

General Journal Transactions

NOTE Only the adjustment for Salaries Expense ($235.00) must be reversed.

May 01   Reversing entries required by April adjustments. Use the adjustment data presented in Sample Problem 4-S as the basis for your reversing entries. Enter Rev.Ent. in the Reference text box.

     02   Returned merchandise purchased on account from Robertson Mfg., Inc., $395.00; the debit memo applies to Voucher No. 5710.

     21   Received merchandise returned on account from Alliance Construction, $1,575.00. The cost of the merchandise returned was $915.00. The credit memo applies to Sales Invoice No. 7593.

10 **Enter the vouchers journal transactions.**

Vouchers Journal Transactions

May 01   Purchased merchandise on account from Clausen Building Co., $1,853.40; Voucher No. 5719.

    08   Purchased merchandise on account from Zimmerman, Inc., $6,000.00; Voucher No. 5720.

    09   Purchased supplies on account from Meyer Office Supply Co., $915.65; no sales tax; Voucher No. 5721. Charge Miscellaneous Expense $65.65 and Supplies $850.00.

    09   Record Voucher No. 5722 to Ormsby Leasing Corporation for monthly rent, $1,100.00.

    15   Purchased merchandise on account from Robertson Mfg., Inc., $6408.30; Voucher No. 5723.

    16   Record Voucher No. 5724 to ACS Gas & Electric Co., for monthly electric bill, $429.27.

    17   Purchased merchandise on account from Gramstad Company, $3,284.00; Voucher No. 5725.

    18   Purchased advertising on account from Sinclair Daily Newspaper, $725.00; Voucher No. 5726.

    21   Record Voucher No. 5727 to Aurora Insurance Co., for theft and fire insurance, $465.50.

    24   Record Voucher No. 5728 to Harrington State Bank for a note payable, $758.79; principal, $591.36; interest, $167.43.

    26   Record Voucher No. 5729 to Midwest Telephone Co., for monthly telephone bill, $398.94.

    27   Record Voucher No. 5730 to reimburse the payroll bank account for monthly salaries expense, $4,103.42.

    28   Record Voucher No. 5731 to Postmaster for postage, $63.15.

    29   Record Voucher No. 5732 to Commissioner of Revenue for sales tax liability, $743.88.

    29   Record Voucher No. 5733 to William Hubbell for the owner's use, $3,000.00.

    30   Purchased merchandise on account from Clausen Building Co., $9,000.00; Voucher No. 5734.

11 **Enter the cash payments journal transactions.**

Cash Payments Journal Transactions

May 01   Paid Voucher No. 5706 to Zimmerman, Inc., $7,600.00, no discount. Check No. 8446.

    04   Paid Voucher No. 5710 to Robertson Mfg., Inc., $1,442.15, no discount. Check No. 8447.

    09   Paid Voucher No. 5722 to Ormsby Leasing Corporation, $1,100.00. Check No. 8448.

    09   Paid Voucher No. 5709 to Gramstad Company, $6,895.00, less 2% discount, $137.90. Check No. 8449.

11   Paid Voucher No. 5655 to Sinclair Daily Newspaper, $1,223.45, no discount. Check No. 8450.

14   Paid Voucher No. 5705 to Meyer Office Supply Co., $146.85, no discount. Check No. 8451.

16   Paid Voucher No. 5724 to ACS Gas & Electric Co., $429.27. Check No. 8452.

18   Paid Voucher No. 5717 to Heritage Mfg. Co., Inc., $9,025.00, less 2% discount, $180.50. Check No. 8453.

24   Paid Voucher No. 5728 to Harrington State Bank, $758.79. Check No. 8454.

26   Paid Voucher No. 5729 to Midwest Telephone Co., $398.94. Check No. 8455.

27   Paid Voucher No. 5730 to Payroll Bank Account, $4,103.42. Check No. 8456.

28   Paid Voucher No. 5731 to Postmaster, $63.15. Check No. 8457.

29   Paid Voucher No. 5732 to Commissioner of Revenue, $743.88. Check No. 8458.

29   Paid Voucher No. 5733 to William Hubbell, $3,000.00. Check No. 8459.

12   Enter the sales journal transactions.

Sales Journal Transactions

May 03   Sold merchandise on account to Chatfield Building Company, $7,585.00, no sales tax. Sales Invoice No. 7597. The cost of the merchandise sold was $4,350.00.

05   Sold merchandise on account to Lasker Window Co., $6,650.00, plus 6% sales tax, $399.00; total, $7,049.00. Sales Invoice No. 7598. The cost of the merchandise sold was $3,950.00.

08   Sold merchandise on account to Osborn Company, $7,000.00, no sales tax. Sales Invoice No. 7599. The cost of the merchandise sold was $4,195.00.

10   Sold merchandise on account to Schaefer Roofing, Inc., $38,095.00, no sales tax. Sales Invoice No. 7600. The cost of the merchandise sold was $21,345.00.

14   Sold merchandise on account to Fuller Construction Co., $11,500.00, no sales tax. Sales Invoice No. 7601. The cost of the merchandise sold was $6,700.00.

21   Sold merchandise on account to Elcor Contractors, $11,050.00, no sales tax. Sales Invoice No. 7602. The cost of the merchandise sold was $6,310.00.

25   Sold merchandise on account to Lewis Builders Supply, $7,675.00, no sales tax. Sales Invoice No. 7603. The cost of the merchandise sold was $4,432.60.

13   Enter the cash receipts journal transactions.

Cash Receipts Journal Transactions

May 01   Received cash on account from Osborn Company, covering Sales Invoice No. 7591 for $3,528.50, no discount.

07   Received cash on account from Lasker Window Co., covering Sales Invoice No. 7592 for $4,823.00, no discount.

10 Received cash on account from Designer Building Supply, covering Sales Invoice No. 7594 for $36,648.00, less 2% discount, $732.96.

15 Sold merchandise for cash, $5,125.00, plus 6% sales tax, $307.50; total, $5,432.50. Cash Receipts No. 822. The cost of the merchandise sold was $3,055.80.

17 Received cash on account from Elcor Contractors, covering Sales Invoice No. 7596 for $4,995.00, no discount.

21 Received cash on account from Lewis Builders Supply, covering Sales Invoice No. 7595 for $24,760.00, no discount.

28 Received cash on account from Alliance Construction, covering Sales Invoice No. 7593 for $7,400.00, no discount.

30 Sold merchandise for cash, $6,250.00, plus 6% sales tax, $375.00; total, $6,625.00. Cash Receipts No. 823. The cost of the merchandise sold was $3,725.00.

14 **Display the vendor list.**

15 **Display the journal entries and make corrections if necessary.**

16 **Display the trial balance.**

17 **Display the schedule of accounts payable and schedule of accounts receivable.**

End-of-Month Activities

After the monthly transactions have been processed, the adjusting entries must be entered into the computer and displayed. The adjustment data for the month of May for Hubbell Building Supplies are listed here.

Insurance expired during May $406.50
Inventory of supplies on May 31 ....$1,267.00
Depreciation for May:
    Store Equipment...$264.50
    Office Equipment..$152.00
    Salaries Payable $389.75

Use the trial balance report prepared in Step 16 as the basis for preparing the adjusting entries.

1 **Enter the adjusting entries in the general journal. Enter a reference of Adj.Ent. in the Reference text box.**

2 **Display the adjusting entries.**

3 **Check your work.**

Click Check on the toolbar. If errors appear, use the Explorer and other error corrections features of the software to correct your errors.

4 Display the income statement.

5 Display the statement of owner's equity.

6 Display the balance sheet.

7 Display the budget report.

8 Generate an actual versus budget graph.

9 Click Save on the toolbar to save the data file.

10 Use the Retirement Planner to calculate the annual contribution toward retirement using the information:

> Beginning Retirement Savings..........................$8,000.00
> Annual Yield (Percent)...................................7.25
> Current Age...25
> Retirement Age...65
> Withdraw until Age...85
> Annual Retirement Income $80,000.00

11 **Optional spreadsheet and word processing integration activity.**

Use a spreadsheet to create a business summary report, then use a word processor to format and enhance the appearance of the report for management. The report should contain the cash balance, accounts receivable balance, vouchers payable balance, net sales (sales minus sales discounts and sales returns and allowances), and cost of merchandise sold from the current trial balance.

Spreadsheet:

a. Display and copy the trial balance to the clipboard in spreadsheet format.

b. Start your spreadsheet software and load template file IA6 Spreadsheet 04-S.(If you completed the optional spreadsheet activity in Sample Problem 4-S, load your solution spreadsheet template file.)

c. Select cell A1 as the current cell, then paste the trial balance (copied to the clipboard in Step a) into the spreadsheet.

d. Enter the appropriate label(s), cell references, and formulas (see Figure 4.24).

e. Print the summary report.

f. Save the completed spreadsheet with a file name of 04-A Your Name.

Word Processing:

a. Start your word processing application software and create a new document. (Use a fixed font such as Courier.)

b. Copy and paste the spreadsheet summary report into the new document.

c. Format and enhance the report's appearance similar to Figure 4.24.

d. Print the report.

e. Save the document to your disk with a file name of 04-A Your Name.

f. End your spreadsheet and word processing sessions.

If you have access to the Internet, use the browser to locate your state's web page or link (use URL: "state-name US"—in Florida use www.Florida-US.com with the hyphen). Find the link to your state government's Department of Finance. Report on the information provided. Be sure to include the source and the URL (Web address) of your search.

12 **End the *Integrated Accounting* 6e session.**

Audit Questions 4-A

NAME

1. What are the totals of the debit and credit columns from the vouchers journal for the month of May?

   Debit amount: _____

   Credit amount: _____

2. What are the totals of the debit and credit columns from the cash payments journal for the month of May?

   Debit amount: _____

   Credit amount: _____

3. What are the totals of the debit and credit columns from the sales journal for the month of May?

   Debit amount: _____

   Credit amount: _____

4. What are the totals of the debit and credit columns from the cash receipts journal for the month of May?

   Debit amount: _____

   Credit amount: _____

5. What is the amount owed to Gramstad Company at the end of May from the schedule of accounts payable?   _____

   _____

6. What is the total amount payable shown on the schedule of accounts payable report at the end of May?   _____

   _____

7. What is the total amount receivable shown on the schedule of accounts receivable report at the end of May?   _____

   _____

8. What is the net income from operations for the month from the income statement?   _____

   _____

9. What is the gross profit for the month expressed as a percentage of operating revenue?

   _____

10. What are the total operating expenses for the year?   _____

    _____

11. What is the owner's capital as of the end of May?   _____

    _____

12.   What are the total assets? _____

_____

13.   What are the total liabilities? _____

_____

14.   What is the amount of budgeted gross profit? _____

_____

15.   How much under budget are salaries at this point in the fiscal year? _____

_____

16.   From the Retirement Plan, what is the annual contribution required for an annual income of
       $80,000.00? _____

_____

17.   What is the retirement savings balance at the time of retirement (age 65)? _____

_____

Problem 4-B

Problem 4-B is a continuation of Sample Problem 4-S. Follow the step-by-step procedures provided to complete this problem for Hubbell Building Supplies for the month of May of the current year. Answer audit questions 4-B on page 185 as you complete this problem. Display reports as necessary to answer the questions.

1 Start *Integrated Accounting* 6e.

2 Open the file named IA6 Problem 04-B.

3 Enter your name in the Your Name text box.

4 Use Save As to save the data to your disk with a file name of 04-B Your Name.

5 Delete Byron, Inc., from the vendor list.

6 Change the name of the vendor Schroeder Manufacturing to Gramstad Company.

7 Add Clausen Building Co., to the vendor list.

8 Enter the following budget amount changes resulting from an anticipated increase in sales projected by management.

Account Title	Budget
Total Revenue	$565,000.00
Cost of Merchandise Sold	$300,000.00
Salaries Expense	$70,000.00
Advertising Expense	$25,000.00

9 Enter the general journal transactions.

General Journal Transactions

NOTE Only the adjustment for Salaries Expense ($235.00) must be reversed.

May 01 Reversing entries required by April adjustments. Use the adjustment data presented in Sample Problem 4-S as the basis for your reversing entries. Enter Rev.Ent. in the Reference text box.

02 Returned merchandise purchased on account from Robertson Mfg., Inc., $425.00; the debit memo applies to Voucher No. 5710.

21 Received merchandise returned on account from Alliance Construction, $1,595.00. The cost of the merchandise returned was $950.00. The credit memo applies to Sales Invoice No. 7593.

10   **Enter the vouchers journal transactions.**

Vouchers Journal Transactions

May 01   Purchased merchandise on account from Clausen Building Co., $2,035.00; Voucher No. 5719.

08   Purchased merchandise on account from Zimmerman, Inc., $6,212.85; Voucher No. 5720.

09   Purchased supplies on account from Meyer Office Supply Co., $1,250.00; no sales tax; Voucher No. 5721. Charge Miscellaneous Expense $75.00 and Supplies $1,175.00.

09   Record Voucher No. 5722 to Ormsby Leasing Corporation for monthly rent, $1,100.00.

15   Purchased merchandise on account from Robertson Mfg., Inc., $5,635.00; Voucher No. 5723.

16   Record Voucher No. 5724 to ACS Gas & Electric Co., for monthly electric bill, $402.37.

17   Purchased merchandise on account from Gramstad Company, $3,049.00; Voucher No. 5725.

18   Purchased advertising on account from Sinclair Daily Newspaper, $750.00; Voucher No. 5726.

21   Record Voucher No. 5727 to Aurora Insurance Co., for theft and fire insurance, $506.00.

24   Record Voucher No. 5728 to Harrington State Bank for a note payable, $758.79; principal, $591.36; interest, $167.43.

26   Record Voucher No. 5729 to Midwest Telephone Co., for monthly telephone bill, $436.76.

27   Record Voucher No. 5730 to reimburse the payroll bank account for monthly salaries expense, $4,201.73.

28   Record Voucher No. 5731 to Postmaster for postage, $46.53.

29   Record Voucher No. 5732 to Commissioner of Revenue for sales tax liability, $743.88.

29   Record Voucher No. 5733 to William Hubbell for the owner's use, $3,500.00.

30   Purchased merchandise on account from Clausen Building Co., $9,275.00; Voucher No. 5734.

11   **Enter the cash payments journal transactions.**

Cash Payments Journal Transactions

May 01   Paid Voucher No. 5706 to Zimmerman, Inc., $7,600.00, no discount. Check No. 8446.

04   Paid Voucher No. 5710 to Robertson Mfg., Inc., $1,412.15, no discount. Check No. 8447.

09   Paid Voucher No. 5722 to Ormsby Leasing Corporation, $1,100.00. Check No. 8448.

09   Paid Voucher No. 5709 to Gramstad Company, $6,895.00, less 2% discount, $137.90. Check No. 8449.

| 11 | Paid Voucher No. 5655 to Sinclair Daily Newspaper, $1,223.45, no discount. Check No. 8450. |

11   Paid Voucher No. 5655 to Sinclair Daily Newspaper, $1,223.45, no discount. Check No. 8450.

14   Paid Voucher No. 5705 to Meyer Office Supply Co., $146.85, no discount. Check No. 8451.

16   Paid Voucher No. 5724 to ACS Gas & Electric Co., $402.37. Check No. 8452.

18   Paid Voucher No. 5717 to Heritage Mfg. Co., Inc., $9,025.00, less 2% discount, $180.50. Check No. 8453.

24   Paid Voucher No. 5728 to Harrington State Bank, $758.79. Check No. 8454.

26   Paid Voucher No. 5729 to Midwest Telephone Co., $436.76. Check No. 8455.

27   Paid Voucher No. 5730 to Payroll Bank Account, $4,201.73. Check No. 8456.

28   Paid Voucher No. 5731 to Postmaster, $46.53. Check No. 8457.

29   Paid Voucher No. 5732 to Commissioner of Revenue, $743.88. Check No. 8458.

29   Paid Voucher No. 5733 to William Hubbell, $3,500.00. Check No. 8459.

12 Enter the sales journal transactions.

Sales Journal Transactions

May 03   Sold merchandise on account to Chatfield Building Company, $8,195.50, no sales tax. Sales Invoice No. 7597. The cost of the merchandise sold was $4,756.00.

05   Sold merchandise on account to Lasker Window Co., $5,689.00, plus 6% sales tax, $341.34; total, $6,030.34. Sales Invoice No. 7598. The cost of the merchandise sold was $3,410.00.

08   Sold merchandise on account to Osborn Company, $7,105.00, no sales tax. Sales Invoice No. 7599. The cost of the merchandise sold was $4,260.00.

10   Sold merchandise on account to Schaefer Roofing, Inc., $37,980.00, no sales tax. Sales Invoice No. 7600. The cost of the merchandise sold was $22,078.00.

14   Sold merchandise on account to Fuller Construction Co., $11,295.00, no sales tax. Sales Invoice No. 7601. The cost of the merchandise sold was $6,575.00.

21   Sold merchandise on account to Elcor Contractors, $11,000.00, no sales tax. Sales Invoice No. 7602. The cost of the merchandise sold was $6,176.50.

28   Sold merchandise on account to Lewis Builders Supply, $7,825.00, no sales tax. Sales Invoice No. 7603. The cost of the merchandise sold was $4,589.00.

13 Enter the cash receipts journal transactions.

Cash Receipts Journal Transactions

May 01   Received cash on account from Osborn Company, covering Sales Invoice No. 7591 for $3528.50, no discount.

07   Received cash on account from Lasker Window Co., covering Sales Invoice No. 7592 for $4,823.00, no discount.

10   Received cash on account from Designer Building Supply, covering Sales Invoice No. 7594 for $36,648.00, less 2% discount, $732.96.

15   Sold merchandise for cash, $4,915.00, plus 6% sales tax, $294.90; total, $5,209.90. Cash Receipts No. 822. The cost of the merchandise sold was $2,885.30.

17   Received cash on account from Elcor Contractors, covering Sales Invoice No. 7596 for $4,995.00, no discount.

21   Received cash on account from Lewis Builders Supply, covering Sales Invoice No. 7595 for $24,760.00, no discount.

28   Received cash on account from Alliance Construction, covering Sales Invoice No. 7593 for $7,380.00, no discount.

30   Sold merchandise for cash, $6,350.00, plus 6% sales tax, $381.00; total, $6,731.00. Cash Receipts No. 823. The cost of the merchandise sold was $3,710.00.

14   Display the vendor list.

15   Display the journal entries and make corrections if necessary.

16   Display the trial balance.

17   Display the schedule of accounts payable and schedule of accounts receivable.

End-of-Month Activities

After the monthly transactions have been processed, the adjusting entries must be entered into the computer. The adjustment data for the month of May for Hubbell Building Supplies are listed next.

Insurance expired during May................................$426.00
Inventory of supplies on May 31.........................$1,425.00
Depreciation for May:
    Store Equipment..$264.50
    Office Equipment...$152.00
    Salaries Payable $370.00

Use the trial balance report prepared in Step 16 as the basis for preparing the adjusting entries.

1   Enter the adjusting entries in the general journal. Enter a reference of Adj.Ent. in the Reference text box.

2   Display the adjusting entries.

3   Display the income statement.

4   Display the statement of owner's equity.

5   Display the balance sheet.

6   Display the budget report.

7   **Generate an actual versus budget graph.**

8   **Click Save on the toolbar to save the data file.**

9   **Use the Retirement Planner to calculate annual retirement income using the information:**

Beginning Retirement Savings	$6,250.00
Annual Yield (Percent)	7.75
Current Age	25
Retirement Age	65
Withdraw until Age	85
Annual Contribution	$3,200.00

10   **Optional spreadsheet and word processing integration activity.**

Use a spreadsheet to create a business summary report, then use a word processor to format and enhance the appearance of the report for management. The report should contain the cash balance, accounts receivable balance, vouchers payable balance, net sales (sales minus sales discounts and sales returns and allowances), and cost of merchandise sold from the current trial balance.

Spreadsheet:

a. Display and copy the trial balance to the clipboard in spreadsheet format.

b. Start your spreadsheet software and load template file IA6 Spreadsheet 04-S. (If you completed the optional spreadsheet activity in Sample Problem 4-S, load your solution spreadsheet template file.)

c. Select cell A1 as the current cell, then paste the trial balance (copied to the clipboard in Step a) into the spreadsheet.

d. Enter the appropriate label(s), cell references, and formulas (see Figure 4.24).

e. Print the summary report.

f. Save the completed spreadsheet with a file name of 04-B Your Name.

Word Processing:

a. Start your word processing application software and create a new document. (Use a fixed font such as Courier.)

b. Copy and paste the spreadsheet summary report into the new document.

c. Format and enhance the report's appearance similar to Figure 4.24.

d. Print the report.

e. Save the document to your disk with a file name of 04-B Your Name.

f. End your spreadsheet and word processing sessions.

INTERNET ACTIVITY

If you have access to the Internet, use the browser to locate your state's web page or link (use URL: "state-name US"—in Florida use www.Florida-US.com with the hyphen). Find the link to your state government's Department of Finance. Report on your state's taxes, tax incentives for new businesses, or any other information regarding the business climate of your state. Be sure to include the source and the URL (Web address) of your search.

11 End the *Integrated Accounting* 6e session.

Audit Questions 4-B

NAME

1. What are the totals of the debit and credit columns from the vouchers journal for the month of May?

    Debit amount: _____

    Credit amount: _____

2. What are the totals of the debit and credit columns from the cash payments journal for the month of May?

    Debit amount: _____

    Credit amount: _____

3. What are the totals of the debit and credit columns from the sales journal for the month of May?

    Debit amount: _____

    Credit amount: _____

4. What are the totals of the debit and credit columns from the cash receipts journal for the month of May?

    Debit amount: _____

    Credit amount: _____

5. What is the amount owed to Gramstad Company at the end of May from the schedule of accounts payable? _____

    _____

6. What is the total amount payable shown on the schedule of accounts payable report at the end of May? _____

    _____

7. What is the total amount receivable shown on the schedule of accounts receivable report at the end of May? _____

    _____

8. What is the net income from operations for the month from the income statement? _____

    _____

9. What is the gross profit for the month expressed as a percentage of operating revenue?

    _____

10. What are the total operating expenses for the year? _____

    _____

11. What is the owner's capital as of the end of May? _____

    _____

12.   What are the total assets?   _____

_____

13.   What are the total liabilities?   _____

_____

14.   How much under budget is operating revenue at this point in the fiscal year?   _____

_____

15.   How much under budget is the total operating expenses at this point in the fiscal year?

_____

16.   From the Retirement Plan, what is the amount of the annual retirement income?   _____

_____

17.   What is the retirement savings balance at the time of retirement (age 65)?   _____

_____

COMPREHENSIVE PROBLEM 1

This comprehensive problem involves completing the accounting cycle for GSE Health Care Products for the months of June and July of the current year. GSE Health Care Products uses a voucher system.

This problem is longer than the problems that were in the chapters. You should follow the instructions carefully and enter the transactions accurately and in the suggested sequence. Be sure to use the correct transaction dates. If you enter transactions using the wrong month, the monthly income statement data will be incorrect. You must also specify the current date ranges when printing reports because only data within the specified date ranges will be included on the reports.

This comprehensive problem contains many transactions and involves a considerable amount of work, which will be lost if your data file is damaged or destroyed. For this reason, you should periodically make a backup (duplicate copy) of your data file. A convenient point to make a backup copy of your data would be before beginning processing for July. Then, if you need to restart the problem, simply load the backup file and proceed from the point you last saved your data.

Audit questions for each month are provided at the end of each month's processing. Complete the audit questions after finishing the month's work.

 To conserve paper, print only those reports identified in the step-by-step instructions. Complete the audit questions from screen displays.

June

1   Start *Integrated Accounting* 6e.

2   Load the opening balance template file, IA6 Comp Problem 01.

3   Enter your name in the Your Name text box.

4   Save the file to your disk or folder with a file name of Comp01-June Your Name (where Comp01 identifies the problem, and June represents the June transactions).

5   Perform the following customer maintenance: (1) Delete Metro Nutrition Center, (2) Change the name of Webb Health Supplies to Webb Nutrition Supplies, and (3) Add Catherine Meier to the customer list.

6   Enter the following budget data.

Account Title	Budget
Total Revenue	$500,000.00
Cost of Goods Sold	$275,000.00
Salaries Expense	$52,000.00
Advertising Expense	$20,000.00
Rent Expense	$15,000.00
Heating & Lighting Exp.	$8,000.00
Telephone Expense	$7,000.00
Supplies Expense	$3,000.00

Postage Expense	$1,500.00
Insurance Expense	$3,500.00
Deprec. Exp. Store Eq.	$7,500.00
Deprec. Exp. Office Eq.	$3,000.00
Miscellaneous Expense	$1,000.00
Interest Expense	$8,500.00

7 **Enter the general journal transactions.**

General Journal Transactions

June 02   Returned merchandise purchased on account from Upton Health Solutions, $1,000.00; the debit memo applies to Voucher No. 4520.

20   Received merchandise returned on account from Vetter Health Products, $1,525.00. The cost of the merchandise returned was $835.00. The credit memo applies to Sales Invoice No. 5798.

8 **Enter the vouchers journal transactions.**

Vouchers Journal Transactions

June 01   Purchased merchandise on account from Golden Crown, Inc., $2,348.50; Voucher No. 4535.

08   Purchased merchandise on account from Upton Health Solutions, $6,000.00; Voucher No. 4536.

09   Purchased advertising on account from Fleming Publications, $1,305.00; Voucher No. 4537.

09   Record Voucher No. 4538 to Edwards Leasing Corp., for monthly rent, $1,200.00.

16   Record Voucher No. 4539 to Quintero Utility Co., for monthly electric bill, $637.17.

19   Purchased merchandise on account from Langdon Products, Inc., $3,810.00; Voucher No. 4540.

21   Purchased supplies on account from Nessler Office Supplies, $700.00; Voucher No. 4541. Charge Miscellaneous Expense, $125.00, and Supplies, $575.00.

23   Purchased merchandise on account from Theissen Company, $7,200.00; Voucher No. 4542.

23   Record Voucher No. 4543 to Postmaster for postage, $108.76.

23   Record Voucher No. 4544 to Drake State Bank for a note payable, $945.00; principal, $669.91; interest, $275.09.

27   Record Voucher No. 4545 to Bristol Telephone Co., for monthly telephone bill, $589.24.

28   Record Voucher No. 4546 to reimburse the payroll bank account for monthly salaries expense, $4,102.43.

29   Record Voucher No. 4547 to Bauer Insurance for liability insurance, $805.00.

30   Record Voucher No. 4548 to Commissioner of Revenue for sales tax liability, $1,077.06.

30   Record Voucher No. 4549 to James Stelter for the owner's use, $3,000.00.

30   Purchased merchandise on account from Ostendorf Mfg., Inc., $9,185.95; Voucher No. 4550.0.

9 **Enter the cash payments journal transactions and display checks.**

Cash Payments Journal Transactions

June 01   Paid Voucher No. 4519 to Langdon Products, Inc., $2,250.00, no discount. Check No. 7260.

02   Paid Voucher No. 4525 to Golden Crown, Inc., $2,938.04, no discount. Check No. 7261.

05   Paid Voucher No. 4521 to Nessler Office Supplies, $937.50, no discount. Check No. 7262.

09   Paid Voucher No. 4538 to Edwards Leasing Corp., $1,200.00. Check No. 7263.

09	Paid Voucher No. 4480 to Fleming Publications, $700.00, no discount. Check No. 7264.
12	Paid Voucher No. 4520 to Upton Health Solutions, $4,912.00, no discount. Check No. 7265.
16	Paid Voucher No. 4539 to Quintero Utility Co., $637.17. Check No. 7266.
16	Paid Voucher No. 4536 to Upton Health Solutions, $6,000.00, less 2% discount, $120.00. Check No. 7267.
23	Paid Voucher No. 4543 to Postmaster, $108.76. Check No. 7268.
23	Paid Voucher No. 4544 to Drake State Bank, $945.00. Check No. 7269.
27	Paid Voucher No. 4545 to Bristol Telephone Co., $589.24. Check No. 7270.
28	Paid Voucher No. 4546 to Payroll Bank Account, $4,102.43. Check No. 7271.
29	Paid Voucher No. 4527 and Voucher No. 4547 to Bauer Insurance, $1,294.40. Check No. 7272.
30	Paid Voucher No. 4548 to Commissioner of Revenue, $1,077.06. Check No. 7273.
30	Paid Voucher No. 4549 to James Stelter, $3,000.00. Check No. 7274.
30	Paid Voucher No. 4542 to Theissen Company, $7,200.00, less 2% discount, $144.00. Check No. 7275.

10 Enter the sales journal transactions.

Sales Journal Transactions

June 02	Sold merchandise on account to Warner Supply Store, $7,865.00, no sales tax. Sales Invoice No. 5804. The cost of the merchandise sold was $4,325.00.
06	Sold merchandise on account to Hartwell, Inc., $7,595.00, no sales tax. Sales Invoice No. 5805. The cost of the merchandise sold was $4,180.00.
09	Sold merchandise on account to Gartner Natural Foods, $8,985.00, no sales tax. Sales Invoice No. 5806. The cost of the merchandise sold was $4,950.00.
16	Sold merchandise on account to Carr Health & Fitness, $12,000.00, no sales tax. Sales Invoice No. 5807. The cost of the merchandise sold was $6,505.00.
20	Sold merchandise on account to Catherine Meier, $7,678.00, plus 6% sales tax, $460.68; total $8,138.68. Sales Invoice No. 5808. The cost of the merchandise sold was $4,225.00.
23	Sold merchandise on account to Schaeffer Outlet, $2,499.95, no sales tax. Sales Invoice No. 5809. The cost of the merchandise sold was $1,375.00.
28	Sold merchandise on account to Ahmed Supply Center, $9,200.00, no sales tax. Sales Invoice No. 5810. The cost of the merchandise sold was $5,060.00.

11 Enter the cash receipts journal transactions.

Cash Receipts Journal Transactions

June 01	Received cash on account from Sommers Health Care, covering Sales Invoice No. 5802 for $1,047.00, less 2% discount, $20.94.
05	Received cash on account from Schaeffer Outlet, covering Sales Invoice No. 5803 for $7,705.15, less 2% discount, $154.10.
12	Received cash on account from Warner Supply Store, covering Sales Invoice No. 5804 for $7,865.00, less 2% discount, $157.30.
15	Sold merchandise for cash, $4,120.00, plus 6% sales tax, $247.20; total, $4,367.20. Cash Receipts No. 1220. The cost of the merchandise sold was $2,265.00.
16	Received cash on account from Ahmed Supply Center, covering Sales Invoice No. 5797 for $7,763.12, no discount.
19	Received cash on account from Gartner Natural Foods, covering Sales Invoice No. 5806 for $8,985.00, less 2% discount, $179.70.

22   Received cash on account from Hartwell, Inc., covering Sales Invoice No. 5800 for $8,214.57, no discount.

30   Sold merchandise for cash, $5,126.00, plus 6% sales tax, $307.56; total, $5,433.56. Cash Receipts No. 1221. The cost of the merchandise sold was $2,820.00.

12   Display the customer list.

13   Display the June journal entries and make corrections if necessary.

14   Display the trial balance.

15   Display the schedule of accounts payable.

16   Display the schedule of accounts receivable.

End-of-Month Activities

The following adjustment data are for the month of June for GSE Health Care Products. Use the trial balance report as the basis for preparing the adjusting entries.

Insurance expired during June..........................$985.00
Inventory of supplies on June 30.................$1,205.00
Depreciation for June:
    Store Equipment $363.82
    Office Equipment $215.50
Salaries Payable $469.35

1   Enter the adjusting entries in the general journal.

Enter a reference of Adj.Ent. in the Reference text box.

2   Display the adjusting entries for June.

3   Display the income statement.

4   Display the statement of owner's equity.

5   Display the balance sheet.

6   Display the budget report.

7   Generate an income statement graph.

8   Save the data file.

9   Complete Audit Questions for Comprehensive Problem 1 (June) on page 191. Display reports as necessary to answer the questions.

Audit Questions for Comprehensive Problem 1 (June)

NAME

Directions   *Write the answers to the following questions in the space provided.*

1.   What are the totals of the debit and credit columns from the vouchers journal for the month of June?

Total debits: _____

Total credits: _____

2.   What are the totals of the debit and credit columns from the cash payments journal for the month of June?

Total debits: _____

Total credits: _____

3.   What are the totals of the debit and credit columns from the sales journal for the month of June?

Total debits: _____

Total credits: _____

4.   What are the totals of the debit and credit columns from the cash receipts journal for the month of June?

Total debits: _____

Total credits: _____

5.   What is the total of Vouchers Payable account as of the end of June? _____

_____

6.   What is the total of Accounts Receivable account as of the end of June? _____

_____

7.   What is the amount of gross profit for the month of June? _____

_____

8.   What are the total operating expenses for the month of June? _____

_____

9.   What is the amount of net income for the month of June? _____

_____

10.   What is the amount of net income for the year to date? _____

_____

11.   What is the total amount of owner's equity at the end of June? _____

_____

12.   What are the total assets? _____

_____

13.   What are the total liabilities?   _____

_____

14.   What is the difference between the budgeted and actual total operating expenses as of the end of June?   _____

_____

July

1 **Open the file you saved as Comp01-June and choose Save As to save your data file with a file name of Comp01-July (where Comp01 identifies the problem, and July represents the July transactions).**

2 **Add Stevens Supply, Inc., to the vendor list.**

3 **Add Bonnie Lorentz to the customer list.**

4 **Enter the general journal transactions.**

General Journal Transactions

July 01   Reversing entries required by June adjustments. Use the adjustment data as of June 30 as the basis for your reversing entries. Enter Rev.Ent. in the Reference text box.

02   Received merchandise returned on account from Webb Nutrition Supplies, $1,500.00. The cost of the merchandise returned was $825.00. The credit memo applies to Sales Invoice No. 5790.

03   Returned merchandise purchased on account from Ostendorf Mfg., Inc., $565.50; the debit memo applies to Voucher No. 4521.

5 **Enter the vouchers journal transactions.**

Vouchers Journal Transactions

July 01   Purchased merchandise on account from Theissen Company, $2,900.00; Voucher No. 4551.

03   Purchased equipment on account from Nessler office Supplies, $4,375.50; Voucher No. 4552. Charge Store Equipment, $3,765.50, and Office Equipment, $610.00.

10   Purchased merchandise on account from Golden Crown, Inc., $7,000.00; Voucher No. 4553.

11   Record Voucher No. 4554 to Postmaster for postage, $146.76.

13   Purchased merchandise on account from Langdon Products, Inc., $4,550.00; Voucher No. 4555.

15   Record Voucher No. 4556 to Edwards Leasing Corp., for monthly rent, $1,200.00.

16   Record Voucher No. 4557 to Quintero Utility Co., for monthly electric bill, $689.13.

18   Purchased merchandise on account from Upton Health Solutions, $7,485.00; Voucher No. 4558.

20   Purchased advertising on account from Fleming Publications, $1,475.00; Voucher No. 4559.

23   Purchased supplies on account from Stevens Supply, Inc., $499.95; Voucher No. 4560. Charge Supplies, $404.95, and Miscellaneous Expense, $95.00.

24   Record Voucher No. 4561 to Drake State Bank for a note payable, $945.00; principal, $681.99; interest, $263.01.

25   Record Voucher No. 4562 to Bristol Telephone Co., for monthly telephone bill, $503.91.

26   Record Voucher No. 4563 to Bauer Insurance for fire and theft insurance, $450.00.

27   Purchased merchandise on account from Theissen Company, $11,000.00; Voucher No. 4564.

29   Record Voucher No. 4565 to reimburse the payroll bank account for monthly salaries expense, $4,257.66.

31   Record Voucher No. 4566 to Commissioner of Revenue for sales tax liability, $1,015.44.

31   Record Voucher No. 4567 to James Stelter for the owner's use, $3,500.00.

6   **Enter the cash payments journal transactions and display checks.**

Cash Payments Journal Transactions

July 01   Paid Voucher No. 4490 to Fleming Publications, $761.65, no discount. Check No. 7276.

01   Paid Voucher No. 4541 to Nessler Office Supplies, $700.00, no discount. Check No. 7277.

02   Paid Voucher No. 4535 to Golden Crown, Inc., $2,348.50, no discount. Check No. 7278.

03   Paid Voucher No. 4485 and Voucher No. 4540 to Langdon Products, Inc., $12,467.42, no discount. Check No. 7279.

03   Paid Voucher No. 4521 to Ostendorf Mfg., Inc., $5,884.41, no discount. Check No. 7280.

10   Paid Voucher No. 4551 to Theissen Company, $2,900.00, less 2% discount, $58.00. Check No. 7281.

11   Paid Voucher No. 4554 to Postmaster, $146.76. Check No. 7282.

13   Paid Voucher No. 4552 to Nessler Office Supplies, $4,375.50, no discount. Check No. 7283.

15   Paid Voucher No. 4556 to Edwards Leasing Corp., $1,200.00. Check No. 7284.

16   Paid Voucher No. 4557 to Quintero Utility Co., $689.13. Check No. 7285.

20   Paid Voucher No. 4555 to Langdon Products, Inc., $4,550.00, less 2% discount, $91.00. Check No. 7286.

20   Paid Voucher No. 4537 and Voucher No. 4559 to Fleming Publications, $2,780.00. Check No. 7287.

24   Paid Voucher No. 4561 to Drake State Bank, $945.00. Check No. 7288.

25   Paid Voucher No. 4562 to Bristol Telephone Co., $503.91. Check No. 7289.

26   Paid Voucher No. 4563 to Bauer Insurance, $450.00. Check No. 7290.

27   Paid Voucher No. 4558 to Upton Health Solutions, $7,485.00, less 2% discount, $149.70. Check No. 7291.

29   Paid Voucher No. 4565 to Payroll Bank Account, $4,257.66. Check No. 7292.

31   Paid Voucher No. 4566 to Commissioner of Revenue, $1,015.44. Check No. 7293.

31   Paid Voucher No. 4567 to James Stelter, $3,500.00. Check No. 7294.

7   **Enter the sales journal transactions.**

Sales Journal Transactions

July 01   Sold merchandise on account to Gartner Natural Foods, $8,950.00, no sales tax. Sales Invoice No. 5811. The cost of the merchandise sold was $4,925.00.

05   Sold merchandise on account to Bonnie Lorentz, $8,076.00, plus 6% sales tax, $484.56; total, $8,560.56. Sales Invoice No. 5812. The cost of the merchandise sold was $4,442.00.

08   Sold merchandise on account to Hartwell, Inc., $9,425.00, no sales tax. Sales Invoice No. 5813. The cost of the merchandise sold was $5,180.00.

12   Sold merchandise on account to Vetter Health Products, $12,795.00, no sales tax. Sales Invoice No. 5814. The cost of the merchandise sold was $7,037.25.

18   Sold merchandise on account to Carr Health & Fitness, $8,685.00, no sales tax. Sales Invoice No. 5815. The cost of the merchandise sold was $4,776.75.

23   Sold merchandise on account to Ahmed Supply Center, $3,835.00, no sales tax. Sales Invoice No. 5816. The cost of the merchandise sold was $2,110.00.

30   Sold merchandise on account to Schaeffer Outlet, $10,000.00, no sales tax. Sales Invoice No. 5817. The cost of the merchandise sold was $5,500.00.

8   Enter the cash receipts journal transactions.

Cash Receipts Journal Transactions

July 01   Received cash on account from Catherine Meier, covering Sales Invoice No. 5808 for $8,138.68, no discount.

01   Received cash on account from Schaeffer Outlet, covering Sales Invoice No. 5809 for $2,499.95, less 2% discount, $50.00.

02   Received cash on account from Carr Health & Fitness, covering Sales Invoice No. 5751 for $393.00, no discount.

06   Received cash on account from Rasmussen Company, covering Sales Invoice No. 5783 for $11,280.00, no discount.

08   Received cash on account from Ahmed Supply Center, covering Sales Invoice No. 5810 for $9,200.00, less 2% discount, $184.00.

12   Received cash on account from Carr Health & Fitness, covering Sales Invoice No. 5807 for $12,000.00, no discount.

18   Received cash on account from Bonnie Lorentz, covering Sales Invoice No. 5812 for $8,560.56, no discount.

20   Sold merchandise for cash, $3,580.00, plus 6% sales tax, $214.80; total, $3,794.80. Cash Receipts No. 1222. The cost of the merchandise sold was $1,970.00.

23   Received cash on account from Hartwell, Inc., covering Sales Invoice No. 5805 for $7,595.00, no discount.

28   Received cash on account from Carr Health & Fitness, covering Sales Invoice No. 5815 for $8,685.00, less 2% discount, $173.70.

30   Sold merchandise for cash, $1,278.00, plus 6% sales tax, $76.68; total, $1,354.68. Cash Receipts No. 1223. The cost of the merchandise sold was $703.00.

9   Display the vendor list.

10   Display the customer list.

11   Display the July journal entries and make corrections if necessary.

12   Display the trial balance.

13   Display the schedule of accounts payable.

14   Display the schedule of accounts receivable.

End-of-Month Activities

The following adjustment data are for the month of July for GSE Health Care Products. Use the trial balance report as the basis for preparing the adjusting entries.

Insurance expired during July $638.50
Inventory of supplies on July 31 ....$1,195.00
Depreciation for July:
    Store Equipment $446.19
    Office Equipment $228.65
Salaries Payable $518.32

1   **Enter the adjusting entries in the general journal.**

Enter a reference of Adj.Ent. in the Reference text box.

2   **Display the adjusting entries for July.**

3   **Display the income statement.**

4   **Display the statement of owner's equity.**

5   **Display the balance sheet.**

6   **Display the budget report.**

7   **Generate an actual versus budget graph.**

8   **Save the data file.**

9   **Complete the Audit Questions for Comprehensive Problem 1 (July) on page 197. Display reports as necessary to answer the questions.**

10   **End the *Integrated Accounting 6e* session.**

Audit Questions for Comprehensive Problem 1 (July)

NAME

Directions   *Write the answers to the following questions in the space provided.*

1.   What are the totals of the debit and credit columns from the vouchers journal for the month of July?

   Total debits: _____

   Total credits: _____

2.   What are the totals of the debit and credit columns from the cash payments journal for the month of July?

   Total debits: _____

   Total credits: _____

3.   What are the totals of the debit and credit columns from the sales journal for the month of July?

   Total debits: _____

   Total credits: _____

4.   What are the totals of the debit and credit columns from the cash receipts journal for the month of July?

   Total debits: _____

   Total credits: _____

5.   What is the total of vouchers payable as of the end of July?   _____

6.   What is the total of accounts receivable as of the end of July?   _____

7.   What is the amount of gross profit for the month of July?   _____

8.   What are the total operating expenses for the month of July?   _____

9.   What is the amount of net income for the month of July?   _____

10. What is the amount of net income for the year to date?   _____

11. What is the total owner's equity at the end of July?   _____

12. What are the total assets?   _____

13. What are the total liabilities? _____

_____

14. What is the difference between the budgeted and actual total operating expenses as of the end of July? _____

_____

Accounts Payable: Purchase Order Processing and Inventory Control

Upon completion of this chapter, you will be able to:

- Identify the components and procedures of a purchase order processing and inventory control system.

- Enter inventory maintenance data.

- Enter purchase order transactions and generate purchase orders.

- Enter voucher transactions.

- Explain accounting and inventory systems integration.

- Display reports reflecting purchase order processing and inventory integration.

Key Terms

Introduction

In this chapter you will maintain the inventory stock items, enter purchase orders, and voucher/purchases invoice transactions for Hagan Appliances. Hagan Appliances is a retail business that sells household appliances such as washers, dryers, refrigerators, freezers, ranges, dishwashers, and trash compactors.

Inventory

Merchandise inventory is often one of the costliest assets and most difficult to manage within a retail business. Successful control of merchandise inventory translates into greater profitability; however, managing merchandise inventory presents many challenges. Merchandise inventory can consist of thousands of different items that may be difficult to manage. The inventory is subject to pilferage and theft. Some inventory items may spoil or become obsolete. Inventory expenses include the cost of storage space and the taxes and insurance premiums that must be paid on inventory. Businesses must often borrow money to purchase inventory, which results in interest payments and reduced profits.

Because the costs associated with merchandise inventory are high, a business must try to keep the stock levels as low as possible. While trying to keep the stock levels low, the business must also maintain sufficient inventory to meet customer demand. If the inventory is too low, out-of-stock conditions may occur, resulting in lost sales, loss of customer confidence, and reduced profits. Therefore, the business must keep the inventory as low as possible while avoiding out-of-stock conditions.

The merchandising business is faced with other difficult decisions related to merchandise inventory. A business must decide when and how many items to reorder. A business must also know which items are selling well and which are not. Without this information, the inventory might contain items that are not selling well yet are quite expensive to maintain.

The large number of items and high volume of transactions in merchandise inventory can make manual record keeping a rather time-consuming, error-prone, and cumbersome process. The computer, on the other hand, lends itself well to the task. Computers can store and retrieve data, make computations quickly and accurately, and sort, organize, and report information.

In a computerized inventory system, the computer stores relevant data for each stock item (**stock number**, description of the item, **unit of measure**,

reorder point, and **retail price**) on disk. Periodically (daily, weekly, etc.), this data file is updated. New stock items are added to the file, data in existing stock items are changed as necessary, and inactive stock items are deleted. Once the stock item file has been maintained (updated), the inventory and accounting system is updated when purchase orders, voucher/purchases invoices, purchases returns, sales, and sales returns transactions for the period are entered. Finally, the appropriate accounting and inventory system reports are generated.

Inventory Stock Item Maintenance

Inventory stock items may be added, changed, or deleted from the inventory system. Choosing Maintain Accounts from the Data menu, clicking Accts. on the toolbar or clicking on the Purchases navigation button and then the Maintain Vendors menu button opens the Account Maintenance window. Click the Inventory tab to display the Inventory stock items shown in Figure 5.1.

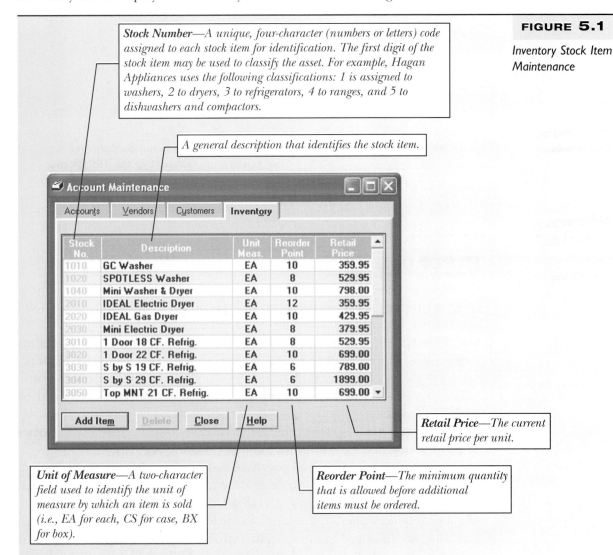

Stock Number—A unique, four-character (numbers or letters) code assigned to each stock item for identification. The first digit of the stock item may be used to classify the asset. For example, Hagan Appliances uses the following classifications: 1 is assigned to washers, 2 to dryers, 3 to refrigerators, 4 to ranges, and 5 to dishwashers and compactors.

A general description that identifies the stock item.

FIGURE 5.1

Inventory Stock Item Maintenance

Retail Price—The current retail price per unit.

Unit of Measure—A two-character field used to identify the unit of measure by which an item is sold (i.e., EA for each, CS for case, BX for box).

Reorder Point—The minimum quantity that is allowed before additional items must be ordered.

Enter, Change, and Delete Inventory Stock Items

To add a new inventory stock item, simply enter the stock number and complete the remaining data fields in the grid cell boxes and click on the Add Item button. To change existing stock item data, select the stock item by clicking on the grid cell containing the data you wish to change. The

Add Item button will change to Change Item when the insertion point is positioned anywhere within an existing stock item. Enter the correct data for the stock item and click on Change Item. To delete an inventory stock item, click on the stock item to be deleted and click Delete.

 You will not be allowed to delete a stock item that has current transaction data.

Table 5.1 contains a description of additional data fields that are stored with each inventory stock item. These fields start out with values of zero. As transactions are entered, these fields are updated.

TABLE 5.1

Descriptions of Additional Inventory Data Fields Stored by the Computer

Field Name	Description
Quantity on Hand	This field stores a count of the quantity that is included in the merchandise inventory at the present time.
Quantity on Order	This field contains the quantity that is currently on order but has not yet arrived.
Yearly Quantity Sold	This field stores an accumulation of the number of items sold so far this year.
Yearly Dollars Sold	This field contains an accumulation of the dollar value of items sold so far this year.
Last Cost Price	This field contains the price paid per unit for the most recent purchase of this stock item.
Average Cost	This field is used by the computer to maintain a per-unit average cost for this stock item.

Purchase Orders

Because cash disbursements are especially susceptible to fraud and embezzlement, the merchandising business must support all claims with valid documents. In addition, separation of employee duties in the purchase of merchandise and the recording and payment of merchandise received by the business help curtail this kind of theft. The degree of employee separation of duties varies depending on the size and complexities of the business and the products or services provided. Many businesses have turned to the computer to help them control their purchases and cash disbursements as a result of the large volume of transactions and the complexities of maintaining accurate inventory and accounting records.

In general, a **computerized purchase order processing system** comprises the procedures involved in automatically integrating the purchase order, voucher (or purchases invoice), and cash disbursement data into the inventory and general ledger. In the purchase order processing system used in this text, the purchasing department enters formal requests for purchases, or **purchase requisitions**, into the computerized purchase order system. A **purchase order** is a document containing a purchase order number, the vendor name, the quantity and description, expected price, and terms of the order. As shown in Figure 5.2, when purchase order information is entered into the computer, the Quantity on Order field of the item(s) ordered is increased in the inventory, data are stored for reference when the merchandise is received by the receiving department, and a purchase order document is generated. The purchase order document is then sent to the vendor for fulfillment of the order.

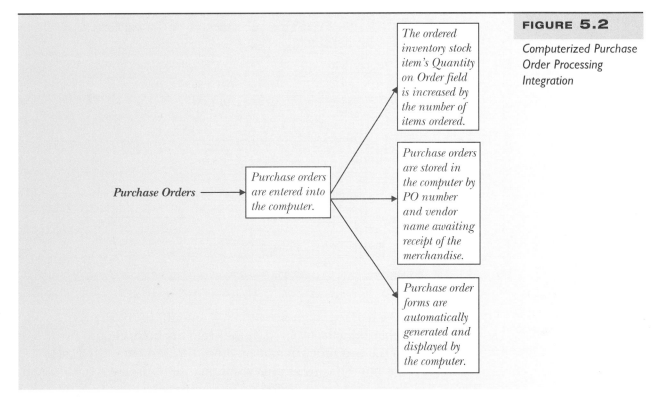

FIGURE 5.2

Computerized Purchase Order Processing Integration

Purchase Order Transactions

The Purch. Order tab is used to enter purchase order transactions for the business. Purchase order transactions that are entered into this window are automatically integrated into the inventory. A purchase order transaction then creates a purchase order record containing the purchase order number, date, vendor, terms, and item(s) ordered. In addition, the Quantity on Order field for said item is increased by the number of items ordered.

Clicking Tasks on the toolbar, choosing Other Tasks from the Data menu, or clicking on the Purchases navigation button and then the Purchase Orders menu button opens the Other Tasks window. Click the Purch. Order tab to reveal a purchase order transaction window as shown in Figure 5.3. The data used in Figure 5.3 is from the purchase order transaction:

> Mar. 01   Ordered the following merchandise from SPOTLESS Mfg., Inc., terms 2/10, n/30. Purchase Order No. 501.
>
> | Description | Quantity | Unit Cost |
> | --- | --- | --- |
> | SPOTLESS Washer | 6 | $319.00 |

Enter Purchase Order Transactions   To enter a purchase order transaction, enter the purchase order number, the date, the vendor name, and the terms of the sale. The terms 2/10, n/30 (read as "two ten, net thirty") shown in Figure 5.3 mean that the business either can pay the invoice within 10 days of the invoice date and take a 2 percent discount or can wait a maximum of

FIGURE 5.3

Purchase Order Transaction

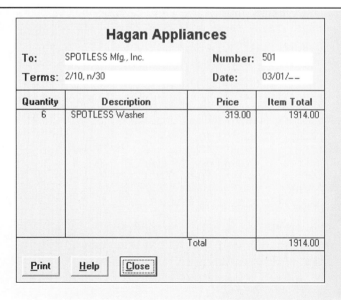

30 days from the invoice date to pay the full amount of the invoice. Finally, enter the number of items ordered in the Quantity field, choose the inventory item from the Inventory Item drop-down list, and enter the cost in the Price field if it is not the same as what is automatically displayed for the item. Repeat this procedure for each item to be purchased.

The computer will multiply the quantity by the price and place the amount in the Item Total column. The computer will also automatically place the Merchandise Inventory general ledger account number in the GL Account column.

After entering the purchase order transaction, click OK and a computer-generated purchase order, similar to the example shown in Figure 5.4 will appear.

FIGURE 5.4

Computer-Generated Purchase Order

Hagan Appliances

| To: | SPOTLESS Mfg., Inc. | Number: | 501 |
| Terms: | 2/10, n/30 | Date: | 03/01/-- |

Quantity	Description	Price	Item Total
6	SPOTLESS Washer	319.00	1914.00
		Total	1914.00

Print   Help   Close

Purchase Order Transaction Integration   The quantity 6, shown in Purchase Order No. 501 (Figures 5.3 and 5.4), is added to the SPOTLESS Washer stock item's Quantity on Order field in the Inventory system. The entire purchase order transaction is stored by the computer for reporting, for future reference, and for potential changes.

Change a Purchase Order Transaction   To change a previously entered purchase order transaction, click on List to the right of the Purch. Ord. # text box to display a list of purchase orders. A sample purchase order list is shown in Figure 5.5.

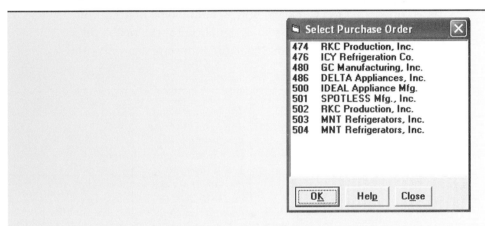

FIGURE 5.5

Purchase Order List

Choose the purchase order to be changed from the list and click OK. Select the text box for the data you wish to change, enter the correction, and click OK to record your change.

Delete a Purchase Order Transaction   To delete a previously entered purchase order transaction, click on List to the right of the Purch. Ord. # text box and choose the purchase order to be deleted. Click on Delete. When the Delete Confirmation dialog box appears, click Yes.

Purchase Invoices and Vouchers

After receiving a purchase order, the vendor ships the merchandise and sends a purchase invoice to the business's accounting department. The **purchase invoice** contains the vendor's name, original purchase order number, quantity and description of the merchandise, price, and terms of sale.

When the merchandise is received, the receiving department writes the description, quantity, and condition of the merchandise received on a form called a **receiving report**. They send the receiving report to the accounting department where it is checked against the purchase order and purchase invoice and then is used to initiate payment. The receiving department typically does not receive a copy of either the purchase order or the purchase invoice as a further separation of employee duties to protect against theft.

In the purchase order processing system used in this text, the accounting department enters the information about the merchandise received (or returned) into the computerized purchase order system. Figure 5.6 shows that when the purchases (or purchases return) information is entered into the computer, the quantity in the Quantity on Order field of the item(s) ordered is reduced and the Quantity on Hand field is increased in the inventory. Purchases (or voucher) journal entries are automatically created and posted to the general ledger, and a voucher (or internal purchase invoice) document is generated. The voucher (or internal purchase invoice) document is used to authorize cash payment.

Integrated Accounting 6e has been designed to handle both standard and voucher accounting systems. When the standard accounting system is designated, the computer displays window tabs, title bars, and related reports as purchase invoices. When the voucher accounting system option is designated, the computer displays window tabs, title bars, and related reports as vouchers. (You will learn how to set the type of accounting system in Chapter 12.) The accounting system designation for the problems in this chapter is set to voucher system; therefore, all the following examples and problems will use the term *voucher.*

FIGURE 5.6

Computerized Voucher/Purchase Invoice Integration

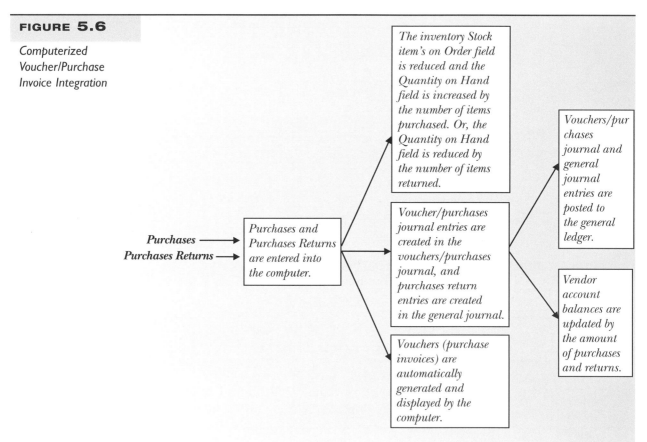

Voucher Transactions

The Voucher tab is used to enter purchase orders received and purchases returns transactions and to generate vouchers for the business. Purchase orders received and purchases returns transactions entered into this window are automatically integrated into the general ledger and inventory. A **voucher transaction** automatically creates and posts the respective journal entry in the vouchers journal, updates the vendor account balance, reduces the number of inventory items on order, increases the number of inventory items on hand, and generates a voucher document. A **purchases return transaction** automatically creates and posts the respective journal entry in the general journal and decreases the number of inventory items on hand.

Click Tasks on the toolbar, select Other Tasks from the Data menu, or click on the Purchases navigation button and then the Purchase Invoices menu button to open the Other Tasks window. Click the Voucher tab to reveal the voucher transaction window as shown in Figure 5.7. The data shown in Figure 5.7 are from the following voucher:

> Mar. 02   Received the following merchandise for Purchase Order No. 474 from RKC Production, Inc., terms 2/10, n/30. Voucher No. 916.

Description	Quantity	Unit Cost
Mini Washer & Dryer	4	$540.00

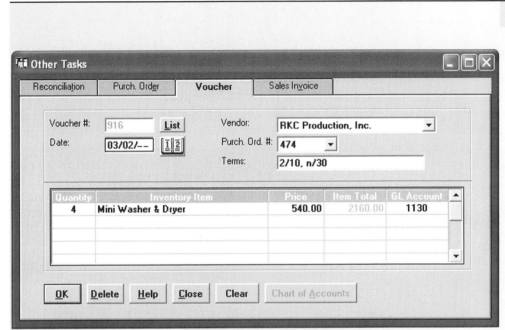

FIGURE 5.7

Voucher Transaction

Enter Voucher Transactions   To enter a voucher transaction, enter the voucher number, the date, and the vendor name. As soon as the vendor name is entered, a Purch. Ord. # drop-down list box will appear immediately under the vendor name. Select the appropriate purchase order number from the list. The terms and item(s) ordered will appear in the respective grid cells. Enter any changes to the quantity received or price. If the transaction is a purchases return, enter the voucher number (with a prefix of *R* to designate Return), the date, and the vendor name. Next, enter the quantity returned as a *negative* value, choose the inventory item from the Inventory Item drop-down list, and enter the cost of the item in the Price field if it is not the same as what is automatically displayed for the item. Repeat this procedure for each order received from the vendor or each item returned to the vendor.

The computer will then multiply the quantity by the price and place the amount in the Item Total column. The computer will also automatically place the merchandise inventory general ledger account number in the GL Account column.

After entering the voucher or purchases return transaction, click OK to open a computer-generated voucher, similar to the example shown in Figure 5.8.

FIGURE 5.8

Computer-Generated Voucher

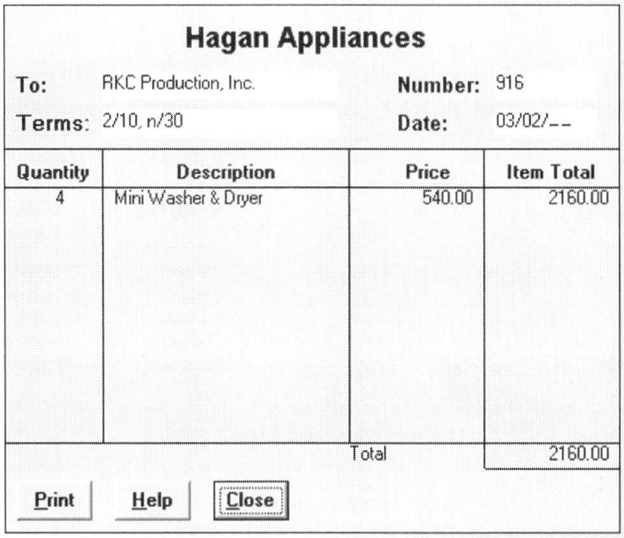

Hagan Appliances

| To: | RKC Production, Inc. | | **Number:** | 916 |
| **Terms:** | 2/10, n/30 | | **Date:** | 03/02/__ |

Quantity	Description	Price	Item Total
4	Mini Washer & Dryer	540.00	2160.00
		Total	2160.00

Print Help Close

Voucher Transaction Integration When Voucher No. 916 (Figures 5.7 and 5.8) is entered, the computer performs the following integration to the Inventory System: The quantity 4, is deducted from the Quantity on Order field and added to the Quantity on Hand field of the Mini Washer and Dryer's inventory stock item.

In the integration to the Accounting System, the computer generates and posts the following Vouchers journal entry:

	Debit	Credit
Merchandise Inventory	$2,160.00	
Vouchers Payable		$2,160.00

In addition, $2,160.00 is added to the RKC Production, Inc., account balance in the Vendor file. Finally, the entire Voucher Transaction is stored for reporting, future reference, and potential changes.

Change a Voucher Transaction To change a previously entered voucher or purchases return transaction, click on List to the right of the Voucher # text box to display a list of vouchers. A sample voucher list is shown in Figure 5.9.

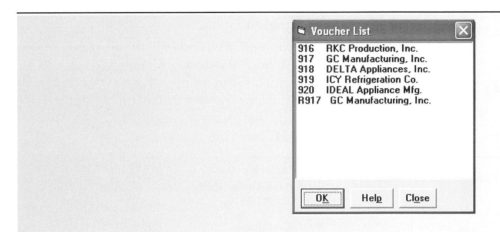

FIGURE 5.9

Voucher List

Choose the voucher to be changed from the list and click OK. Select the text box for the data you wish to change, enter the correction, and click OK to record your change.

Delete a Voucher Transaction   To delete a previously entered voucher or purchases return transaction, click on List to the right of the Voucher # text box and choose the voucher to be deleted. Click Delete. When the Delete Confirmation dialog box appears, click Yes.

Purge Invoices and Purchase Orders

Integrated Accounting 6e has a capacity of 50 purchase order and 50 voucher/purchase invoice transactions. If either of these capacities is exceeded, an Alert dialog box will appear informing you of this condition. Before additional purchase orders or voucher/purchase invoices can be entered, the previously entered data must be erased by choosing **purge invoices and purchase orders** from the Options menu. A dialog box will appear asking you to confirm whether you indeed want to purge vouchers/invoices and purchase orders in the event you accidentally chose this menu item. Because the data from the purchase orders and vouchers/invoices previously entered were automatically integrated into the inventory and general ledger, purging them will not cause any information to be lost. A backup file should be made before the purchase orders and vouchers/invoices are purged. This procedure should not be necessary in this text-workbook because none of the problems exceed the system capacity.

Reports

The general journal, vouchers journal, cash payments journal, schedule of accounts payable, and accounts payable ledger reports you worked with in previous chapters will be used for purchase order reporting. In addition, purchase order and voucher registers will be used for purchase order reporting, and the inventory list, inventory transactions, and inventory exceptions reports will be used for inventory reporting. The procedure to display and print the registers and inventory reports is identical to that used in previous chapters.

Reports

Purchase Order Register

After purchase order transactions have been entered into the computerized purchase order processing system, a **purchase order register** should be displayed. Purchase orders are displayed in numerical and date order. Each purchase order is shown with the total amount ordered from each vendor during the processing period. In the example shown in Figure 5.10, the processing period is one week—March 1 through March 7.

FIGURE 5.10

Purchase Order Register

Hagan Appliances
Purchase Order Register
03/07/—

P.O. Number	P.O. Date	Vendor Name	P.O. Amount
501	03/01/—	SPOTLESS Mfg., Inc.	1,914.00
502	03/02/—	RKC Production, Inc.	2,170.00
503	03/04/—	MNT Refrigerators, Inc.	7,007.00
504	03/07/—	MNT Refrigerators, Inc.	1,820.00
		Total Amount	12,911.00

Voucher Register

After voucher transactions have been entered into the computerized purchase order processing system, a **voucher register** should be displayed. Vouchers are displayed in numerical order, except for returns, which are listed last. Each voucher is shown with the total amount of expenditure due (or credited) each vendor during the processing period. In the example shown in Figure 5.11, the processing period is one week—March 1 through March 7.

FIGURE 5.11

Voucher Register

Hagan Appliances
Voucher Register
03/07/—

Invoice Number	Invoice Date	Vendor Name	Invoice Amount
916	03/02/—	RKC Production, Inc.	2,160.00
917	03/03/—	GC Manufacturing, Inc.	1,590.00
918	03/05/—	DELTA Appliances, Inc.	1,750.00
919	03/06/—	ICY Refrigeration Co.	2,855.40
920	03/07/—	IDEAL Appliance Mfg.	710.25
R917	03/06/—	GC Manufacturing, Inc.	−530.00
		Total Amount	8,535.65

Inventory List

The inventory list report provides the current status of each inventory item for reference. The report is also useful for verifying the accuracy of inventory maintenance. Figure 5.12 shows an example of an inventory list report.

FIGURE 5.12

Inventory List Report

Hagan Appliances
Inventory List
03/07/—

Stock No.	Description	Unit Meas.	On Hand	On Order	Reorder Point	Last Cost	Retail Price
1010	GC Washer	EA	19	0	10	241.00	359.95
1020	SPOTLESS Washer	EA	13	6	8	319.00	529.95
1040	Mini Washer & Dryer	EA	19	0	10	540.00	798.00
2010	IDEAL Electric Dryer	EA	24	0	12	220.00	359.95
2020	IDEAL Gas Dryer	EA	9	0	10	305.00	429.95
2030	Mini Electric Dryer	EA	11	0	8	225.00	379.95
3010	1 Door 18 CF. Refrig.	EA	18	0	8	350.00	529.95
3020	1 Door 22 CF. Refrig.	EA	11	6	10	435.00	699.00
3030	S by S 19 CF. Refrig.	EA	15	0	6	530.00	789.00
3040	S by S 29 CF. Refrig.	EA	7	4	6	1135.00	1899.00
3050	Top MNT 21 CF. Refrig.	EA	13	4	10	455.00	699.00
3060	Top MNT 25 CF. Refrig.	EA	14	0	6	510.00	859.95
3070	Mini FR. & Refrig.	EA	15	0	8	237.95	349.95
3080	ICY 20 CF. Freezer	EA	6	0	10	285.00	428.00
3090	Micro Refrig.	EA	0	0	10		380.00
4010	RKC Electric Range	EA	21	0	8	216.00	349.99
4020	RKC Gas Range	EA	7	7	6	310.00	435.95
5010	DELTA Dishwasher	EA	15	0	10	350.00	549.95
5020	IDEAL Dishwasher	EA	20	0	10	236.75	329.95
5030	Trash Compactor	EA	13	0	6	233.90	389.95

Inventory Transactions

The Inventory Transactions report lists all transactions that affected inventory items during the processing period. You should display this report whenever you enter, correct, or delete purchase orders or voucher transactions to verify that all data were recorded and entered correctly in the inventory system. An example of an Inventory Transactions report is shown in Figure 5.13. (The item's quantity sold and selling price data will be discussed in Chapter 6.)

FIGURE 5.13

Inventory Transactions Report

Hagan Appliances
Inventory Transactions
03/07/—

Date	Description	Inv./ P.O.	Quantity Sold	Selling Price	Quan. Ord.	Quan. Recd.	Cost Price
Purchase Orders							
03/01	SPOTLESS Washer	501			6		
03/02	RKC Gas Range	502			7		
03/04	1 Door 22 CF. Refrig.	503			6		
	S by S 29 CF. Refrig.				4		
03/07	Top MNT 21 CF. Refrig.	504			4		

(continued)

FIGURE 5.13

(Concluded)

Vouchers					
03/02	Mini Washer & Dryer	916		4	540.00
03/03	S by S 19 CF. Refrig.	917		3	530.00
03/05	DELTA Dishwasher	918		5	350.00
03/06	Mini FR. & Refrig.	919		12	237.95
03/07	IDEAL Dishwasher	920		3	236.75
03/06	S by S 19 CF. Refrig.	R917		−1	530.00
	Totals		24	26	

Inventory Exceptions

The inventory exceptions report lists items in the inventory that are out of stock (quantity on hand of zero or less) and items that are at or below the reorder point (quantity on hand less than or equal to the reorder point). This report alerts management to items in the inventory that need attention. An inventory exceptions report is shown in Figure 5.14.

FIGURE 5.14

Inventory Exceptions Report

Hagan Appliances
Inventory Exceptions
03/07/—

Stock No.	Description	Unit Meas	On Hand	On Order	Reorder Point	Exception
2020	IDEAL Gas Dryer	EA	9		10	At/below reorder point
3080	ICY 20 CF. Freezer	EA	6		10	At/below reorder point
3090	Micro Refrig.	EA	0		10	Out of stock

Chapter Summary

■ A business's success in controlling merchandise inventory relates directly to its profitability.

■ Because costs associated with merchandise inventory are high, a business must try to keep the stock levels as low as possible yet maintain sufficient inventory to meet customer demand.

■ Inventory stock items may be added, changed, or deleted from the inventory system.

■ A stock number is a unique, four-character code that is assigned to each inventory item for identification.

■ The unit of measure is a two-character abbreviation that indicates how the item is sold (i.e., each, by the case, by the box, etc.).

■ The minimum quantity that is allowed before additional items must be ordered is referred to as the reorder point.

■ The quantity on hand is the quantity that is included in the inventory at the present time.

■ The quantity on order is the quantity of additional merchandise that has been ordered but not yet arrived.

- The current selling price per unit is called the retail price.

- A computerized purchase order processing system comprises the procedures involved in automatically integrating the purchase order, voucher (or purchases invoice), and cash disbursement data into the inventory and general ledger.

- A purchase requisition is a formal request for the purchase of merchandise.

- A purchase order is a document containing a purchase order number, vendor name, quantity and description, expected price, and terms of the order.

- A purchase invoice contains the vendor's name, original purchase order number, quantity and description of the merchandise, price, and terms of the order.

- A receiving report is created by the receiving department and contains the description, quantity, and condition of the merchandise.

- A voucher transaction automatically creates and posts the respective journal entry in the vouchers journal, updates the vendor account balance, reduces the number of inventory items on order, increases the number of inventory items on hand, and generates a voucher document.

- A purchases return transaction automatically creates and posts the appropriate journal entry in the general journal and decreases the number of inventory items on hand.

- A purchase order register lists the total amount ordered from each vendor in numerical and date order for the processing period.

- A voucher register lists the total amount of expenditure due (or credited for purchase returns) each vendor during the processing period.

- The inventory list report provides the current status of each inventory item for reference and is useful for verifying the accuracy of inventory maintenance.

- The inventory transactions report lists all the transactions that affected the inventory items during the processing period.

- The inventory exceptions report alerts management to items in the inventory that need attention by listing items that are out of stock (quantity on hand of zero or less) and items that are at or below the reorder point (quantity on hand less than or equal to the reorder point).

Sample Problem 5-S

In this problem, you will perform the operating procedures necessary to add new inventory stock items, make changes to existing inventory stock items, and delete an inventory stock item. In addition, you will process the purchase orders, vouchers, and cash payment transactions for the week of March 1 through March 7 of the current year for Hagan Appliances.

1   **Start *Integrated Accounting* 6e.**

2   **Load opening balances file IA6 Problem 05-S.**

3   **Enter your name in the Your Name text box and click OK.**

4   **Save the file with a file name of 05-S Your Name.**

5   **Enter the inventory stock item maintenance data.**

Click on the Inventory navigation button, and then the Maintain Inventory menu button. Enter the following inventory stock item maintenance data:

Add Stock No. 3090; Micro Refrig.; unit of measure, EA; reorder point, 10; retail price, $380.00 to the inventory stock item file.

Change the retail price of 1 Door 18 CF. Refrig. (Stock No. 3010) to $529.95.

Change the retail price of Mini FR. & Refrig. (Stock No. 3070) to $349.95.

Change the reorder point of DELTA Dishwasher (Stock No. 5010) to 10.

Delete Mini Washer (Stock No. 1030) from the stock item file.

6   **Enter the following purchase order and voucher transactions. The March 1 Purchase Order No. 501 is shown in Figure 5.15(a), the March 2 Voucher No. 916 is shown in Figure 5.15(b), and the March 6 Purchase Return No. R917 is shown in Figure 5.15(c).**

Click on the Purchases navigation button, and then the appropriate Purchase Orders or Purchase Invoices menu buttons. Enter the following March 1 through March 7 transactions. If the unit cost differs (e.g., March 4 Purchase Order No. 503), make sure you enter the data shown in the transaction.

 It is important that you enter the transactions in date sequence; otherwise, your reports may be incorrect because the computer calculates perpetual inventory according to the transactions' dates.

Weekly Purchase Order and Voucher Transactions

Mar. 01   Ordered the following merchandise from SPOTLESS Mfg., Inc., terms 2/10, n/30. Purchase Order No. 501.

Description	Quantity	Unit Cost
SPOTLESS Washer	6	$319.00

02   Ordered the following merchandise from RKC Production, Inc., terms 2/10. n/30. Purchase Order No. 502.

Description	Quantity	Unit Cost
RKC Gas Range	7	$310.00

02   Received the following merchandise for Purchase Order No. 474 from RKC Production, Inc., terms 2/10, n/30. Voucher No. 916.

Description	Quantity	Unit Cost
Mini Washer & Dryer	4	$540.00

03   Received the following merchandise for Purchase Order No. 480 from GC Manufacturing, Inc., terms 2/10, n/30. Voucher No. 917.

Description	Quantity	Unit Cost
S by S 19 CF. Refrig.	3	$530.00

04   Ordered the following merchandise from MNT Refrigerators, Inc., terms 2/10, n/30. Purchase Order No. 503. (Be sure to enter the unit cost difference.)

Description	Quantity	Unit Cost
1 Door 22 CF. Refrig.	6	$426.30
S by S 29 CF. Refrig.	4	1,112.30

05   Received the following merchandise for Purchase Order No. 486 from DELTA Appliances, Inc., terms 2/10, n/30. Voucher No. 918.

Description	Quantity	Unit Cost
DELTA Dishwasher	5	$350.00

06   Returned the following merchandise to GC Manufacturing, Inc., Voucher No. R917. (Be sure to enter a quantity of −1 to indicate a return of one item.)

Description	Quantity	Unit Cost
S by S 19 CF. Refrig.	1	$530.00

06   Received the following merchandise from Purchase Order No. 476 from ICY Refrigeration Co., terms 2/10, n/30. Voucher No. 919.

Description	Quantity	Unit Cost
Mini FR. & Refrig.	12	$237.95

07   Received the following merchandise for Purchase Order No. 500 from IDEAL Appliance Mfg., terms 2/10, n/30. Voucher No. 920.

Description	Quantity	Unit Cost
IDEAL Dishwasher	3	$236.75

07   Ordered the following merchandise from MNT Refrigerators, Inc., terms 2/10, n/30. Purchase Order No. 504.

Description	Quantity	Unit Cost
Top MNT 21 CF. Refrig.	4	$455.00

FIGURE 5.15(A)

Purchase Order No. 501

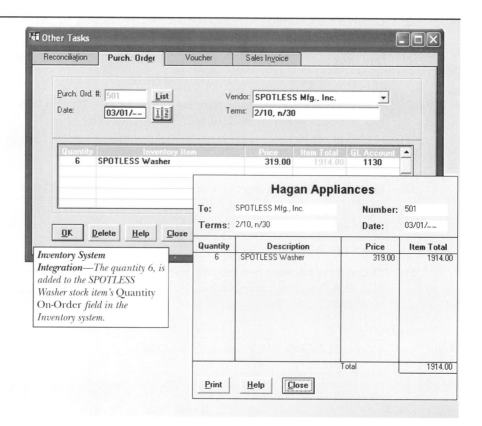

Inventory System Integration—The quantity 6, is added to the SPOTLESS Washer stock item's Quantity On-Order *field in the Inventory system.*

FIGURE 5.15(B)

Voucher No. 916

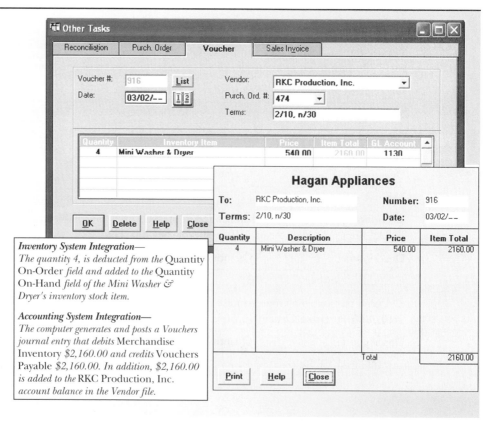

Inventory System Integration— The quantity 4, is deducted from the Quantity On-Order *field and added to the* Quantity On-Hand *field of the Mini Washer & Dryer's inventory stock item.*

Accounting System Integration— The computer generates and posts a Vouchers journal entry that debits Merchandise Inventory $2,160.00 *and credits* Vouchers Payable $2,160.00. *In addition, $2,160.00 is added to the* RKC Production, Inc. *account balance in the Vendor file.*

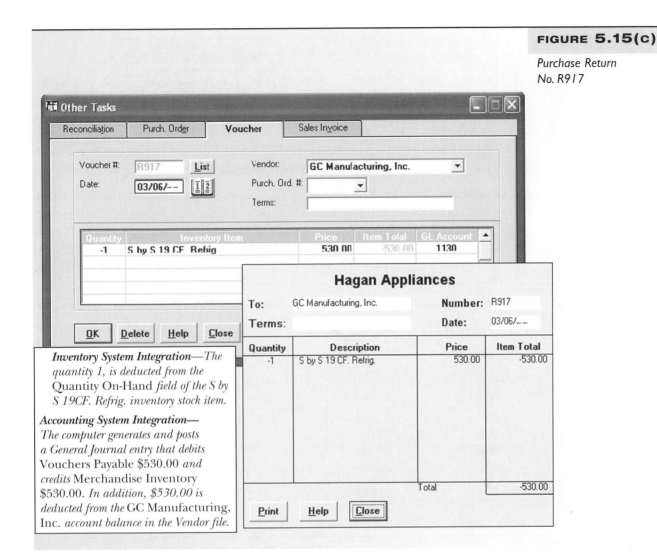

FIGURE 5.15(c)

*Purchase Return
No. R917*

Inventory System Integration—The quantity 1, is deducted from the Quantity On-Hand *field of the S by S 19CF. Refrig. inventory stock item.*

Accounting System Integration— The computer generates and posts a General Journal entry that debits Vouchers Payable $530.00 *and credits* Merchandise Inventory $530.00. *In addition, $530.00 is deducted from the* GC Manufacturing, Inc. *account balance in the Vendor file.*

---

(7)   Enter the following cash payments journal transactions as illustrated in Figure 5.16.

Click on the Purchases navigation button and then the Purchases Journal menu button. When the Journal Entries window appears, click on the Cash Payments tab.

Weekly Cash Payment Transactions

Mar. 05   Paid invoice 916 to RKC Production, Inc., $2,160.00, no discount. Check No. 4732.

06   Paid invoice 918 to DELTA Appliances, Inc., $1,750.00, less 2% discount, $35.00. Check No. 4733.

07   Paid invoice 919 to ICY Refrigeration Co., $2,855.40, less 2% discount, $57.10. Check No. 4734.

FIGURE 5.16

Cash Payments

Date	Refer.	V.P. Debit	Mrch. Inv. Cr.	Cash Credit	Vendor
03/05/	4732	2160.00		2160.00	RKC Production, Inc.
03/06/	4733	1750.00	35.00	1715.00	DELTA Appliances, Inc.
03/07/	4734	2855.40	57.10	2798.30	ICY Refrigeration Co.

8 **Display the purchase order and voucher registers for the period of March 1 through March 7.**

Click on the Purchases navigation button and then the Purchase Orders/Invoices Reports menu button. Choose the Purchase Orders and Invoices option, then select the Purch. Orders (if not already selected), and the purchase order register report will be displayed. Then select Vouchers, and the voucher register report will be displayed. The reports appear in Figure 5.17(a) and (b), respectively.

FIGURE 5.17(A)

Purchase Order Register

Hagan Appliances
Purchase Order Register
03/07/—

P.O. Number	P.O. Date	Vendor Name	P.O. Amount
501	03/01/—	SPOTLESS Mfg., Inc.	1,914.00
502	03/02/—	RKC Production, Inc.	2,170.00
503	03/04/—	MNT Refrigerators, Inc.	7,007.00
504	03/07/—	MNT Refrigerators, Inc.	1,820.00
		Total Amount	12,911.00

FIGURE 5.17(B)

Voucher Register

Hagan Appliances
Voucher Register
03/07/—

Invoice Number	Invoice Date	Vendor Name	Invoice Amount
916	03/02/—	RKC Production, Inc.	2,160.00
917	03/03/—	GC Manufacturing, Inc.	1,590.00
918	03/05/—	DELTA Appliances, Inc.	1,750.00
919	03/06/—	ICY Refrigeration Co.	2,855.40
920	03/07/—	IDEAL Appliance Mfg.	710.25
R917	03/06/—	GC Manufacturing, Inc.	−530.00
		Total Amount	8,535.65

9 **Display an Inventory List report.**

Choose the Inventory Reports option, select the Inventory List report, and click OK. The report appears in Figure 5.18.

Hagan Appliances
Inventory List
03/07/—

Stock No.	Description	Unit Meas.	On Hand	On Order	Reorder Point	Last Cost	Retail Price
1010	GC Washer	EA	19	0	10	241.00	359.95
1020	SPOTLESS Washer	EA	13	6	8	319.00	529.95
1040	Mini Washer & Dryer	EA	19	0	10	540.00	798.00
2010	IDEAL Electric Dryer	EA	24	0	12	220.00	359.95
2020	IDEAL Gas Dryer	EA	9	0	10	305.00	429.95
2030	Mini Electric Dryer	EA	11	0	8	225.00	379.95
3010	1 Door 18 CF. Refrig.	EA	18	0	8	350.00	529.95
3020	1 Door 22 CF. Refrig.	EA	11	6	10	435.00	699.00
3030	S by S 19 CF. Refrig.	EA	15	0	6	530.00	789.00
3040	S by S 29 CF. Refrig.	EA	7	4	6	1135.00	1899.00
3050	Top MNT 21 CF. Refrig.	EA	13	4	10	455.00	699.00
3060	Top MNT 25 CF. Refrig.	EA	14	0	6	510.00	859.95
3070	Mini FR. & Refrig.	EA	15	0	8	237.95	349.95
3080	ICY 20 CF. Freezer	EA	6	0	10	285.00	428.00
3090	Micro Refrig.	EA	0	0	10		380.00
4010	RKC Electric Range	EA	21	0	8	216.00	349.99
4020	RKC Gas Range	EA	7	7	6	310.00	435.95
5010	DELTA Dishwasher	EA	15	0	10	350.00	549.95
5020	IDEAL Dishwasher	EA	20	0	10	236.75	329.95
5030	Trash Compactor	EA	13	0	6	233.90	389.95

FIGURE 5.18

Inventory List Report

10 **Display the general journal for the period of March 1 through March 7.**

The report appears in Figure 5.19.

Hagan Appliances
General Journal
03/07/—

Date	Refer.	Acct.	Title	Debit	Credit
03/06	R917	1130	Merchandise Inventory		530.00
03/06	R917	2110	VP/GC Manufacturing, Inc.	530.00	
			Totals	530.00	530.00

FIGURE 5.19

General Journal

11   **Display the vouchers journal for the period of March 1 through March 7.**

The report appears in Figure 5.20.

FIGURE **5.20**

Vouchers Journal

Hagan Appliances
Vouchers Journal
03/07/—

Date	Inv. No.	Acct.	Title	Debit	Credit
03/02	916	1130	Merchandise Inventory	2,160.00	
03/02	916	2110	VP/RKC Production, Inc.		2,160.00
03/03	917	1130	Merchandise Inventory	1,590.00	
03/03	917	2110	VP/GC Manufacturing, Inc.		1,590.00
03/05	918	1130	Merchandise Inventory	1,750.00	
03/05	918	2110	VP/DELTA Appliances, Inc.		1,750.00
03/06	919	1130	Merchandise Inventory	2,855.40	
03/06	919	2110	VP/ICY Refrigeration Co.		2,855.40
03/07	920	1130	Merchandise Inventory	710.25	
03/07	920	2110	VP/IDEAL Appliance Mfg.		710.25
			Totals	9,065.65	9,065.65

12   **Display the cash payments journal for the period of March 1 through March 7.**

The report appears in Figure 5.21.

FIGURE **5.21**

Cash Payments Journal

Hagan Appliances
Cash Payments Journal
03/07/—

Date	Ck. No.	Acct.	Title	Debit	Credit
03/05	4732	2110	VP/RKC Production, Inc.	2,160.00	
03/05	4732	1110	Cash		2,160.00
03/06	4733	2110	VP/DELTA Appliances, Inc.	1,750.00	
03/06	4733	1110	Cash		1,715.00
03/06	4733	1130	Merchandise Inventory		35.00
03/07	4734	2110	VP/ICY Refrigeration Co.	2,855.40	
03/07	4734	1110	Cash		2,798.30
03/07	4734	1130	Merchandise Inventory		57.10
			Totals	6,765.40	6,765.40

13   **Display a general ledger report for the Merchandise Inventory and Vouchers Payable accounts.**

In the Report Selection window, choose Ledger Reports and General Ledger, and then click OK. Enter the Merchandise Inventory account (1130) in both the From and To drop-down text boxes in the Account Range dialog box. To display the Vouchers Payable account, enter (2110) in the From and To text box. The reports appear in Figures 5.22(a) and (b), respectively.

Hagan Appliances
General Ledger
03/07/—

Account	Journal	Date	Refer.	Debit	Credit	Balance
1130-Merchandise Inventory						
	Balance Forward					85,965.84Dr
	Vouchers	03/02	916	2,160.00		88,125.84Dr
	Vouchers	03/03	917	1,590.00		89,715.84Dr
	Vouchers	03/05	918	1,750.00		91,465.84Dr
	Cash Payments	03/06	4733		35.00	91,430.84Dr
	Vouchers	03/06	919	2,855.40		94,286.24Dr
	General	03/06	R917		530.00	93,756.24Dr
	Cash Payments	03/07	4734		57.10	93,699.14Dr
	Vouchers	03/07	920	710.25		94,409.39Dr

FIGURE 5.22(A)

Merchandise Inventory Account

Hagan Appliances
General Ledger
03/07/—

Account	Journal	Date	Refer.	Debit	Credit	Balance
2110-Vouchers Payable						
	Balance Forward					24,240.00Cr
	Vouchers	03/02	916		2,160.00	26,400.00Cr
	Vouchers	03/03	917		1,590.00	27,990.00Cr
	Cash Payments	03/05	4732	2,160.00		25,830.00Cr
	Vouchers	03/05	918		1,750.00	27,580.00Cr
	Cash Payments	03/06	4733	1,750.00		25,830.00Cr
	Vouchers	03/06	919		2,855.40	28,685.40Cr
	General	03/06	R917	530.00		28,155.40Cr
	Cash Payments	03/07	4734	2,855.40		25,300.00Cr
	Vouchers	03/07	920		710.25	26,010.25Cr

FIGURE 5.22(B)

Vouchers Payable Account

14   Display a trial balance report.

The trial balance report is shown in Figure 5.23.

FIGURE 5.23			
Trial Balance.			

Hagan Appliances
Trial Balance
03/07/—

Acct. Number	Account Title	Debit	Credit
1110	Cash	9,386.76	
1120	Accounts Receivable	69,260.00	
1130	Merchandise Inventory	94,409.39	
1140	Supplies	2,460.64	
1150	Prepaid Insurance	1,546.07	
2110	Vouchers Payable		26,010.25
3110	Kimberly Hagan, Capital		153,498.76
3120	Kimberly Hagan, Drawing	24,000.00	
4110	Sales		206,237.99
5110	Cost of Merchandise Sold	164,054.70	
6110	Advertising Expense	1,800.00	
6120	Miscellaneous Expense	637.65	
6140	Rent Expense	10,000.00	
6160	Telephone Expense	3,973.50	
6170	Utilities Expense	4,218.29	
	Totals	385,747.00	385,747.00

15   Display a schedule of accounts payable.

The report is shown in Figure 5.24.

FIGURE 5.24	
Schedule of Accounts Payable	

Hagan Appliances
Schedule of Accounts Payable
03/07/—

Name	Balance
DELTA Appliances, Inc.	3,995.00
GC Manufacturing, Inc.	5,230.65
ICY Refrigeration Co.	5,485.50
IDEAL Appliance Mfg.	4,185.25
RKC Production, Inc.	2,235.85
SPOTLESS Mfg., Inc.	4,878.00
Total	26,010.25

16 Display the accounts payable ledger.

The report is shown in Figure 5.25.

Account	Journal	Date	Refer.	Debit	Credit	Balance
Hagan Appliances						
Accounts Payable Ledger						
03/07/—						
DELTA Appliances, Inc.						
	Balance Forward					3,995.00Cr
	Vouchers	03/05	918		1,750.00	5,745.00Cr
	Cash Payments	03/06	4733	1,750.00		3,995.00Cr
GC Manufacturing, Inc.						
	Balance Forward					4,170.65Cr
	Vouchers	03/03	917		1,590.00	5,760.65Cr
	General	03/06	R917	530.00		5,230.65Cr
ICY Refrigeration Co.						
	Balance Forward					5,485.50Cr
	Vouchers	03/06	919		2,855.40	8,340.90Cr
	Cash Payments	03/07	4734	2,855.40		5,485.50Cr
IDEAL Appliance Mfg.						
	Balance Forward					3,475.00Cr
	Vouchers	03/07	920		710.25	4,185.25Cr
MNT Refrigerators, Inc.						
	*** No Activity ***					.00
RKC Production, Inc.						
	Balance Forward					2,235.85Cr
	Vouchers	03/02	916		2,160.00	4,395.85Cr
	Cash Payments	03/05	4732	2,160.00		2,235.85Cr
SPOTLESS Mfg., Inc.						
	Balance Forward					4,878.00Cr

FIGURE 5.25

Accounts Payable Ledger

17 Display the inventory transactions report.

In the Report Selection window, choose Inventory Reports and Inventory Transactions, and then click OK. The report appears in Figure 5.26.

Date	Description	Inv./ P.O.	Quantity Sold	Selling Price	Quan. Ord.	Quan. Recd.	Cost Price
Hagan Appliances							
Inventory Transactions							
03/07/—							
Purchase Orders							
03/01	SPOTLESS Washer	501			6		
03/02	RKC Gas Range	502			7		

(continued)

FIGURE 5.26

Inventory Transaction Report

FIGURE 5.26

(Concluded)

03/04	1 Door 22 CF. Refrig.	503	6		
	S by S 29 CF. Refrig.		4		
03/07	Top MNT 21 CF. Refrig.	504	4		
Vouchers					
03/02	Mini Washer & Dryer	916		4	540.00
03/03	S by S 19 CF. Refrig.	917		3	530.00
03/05	DELTA Dishwasher	918		5	350.00
03/06	Mini FR. & Refrig.	919		12	237.95
03/07	IDEAL Dishwasher	920		3	236.75
03/06	S by S 19 CF. Refrig.	R917		−1	530.00
	Totals		27	26	

18 **Display the inventory exceptions report.**

Select Inventory Exceptions and click OK. The report appears in Figure 5.27.

FIGURE 5.27

Inventory Exceptions Report

Hagan Appliances
Inventory Exceptions
03/07/—

Stock No.	Description	Unit Meas	On Hand	On Order	Reorder Point	Exception
2020	IDEAL Gas Dryer	EA	9		10	At/below reorder point
3080	ICY 20 CF. Freezer	EA	6		10	At/below reorder point
3090	Micro Refrig.	EA	0		10	Out of stock

19 **Generate a most profitable inventory items graph and a least profitable inventory items graph.**

The graphs are shown in Figures 5.28(a) and (b), respectively.

FIGURE 5.28(A)

Most Profitable Inventory Items Graph

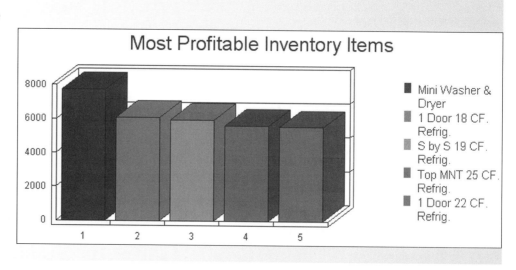

FIGURE 5.28(B)

Least Profitable Inventory Items Graph

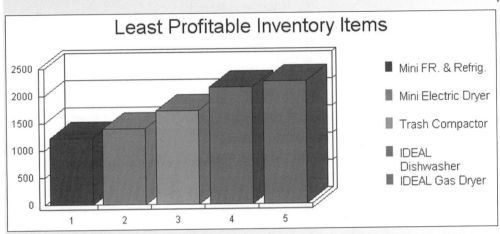

20 **Save your data to disk.**

21 **Use Check on the toolbar to check your work.**

22 **Optional spreadsheet integration activity.**

The management at Hagan Appliances asked you to use a spreadsheet to prepare a report that shows each inventory stock item's value at retail. (Because Hagan Appliances uses a perpetual inventory system, the inventory value is reflected at cost in the merchandise inventory account.)

a. Display and copy the inventory list report to the clipboard in spreadsheet format.

b. Start your spreadsheet software and load template file IA6 Spreadsheet 05-S.

c. Select cell A1 as the current cell, and paste the inventory list report from the clipboard into the spreadsheet.

d. In cell B4 enter: Value at Retail.

   In cell I7, enter: Value, and in cell I8 enter: At Retail.

   Enter the formula to calculate the Value at Retail in cell I10, then copy it to cells I11 through I29 (Value at Retail = On Hand × Retail Price).

   Enter the appropriate formula for your spreadsheet software to sum the Value At Retail column in cell I31.

e. The completed report is shown in Figure 5.29.

f. Print the spreadsheet report.

g. Save your spreadsheet data with a file name of 05-S Your Name.

h. End your spreadsheet session.

FIGURE 5.29

Spreadsheet Inventory Value At Retail Report

Student Name

Hagan Appliances
Value at Retail
As Of 03/07/—

Stock No.	Description	Unit Meas.	On Hand	On Order	Reorder Point	Last Cost	Retail Price	Value at Retail
1010	GC Washer	EA	19	0	10	$241.00	$359.95	$6,839.05
1020	SPOTLESS Washer	EA	13	6	8	$319.00	$529.95	$6,889.35
1040	Mini Washer & Dryer	EA	19	0	10	$540.00	$798.00	$15,162.00
2010	IDEAL Electric Dryer	EA	24	0	12	$220.00	$359.95	$8,638.80
2020	IDEAL Gas Dryer	EA	9	0	10	$305.00	$429.95	$3,869.55
2030	Mini Electric Dryer	EA	11	0	8	$225.00	$379.95	$4,179.45
3010	1 Door 18 C.F. Refrig	EA	18	0	8	$350.00	$529.95	$9,539.10
3020	1 Door 22 C.F. Refrig.	EA	11	6	10	$435.00	$699.00	$7,689.00
3030	S by S 19 C.F. Refrig.	EA	15	0	6	$530.00	$789.00	$11,835.00
3040	S by S 29 C.F. Refrig.	EA	7	4	6	$1135.00	$1899.00	$13,293.00
3050	Top MNT 21 C.F. Refrig.	EA	13	4	10	$455.00	$699.00	$9,087.00
3060	Top MNT 25 C.F. Refrig.	EA	14	0	6	$510.00	$859.95	$12,039.30
3070	Mini FR. & Refrig.	EA	15	0	8	$237.95	$349.95	$5,249.25
3080	ICY 20 C.F. Freezer	EA	6	0	10	$285.00	$428.00	$2,568.00
3090	Micro Refrig.	EA	0	0	10		$380.00	$0.00
4010	RKC Electric Range	EA	21	0	8	$216.00	$349.99	$7,349.79
4020	RKC Gas Range	EA	7	7	6	$310.00	$435.95	$3,051.65
5010	DELTA Dishwasher	EA	15	0	10	$350.00	$549.95	$8,249.25
5020	IDEAL Dishwasher	EA	20	0	10	$236.75	$329.95	$6,599.00
5030	Trash Compactor	EA	13	0	6	$233.90	$389.95	$5,069.35

147,196.89

㉓   Optional word processing integration activity.

The manager of the accounting department asked you to provide a list of all inventory items currently on order. The list should include the average and last cost paid for each item on the list. A memorandum with space left for the inventory on-order information has already been prepared.

a.   Display and copy the inventory list report to the clipboard in word processor format.

b.   Start your word processing software and load template file IA6 Word-processing 05-S (load as a text file).

c.   Paste the contents of the clipboard into the memorandum at the location specified.

d.   Enter your name and today's date where indicated.

e.   Remove the report heading and align the column headings. Remove all inventory items that do not have on-order quantities and format the information as necessary to match the completed memorandum shown in Figure 5.30.

f.　Save the memorandum document with a file name of 05-S Your Name.

g.　End your word processing session.

FIGURE 5.30

Word Processing Memorandum

MEMORANDUM

TO:　Hagan Appliances

FROM:　Students Name

DATE:　(Today's Date)

SUBJECT:　Inventory items that are on order

As of the end of the current week, Hagan Appliances inventory items that are on order are listed below. I have included that last cost and retail price of each item as well as additional information for your financial planning.

Stock No.	Description	Unit Meas.	On Hand	On Order	Reorder Point	Last Cost	Retail Price
1020	SPOTLESS Washer	EA	13	6	8	319.00	529.95
3020	I Door 22 CF. Refrig.	EA	11	6	10	435.00	699.00
3040	S by S 29 CF. Refrig.	EA	7	4	6	1135.00	1899.00
3050	Top MNT 21 CF. Refrig.	EA	13	4	10	455.00	699.00
4020	RKC Gas Range	EA	7	7	6	310.00	435.95

If you have access to the Internet, use your browser to find information about international entrepreneur business trends and opportunities. *Hint:* Use business opportunities entrepreneur as your search string. Report on your findings. Be sure to include the source and the URL (Web address) of your search.

INTERNET ACTIVITY

24　**End the *Integrated Accounting* 6e session.**

Chapter 5 Student Exercises

NAME

I Matching

Directions *For each of the definitions, write the letter of the appropriate term in the space provided.*

a. purge invoices and purchase orders
b. account maintenance/inventory
c. computerized purchase order processing system
d. unit of measure
e. purchase requisition
f. reorder point
g. purchase order transaction

h. quantity on hand
i. quantity on order
j. purchase invoice
k. receiving report
l. retail price
m. voucher transaction
n. purchases return transaction

1.____ A two-character abbreviation that indicates how the item is sold (each, by the dozen, by the box, etc.).

2.____ A count of the quantity of this particular item currently contained in the merchandise inventory.

3.____ A transaction that creates and posts an entry in the general journal, updates the vendor account balance, and decreases an inventory item's quantity on hand.

4.____ A transaction that increases an inventory item's quantity on order.

5.____ A transaction that creates and posts an entry in the vouchers journal, updates the vendor account balance, decreases inventory item(s) quantity on order, increases an inventory item(s) quantity on hand, and generates a voucher document.

6.____ The current selling price per unit for this item.

7.____ The window used to enter additions, changes, and deletions to inventory items.

8.____ A document sent to the business's accounting department by a vendor containing the original purchase order number, quantity and description of the merchandise, price, and terms of the merchandise sent.

9.____ When the quantity on hand reaches this point, additional items are to be ordered.

10.____ The process in which previously entered transactions are erased when capacity is exceeded.

11.____ A document prepared by the receiving department, containing the description, quantity, and condition of the merchandise received.

12.____ A formal document requesting a purchase of merchandise.

13.____ The quantity of this item for which stock is ordered but not yet received.

14.____ Comprises the procedures involved in automatically integrating the purchase order, voucher (or purchases invoice), and cash disbursement data into the inventory and general ledger.

II Questions

Directions   *Answer each of the following questions in the space provided.*

1.   What problem(s) may occur if the merchandise inventory is too low? _____

_____

2.   Why is data not lost when invoices and purchase orders are purged? _____

_____

3.   Make use of the data in Sample Problem 5-S to describe the integration that would take place when the following transaction is entered into the computer:

Ordered—3 SPOTLESS Washers at $300.00 each from SPOTLESS Mfg., Inc.

_____

4.   Make use of the data in Sample Problem 5-S to describe the integration that would take place when the following transaction is entered into the computer:

Received—2 Mini Washer & Dryers at $525.00 each from RKC Production, Inc.

Inventory System Integration: _____

_____

Accounting System Integration: _____

_____

5.   Make use of the data in Sample Problem 5-S to describe the integration that would take place when the following transaction is entered into the computer:

Returned—2 S by S 19 CF. Refrig. at $500.00 each to GC Manufacturing, Inc.

Inventory System Integration: _____

_____

Accounting System Integration: _____

_____

6.   What information is contained on the purchase order register?

_____

7.   What information is contained on the voucher register?

_____

8.   What is the purpose of the inventory list report?

_____

9.   What is the purpose of the inventory transactions report?

_____

10.   What is the purpose of the inventory exceptions report?

_____

Problem 5-A

In this problem, you will perform the operating procedures necessary to maintain inventory stock items and process purchase orders, vouchers, and cash payment transactions for the week of March 8 through March 14 for Hagan Appliances. Answer Audit Questions 5-A on pages 235–236 as you complete this problem. Display reports as necessary to answer the questions, and click Info. on the toolbar for helpful check figures to audit your work.

1 Start *Integrated Accounting* 6e.

2 Load opening balances file IA6 Problem 05-A.

3 Enter your name in the Your Name text box and click OK.

4 Save the file with a file name of 05-A Your Name.

5 Enter the inventory stock item maintenance data.

Add Stock No. 4030; GC Electric Range; unit of measure, EA (Each); reorder point, 5; retail price, $465.50 to the stock item file.

Add Stock No. 4040; GC Gas Range; unit of measure, EA (Each); reorder point, 5; retail price, $538.79 to the stock item file.

Change the retail price of S by S 29 CF. Refrig. (Stock No. 3040) to $1,859.00.

Change the reorder point of GC Washer (Stock No. 1010) to 12 and the retail price to $339.95.

6 Enter the following purchase order and voucher transactions.

Weekly Purchase Order and Voucher Transactions

Mar. 08 Ordered the following merchandise from ICY Refrigeration Co., terms 2/10, n/30. Purchase Order No. 505.

Description	Quantity	Unit Cost
Micro Refrig.	12	$225.00

08 Received the following merchandise for Purchase Order No. 501 from SPOTLESS Mfg., Inc., terms 2/10, n/30. Voucher No. 921.

Description	Quantity	Unit Cost
SPOTLESS Washer	6	$319.00

08 Ordered the following merchandise from IDEAL Appliance Mfg., terms 2/10. N/30. Purchase Order No. 506.

Description	Quantity	Unit Cost
IDEAL Gas Dryer	6	$305.00

09   Received the following merchandise for Purchase Order No. 503 from MNT Refrigerators, Inc., terms 2/10, n/30. Voucher No. 922.

Description	Quantity	Unit Cost
I Door 22 CF. Refrig.	6	$426.30
S by S 29 CF. Refrig.	4	$1,112.30

10   Ordered the following merchandise from RKC Production, Inc., terms 2/10, n/30. Purchase Order No. 507.

Description	Quantity	Unit Cost
Trash Compactor	3	$230.00
Mini Electric Dryer	3	$220.00

11   Returned the following merchandise to ICY Refrigeration, Co. Voucher No. R919.

Description	Quantity	Unit Cost
Mini Fr. & Refrig.	2	$237.95

12   Received the following merchandise from Purchase Order No. 502 from RKC Production, Inc., terms 2/10, n/30. Voucher No. 923.

Description	Quantity	Unit Cost
RKC Gas Range	7	$310.00

13   Ordered the following merchandise from ICY Refrigeration, Co., terms 2/10, n/30. Purchase Order No. 508.

Description	Quantity	Unit Cost
ICY 20 CF. Freezer	12	$285.00

14   Received the following merchandise for Purchase Order No. 504 from MNT Refrigerators, Inc., terms 2/10, n/30. Voucher No. 924.

Description	Quantity	Unit Cost
Top MNT 21 CF. Refrig.	4	$455.00

7   **Enter the Cash Payments Journal Transactions listed here.**

Weekly Cash Payment Transactions

Mar. 12   Paid invoice 917 to GC Manufacturing, Inc., $1,590.00, no discount. Check No. 4735.

13   Paid invoice 920 to IDEAL Appliance Mfg., $710.25, less 2% discount, $14.21. Check No. 4736.

14   Paid invoice 921 to SPOTLESS Mfg., Inc., $1,914.00, less 2% discount, $38.28. Check No. 4737.

8   **Display the purchase order and voucher registers for the period of March 8 through March 14.**

9   **Display an inventory list report.**

10   **Display the general, vouchers, and cash payments journals for the period of March 8 through March 14.**

11   **Display a general ledger report for the Merchandise Inventory and Vouchers Payable accounts.**

12   **Display a schedule of accounts payable.**

13   **Display an accounts payable ledger.**

14   **Display the inventory transactions report for the period of March 8 through March 14.**

15   **Display the inventory exceptions report.**

16   **Generate a most profitable inventory items graph and a least profitable Inventory Items graph.**

17   **Save your data to disk.**

18   **Use the Check toolbar button to check your work.**

19   **Optional spreadsheet integration activity.**

Use a spreadsheet to prepare a report showing the current retail value of each stock item in Hagan Appliances' inventory. Use the optional spreadsheet integration activity in Sample Problem 5-S and Figure 5.29 as a guide if necessary.

a. Display and copy the inventory list report to the clipboard in spreadsheet format.

b. Start your spreadsheet software and load template file IA6 Spreadsheet 05-S.

c. Select cell A1 as the current cell, and paste the inventory list report from the clipboard into the spreadsheet.

d. In Cell B4 enter: Value at Retail.

In cell I7 enter: Value, and in cell I8 enter: At Retail.

Enter the formula to calculate the value at retail in cell I10, and then copy it to each of the following inventory items.

Enter the appropriate formula for your spreadsheet software to sum the Value At Retail column at the end of the report.

e. Print the spreadsheet report.

f. Save your spreadsheet data with a file name of 05-A Your Name.

g. End your spreadsheet session.

20   **Optional word processing integration activity.**

Complete a memorandum that lists inventory items currently on order. The list should include the last cost and retail price for each item on the list. Refer to Figure 5.30 as a guide if necessary.

a. Display and copy the inventory list report to the clipboard in word processor format.

b. Start your word processing software and load template file IA6 Word-processing 05-S (load as a text file).

c. Paste the contents of the clipboard into the memorandum at the location specified.

d. Enter your name and today's date where indicated.

e. Remove the report heading and align the column headings. Remove all inventory items that do not have on-order quantities and format the information as necessary.

f. Print the memorandum.

g. Save the memorandum document with a file name of 05-A Your Name.

h. End your word processing session.

If you have access to the Internet, use your browser to find information about entrepreneur start-up businesses or a list of some of the top small businesses in the United States. *Hint:* Use business opportunities entrepreneur as your search string. Report on your findings. Be sure to include the source and the URL (Web address) of your search.

21 End the *Integrated Accounting* **6e session.**

Audit Questions 5-A

NAME

Directions   *Write the answers to the following questions in the space provided. Note: all the following questions relate to March 8 through 14.*

Register Reports

1.   What is the total amount of purchase orders for the period?   _____

2.   What is the total amount of vouchers for the period?   _____

Inventory List Report

3.   What is the last cost for the RKC Electric Range?   _____

4.   What is the reorder point for the ICY 20 C.F. Freezer?   _____

5.   How many Trash Compactors are on hand?   _____

Journal and Ledger Reports

6.   What are the total debits and credits shown on the vouchers journal?   _____

7.   What are the total debits and credits shown on the cash payments journal?   _____

8.   From the general ledger report, what was the Merchandise Inventory account balance on March 14?   _____

9.   From the general ledger report, what was the Vouchers Payable account balance on March 13?   _____

10.   From the schedule of accounts payable, what is the total amount owed?   _____

Inventory Reports and Graph

11. How many items were ordered during the period? _____

_____

12. How many items were received during the period? _____

_____

13. List the item(s) that are out of stock for which no items are currently on order. _____

_____

14. From the graph, what is the most profitable inventory item? _____

_____

Problem 5-B

In this problem, you will perform the operating procedures necessary to maintain inventory stock items and process purchase orders, vouchers, and cash payment transactions for the week of March 8 through March 14 for Hagan Appliances. Answer Audit Questions 5-B on pages 241–242 as you complete this problem. Display reports as necessary to answer the questions.

1 Start *Integrated Accounting* 6e.

2 Load opening balances file IA6 Problem 05-B.

3 Enter your name in the Your Name text box and click OK.

4 Save the file with a file name of 05-B Your Name.

5 Enter the inventory stock item maintenance data.

Add Stock No. 4030; Mini Gas Range; unit of measure, EA (Each); reorder point, 6; retail price, $189.95 to the stock item file.

Add Stock No. 5040; Garbage Disposal; unit of measure, EA (Each); reorder point, 8; retail price, $129.95 to the stock item file.

Change the retail price of DELTA Dishwasher (Stock No. 5010) to $529.95.

Change the reorder point of 1 Door 18 CF. Refrig. (Stock No. 3010) to 10 and the retail price to $499.95.

6 Enter the purchase order and voucher transactions listed here.

Weekly Purchase Order and Voucher Invoice Transactions

Mar. 08   Ordered the following merchandise from ICY Refrigeration Co., terms 2/10, n/30. Purchase Order No. 505.

Description	Quantity	Unit Cost
Micro Refrig.	16	$225.00

08   Received the following merchandise for Purchase Order No. 501 from SPOTLESS Mfg., Inc., terms 2/10, n/30. Voucher No. 921.

Description	Quantity	Unit Cost
SPOTLESS Washer	4	$319.00

08   Ordered the following merchandise from IDEAL Appliance Mfg., terms 2/10. N/30. Purchase Order No. 506.

Description	Quantity	Unit Cost
IDEAL Gas Dryer	5	$305.00

09   Received the following merchandise for Purchase Order No. 503 from MNT Refrigerators, Inc., terms 2/10, n/30. Voucher No. 922.

Description	Quantity	Unit Cost
1 Door 22 CF. Refrig.	5	$426.30
S by S 29 CF. Refrig.	3	$1,112.30

10   Ordered the following merchandise from RKC Production, Inc., terms 2/10, n/30. Purchase Order No. 507.

Description	Quantity	Unit Cost
Trash Compactor	2	$230.00
Mini Electric Dryer	3	$220.00

11   Returned the following merchandise to ICY Refrigeration, Co. Voucher No. R919.

Description	Quantity	Unit Cost
Mini Fr. & Refrig.	3	$237.95

12   Received the following merchandise from Purchase Order No. 502 from RKC Production, Inc., terms 2/10, n/30. Voucher No. 923.

Description	Quantity	Unit Cost
RKC Gas Range	7	$310.00

13   Ordered the following merchandise from ICY Refrigeration, Co., terms 2/10, n/30. Purchase Order No. 508.

Description	Quantity	Unit Cost
ICY 20 C.F. Freezer	10	$285.00

14   Received the following merchandise for Purchase Order No. 504 from MNT Refrigerators, Inc., terms 2/10, n/30. Voucher No. 924.

Description	Quantity	Unit Cost
Top MNT 21 C.F. Refrig.	4	$455.00

7   **Enter the Cash Payments Journal Transactions listed here.**

Weekly Cash Payment Transactions

Mar. 12   Paid invoice 917 to GC Manufacturing, Inc., $1,590.00, no discount. Check No. 4735.

13   Paid invoice 920 to IDEAL Appliance Mfg., $710.25, less 2% discount, $14.21. Check No. 4736.

14   Paid invoice 921 to SPOTLESS Mfg., Inc., $1,276.00, less 2% discount, $25.52. Check No. 4737.

8   **Display the purchase order and voucher registers for the period of March 8 through March 14.**

9   **Display an inventory list report.**

10   **Display the general, vouchers, and cash payments journals for the period of March 8 through March 14.**

11   **Display a general ledger report for the Merchandise Inventory and Vouchers Payable accounts.**

12   **Display a schedule of accounts payable.**

13 **Display an accounts payable ledger.**

14 **Display the inventory transactions report for the period of March 8 through March 14.**

15 **Display the inventory exceptions report.**

16 **Generate a most profitable inventory items graph and a least profitable inventory items graph.**

17 **Save your data to disk.**

18 **Optional spreadsheet integration activity.**

Use a spreadsheet to prepare a report showing the current retail value of each stock item in Hagan Appliances's inventory. Use the optional spreadsheet integration activity in Sample Problem 5-S and Figure 5.29 as a guide if necessary.

a. Display and copy the inventory list report to the clipboard in spreadsheet format.

b. Start your spreadsheet software and load template file IA6 Spreadsheet 05-S.

c. Select cell A1 as the current cell, and paste the inventory list report from the clipboard into the spreadsheet.

d. In Cell B4 enter: Value at Retail.
    In cell I7 enter: Value, and in cell I8 enter: At Retail.
    Enter the formula to calculate the value at retail in cell I10, and then copy it to each of the following inventory items.
    Enter the appropriate formula for your spreadsheet software to sum the Value At Retail column at the end of the report.

e. Print the spreadsheet report.

f. Save your spreadsheet data with a file name of 05-B Your Name.

g. End your spreadsheet session.

19 **Optional word processing integration activity.**

Complete a memorandum that lists inventory items currently on order. The list should include the last cost and retail price for each item on the list. Refer to Figure 5.30 as a guide if necessary.

a. Display and copy the inventory list report to the clipboard in word processor format.

b. Start your word processing software and load template file IA6 Word-processing 05-S (load as a text file).

c. Paste the contents of the clipboard into the memorandum at the location specified.

d. Enter your name and today's date where indicated.

e. Remove the report heading and align the column headings. Remove all inventory items that do not have on-order quantities and format the information as necessary.

f. Print the memorandum.

g. Save the memorandum document with a file name of 05-B Your Name.

h. End your word processing session.

If you have access to the Internet, use your browser to find information about franchising or resources for online entrepreneurs. *Hint:* Use business opportunities entrepreneur or business opportunities franchising as your search strings. Report on your findings. Be sure to include the source and the URL (Web address) of your search.

20   **End the *Integrated Accounting* 6e session.**

Audit Questions 5-B

NAME

Directions   *Write the answers to the following questions in the space provided. Note: all the following questions relate to March 8 through 14.*

Register Reports

1.   What is the total amount of purchase orders for the period?   _____

_____

2.   What is the total amount of vouchers for the period?   _____

_____

Inventory List Report

3.   What is the last cost for the SPOTLESS Washer?   _____

_____

4.   What is the retail price of the Top MNT 25 CF. Refrig.?   _____

_____

5.   How many IDEAL Dishwashers are on hand?   _____

_____

Journal and Ledger Reports

6.   What are the total debits and credits shown on the vouchers journal?   _____

_____

7.   What are the total debits and credits shown on the cash payments journal?   _____

_____

8.   From the general ledger report, what was the Merchandise Inventory account balance on March 14?   _____

_____

9.   From the general ledger report, what was the Vouchers Payable account balance on March 11?

_____

10.   From the schedule of accounts payable, what is the total amount owed?   _____

_____

Inventory Reports and Graph

11.   How many items were ordered during the period? _____

_____

12.   How many items were received during the period? _____

_____

13.   List the item(s) that are out of stock for which no items are currently on order. _____

_____

14.   From the graph, what is the least profitable inventory item? _____

_____

Accounts Receivable
Sales Order Processing and Inventory Control

Upon completion of this chapter, you will be able to:

- Identify the components and procedures of a sales order processing and inventory control system.

- Enter sales invoice transactions.

- Generate sales invoices.

- Explain sales transaction accounting and inventory systems integration.

- Display reports reflecting sales order processing and inventory integration.

Introduction

An organization's revenue depends on its ability to sell its products or services to customers. To accomplish this task, a sales order processing system is used. Sales order processing comprises the procedures and controls involved in preparing invoices, updating accounting records, and shipping merchandise.

The complexity of sales order systems, and the procedures they use, vary greatly depending on the size of the business and the products or services provided. Many businesses have turned to the computer to help them control their sales order processing as a result of the large volumes of transactions and the complexities of maintaining accurate inventory and other accounting-related records. In general, a **computerized sales order processing system** comprises the procedures involved in preparing a sales invoice and automatically integrating the data it contains into the inventory and general ledger. A **sales invoice** is a form used to describe the goods sold, the quantity, and the price. It is used as a source document for recording sales on account transactions.

Most computerized sales order processing systems enable businesses to prepare the invoice at the time of sale or at the time an order is received. It may occur in a store, over a telephone, through the mail, the Internet, a facsimile, or by any means the business uses to sell its goods. As the sales invoice is prepared, the computer checks the inventory to make sure the goods are available. If any of the goods ordered are out of stock, the computer immediately notifies the user so action can be taken to replenish the stock. When the computer finds stock on hand, it updates inventory and other accounting related records and generates a sales invoice. Depending on the type of business and merchandise sold, the sales invoice may be given to the customer at the time of sale, included with the merchandise (called a packing slip) when it is shipped, or sent to the warehouse to be used to fill the order and prepare it for shipment (called a pick list or picking slip).

In *Integrated Accounting* 6e, a complete invoice is prepared for each sale on account (or each sales return). The sales invoice contains the customer name, credit terms, revenue account, invoice number, date, sales tax percent, and the quantity, description, and selling price of each inventory item sold. As shown in Figure 6.1, when invoice data are entered into the computer, the inventory records are updated (i.e., quantity on hand is reduced by the quantity sold or increased in the case of a sales return, and other sales information is stored for later reporting purposes). Journal entries resulting from the sale are created and entered into the sales journal and posted to the general ledger. If the merchandising business uses a Cost of Goods Sold account (for a perpetual inventory system) the sales invoice entry will not only record the sale at retail, but also debit Cost of Merchandise Sold account and credit Merchandise Inventory account at cost based on the inventory costing method selected.

Each customer's account in the customers file (subsidiary ledger) is updated to reflect the amount owed. Finally, a sales invoice is generated. A copy may be given to the customer at the time of the sale, packaged with the merchandise, or mailed after the merchandise is shipped. Sometime during the month, a statement of account that shows all account activities and the current account balance is generated and sent to each customer who has an outstanding balance.

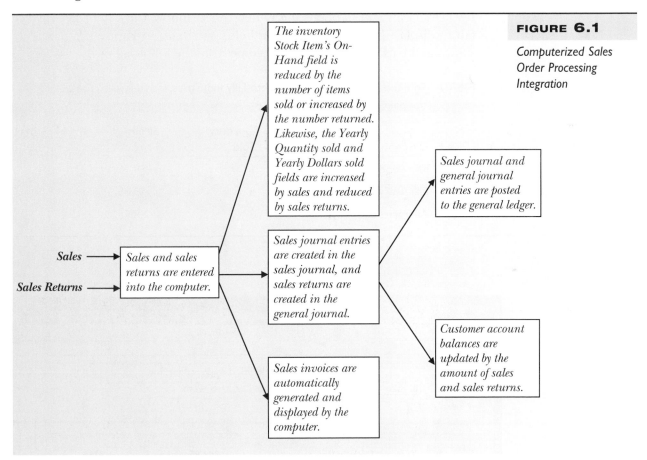

FIGURE 6.1

Computerized Sales Order Processing Integration

The examples used in this chapter are for a retailing business called Palmer Vacuum Center that uses a perpetual inventory system. The business sells vacuum cleaners, supplies, and attachments to local customers. Only information related to sales order processing and related reports will be discussed in this chapter.

Sales and Sales Return Transactions

The Sales Invoice tab is used to enter sales and sales return transactions and to generate sales invoices for the business. Data from sales and sales return transactions entered into this window are automatically integrated into the accounting and inventory systems. A **sales transaction** entered in the Other Tasks/Sales Invoice window automatically creates and posts the respective journal entry in the sales journal and reduces the number of inventory items on hand. A **sales returns and allowances transaction** entered here automatically creates and posts the appropriate journal entry in the general journal and increases the number of inventory items on hand.

Clicking Tasks on the toolbar, clicking the Other Tasks menu item from the Data menu, or clicking on the Sales navigation button and then the Sales Invoices menu button opens the Other Tasks window. Click the Sales Invoice tab to display the sales invoice data fields, as shown in Figure 6.2. The data shown in the example in Figure 6.2 come from the following sales transaction:

Feb. 02   Sold the following merchandise to Lilly Industries, Inc., terms 2/10, n/30, 6% sales tax, Sales Invoice No. 525:

Description	Quantity Sold	Selling Price
Kenwood Canister Vac	1	$689.95
Canister Cleaner Bag	8	$3.85
Allerginci Bag	8	$8.95

FIGURE 6.2

Sales Invoice

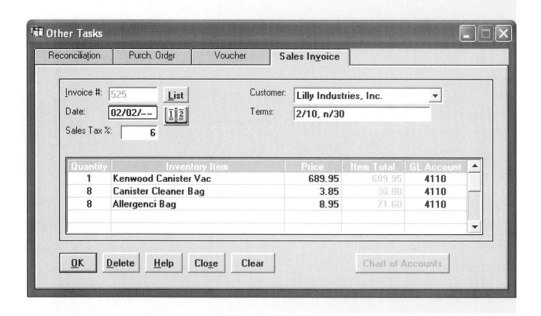

Enter Sales Invoice or Sales Return Transaction

To enter a sales invoice or sales return transaction, enter the invoice number, the date, sales tax percent, the customer name, and the terms of the sale. The terms 2/10, n/30 (read as "two ten, net thirty") mean the customer can either pay the invoice within 10 days of the invoice date and take a 2 percent discount or wait a maximum of 30 days and then pay the full amount of the invoice. Finally, enter the number of items sold in the Quantity field (if the item is a sales return, enter the quantity as a *negative* value), choose the inventory item from the Inventory Item drop-down list, and enter the selling price in the Price field (if it is not the same as what is automatically displayed for the item). Repeat this procedure for each item sold or returned by the customer.

The computer automatically multiplies the quantity by the price and places the amount in the Item Total column. The computer will also automatically place the sales account number in the GL Account column. (If the quantity is entered as a negative number indicating a sales return, the computer will insert the Sales Returns and Allowances account number. If the number is initially entered as a positive and afterward changed to a negative, you will need to adjust the account number rather than relying on the default.)

 If the item chosen has an on-hand quantity at or below its reorder point, a warning message will appear at the bottom of the window indicating this condition.

After the sales invoice or sales return transaction has been entered, click OK, and a computer-generated sales invoice, similar to the example shown in Figure 6.3, will appear.

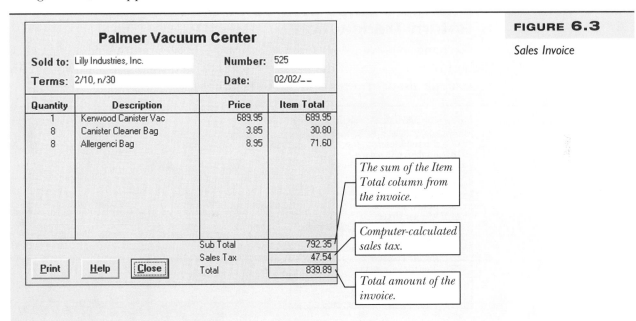

FIGURE 6.3

Sales Invoice

Click on Print to print the invoice to an attached printer, or click on Close to dismiss the invoice and continue.

Sales Transaction Integration

When Sales Invoice No. 525 (Figures 6.2 and 6.3) is entered, the computer performs the following integration to the Inventory System: (1) quantity 1, is deducted from the Quantity on Hand, added to the Yearly Quantity Sold, and $689.95 is added to the Yearly Dollars Sold fields of the Kenwood Canister Vac's inventory stock item, (2) quantity 8, is deducted from the Quantity on Hand field, added to the Yearly Quantity Sold, and $23.10 is added to the Yearly Dollars Sold fields of the Canister Cleaner Bag's inventory stock item, and (3) quantity 8, is deducted from the Quantity on Hand field, added to the Yearly Quantity Sold, and $53.70 is added to the Yearly Dollars Sold fields of the Allergenci Bag's inventory stock item.

In the integration to the Accounting System, the computer generates and posts the following Sales Journal entry:

	Debit	Credit
Accounts Receivable	$839.89	
Sales		$792.35
Sales Tax Payable		$47.54
Cost of Merchandise Sold	$466.20	
Merchandise Inventory		$466.20

Because the business is using the FIFO method of inventory valuation (see page 250) the computer extracts the cost of the first item received into inventory for each of the three inventory items: Kenwood Canister Vac $405.00 + Canister Cleaner Bag (8 × $2.30)$18.40 + Allergenci Bag (8 × $5.35)$42.80 = $466.20.

In addition, $839.89 is added to the Lilly Industries, Inc., account balance in the customer file. Finally, the entire sales invoice transaction is stored for reporting, future reference, and potential changes.

Change a Sales Invoice or Sales Return Transaction

To change a previously entered sales invoice or sales return transaction, click on List to the right of the Invoice # text box to display a list of invoices. An example list of invoices is shown in Figure 6.4.

FIGURE 6.4

Sales Invoice List

Choose the invoice to be changed from the sales invoice list and click OK. Select the text box for the data you wish to change, enter the correction, and click OK to record your change.

Delete a Sales Invoice or Sales Return Transaction

To delete a previously entered sales invoice or sales return transaction, click on List to the right of the Invoice # text box and choose the invoice to be deleted and click OK, then click Delete. When the Delete confirmation dialog box appears, click Yes.

Statements of Account

Statements of account show the customer name; balance forward; invoice number, date, and amount of each outstanding invoice of the current period; and payments received during the current period. A running balance and the total amount due from each customer are also shown. Statements of account are generated by choosing the Statements of Account option from the Ledger Reports list in the Report Selection menu. A computer-generated statement of account for Robert Thorson is shown in Figure 6.5.

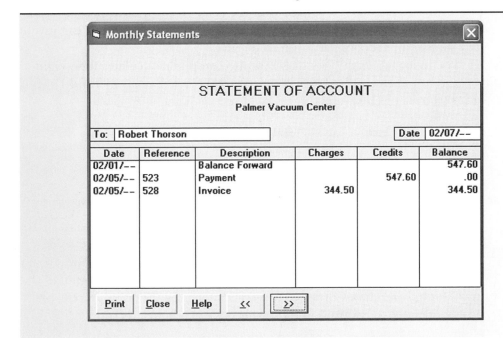

FIGURE 6.5

Statement of Account

Click on Print to print the currently displayed statement of account to an attached printer. Click on the >> button to advance to the next statement, or the << button to return to the previous statement. Click on Close to dismiss the statement of accounts and return to the Report Selection menu.

Purge Sales Invoices

Integrated Accounting 6e has a capacity of 50 sales invoice transactions. If this capacity is exceeded, an Alert dialog box appears informing you of this condition. Before additional invoices can be entered, the previously entered invoices must be erased by choosing the Purge Invoices and Purchase Orders from the Options menu. When this menu item is chosen, a dialog box will appear asking you to confirm whether you indeed want to purge invoices and purchase orders in the event you accidentally chose this menu item. Because the data from the sales and purchases invoices and voucher or purchase orders previously entered were automatically integrated into the inventory and accounting systems, purging them will not cause any information to be lost. A backup file should be made before the invoices and purchase orders are purged. This condition will not occur with this text-workbook because none of the problems you are asked to complete exceed the system capacity.

Inventory Valuation

Three methods of inventory valuation are provided by *Integrated Accounting* 6e: Average Cost; last in, first out (LIFO); and first in, first out (FIFO). You will learn how to specify the valuation method later in Chapter 12.

Average Cost Method

When the **average cost method** is used, the computer updates the Cost of Merchandise Sold and Merchandise Inventory accounts based on the history of the inventory item's weighted average cost. When the invoices and purchases orders are purged, the weighted average cost is stored in the inventory stock item's record for future reference.

The following example shows how the computer calculates the weighted average cost. Assume that 1 unit of a stock item is listed at $275.00 and 11 units at $300.00 each. The average cost would be calculated as follows:

Quantity		Cost		Total	
1	×	$270.00	=	$270.00	
11	×	$300.00	=	$3,300.00	
12				$3,570.00	($3,570.00 ÷ 12 = $297.50 average cost)

The computer uses the history of an item's cost and quantity to calculate the weighted average cost and generate the cost of merchandise sold and merchandise inventory parts of the sales journal entry. In the case where no previous transactions are available (as a result of inactivity or purging of the invoices and purchases orders), the computer uses the average cost previously calculated and stored in the inventory stock item's record.

Last in, Last out Method

With the **LIFO method** of inventory valuation, the assumption is made that the last items received into inventory are the first to be sold. Therefore, any items remaining in the inventory are the first items received. The computer uses the cost of the last item received into inventory to generate the cost of merchandise sold and merchandise inventory parts of the sales journal entry.

First in, First out Method

The **FIFO Method** of inventory valuation assumes that the first items received into inventory are the first sold. Therefore, any items remaining in inventory are the last items received. The computer uses the cost of the first item received into inventory to generate the cost of merchandise sold and merchandise inventory parts of the sales journal entry (see Figure 6.7 on page 256).

Chapter Summary

■ A sales invoice is a form used to record sales-on-account transactions.

■ A computerized sales order processing system comprises the procedures involved in preparing a sales invoice and automatically integrating the data it contains into the inventory and general ledger.

- The sales invoice contains the customer name, credit terms, revenue account, invoice number, date, sales tax percent, and the quantity, description, and selling price of each item from inventory sold.

- When sales invoice (or sales return) data are entered through the Other Tasks/Sales Invoices window, four changes take place: (1) inventory records are updated; (2) journal entries resulting from the sale (sales return) are entered into the sales journal (general journal); (3) the journal entries are posted to the general ledger and customer accounts; and (4) a sales invoice is generated.

- A sales invoice is automatically generated by the computer for sales, and a general journal entry is automatically generated by the computer for sales return transactions entered into the computer.

- Statements of account are generated by choosing the Statements of Account option from the Ledger Report list in the Report Selection menu. Each statement shows the customer name; balance forward; invoice number, date, and amount of each outstanding invoice of the current period; payments received during the current period; and total amount due.

- Purging invoices and purchase orders is the process in which previously entered invoices and purchase orders are erased when capacity is reached.

- Three methods of inventory valuation are provided by *Integrated Accounting* 6e: average cost, LIFO, and FIFO.

- When the average cost method is used, the computer updates the Cost of Merchandise Sold and Merchandise Inventory accounts based on the history of the inventory items' weighted average cost.

- The LIFO method of inventory valuation makes the assumption that the last items received into inventory are the first to be sold.

- The FIFO method of inventory valuation makes the assumption that the first items received into inventory are the first sold.

Sample Problem 6-S

In this problem, you will process the sales and purchases transactions for the week of February 1 through February 7 of the current year for Palmer Vacuum Center. Palmer Vacuum Center uses the FIFO method to value its perpetual inventory system. You will also perform the operating procedures necessary to process sales invoices, sales return, purchase orders, vouchers, and purchase return transactions using the sales order and purchase order processing features of *Integrated Accounting* 6e.

 WARNING The inventory valuation (Merchandise Inventory and Cost of Goods Sold accounts) may be affected by the order in which transactions are entered. Therefore, making corrections to previous transactions or changing the sequence in which transactions are entered may affect the FIFO method of valuation used in this problem. If you must make a correction to a previously entered transaction affecting inventory, it is a good idea to delete all subsequent entries related to the inventory items as well and then reenter the transactions in the order presented.

1   Start *Integrated Accounting* 6e.

2   Load opening balances file IA6 Problem 06-S.

3   Enter your name in the Your Name text box and click OK.

4   Save the file with a file name of 06-S Your Name.

5   Enter the following purchase order and voucher transactions.

Purchase Order No. 275 is shown in Figure 6.6(a), and Voucher No. 856 is shown in Figure 6.6(b) as a guide.

Weekly Purchase Order and Voucher Transactions

Feb. 02   Ordered the following merchandise from Handy Manufacturing, Inc., terms 2/10, n/30. Purchase Order No. 275. (Be sure to key the new Unit Cost amount.)

Description	Quantity	Unit Cost
Allergenci Bag	32	$5.35

04   Received the following merchandise for Purchase Order No. 271 from Kenwood Vacuum Cleaners, terms 2/10, n/30. Voucher No. 856.

Description	Quantity	Unit Cost
Kenwood Canister Vac	7	$405.00

05   Received the following merchandise for Purchase Order No. 272 from Royal Accessories, Inc., terms 2/10, n/30. Voucher No. 857.

Description	Quantity	Unit Cost
Canister Cleaner Bag	64	$2.30

06   Received the following merchandise for Purchase Order No. 273 from
      Nantz Vacuum Cleaner Co., terms 2/10, n/30. Voucher No. 858.

Description	Quantity	Unit Cost
Pile Lifter Brush	5	$31.50

07   Ordered the following merchandise from Royal Accessories, Inc., terms
      2/10, n/30. Purchase Order No. 276.

Description	Quantity	Unit Cost
Attachment Kit	2	$32.95
Upright Cleaner Bag	24	$2.35

FIGURE 6.6(A)

Purchase Order No. 275

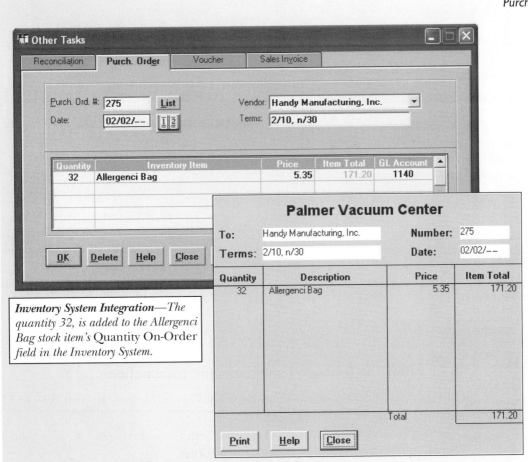

Inventory System Integration—The quantity 32, is added to the Allergenci Bag stock item's Quantity On-Order field in the Inventory System.

FIGURE 6.6(B)

Voucher No. 856

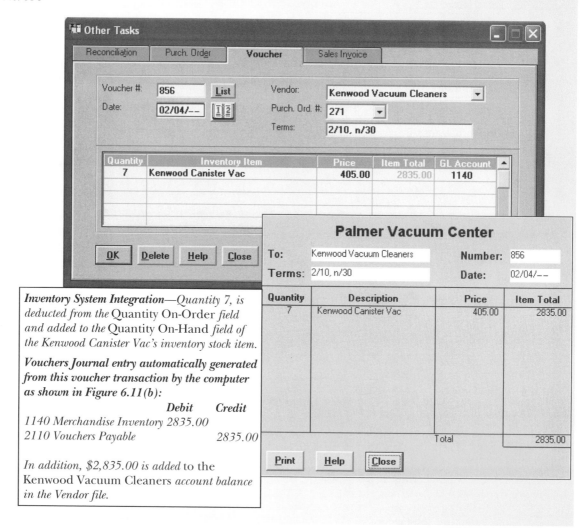

Inventory System Integration—Quantity 7, is deducted from the Quantity On-Order *field and added to the* Quantity On-Hand *field of the Kenwood Canister Vac's inventory stock item.*

Vouchers Journal entry automatically generated from this voucher transaction by the computer as shown in Figure 6.11(b):

	Debit	Credit
1140 Merchandise Inventory	2835.00	
2110 Vouchers Payable		2835.00

In addition, $2,835.00 is added to the Kenwood Vacuum Cleaners account balance in the Vendor file.

⑥ Enter the following sales invoice transactions.

Sales Invoice No. 525 is shown in Figure 6.7(a), and Sales Return No. R517 is shown in Figure 6.7(b) as a guide.

Click on the Sales navigation button, and then the Sales Invoices menu button and enter the sales invoice transactions.

Weekly Sales Transactions

Feb. 02   Sold the following merchandise to Lilly Industries, Inc., terms 2/10, n/30, 6% sales tax, Sales Invoice No. 525:

Description	Quantity Sold	Selling Price
Kenwood Canister Vac	1	$689.95
Canister Cleaner Bag	8	$3.85
Allerginci Bag	8	$8.95

03   Sold the following merchandise to Matthew Cornish, terms 30 days, 6% sales tax, Sales Invoice No. 526:

Description	Quantity Sold	Selling Price
Electric Broom	2	$99.99

04   Sold the following merchandise to Bassett Cleaning, Inc., terms 2/10, n/30, 6% sales tax, Sales Invoice No. 527.

Description	Quantity Sold	Selling Price
Alpha Upright Vacuum	1	$795.95
Allergenci Bag	4	$8.95

05   Sold the following merchandise to Robert Thorson, terms 30 days, 6% sales tax, Sales Invoice No. 528:

Description	Quantity Sold	Selling Price
Wet & Dry Vacuum	1	$325.00

06   The following merchandise was returned to Palmer Vacuum Center by Bassett Cleaning, Inc., 6% sales tax, Sales Return No. R517:

Description	Quantity Sold	Selling Price
Upright Cleaner Bag	6	$3.95

06   Sold the following merchandise to Broderick Company, 2/10, n/30, 6% sales tax, Sales Invoice No. 529:

Description	Quantity Sold	Selling Price
Nantz Canister Vacuum	1	$369.99
Wet & Dry Vacuum	1	$325.00
Steam Cleaner	1	$219.00
Canister Cleaner Bag	24	$3.85

07   Sold the following merchandise to Wingler Motel, terms 2/10, n/30, 6% sales tax, Sales Invoice No. 530:

Description	Quantity Sold	Selling Price
Handy Upright Vacuum	2	$485.00
Upright Cleaner Bag	12	$3.95

FIGURE 6.7(A)

Sales Invoice No. 525

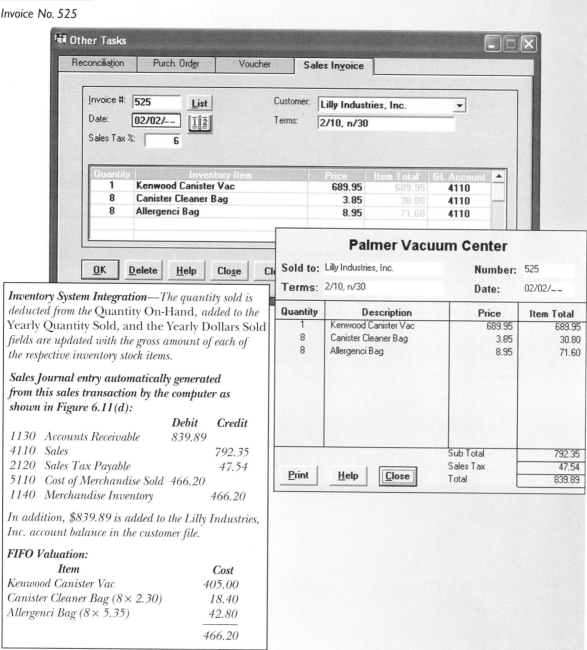

Inventory System Integration—*The quantity sold is deducted from the* Quantity On-Hand, *added to the* Yearly Quantity Sold, *and the* Yearly Dollars Sold *fields are updated with the gross amount of each of the respective inventory stock items.*

Sales Journal *entry automatically generated from this sales transaction by the computer as shown in Figure 6.11(d):*

		Debit	Credit
1130	Accounts Receivable	839.89	
4110	Sales		792.35
2120	Sales Tax Payable		47.54
5110	Cost of Merchandise Sold	466.20	
1140	Merchandise Inventory		466.20

In addition, $839.89 is added to the Lilly Industries, Inc. account balance in the customer file.

FIFO Valuation:

Item	Cost
Kenwood Canister Vac	405.00
Canister Cleaner Bag (8 × 2.30)	18.40
Allergenci Bag (8 × 5.35)	42.80
	466.20

FIGURE 6.7(B)

Sales Return No. R517

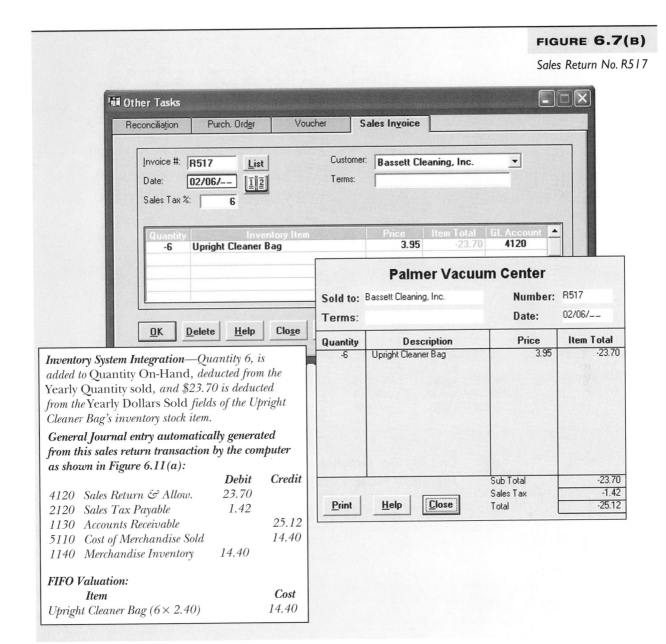

Inventory System Integration—*Quantity 6, is added to* Quantity On-Hand, *deducted from the* Yearly Quantity sold, *and $23.70 is deducted from the* Yearly Dollars Sold *fields of the Upright Cleaner Bag's inventory stock item.*

General Journal entry automatically generated from this sales return transaction by the computer as shown in Figure 6.11(a):

		Debit	Credit
4120	Sales Return & Allow.	23.70	
2120	Sales Tax Payable	1.42	
1130	Accounts Receivable		25.12
5110	Cost of Merchandise Sold		14.40
1140	Merchandise Inventory	14.40	

FIFO Valuation:

Item	Cost
Upright Cleaner Bag (6 × 2.40)	14.40

7 Enter the following cash payments journal transactions as illustrated in Figure 6.8.

Weekly Cash Payment Transactions

Feb. 06 Paid invoice 856 to Kenwood Vacuum Cleaners, $2,835.00, less 2% discount, $56.70. Check No. 3618.

07 Paid invoice 857 to Royal Accessories, Inc., $147.20, less 2% discount, $2.94. Check No. 3619.

07 Paid invoice 852 to Handy Manufacturing, Inc., $191.40, less 2% discount, $3.83. Check No. 3620.

FIGURE 6.8

Cash Payments

Date	Refer.	V.P. Debit	Mrch. Inv. Cr.	Cash Credit	Vendor
02/06/--	3618	2835.00	56.70	2778.30	Kenwood Vacuum Cleaners
02/07/--	3619	147.20	2.94	144.26	Royal Accessories, Inc.
02/07/--	3620	191.40	3.83	187.57	Handy Manufacturing, Inc.

8 **Enter the following cash receipt journal transactions as illustrated in Figure 6.9.**

Weekly Cash Receipt Transactions

Feb. 03   Received cash on account from Wingler Motel, covering Sales Invoice No. 524 for $3,703.19, less 2% discount, $74.06.

05   Received cash on account from Robert Thorson, covering Sales Invoice No. 523 for $547.60, no discount.

07   Received cash on account from Matthew Cornish, covering Sales Invoice No. 526 for $211.98, no discount.

FIGURE 6.9

Cash Receipts

Date	Refer.	A.R. Credit	Sales Disc. Dr	Cash Debit	Customer
02/03/--	524	3703.19	74.06	3629.13	Wingler Motel
02/05/--	523	547.60		547.60	Robert Thorson
02/07/--	526	211.98		211.98	Matthew Cornish

9 **Display the purchase orders, vouchers, and sales invoices registers for the period February 1 through February 7.**

The reports are shown in Figures 6.10(a), (b), and (c), respectively.

FIGURE 6.10(A)

Purchase Order Register

Palmer Vacuum Center
Purchase Order Register
02/07/—

P.O. Number	P.O. Date	Vendor Name	P.O. Amount
275	02/02/—	Handy Manufacturing, Inc.	171.20
276	02/07/—	Royal Accessories, Inc.	122.30
		Total Amount	293.50

FIGURE 6.10(B)

Voucher Register

Palmer Vacuum Center
Voucher Register
02/07/—

Invoice Number	Invoice Date	Vendor Name	Invoice Amount
856	02/04/—	Kenwood Vacuum Cleaners	2,835.00
857	02/05/—	Royal Accessories, Inc.	147.20
858	02/06/—	Nantz Vacuum Cleaner Co.	157.50
		Total Amount	3,139.70

FIGURE 6.10(C)

Sales Invoice Register

Palmer Vacuum Center
Sales Invoice Register
02/07/—

Invoice Number	Invoice Date	Customer Name	Invoice Amount	Sales Tax
525	02/02/—	Lilly Industries, Inc.	792.35	47.54
526	02/03/—	Matthew Cornish	199.98	12.00
527	02/04/—	Bassett Cleaning, Inc.	831.75	49.91
528	02/05/—	Robert Thorson	325.00	19.50
529	02/06/—	Broderick Company	1,006.39	60.38
530	02/07/—	Wingler Motel	1,017.40	61.04
R517	02/06/—	Bassett Cleaning, Inc.	−23.70	−1.42
		Total Amount	4,149.17	248.95

10 **Display the general, vouchers, cash payments, sales, and cash receipts journals for the period February 1 through February 7.**

The journal reports are shown in Figures 6.11(a), (b), (c), (d), and (e), respectively.

FIGURE 6.11(A)

General Journal

Palmer Vacuum Center
General Journal
02/07/—

Date	Refer.	Acct.	Title	Debit	Credit
02/06	R517	4120	Sales Returns & Allow.	23.70	
02/06	R517	2120	Sales Tax Payable	1.42	
02/06	R517	1130	AR/Bassett Cleaning, Inc.		25.12
02/06	R517	5110	Cost of Merchandise Sold		14.40
02/06	R517	1140	Merchandise Inventory	14.40	
			Totals	39.52	39.52

FIGURE 6.11(B)

Vouchers Journal

Palmer Vacuum Center
Vouchers Journal
02/07/—

Date	Inv. No.	Acct.	Title	Debit	Credit
02/04	856	1140	Merchandise Inventory	2,835.00	
02/04	856	2110	VP/Kenwood Vacuum Cleaners		2,835.00
02/05	857	1140	Merchandise Inventory	147.20	
02/05	857	2110	VP/Royal Accessories, Inc.		147.20
02/06	858	1140	Merchandise Inventory	157.50	
02/06	858	2110	VP/Nantz Vacuum Cleaner Co.		157.50
			Totals	3,139.70	3,139.70

FIGURE 6.11(C)

Cash Payments Journal

Palmer Vacuum Center
Cash Payments Journal
02/07/—

Date	Ck. No.	Acct.	Title	Debit	Credit
02/06	3618	2110	VP/Kenwood Vacuum Cleaners	2,835.00	
02/06	3618	1110	Cash		2,778.30
02/06	3618	1140	Merchandise Inventory		56.70
02/07	3619	2110	VP/Royal Accessories, Inc.	147.20	
02/07	3619	1110	Cash		144.26
02/07	3619	1140	Merchandise Inventory		2.94
02/07	3620	2110	VP/Handy Manufacturing, Inc.	191.40	
02/07	3620	1110	Cash		187.57
02/07	3620	1140	Merchandise Inventory		3.83
			Totals	3,173.60	3,173.60

FIGURE 6.11(D)

Sales Journal

Palmer Vacuum Center
Sales Journal
02/07/—

Date	Inv. No.	Acct.	Title	Debit	Credit
02/02	525	1130	AR/Lilly Industries, Inc.	839.89	
02/02	525	4110	Sales		792.35
02/02	525	2120	Sales Tax Payable		47.54
02/02	525	5110	Cost of Merchandise Sold	466.20	
02/02	525	1140	Merchandise Inventory		466.20
02/03	526	1130	AR/Matthew Cornish	211.98	
02/03	526	4110	Sales		199.98
02/03	526	2120	Sales Tax Payable		12.00
02/03	526	5110	Cost of Merchandise Sold	116.00	
02/03	526	1140	Merchandise Inventory		116.00
02/04	527	1130	AR/Bassett Cleaning, Inc.	881.66	
02/04	527	4110	Sales		831.75
02/04	527	2120	Sales Tax Payable		49.91
02/04	527	5110	Cost of Merchandise Sold	501.30	
02/04	527	1140	Merchandise Inventory		501.30
02/05	528	1130	AR/Robert Thorson	344.50	
02/05	528	4110	Sales		325.00
02/05	528	2120	Sales Tax Payable		19.50
02/05	528	5110	Cost of Merchandise Sold	185.00	
02/05	528	1140	Merchandise Inventory		185.00
02/06	529	1130	AR/Broderick Company	1,066.77	
02/06	529	4110	Sales		1,006.39
02/06	529	2120	Sales Tax Payable		60.38
02/06	529	5110	Cost of Merchandise Sold	632.20	
02/06	529	1140	Merchandise Inventory		632.20

(continued)

02/07	530	1130	AR/Wingler Motel	1,078.44	
02/07	530	4110	Sales		1,017.40
02/07	530	2120	Sales Tax Payable		61.04
02/07	530	5110	Cost of Merchandise Sold	659.30	
02/07	530	1140	Merchandise Inventory		659.30
			Totals	6,983.24	6,983.24

FIGURE 6.11(D)

(Concluded)

Palmer Vacuum Center
Cash Receipts Journal
02/07/—

FIGURE 6.11(E)

Cash Receipts Journal

Date	Refer.	Acct.	Title	Debit	Credit
02/03	524	1110	Cash	3,629.13	
02/03	524	4130	Sales Discount	74.06	
02/03	524	1130	AR/Wingler Motel		3,703.19
02/05	523	1110	Cash	547.60	
02/05	523	1130	AR/Robert Thorson		547.60
02/07	526	1110	Cash	211.98	
02/07	526	1130	AR/Matthew Cornish		211.98
			Totals	4,462.77	4,462.77

11   Display a general ledger report for the Accounts Receivable, Sales, Sales Returns and Allowance, and Sales Discount accounts.

The general ledger reports appear in Figures 6.12(a) and (b), respectively.

Palmer Vacuum Center
General Ledger
02/07/—

FIGURE 6.12(A)

Accounts Receivable

Account	Journal	Date	Refer.	Debit	Credit	Balance
1130-Accounts Receivable						
	Sales	01/24	517	8,968.82		8,968.82Dr
	Sales	01/25	518	7,594.73		16,563.55Dr
	Sales	01/26	519	1,884.78		18,448.33Dr
	Cash Receipts	01/27	519		1,884.78	16,563.55Dr
	Sales	01/27	520	108.81		16,672.36Dr
	Cash Receipts	01/28	520		108.81	16,563.55Dr
	Sales	01/28	521	8,540.84		25,104.39Dr
	Sales	01/29	522	868.83		25,973.22Dr
	Sales	01/30	523	547.60		26,520.82Dr
	Cash Receipts	01/31	522		868.83	25,651.99Dr
	Sales	01/31	524	3,703.19		29,355.18Dr
	Sales	02/02	525	839.89		30,195.07Dr
	Sales	02/03	526	211.98		30,407.05Dr
	Cash Receipts	02/03	524		3,703.19	26,703.86Dr
	Sales	02/04	527	881.66		27,585.52Dr

(continued)

FIGURE 6.12(A)

(Concluded)

Sales	02/05	528	344.50		27,930.02Dr
Cash Receipts	02/05	523		547.60	27,382.42Dr
Sales	02/06	529	1,066.77		28,449.19Dr
General	02/06	R517		25.12	28,424.07Dr
Sales	02/07	530	1,078.44		29,502.51Dr
Cash Receipts	02/07	526		211.98	29,290.53Dr

FIGURE 6.12(B)

Sales, Sales Returns and Allowances, and Sales Discounts

Palmer Vacuum Center
General Ledger
02/07/—

Account	Journal	Date	Refer.	Debit	Credit	Balance
4110-Sales						
	Sales	01/24	517		8,461.15	8,461.15Cr
	Sales	01/25	518		7,164.84	15,625.99Cr
	Sales	01/26	519		1,778.09	17,404.08Cr
	Sales	01/27	520		102.65	17,506.73Cr
	Sales	01/28	521		8,057.40	25,564.13Cr
	Sales	01/29	522		819.65	26,383.78Cr
	Sales	01/30	523		516.60	26,900.38Cr
	Sales	01/31	524		3,493.58	30,393.96Cr
	Sales	02/02	525		792.35	31,186.31Cr
	Sales	02/03	526		199.98	31,386.29Cr
	Sales	02/04	527		831.75	32,218.04Cr
	Sales	02/05	528		325.00	32,543.04Cr
	Sales	02/06	529		1,006.39	33,549.43Cr
	Sales	02/07	530		1,017.40	34,566.83Cr
4120-Sales Returns & Allow.						
	General	02/06	R517	23.70		23.70Dr
4130-Sales Discount						
	Cash Receipts	01/27	519	37.70		37.70Dr
	Cash Receipts	02/03	524	74.06		111.76Dr

12 Display a trial balance report.

The trial balance report is shown in Figure 6.13.

FIGURE 6.13

Trial Balance

Palmer Vacuum Center
Trial Balance
02/07/—

Acct. Number	Account Title	Debit	Credit
1110	Cash	29,631.43	
1120	Petty Cash	150.00	
1130	Accounts Receivable	29,290.53	
1140	Merchandise Inventory	35,099.32	
1150	Supplies	2,500.00	

(continued)

1160	Prepaid Insurance	1,500.00	
2110	Vouchers Payable		11,136.45
2120	Sales Tax Payable		2,072.59
3110	Diane Palmer, Capital		79,645.44
3120	Diane Palmer, Drawing	6,000.00	
4110	Sales		34,566.83
4120	Sales Returns & Allow.	23.70	
4130	Sales Discount	111.76	
5110	Cost of Merchandise Sold	21,500.80	
6110	Advertising Expense	130.00	
6120	Miscellaneous Expense	105.00	
6130	Rent Expense	850.00	
6140	Telephone Expense	207.60	
6150	Utilities Expense	321.17	
	Totals	127,421.31	127,421.31

FIGURE 6.13

(Concluded)

13 **Display a schedule of accounts receivable and an accounts receivable ledger report for all customers.**

The schedule of accounts receivable and accounts receivable ledger reports are shown in Figure 6.14(a) and (b), respectively.

Palmer Vacuum Center
Schedule of Accounts Receivable
02/07/—

Name	Balance
Bassett Cleaning, Inc.	9,825.36
Broderick Company	8,661.50
Lilly Industries, Inc.	9,380.73
Robert Thorson	344.50
Wingler Motel	1,078.44
Total	29,290.53

FIGURE 6.14(A)

Schedule of Accounts Receivable

Palmer Vacuum Center
Accounts Receivable Ledger
02/07/—

Account	Journal	Date	Refer.	Debit	Credit	Balance
Bassett Cleaning, Inc.						
	Sales	01/24	517	8,968.82		8,968.82Dr
	Sales	02/04	527	881.66		9,850.48Dr
	General	02/06	R517		25.12	9,825.36Dr
Broderick Company						
	Sales	01/25	518	7,594.73		7,594.73Dr
	Sales	02/06	529	1,066.77		8,661.50Dr
						(continued)

FIGURE 6.14(B)

Accounts Receivable Ledger

FIGURE 6.14(B)

(Concluded)

Fraze Department Stores

Sales	01/26	519	1,884.78		1,884.78Dr
Cash Receipts	01/27	519		1,884.78	.00

Jennifer Martens

Sales	01/27	520	108.81		108.81Dr
Cash Receipts	01/28	520		108.81	.00

Lilly Industries, Inc.

Sales	01/28	521	8,540.84		8,540.84Dr
Sales	02/02	525	839.89		9,380.73Dr

Matthew Cornish

Sales	01/29	522	868.83		868.83Dr
Cash Receipts	01/31	522		868.83	.00
Sales	02/03	526	211.98		211.98Dr
Cash Receipts	02/07	526		211.98	.00

Robert Thorson

Sales	01/30	523	547.60		547.60Dr
Sales	02/05	528	344.50		892.10Dr
Cash Receipts	02/05	523		547.60	344.50Dr

Wingler Motel

Sales	01/31	524	3,703.19		3,703.19Dr
Cash Receipts	02/03	524		3,703.19	.00
Sales	02/07	530	1,078.44		1,078.44Dr

14 **Display a statement of account for Robert Thorson.**

Select Statements of Account and click OK. Advance through the statements by clicking on the >> button until Robert Thorson appears as shown in Figure 6.15.

FIGURE 6.15

*Robert Thorson
Statement of Account*

STATEMENT OF ACCOUNT
Palmer Vacuum Center

To: Robert Thorson   Date 02/07/——

Date	Reference	Description	Charges	Credits	Balance
02/01/——		Balance Forward			547.60
02/05/——	528	Invoice	344.50		892.10
02/05/——	523	Payment		547.60	344.50

15   Display an inventory list report.

The report appears in Figure 6.16.

Palmer Vacuum Center
Inventory List
02/07/—

Stock No.	Description	Unit Meas.	On Hand	On Order	Reorder Point	Last Cost	Retail Price
1010	Alpha Upright Vacuum	EA	12	0	6	480.00	795.95
1020	Handy Upright Vacuum	EA	22	0	8	315.25	485.00
1030	Kenwood Canister Vac	EA	11	0	5	405.00	689.95
1040	Nantz Canister Vacuum	EA	15	0	8	240.00	369.99
1050	Steam Cleaner	EA	26	0	10	152.00	219.00
1060	Rug Machine	EA	22	0	10	135.00	189.99
1070	Wet & Dry Vacuum	EA	18	0	12	199.00	325.00
1080	Electric Broom	EA	15	10	10	58.00	99.99
1090	Battery Powered Vac	EA	30	0	15	22.80	38.95
1100	Car Vac	EA	26	0	15	20.95	29.95
2010	Upright Cleaner Bag	EA	110	24	32	2.35	3.95
2020	Canister Cleaner Bag	EA	64	0	32	2.30	3.85
2030	Allergenci Bag	EA	4	32	12	5.30	8.95
2040	Pile Lifter Brush	EA	24	0	10	31.50	49.00
2050	Shampoo Attachment	EA	25	0	8	25.70	38.95
2060	Attachment Kit	EA	27	2	10	32.95	49.95

FIGURE 6.16

Inventory List Report

16   Display the inventory transactions for the period of February 1 through February 7.

The report appears in Figure 6.17.

Palmer Vacuum Center
Inventory Transactions
02/07/—

Date	Description	Inv./ P.O.	Quantity Sold	Selling Price	Quan. Ord.	Quan. Recd.	Cost Price
Sales Invoices							
02/02	Kenwood Canister Vac	525	1	689.95			
	Canister Cleaner Bag		8	3.85			
	Allergenci Bag		8	8.95			
02/03	Electric Broom	526	2	99.99			
02/04	Alpha Upright Vacuum	527	1	795.95			
	Allergenci Bag		4	8.95			
02/05	Wet & Dry Vacuum	528	1	325.00			
02/06	Nantz Canister Vacuum	529	1	369.99			
	Wet & Dry Vacuum		1	325.00			
	Steam Cleaner		1	219.00			
	Canister Cleaner Bag		24	3.85			

(continued)

FIGURE 6.17

Inventory Transactions Report

FIGURE 6.17

(Concluded)

02/07	Handy Upright Vacuum	530	2	485.00			
	Upright Cleaner Bag		12	3.95			
02/06	Upright Cleaner Bag	R517	−6	3.95			

Purchase Orders
02/02	Allergenci Bag	275		32	
02/07	Attachment Kit	276		2	
	Upright Cleaner Bag			24	

Vouchers
02/04	Kenwood Canister Vac	856		7	405.00
02/05	Canister Cleaner Bag	857		64	2.30
02/06	Pile Lifter Brush	858		5	31.50
	Totals		60	58	76

17   **Display the inventory exceptions report.**

The report appears in Figure 6.18.

FIGURE 6.18

Inventory Exceptions Report

Palmer Vacuum Center
Inventory Exceptions
02/07/—

Stock No.	Description	Unit Meas.	On Hand	On Order	Reorder Point	Exception
2030	Allergenci Bag	EA	4	32	12	At/below reorder point

18   **Display the yearly sales report.**

The report appears in Figure 6.19.

FIGURE 6.19

Yearly Sales Report

Palmer Vacuum Center
Yearly Sales
02/07/—

Stock No.	Description	Unit Meas.	Yearly Quantity	Yearly Amount
1010	Alpha Upright Vacuum	EA	12	9,551.40
1020	Handy Upright Vacuum	EA	18	8,730.00
1030	Kenwood Canister Vac	EA	6	4,139.70
1040	Nantz Canister Vacuum	EA	9	3,329.91
1050	Steam Cleaner	EA	6	1,314.00
1060	Rug Machine	EA	10	1,899.90
1070	Wet & Dry Vacuum	EA	8	2,600.00
1080	Electric Broom	EA	13	1,299.87
1090	Battery Powered Vac	EA	6	233.70
1100	Car Vac	EA	1	29.95
2010	Upright Cleaner Bag	EA	32	126.40

(continued)

2020	Canister Cleaner Bag	EA	64	246.40	**FIGURE 6.19**
2030	Allergenci Bag	EA	28	250.60	*(Concluded)*
2040	Pile Lifter Brush	EA	3	147.00	
2050	Shampoo Attachment	EA	5	194.75	
2060	Attachment Kit	EA	9	449.55	
			230	34,543.13	

19 Display the top customers graph.

The top customers graph is shown in Figure 6.20.

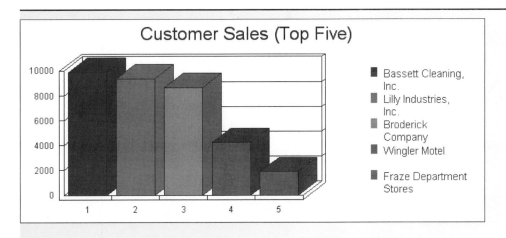

FIGURE 6.20

Top Customers Graph

20 Save your data to disk.

21 Use Check on the toolbar to check your work.

22 Optional spreadsheet integration activity.

The owner of Palmer Vacuum Center asked you to prepare a spreadsheet based on the current inventory data, that can be used to provide information about items with low gross sales. You are to prepare a list of inventory items with year-to-date gross sales of less than $500.00.

a. Display and copy the yearly sales report to the clipboard in spreadsheet format.

b. Start your spreadsheet software and load file IA6 Spreadsheet 06-S.

c. Select cell A1 as the current cell (if not already selected) and paste the yearly sales report into the spreadsheet.

d. In cell B35, enter the IF function appropriate for your spreadsheet software to display the description of each inventory item with yearly sales less than $500.00—if not, display "Delete this row." For example, @IF(E10<500,B10,"Delete this row"). Copy the formula from cell B35 to cells B36–B50.

e. In cell C35, enter the IF function appropriate for your spreadsheet software to display the amount of each inventory item with yearly sales less than $500.00—if not, display a blank. For example, @IF(E10<500,E10," "). Copy the formula from cell C35 to cells C36–C50.

f. Delete the rows in cells B35–B50 that contain "Delete this row" (items that do not match the criteria).

g. Sum the amount (column C) of the items that match the criteria, and use this sum to calculate and display the percent of yearly total sales.

h. Print the item list and percentage of total sales. The competed spreadsheet is shown in Figure 6.21.

i. Save your spreadsheet data with a file name of 06-S Your Name.

FIGURE 6.21

Inventory Items with Year-to-Date Sales Less than $500.00

Battery powered Vac	$233.70
Car Vac	$29.95
Upright Cleaner Bag	$126.40
Canister Cleaner Bag	$246.40
Allergenci Bag	$250.60
Pile Lifter Brush	$147.00
Shampoo Attachment	$194.75
Attachment Kit	$449.55
	$1,678.35
Percent of Total Sales	4.86%

23 **Optional word processing integration activity.**

Prepare a memorandum to the Owner of Palmer Vacuum Center (Diane Palmer) listing the items of inventory with gross year-to-date sales less than $500.00 and their percentage of total sales. A memorandum with space left for this information has already been prepared.

a. Copy the list of inventory items with gross sales less than $500.00 and the percentage of total sales from the spreadsheet.

b. Start your word processing software and load template file IA6 Word-processing 06-S (load as a text file).

c. Paste the contents of the clipboard into the memorandum at the location specified.

d. Format the document as necessary (i.e., choose smaller font size for spreadsheet pasted data, center data, etc.).

e. Enter your name and today's date where indicated.

f. Print the memorandum. The completed memorandum is shown in Figure 6.22.

g. Save the memorandum document with a file name of 06-S Your Name.

FIGURE 6.22

Word Processing Memorandum

MEMORANDUM

TO:	Diane Palmer
FROM:	Your Name
DATE:	(Today's Date)
SUBJECT:	Year-to-Date Gross Sales Data

The following inventory items have year-to-date gross sales less than $500.00. Note the percent of total sales these items generate.

Battery powered Vac	$233.70
Car Vac	$29.95
Upright Cleaner Bag	$126.40
Canister Cleaner Bag	$246.40
Allergenci Bag	$250.60
Pile Lifter Brush	$147.00
Shampoo Attachment	$194.75
Attachment Kit	$449.55
	$1,678.35
Percent of Total Sales	4.86%

If you have access to the Internet, use your browser to access the U.S. Chamber of Commerce web site to find information about international trading. *Hint:* Use U.S. Chamber of Commerce as your search string to find the site, and then choose International links to find information about Asia-Pacific economic cooperation, Trans-Atlantic economic cooperation, free trade area of the Americas, and other trade agreements. Report on your findings.

24 **End the *Integrated Accounting* 6e session.**

Chapter 6 Student Exercises

NAME

I Matching

Directions   *For each of the definitions, write the letter of the appropriate term in the space provided.*

a. purge invoices and purchase orders
b. sales invoice
c. computerized sales order processing
d. sales returns and allowances
e. sales
f. sales order processing
g. statement of account

1.____ The revenue account used to record a sale.

2.____ The revenue account used to record a sales return.

3.____ Window used to enter sales-on-account transactions.

4.____ A system that comprises the procedures involved in preparing a sales invoice and automatically integrating the data it contains into the inventory and general ledger.

5.____ The process in which previously entered invoices and purchase orders are erased when capacity is exceeded.

6.____ The procedures and controls involved in preparing invoices, updating accounting records, and shipping merchandise.

7.____ A computer-generated output for each customer that shows the customer's name, balance brought forward, sales invoices of the current period, payments received in the current period, and balance owed.

II Questions

Directions   *Write the answers to the following questions in the space provided.*

1. Identify the tasks performed by the computer when sales invoice data are entered through the Sales Invoice window. _____

_____

2. How is the quantity entered in the Sales Invoice window for a sales return transaction?

_____

3. Itemize the steps required to make a change to an existing sales invoice. _____

_____

4. What do the terms 2/10, n/30 mean? _____

_____

5. What totals are contained at the bottom of the computer-generated sales invoice? _____

_____

6.   Make use of the data in Sample Problem 6-S to describe the integration that would take place when the following sales invoice is entered into the computer:

Sold—1 Wet & Dry Vacuum at $325.00, $19.50 sales tax, to Robert Thorson (use a FIFO cost of $185.00).

Inventory System Integration: _____

_____

_____

Accounting System Integration: _____

_____

_____

7.   List the information contained on the computer-generated statements of account.   _____

_____

8.   Why are data not lost when sales invoices are purged?   _____

_____

9.   How does the computer determine the value of an inventory item based on average cost?

_____

10.   What assumption does the computer make to determine the value of an inventory item based on the LIFO method?   _____

_____

11.   What assumption does the computer make to determine the value of an inventory item based on the FIFO method?   _____

_____

Problem 6-A

In this problem, you will process the sales and purchases transactions for the week of February 8 through February 14 for Palmer Vacuum Center. Answer Audit Questions 6-A on pages 278–279 as you complete this problem. Display reports as necessary to answer the questions, and click Info. on the toolbar for helpful check figures to audit your work.

 The inventory valuation (Merchandise Inventory and Cost of Goods Sold accounts) may be affected by the order in which transactions are entered. Therefore, making corrections to previous transactions or changing the sequence in which transactions are entered may affect the FIFO method of valuation used in this problem. If you must make a correction to a previously entered transaction affecting inventory, it is a good idea to delete all subsequent entries related to the inventory items as well and then reenter the transactions in the order presented.

1   Start *Integrated Accounting* 6e.

2   Load opening balances file IA6 Problem 06-A.

3   Enter your name in the Your Name text box and click OK.

4   Save the file with a file name of 06-A Your name.

5   Enter the following purchase order and voucher transactions.

Weekly Purchase Order and Voucher Transactions

Feb. 08   Ordered the following merchandise from Handy Manufacturing, Inc., terms 2/10, n/30. Purchase Order No. 277.

Description	Quantity	Unit Cost
Wet & Dry Vacuum	6	$199.00

11   Received the following merchandise for Purchase Order No. 275 from Handy Manufacturing, Inc., terms 2/10, n/30. Voucher No. 859.

Description	Quantity	Unit Cost
Allergenci Bag	32	$5.35

12   Received the following merchandise for Purchase Order No. 276 from Royal Accessories, Inc., terms 2/10, n/30. Voucher No. 860.

Description	Quantity	Unit Cost
Attachment Kit	2	$32.95
Upright Cleaner Bag	24	$2.35

14   Ordered the following merchandise from Nantz Vacuum Cleaner Co., terms 2/10, n/30. Purchase Order No. 278.

Description	Quantity	Unit Cost
Nantz Canister Vacuum	5	$240.00

6   **Enter the following sales invoice transactions.**

Weekly Sales Transactions

Feb. 08   Sold the following merchandise to Fraze Department Stores, terms 2/10, n/30, 6% sales tax, Sales Invoice No. 531:

Description	Quantity Sold	Selling Price
Attachment Kit	2	$49.95
Steam Cleaner	1	$219.00
Alpha Upright Vacuum	1	$795.95
Upright Cleaner Bag	8	$3.95

Feb. 09   Sold the following merchandise to Jennifer Martens, terms 30 days, 6% sales tax, Sales Invoice No. 532:

Description	Quantity Sold	Selling Price
Rug Machine	1	$189.99
Pile Lifter Brush	1	$49.00

Feb. 10   The following merchandise was returned to Palmer Vacuum Center by Wingler Motel, 6% sales tax, Sales Return No. R530:

Description	Quantity Sold	Selling Price
Handy Upright Vacuum	1	$485.00

Feb. 10   Sold the following merchandise to Wingler Motel, terms 2/10, n/30, 6% sales tax, Sales Invoice No. 533:

Description	Quantity Sold	Selling Price
Alpha Upright Vacuum	2	$795.95
Electric Broom	2	$99.99
Shampoo Attachment	1	$38.95

Feb. 11   Sold the following merchandise to Robert Thorson, terms 30 days, 6% sales tax, Sales Invoice No. 534:

Description	Quantity Sold	Selling Price
Car Vac	1	$29.95
Battery Powered Vac	1	$38.95

Feb. 12   Sold the following merchandise to Bassett Cleaning, Inc., terms 2/10, n/30, 6% sales tax, Sales Invoice No. 535:

Description	Quantity Sold	Selling Price
Upright Cleaner Bag	6	$3.95
Steam Cleaner	2	$219.00

Feb. 13   Sold the following merchandise to Lilly Industries, Inc., terms 2/10, n/30, 6% sales tax, Sales Invoice No. 536:

Description	Quantity Sold	Selling Price
Wet & Dry Vacuum	2	$325.00
Allergenci Bag	12	$8.95
Attachment Kit	1	$49.95
Rug Machine	1	$189.99

Feb. 14   Sold the following merchandise to Matthew Cornish, terms 30 days, 6% sales tax, Sales Invoice No. 537:

Description	Quantity Sold	Selling Price
Wet & Dry Vacuum	1	$325.00

7   **Enter the following cash payments journal transactions.**

Weekly Cash Payment Transactions

Feb. 13   Paid invoice 859 to Handy Manufacturing, Inc., $171.20, less 2% discount, $3.42. Check No. 3621.

14   Paid invoice 855 to Royal Accessories, Inc., $511.20, no discount. Check No. 3622.

8   **Enter the following cash receipt journal transactions.**

Weekly Cash Receipt Transactions

Feb. 10   Received cash on account from Lilly Industries, Inc., covering Sales Invoice No. 525 for $839.89, less 2% discount, $16.80.

12   Received cash on account from Bassett Cleaning, Inc., covering Sales Invoice No. 527 for $881.66, less 2% discount, $17.63.

13   Received cash on account from Broderick Company, covering Sales Invoice No. 518 for $7,594.73, no discount.

9   **Display the purchase order, voucher, and sales invoice registers for the period February 8 through February 14.**

10   **Display the general, vouchers, cash payments, sales, and cash receipts journals for the period February 8 through February 14.**

11   **Display a general ledger report for the Accounts Receivable, Sales, Sales Returns and Allowance, and Sales Discount accounts.**

12   **Display a trial balance report.**

13   **Display a schedule of accounts receivable and an accounts receivable ledger report for all customers.**

14   **Display a statement of account for Bassett Cleaning, Inc.**

15   **Display an inventory list report.**

16   **Display the inventory transactions for the period of February 8 through February 14.**

17   **Display the yearly sales report.**

18   **Display the top customers graph.**

19   **Save your data to disk.**

20   **Use Check on the toolbar to check your work.**

21   **Optional spreadsheet integration activity.**

Use a spreadsheet to prepare a list of inventory items with year-to-date gross sales greater than $2,000.00. Use Figure 6.21 as a guide if necessary.

a. Display and copy the yearly sales report to the clipboard in spreadsheet format.

b. Start your spreadsheet software and load file IA6 Spreadsheet 06-S.

c. Select cell A1 as the current cell (if not already selected) and paste the yearly sales report into the spreadsheet.

d. In cell B35, enter the IF function appropriate for your spreadsheet software to display the description of each inventory item with year-to-date gross sales greater than $2,000.00—if not, display "Delete this row." For example, @IF(E10>2000,B10,"Delete this row"). Copy the formula from cell B35 to cells B36–B50.

e. In cell C35, enter the IF function appropriate for your spreadsheet software to display the amount of each inventory item with year-to-date gross sales greater than $2,000.00—if not, display a blank. For example, @IF(E10>2000,E10," "). Copy the formula from cell C35 to cells C36–C50.

f. Delete the rows in cells B35–B50 that contain "Delete this row."

g. Sum the amount (column C) of the items that match the criteria, and use this sum to calculate and display the percent of yearly total sales.

h. Print the list of items that meet the criteria.

i. Save your spreadsheet data with a file name of 06-A Your Name.

22   **Optional word processing integration activity.**

Prepare a memorandum to the Owner of Palmer Vacuum Center (Diane Palmer) listing the items of inventory with year-to-date gross sales greater than $2,000.00 and their percentage of total sales.

a. Copy the list of inventory items from the spreadsheet.

b. Start your word processing software and load template file IA6 Word-processing 06-S (load as a text file).

c. Paste the contents of the clipboard into the memorandum at the location specified and change the text reference from less than $500.00 to greater than $2,000.00.

d. Format the document as necessary.

e. Enter your name and today's date where indicated.

f. Print the memorandum.

g. Save the memorandum document with a file name of 06-A Your Name.

If you have access to the Internet, use your browser to find information or examples of Incoterms. (Incoterms are interpretations of common sales terms used in foreign trade, which are adopted by most international trade associations.) *Hint:* Use Incoterms as your search string. Report on your findings. Be sure to include the sources, including URLs (Web addresses) of your reported findings.

INTERNET ACTIVITY

23   **End the *Integrated Accounting* 6e session.**

Audit Questions 6-A

NAME _____

Directions *Write the answers to the following questions in the space provided.*

 All of the following questions relate to February 8 through 14.

Register Reports

1. What is the total amount of purchase orders for the period? _____

    _____

2. What is the total amount of vouchers for the period? _____

    _____

3. What is the total amount of sales for the period? _____

    _____

Journal and Ledger Reports

4. What are the total debits and credits shown on the vouchers journal? _____

    _____

5. What are the total debits and credits shown on the cash payments journal? _____

    _____

6. What are the total debits and credits shown on the sales journal? _____

    _____

7. What are the total debits and credits shown on the cash receipts journal? _____

    _____

8. From the general ledger report, what was the Accounts Receivable account balance on February 14? _____

    _____

9. What is the account balance of the following accounts as of February 14?

    Sales _____

    Sales returns and allowances _____

    Sales discounts _____

10. From the trial balance, what is the net amount of sales (sales minus sales returns and allowances)? Does it equal the total amount of yearly sales shown on the inventory yearly sales report? _____

    _____

11.   From the schedule of accounts receivable, what is the total due from all customers as of February 14? Does it equal the current balance in the Accounts Receivable account?   _____

      _____

12.   From the statement of account for Bassett Cleaning, Inc., what is the current account balance?

      _____

Inventory Reports and Graph

13.   How many items were sold during the period?

      _____

14.   Which item has the greatest sales volume based on the dollar amount?

      _____

15.   What is the total amount of yearly sales?

      _____

16.   From the graph, what customer has the greatest amount of sales to date?

      _____

Problem 6-B

In this problem, you will process the sales and purchases transactions for the week of February 8 through February 14 for Palmer Vacuum Center. Answer Audit Questions 6-B on pages 285–286 as you complete this problem. Display reports as necessary to answer the questions.

 The inventory valuation (Merchandise Inventory and Cost of Goods Sold accounts) may be affected by the order in which transactions are entered. Therefore, making corrections to previous transactions or changing the sequence in which transactions are entered may affect the FIFO method of valuation used in this problem. If you must make a correction to a previously entered transaction affecting inventory, it is a good idea to delete all subsequent entries related to the inventory items as well and then reenter the transactions in the order presented.

1   Start *Integrated Accounting* 6e.

2   Load opening balances file IA6 Problem 06-B.

3   Enter your name in the Your Name text box and click OK.

4   Save the file with a file name of 06-B Your name.

5   Enter the following purchase order and voucher transactions.

Weekly Purchase Order and Voucher Transactions

Feb. 08   Ordered the following merchandise from Nantz Vacuum Cleaner Co., terms 2/10, n/30. Purchase Order No. 277.

Description	Quantity	Unit Cost
Nantz Canister Vacuum	8	$240.00

09   Ordered the following merchandise from Alpha Vacuum Mfg., Inc., terms 2/10. N/30. Purchase Order No. 278.

Description	Quantity	Unit Cost
Alpha Upright Vacuum	4	$480.00

12   Received the following merchandise for Purchase Order No. 275 from Handy Manufacturing, Inc., terms 2/10, n/30. Voucher No. 859.

Description	Quantity	Unit Cost
Allergenci Bag	24	$5.35

14   Received the following merchandise for Purchase Order No. 276 from Royal Accessories, Inc., terms 2/10, n/30. Voucher No. 860.

Description	Quantity	Unit Cost
Attachment Kit	2	$32.95
Upright Cleaner Bag	24	$2.35

6   **Enter the following sales invoice transactions.**

Weekly Sales Transactions

Feb. 08   The following merchandise was returned to Palmer Vacuum Center by Wingler Motel, 6% sales tax, Sales Return No. R530:

Description	Quantity Returned	Price
Handy Upright Vacuum	1	$485.00

Feb. 08   Sold the following merchandise to Wingler Motel, terms 2/10, n/30, 6% sales tax, Sales Invoice No. 531:

Description	Quantity Sold	Selling Price
Kenwood Canister Vac	2	$689.95
Canister Cleaner Bag	10	$3.85
Attachment Kit	1	$49.95

Feb. 09   Sold the following merchandise to Fraze Department Stores, terms 2/10, n/30, 6% sales tax, Sales Invoice No. 532:

Description	Quantity Sold	Selling Price
Battery Powered Vac	2	$38.95
Steam Cleaner	1	$219.00
Handy Upright Vacuum	1	$485.00
Upright Cleaner Bag	12	$3.95

Feb. 10   Sold the following merchandise to Robert Thorson, terms 30 days, 6% sales tax, Sales Invoice No. 533:

Description	Quantity Sold	Selling Price
Steam Cleaner	1	$219.00

Feb. 11   Sold the following merchandise to Jennifer Martens, terms 30 days, 6% sales tax, Sales Invoice No. 534:

Description	Quantity Sold	Selling Price
Nantz Canister Vac	1	$369.99
Canister Cleaner Bag	12	$3.85
Pile Lifter Brush	1	$49.00

Feb. 12   Sold the following merchandise to Broderick Company, terms 2/10, n/30, 6% sales tax, Sales Invoice No. 535:

Description	Quantity Sold	Selling Price
Shampoo Attachment	1	$38.95
Allergenci Bag	6	$8.95

Feb. 13   Sold the following merchandise to Lilly Industries, Inc., terms 2/10, n/30, 6% sales tax, Sales Invoice No. 536:

Description	Quantity Sold	Selling Price
Wet & Dry Vacuum	1	$325.00
Steam Cleaner	1	$219.00

Feb. 14   Sold the following merchandise to Matthew Cornish, terms 30 days, 6% sales tax, Sales Invoice No. 537:

Description	Quantity Sold	Selling Price
Rug Machine	2	$189.99
Pile Lifter Brush	1	$49.00
Shampoo Attachment	1	$38.95

7   **Enter the following cash payments journal transactions.**

Weekly Cash Payment Transactions

Feb. 13   Paid invoice 858 to Nantz Vacuum Cleaner Co., $157.50, less 2% discount, $3.15. Check No. 3621.

14   Paid invoice 850 to Alpha Vacuum Mfg., Inc., $3,314.75, no discount. Check No. 3622.

8   **Enter the following cash receipt journal transactions.**

Weekly Cash Receipt Transactions

Feb. 10   Received cash on account from Bassett Cleaning, Inc., covering Sales Invoice No. 527 for $881.66, less 2% discount, $17.63.

13   Received cash on account from Robert Thorson, covering Sales Invoice No. 528 for $344.50, no discount.

14   Received cash on account from Broderick Company, covering Sales Invoice No. 529 for $1,066.77, less 2% discount, $21.34.

9   **Display the purchase order, voucher, and sales invoice registers for the period February 8 through February 14.**

10   **Display the general, vouchers, cash payments, sales, and cash receipts journals for the period February 8 through February 14.**

11   **Display a general ledger report for the Accounts Receivable, Sales, Sales Returns and Allowance, and Sales Discount accounts.**

12   **Display a trial balance report.**

13   **Display a schedule of accounts receivable and an accounts receivable ledger report for all customers.**

14   **Display a statement of account for Wingler Motel.**

15   **Display an inventory list report.**

16   **Display the inventory transactions for the period of February 8 through February 14.**

17 **Display the yearly sales report.**

18 **Display the top customers graph.**

19 **Save your data to disk.**

20 **Optional spreadsheet integration activity.**

Use a spreadsheet to prepare a list of inventory items with year-to-date gross sales greater than $3,500.00. Use Figure 6.21 as a guide if necessary.

a. Display and copy the yearly sales report to the clipboard in spreadsheet format.

b. Start your spreadsheet software and load file IA6 Spreadsheet 06-S.

c. Select cell A1 as the current cell (if not already selected) and paste the yearly sales report into the spreadsheet.

d. In cell B35, enter the IF function appropriate for your spreadsheet software to display the description of each inventory item with year-to-date gross sales greater than $3,500.00—if not, display "Delete this row." For example, @IF(E10>3500,B10,"Delete this row"). Copy the formula from cell B35 to cells B36–B50.

e. In cell C35, enter the IF function appropriate for your spreadsheet software to display the amount of each inventory item with year-to-date gross sales greater than $3,500.00—if not, display a blank. For example, @IF(E10>3500,E10," "). Copy the formula from cell C35 to cells C36–C50.

f. Delete the rows in cells B35–B50 that contain "Delete this row."

g. Sum the amount (column C) of the items that match the criteria, and use this sum to calculate and display the percent of yearly total sales.

h. Print the list of items that meet the criteria.

i. Save your spreadsheet data with a file name of 06-B Your Name.

21 **Optional word processing integration activity.**

Prepare a memorandum to the Owner of Palmer Vacuum Center (Diane Palmer) listing the items of inventory with year-to-date gross sales greater than $3,500.00 and their percentage of total sales.

a. Copy the list of inventory items from the spreadsheet.

b. Start your word processing software and load template file IA6 Word-processing 06-S (load as a text file).

c. Paste the contents of the clipboard into the memorandum at the location specified and change the text reference from less than $500.00 to greater than $3,500.00.

d. Format the document as necessary.

e. Enter your name and today's date where indicated.

f. Print the memorandum.

g. Save the memorandum document with a file name of 06-B Your Name.

INTERNET
ACTIVITY

If you have access to the Internet, use your browser to find information about value added tax (VAT) in another country. *Hint:* Use international taxation as a search string, then use search argument VAT. Report on your findings. Be sure to include the sources, including URLs (Web addresses) of your reported findings.

22   **End the *Integrated Accounting* 6e session.**

Audit Questions 6-B

NAME

Directions *Write the answers to the following questions in the space provided.*

 All of the following questions relate to February 8 through 14.

Register Reports

1. What is the total amount of purchase orders for the period? _____

2. What is the total amount of vouchers for the period? _____

3. What is the total amount of sales for the period? _____

Journal and Ledger Reports

4. What are the total debits and credits shown on the vouchers journal? _____

5. What are the total debits and credits shown on the cash payments journal? _____

6. What are the total debits and credits shown on the sales journal? _____

7. What are the total debits and credits shown on the cash receipts journal? _____

8. From the general ledger report, what was the Accounts Receivable account balance on February 14? _____

9. What is the account balance of the following accounts as of February 14?

    Sales _____

    Sales returns and allowances _____

    Sales discounts _____

10. From the trial balance, what is the net amount of sales (sales minus sales returns and allowances)? Does it equal the total amount of yearly sales shown on the inventory yearly sales report? _____

11. From the schedule of accounts receivable, what is the total due from all customers as of February 14? Does it equal the current balance in the Accounts Receivable account?   _____

_____

12. From the statement of account for Wingler Motel, what is the current account balance?

_____

Inventory Reports and Graph

13. How many items were sold during the period?   _____

_____

14. Which item has the greatest sales volume based on the dollar amount?   _____

_____

15. What is the total amount of yearly sales?   _____

_____

16. From the graph, what customer has greatest amount of sales to date?

_____

Fixed Assets

Upon completion of this chapter, you will be able to:

- Identify the differences between the following methods of depreciation: straight-line method, double declining-balance method, sum-of-the-years-digits method, and the modified accelerated cost recovery system.

- Maintain fixed assets records.
- Display the fixed assets list.
- Display depreciation schedules.
- Generate and post the depreciation adjusting entries.

Introduction

Assets used for a number of years in the operation of a business are called **fixed assets** (also commonly referred to as plant assets). Accounting uses fixed assets information to show costs, to show an asset's reduction in value as a result of usage, and to dispose of assets. **Asset disposition** occurs when an asset is removed from use in the business.

As assets wear out with time, they decrease in value. Therefore, during their useful life, they must be systematically depreciated for proper accounting and tax reporting purposes. The amount of the depreciation is recorded as adjusting entries at the end of the month or year.

Fixed asset information can also be used in many areas other than accounting. For example, fixed assets reports are used to ensure adequate insurance coverage and to determine the amount of the settlement in insurance claims. The information can also be used to estimate the worth of an asset for **trade-in value**. Trade-in value is considered as payment or partial payment toward another asset.

In a **computerized fixed assets system**, the computer maintains and stores relevant data for each asset in a file on an auxiliary storage device (e.g., disk). When new assets are acquired, they are added to the file. Likewise, they are deleted from the file at the time of disposition. Changes and corrections are made as needed.

Once the fixed assets data have been updated, a fixed assets report is generated to list all the information stored for each asset in the file. A depreciation schedule can be displayed for an individual asset or a range of assets. Finally, when directed to do so, the computer will analyze the fixed assets data and generate the depreciation adjusting entries.

This text and the accompanying software provide four methods of calculating depreciation: (1) straight-line, (2) double declining-balance, (3) sum-of-the-years-digits, and (4) modified accelerated cost recovery system.

Straight-Line Method

In the **straight-line method** of depreciation, the same amount of depreciation is recorded for each accounting period over the useful life of the asset. To obtain annual depreciation using the straight-line method, the program subtracts the **salvage value** (the amount representing the remaining value of an asset after the end of its useful life) from the original cost of the asset and then divides the difference by the asset's useful life (expressed in years). The same amount is subtracted for each year of the asset's useful life.

Double Declining-Balance Method

The **double declining-balance method** (also commonly called declining-balance method) requires similar calculations to those used to computing straight-line depreciation, with two important exceptions. First, the depreciation rate for the double declining-balance method is twice the rate of the straight-line method. Under the straight-line method, an asset depreciated over a useful life of 10 years, would have an annual depreciation rate of 1/10 per year, or 10 percent. On the other hand, the double declining-balance rate would be 2/10 or 20 percent per year.

The second exception is that the salvage value is not considered when using the double declining-balance method. However, an asset should not be depreciated below the estimated salvage value. If the difference between the final book value and salvage value is substantial, many users would switch to another method to depreciate the asset down to the salvage value. This switch should be made near the end of the asset's useful life when the straight-line or sum-of-the-years-digits method provides a higher annual depreciation.

Sum-of-the-Years-Digits Method

The **sum-of-the-years-digits method** calculates depreciation amounts as a fractional portion of the original cost of the asset. The denominator of the fraction is obtained by adding the digits of the years of the asset's useful life. For example, if the asset's useful life is 5 years, the sum of the years digits used in the denominator would be 15 (1 + 2 + 3 + 4 + 5 = 15). The numerator used for calculating any one year of depreciation is simply the number of remaining years of useful life. The computer then multiplies the sum-of-the-years-digits fraction by the original cost of the asset, minus any salvage value, to calculate the annual depreciation. The fraction is then adjusted and the process continues until the numerator reaches zero, indicating that the useful life of the asset has been reached. With the number of remaining years of life of the asset as the numerator, the first year's depreciation for a 5-year asset would be 5/15, the second year's would be 4/15, and so on.

Modified Accelerated Cost Recovery System

The Economic Recovery Tax Act of 1981 allows businesses to take accelerated cost recovery deductions under the Accelerated Cost Recovery System (ACRS). The purpose of ACRS is to reduce federal tax on businesses and encourage reinvestment of capital in depreciable assets. The Tax Reform Act of 1986 modified the rates for those assets acquired after 1986. The **modified accelerated cost recovery system (MACRS)** increases the number of property classes and lengthens the time periods of most assets. The 1986 Act allows for the recovery of expenditures for assets over periods of 3, 5, 7, 10, 15, 20, 27.5, and 31.5 years depending on the type of property. Because most of the common assets (other than buildings) are classified as 5-year or 7-year assets, the *Integrated Accounting* 6e software includes only those two classes.

Buildings are depreciated using either 27.5 or 31.5 years under straight-line depreciation. Types of assets included in the 5-year and 7-year classes are described in Table 7.1.

TABLE 7.1 *Classes of Assets*		
	5-year class	This class includes automobiles, trucks, computers, office equipment, and technological equipment.
	7-year class	This class includes office furniture and fixtures, commercial aircraft, and most manufacturing machinery.

Several conventions may be used with the MACRS rates. The most commonly used convention is the half-year convention, which assumes that all assets are placed into service in the middle of the year and taken out of service in the middle of the year. *Integrated Accounting* software uses this convention.

When you use the MACRS depreciation method in *Integrated Accounting*, remember the following three items: (1) only periods of 5 and 7 years can be used when determining useful life of an asset; (2) any salvage value of an asset is disregarded; and (3) the asset is assumed to be placed in service in the middle of the year.

To calculate the annual cost recovery deduction using this system, the computer references the appropriate percentage from the MACRS rate schedule based on the recovery period. This method approximates the double declining-balance method. Table 7.2 shows the MACRS rate schedules for the 5-year and 7-year rates.

TABLE 7.2 *Modified Acclerated Cost Recovery System Rate Schedules*	Recovery Year	5-Year Rate (%)	7-Year Rate (%)
	1	20.00	14.29
	2	32.00	24.49
	3	19.20	17.49
	4	11.52	12.49
	5	11.52	8.93
	6	5.76	8.92
	7	—	8.93
	8	—	4.46

Maintaining Fixed Assets Data

The process of adding, changing, and deleting assets is referred to as **maintaining fixed assets data**. Choosing Maintain Accounts from the Data menu, clicking Accts. on the toolbar, or clicking on the Assets navigation button and then the Maintain Fixed Assets menu button opens the Account Maintenance window. Click the Fixed Assets tab (if not already selected) and enter the maintenance data. Figure 7.1 shows the Fixed Assets tab containing fixed asset data.

FIGURE 7.1

Fixed Assets Maintenance

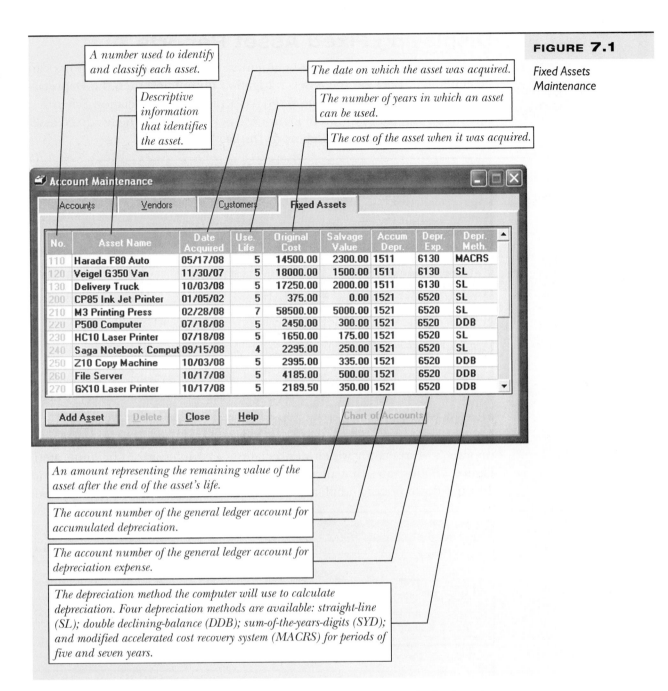

New assets may be added after the last fixed asset in the list by keying the asset number, description, and each of the remaining columns of information shown in Figure 7.1 and clicking Add Asset. The new asset will be inserted into the existing fixed assets in asset number sequence. Existing fixed assets may be changed by selecting the asset you wish to change, keying the correct data (or selecting a different depreciation method), and clicking Change Asset (the Add Asset button changes to Change Asset). An existing fixed asset may be deleted by simply selecting the asset to be deleted and clicking Delete.

 NOTE The asset number cannot be changed. A fixed asset with an incorrect asset number must be deleted and then added back as a new fixed asset with the correct number.

Reports

Displaying Fixed Asset Reports

Once the fixed asset data have been entered, the depreciation reports can be generated. Click on the Assets navigation button and then the Depreciation Reports menu button. The Fixed Asset List and Depreciation Schedules options will appear as shown in Figure 7.2. Select either of the two fixed asset reports from the Choose a Report to Display list.

FIGURE 7.2

Report Selection (Fixed Asset Reports)

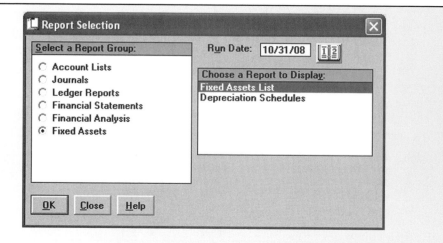

When the Depreciation Schedules option is selected, the Depreciation Schedules window shown in Figure 7.3 appears, allowing you to select the range of assets for which depreciation schedules are to be generated. Figure 7.3 illustrates that all assets, including those shown in the From and To drop-down boxes and all assets between these two, are to be generated.

FIGURE 7.3

Depreciation Schedule Range Selection

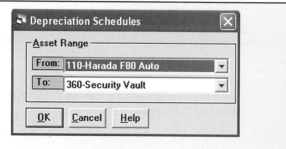

Fixed Assets List Report

The **fixed assets list report** is useful in detecting typing errors and verifying the accuracy of your input. The report also provides information concerning the costs of assets, which is useful in determining current asset value. An example of a fixed assets list report is shown in Figure 7.4.

FIGURE 7.4

Fixed Assets List Report

Sherwood Merchandise Co.
Fixed Assets List
10/31/08

	Asset	Date Acquired	Depr. Method	Useful Life	Original Cost	Salvage Value	Depr. Accts
110	Harada F80 Auto	05/17/08	MACRS	5	14,500.00	2,300.00	1511 6130
120	Veigel G350 Van	11/30/07	SL	5	18,000.00	1,500.00	1511 6130
130	Delivery Truck	10/03/08	SL	5	17,250.00	2,000.00	1511 6130
200	CP85 Ink Jet Printer	01/05/02	SL	5	375.00	0.00	1521 6520
210	M3 Printing Press	02/28/08	SL	7	58,500.00	5,000.00	1521 6520
220	P500 Computer	07/18/08	DDB	5	2,450.00	300.00	1521 6520
230	HC10 Laser Printer	07/18/08	SL	5	1,650.00	175.00	1521 6520
240	Saga Notebook Computer	09/15/08	SL	4	2,295.00	250.00	1521 6520
250	Z10 Copy Machine	10/03/08	DDB	5	2,995.00	335.00	1521 6520
260	File Server	10/17/08	DDB	5	4,185.00	500.00	1521 6520
270	GX10 Laser Printer	10/17/08	DDB	5	2,189.50	350.00	1521 6520
280	Alpha-5 Fax Machine	10/21/08	MACRS	5	3,899.00	400.00	1521 6520
310	Conf. Table & Chairs	01/31/08	MACRS	7	6,200.00	950.00	1531 6525
320	Receptionist Station	08/22/08	SYD	6	2,195.00	350.00	1531 6525
330	Office Desk & Chair	06/16/08	SL	6	3,085.00	650.00	1531 6525
340	Storage Cabinet	10/09/08	SL	10	2,360.00	225.00	1531 6525
350	Office Desk	10/14/08	SYD	10	1,495.00	260.00	1531 6525
360	Security Vault	10/27/08	SYD	20	5,975.00	450.00	1531 6525
	Total Fixed Assets				149,598.50		

Depreciation Schedules

Depreciation schedules can be generated for any range of assets. The depreciation schedule provides annual depreciation for each year of the asset's useful life. The depreciation is calculated based on the date the asset was acquired and one of the four depreciation methods. An asset purchased in any month other than January has first-year and last-year amounts that are prorated from the month the asset was purchased. In the example shown in Figure 7.5, which uses the straight-line method, the asset was purchased on October 3. Therefore the first year's depreciation is prorated for October through December, which is three months or three twelfths of the annual depreciation of $3,050.00 (3/12 × $3,050.00 = $762.50). Likewise, the depreciation for the last year is $2,287.50 (9/12 × $3,050.00 = $2,287.50).

FIGURE 7.5

Depreciation Schedule

Sherwood Merchandise Co.
Depreciation Schedules
10/31/08

	Year	Annual Deprec.	Accum. Deprec.	Book Value
(130) Delivery Truck	2008	762.50	762.50	16,487.50
Acquired on 10/03/08	2009	3,050.00	3,812.50	13,437.50
Straight-Line	2010	3,050.00	6,862.50	10,387.50
Useful Life = 5	2011	3,050.00	9,912.50	7,337.50
Original Cost = 17,250.00	2012	3,050.00	12,962.50	4,287.50
Salvage Value = 2,000.00	2013	2,287.50	15,250.00	2,000.00

Generating and Posting Depreciation Adjusting Entries

When the Depreciation Adjusting Entries menu button is selected from the Assets navigation button (or Depreciation Adjusting Entries is selected from the Options menu), the computer will analyze the fixed assets records, determine the depreciation for the period, and generate the depreciation adjusting entries. The depreciation adjusting entries can be generated for either a monthly or yearly period depending on how the Income Statement option is set. (This setting is usually determined during system setup and will be covered in Chapter 12.) For the problems in this text-workbook, the computer will generate monthly adjusting entries.

To generate the depreciation adjusting entries, click on the Assets navigation button and then the Depreciation Adjusting Entries menu button (or choose Depreciation Adjusting Entries from the Options menu). The confirmation dialog box shown in Figure 7.6 will appear.

FIGURE 7.6

Confirmation Dialog Box

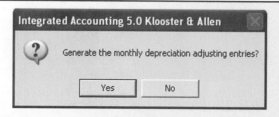

Click Yes. The computer-generated depreciation adjusting entries shown in Figure 7.7 will appear. The three entries for the three classifications of fixed assets (used in the problems in this chapter) will appear as one compound entry.

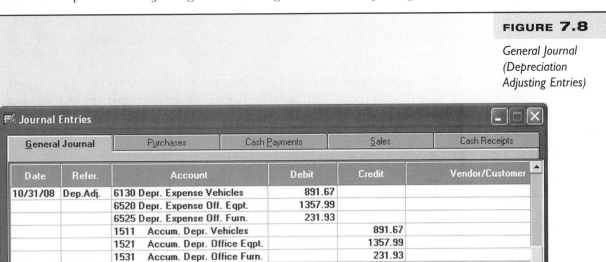

FIGURE 7.7

Depreciation Adjusting Entries Dialog Box

Click Post to post the entries to the general journal. Finally, the adjusting entries will appear in the general journal as illustrated in Figure 7.8. Verify the accuracy of the entries and click Close. If the adjusting entries are incorrect, return to the Fixed Assets tab in the Account Maintenance window and make the necessary corrections. Then select the General Journal, delete the incorrect depreciation adjusting entries, and generate new adjusting entries.

FIGURE 7.8

General Journal (Depreciation Adjusting Entries)

Chapter Summary

- Assets used for a number of years in the operation of a business are called fixed assets.

- Disposing of an asset is referred to as asset disposition.

- The amount of depreciation is recorded as adjusting entries at the end of the month or year.

- A trade-in value is the worth of an asset used as payment or partial payment toward another asset.

- A computerized fixed asset system is used to maintain and store records for all fixed assets for a business.

- When new assets are acquired, they are added to the file. When assets are disposed of, they are deleted from the file. Changes and corrections are made as needed.

- The number of years in which an asset can be used in the operation of a business is referred to as its useful life.

- The method the computer uses to calculate an asset's decrease in value is called the depreciation method. Four depreciation methods are available: straight-line; double declining-balance; sum-of-the-years-digits; and MACRS.

- The cost of the asset when it was acquired is called original cost.

- The amount representing the remaining value of an asset after the end of its useful life is referred to as salvage value.

- Fixed asset maintenance is the process of adding, changing, and deleting assets.

- The fixed assets list report provides information concerning the costs of assets. It is useful in detecting typing errors and verifying the accuracy of input.

- Depreciation schedules provide annual depreciation for each year of the asset's useful life.

- The computer automatically generates the depreciation adjusting entries by analyzing the fixed assets records and determining the depreciation for the period.

Sample Problem 7-S

In this sample problem, all of the monthly journal entries not related to fixed assets have already been entered and posted. You will enter the fixed assets transactions, display depreciation schedules, and generate and post the depreciation adjusting entries for Sherwood Merchandise Co. Sherwood Merchandise Co., has three types of assets: (1) vehicles, (2) office equipment, and (3) office furniture. You will enter the rest of the adjusting entries for the end of the period and complete the end-of-period processing.

1 **Start *Integrated Accounting* 6e.**

2 **Load the opening balances template file, IA6 Problem 07-S.**

3 **Enter your name in the Your Name text box and click OK.**

4 **Save the data to your disk as 07-S Your Name.**

5 **Delete Asset No. 211, Atwood Copy Machine.**

Click the Assets navigation button and then the Maintain Fixed Assets menu button. When the Fixed Assets tab in the Accounts Maintenance window appears, select 211, Atwood Copy Machine. Click Delete and then OK when the Delete dialog box appears.

6 **Change the name of Asset No. 220 to P500 Computer.**

Select 220, P400 Computer. Enter the new asset name then click Change Asset.

7 **Enter the fixed asset data in Account Maintenance.**

It is critical that you accurately enter the entire data *(including year acquired)* for each fixed asset. Many of the calculated depreciation amounts are date sensitive and will display incorrectly if not entered incorrectly.

Fixed Assets Transactions

Oct. 03, 2008 Purchased a Delivery Truck for $17,250.00; asset number, 130; depreciation method, straight-line; useful life, 5 years; salvage value, $2,000.00; accumulated depreciation, account number 1511; depreciation expense, account number 6130.

Oct. 03, 2008 Purchased a Z10 Copy Machine for $2,995.00; asset number, 250; depreciation method, double declining-balance; useful life, 5 years; salvage value, $335.00; accumulated depreciation, account number 1521; depreciation expense, account number 6520.

Oct. 09, 2008 Purchased a Storage Cabinet for $2,360.00; asset number, 340; depreciation method, straight-line; useful life, 10 years; salvage value, $225.00; accumulated depreciation, account number 1531; depreciation expense, account number 6525.

Oct. 14, 2008 Purchased an Office Desk for $1,495.00; asset number 350; depreciation method, sum-of-the-years-digits; useful life, 10 years; salvage value, $260.00; accumulated depreciation, account number 1531; depreciation expense, account number 6525.

Oct. 17, 2008 Purchased a File Server for $4,185.00; asset number, 260; depreciation method, double declining-balance; useful life, 5 years; salvage value, $500.00; accumulated depreciation, account number 1521; depreciation expense, account number 6520.

Oct. 17, 2008   Purchased a GX10 Laser Printer for $2,189.50; asset number, 270; depreciation method, double declining-balance; useful life, 5 years; salvage value, $350.00; accumulated depreciation, account number 1521; depreciation expense, account number 6520.

Oct. 21, 2008   Purchased an Alpha-5 Fax Machine for $3,899.00; asset number, 280; depreciation method, MACRS; useful life, 5 years; salvage value, $400.00; accumulated depreciation, account number 1521; depreciation expense, account number 6520.

Oct. 27, 2008   Purchased a Security Vault for $5,975.00; asset number 360; depreciation method, sum-of-the-years-digits; useful life, 20 years; salvage value, $450.00; accumulated depreciation, account number 1531; depreciation expense, account number 6525.

8   **Use the general journal to enter and post the following assets to the general ledger.**

Be sure that you accurately enter the entire data *(including year)* for each transaction's type of asset (vehicles, office equipment, and office furniture) as shown in Figure 7.9.

General Journal Transactions

Oct. 01, 2008   Discarded asset no. 211, Atwood Copy Machine (Office Equipment) bought in January, 2002: cost, $760.00; total accumulated depreciation recorded to December 31, 2006, $760.00. Memo No. 112.

Oct. 03, 2008   Paid cash for Delivery Truck, $17,250.00; Check No. 3831.

Oct. 03, 2008   Paid cash for Z10 Copy Machine, $2,995.00; Check No. 3832.

Oct. 09, 2008   Paid cash for Storage Cabinet, $2,360.00; Check No. 3833.

Oct. 14, 2008   Paid cash for Office Desk, $1,495.00; Check No. 3834.

Oct. 17, 2008   Paid cash for File Server, $4,185.00; Check No. 3835.

Oct. 17, 2008   Paid cash for GX10 Laser Printer, $2,189.50; Check No. 3836.

Oct. 21, 2008   Paid cash for Alpha-5 Fax Machine, $3,899.00; Check No. 3837.

Oct. 27, 2008   Paid cash for Security Vault, $5,975.00; Check No. 3838.

FIGURE 7.9

General Journal Entries

Date	Refer.	Account	Debit	Credit	Vendor/Customer
10/01/08	112	1521 Accum. Depr. Office Eqpt.	760.00		
		1520 Office Equipment		760.00	
10/03/08	3831	1510 Vehicles	17250.00		
		1110 Cash		17250.00	
10/03/08	3832	1520 Office Equipment	2995.00		
		1110 Cash		2995.00	
10/09/08	3833	1530 Office Furniture	2360.00		
		1110 Cash		2360.00	
10/14/08	3834	1530 Office Furniture	1495.00		
		1110 Cash		1495.00	
10/17/08	3835	1520 Office Equipment	4185.00		
		1110 Cash		4185.00	
10/17/08	3836	1520 Office Equipment	2189.50		
		1110 Cash		2189.50	
10/21/08	3837	1520 Office Equipment	3899.00		
		1110 Cash		3899.00	
10/27/08	3838	1530 Office Furniture	5975.00		
		1110 Cash		5975.00	

9   **Display a General Journal report.**

The General Journal report is shown in Figure 7.10. (Make sure the date on the Report Selection menu is set to 10/31/08.)

FIGURE 7.10

General Journal Report

Sherwood Merchandise Co.
General Journal
10/31/08

Date	Refer.	Acct.	Title	Debit	Credit
10/01	112	1521	Accum. Depr. Office Eqpt.	760.00	
10/01	112	1520	Office Equipment		760.00
10/03	3831	1510	Vehicles	17,250.00	
10/03	3831	1110	Cash		17,250.00
10/03	3832	1520	Office Equipment	2,995.00	
10/03	3832	1110	Cash		2,995.00
10/09	3833	1530	Office Furniture	2,360.00	
10/09	3833	1110	Cash		2,360.00
10/14	3834	1530	Office Furniture	1,495.00	
10/14	3834	1110	Cash		1,495.00
10/17	3835	1520	Office Equipment	4,185.00	
10/17	3835	1110	Cash		4,185.00
10/17	3836	1520	Office Equipment	2,189.50	
10/17	3836	1110	Cash		2,189.50
10/21	3837	1520	Office Equipment	3,899.00	
10/21	3837	1110	Cash		3,899.00
10/27	3838	1530	Office Furniture	5,975.00	
10/27	3838	1110	Cash		5,975.00
			Totals	41,108.50	41,108.50

10   **Display a Fixed Assets List report.**

Click the Assets Navigation button and then the Depreciation Reports menu button. With the Fixed Assets List selected, click OK. (Make sure the date on the Report Selection menu is set to 10/31/08.) The report is shown in Figure 7.11.

FIGURE 7.11

Fixed Assets List

Sherwood Merchandise Co.
Fixed Assets List
10/31/08

	Asset	Date Acquired	Depr. Method	Useful Life	Original Cost	Salvage Value	Depr. Accts
110	Harada F80 Auto	05/17/08	MACRS	5	14,500.00	2,300.00	1511 6130
120	Veigel G350 Van	11/30/07	SL	5	18,000.00	1,500.00	1511 6130

(continued)

FIGURE 7.11

(Concluded)

130	Delivery Truck	10/03/08	SL	5	17,250.00	2,00.00	1511 6130
200	CP85 Ink Jet Printer	01/05/02	SL	5	375.00	0.00	1521 6520
210	M3 Printing Press	02/28/08	SL	7	58,500.00	5,000.00	1521 6520
220	P500 Computer	07/18/08	DDB	5	2,450.00	300.00	1521 6520
230	HC10 Laser Printer	07/18/08	SL	5	1,650.00	175.00	1521 6520
240	Saga Notebook Computer	09/15/08	SL	4	2,295.00	250.00	1521 6520
250	Z10 Copy Machine	10/03/08	DDB	5	2,995.00	335.00	1521 6520
260	File Server	10/17/08	DDB	5	4,185.00	500.00	1521 6520
270	GX10 Laser Printer	10/17/08	DDB	5	2,189.50	350.00	1521 6520
280	Alpha-5 Fax Machine	10/21/08	MACRS	5	3,899.00	400.00	1521 6520
310	Conf. Table & Chairs	01/31/08	MACRS	7	6,200.00	950.00	1531 6525
320	Receptionist Station	08/22/08	SYD	6	2,195.00	350.00	1531 6525
330	Office Desk & Chair	06/16/08	SL	6	3,085.00	650.00	1531 6525
340	Storage Cabinet	10/09/08	SL	10	2,360.00	225.00	1531 6525
350	Office Desk	10/14/08	SYD	10	1,495.00	260.00	1531 6525
360	Security Vault	10/27/08	SYD	20	5,975.00	450.00	1531 6525
	Total Fixed Assets				149,598.50		

11 **Display depreciation schedules for the new assets by type: vehicles, office equipment, and office furniture.**

Choose Fixed Assets and then Depreciation Schedules from the Choose a Report to Display list, then click OK. When the Depreciation Schedules dialog box shown in Figure 7.12 appears, select a range of assets to include all new vehicles (select Delivery Truck from the drop-down lists for both the From and To ranges). Click OK. The depreciation schedule for the Delivery Truck is shown in Figure 7.13.

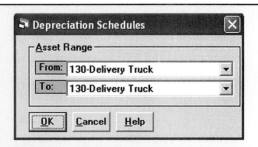

FIGURE 7.12

Depreciation Schedules Dialog Box

Sherwood Merchandise Co.
Depreciation Schedules
10/31/08

FIGURE 7.13

Depreciation Schedule for Vehicle

	Year	Annual Deprec.	Accum. Deprec.	Book Value
(130) Delivery Truck	2008	762.50	762.50	16,487.50
Acquired on 10/03/08	2009	3,050.00	3,812.50	13,437.50
Straight-Line	2010	3,050.00	6,862.50	10,387.50
Useful Life = 5	2011	3,050.00	9,912.50	7,337.50
Original Cost = 17,250.00	2012	3,050.00	12,962.50	4,287.50
Salvage Value = 20,000.00	2013	2,287.50	15,250.00	2,000.00

Select Depreciation Schedules from the Report Selection window.

When the Depreciation Schedules dialog box appears, select a range of assets from Z10 Copy Machine to Alpha-5 Fax Machine. The schedules for the new office equipment appear in Figure 7.14.

Sherwood Merchandise Co.
Depreciation Schedules
10/31/08

FIGURE 7.14

Depreciation Schedules for Office Equipment

	Year	Annual Deprec.	Accum. Deprec.	Book Value
(250) Z10 Copy Machine	2008	299.50	299.50	2,695.50
Acquired on 10/03/08	2009	1,078.20	1,377.70	1,617.30
Double Declining-Balance	2010	646.92	2,024.62	970.38
Useful Life = 5	2011	388.15	2,412.77	582.23
Original Cost = 2,995.00	2012	232.89	2,645.66	349.34
Salvage Value = 335.00	2013	14.34	2,660.00	335.00
(260) File Server	2008	418.50	418.50	3,766.50
Acquired on 10/17/08	2009	1,506.60	1,925.10	2,259.90
Double Declining-Balance	2010	903.96	2,829.06	1,355.94
Useful Life = 5	2011	542.38	3,371.44	813.56
Original Cost = 4,185.00	2012	313.56	3,685.00	500.00
Salvage Value = 500.00				

(continued)

FIGURE 7.14

(Concluded)

(270) GX10 Laser Printer	2008	218.95	218.95	1,970.55
Acquired on 10/17/08	2009	788.22	1,007.17	1,182.33
Double Declining-Balance	2010	472.93	1,480.10	709.40
Useful Life = 5	2011	283.76	1,763.86	425.64
Original Cost = 2,189.50	2012	75.64	1,839.50	350.00
Salvage Value = 350.00				
(280) Alpha-5 Fax Machine	2008	779.80	779.80	3,119.20
Acquired on 10/21/08	2009	1,247.68	2,027.48	1,871.52
MACRS	2010	748.61	2,776.09	1,122.91
Useful Life = 5	2011	449.16	3,225.25	673.75
Original Cost = 3,899.00	2012	449.16	3,674.41	224.59
Salvage Value = 400.00	2013	224.59	3,899.00	0.00

Select Depreciation Schedules from the Report Selection window.

When the Depreciation Schedules dialog box appears, select a range of assets from Storage Cabinet to Security Vault to display schedules for the new office furniture. The schedules for the new office furniture appear in Figure 7.15.

FIGURE 7.15

Depreciation Schedules for Office Furniture

Sherwood Merchandise Co.
Depreciation Schedules
10/31/08

	Year	Annual Deprec.	Accum. Deprec.	Book Value
(340) Storage Cabinet	2008	53.38	53.38	2,306.62
Acquired on 10/09/08	2009	213.50	266.88	2,093.12
Straight-Line	2010	213.50	480.38	1,879.62
Useful Life = 10	2011	213.50	693.88	1,666.12
Original Cost = 2,360.00	2012	213.50	907.38	1,452.62
Salvage Value = 225.00	2013	213.50	1,120.88	1,239.12
	2014	213.50	1,334.38	1,025.62
	2015	213.50	1,547.88	812.12
	2016	213.50	1,761.38	598.62
	2017	213.50	1,974.88	385.12
	2018	160.12	2,135.00	225.00
(350) Office Desk	2008	56.14	56.14	1,438.86
Acquired on 10/14/08	2009	218.93	275.07	1,219.93
Sum-of-the-Years-Digits	2010	196.48	471.55	1,023.45
Useful Life = 10	2011	174.03	645.58	849.42
Original Cost = 1,495.00	2012	151.57	797.15	697.85
Salvage Value = 260.00	2013	129.12	926.27	568.73
	2014	106.65	1,032.92	462.08
	2015	84.20	1,117.12	377.88
	2016	61.75	1,178.87	316.13
	2017	39.29	1,218.16	276.84
	2018	16.84	1,235.00	260.00
(360) Security Vault	2008	131.55	131.55	5,843.45
Acquired on 10/27/08	2009	519.61	651.16	5,323.84
Sum-of-the-Years-Digits	2010	493.30	1,144.46	4,830.54

(continued)

Useful Life = 20	2011	467.00	1,611.46	4,363.54
Original Cost = 5,975.00	2012	440.69	2,052.15	3,922.85
Salvage Value = 450.00	2013	414.37	2,466.52	3,508.48
	2014	388.06	2,854.58	3,120.42
	2015	361.76	3,216.34	2,758.66
	2016	335.45	3,551.79	2,423.21
	2017	309.14	3,860.93	2,114.07
	2018	282.82	4,143.75	1,831.25
	2019	256.52	4,400.27	1,574.73
	2020	230.21	4,630.48	1,344.52
	2021	203.90	4,834.38	1,140.62
	2022	177.59	5,011.97	963.03
	2023	151.28	5,163.25	811.75
	2024	124.97	5,288.22	686.78
	2025	98.66	5,386.88	588.12
	2026	72.35	5,459.23	515.77
	2027	46.04	5,505.27	469.73
	2028	19.73	5,525.00	450.00

FIGURE 7.15

(Concluded)

12 Display a trial balance.

The trial balance is shown in Figure 7.16.

Sherwood Merchandise Co.
Trial Balance
10/31/08

FIGURE 7.16

Trial Balance

Acct. Number	Account Title	Debit	Credit
1110	Cash	52,541.49	
1120	Accounts Receivable	61,988.54	
1130	Merchandise Inventory	133,300.00	
1140	Prepaid Insurance	3,642.30	
1150	Supplies	3,673.41	
1510	Vehicles	49,750.00	
1511	Accum. Depr. Vehicles		4,498.04
1520	Office Equipment	78,538.50	
1521	Accum. Depr. Office Eqpt.		5,032.08
1530	Office Furniture	21,310.00	
1531	Accum. Depr. Office Furn.		855.46
2110	Accounts Payable		46,736.17
2120	Sales Tax Payable		483.32
2510	Note Payable		30,309.00
3110	Emily Madigan, Capital		306,050.60
3120	Emily Madigan, Drawing	15,600.00	
3130	Income Summary	4,093.20	
4110	Sales		323,415.28
4111	Sales Returns & Allow.	5,728.43	
4112	Sales Discounts	3,751.44	
5110	Cost of Merchandise Sold	209,940.29	
6110	Sales Salary Expense	20,580.78	

(continued)

FIGURE 7.16

(Concluded)

6120	Advertising Expense	12,215.50	
6125	Delivery Expense	385.00	
6130	Depr. Expense Vehicles	6,372.15	
6140	Supplies Expense	1,657.51	
6150	Misc. Selling Expense	570.00	
6510	Rent Expense	3,603.00	
6520	Depr. Expense Off. Eqpt.	6,000.50	
6525	Depr. Expense Off. Furn.	1,006.60	
6530	Misc. General Expense	332.20	
6540	Office Salary Expense	11,977.74	
6550	Insurance Expense	332.00	
6560	Telephone Expense	1,390.46	
6570	Heating & Lighting Exp.	1,921.33	
6580	Legal & Prof. Fees Exp.	3,925.00	
7110	Interest Income		189.10
8110	Interest Expense	1,441.68	
	Totals	717,569.05	717,569.05

End-of-Month Activities

The depreciation adjusting entries are automatically generated from the fixed assets information. The rest of the adjusting entries must be entered separately into the computer. Sherwood Merchandise Co., recorded the following adjustment data for October. The completed adjusting entries are shown in Figure 7.17 as they would appear when entered and posted in the general journal.

> Insurance expired during October $330.00
> Inventory of supplies on October 31 .... $2,680.00

1 **Enter the adjusting entries.**

The adjusting entries are shown in Figure 7.17.

FIGURE 7.17

*General Journal
(Adjusting Entries)*

Date	Refer.	Account	Debit	Credit	Vendor/Customer
10/31/08	Adj.Ent.	6550 Insurance Expense	330.00		
		1140 Prepaid Insurance		330.00	
10/31/08	Adj.Ent.	6140 Supplies Expense	993.41		
		1150 Supplies		993.41	

2 **Generate and post the depreciation adjusting entries.**

Click the Assets navigation button, and then click on the Depreciation Adjusting Entries menu button. Click Yes when asked if you want to generate the monthly depreciation adjusting entries. When the Depreciation Adjusting Entries dialog box appears, click on the Post button. The journal entry will reappear, posted, in the general journal. The depreciation adjusting entries are shown in Figure 7.18.

NOTE If your adjusting entries do not match Figure 7.18, check your fixed assets report for typing errors and make the necessary corrections. Return to the General Journal window, delete the incorrect depreciation adjusting entries (if posted), and generate new adjusting entries.

Acct. #	Account Title	Debit	Credit
6130	Depr. Expense Vehicles	891.67	
6520	Depr. Expense Off. Eqpt.	1357.99	
6525	Depr. Expense Off. Furn.	231.93	
1511	Accum. Depr. Vehicles		891.67
1521	Accum. Depr. Office Eqpt.		1357.99
1531	Accum. Depr. Office Furn.		231.93

FIGURE 7.18

Depreciation Adjusting Entries

3   Display the adjusting entries.

Click the Gen. Leg. navigation button, and then click on the Journal Reports menu button. With the Journals option and the General Journal report already selected, click OK. When the Journal Report Selection window appears, choose Customize Journal Report and then select a date range of October 31, 2008 through October 31, 2008. The report appears in Figure 7.19.

Sherwood Merchandise Co.
General Journal
10/31/08

Date	Refer.	Acct.	Title	Debit	Credit
10/31	Adj.Ent.	6550	Insurance Expense	330.00	
10/31	Adj.Ent.	1140	Prepaid Insurance		330.00
10/31	Adj.Ent.	6140	Supplies Expense	993.41	
10/31	Adj.Ent.	1150	Supplies		993.41
10/31	Dep.Adj.	6130	Depr. Expense Vehicles	891.67	
10/31	Dep.Adj.	6520	Depr. Expense Off. Eqpt.	1,357.99	
10/31	Dep.Adj.	6525	Depr. Expense Off. Furn.	231.93	
10/31	Dep.Adj.	1511	Accum. Depr. Vehicles		891.67
10/31	Dep.Adj.	1521	Accum. Depr. Office Eqpt.		1,357.99
10/31	Dep.Adj.	1531	Accum. Depr. Office Furn.		231.93
			Totals	3,805.00	3,805.00

FIGURE 7.19

General Journal Report (Adjusting Entries)

4   Check your work.

Click Check on the toolbar. If errors appear, use the Explorer and other error correction features of the software to correct your errors.

5   Display the income statement.

The income statement is shown in Figure 7.20.

FIGURE 7.20

Income Statement

Sherwood Merchandise Co.
Income Statement
For Period Ended 10/31/08

	Monthly Amount	Monthly Percent	Yearly Amount	Yearly Percent
Operating Revenue				
Sales	58,986.00	100.79	323,415.28	103.02
Sales Returns & Allow.			−5,728.43	−1.82
Sales Discounts	−460.10	−0.79	−3,751.44	−1.20
Total Operating Revenue	58,525.90	100.00	313,935.41	100.00
Cost				
Cost of Merchandise Sold	37,863.00	64.69	209,940.29	66.87
Total Cost	37,863.00	64.69	209,940.29	66.87
Gross Profit	20,662.90	35.31	103,995.12	33.13
Operating Expenses				
Sales Salary Expense	3,760.00	6.42	20,580.78	6.56
Advertising Expense	1,620.00	2.77	12,215.50	3.89
Delivery Expense	185.00	0.32	385.00	0.12
Depr. Expense Vehicles	891.67	1.52	7,263.82	2.31
Supplies Expense	993.41	1.70	2,650.92	0.84
Misc. Selling Expense	90.00	0.15	570.00	0.18
Total Selling Expenses	7,540.08	12.88	43,666.02	13.91
Rent Expense	930.00	1.59	3,603.00	1.15
Depr. Expense Off. Eqpt.	1,357.99	2.32	7,358.49	2.34
Depr. Expense Off. Furn.	231.93	0.40	1,238.53	0.39
Misc. General Expense	25.00	0.04	332.20	0.11
Office Salary Expense	2,915.00	4.98	11,977.74	3.82
Insurance Expense	330.00	0.56	662.00	0.21
Telephone Expense	496.00	0.85	1,390.46	0.44
Heating & Lighting Exp.	545.00	0.93	1,921.33	0.61
Legal & Prof. Fees Exp.	425.00	0.73	3,925.00	1.25
Total Administrative Expense	7,255.92	12.40	32,408.75	10.32
Total Operating Expenses	14,796.00	25.28	76,074.77	24.23
Net Income from Operations	5,866.90	10.02	27,920.35	8.89
Other Revenue				
Interest Income	86.50	0.15	189.10	0.06
Other Expense				
Interest Expense	99.35	0.17	1,441.68	0.46
Net Income	5,854.05	10.00	26,667.77	8.49

6   Display the statement of owner's equity.

The statement of owner's equity is shown in Figure 7.21.

Sherwood Merchandise Co. **Statement of Owner's Equity** **For Period Ended 10/31/08**		

FIGURE 7.21

Statement of Owner's Equity

Emily Madigan, Capital (Beg. of Period)	306,050.60
Emily Madigan, Drawing	−15,600.00
Net Income	22,574.57
Emily Madigan, Capital (End of Period)	313,025.17

7   Display the balance sheet.

The balance sheet is shown in Figure 7.22.

Sherwood Merchandise Co.
Balance Sheet
10/31/08

FIGURE 7.22

Balance Sheet

Assets		
Cash	52,541.49	
Accounts Receivable	61,988.54	
Merchandise Inventory	133,300.00	
Prepaid Insurance	3,312.30	
Supplies	2,680.00	
Total Current Assets	253,822.33	
Vehicles	49,750.00	
Accum. Depr. Vehicles	−5,389.71	
Office Equipment	78,538.50	
Accum. Depr. Office Eqpt.	−6,390.07	
Office Furniture	21,310.00	
Accum. Depr. Office Furn.	−1,087.39	
Total Plant Assets	136,731.33	
Total Assets		390,553.66
Liabilities		
Accounts Payable	46,736.17	
Sales Tax Payable	483.32	
Total Current Liabilities	47,219.49	
Note Payable	30,309.00	
Total Long Term Liabilities	30,309.00	
Total Liabilities		77,528.49
Owner's Equity		
Emily Madigan, Capital	306,050.60	
Emily Madigan, Drawing	−15,600.00	
Net Income	22,574.57	
Total Owner's Equity		313,025.17
Total Liabilities & Equity		390,553.66

8   **Generate Depreciation Comparison graphs for the Delivery Truck and Security Vault.**

Click Graphs on the toolbar button. Click on Depreciation Compare. When the select Asset list box appears (as shown in Figure 7.23), select Delivery Truck, and then click OK. Repeat this procedure to generate the comparison graph for the Security Vault. The generated graphs for the Delivery Truck and Security Vault are illustrated in Figures 7.24(a) and (b), respectively.

FIGURE 7.23

Select Asset List Box

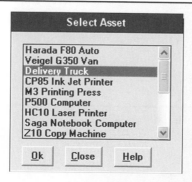

FIGURE 7.24(A)

Delivery Truck Depreciation Comparison Graph

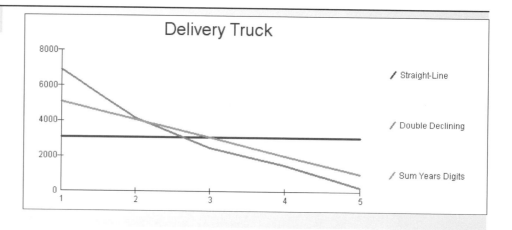

FIGURE 7.24(B)

Security Vault Depreciation Comparison Graph

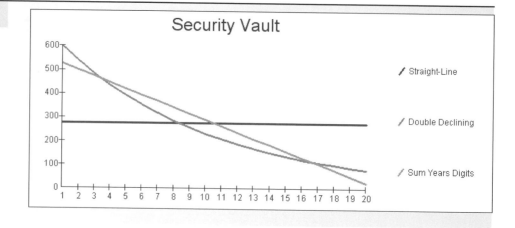

9   **Save the data to your disk.**

10   **Optional spreadsheet integration activity.**

Not all depreciation methods depreciate an asset by the same amount each year. Therefore, the manager of the accounting department wants you to use a spreadsheet template to prepare comparison information. You are to generate depreciation schedules for a given asset using each of the four depreciation methods discussed in this chapter. As each schedule is displayed, it must be copied and pasted into a spreadsheet template to obtain the comparison information.

a.   Display and copy the depreciation schedule for asset 130-Delivery Truck, to the clipboard in spreadsheet format.

b.   Start your spreadsheet software and load template file IA6 Spreadsheet 07-S.

c.   Select cell A1 as the current cell and paste the Delivery Truck depreciation schedule into the spreadsheet.

d.   Copy the year from cells B10–B15 to cells B29–B34. Copy the Annual Depreciation from cells C10–C15 to the appropriate column (i.e., copy to cells C29–C34 if the depreciation schedule uses the straight-line method, copy to cells D29–D34 if the double declining-balance method is used, and so on).

e.   Return to *Integrated Accounting* 6e, click Accts. on the toolbar, and change the Depreciation Method for 130 Delivery Truck. Repeat steps c and d for each of the remaining depreciation methods.

f.   Print the comparison report (cells A22–F34). The completed report is shown in Figure 7.25.

g.   Save the spreadsheet data to your disk with a file name of 07-S Your Name. Do *not* save the changed *Integrated Accounting* 6e data.

Sherwood Merchandise Co. Depreciation Schedules As Of 10/31/08					
	Year	SL Annual Deprec.	DDB Annual Deprec.	SYD Annual Deprec.	MACRS Annual Deprec.
(130) Delivery Truck	2008	$762.50	$1,725.00	$1,270.83	$3,450.00
Acquired on 10/03/08	2009	$3,050.00	$6,210.00	$4,829.17	$5,520.00
Depreciation Methods	2010	$3,050.00	$3,726.00	$3,812.50	$3,312.00
Useful Life = 5	2011	$3,050.00	$2,235.60	$2,795.83	$1,987.20
Original Cost = 17,250.00	2012	$3,050.00	$1,341.36	$1,779.17	$1,987.20
Salvage Value = 2,000.00	2013	$2,287.50	$12.04	$762.50	$993.60

FIGURE 7.25

Spreadsheet Comparison Report

11   Optional word processing integration activity.

Prepare a memorandum to the manager of the accounting department that shows depreciation comparison information from the spreadsheet activity.

a. Start your word processing software application and create a new document. (If your software has templates, load a memorandum format.)

b. Enter the memorandum heading information as shown in Figure 7.26. Copy and paste the spreadsheet comparison report (cells A26–F34) into the body of the memorandum.

c. Print the memorandum.

d. Save the memorandum to your disk with a file name of 07-S Your Name.

e. End your word processing and spreadsheet sessions.

FIGURE 7.26

Depreciation Comparison Memorandum

MEMORANDUM

TO: Manager, Accounting Department

FROM: Your name

DATE: (Today's Date)

SUBJECT: Depreciation Schedule Comparisons

As per your request, the following table depicts a comparison of the straight-line, double declining-balance, sum-of-the-years-digits, and MACRS methods of depreciation for Asset No. 130-Delivery Truck.

	Year	SL Annual Deprec.	DDB Annual Deprec.	SYD Annual Deprec.	MACRS Annual Deprec.
(130) Delivery Truck	2008	$762.50	$1,725.00	$1,270.83	$3,450.00
Acquired on 10/03/08	2009	$3,050.00	$6,210.00	$4,829.17	$5,520.00
Depreciation Methods	2010	$3,050.00	$3,726.00	$3,812.50	$3,312.00
Useful Life = 5	2011	$3,050.00	$2,235.60	$2,795.83	$1,987.20
Original Cost = 17,250.00	2012	$3,050.00	$1,341.36	$1,779.17	$1,987.20
Salvage Value = 2,000.00	2013	$2,287.50	$12.04	$762.50	$993.60

If you have access to the Internet, use your browser to find the current year's IRS Depreciation and Amortization Form No. 4562. *Hint:* Use Depreciation as a search argument. Print the form and be sure to indicate the source, including the URL (Web address), of where you found it.

INTERNET ACTIVITY

12   End the *Integrated Accounting* 6e session (do not save the data).

Chapter 7 Student Exercises

NAME

I True/False

Directions   *If the statement is true, write T in the space provided. If the statement is false, write F in the space provided.*

1.____ Under the sum-of-the-years-digits depreciation method, the same amount of depreciation is recorded for each accounting period over the useful life of the asset.

2.____ The depreciation rate for the double declining-balance method is twice the straight-line rate.

3.____ Under the MACRS depreciation method, office furniture is included in the 7-year class of assets.

4.____ When the MACRS method is used, any salvage value is disregarded.

5.____ When the straight-line method is used, the salvage value is disregarded.

6.____ Under the double declining-balance method, the salvage value is ignored in the calculations; however, the asset is not depreciated below the salvage value.

7.____ Under all methods except MACRS, an asset purchased in any month other than January has first-year and last-year depreciation amounts that are prorated from the month the asset was purchased.

8.____ Under MACRS, all assets are assumed to have been placed into service on January 1, regardless of when they were actually purchased.

9.____ The computer can generate the depreciation adjusting entries from the fixed assets information.

10.____ Depreciation adjusting entries do not need to be posted.

II Questions

Directions   *Write the answers to the following questions in the space provided.*

1. What is the fraction used to calculate the first year's depreciation under the sum-of-the-years-digits method for an asset with a useful life of 6 years? _____

    _____

2. What types of assets are included in the 5-year class for MACRS? _____

    _____

3. Using the straight-line method, what is the amount of depreciation for the first year for an asset purchased on January 1 for $3,000, with a useful life of 5 years, and with a salvage value of $200.00? _____

    _____

4. What are three uses of the information provided by the fixed assets system? _____

   _____

5. What report must be selected in order to obtain a listing of the depreciation adjusting entries generated and posted by the computer? _____

   _____

Problem 7-A

In this problem, you will process transactions involving fixed assets for Sherwood Merchandise Co., for the month of November 2008. In addition, you will complete the monthly accounting cycle. The monthly transactions not related to fixed assets have already been entered and posted into the computer and are included in the opening balance file. Answer audit questions 7-A on page 317 as you complete this problem. Display reports as necessary to answer the questions. Remember to click Info. on the toolbar for helpful check figures to audit your work.

1   Start *Integrated Accounting* 6e.

2   Load the opening balances template file, IA6 Problem 07-A.

3   Enter your name in the Your Name text box and click OK.

4   Save the data to your disk as 07-A Your Name.

5   Delete Asset No. 200, CP85 Ink Jet Printer.

6   Change the name of Asset No. 280 to Facsimile Machine.

7   Enter the fixed asset data in Account Maintenance.

Fixed Assets Transactions

Nov. 04, 2008   Purchased a Binding Machine for $495.95; asset number, 215; depreciation method, double declining-balance; useful life, 6 years; salvage value, $50.00; accumulated depreciation, account number 1521; depreciation expense, account number 6520.

Nov. 10, 2008   Purchased a K6 Telephone System for $5,175.00; asset number, 290; depreciation method, sum-of-the-years-digits; useful life, 7 years; salvage value, $500.00; accumulated depreciation, account number 1521; depreciation expense, account number 6520.

Nov. 12, 2008   Purchased a File Cabinet for $385.00; asset number, 370; depreciation method, MACRS; useful life, 7 years; salvage value, $45.00; accumulated depreciation, account number 1531; depreciation expense, account number 6525.

Nov. 14, 2008   Purchased Shelving for $615.50; asset number 380; depreciation method, straight-line; useful life, 10 years; salvage value, $75.00; accumulated depreciation, account number 1531; depreciation expense, account number 6525.

Nov. 20, 2008   Purchased a Pickup Truck for $11,995.00; asset number, 140; depreciation method, straight-line; useful life, 5 years; salvage value, $1,175.00; accumulated depreciation, account number 1511; depreciation expense, account number 6130.

Nov. 25, 2008   Purchased a HC-2530 Computer for $2,865.00; asset number, 225; depreciation method, double declining-balance; useful life, 5 years; salvage value, $250.00; accumulated depreciation, account number 1521; depreciation expense, account number 6520.

8 **Use the general journal to enter and post the following assets to the general ledger.**

Nov. 01, 2008   Discarded asset no. 200, CP85 Ink Jet Printer (Office Equipment) bought in January, 2002: cost, $375.00; total accumulated depreciation recorded to December 31, 2006, $375.00. Memo No. 113.

Nov. 04, 2008   Paid cash for Binding Machine, $495.95; Check No. 3839.

Nov. 10, 2008   Paid cash for K6 Telephone System, $5,175.00; Check No. 3840.

Nov. 12, 2008   Paid cash for File Cabinet, $385.00; Check No. 3841.

Nov. 14, 2008   Paid cash for Shelving, $615.50; Check No. 3842.

Nov. 20, 2008   Paid cash for Pickup Truck, $11,995.00; Check No. 3843.

Nov. 25, 2008   Paid cash for HC-2530 Computer, $2,865.00; Check No. 3844.

9 **Display a General Journal report.**

(Make sure the date on the Report Selection menu is set to 11/30/08.)

10 **Display a fixed assets list.**

11 **Display a depreciation schedule for each of the new assets purchased in November.**

12 **Display the trial balance.**

End-of-Month Activities

The depreciation adjusting entries are automatically generated from the fixed assets information. The rest of the adjusting entries must be entered separately into the computer. Sherwood Merchandise Co., had the following adjustment data for November.

Insurance expired during November...................$335.00
Inventory of supplies on November 30.............$2,045.50

1 **Enter the adjusting entries.**

2 **Generate and post the depreciation adjusting entries.**

3 **Display the adjusting entries (use 11/30/08 as both the start and end dates).**

4 **Use Check on the toolbar to check your work.**

5 **Display the income statement.**

6 **Display the statement of owner's equity.**

7 **Display the balance sheet.**

8   **Generate Depreciation Comparison graphs for the K6 Telephone System and the Pickup Truck.**

9   **Save your data to disk.**

10   **Optional spreadsheet integration activity.**

Generate depreciation schedules for asset 140, Pickup Truck, using each of the four depreciation methods discussed in this chapter. Copy and paste each schedule into a spreadsheet template to obtain comparison information.

a. Display and copy the depreciation schedule for asset 140-Pickup Truck, to the clipboard in spreadsheet format.

b. Start your spreadsheet software and load template file IA6 Spreadsheet 07-S.

c. Select cell A1 as the current cell and paste the Pickup Truck depreciation schedule into the spreadsheet.

d. Copy the year from cells B10–B15 to cells B29–B34. Copy the annual depreciation from cells C10–C15 to the appropriate column (i.e., copy to cells C29–C34 if the depreciation schedule uses the straight-line method, copy to cells D29–D34 if the double declining-balance method is used, and so on).

e. Return to *Integrated Accounting* 6e, click Accts. on the toolbar, and change the depreciation method for asset 140 Pickup Truck. Repeat steps c and d for each of the remaining depreciation methods.

f. Print the comparison report (cells A22–F34).

g. Save the spreadsheet data to your disk with a file name of 07-A Your Name. Do *not* save the changed *Integrated Accounting* 6e data.

11   **Optional word processing integration activity.**

Prepare a memorandum to the manager of the accounting department that shows depreciation comparison information from the preceding spreadsheet activity.

a. Start your word processing software application and create a new document. (If your software has templates, load a memorandum format.)

b. Enter the memorandum heading information using Figure 7.26 as a guide. Copy and paste the spreadsheet comparison report (cells A26–F34) into the body of the memorandum.

c. Print the memorandum.

d. Save the memorandum to your disk with a file name of 07-A Your Name.

e. End your word processing and spreadsheet sessions.

If you have access to the Internet, use your browser to find fixed asset management software. *Hint:* Use Depreciation as a search argument. Report your findings. Be sure to indicate the sources, including the URLs (Web addresses) of your reported findings.

12 **End the *Integrated Accounting* 6e session. (Do not save the data.)**

Audit Questions 7-A

NAME

Directions   *Write the answers to the following questions in the space provided.*

1.   What is the original cost of asset number 350 (office desk) as shown on the fixed assets list?   _____

_____

2.   What is the salvage value of asset number 280 (Facsimile Machine) as shown on the fixed assets list?   _____

_____

3.   What is the total value of all assets based on original costs as shown on the fixed assets list?

_____

4.   On what date was the K6 Telephone System acquired?   _____

_____

5.   Refer to the depreciation schedule for asset number 215 (Binding Machine). What is the annual depreciation calculated for 2012?   _____

_____

6.   Refer to the depreciation schedule for asset number 380 (Shelving). What is the book value at the end of 2014?   _____

_____

7.   What are the depreciation journal entries on November 30, 2008, for each of the following accounts?

	Debit	Credit
Depr. Expense Vehicles	_____	_____
Accum. Depr. Vehicles	_____	_____
Depr. Expense Off. Eqpt.	_____	_____
Accum. Depr. Office Eqpt.	_____	_____
Depr. Expense Off. Furn.	_____	_____
Accum. Depr. Office Furn.	_____	_____

8.   What is the amount of net income for the month as shown on the income statement?

_____

9.   What is the net income for the year as shown on the income statement expressed as a percentage?   _____

_____

10.   What is the amount of total owner's equity at the end of the period?   _____

_____

11.   What is the amount of total assets as shown on the balance sheet?   _____

_____

12.   Refer to the depreciation comparison graph for the K6 Telephone System. Which depreciation method yields the highest amount of depreciation during the first year?   _____

_____

13.   Refer to the depreciation comparison graph for the Pickup Truck. Which depreciation method yields the lowest amount of depreciation in the last year?   _____

_____

Problem 7-B

In this problem, you will process transactions involving fixed assets for Sherwood Merchandise Co., for the month of November 2008. In addition, you will complete the monthly accounting cycle. The monthly transactions not related to fixed assets have already been entered and posted into the computer and are included in the opening balance file. Answer audit questions 7-B on page 323 as you complete this problem.

1 Start *Integrated Accounting* 6e.

2 Load the opening balances template file, IA6 Problem 07-B.

3 Enter your name in the Your Name text box and click OK.

4 Save the data to your disk as 07-B Your Name.

5 Delete Asset No. 200, CP85 Ink Jet Printer.

6 Change the name of Asset No. 270 to CB10 Laser Printer.

7 Enter the fixed asset data in Account Maintenance.

Fixed Assets Transactions

Nov. 04, 2008 — Purchased a Typesetting Machine for $1,035.00; asset number, 215; depreciation method, sum-of-the-years-digits; useful life, 6 years; salvage value, $50.00; accumulated depreciation, account number 1521; depreciation expense, account number 6520.

Nov. 10, 2008 — Purchased a Voice Mail System for $4,775.50; asset number, 290; depreciation method, double declining-balance; useful life, 7 years; salvage value, $475.00; accumulated depreciation, account number 1521; depreciation expense, account number 6520.

Nov. 12, 2008 — Purchased a Bookshelf for $489.00; asset number, 370; depreciation method, MACRS; useful life, 7 years; salvage value, $50.00; accumulated depreciation, account number 1531; depreciation expense, account number 6525.

Nov. 14, 2008 — Purchased Glass Shelving for $625.00; asset number 380; depreciation method, straight-line; useful life, 10 years; salvage value, $65.00; accumulated depreciation, account number 1531; depreciation expense, account number 6525.

Nov. 20, 2008 — Purchased a Utility Vehicle for $12,350.00; asset number, 140; depreciation method, straight-line; useful life, 5 years; salvage value, $1,250.00; accumulated depreciation, account number 1511; depreciation expense, account number 6130.

Nov. 25, 2008 — Purchased a Web Site Server for $3,189.00; asset number, 225; depreciation method, double declining-balance; useful life, 5 years; salvage value, $245.00; accumulated depreciation, account number 1521; depreciation expense, account number 6520.

8 **Use the general journal to enter and post the following assets to the general ledger.**

Nov. 01, 2008   Discarded asset no. 200, CP85 Ink Jet Printer (Office Equipment) bought in January, 2002: cost, $375.00; total accumulated depreciation recorded to December 31, 2006, $375.00. Memo No. 113.

Nov. 04, 2008   Paid cash for Typesetting Machine, $1,035.00; Check No. 3839.

Nov. 10, 2008   Paid cash for Voice Mail System, $4,775.50; Check No. 3840.

Nov. 12, 2008   Paid cash for Bookshelf, $489.00; Check No. 3841.

Nov. 14, 2008   Paid cash for Glass Shelving, $625.00; Check No. 3842.

Nov. 20, 2008   Paid cash for Utility Vehicle, $12,350.00; Check No. 3843.

Nov. 25, 2008   Paid cash for Web Site Server, $3,189.00; Check No. 3844.

9 **Display a General Journal report.**

(Make sure the date on the Report Selection menu is set to 11/30/08.)

10 **Display a fixed assets list.**

11 **Display a depreciation schedule for each of the new assets purchased in November.**

12 **Display the trial balance.**

End-of-Month Activities

The depreciation adjusting entries are automatically generated from the fixed assets information. The rest of the adjusting entries must be entered separately into the computer. Sherwood Merchandise Co., had the following adjustment data for November.

Insurance expired during November...................$340.00
Inventory of supplies on November 30............$1,990.60

1 **Enter the adjusting entries.**

2 **Generate and post the depreciation adjusting entries.**

3 **Display the adjusting entries (use 11/30/08 as both the Start and End dates).**

4 **Display the income statement.**

5 **Display the statement of owner's equity.**

6 **Display the balance sheet.**

7 **Generate Depreciation Comparison graphs for the Bookshelf and the Web Site Server.**

8   **Save your data to disk.**

9   **Optional spreadsheet integration activity.**

Generate depreciation schedules for asset 225-Web Site Server, using each of the four depreciation methods discussed in this chapter. Copy and paste each schedule into a spreadsheet template to obtain comparison information.

a. Display and copy the depreciation schedule for asset 225-Web Site Server, to the clipboard in spreadsheet format.

b. Start your spreadsheet software and load template file IA6 Spreadsheet 07-S.

c. Select cell A1 as the current cell and paste the Web Site Server depreciation schedule into the spreadsheet.

d. Copy the Year from cells B10–B15 to cells B29–B34. Copy the annual depreciation from cells C10–C15 to the appropriate column (i.e., copy to cells C29–C34 if the depreciation schedule uses the straight-line method, copy to cells D29–D34 if the double declining-balance method is used, and so on).

e. Return to *Integrated Accounting* 6e, click on Accts. on the toolbar, and change the Depreciation Method for asset 225-Web Site Server. Repeat steps c and d for each of the remaining depreciation methods.

f. Print the comparison report (cells A22–F34).

g. Save the spreadsheet data to your disk with a file name of 07-B Your Name. Do *not* save the changed *Integrated Accounting* 6e data.

10   **Optional word processing integration activity.**

Prepare a memorandum to the manager of the accounting department that shows depreciation comparison information from the preceding spreadsheet activity.

a. Start your word processing software application and create a new document. (If your software has templates, load a memorandum format.)

b. Enter the memorandum heading information using Figure 7.26 as a guide. Copy and paste the spreadsheet comparison report (cells A26–F34) into the body of the memorandum.

c. Print the memorandum.

d. Save the memorandum to your disk with a file name of 07-B Your Name.

e. End your word processing and spreadsheet sessions.

If you have access to the Internet, use your browser to find financial wizard application software that includes various depreciation method calculations. *Hint:* Use Depreciation as a search argument. Report your findings. Be sure to indicate the sources, including the URLs (Web addresses), of your reported findings.

11 **End the *Integrated Accounting* 6e session. (Do not save the data.)**

Audit Questions 7-B

NAME

Directions   *Write the answers to the following question in the space provided.*

1.   What is the original cost of asset number 120 (Veigel G350 Van) as shown on the fixed assets list? _____

   _____

2.   What is the salvage value of asset number 340 (Storage Cabinet) as shown on the fixed assets list? _____

   _____

3.   What is the total value of all assets based on original costs as shown on the fixed assets list?

   _____

4.   On what date was the Voice Mail System acquired? _____

   _____

5.   Refer to the depreciation schedule for asset number 215 (Typesetting Machine). What is the annual depreciation calculated for 2012? _____

   _____

6   Refer to the depreciation schedule for asset number 290 (Voice Mail System). What is the book value at the end of 2012? _____

   _____

7.   What are the depreciation journal entries on November 30, 2008, for each of the following accounts?

	Debit	Credit
Depr. Expense Vehicles	_____	_____
Accum. Depr. Vehicles	_____	_____
Depr. Expense Off. Eqpt.	_____	_____
Accum. Depr. Office Eqpt.	_____	_____
Depr. Expense Off. Furn.	_____	_____
Accum. Depr. Office Furn.	_____	_____

8.   What is the amount of gross profit for the month as shown on the income statement?

   _____

9.   What are the total operating expenses for the year as shown on the income statement expressed as a percentage? _____

   _____

10.   What is the amount of total owner's equity at the end of the period?   _____

_____

11.   What is the amount of total liabilities as shown on the balance sheet?   _____

_____

12.   Refer to the depreciation comparison graph for the Bookshelf. Which depreciation method yields the greatest amount of depreciation during the first year?   _____

_____

13   Refer to the depreciation comparison graph for the Web Site Server. Which depreciation method yields the greatest amount of depreciation in the last year?   _____

_____

Payroll

Upon completion of this chapter, you will be able to:

- Identify the components and procedures of a computerized payroll system.

- Add, change, and delete employees from the payroll.

- Enter and correct payroll transactions.

- Display payroll reports.

- Generate and post the payroll journal entries.

Introduction

In a **computerized payroll system**, the computer stores data such as an employee's name, address, Social Security number, marital status, number of withholding allowances, pay rate, and voluntary deductions. At the end of each pay period, all payroll transaction data, such as gross pay and deductions, are entered into the computer. The computer can calculate the withholding taxes and create the resulting journal entries.

After entering the employee data, an employee list report verifies the accuracy of input data. A payroll report displays earnings and withholdings for the month, quarter, and year at any time. *Integrated Accounting* 6e can generate both the current payroll and employer's payroll tax expenses journal entries. The quarterly report is produced at the end of the quarter, whereas the W-2 statements of earnings and withholdings are provided at the end of the year.

The computer uses the payroll transactions dates to accumulate totals and process the end-of-quarter and end-of-year reports. Therefore, it is especially important that the correct payroll transaction dates be entered *each* pay period.

Employee Maintenance

Click on the Payroll navigation button and then the Maintain Employees menu button (or click Accts. on the toolbar) to open the Account Maintenance window. Click the Employees tab (if not already selected) and enter the maintenance data. Figure 8.1 shows the Employees tab containing employee data and gives a description of each data field.

New employees may be added by keying the data into the grid cell boxes and choosing the employee's marital status. When the focus moves to the marital status, choose Single or Married from the drop-down list or type the first letter of the desired marital status (S or M). Click on Add Employee or press Enter and the new employee will be inserted into the existing employee list in employee number sequence. Existing employee data may be changed by selecting the employee you wish to change, keying the correct data (or selecting a different marital status), and clicking the Change Employee button. (The Add Employee button changes to Change Employee when an existing employee has the focus.) An existing employee may be deleted by simply selecting the desired employee and clicking Delete.

NOTE You will not be allowed to delete an employee with cumulative earnings for the current year until after the end of the calendar year.

326

FIGURE 8.1

Employee Maintenance

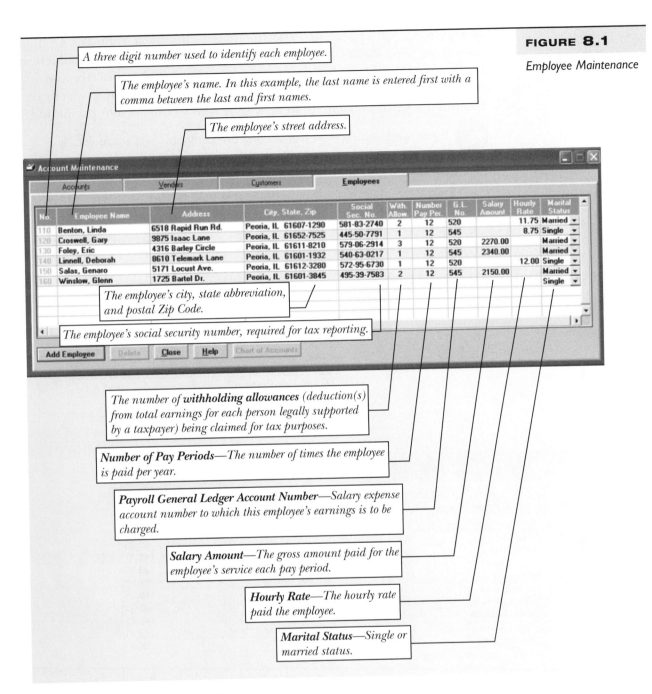

A three digit number used to identify each employee.

The employee's name. In this example, the last name is entered first with a comma between the last and first names.

The employee's street address.

The employee's city, state abbreviation, and postal Zip Code.

The employee's social security number, required for tax reporting.

*The number of **withholding allowances** (deduction(s) from total earnings for each person legally supported by a taxpayer) being claimed for tax purposes.*

***Number of Pay Periods**—The number of times the employee is paid per year.*

***Payroll General Ledger Account Number**—Salary expense account number to which this employee's earnings is to be charged.*

***Salary Amount**—The gross amount paid for the employee's service each pay period.*

***Hourly Rate**—The hourly rate paid the employee.*

***Marital Status**—Single or married status.*

Payroll Transactions

Employee payroll transaction data are entered into the Payroll tab of the Other Tasks window. Entering the payroll transactions identifies the employees to be paid for the current pay period and records the employee's pay-period transaction data. For each employee's payroll transaction, the payroll date, pay information, and employee deductions (if different from the previous pay period) are entered. The employee taxes can be either entered or automatically calculated by the computer. The payroll taxes for problems in this textbook will be automatically calculated by the computer.

Click on the Payroll navigation button and then the Pay Employees menu button (or Tasks on the toolbar), and the Other Tasks window will appear. Click the Payroll tab (if not already selected) and the screen shown in Figure 8.2 will appear. Click Deductions to display a Voluntary Deductions dialog box similar to that shown in Figure 8.3. A **voluntary deduction** is an amount withheld from the employee's pay at his or her option for items such as insurance or savings. This dialog box allows you to specify the voluntary deductions that are to be withheld from the current pay period.

 NOTE If you forget to click on Deductions, the computer will automatically display the Voluntary Deductions dialog box during entry of the first employee's data for the current pay period.

Deselect the deduction(s) that are *not* to be withheld from the current pay period by clicking on the appropriate check box to remove the checkmark. Only deductions with a check mark (✓) are withheld from the current pay period.

FIGURE 8.2

Payroll Tab

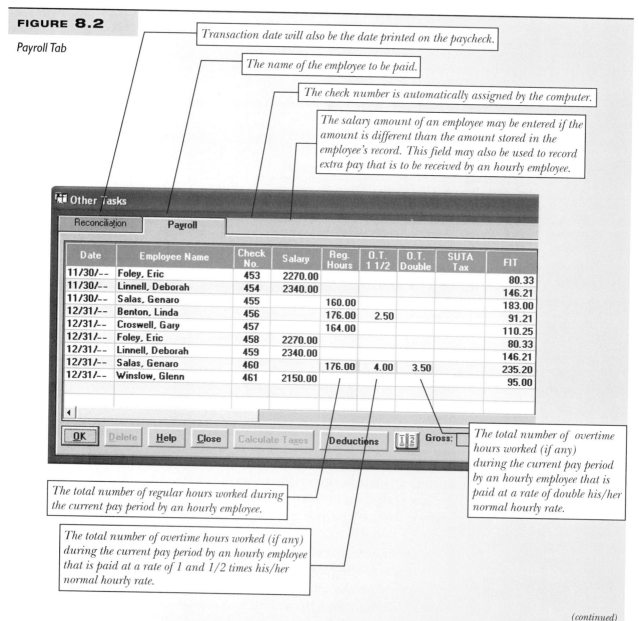

Transaction date will also be the date printed on the paycheck.

The name of the employee to be paid.

The check number is automatically assigned by the computer.

The salary amount of an employee may be entered if the amount is different than the amount stored in the employee's record. This field may also be used to record extra pay that is to be received by an hourly employee.

Other Tasks

Date	Employee Name	Check No.	Salary	Reg. Hours	O.T. 1 1/2	O.T. Double	SUTA Tax	FIT
11/30/--	Foley, Eric	453	2270.00					80.33
11/30/--	Linnell, Deborah	454	2340.00					146.21
11/30/--	Salas, Genaro	455		160.00				183.00
12/31/--	Benton, Linda	456		176.00	2.50			91.21
12/31/--	Croswell, Gary	457		164.00				110.25
12/31/--	Foley, Eric	458	2270.00					80.33
12/31/--	Linnell, Deborah	459	2340.00					146.21
12/31/--	Salas, Genaro	460		176.00	4.00	3.50		235.20
12/31/--	Winslow, Glenn	461	2150.00					95.00

OK **Delete** **Help** **Close** **Calculate Taxes** **Deductions** **Gross:**

The total number of regular hours worked during the current pay period by an hourly employee.

The total number of overtime hours worked (if any) during the current pay period by an hourly employee that is paid at a rate of 1 and 1/2 times his/her normal hourly rate.

The total number of overtime hours worked (if any) during the current pay period by an hourly employee that is paid at a rate of double his/her normal hourly rate.

(continued)

FIGURE **8.2**

(Concluded)

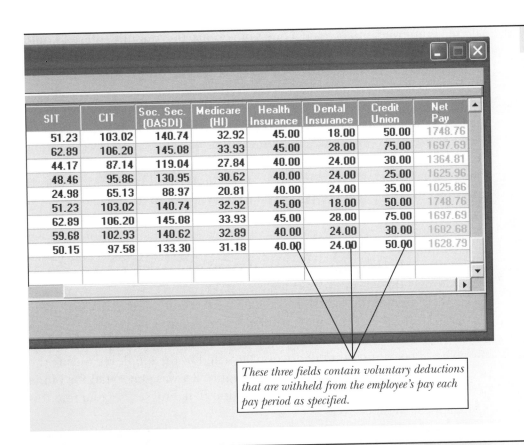

SIT	CIT	Soc. Sec. (OASDI)	Medicare (HI)	Health Insurance	Dental Insurance	Credit Union	Net Pay
51.23	103.02	140.74	32.92	45.00	18.00	50.00	1748.76
62.89	106.20	145.08	33.93	45.00	28.00	75.00	1697.69
44.17	87.14	119.04	27.84	40.00	24.00	30.00	1364.81
48.46	95.86	130.95	30.62	40.00	24.00	25.00	1625.96
24.98	65.13	88.97	20.81	40.00	24.00	35.00	1025.86
51.23	103.02	140.74	32.92	45.00	18.00	50.00	1748.76
62.89	106.20	145.08	33.93	45.00	28.00	75.00	1697.69
59.68	102.93	140.62	32.89	40.00	24.00	30.00	1602.68
50.15	97.58	133.30	31.18	40.00	24.00	50.00	1628.79

These three fields contain voluntary deductions that are withheld from the employee's pay each pay period as specified.

FIGURE **8.3**

Voluntary Deductions Dialog Box

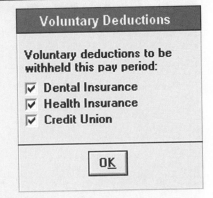

Voluntary Deductions

Voluntary deductions to be withheld this pay period:

☑ Dental Insurance
☑ Health Insurance
☑ Credit Union

<u>O</u>K

After the voluntary deductions are specified and the dialog box is dismissed, the payroll transaction data may be entered. Be careful to enter the correct date of the check because payroll processing is date sensitive and will accumulate and display incorrectly if the dates are entered incorrectly. Also, verify that the check number displayed by the computer is correct. Reenter the correct check number if necessary.

 NOTE The check number is automatically sequenced and generated by the computer. However, if the check number must be changed (e.g., for a special check) or the check numbering sequence needs to be changed (e.g., switched banks or checking accounts), you may enter the desired check number in this text box.

If the employee is salaried, the salary amount will be displayed. You may enter a different salary amount that will override the amount shown. If a salaried employee is to be paid a one-time bonus, the amount entered would be the employee's normal salary plus the bonus amount. Also, the salary grid cell may be used to enter extra pay earned by hourly employees. The computer will add the amount entered to the hourly employee's earnings.

If the employee is paid hourly, enter the regular hours worked in the Reg. Hours grid cell. If the employee is paid hourly and is to be paid overtime at a rate of one-and-a-half times his or her normal hourly rate, enter the overtime hours worked in the O.T. 1 1/2 grid cell. If the employee is paid hourly and is to be paid overtime at a rate of double his or her normal hourly rate, enter the overtime hours worked in the O.T. Double grid cell.

Enter the employee voluntary deductions if different than those shown, or if the employee is new, then click on the Calculate Taxes button to direct the computer to calculate the employee taxes. The taxes will be calculated and displayed in the employee taxes grid cells. You could also enter the tax withholding amounts in the text boxes.

Finally, after all the employee's data have been entered and taxes calculated, click OK. A payroll check will be generated and displayed. A **payroll check** generated by the computer shows the net amount of pay (earnings after payroll taxes and other deductions) earned by the employee during the pay period. The payroll check shown in Figure 8.4 was generated for Linda Benton on 12/31/—. The payroll transaction data entered to generate this check appear in Figure 8.2.

FIGURE 8.4

Payroll Check

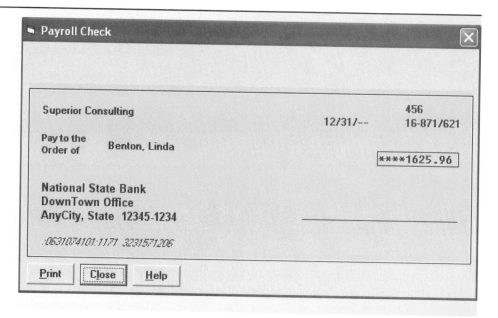

A previously entered payroll transaction may be corrected by simply selecting the incorrect payroll transaction, keying the correction, and clicking OK. The computer will update the employee's record and display a new check. The previously generated check should be marked void and filed as an audit trail document. Likewise, an existing payroll transaction may be deleted by selecting the payroll transaction to be deleted and clicking Delete. Again, the previously written check should be marked void and filed as an audit trail document.

Generate and Post Payroll Journal Entries

Integrated Accounting can automatically generate the **current payroll journal entry** (salary expenses, employee federal tax payable, employee state tax payable, employee city tax payable, Social Security—old-age, survivors, and disability insurance [OASDI], Medicare—hospital insurance [HI], and voluntary deductions). It can also generate the **employer's payroll taxes** journal entry (Social Security—OASDI, Medicare—HI, federal unemployment, and state unemployment).

The current payroll journal entry can be generated by clicking on the Payroll navigation button and then the Current Payroll Journal Entry menu button (or by choosing Current Payroll Journal Entry from the Options menu). The employer's payroll taxes journal entry can be generated by clicking on the Payroll navigation button and then the Employer's Payroll Taxes Journal Entry menu button (or by choosing the Employer's Payroll Taxes from the Options menu). The chosen journal entry will appear in a dialog box for your verification. When it is posted to the general ledger, the general journal appears showing the posted entry.

If you must make a change or correction to a payroll transaction after the journal entry has been generated and posted, you must first delete the old journal entry and again generate the corrected journal entry.

Generating the Current Payroll Journal Entries

Click on the Current Payroll Journal entry menu button from the Payroll navigation button (or select Current Payroll Journal Entry from the Options menu). When the confirmation dialog box shown in Figure 8.5 appears, click Yes.

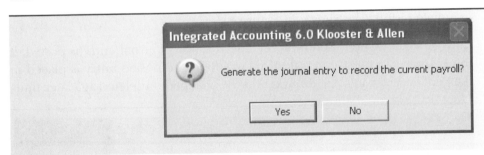

FIGURE 8.5

Generate the Journal Entry to Record the Current Payroll

The generated journal entry for the current payroll will appear in a dialog window as illustrated in Figure 8.6.

Click on Post   When the current payroll journal entry is posted, the general journal window appears showing that the entry has been automatically entered and posted. This entry is placed in the general journal should it become necessary to change or delete it at a later time.

Generating the Employer's Payroll Taxes Journal Entries

Click on the Employer's Payroll Taxes Journal Entry menu button from the Payroll navigation button (or select Employer's Payroll Taxes from the Options menu). When the confirmation dialog box shown in Figure 8.7 appears, click Yes.

FIGURE 8.6

*Current Payroll
Journal Entry*

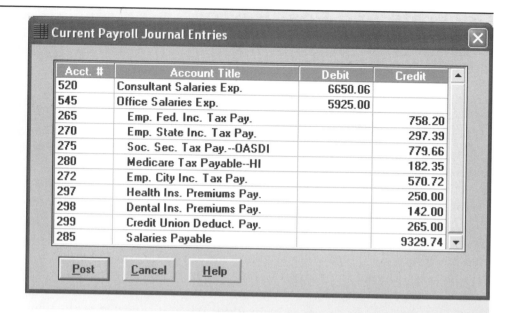

FIGURE 8.6

*Current Payroll
Journal Entry*

FIGURE 8.7

*Employer's Payroll Taxes
Confirmation Dialog Box*

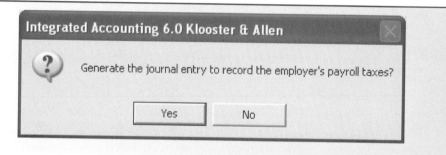

The generated journal entry for the employer's payroll taxes will appear in a dialog window as shown in Figure 8.8.

Click on Post   When the employer's payroll taxes journal entry is posted, it will reappear in the General Journal window. The posted entry is placed in the general journal in the event it must be changed or deleted at a later time.

FIGURE 8.8

*Employer's Payroll Taxes
Journal Entry*

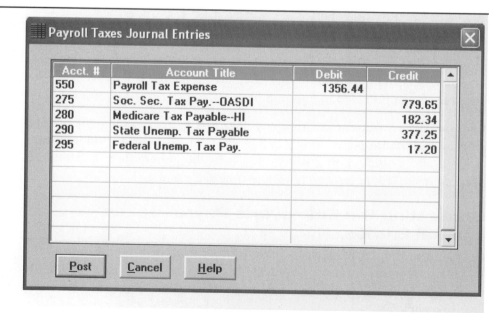

Payroll Reports

Once the payroll transaction data have been entered, the payroll reports can be generated. Click on the Payroll navigation button and then the Payroll Reports menu button (or select Reports from the toolbar, then choose the Payroll Reports option). A list of payroll reports will appear as shown in Figure 8.9. Select the desired report from the Choose a Report to Display list.

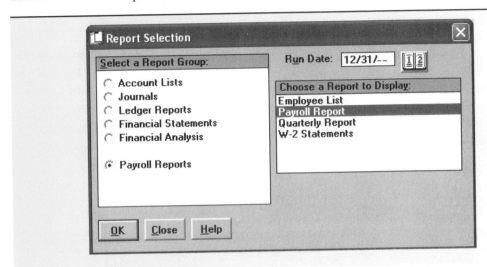

FIGURE 8.9

Report Selection (Payroll Reports)

Employee List Report

The **employee list** report provides a listing of the employee information entered into the computer via the Employees Account Maintenance window. This report is useful in verifying the accuracy of data entered. An example of an employee list report is shown in Figure 8.10.

FIGURE 8.10

Employee List Report

Superior Consulting
Employee List
12/31/—

Emp. No.	Employee Name/Address	Soc. Sec./ Mar. Stat.	# Pay Periods	G.L. Acct.	Salary/ Rate
110	Benton, Linda 6518 Rapid Run Rd. Peoria, IL 61607-1290	581-83-2740 Married W/H 2	12	520	11.75
120	Croswell, Gary 9875 Isaac Lane Peoria, IL 61652-7525	445-50-7791 Single W/H 1	12	545	8.75
130	Foley, Eric 4316 Barley Circle Peoria, IL 61611-8210	579-06-2914 Married W/H 3	12	520	2,270.00
140	Linnell, Deborah 8610 Telemark Lane Peoria, IL 61601-1932	540-63-0217 Married W/H 1	12	545	2,340.00

(continued)

FIGURE 8.10	150	Salas, Genaro	572-95-6730	12	520	
		5171 Locust Ave.	Single			12.00
(Concluded)		Peoria, IL 61612-3280	W/H 1			
	160	Winslow, Glenn	495-39-7583	12	545	2,150.00
		1725 Bartel Dr.	Married			
		Peoria, IL 61601-3845	W/H 2			

Payroll Report

The **payroll report**, which should be generated each pay period, provides earnings and withholding information for each employee for the month, quarter, and year. A summary of the total earnings and withholdings for all employees appears at the end of the report. An example of a payroll report is shown in Figure 8.11.

FIGURE 8.11

Payroll Report (Showing Only First Employee and Payroll Summary)

Superior Consulting
Payroll Report
12/31/—

		Current	Quarterly	Yearly
110-Benton, Linda	Gross Pay	2,112.06	6,104.12	24,534.00
520-Consultant	FIT	91.21	480.02	2,303.25
Married Acct. 520	SIT	48.46	143.58	592.38
W/H 2 581-83-2740	Soc. Sec.—OASDI	130.95	378.46	1,521.13
Pay Periods 12	Medicare—HI	30.62	88.50	355.74
Salary	CIT	95.86	277.04	1,113.51
Hourly Rate 11.75	Health Insurance	40.00	120.00	480.00
Reg. Hours 176.00	Dental Insurance	24.00	72.00	288.00
O.T. Hours 2.50	Credit Union	25.00	75.00	300.00
Check Number 456	Employee SUTA			
Check Date 12/31/—	Net Pay	1,625.96	4,469.52	17,579.99

/\

Payroll Summary	Gross Pay	12,575.06	32,803.12	125,261.32
	FIT	758.20	2,232.49	9,095.54
	SIT	297.39	771.13	2,967.47
	Soc. Sec.—OASDI	779.66	2,033.80	7,766.22
	Medicare—HI	182.35	475.66	1,816.36
	CIT	570.72	1,488.76	5,684.96
	Health Insurance	250.00	670.00	2,560.00
	Dental Insurance	142.00	378.00	1,440.00
	Credit Union	265.00	695.00	2,630.00
	Employee SUTA			
	Net Pay	9,329.74	24,058.28	91,300.77

Quarterly Report

At the end of each quarter, the **quarterly report** must be run. The company uses it to report Social Security and Medicare taxable wages to the Internal Revenue Service (IRS). A quarterly report is shown in Figure 8.12.

FIGURE 8.12

Quarterly Report

Superior Consulting
Quarterly Report
12/31/—

Soc. Sec. Number	Employee Name	Taxable Soc. Sec.	Taxable Medicare
581-83-2740	Benton, Linda	6,104.12	6,104.12
445-50-7791	Croswell, Gary	4,515.00	4,515.00
579-06-2914	Foley, Eric	6,810.00	6,810.00
540-63-0217	Linnell, Deborah	7,020.00	7,020.00
572-95-6730	Salas, Genaro	6,204.00	6,204.00
495-39-7583	Winslow, Glenn	2,150.00	2,150.00
	Totals	32,803.12	32,803.12

Total Employees 6

W-2 Statements

At the end of the year, the company must provide a **W-2 statement** to each employee paid during the past year. The W-2 statement is used for individual tax reporting purposes. An example of an employee's W-2 statement is shown in Figure 8.13.

FIGURE 8.13

W-2 Statement

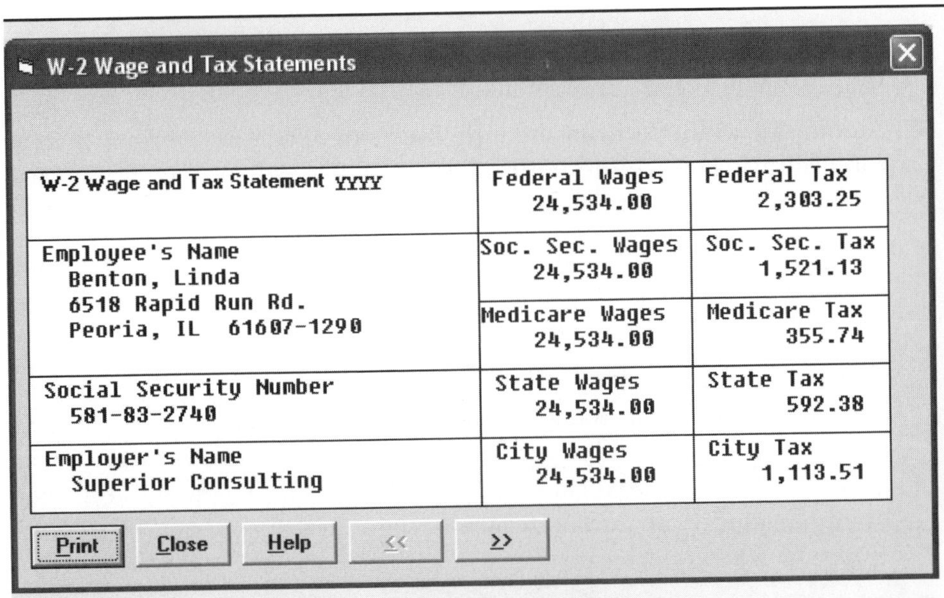

Click Print to print the currently displayed statement to an attached printer. Click the >> button to advance to the next statement, or the << button to return to the previous statement.

Purge Payroll Transactions (Year End)

The Purge Payroll Transactions (Year End) menu item, located in the Options menu, may be used to remove all payroll transactions at the end of the fiscal year. Before selecting this menu item, make sure all year-end reports have been printed and a backup copy of the last payroll for the calendar year has been made. Once this menu item is executed, all payroll transactions will be erased from the accounting file currently loaded in memory.

Chapter Summary

■ A computerized payroll system stores data for each employee, permits pay-period transaction data to be entered, processes the data, and generates the required reports, checks, and statements.

■ The withholding allowances are the number of deductions from total earnings for each person legally supported by a taxpayer.

■ The number of pay periods is the number of times the employee is paid per year.

■ The general ledger account entered in the G.L. No. column of the Account Maintenance/Employees window indicates the salary expense account to which the employee's earnings is to be charged.

■ A designation of whether the employee is single or married is referred to as the employee's marital status.

■ The salary amount is the gross amount paid for employee services each pay period.

■ The hourly rate is the gross amount an hourly employee is paid for each hour worked.

■ Amount(s) withheld from the employee's pay each pay period, such as for health insurance, dental insurance, and credit union savings, are called voluntary deductions.

■ A payroll check is a paycheck generated by the computer showing the net amount of pay (earnings after payroll taxes and other deductions) earned by each employee during the pay period.

■ The current payroll journal entry (salary expenses, employee federal and state tax payable, Social Security—OASDI, Medicare—HI, and voluntary deductions) and employer's payroll taxes journal entry (Social Security—OASDI, Medicare—HI, federal unemployment, and state unemployment) can automatically be generated and posted by the *Integrated Accounting* software.

■ The employee list report verifies the accuracy of data entered into the computer via the Account Maintenance/Employees window.

■ The payroll report provides earnings and withholding information for each employee for the month, quarter, and year.

■ The quarterly report, created at the end of each quarter, is used by the company to report Social Security and Medicare taxable wages to the IRS.

■ W-2 statements are used for individual tax reporting purposes and are provided to each employee at the end of the year.

Sample Problem 8-S

In this sample problem, you will process the December payroll for Superior Consulting. You will perform the operating procedures necessary to add new employees, make changes to employee data, and delete employees. In addition, you will process the monthly payroll and generate the payroll journal entries. Because this is the last payroll of the year it will include the end-of-quarter and W-2 statements.

1   **Start *Integrated Accounting* 6e.**

2   **Load file IA6 Problem 08-S.**

3   **Enter your name in the Your Name text box and click OK.**

4   **Save the file as 08-S Your Name.**

5   **Enter the employee maintenance data.**

Click on the Payroll navigation button and then click the Maintain Employees menu button. Enter the following employee maintenance data:

Add new employee Winslow, Glenn; 1725 Bartel Dr.; Peoria, IL 61601-3845; Assign employee number 160; Social Security number, 495-39-7583; withholding allowances, 2; pay periods per year, 12; G.L. Account, 545 (Office Salaries Exp.); salaried, $2,150.00; married.

Change the marital status of Linda Benton to married and the number of withholding allowances to 2.

Change the street address of Deborah Linnell to 8610 Telemark Lane.

Delete employee no. 100 (Acker, Gregory)

6   **Enter the payroll transactions and generate paychecks. Withhold all three voluntary deductions this pay period (health insurance, dental insurance, and credit union deductions).**

Click on the Payroll navigation button and then the Pay Employees menu button. Click Deductions, then click on all three deductions (if not already checked) to indicate that they are to be withheld this pay period, and then click OK. Enter the following payroll transaction data (illustrated in Figure 8.14) and have the computer calculate taxes. The first paycheck appears in Figure 8.15.

 NOTE   You must enter the correct date (December 31, —) when entering the payroll transactions. Payroll processing is date sensitive and will accumulate and display incorrectly if the dates are not entered correctly.

Dec. 31   Record the monthly payroll check to Benton, Linda; Check No. 456; regular hours, 176.0; one-and-a-half times overtime hours, 2.5; health insurance, $40.00; dental insurance, $24.00; credit union, $25.00.

     31   Record the monthly payroll check to Croswell, Gary; Check No. 457; regular hours, 164.0; health insurance, $40.00; dental insurance, $24.00; credit union, $35.00.

31 Record the monthly payroll check to Foley, Eric; Check No. 458; salary amount, $2,270.00; health insurance, $45.00; dental insurance, $18.00; credit union, $50.00.

31 Record the monthly payroll check to Linnell, Deborah; Check No. 459; salary amount, $2,340.00; health insurance, $45.00; dental insurance, $28.00; credit union, $75.00.

31 Record the monthly payroll check to Salas, Genaro; Check No. 460; regular hours, 176.0; one-and-a-half times overtime hours, 4.0; double overtime hours, 3.5; health insurance, $40.00; dental insurance, $24.00; credit union, $30.00.

31 Record the monthly payroll check to Winslow, Glenn; Check No. 461; salary amount, $2,150.00; health insurance, $40.00; dental insurance, $24.00; credit union, $50.00. (Because this is a new employee be sure to key the health insurance, dental insurance, and credit union amounts.)

FIGURE 8.14

Completed Employee Transactions

Date	Employee Name	Check No.	Salary	Reg. Hours	O.T. 1 1/2	O.T. Double	SUTA Tax	FIT	SIT
12/31/--	Benton, Linda	456		176.00	2.50			91.21	48.46
12/31/--	Croswell, Gary	457		164.00				110.25	24.98
12/31/--	Foley, Eric	458	2270.00					80.33	51.23
12/31/--	Linnell, Deborah	459	2340.00					146.21	62.89
12/31/--	Salas, Genaro	460		176.00	4.00	3.50		235.20	59.68
12/31/--	Winslow, Glenn	461	2150.00					95.00	50.15

CIT	Soc. Sec. (OASDI)	Medicare (HI)	Health Insurance	Dental Insurance	Credit Union	Net Pay
95.86	130.95	30.62	40.00	24.00	25.00	1625.96
65.13	88.97	20.81	40.00	24.00	35.00	1025.86
103.02	140.74	32.92	45.00	18.00	50.00	1748.76
106.20	145.08	33.93	45.00	28.00	75.00	1697.69
102.93	140.62	32.89	40.00	24.00	30.00	1602.68
97.58	133.30	31.18	40.00	24.00	50.00	1628.79

FIGURE 8.15

First Paycheck

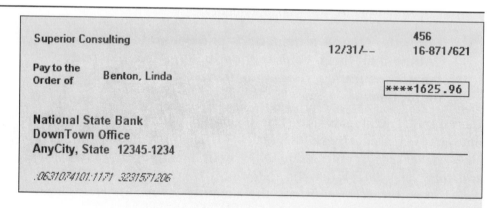

Superior Consulting

12/31/--   456   16-871/621

Pay to the Order of   Benton, Linda

****1625.96

National State Bank
DownTown Office
AnyCity, State 12345-1234

⦙063107410⦙ 1171 323157 1206

---

7 **Display the employee list report.**

Click on the Payroll navigation button and then the Payroll Reports menu button. Select the Employee List report and click OK. The report is shown in Figure 8.16. Verify the accuracy of the maintenance input and make any corrections via the Employees tab in the Account Maintenance window.

FIGURE **8.16**

Employee List

Superior Consulting
Employee List
12/31/—

Emp. No.	Employee Name/Address	Soc. Sec./ Mar. Stat.	# Pay Periods	G.L. Acct.	Salary/ Rate
110	Benton, Linda 6518 Rapid Run Rd. Peoria, IL 61607-1290	581-83-2740 Married W/H 2	12	520	11.75
120	Croswell, Gary 9875 Isaac Lane Peoria, IL 61652-7525	445-50-7791 Single W/H 1	12	545	8.75
130	Foley, Eric 4316 Barley Circle Peoria, IL 61611-8210	579-06-2914 Married W/H 3	12	520	2,270.00
140	Linnell, Deborah 8610 Telemark Lane Peoria, IL 61601-1932	540-63-0217 Married W/H 1	12	545	2,340.00
150	Salas, Genaro 5171 Locust Ave. Peoria, IL 61612-3280	572-95-6730 Single W/H 1	12	520	12.00
160	Winslow, Glenn 1725 Bartel Dr. Peoria, IL 61601-3845	495-39-7583 Married W/H 2	12	545	2,150.00

8   Display the payroll report.

Make sure the Run Date is set to 12/31/—, choose the Payroll Report option, and click OK. The Payroll Report is shown in Figure 8.17. Verify the accuracy of the transaction input and make any corrections via the Payroll tab in the Other Tasks window.

FIGURE **8.17**

Payroll Report

Superior Consulting
Payroll Report
12/31/—

		Current	Quarterly	Yearly
110-Benton, Linda	Gross Pay	2,112.06	6,104.12	24,534.00
520-Consultant	FIT	91.21	480.02	2,303.25
Married Acct. 520	SIT	48.46	143.58	592.38
W/H 2 581-83-2740	Soc. Sec.—OASDI	130.95	378.46	1,521.13
Pay Periods 12	Medicare—HI	30.62	88.50	355.74
Salary	CIT	95.86	277.04	1,113.51
Hourly Rate 11.75	Health Insurance	40.00	120.00	480.00
Reg. Hours 176.00	Dental Insurance	24.00	72.00	288.00
O.T. Hours 2.50	Credit Union	25.00	75.00	300.00
Check Number 456	Employee SUTA			
Check Date 12/31/—	Net Pay	1,625.96	4,469.52	17,579.99

(continued)

FIGURE 8.17

(Concluded)

120-Croswell, Gary	Gross Pay	1,435.00	4,515.00	18,285.32
545-Office	FIT	110.25	362.25	1,482.80
Single Acct. 545	SIT	24.98	82.74	339.35
W/H 1 445-50-7791	Soc. Sec.—OASDI	88.97	279.93	1,133.70
Pay Periods 12	Medicare—HI	20.81	65.47	265.15
Salary	CIT	65.13	204.91	829.88
Hourly Rate 8.75	Health Insurance	40.00	120.00	480.00
Reg. Hours 164.00	Dental Insurance	24.00	72.00	288.00
O.T. Hours	Credit Union	35.00	105.00	420.00
Check Number 457	Employee SUTA			
Check Date 12/31/—	Net Pay	1,025.86	3,222.70	13,046.44
130-Foley, Eric	Gross Pay	2,270.00	6,810.00	27,240.00
520-Consultant	FIT	80.33	240.99	963.96
Married Acct. 520	SIT	51.23	153.69	614.76
W/H 3 579-06-2914	Soc. Sec.—OASDI	140.74	422.22	1,688.88
Pay Periods 12	Medicare—HI	32.92	98.76	395.04
Salary 2,270.00	CIT	103.02	309.06	1,236.24
Hourly Rate	Health Insurance	45.00	135.00	540.00
Reg. Hours	Dental Insurance	18.00	54.00	216.00
O.T. Hours	Credit Union	50.00	150.00	600.00
Check Number 458	Employee SUTA			
Check Date 12/31/—	Net Pay	1,748.76	5,246.28	20,985.12
140-Linnell, Deborah	Gross Pay	2,340.00	7,020.00	28,080.00
545-Office	FIT	146.21	438.63	1,760.98
Married Acct. 545	SIT	62.89	188.67	754.68
W/H 1 540-63-0217	Soc. Sec.—OASDI	145.08	435.24	1,740.96
Pay Periods 12	Medicare—HI	33.93	101.79	407.16
Salary 2,340.00	CIT	106.20	318.60	1,274.40
Hourly Rate	Health Insurance	45.00	135.00	540.00
Reg. Hours	Dental Insurance	28.00	84.00	336.00
O.T. Hours	Credit Union	75.00	225.00	900.00
Check Number 459	Employee SUTA			
Check Date 12/31/—	Net Pay	1,697.69	5,093.07	20,365.82
150-Salas, Genaro	Gross Pay	2,268.00	6,204.00	24,972.00
520-Consultant	FIT	235.20	615.60	2,489.55
Single Acct. 520	SIT	59.68	152.30	616.15
W/H 1 572-95-6730	Soc. Sec.—OASDI	140.62	384.65	1,548.25
Pay Periods 12	Medicare—HI	32.89	89.96	362.09
Salary	CIT	102.93	281.57	1,133.35
Hourly Rate 12.00	Health Insurance	40.00	120.00	480.00
Reg. Hours 176.00	Dental Insurance	24.00	72.00	288.00
O.T. Hours 4.00 3.50	Credit Union	30.00	90.00	360.00
Check Number 460	Employee SUTA			
Check Date 12/31/—	Net Pay	1,602.68	4,397.92	17,694.61
160-Winslow, Glenn	Gross Pay	2,150.00	2,150.00	2,150.00
545-Office	FIT	95.00	95.00	95.00
Married Acct. 545	SIT	50.15	50.15	50.15
W/H 2 495-39-7583	Soc. Sec.—OASDI	133.30	133.30	133.30
Pay Periods 12	Medicare—HI	31.18	31.18	31.18
Salary 2,150.00	CIT	97.58	97.58	97.58
Hourly Rate	Health Insurance	40.00	40.00	40.00
Reg. Hours	Dental Insurance	24.00	24.00	24.00

(continued)

O.T. Hours	Credit Union	50.00	50.00	50.00	**FIGURE 8.17**
Check Number 461	Employee SUTA				*(Concluded)*
Check Date 12/31/—	Net Pay	1,628.79	1,628.79	1,628.79	
Payroll Summary	Gross Pay	12,575.06	32,803.12	125,261.32	
	FIT	758.20	2,232.49	9,095.54	
	SIT	297.39	771.13	2,967.47	
	Soc. Sec.—OASDI	779.66	2,033.80	7,766.22	
	Medicare—HI	182.35	475.66	1,816.36	
	CIT	570.72	1,488.76	5,684.96	
	Health Insurance	250.00	670.00	2,560.00	
	Dental Insurance	142.00	378.00	1,440.00	
	Credit Union	265.00	695.00	2,630.00	
	Employee SUTA				
	Net Pay	9,329.74	24,058.28	91,300.77	

9   **Generate and post the journal entry for the current payroll.**

Click on the Payroll navigation button and then the Current Payroll Journal Entry. Click Yes when asked if you want to generate the journal entry. When the entry appears in the Current Payroll Journal Entries dialog box, as shown in Figure 8.18, click Post. The journal entry will reappear, posted in the general journal.

Acct. #	Account Title	Debit	Credit	**FIGURE 8.18**
520	Consultant Salaries Exp.	6650.06		*Current Payroll Journal Entries Dialog Box*
545	Office Salaries Exp.	5925.00		
265	Emp. Fed. Inc. Tax Pay.		758.20	
270	Emp. State Inc. Tax Pay.		297.39	
275	Soc. Sec. Tax Pay.--OASDI		779.66	
280	Medicare Tax Payable--HI		182.35	
272	Emp. City Inc. Tax Pay.		570.72	
297	Health Ins. Premiums Pay.		250.00	
298	Dental Ins. Premiums Pay.		142.00	
299	Credit Union Deduct. Pay.		265.00	
285	Salaries Payable		9329.74	

If your journal entries do not match those shown in Figure 8.18, check your employee list and payroll report for keying errors and make the necessary corrections. Return to the General Journal window, delete the incorrect entries, and generate new entries.

10   **Generate and post the employer's payroll taxes journal entry.**

Click on the Payroll navigation button, and then click on the Employer's Payroll Taxes Journal Entry menu button. Click Yes when asked if you want to generate the journal entry. When the entries appear in the Payroll Taxes Journal Entries dialog box, as shown in Figure 8.19, click Post. The journal entries will reappear, posted in the general journal.

FIGURE 8.19

Employer's Payroll Taxes Journal Entries Dialog Box

Acct. #	Account Title	Debit	Credit
550	Payroll Tax Expense	1356.44	
275	Soc. Sec. Tax Pay.--OASDI		779.65
280	Medicare Tax Payable--HI		182.34
290	State Unemp. Tax Payable		377.25
295	Federal Unemp. Tax Pay.		17.20

11   **Display the payroll journal entries.**

Click on the Payroll navigation button and then the Payroll Reports menu button. Choose the Journals option. Select the General Journal report and click OK. When the Journal Report selection window appears, choose the Customize Journal Report option and click OK. If necessary, set the date range to 12/31/—through 12/31/—. The report appears in Figure 8.20.

FIGURE 8.20

General Journal Report (Payroll Journal Entries)

**Superior Consulting
General Journal
12/31/—**

Date	Refer.	Acct.	Title	Debit	Credit
12/31	Payroll	520	Consultant Salaries Exp.	6,650.06	
12/31	Payroll	545	Office Salaries Exp.	5,925.00	
12/31	Payroll	265	Emp. Fed. Inc. Tax Pay.		758.20
12/31	Payroll	270	Emp. State Inc. Tax Pay.		297.39
12/31	Payroll	275	Soc. Sec. Tax Pay.—OASDI		779.66
12/31	Payroll	280	Medicare Tax Payable—HI		182.35
12/31	Payroll	272	Emp. City Inc. Tax Pay.		570.72
12/31	Payroll	297	Health Ins. Premiums Pay.		250.00
12/31	Payroll	298	Dental Ins. Premiums Pay.		142.00
12/31	Payroll	299	Credit Union Deduct. Pay.		265.00
12/31	Payroll	285	Salaries Payable		9,329.74
12/31	Pay. Tax	550	Payroll Tax Expense	1,356.44	
12/31	Pay. Tax	275	Soc. Sec. Tax Pay.—OASDI		779.65
12/31	Pay. Tax	280	Medicare Tax Payable—HI		182.34
12/31	Pay. Tax	290	State Unemp. Tax Payable		377.25
12/31	Pay. Tax	295	Federal Unemp. Tax Pay		17.20
			Totals	13,931.50	13,931.50

12   **Use Check on the toolbar to check your work.**

13   **Generate a labor distribution graph.**

Click Graphs on the toolbar. Click on Labor Distribution to generate the graph shown in Figure 8.21.

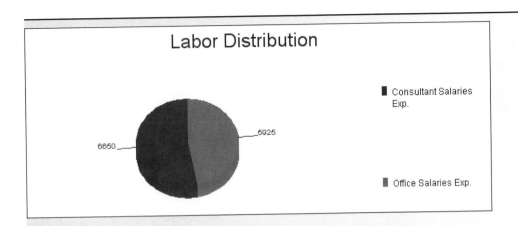

FIGURE 8.21

Labor Distribution Graph

14 **Display the quarterly report.**

Choose the Payroll Reports menu button from the Payroll navigation button, select the Quarterly Report, and click OK. The quarterly report appears in Figure 8.22.

Superior Consulting
Quarterly Report
12/31/—

Soc. Sec. Number	Employee Name	Taxable Soc. Sec.	Taxable Medicare
581-83-2740	Benton, Linda	6,104.12	6,104.12
445-50-7791	Croswell, Gary	4,515.00	4,515.00
579-06-2914	Foley, Eric	6,810.00	6,810.00
540-63-0217	Linnell, Deborah	7,020.00	7,020.00
572-95-6730	Salas, Genaro	6,204.00	6,204.00
495-39-7583	Winslow, Glenn	2,150.00	2,150.00
	Totals	32,803.12	32,803.12

Total Employees 6

FIGURE 8.22

Quarterly Report

15 **Display the W-2 statements.**

Select the W-2 Statements and click OK. The first statement is shown in Figure 8.23.

W-2 Wage and Tax Statement yyyy	Federal Wages 24,534.00	Federal Tax 2,303.25
Employee's Name Benton, Linda 6518 Rapid Run Rd. Peoria, IL 61607-1290	Soc. Sec. Wages 24,534.00	Soc. Sec. Tax 1,521.13
	Medicare Wages 24,534.00	Medicare Tax 355.74
Social Security Number 581-83-2740	State Wages 24,534.00	State Tax 592.38
Employer's Name Superior Consulting	City Wages 24,534.00	City Tax 1,113.51

FIGURE 8.23

W-2 Statement

16   **Save your data to disk.**

17   **Calculate the amount of savings over a given period of time using the Savings Planner.**

Superior Consulting is considering purchasing land and a building. Based on their financial condition, they can transfer $15,000.00 from their cash account to a savings account and contribute $1,800.00 into the account monthly with an interest rate of 7.5% over the next 5 years (60 months).

Click the Tools toolbar button. When the Planning Tools window appears, click the Savings Planner tab. With the Ending Savings Balance option in the Calculate grouping set to on, enter the following savings information and generate the Savings Planner schedule shown in Figure 8.24.

Beginning savings.......................................$15,000.00
Annual yield..7.50%
Number of months.....................................60
Monthly contribution...............................$1,800.00

FIGURE 8.24

Savings Plan Report

Savings Plan
12/31/—

Savings Planner Schedule

Month Number	Monthly Contribution	Monthly Yield	Cumulative Total
(Beginning Balance)			15,000.00
1	1,800.00	93.75	16,893.75
2	1,800.00	105.59	18,799.34
3	1,800.00	117.50	20,716.84
4	1,800.00	129.48	22,646.32
5	1,800.00	141.54	24,587.86
6	1,800.00	153.67	26,541.53
7	1,800.00	165.88	28,507.41
8	1,800.00	178.17	30,485.58
9	1,800.00	190.53	32,476.11
10	1,800.00	202.98	34,479.09
/\			
55	1,800.00	851.19	138,841.63
56	1,800.00	867.76	141,509.39
57	1,800.00	884.43	144,193.82
58	1,800.00	901.21	146,895.03
59	1,800.00	918.09	149,613.12
60	1,800.00	935.09	152,348.21

18   **Optional spreadsheet integration activity.**

Superior Consulting asked you to use a spreadsheet to estimate of the cost of giving each employee a 4 percent raise next year.

a. Copy the payroll report to the clipboard in spreadsheet format.

b. Start up your spreadsheet software and load the template file IA6 Spreadsheet 08-S.

c. Select cell A1 as the current cell and paste the report copied in step a into the spreadsheet.

d. Enter: 4% in cell C94 (percent of increase in gross pay); 6.2% in cell C95 (Social Security withholding rate); 1.45% in cell C96 (Medicare withholding rate); in cell C99, enter the appropriate formula to calculate the 4-percent increase in amount of gross pay.

In cell C100, enter the appropriate formula to calculate the amount of Social Security; in cell C101, enter the appropriate formula to calculate the amount of Medicare; in cell D99, enter the appropriate formula to calculate the difference between last year's gross pay and the 4-percent increased gross pay amount.

In cell D100, enter the appropriate formula to calculate the difference between last year's Social Security and the projected Social Security amount; in cell D101, enter the appropriate formula to calculate the difference between last year's Medicare and the projected Medicare amount; in cell D103, enter the appropriate formula to sum the total effect of a 4-percent increase in gross pay.

e. Print the results of a 4-percent increase in gross pay. The completed spreadsheet is shown in Figure 8.25.

f. Save the spreadsheet with a file name of 08-S Your Name.

g. What would the estimated cost to Superior Consulting be for a 5-percent raise? What if the Social Security rate increases to 6.5 percent or the Medicare rate increases to 1.75 percent?

h. End your spreadsheet session.

FIGURE 8.25

Estimated Cost of 4-Percent Raise

		Projections	Difference
Pay Increase:	4.00%		
Soc. Sec. Rate:	6.20%		
Medicare Rate:	1.45%		
		Projections	Difference
Gross Pay		$130,271.77	$5,010.45
Soc. Sec. W/H		$8,076.85	$310.63
Medicare W/H		$1,888.94	$72.58
Total			$5,393.66

19 **Optional word processing activity.**

Prepare an address list of the current active employees for the personal department.

a. Display and copy the employee list to the clipboard in word processing format.

b. Start up your word processing application software and create a new document. (Use a fixed type font such as Courier.)

c. Paste the employee list report into the document.

d. Enter headings, delete unwanted data, and format the document to match Figure 8.26.

e. Print the completed address list.

f. Save the document with a file name of 08-S Your Name.

g. End your word processing session.

FIGURE 8.26

Employee Address List

Superior Consulting
Employee List
12/31/—

Employee Name	Address	City,	State,	& Zip
Benton, Linda	6518 Rapid Run Rd	Peoria,	IL	61607-1290
Croswell, Gary	9875 Isaac Lane	Peoria,	IL	61652-7525
Foley, Eric	4316 Barley Circle	Peoria,	IL	61611-8210
Linnell, Deborah	8610 Telemark Lane	Peoria,	IL	61601-1932
Salas, Genaro	5171 Locust Ave.	Peoria,	IL	61612-3280
Winslow, Glenn	1725 Bartel Dr.	Peoria,	IL	61601-3845

INTERNET ACTIVITY

If you have access to the Internet, use your browser to access the U.S. IRS Internet site. Use the IRS Publications link to obtain instructions and a W-2 statement form.

20 **End the *Integrated Accounting* 6e session.**

Chapter 8 Student Exercises

NAME

I True/False

Directions   *If the statement is true, write T in the space provided. If the statement is false, write F in the space provided.*

1.____   The computer permits the user to delete an employee at anytime during the calendar year.

2.____   You cannot make corrections to the payroll transactions once they have been entered into the computer.

3.____   When a payroll transaction is entered, the computer can be instructed to calculate payroll taxes.

4.____   The computer can automatically generate an employee's paycheck.

5.____   The payroll software is date sensitive, and it depends on the payroll transaction dates to accurately accumulate and process payroll data.

6.____   Payroll journal entries must be manually entered into the general journal to update the general ledger payroll account balances.

7.____   The general journal report provides a listing of the journal entries posted during payroll processing.

II Questions

Directions   *Write the answers to the following questions in the space provided.*

1.   If an employee is paid biweekly (every 2 weeks), what would you record in the employee data field, Number Pay Per? _____

_____

2.   What is the difference between the Current Payroll Journal Entry and the Employer's Payroll Taxes menu items? _____

_____

3.   What steps must be taken to delete a payroll transaction already entered to prevent an employee from being paid. _____

_____

4.   How does the computer know what check numbers to assign to current payroll checks?

_____

5.   What is the purpose of the quarterly report? _____

_____

Problem 8-A

In this problem, you will process the November and December monthly payrolls for Wilker Merchandising Co. You will perform the operating procedures necessary to add new employees, make changes to employee data, and delete employees. Because December 31st is the end of the year, you will also display the quarterly report and W-2 statements. Answer audit questions 8-A on pages 354–356 as you complete this problem. Display reports as necessary to answer the questions. As you complete this problem, click Info. on the toolbar for helpful check figures to audit your work.

1 **Start *Integrated Accounting* 6e.**

2 **Load file IA6 Problem 08-A.**

3 **Enter your name in the Your Name text box.**

4 **Save the file as 08-A1 Your Name.**

5 **Enter the employee maintenance data:**

Add new employee Zinser, Richard; 857 Shaffer Ave.; Atlanta, GA 30327-4835; Assign employee number 290; Social Security number, 520-69-8573; withholding allowances, 2; pay periods per year, 12; G.L. Account, 6210 (Sales Salaries Exp.); hourly, $10.25; married.
    Change the marital status of Griffith, Phillip to married.
    Change the street address of Schilling, Frank to 7576 Deercross Dr.
Delete employee no. 230 (Kastella, Earl)

6 **Enter the following November payroll transactions and generate paychecks. Withhold all three voluntary deductions this pay period (health insurance, dental insurance, and credit union deductions) and use a transaction date of 11/30/—. Calculate taxes using the Calculate Taxes button.**

November Payroll

Nov. 30   Record the monthly payroll check to Falgren, Eunice; Check No. 562; salary amount, $5,000.00; health insurance, $75.00; dental insurance, $35.00; credit union, $350.00.

     30   Record the monthly payroll check to Griffith, Phillip; Check No. 563; regular hours, 160.0; health insurance, $65.00; dental insurance, $25.00; credit union, $75.00.

     30   Record the monthly payroll check to Mettler, Mary; Check No. 564; regular hours, 168.0; one-and-a-half times overtime hours, 3.5; health insurance, $85.00; dental insurance, $35.00; credit union, $100.00.

     30   Record the monthly payroll check to Phelps, Donna; Check No. 565; regular hours, 168.0; health insurance, $65.00; dental insurance, $25.00; credit union, $100.00.

30 Record the monthly payroll check to Schilling, Frank; Check No. 566; salary amount, $4,324.00; health insurance, $80.00; dental insurance, $30.00; credit union, $300.00.

30 Record the monthly payroll check to Winters, Annette; Check No. 567; regular hours, 168.0; one-and-a-half times overtime hours, 3.0; double overtime hours, 2.5; health insurance, $65.00; dental insurance, $25.00; credit union, $50.00.

30 Record the monthly payroll check to Yoshino, Sumio; Check No. 568; salary amount, $2,850.00; health insurance, $70.00; dental insurance, $28.00; credit union, $50.00.

30 Record the monthly payroll check to Zinser, Richard; Check No. 569; regular hours, 136.0; health insurance, $70.00; dental insurance, $25.00; credit union, $60.00.

7 **Display the employee list report.**

8 **Display the payroll report.**

9 **Generate and post the journal entry for the current payroll.**

10 **Generate and post the employer's payroll taxes journal entry.**

11 **Display the November payroll journal entries.**

12 **Save your data to disk (with file name 08-A1 Your Name).**

13 **Use Save As to save to save the data with a file name of 08-A2 Your Name).**

14 **Enter the following December payroll transactions and generate paychecks. Withhold all three voluntary deductions this pay period (health insurance, dental insurance, and credit union deductions) and use a transaction date of 12/31/—.**

December Payroll

Dec. 31 Record the monthly payroll check to Falgren, Eunice; Check No. 570; salary amount, $5,000.00; health insurance, $75.00; dental insurance, $35.00; credit union, $350.00.

31 Record the monthly payroll check to Griffith, Phillip; Check No. 571; regular hours, 176.0; one-and-a-half times overtime hours, 2.5; health insurance, $65.00; dental insurance, $25.00; credit union, $75.00.

31   Record the monthly payroll check to Mettler, Mary; Check No. 572; regular hours, 176.0; health insurance, $85.00; dental insurance, $35.00; credit union, $100.00.

31   Record the monthly payroll check to Phelps, Donna; Check No. 573; regular hours, 152.0; health insurance, $65.00; dental insurance, $25.00; credit union, $100.00.

31   Record the monthly payroll check to Schilling, Frank; Check No. 574; salary amount, $4,324.00; health insurance, $80.00; dental insurance, $30.00; credit union, $300.00.

31   Record the monthly payroll check to Winters, Annette; Check No. 575; regular hours, 176.0; health insurance, $65.00; dental insurance, $25.00; credit union, $50.00.

31   Record the monthly payroll check to Yoshino, Sumio; Check No. 576; salary amount, $2,850.00; health insurance, $70.00; dental insurance, $28.00; credit union, $50.00.

31   Record the monthly payroll check to Zinser, Richard; Check No. 577; regular hours, 176.0; one-and-a-half times overtime hours, 4.0; double overtime hours, 2.0; health insurance, $70.00; dental insurance, $25.00; credit union, $60.00.

15   **Display the payroll report.**

16   **Generate and post the journal entry for the current payroll.**

17   **Generate and post the employer's payroll taxes journal entry.**

18   **Display the December payroll journal entries.**

19   **Use Check on the toolbar to check your work.**

20   **Generate a labor distribution graph.**

21   **Display the quarterly report.**

22   **Display the W-2 statements.**

23   **Save your data to disk with a file name of 08-A2 Your Name.**

24   **Use the Savings Planner to calculate the number of months needed for an ending balance given the following information:**

Beginning savings.................................$25,000.00

Annual yield...8.00%

Monthly contribution...............................$2,000.00

Ending savings balance...........................$200,000.00

25 **Optional spreadsheet integration activity.**

The management of Wilker Merchandising Co., asked you to use a spreadsheet to prepare a payroll distribution of gross earnings report for the year.

a. Copy the payroll report to the clipboard in spreadsheet format.

b. Start up your spreadsheet software and load the template file IA6 Spreadsheet 08-A.

c. Select cell A1 as the current cell (if not already selected) and paste the report copied in step a into the spreadsheet.

d. Enter *+A3* in cell A120.

   Enter *Payroll Distribution (Gross Earnings)* in cell A121.

   Enter *+A5* in cell A122.

   Enter *Employee* in cell A124.

   Enter *Gross Earnings* in cell B124.

   Enter the cell references to each employee and their corresponding yearly gross earnings in the columns under the respective headings.

   Enter the appropriate formula to sum the gross earnings.

   Format the report (align headings, format currency cells, etc.).

e. Generate a pie chart.

   Select the range of cells containing the employee number/name and corresponding gross earnings, then choose the Chart or Graph menu item from the spreadsheet program you are using. If the computer asks for a graph name, etc., enter *Payroll Distribution* and click OK. Choose Pie Chart from the toolbar if the graph that appears is not a pie chart. Finally, if the spreadsheet software you are using permits copying and pasting the chart into the worksheet, copy and paste the chart immediately after the payroll distribution report cells.

f. Print the payroll distribution report portion of the spreadsheet and pie chart.

g. Save the spreadsheet data with a file name of 08-A Your Name.

h. End your spreadsheet session.

26 **Optional word processing integration activity.**

The personnel department asked you to prepare a report showing each employee's general ledger salary expense account number and salary/hourly rate.

a. Display and copy the employee list to the clipboard in word processing format.

b. Start up your word processing application software and create a new document. (Use a fixed type font such as Courier.)

c. Paste the employee list report into the document.

d. Enter headings, delete unwanted data, and so on, and then format the report for the desired data.

e. Print the completed report.

f. Save the document with a file name of 08-A Your Name.

g. End your word processing session.

If you have access to the Internet, use your browser to find the most recent year's payroll tax rates for the state in which you reside. *Hint*: Use U.S. IRS, regional services, or state and local tax as your search strings. Report your findings. Be sure to indicate the sources, including URLs (Web addresses), of your reported findings.

INTERNET ACTIVITY

27   **End the *Integrated Accounting* 6e session.**

Audit Questions 8-A

NAME

November Payroll   *Use the payroll file you saved under file name 08-A1 Your Name to answer the following questions for the November payroll.*

Employee List

1.   What is the number of withholding allowances for Mary Mettler? _____

2.   What is Eunice Falgren's street address? _____

Payroll Report

3.   What is Phillip Griffith's hourly rate? _____

4.   What is the current gross pay for Donna Phelps? _____

5.   What is the Medicare amount withheld for the quarter for Annette Winters? _____

6.   What is Sumio Yoshino's gross pay for the quarter? _____

7.   What is Richard Zinser's current net pay? _____

8.   What is the total current net pay for all employees? _____

9.   What is the total yearly gross pay for all employees? _____

Journal Entries Report

10.   What is the amount of the credit to employee federal income tax payable? _____

11.   What is the amount of the credit to Medicare tax payable–HI? _____

12.   What is the amount of the credit to employee city income tax payable? _____

December Payroll   *Use the payroll file you saved under file name 08-A2 Your Name to answer the following questions for the December payroll.*

Payroll Report

1. What is the current net pay for Phillip Griffith? _____

_____

2. What is the current federal withholding amount for Donna Phelps? _____

_____

3. What is the Medicare amount withheld for the year for Frank Schilling? _____

_____

4. What is the check number for the check written to Annette Winters? _____

_____

5. What is the total current amount withheld for dental insurance for all employees?

_____

6. What is the total yearly Social Security–OASDI withheld for all employees? _____

_____

Journal Entries Report

7. What is the amount of the credit to Medicare tax payable–HI? _____

_____

8. What is the amount of the debit to payroll taxes expense? _____

_____

9. What is the amount of the credit to salaries payable? _____

_____

Quarterly Report

10. What is the taxable Social Security amount for Mary Mettler? _____

_____

11. What is the total taxable Medicare amount for all employees for the quarter? _____

_____

W-2 Statements

12. What is the amount of state tax shown for Eunice Falgren? _____

_____

13. What is the federal tax shown for Frank Schilling? _____

_____

Savings Planner

14. How many months does it take to save $200,000.00 based on the information provided in this problem? _____

_____

15. What is the monthly yield for month 6? _____

_____

Problem 8-B

In this problem, you will process the November and December monthly payrolls for Wilker Merchandising Co. You will perform the operating procedures necessary to add new employees, make changes to employee data, and delete employees. Because December 31st is the end of the year, you will also display the quarterly report and W-2 statements. Answer audit questions 8-B on pages 362–364 as you complete this problem. Display reports as necessary to answer the questions.

1 Start *Integrated Accounting* 6e.

2 Load file IA6 Problem 08-B.

3 Enter your name in the Your Name text box.

4 Save the file as 08-B1 Your Name.

5 Enter the employee maintenance data:

Add new employee Zachary, Sarah; 11732 Kettering Dr.; Atlanta, GA 30345-0060; Assign employee number 290; Social Security number, 596-35-7381; withholding allowances, 1; pay periods per year, 12; G.L. Account, 6210 (Sales Salaries Exp.); hourly, $10.00; single.

Change the marital status of Griffith, Phillip to married and the withholding allowances to 2.

Change the street address of Schilling, Frank to 8416 Pinnacle Ct.

Delete employee no. 230 (Kastella, Earl).

6 Enter the following November payroll transactions and generate paychecks. Withhold all three voluntary deductions this pay period (health insurance, dental insurance, and credit union deductions) and use a transaction date of 11/30/—. Calculate taxes using the Calculate Taxes button.

November Payroll

Nov. 30   Record the monthly payroll check to Falgren, Eunice; Check No. 562; salary amount, $5,000.00; health insurance, $75.00; dental insurance, $35.00; credit union, $350.00.

30   Record the monthly payroll check to Griffith, Phillip; Check No. 563; regular hours, 140.0; health insurance, $65.00; dental insurance, $25.00; credit union, $75.00.

30   Record the monthly payroll check to Mettler, Mary; Check No. 564; regular hours, 168.0; one-and-a-half times overtime hours, 4.5; health insurance, $85.00; dental insurance, $35.00; credit union, $100.00.

30   Record the monthly payroll check to Phelps, Donna; Check No. 565; regular hours, 168.0; health insurance, $65.00; dental insurance, $25.00; credit union, $100.00.

30   Record the monthly payroll check to Schilling, Frank; Check No. 566; salary amount, $4,324.00; health insurance, $80.00; dental insurance, $30.00; credit union, $300.00.

30   Record the monthly payroll check to Winters, Annette; Check No. 567; regular hours, 168.0; one-and-a-half times overtime hours, 2.5; double overtime hours, 2.0; health insurance, $65.00; dental insurance, $25.00; credit union, $50.00.

30   Record the monthly payroll check to Yoshino, Sumio; Check No. 568; salary amount, $2,850.00; health insurance, $70.00; dental insurance, $28.00; credit union, $50.00.

30   Record the monthly payroll check to Zachary, Sarah; Check No. 569; regular hours, 148.0; health insurance, $65.00; dental insurance, $25.00; credit union, $85.00.

7   **Display the employee list report.**

8   **Display the payroll report.**

9   **Generate and post the journal entry for the current payroll.**

10   **Generate and post the employer's payroll taxes journal entry.**

11   **Display the November payroll journal entries.**

12   **Save your data to disk with file name 08-B1 Your Name.**

13   **Use Save As to save the data with a file name of 08-B2 Your Name.**

14   **Enter the following December payroll transactions and generate paychecks. Withhold all three voluntary deductions this pay period (health insurance, dental insurance, and credit union deductions) and use a transaction date of 12/31/—.**

December Payroll

Dec. 31   Record the monthly payroll check to Falgren, Eunice; Check No. 570; salary amount, $5,000.00; health insurance, $75.00; dental insurance, $35.00; credit union, $350.00.

31   Record the monthly payroll check to Griffith, Phillip; Check No. 571; regular hours, 176.0; one-and-a-half times overtime hours, 1.5; health insurance, $65.00; dental insurance, $25.00; credit union, $75.00.

31   Record the monthly payroll check to Mettler, Mary; Check No. 572; regular hours, 176.0; health insurance, $85.00; dental insurance, $35.00; credit union, $100.00.

31   Record the monthly payroll check to Phelps, Donna; Check No. 573; regular hours, 168.0; health insurance, $65.00; dental insurance, $25.00; credit union, $100.00.

31   Record the monthly payroll check to Schilling, Frank; Check No. 574; salary amount, $4,324.00; health insurance, $80.00; dental insurance, $30.00; credit union, $300.00.

31   Record the monthly payroll check to Winters, Annette; Check No. 575; regular hours, 176.0; health insurance, $65.00; dental insurance, $25.00; credit union, $50.00.

31   Record the monthly payroll check to Yoshino, Sumio; Check No. 576; salary amount, $2,850.00; health insurance, $70.00; dental insurance, $28.00; credit union, $50.00.

31   Record the monthly payroll check to Zachary, Sarah; Check No. 577; regular hours, 176.0; one-and-a-half times overtime hours, 4.5; double overtime hours, 3.0; health insurance, $65.00; dental insurance, $25.00; credit union, $85.00.

15   **Display the December payroll report.**

16   **Generate and post the journal entry for the current payroll.**

17   **Generate and post the employer's payroll taxes journal entry.**

18   **Display the December payroll journal entries.**

19   **Generate a labor distribution graph.**

20   **Display the quarterly report.**

21   **Display the W-2 statements.**

22   **Save your data to disk with a file name of 08-B2 Your Name.**

23   **Use the Savings Planner to calculate the monthly contribution given the following information:**

Beginning savings...$17,500.00

Annual yield...8.25%

Number of months...60

Ending savings balance.........................$175,000.00

24   **Optional spreadsheet integration activity.**

The management at Wilker Merchandising Co., asked you to use a spreadsheet to prepare a payroll distribution of gross earnings report for the year.

a.   Copy the payroll report to the clipboard in spreadsheet format.

b.   Start up your spreadsheet software and load the template file IA6 Spreadsheet 08-A.

c. Select cell A1 as the current cell (if not already selected) and paste the report copied in step a into the spreadsheet.

d. Enter *+A3* in cell A120.

Enter *Payroll Distribution (Gross Earnings)* in cell A121.

Enter *+A5* in cell A122.

Enter *Employee* in cell A124.

Enter *Gross Earnings* in cell B124.

Enter the cell references to each employee and their corresponding yearly gross earnings in the columns under the respective headings.

Enter the appropriate formula to sum the gross earnings.

Format the report (align headings, format currency cells, etc.).

e. Generate a pie chart.

Select the range of cells containing the employee number/name and corresponding gross earnings, then choose the Chart or Graph menu items from the spreadsheet program you are using. If the computer asks for a graph name, etc., enter *Payroll Distribution* and click OK. Choose Pie Chart from the toolbar if the graph that appears is not a pie chart. Finally, if the spreadsheet you are using permits copying and pasting the chart into the worksheet, copy and paste the chart immediately after the payroll distribution report cells.

f. Print the payroll distribution report portion of the spreadsheet and pie chart.

g. Save the spreadsheet data with a file name of 08-B Your Name.

h. End your spreadsheet session.

25 **Optional word processing integration activity.**

The personal department asked you to prepare a report showing each employee's general ledger salary expense account number and salary/hourly rate.

a. Display and copy the employee list to the clipboard in word processing format.

b. Start up your word processing application software and create a new document. (Use a fixed type font such as Courier.)

c. Paste the employee list report into the document.

d. Enter headings, delete unwanted data, and so on, and then format the report for the desired data.

e. Print the completed report.

f. Save the document with a file name of 08-B Your Name.

g. End your word processing session.

If you have access to the Internet, use your browser to find information about tax preparation or tax preparation assistance that is available via the Internet. *Hint*: Use U.S. IRS and its appropriate links to obtain the information. Report your findings. Be sure to indicate the sources, including the URLs (Web addresses), of your reported findings.

26   **End the *Integrated Accounting* 6e session.**

Audit Questions 8-B

NAME

November Payroll   *Use the payroll file you saved under file name 08-B1 Your Name to answer the following questions for the November payroll.*

Employee List

1. What is the number of withholding allowances for Eunice Falgren? _____
    _____

2. What is Phillip Griffith's street address? _____
    _____

Payroll Report

3. What is Mary Mettler's hourly rate? _____
    _____

4. What is the current gross pay for Mary Mettler? _____
    _____

5. What is the Medicare amount withheld for the quarter for Frank Schilling? _____
    _____

6. What is Annette Winter's gross pay for the quarter? _____
    _____

7. What is Sarah Zachary's current net pay? _____
    _____

8. What is the total current net pay for all employees? _____
    _____

9. What is the total yearly gross pay for all employees? _____
    _____

Journal Entries Report

10. What is the amount of the credit to employee state income tax payable? _____
    _____

11. What is the amount of the credit to health insurance premiums payable? _____
    _____

12. What is the amount of the credit to salaries payable? _____
    _____

December Payroll   *Use the payroll file you saved under file name 08-B2 Your Name to answer the following questions for the December payroll.*

Payroll Report

1.   What is the current net pay for Mary Mettler? _____

2.   What is the current federal withholding amount for Frank Schilling? _____

3.   What is the Medicare amount withheld for the year for Frank Schilling? _____

4.   What is the check number for the check written to Sumio Yoshino? _____

5.   What is the total current credit union amount withheld for all employees? _____

6.   What is the total yearly Social Security–OASDI withheld for all employees? _____

Journal Entries Report

7.   What is the amount of the credit to Social Security tax payable–OASDI? _____

8.   What is the amount of the debit to payroll taxes expense? _____

9.   What is the amount of the credit to salaries payable? _____

Quarterly Report

10.   What is the taxable Social Security amount for Frank Schilling? _____

11.   What is the total taxable Medicare amount for all employees for the quarter? _____

W-2 Statements

12.   What is the amount of Social Security tax shown for Eunice Falgren? _____

13.   What is the city tax shown for Donna Phelps? _____

Savings Planner

14.   What is the amount of monthly contribution required to accumulate a savings of $175,000.00 based on the information provided in this problem? _____

_____

15.   What is the monthly yield for month 60? _____

_____

Partnerships and Corporations

Upon completion of this chapter, you will be able to:

- Identify the basic differences among businesses organized as sole proprietorships, partnerships, and corporations.

- Identify the components and procedures used in the accounting cycle for partnerships and corporations.

- Complete the period-end closing procedure for a partnership.

- Enter journal transactions for a corporation.

- Identify some key differences between the financial statements of partnerships and corporations.

Introduction

In the previous chapters, you performed computerized accounting activities for businesses that were organized as **sole proprietorships**. A sole proprietorship has one owner. In this chapter, you will use *Integrated Accounting* 6e to process an accounting cycle for a partnership and a corporation. A **partnership** is a business that is owned by two or more persons. Many small businesses are organized as partnerships to take advantage of combined capital, managerial experience, and the expertise of two or more individuals. A **corporation** is a business that exists as a separate legal entity and is owned by stockholders. Most large U.S. businesses are organized as corporations. Table 9.1 shows some of the characteristics of sole proprietorships, partnerships, and corporations.

	Sole Proprietorship	Partnership	Corporation
Owner	One individual	Two or more persons	Stockholders
Advantage	Owner makes all decisions	Owners share managerial and technical expertise	Owners have limited risk
Disadvantages	Owner assumes all risks	Owners may disagree on best way to manage	Owners have little influence on business decisions

TABLE 9.1

Characteristics of Business Organizations

   This accounting software is designed to recognize the various types of business organizations and to tailor its output to the proper business organization. For example, the balance sheet for a partnership is similar to that of a sole proprietorship except that the capital section lists the capital and drawing account balances of each partner. In contrast, the balance sheet for a corporation contains a stockholders' equity section instead of a capital section. Also, a retained earnings statement is available for corporations. Chapter 12 will explain how to specify the type of business organization during system setup.

   The operational procedures used in performing computerized accounting processing for sole proprietorships in the previous chapters are the same as those for a partnership or a corporation. However, this chapter will identify input transactions that are unique to partnerships and corporations. Examples taken from two computer problems at the end of this chapter will enhance your understanding of this material and assist in solving these problems.

Partnerships

Tate Architecture Inc., is a partnership that will be used as an example in the following discussion and in Problem 9-A. For a partnership with equal distribution of income or loss, the computer will automatically generate and post the entries to distribute the balance in the Income Summary account to the partners' capital accounts and close the partners' Drawing accounts. If the distribution is unequal (as in the problem in this chapter), entries will be generated and posted that will close the net income or loss to the Income Summary account by clicking on the Gen. Led. navigation button and then the Generate Closing Entries menu button (or by choosing Generate Closing Journal Entries from the Options menu). Journal entries must then be made to distribute the income or loss from the Income Summary account to the partners' Capital accounts and to close the partners' Drawing accounts to their respective Capital accounts.

Three partners own Tate Architecture Inc. Notice that each partner has a Capital and a Drawing account as listed in the chart of accounts for Tate Architecture Inc., in Figure 9.1.

FIGURE 9.1

Chart of Accounts for Tate Architecture Inc.

Tate Architecture Inc.
Chart of Accounts
12/31/—

Assets

1110	Cash
1120	Accounts Receivable
1130	Supplies
1140	Prepaid Insurance
1510	Office Equipment
1520	Accum. Deprec. Off. Eq.

Liabilities

2110	Accounts Payable

Owners' Equity

3110	Douglas Foster, Capital
3120	Douglas Foster, Drawing
3130	Karen Knutson, Capital
3140	Karen Knutson, Drawing
3150	Gary Sabin, Capital
3160	Gary Sabin, Drawing
3170	Income Summary

Revenue

4110	Fees

Expenses

5110	Advertising Expense
5120	Salaries Expense
5130	Rent Expense
5140	Utilities Expense
5150	Insurance Expense
5160	Supplies Expense
5170	Telephone Expense
5180	Travel Expense
5190	Deprec. Exp.—Off. Eq.
5200	Miscellaneous Expense

The partnership agreement for Tate Architecture Inc., states that Douglas Foster will receive 35 percent, Karen Knutson will receive 35 percent, and Gary Sabin will receive 30 percent of net income or loss. Figure 9.2 shows a trial balance for the company after the computer performs the closing. Notice that during the closing process, the computer brings forward the net income to the Income Summary account (account number 3170). Figure 9.3 shows the entries that you would make to complete the closing process. Figure 9.4 shows the trial balance after these general journal entries have been entered and posted in the general journal.

FIGURE 9.2

Trial Balance After Closing Entries Are Generated and Posted

Tate Architecture Inc.
Trial Balance
12/31/—

Acct. Number	Account Title	Debit	Credit
1110	Cash	7,956.77	
1120	Accounts Receivable	14,500.00	
1130	Supplies	2,056.00	
1140	Prepaid Insurance	240.00	
1510	Office Equipment	13,550.00	
1520	Accum. Deprec. Off. Eq.		5,423.74
2110	Accounts Payable		985.00
3110	Douglas Foster, Capital		7,800.00
3120	Douglas Foster, Drawing	35,450.00	
3130	Karen Knutson, Capital		7,800.00
3140	Karen Knutson, Drawing	35,450.00	
3150	Gary Sabin, Capital		3,900.00
3160	Gary Sabin, Drawing	18,600.00	
3170	Income Summary		101,894.03
	Totals	127,802.77	127,802.77

NOTE The computer has closed the net income to the Income Summary account.

FIGURE 9.3

Closing Entries for Income Summary and Drawing Accounts

Tate Architecture Inc.
General Journal
12/31/—

Date	Refer.	Acct.	Title	Debit	Credit
12/31	Clo.Ent.	3110	Douglas Foster, Capital	35,450.00	
12/31	Clo.Ent.	3120	Douglas Foster, Drawing		35,450.00
12/31	Clo.Ent.	3130	Karen Knutson, Capital	35,450.00	
12/31	Clo.Ent.	3140	Karen Knutson, Drawing		35,450.00
12/31	Clo.Ent.	3150	Gary Sabin, Capital	18,600.00	
12/31	Clo.Ent.	3160	Gary Sabin, Drawing		18,600.00
12/31	Clo.Ent.	3170	Income Summary	101,894.03	
12/31	Clo.Ent.	3110	Douglas Foster, Capital		35,662.91
12/31	Clo.Ent.	3130	Karen Knutson, Capital		35,662.91
12/31	Clo.Ent.	3150	Gary Sabin, Capital		30,568.21
			Totals	191,394.03	191,394.03

The drawing accounts are closed to their respective capital accounts. The net income is distributed to the partners: 35 percent of net income to Douglas Foster ($101,894.03 × .35 = $35,662.91), 35 percent to Karen Knutson ($101,894.03 × .35 = $35,662.91), and 30 percent to Gary Sabin ($101,894.03 × .30 = $30,568.21).

FIGURE 9.4

Trial Balance After Closing Entries

Tate Architecture Inc.
Trial Balance
12/31/—

Acct. Number	Account Title	Debit	Credit
1110	Cash	7,956.77	
1120	Accounts Receivable	14,500.00	
1130	Supplies	2,056.00	
1140	Prepaid Insurance	240.00	
1510	Office Equipment	13,550.00	
1520	Accum. Deprec. Off. Eq.		5,423.74
2110	Accounts Payable		985.00
3110	Douglas Foster, Capital		8,012.91
3130	Karen Knutson, Capital		8,012.91
3150	Gary Sabin, Capital		15,868.21
	Totals	38,302.77	38,302.77

The partner's capital accounts have been updated, and the Income Summary and Drawing accounts now have zero balances (and thus do not appear on the post-closing trial balance).

Corporations

Mellen Corporation will be used as an example in the following discussion and in Problem 9-B. Examples of general journal and cash payments journal transactions and report information generated by the computer that are unique for corporations will be provided.

Figure 9.5 shows the chart of accounts for Mellen Corporation. Notice the addition of several accounts in the equity section that were not included for either the sole proprietorship or partnership. Also notice that an account is included for corporate federal income tax.

FIGURE 9.5

Chart of Accounts for Mellen Corporation

Mellen Corporation
Chart of Accounts
12/31/—

Assets
1110	Cash
1120	Accounts Receivable
1130	Merchandise Inventory
1140	Supplies
1510	Equipment
1520	Accum. Deprec. Equipment

Liabilities
2110	Accounts Payable

Stockholders' Equity
3110	Common Stock
3115	Treasury Stock
3120	Retained Earnings
3130	Cash Dividends
3140	Stock Dividends
3150	Approp. for Plant Expan.
3160	Approp. for Treas. Stock
3170	Pd-In Cap. Ex. Par—Com.
3180	Stock Dividends Distrib.
3210	Income Summary

Revenue
4110	Sales

Cost
5110	Cost of Merchandise Sold

Expenses
6110	Advertising Expense
6120	Rent Expense
6130	Utilities Expense
6140	Salaries Expense
6150	Supplies Expense
6160	Miscellaneous Expense
6170	Deprec. Exp. Equipment

Corporate Income Tax
9110	Corporate Income Tax

General Journal Entries

Mellen Corporation requires several different types of journal transactions. These transactions are discussed in detail to provide examples of how stock dividends, issuances of stock certificates, appropriations for treasury stock, appropriations for plant expansion, paying of a cash dividend, and purchases of treasury stock are entered.

Stock Dividend   A **stock dividend** is a proportional issuance of additional stock shares to a corporation's stockholders. Figure 9.6 is an example of a stock dividend transaction. On December 5th, Mellen Corporation declared

a 5-percent common stock dividend on common stock outstanding (55,000 ×
0.05 = 2,750 shares). The current market value of the common stock is $31.50
per share. The market value is used for the debit to Stock Dividends. Before to
this transaction, 55,000 shares of $25.20 **par value** (the amount printed on
each share of stock) common stock were outstanding.

To record this transaction, debit Stock Dividends for $86,625.00 (2,750
shares × $31.50 per share = $86,625.00), credit Stock Dividends Distributable for $69,300.00 (2,750 shares × $25.20 par value = $69,300.00), and
credit Paid-In Capital in Excess of Par—Common Stock for the difference
($86,625.00 − 69,300.00 = $17,325.00). Notice that the market value of the
stock is used for the debit to Stock Dividends, and the par value is used for
the credit to Stock Dividends Distributable. Retained Earnings may be
debited instead of Stock Dividends, but using a separate Stock Dividends
account provides more information. The computer closes Stock Dividends
to Retained Earnings at the end of the accounting period.

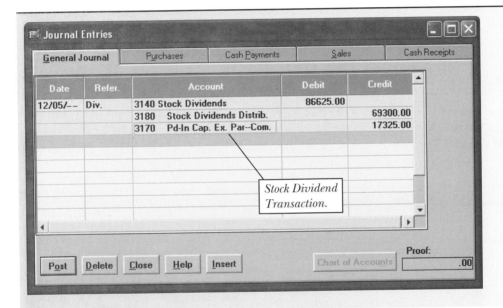

FIGURE 9.6

*Example of Stock
Dividend Transaction*

Issuance of Stock Certificates for Previously Declared Stock Dividend　The
second transaction (shown in Figure 9.7) is an example of issuing common
stock certificates for previously declared stock dividends. On December 8th,
Mellen Corporation issued the stock certificates for the common stock
dividend declared on December 5th. To record this transaction, debit Stock
Dividends Distributable for $69,300.00 and credit Common Stock for
$69,300.00 as illustrated in Figure 9.7.

FIGURE 9.7

*Issuance of Stock
Certificates Transaction*

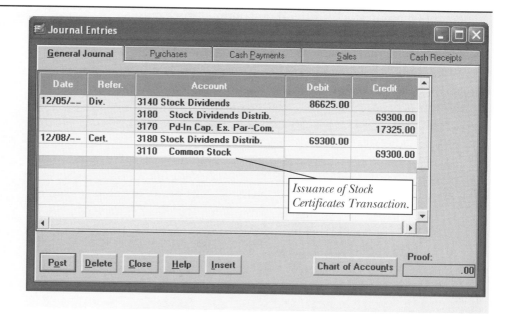

Appropriation for Treasury Stock Shares of stock previously issued and then bought back and held by the corporation are called **treasury stock**. The third transaction (shown in Figure 9.8) is an example of an appropriation to purchase treasury stock. On December 31, the Mellen Corporation's board of directors authorized an appropriation of $30,000.00 for treasury stock. To record this transaction, debit Retained Earnings for $30,000.00 and credit Appropriation for Treasury Stock for $30,000.00.

FIGURE 9.8

*Appropriation for
Treasury Stock
Transaction*

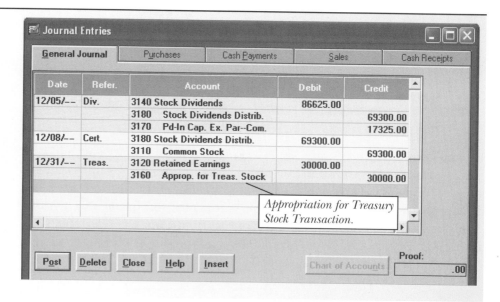

Appropriation for Plant Expansion   The last general journal transaction is an example of an appropriation for plant expansion. On December 31, the Mellen Corporation's board of directors authorized an appropriation of $300,000.00 for plant expansion. To record this transaction, debit Retained Earnings for $300,000.00 and credit Appropriation for Plant Expansion for $300,000.00 as illustrated in Figure 9.9.

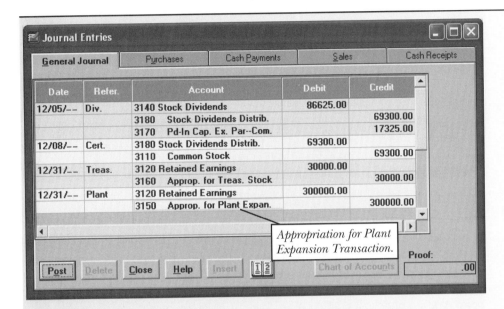

FIGURE 9.9

Appropriation for Plant Expansion Transaction

Cash Payments

Cash payment transactions for Mellen Corporation for entering cash dividends and for purchasing treasury stock are discussed next.

Payment of Cash Dividend   The transaction shown in Figure 9.10 is an example of the payment of a cash dividend. On December 2nd, Mellen Corporation declared and paid an annual dividend of $3.25 per share on the 55,000 shares of common stock outstanding to stockholders of record (Check No. 4253).

To record a cash payment for a dividend, enter the date and check number in the appropriate grid cells. Debit Cash Dividends (account number 3130) for $178,750.00 ($3.25 × 55,000). The computer will automatically credit Cash for $178,750.00.

 If a dividend is declared but not paid, a liability account for Dividends Payable would be used.

FIGURE **9.10**

*Payment of Cash
Dividend Transaction*

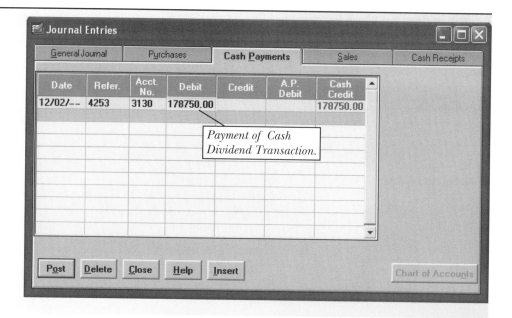

Payment for Purchase of Common Stock   The second transaction (shown in Figure 9.11) is the payment for the purchase of the business's own common stock. This common stock is now called treasury stock because the corporation reacquired it. On December 24th, Mellen Corporation purchased 2,500 shares of its own common stock at $30.25, recording the stock at cost (Check No. 4260). To record the transaction, debit Treasury Stock (account number 3115) for $75,625.00 ($30.25 × 2,500). The computer will automatically credit Cash for $75,625.00.

FIGURE **9.11**

*Purchase of Treasury
Stock Transaction*

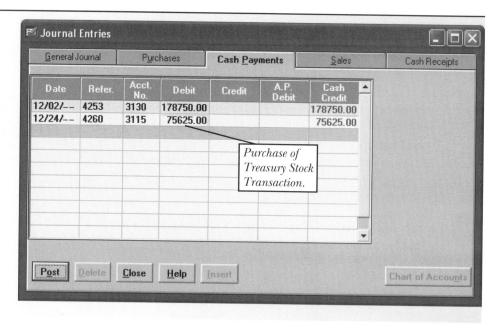

Reports

The financial statements for a corporation are slightly different from those of a business organized as a sole proprietorship or partnership. The retained earnings statement is only available for a corporation.

Income Statement for a Corporation

When the income statement report is chosen, a section referred to as income tax will be included at the end of the statement as shown in Figure 9.12. This section reports the amount of income tax expense for the corporation. The final amount shown on the statement is the net income after the income tax is deducted. Other than these minor changes, the format of the income statement of a corporation is the same as that of a sole proprietorship or partnership.

Mellen Corporation Income Statement For Year Ended 12/31/—	Monthly Amount	Monthly Percent	Yearly Amount	Yearly Percent
Operating Revenue				
Sales	465,125.00	100.00	5,636,905.00	100.00
Total Operating Revenue	465,125.00	100.00	5,636,905.00	100.00
Cost				
Cost of Merchandise Sold	148,839.20	32.00	3,543,865.20	62.87
Total Cost	148,839.20	32.00	3,543,865.20	62.87
Gross Profit	316,285.80	68.00	2,093,039.80	37.13
Operating Expenses				
Advertising Expense	7,500.00	1.61	143,200.00	2.54
Rent Expense	13,250.00	2.85	161,750.00	2.87
Utilities Expense	3,045.00	0.65	31,222.00	0.55
Salaries Expense	65,565.70	14.10	800,256.00	14.20
Supplies Expense	1,280.00	0.28	20,237.00	0.36
Miscellaneous Expense	425.00	0.09	3,875.00	0.07
Deprec. Exp. Equipment	810.20	0.17	9,262.20	0.16
Total Operating Expenses	91,875.90	19.75	1,169,802.20	20.75
Net Income from Operations	224,409.90	48.25	923,237.60	16.38
Net Income before Income Tax	224,409.90	48.25	923,237.60	16.38
Income Tax				
Corporate Income Tax	35,750.00	7.69	222,650.00	3.95
Net Income after Income Tax	188,659.90	40.56	700,587.60	12.43

FIGURE 9.12

Mellen Corporation Income Statement

Retained Earnings Statement for a Corporation

A retained earnings statement reports changes in a corporation's retained earnings. Notice that the statement is divided into two major sections: (1) appropriated and (2) unappropriated. The appropriated section reports the additions or deductions during the period and ends with the total retained earnings appropriated. The unappropriated section begins with the opening balance and is then followed by dividends, transfers to and from the appropriation accounts, net income, and total retained earnings unappropriated. The final amount shown on the statement is the total retained earnings at the end of the period. A retained earnings statement for Mellen Corporation is shown in Figure 9.13.

FIGURE 9.13

Mellen Corporation Retained Earnings Statement

Mellen Corporation
Retained Earnings Statement
For Year Ended 12/31/—

Appropriated	
Approp. for Plant Expan. (Additional)	300,000.00
Approp. for Treas. Stock (Additional)	30,000.00
Retained Earnings Appropriated	330,000.00
Unappropriated	
Retained Earnings (Beg. of Period)	995,551.00
Cash Dividends	−178,750.00
Stock Dividends	−86,625.00
Transfer Approp. for Plant Expan.	−300,000.00
Transfer Approp. for Treas. Stock	−30,000.00
Net Income	700,587.60
Retained Earnings Unappropriated	1,100,763.60
Retained Earnings (End of Period)	1,430,763.60

Balance Sheet for a Corporation

The balance sheet of a corporation contains a section referred to as the stockholders' equity section. This section reports the investment of the stockholders and the net income retained in the business. A balance sheet for Mellen Corporation is shown in Figure 9.14.

FIGURE 9.14

Mellen Corporation Balance Sheet

Mellen Corporation
Balance Sheet
12/31/—

Assets		
Cash	463,049.00	
Accounts Receivable	175,135.00	
Merchandise Inventory	2,202,224.80	
Supplies	7,540.00	
Equipment	46,125.00	
Accum. Deprec. Equipment	−19,260.20	
Total Assets		2,874,813.60

(continued)

FIGURE 9.14

(Concluded)

Liabilities		
Accounts Payable	173,050.00	
Total Liabilities		173,050.00
Stockholders' Equity		
Common Stock	1,329,300.00	
Treasury Stock	−75,625.00	
Retained Earnings	665,551.00	
Cash Dividends	−178,750.00	
Stock Dividends	−86,625.00	
Approp. for Plant Expan.	30,000.00	
Approp. for Treas. Stock	300,00.00	
Pd-In Cap. Ex. Par—Com.	17,325.00	
Net Income	700,587.60	
Total Stockholders' Equity		2,701,763.60
Total Liabilities & Equity		2,874,813.60

Chapter Summary

■ A business that is owned by one individual is called a sole proprietorship.

■ A business that is owned by two or more persons is called a partnership.

■ A corporation is a business that exists as a separate legal entity and is owned by stockholders.

■ The accounting software is designed to recognize the various types of business organizations and to perform its processing according to the business type that is set up on the computer.

■ The balance sheet for a partnership is similar to that of a sole proprietorship except that the capital section lists the capital and drawing account balances of each partner.

■ The balance sheet for a corporation contains a stockholders' equity section instead of a capital section.

■ A retained earnings statement report is available as an option when the business is organized as a corporation.

■ For a partnership with equal distribution of income or loss, the computer will automatically generate and post the entries to distribute the balance in the Income Summary account to the partners' capital accounts and close the partners' drawing accounts.

■ For a partnership with unequal distribution of income or loss, entries will be generated and posted that will close the net income or loss to the Income Summary account. Journal entries must then be made to distribute the income or loss from the Income Summary account to the partners' capital accounts and to close the partners' drawing accounts to their respective capital accounts.

■ A stock dividend is a proportional issuance of additional stock shares to a corporation's stockholders.

- Par value is the amount printed on each share of stock.

- Stock dividends are recorded in the computer by debiting Stock Dividends, crediting Stock Dividends Distributable, and crediting Paid-In Capital in Excess of Par—Common Stock in the general journal.

- Issuance of stock certificates for a previously declared stock dividend is recorded by debiting Stock Dividends Distributable and crediting Common Stock in the Journal Entries/General Journal window.

- Issued shares of stock that have been bought back and held by the corporation are called treasury stock.

- An appropriation to purchase treasury stock is recorded by debiting Retained Earnings and crediting Appropriation for Treasury Stock in the Journal Entries/General Journal window.

- An appropriation for plant expansion is recorded by debiting Retained Earnings and crediting Appropriation for Plant Expansion in the Journal Entries/General Journal window.

- The payment of a cash dividend is recorded in the computer by debiting Cash Dividends and crediting Cash in the cash payments journal.

- The payment for the purchase of the business's own common stock is recorded in the computer by debiting Treasury Stock and crediting Cash in the cash payments journal.

Chapter 9 Student Exercises

NAME

I Matching
Directions *For each of the definitions, write the letter of the appropriate term in the space provided.*

a. corporation
b. retained earnings statement
c. stock dividend
d. sole proprietorship
e. balance sheet
f. partnership
g. cash dividend
h. income statement

1.____ A business that is owned by one individual.

2.____ A business that is owned by two or more individuals.

3.____ A business that is owned by stockholders.

4.____ A transaction that is entered into the computer via the Journal Entries/General Journal window.

5.____ A transaction that is entered into the computer via the cash payments journal.

6.____ A report that contains a section referred to as the stockholders' equity section, which reports the investment of the stockholders and the net income retained in the business.

7.____ A report that contains the amount of income tax expense for a corporation.

8.____ A report that shows the changes in a corporation's retained earnings from one period to the next.

II Questions
Directions *Answer each of the following questions in the space provided.*

1. What procedure is used to perform period-end closing for a business organized as a partnership with unequal partner distribution of income or loss? _____

_____

_____

2. What information is provided on a corporation's income statement that is not contained on a sole proprietorship or partnership income statement? _____

_____

_____

3. What is the purpose of the retained earnings statement? _____

_____

_____

4. What is the purpose of the stockholders' equity section of the balance sheet? _____

_____

_____

Problem 9-A (Partnerships)

The following transactions for Tate Architecture Inc., occurred during December of the current year. Follow the step-by-step instructions to process the transactions, process the adjusting entries, and prepare the financial statements. You may click Info. on the toolbar for helpful check figures to audit your work.

1   **Start *Integrated Accounting* 6e.**

2   **Open file IA6 Problem 09-A.**

3   **Enter your name in the Your Name text box.**

4   **Use Save As to save your file with a file name of 09-ABC Your Name (where 09-A identifies the problem, and BC represents Before Closing).**

5   **Enter the purchases journal transactions.**

Purchases Journal Transactions

Dec. 02   Purchased supplies on account from Lerner Supply Company, $325.00; Vendor Invoice No. 576.

12   Purchased supplies on account from Stolle Office Products, $160.00; Vendor Invoice No. 577.

21   Purchased office equipment on account from Parker Office Products, $500.00; Vendor Invoice No. 578.

6   **Enter the cash payments journal transactions.**

Cash Payments Journal Transactions

Dec. 06   Paid cash for electric bill, $128.16. Check No. 810.

08   Reimbursed a partner for business travel expense, $155.00. Check No. 811.

 Debit Travel Expense and credit Cash.

10   Paid cash on account to Riverview Media, Inc., $902.00. Check No. 812.

16   Paid cash for advertising, $750.00. Check No. 813.

18   Paid cash on account to Stolle Office Products, $456.00. Check No. 814.

20   Paid cash for telephone bill, $509.73. Check No. 815.

22   Reimbursed a partner for travel expenses, $315.00. Check No. 816.

23   Douglas Foster, a partner, withdrew cash for personal use, $2,450.00. Check No. 817.

23   Karen Knutson, a partner, withdrew cash for personal use, $2,450.00. Check No. 818.

23   Gary Sabin, a partner, withdrew cash for personal use, $2,100.00. Check No. 819.

28   Paid cash for miscellaneous expense, $75.00. Check No. 820.

30   Paid salaries expense, $1,810.62. Check No. 821.

30   Paid cash for rent expense, $935.00. Check No. 822.

7   Enter the sales journal transactions.

Sales Journal Transactions

Dec. 04   Billed Rockmore Construction for consulting services, $4,000.00; Invoice No. 951.

10   Billed Foley Associates, Inc., for consulting services, $3,200.00; Invoice No. 952.

18   Billed Security Engineering Co., for consulting services, $4,800.00; Invoice No. 953.

28   Billed Randall Development Co., for consulting services, $2,500.00; Invoice No. 954.

8   Enter the cash receipts journal transactions.

Cash Receipts Journal Transactions

Dec. 03   Received cash on account from Foley Associates, Inc., covering Invoice No. 930 for $5,554.00.

18   Received cash on account from Security Engineering Co., covering Invoice No. 935 for $7,996.00.

9   Display the journal entries and make corrections, if necessary.

10   Display the trial balance.

11   Display the schedule of accounts payable.

12   Display the schedule of accounts receivable.

End-of-Month Activities

Use the following adjustment data for the month of December for Tate Architecture Inc., and the trial balance report as the basis for preparing the adjusting entries.

Inventory of supplies on December 31.................................$2,056.00

Insurance expired during December...$110.00

Depreciation on office equipment for December $228.74

1   Enter the adjusting entries in the general journal. Enter a reference of Adj.Ent. in the Reference text box.

2   Display the adjusting entries.

3   Display the income statement.

4   **Display the balance sheet.**

5   **Generate an income statement graph.**

6   **Save your data to disk with file name 09-ABC Your Name.**

7   **Optional spreadsheet integration activity.**

The partners at Tate Architecture Inc., asked you to use a spreadsheet to prepare a distribution of net income statement for the current year. For the partially constructed spreadsheet template file, you must complete the following steps:

a. Display and copy the income statement to the clipboard in spreadsheet format.

b. Start your spreadsheet software and load template file IA6 Spreadsheet 09-A.

c. Select cell A1 as the current cell (if not already selected) and paste the income statement into the spreadsheet.

d. Enter the formulas appropriate for your spreadsheet software to calculate the distribution of net income (or loss) for each partner for the year. Also enter the formula to obtain a sum of the partner's distribution.

Douglas Foster = 35 percent

Karen Knutson = 35 percent

Gary Sabin = 30 percent

e. Format the amounts in currency format if necessary.

f. Print the spreadsheet distribution of net income statement.

g. Save your spreadsheet with a file name of 09-A Your Name.

h. What if the distribution of net income were changed as follows:

Douglas Foster = 38 percent

Karen Knutson = 38 percent

Gary Sabin = 24 percent

Change the distribution of net income statement to reflect these partnership percentages. Do not save this data.

i. Exit your spreadsheet session and return to the *Integrated Accounting* 6e application.

8   **Optional word processing integration activity.**

Prepare a memo addressed to each partner of Tate Architecture Inc., showing their distribution of net income for the year ended December 31.

a. Start your word processing software application and create a new document.

b. Enter a memorandum to Douglas Foster, Karen Knutson, and Gary Sabin. If you completed the optional spreadsheet activity in Step 8, copy and paste the distribution of net income from your spreadsheet into your document.

c. Print the memorandum.

d. Save the memorandum with a file name of 09-A Your Name.

e. End your word processing session.

9   **Generate and post the closing journal entries.**

10   **Display the computer-generated closing entries.**

11   **Display a trial balance.**

12   **Enter the journal entries to close the partners' Drawing accounts to their Capital accounts. Also enter the journal entry to close the Income Summary account to the partners' capital accounts based on the method of income distribution: 35 percent to Douglas Foster, 35 percent to Karen Knutson, and 30 percent to Gary Sabin. Enter a reference of Clo.Ent. in the Reference text box.**

13   **Display all the closing entries.**

14   **Display a post-closing trial balance.**

15   **Use Save As to save your data with a file name of 09-AAC (where 09-A identifies the problem, and AC represents After Closing).**

16   **Calculate maturity dates, interest, and value on notes.**

Use the Notes & Interest Planner to calculate the maturity date, interest, and maturity value for each of the following notes. Use the current year for the date of each note.

Note	Date of Note	Principal of Note ($)	Interest Rate (%)	Time of Note
1	Jan. 15	6,000.00	8.25	60 days (based on 360 days)
2	Apr. 20	3,500.00	7.75	30 days (based on 365 days)
3	July 12	9,500.00	10.25	1 year (number of months)
4	Oct. 05	4,000.00	11.50	6 months (number of months)
5	Nov. 01	5,000.00	12.75	120 days (based on 360 days)

INTERNET ACTIVITY

If you have access to the Internet, use your browser to obtain information about the Uniform Partnership Act. *Hint:* Use Uniform Partnership Act as your search string. Report your findings. Be sure to indicate the sources, including the URLs (Web addresses), of your reported findings.

17   **End the *Integrated Accounting* 6e session.**

Audit Questions 9-A

NAME

Directions   *Write the answers to the following questions in the space provided.*

1.   What are the total fees for the month of December?   _____

   _____

   _____

2.   What is the total amount owed to Parker Office Products?   _____

   _____

   _____

3.   What is the total amount of accounts payable at the end of December?   _____

   _____

   _____

4.   What is the total amount of accounts receivable at the end of December?   _____

   _____

   _____

5.   What is the net income for the current month?   _____

   _____

   _____

6.   What is the net income expressed as a percentage of total operating revenue for the current
   year?   _____

   _____

   _____

7.   What are the amounts withdrawn by each of the three partners as shown on the balance sheet?

   _____

   _____

8.   What is the amount of total assets as shown on the balance sheet?   _____

   _____

   _____

9.   What is the amount of capital for each of the three partners as shown on the post-closing trial
   balance?   _____

   _____

   _____

10.   What is the amount of interest for note 3?   _____

_____

_____

11.   What is the maturity date of note 4?   _____

_____

_____

12.   What is the maturity value of note 5?   _____

_____

_____

Problem 9-B (Corporations)

The following transactions for Mellen Corporation occurred during December of the current year. Follow the step-by-step instructions to enter the transactions, process the adjusting entries, and prepare the financial statements. The transactions in this problem do not require vendor or customer names. (Mellen Corporation does not maintain vendor and customer ledgers). You may click Info. on the toolbar for helpful check figures to audit your work.

1   Start *Integrated Accounting* 6e.

2   Open file IA6 Problem 09-B.

3   Enter your name in the Your Name text box.

4   Use Save As to save your file with a file name of 09-BBC Your Name (where 09-B identifies the problem, and BC represents Before Closing).

5   Enter the general journal transactions.

General Journal Transactions

Dec. 05   Declared a 5-percent common stock dividend on common stock outstanding (55,000 × 5% = 2,750 shares). The market value of the common stock is $31.50; Reference, Div.

NOTE   Before this transaction, 55,000 shares of common stock with a par value of $25.20 were outstanding.

08   Issued the stock certificates for the common stock dividend declared on December 5th; Reference, Cert.

31   The board of directors authorized an appropriation for treasury stock, $30,000.00; Reference, Treas.

31   The board of directors authorized an appropriation for plant expansion, $300,000.00; Reference, Plant.

6   Enter the purchases journal transactions.

Purchases Journal Transactions

Dec. 11   Purchased merchandise on account, $134,798.00; Invoice No. 5511.

27   Purchased merchandise on account, $173,050.00; Invoice No. 5512.

7   Enter the cash payments journal transactions.

Cash Payments Journal Transactions

Dec. 02   Declared and paid an annual dividend of $3.25 per share on the 55,000 shares of common stock outstanding to stockholders of record; Check No. 4253.

08   Paid cash on account, $140,665.00; Check No. 4254.

09   Paid for advertising, $7,500.00; Check No. 4255.

15 Paid additional federal income tax, $35,750.00; Check No. 4256.

15 Paid salaries, $65,565.70; Check No. 4257.

18 Paid utilities, $3,045.00; Check No. 4258.

21 Paid cash on account, $134,798.00; Check No. 4259.

24 Purchased 2,500 shares of own common stock (treasury stock) at $30.25, recording the stock at cost; Check No. 4260.

27 Paid monthly rent, $13,250.00; Check No. 4261.

29 Paid miscellaneous expense, $425.00; Check No. 4262.

8 **Enter the sales journal transactions.**

Sales Journal Transactions

Dec. 06 Sold merchandise on account, $289,990.00; Sales Invoice No. 3135. The cost of the merchandise sold was $92,796.00.

19 Sold merchandise on account, $175,135.00; Sales Invoice No. 3136. The cost of the merchandise sold was $56,043.20.

9 **Enter the cash receipts journal transactions.**

Cash Receipts Journal Transactions

Dec. 04 Received cash on account, covering Sales Invoice No. 3101 for $50,411.00.

09 Received cash on account, covering Sales Invoice No. 3105 for $289,990.00.

10 **Display the journal entries and make corrections, if necessary.**

11 **Display the trial balance.**

End-of-Month Activities

Use the following adjustment data for the month of December for Mellen Corporation and the trial balance report as the basis for preparing the adjusting entries.

Inventory of supplies on December 31 ....$7,540.00

Depreciation on equipment for December $810.20

1 **Enter the adjusting entries in the general journal. Enter a reference of Adj.Ent. in the Reference text box.**

2 **Display the adjusting entries.**

3 **Display the income statement.**

4 **Display the retained earnings statement.**

5   **Display the balance sheet.**

6   **Generate an expense distribution graph.**

7   **Save your data to disk with a file name of 09-BBC Your Name.**

8   **Optional spreadsheet integration activity.**

Corporations may sell bonds to the investing public to finance operations and expansion. Bonds must be repaid at a certain time and require periodic payments of interest. (In this problem interest will be paid annually.) Use a spreadsheet template to calculate the interest and amortization of a bond issue (sold at a discount) using the effective interest method.

a. Start your spreadsheet software.

b. Open and load the spreadsheet template file: IA6 Spreadsheet 09-B.

c. Enter your name in cell A1.

d. Enter the data about the following bond issue sold at a discount in appropriate cells C5–C9:
    Bond issue: $205,000.00
    Carrying value: $197,179.00
    Length (years): 5
    Face interest rate: 8.75%
    Effective interest rate: 9.75%

e. Highlight and copy cells A14–F14 to the clipboard.

f. Highlight and paste the number of the following rows corresponding to the number of years (minus one) of amortization. For example, in this problem highlight and paste the following four rows: A15–F18.

g. Print the completed spreadsheet.

h. Save the spreadsheet to your disk and folder with a file name of 09-B Your Name. Experiment using different bond issue data.

9   **Optional word processing integration activity.**

Use the company's word processing memorandum template to prepare a memorandum to the accounting department containing the interest and amortization of the bond discount calculated in the spreadsheet.

a. Copy the interest and amortization headings and data for each of the 5 years from the spreadsheet to the clipboard.

b. Start your word processing application software and load template file IA6 Wordprocessing 09-B (load as a text file).

c. Enter your name in the FROM field and complete the remainder of the top portion of the memorandum.

d. Position the insertion point at the location indicated and paste the report. Format the document as necessary.

e. Print the completed document.

f. Save the document to your disk and folder with a file name of 09-B Your Name.

10 **Generate and post the closing journal entries.**

11 **Display the computer-generated closing entries.**

12 **Display the post-closing trial balance.**

13 **Save your data with a file name of 09-BAC Your Name (where 09-B identifies the problem, and AC represents After Closing).**

14 **Calculate maturity dates, interest, and value on notes.**

Use the Notes & Interest Planner to calculate the maturity date, interest, and maturity value for each of the following notes. Use the current year for the date of each note.

Note	Date of Note	Principal of Note ($)	Interest Rate (%)	Time of Note
1	Feb. 10	6,000.00	8.25	60 days (based on 360 days)
2	May 21	5,000.00	9.50	30 days (based on 365 days)
3	June 07	10,000.00	9.75	1 year (number of months)
4	Oct. 25	5,000.00	10.50	6 months (number of months)
5	Dec. 01	8,000.00	11.00	120 days (based on 360 days)

INTERNET ACTIVITY

If you have access to the Internet, use your browser to obtain an incorporation form from a state or city. *Hint:* Use incorporation form as your search string. Print a copy of the form you find. Be sure to note the source and the URL (Web address) where you found the form.

15 **End the *Integrated Accounting* 6e session.**

Audit Questions 9-B

NAME

Directions   *Write the answers to the following questions in the space provided.*

1. What are the totals of the Debit and Credit columns of the general journal (before adjusting entries) for the month of December?

    Total debits: _____

    Total credits: _____

2. What are the totals of the Debit and Credit columns from the purchases journal for the month of December?

    Total debits: _____

    Total credits: _____

3. What are the totals of the Debit and Credit columns from the cash payments journal for the month of December?

    Total debits: _____

    Total credits: _____

4. What are the totals of the Debit and Credit columns from the sales journal for the month of December?

    Total debits: _____

    Total credits: _____

5. What are the totals of the Debit and Credit columns from the cash receipts journal for the month of December?

    Total debits: _____

    Total credits: _____

6. What is the amount of gross profit for the month?   _____

    _____

7. What are the total operating expenses for the year?   _____

    _____

8. What is the net income after income tax for the year?   _____

    _____

9. What is the amount of total retained earnings at the end of the period?   _____

    _____

10. What are the total assets?   _____

    _____

11. What are the total liabilities?   _____

    _____

12. What is the total stockholders' equity? _____

_____

13. What is the amount of unappropriated retained earnings shown on the post-closing trial balance? _____

_____

14. What is the amount of interest for note 3? _____

_____

15. What is the maturity value of note 4? _____

_____

16. What is the maturity date of note 5? _____

_____

COMPREHENSIVE PROBLEM 2

In Comprehensive Problem 2, you will complete the accounting cycle for Herzog Clock Center, a merchandising business organized as a sole proprietorship. You will process the transactions for the month of April 2008, including payroll and fixed assets.

Because the fixed asset system is date sensitive, it is *imperative* that you use a year of 2008. Otherwise, the depreciation reports and the depreciation adjusting entries will be incorrect.

This problem is longer than the problems that were in the chapters. Follow the instructions carefully and enter the transactions accurately. A considerable amount of work will be lost if your data file is damaged or destroyed. For this reason, you should periodically make a backup (duplicate copy) of your data file. If you need to restart the problem, simply load your backup data file. Complete the Audit Questions after finishing the month's work.

1 **Start *Integrated Accounting* 6e.**

2 **Open the file named IA6 Comp Problem 02.**

3 **Enter your name in the Your Name text box.**

4 **Save the file to your disk or folder with a file name of C-2 Your Name.**

5 **Enter the following purchase order and purchase invoice transactions.**

Apr. 03 Ordered the following merchandise from Accurate Clocks, Inc., terms 2/10, n/30. Purchase Order No. 713.

Description	Quantity	Unit Cost
Travel Alarm Clock	20	$16.50

18 Received the following merchandise for Purchase Order No. 711 from Clock Assembly Co., terms 2/10, n/30. Purchase Invoice No. 1273.

Description	Quantity	Unit Cost
Pen & Pencil Desk Clock	5	$41.50

21 Received the following merchandise for Purchase Order No. 712 from Clock Shop, Inc., terms 2/10, n/30. Purchase Invoice No. 1274.

Description	Quantity	Unit Cost
Pendulum Table Clock	10	$63.75

22 Returned the following merchandise to Precision Clock, Mfg., Purchase Invoice No. R1264. (Be sure to enter a quantity of −1 to indicate a return of one item.)

Description	Quantity	Unit Cost
Wood Table Clock	1	$71.35

29 Ordered the following merchandise from Clock Assembly Co., terms 2/10, n/30. Purchase Order No. 714.

Description	Quantity	Unit Cost
Cherry Grandfather Clock	1	$2,125.00
Cuckoo Clock	3	$128.50

6 **Enter the following cash payment transactions.**

Apr. 01   Paid cash for the liability for monthly salaries, $7,819.77; Check No. 3023.

05   Paid cash for the liability for the health insurance deductions withheld from employees, $270.00; Check No. 3024.

05   Paid cash for the liability for the life insurance deductions withheld from employees, $130.00; Check No. 3025.

07   Paid cash for store equipment, $1,225.00; Check No. 3026.

10   Paid cash for the liability for the credit union deductions withheld from employees, $420.00; Check No. 3027.

13   Paid cash for store supplies, $165.58; Check No. 3028.

15   Paid cash for the liability for federal income tax, $903.96; Soc. Sec. Tax—OASDI, $677.04; and Medicare tax—HI, $158.35; Check No. 3029.

15   Paid cash for the liability for state income tax, $304.68; Check No. 3030.

15   Paid cash for the liability for city income tax, $109.20; Check No. 3031.

16   Paid cash for office equipment, $430.00; Check No. 3032.

17   Paid cash for store equipment, $535.00; Check No. 3033.

18   Paid cash for monthly telephone expense, $341.35; Check No. 3034.

22   Paid cash for the liability for federal unemployment tax, $33.36; Check No. 3035.

25   Paid cash for utilities, $405.87; Check No. 3036.

25   Paid purchase invoice no. 1268 to Precision Clock, Mfg., $1,924.35, no discount; Check No. 3037.

28   Paid cash for the liability for state unemployment tax, $327.60; Check No. 3038.

28   Paid cash for office supplies, $125.00; Check No. 3039.

29   Paid cash for office equipment, $1,495.00; Check No. 3040.

29   Nadine Herzog, owner, withdrew cash for personal use, $500.00; Check No. 3041.

30   Paid Purchase Invoice No. 1272 to Precision Clock, Mfg., $1,376.90, less 2% discount, $27.54. Check No. 3042.

7 **Enter the following sales invoice transactions.**

Apr. 02   Sold the following merchandise to Mayfield Golf Club, terms 2/10, n/30, 6% sales tax, Sales Invoice No. 4525:

Description	Quantity Sold	Selling Price
Oak Grandfather Clock	6	$1,589.00
Pen & Pencil Desk Clock	10	$75.00
Paper Weight Clock	4	$35.95
Pocket Watch	5	$50.00

06   Sold the following merchandise to Schaefer Decorating, terms 2/10, n/30, 6% sales tax, Sales Invoice No. 4526:

Description	Quantity Sold	Selling Price
Cherry Grandfather Clock	4	$3,895.00

16   Sold the following merchandise to Kuhl Manufacturing, terms 2/10, n/30, 6% sales tax, Sales Invoice No. 4527:

Description	Quantity Sold	Selling Price
Pendulum Clock	1	$1,695.00
Electric Wall Clock	4	$145.00

21   The following merchandise was returned to Herzog Clock Center by Milner & Son Law Offices, 6% sales tax, sales return no. R4524: (Be sure to enter a quantity of −1 to indicate a return of one item.)

Description	Quantity Returned	Price
Pocket Watch	1	$50.00

25   Sold the following merchandise to Foster Clinic, terms 2/10, n/30, 6% sales tax, Sales Invoice No. 4528:

Description	Quantity Sold	Selling Price
Pendulum Clock	4	$1,695.00
Digital Alarm Clock	3	$34.85
Radio Alarm Clock	1	$39.99
Marble Desk Clock	5	$45.00

8   **Enter the following cash receipt transactions.**

Apr. 03   Received cash on account from Foster Clinic, covering Sales Invoice No. 4522 for $4,991.54, less 2% discount, $99.83.

16   Received cash on account from Mayfield Golf Club, covering Sales Invoice No. 4520 for $10,333.36, less 2% discount, $206.67.

21   Received cash on account from Mayfield Golf Club, covering Sales Invoice No. 4525 for $11,318.47, less 2% discount, $226.37.

28   Received cash on account from Schaefer Decorating, covering Sales Invoice No. 4526 for $16,514.80 less 2% discount, $330.30.

9   **Display the purchase order, purchase invoice, and sales invoice registers for the month of April.**

10   **Display the journal reports (general, purchases, cash payments, sales, and cash receipts).**

11   **Display the schedule of accounts payable and schedule of accounts receivable.**

12   **Display the statement of account for Foster Clinic.**

13   **Display the inventory transactions report for the month of April.**

14   **Enter the following April payroll transactions and generate paychecks. Withhold all three voluntary deductions this pay period (health insurance, life insurance, and credit union deductions). For all payroll transactions, direct the computer to calculate the employee taxes.**

Apr. 30   Record the monthly payroll check to James Forster; gross pay, $3,275.00; health insurance, $50.00; life insurance, $25.00; credit union, $150.00; Check No. 853.

     30   Record the monthly payroll check to Luis Ramos, $3,500.00; health insurance, $85.00; life insurance, $40.00; credit union, $120.00; Check No. 854.

     30   Record the monthly payroll check to Charles Sieberg; gross pay, $2,475.00; health insurance, $85.00; life insurance, $40.00; credit union, $100.00; Check No. 855.

     30   Record the monthly payroll check to Karla Visser; gross pay, $1,670.00; health insurance, $50.00; life insurance, $25.00; credit union, $50.00; Check No. 856.

15   **Display the payroll report.**

16   **Generate and post the current payroll journal entry for April.**

17   **Generate and post the employer's payroll taxes journal entry for April.**

18   **Enter the following fixed assets purchased during April.**

Apr. 07   Display Case for $1,225.00, asset number, 170; depreciation method, straight-line; useful life, 5 years; salvage value, $100.00; accumulated depreciation, account number 1520; depreciation expense, account number 6140.

     16   Binding Machine for $430.00, asset number, 280; depreciation method, sum-of-the-years-digits; useful life, 5 years; salvage value, $35.00; accumulated depreciation, account number 1540; depreciation expense, account number 6560.

     17   Color Monitor for $535.00, asset number, 180; depreciation method, double declining-balance; useful life, 4 years; salvage value, $50.00; accumulated depreciation, account number 1520; depreciation expense, account number 6140.

     29   Notebook Computer for $1,495.00, asset number, 290; depreciation method, MACRS; useful life, 5 years; salvage value, $300.00; accumulated depreciation, account number 1540; depreciation expense, account number 6560.

19   **Display a fixed assets list.**

20   **Display a depreciation schedule for each of the new assets purchased in April.**

21   **Display the trial balance.**

End-of-Month Activities

The depreciation adjusting entries can be generated automatically from the Options menu. The rest of the adjusting entries must be entered into the computer. The following adjustment data are for the month of April for Herzog Clock Center.

Insurance expired during April $80.00
Inventory of supplies on April 30
    Store Supplies $3,260.00
    Office Supplies $2,075.00

1   **Enter and post the adjusting entries in the general journal. Enter Adj.Ent. in the Reference text box.**

2   **Generate and post the depreciation adjusting entries.**

3   **Display the adjusting entries (references of Adj.Ent. and Dep.Adj.).**

4   **Display the income statement.**

5   **Display the statement of owner's equity.**

6   **Display the balance sheet.**

7   **Generate and compare graphs for labor distribution and depreciation for the Notebook Computer.**

8   **Click Save on the toolbar to save the data file.**

9   **End the *Integrated Accounting* 6e session.**

Audit Questions for Comprehensive Problem 2

NAME

Directions   *Write the answers to the following questions in the space provided.*

1.   What are the totals of the purchase order, purchase invoice, and sales invoice registers?

   Purchase order register: _____

   Purchase invoice register: _____

   Sales invoice register: _____

2.   What is the total of the debit and credit columns from the cash payments journal for the month of April?

   Total debits: _____

   Total credits: _____

3.   How many items were sold during the month of April as shown on the inventory transaction report?   _____

   _____

4.   To what account number is James Forster's salary charged?   _____

   _____

5.   What is the amount of net pay for Karla Visser for the year?   _____

   _____

6.   What is the amount of the total social security—OASDI withholding for the year for all employees?   _____

   _____

7.   What is the total amount of the original cost for all assets at the end of April as shown on the fixed assets list?   _____

   _____

8.   What is the amount of depreciation for 2008 for asset number 180, Color Monitor?   _____

   _____

9.   What is the book value at the end of 2009 for asset number 280, Binding Machine?   _____

   _____

10.   What is the total of the debit and credit columns from the general journal for the adjusting entries you entered (reference Adj.Ent.)?

   Total debits: _____

   Total credits: _____

11.   What is the total of the debit and credit columns from the general journal for the depreciation adjusting entries (reference Dep.Adj.)?

Total debits: _____

Total credits: _____

12.   What is the amount of gross profit for the month expressed as a percent of sales as shown on the income statement?   _____

_____

13.   What is the amount of net income for the year as shown on the income statement?   _____

_____

14.   What is the amount of capital at the end of April as shown on the statement of owner's equity?

_____

15.   What is the amount of total assets as shown on the balance sheet?   _____

_____

16.   What is the amount of total liabilities as shown on the balance sheet?   _____

_____

Financial Statement Analysis

Upon completion of this chapter, you will be able to:

- Display and interpret a comparative income statement with horizontal analysis.

- Display and interpret a comparative income statement with vertical analysis.

- Display and interpret a comparative balance sheet with horizontal analysis.

- Display and interpret a comparative balance sheet with vertical analysis.

- Display and interpret financial information regarding earnings performance, efficiency, short-term strength, and long-term strength.

- Display and interpret a statement of cash flows.

Introduction

This chapter will cover several types of financial analysis. The bases for analysis will be the account balances at the end of the current and previous years. In addition, the detailed accounting transactions are used to prepare the statement of cash flows.

Information provided on the financial analysis reports is important for managers when making decisions that affect the future of the company. This information is also valuable to other groups, such as investors, owners, and lenders.

Financial Statement Analysis Reports

The *Integrated Accounting* 6e software provides six financial statement analysis reports: (1) a comparative income statement with horizontal analysis, (2) a comparative income statement with vertical analysis, (3) a comparative balance sheet with horizontal analysis, (4) a comparative balance sheet with vertical analysis, (5) a ratio analysis, and (6) a statement of cash flows. In this chapter, the financial statements for Fossen Corporation will be discussed and illustrated.

Horizontal Analysis

Horizontal analysis compares the ending balance of each account for the current year with the ending balance for the previous year and shows the percentage of change. For example, assume that Fossen Corporation's sales for the current year are $835,395.00 and sales for the previous year were $786,150.00. A horizontal analysis for this item provides the following information:

Current Year	Previous Year	Change	Percent
$836,490.00	$786,150.00	$50,340.00	6.40

When an income statement or balance sheet with horizontal analysis is displayed, the computer calculates the change and the percentage of change for each item on the statement.

Vertical Analysis

Vertical analysis shows the relationship of the component parts to the total. On the income statement, for example, each item is expressed as a percentage of total operating revenue. On the balance sheet, each item is expressed as a percentage of total assets. When the computer displays the statements for Fossen Corporation, the current and previous years' amounts and percentages will be shown.

Ratio Analysis

The **ratio analysis** reports information about the earnings, efficiency, and financial strength of a business. The report classifies the information into four different groups: (1) earnings performance analysis, (2) efficiency analysis, (3) short-term financial strength analysis, and (4) long-term financial strength analysis. The formulas used to compute the information provided in the ratio analysis report are illustrated in Table 10.1.

Ratio Analysis	Formula
Earnings Performance Analysis	
Rate earned on average total assets	net income after federal income tax ÷ average total assets
Rate earned on average stockholders' equity	net income after federal income tax ÷ average stockholders' equity
Rate earned on net sales	net income after federal income tax ÷ net sales
Earnings per share	net income after federal income tax ÷ shares of stock outstanding
Price-earnings ratio	market price per share ÷ earnings per share
Efficiency Analysis	
Accounts receivable turnover ratio	net sales on account ÷ average book value of accounts receivable
Average days for payment	days in year ÷ accounts receivable turnover ratio
Merchandise inventory turnover ratio	cost of merchandise sold ÷ average merchandise inventory
Average number of days sales in merchandise inventory	days in year ÷ merchandise inventory turnover ratio
Short-Term Financial Strength	
Working capital	total current assets − total current liabilities
Current ratio	total current assets ÷ total current liabilities
Acid-test ratio	cash + accounts receivable ÷ total current liabilities
Long-Term Financial Strength	
Debt ratio	total liabilities ÷ total assets
Equity ratio	total stockholders' equity ÷ total assets
Equity per share	total stockholders' equity ÷ shares of capital stock outstanding

TABLE 10.1

Ratio Analysis Report Formulas

Statement of Cash Flows

The **statement of cash flows** reports cash receipts, cash payments, and the change in cash for a business. The report classifies the cash flows into three different groups: (1) cash flows from operating activities, (2) cash flows from investing activities, and (3) cash flows from financing activities. Each cash receipt or payment transaction falls into one of these categories according to its purpose as illustrated in Table 10.2.

TABLE **10.2**	Classsification	Transactions Included
Classification of Cash Flows	Cash flows from operating activities	Cash transactions that determine net income, including cash receipts for sales, interest and dividend revenue, and cash payments for purchases of inventory and operating expenses
	Cash flows from investing activities	Receipts from the sale of investments and long-term assets and payments for the acquisition of investments and long-term assets
	Cash flows from financing activities	Receipts from issuance of equity and debt, dividend payments, purchases of treasury stock, and repayment of the principal on debt

Reports

Financial Analysis Reports

The financial analysis reports are chosen from the Report Selection dialog box shown in Figure 10.1. Each of the financial analysis reports will be explained in sequence.

FIGURE 10.1

Report Selection Dialog Box

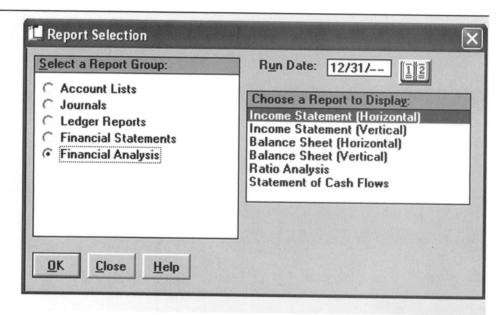

Comparative Income Statement—Horizontal Analysis

The **comparative income statement** compares the income statement for the current year to the income statement for the previous year. With horizontal analysis the amount of increase or decrease is provided for each line of the report. A comparative income statement with horizontal analysis for Fossen Corporation is shown in Figure 10.2.

FIGURE 10.2

*Income Statement
(Horizontal Analysis)*

**Fossen Corporation
Income Stmt. Horizontal Analysis
For Years Ended 12/31/— and 12/31/—**

	Current Period	Previous Period	Change	Percent
Operating Revenue				
Sales	836,490.00	786,150.00	50,340.00	6.40
Sales Returns & Allow.	−6,000.00	−5,645.00	−355.00	6.29
Sales Discounts	−3,595.00	−6,070.94	2,475.94	−40.78
Total Operating Revenue	826,895.00	774,434.06	52,460.94	6.77
Cost				
Cost of Merchandise Sold	593,255.00	577,285.62	15,969.38	2.77
Total Cost	593,255.00	577,285.62	15,969.38	2.77
Gross Profit	233,640.00	197,148.44	36,491.56	18.51
Operating Expenses				
Sales Salaries Expense	63,873.10	66,477.00	−2,603.90	−3.92
Advertising Expense	11,500.00	10,250.00	1,250.00	12.20
Depr. Exp. Store Eqpt.	2,960.00	2,644.00	316.00	11.95
Insurance Expense Selling	3,350.00	2,970.00	380.00	12.79
Store Supplies Expense	1,729.30	2,360.00	−630.70	−26.72
Misc. Selling Expense	1,525.00	704.00	821.00	116.62
Selling Expenses	84,937.40	85,405.00	−467.60	−0.55
Office Salaries Expense	20,377.00	18,605.00	1,772.00	9.52
Utilities Expense	8,776.72	8,956.00	−179.28	−2.00
Depr. Exp. Building	17,000.00	10,845.00	6,155.00	56.75
Depr. Exp. Office Eqpt.	1,135.00	1,425.00	−290.00	−20.35
Insurance Expense General	1,800.00	1,540.00	260.00	16.88
Office Supplies Expense	613.40	601.00	12.40	2.06
Misc. General Expense	415.00	345.00	70.00	20.29
Administrative Expenses	50,117.12	42,317.00	7,800.12	18.43
Total Operating Expenses	135,054.52	127,722.00	7,332.52	5.74
Net Income from Operations	98,585.48	69,426.44	29,159.04	42.00
Other Revenue				
Interest Income	1,833.00	3,470.00	−1,637.00	−47.18
Gain on Sale Office Eqpt.	130.00	200.00	−70.00	−35.00
Other Expense				
Interest Expense	6,211.14	4,650.00	1,561.14	33.57
Net Income before Income Tax	94,337.34	68,446.44	25,890.90	37.83
Income Tax				
Corporate Income Tax	24,872.00	22,655.00	2,217.00	9.79
Net Income after Income Tax	69,465.34	45,791.44	23,673.90	51.70

Comparative Income Statement—
Vertical Analysis

The vertical analysis of the income statement also compares the income statement for the current and previous years. Each item for this year and last year is expressed as a percentage of the **total operating revenue** for the respective year. This statement is similar to the income statement that you have already prepared in the previous chapters. However, it compares the results for 2 years rather than for the month to date and year to date. A comparative income statement with vertical analysis for Fossen Corporation is shown in Figure 10.3.

FIGURE 10.3

Income Statement (Vertical Analysis)

Fossen Corporation
Income Stmt. Vertical Analysis
For Years Ended 12/31/— and 12/31/—

	Current Amount	Current Percent	Previous Amount	Previous Percent
Operating Revenue				
Sales	836,490.00	101.16	786,150.00	101.51
Sales Returns & Allow.	−6,000.00	−0.73	−5,645.00	−0.73
Sales Discounts	−3,595.00	−0.43	−6,070.94	−0.78
Total Operating Revenue	826,895.00	100.00	774,434.06	100.00
Cost				
Cost of Merchandise Sold	593,255.00	71.74	577,285.62	74.54
Total Cost	593,255.00	71.74	577,285.62	74.54
Gross Profit	233,640.00	28.26	197,148.44	25.46
Operating Expenses				
Sales Salaries Expense	63,873.10	7.72	66,477.00	8.58
Advertising Expense	11,500.00	1.39	10,250.00	1.32
Depr. Exp. Store Eqpt.	2,960.00	0.36	2,644.00	0.34
Insurance Expense Selling	3,350.00	0.41	2,970.00	0.38
Store Supplies Expense	1,729.30	0.21	2,360.00	0.30
Misc. Selling Expense	1,525.00	0.18	704.00	0.09
Selling Expenses	84,937.40	10.27	85,405.00	11.03
Office Salaries Expense	20,377.00	2.46	18,605.00	2.40
Utilities Expense	8,776.72	1.06	8,956.00	1.16
Depr. Exp. Building	17,000.00	2.06	10,845.00	1.40
Depr. Exp. Office Eqpt.	1,135.00	0.14	1,425.00	0.18
Insurance Expense General	1,800.00	0.22	1,540.00	0.20
Office Supplies Expense	613.40	0.07	601.00	0.08
Misc. General Expense	415.00	0.05	345.00	0.04
Administrative Expenses	50,117.12	6.06	42,317.00	5.46
Total Operating Expenses	135,054.52	16.33	127,722.00	16.49
Net Income from Operations	98,585.48	11.92	69,426.44	8.96
Other Revenue				
Interest Income	1,833.00	0.22	3,470.00	0.45
Gain on Sale Office Eqpt.	130.00	0.02	200.00	0.03
Other Expense				
Interest Expense	6,211.14	0.75	4,650.00	0.60
Net Income before Income Tax	94,337.34	11.41	68,446.44	8.84
Income Tax				
Corporate Income Tax	24,872.00	3.01	22,655.00	2.93
Net Income after Income Tax	69,465.34	8.40	45,791.44	5.91

Each item in this statement can be analyzed for favorable or unfavorable changes. This vertical analysis can be used in conjunction with the horizontal analysis to determine the significance of any unfavorable changes. For example, the horizontal analysis in Figure 10.2 showed an increase in Fossen Corporation's operating expenses for the current year. However, the vertical analysis reveals that operating expenses expressed as a percentage of total operating revenue have remained about the same.

Comparative Balance Sheet—Horizontal Analysis

The **comparative balance sheet** compares the balance sheet at the end of the current year to the balance sheet at the end of the previous year. In a horizontal comparative balance sheet, the amount and percentage of increase or decrease for each item are shown. This statement can also be used to analyze some of the amounts on the statement of cash flows. A comparative balance sheet using horizontal analysis for Fossen Corporation is shown in Figure 10.4.

FIGURE 10.4

Balance Sheet (Horizontal Analysis)

Fossen Corporation Balance Sheet Horizontal Analysis For Years Ended 12/31/— and 12/31/—	Current Period	Previous Period	Change	Percent
Assets				
Cash	67,534.52	8,216.44	59,318.08	721.94
Notes Receivable	15,091.00	15,143.00	−52.00	−0.34
Interest Receivable	335.00	450.00	−115.00	−25.56
Accounts Receivable	59,650.00	45,255.00	14,395.00	31.81
Merchandise Inventory	77,933.00	69,508.00	8,425.00	12.12
Store Supplies	1,520.00	962.00	558.00	58.00
Office Supplies	1,835.50	414.00	1,421.50	343.36
Prepaid Insurance	3,063.00	963.00	2,100.00	218.07
Total Current Assets	226,962.02	140,911.44	86,050.58	61.07
Land	94,500.00	73,000.00	21,500.00	29.45
Building	286,500.00	212,000.00	74,500.00	35.14
Accum. Depr. Building	−38,479.00	−21,479.00	−17,000.00	79.15
Office Equipment	11,145.00	13,600.00	−2,455.00	−18.05
Accum. Depr. Office Eqpt.	−3,587.00	−2,987.00	−600.00	20.09
Store Equipment	31,200.00	29,700.00	1,500.00	5.05
Accum. Depr. Store Eqpt.	−8,904.00	−5,944.00	−2,960.00	49.80
Total Plant Assets	372,375.00	297,890.00	74,485.00	25.00
Total Assets	599,337.02	438,801.44	160,535.58	36.59

(continued)

FIGURE 10.4

(Concluded)

Liabilities				
Interest Payable	1,325.00	650.00	675.00	103.85
Accounts Payable	97,111.00	19,761.00	77,350.00	391.43
Salaries Payable	1,454.00	1,250.00	204.00	16.32
Notes Payable	4,950.00	10,000.00	−5,050.00	−50.50
Current Liabilities	104,840.00	31,661.00	73,179.00	231.13
Mortgage Note Payable	161,391.24	123,500.00	37,891.24	30.68
Long-Term Liabilities	161,391.24	123,500.00	37,891.24	30.68
Total Liabilities	266,231.24	155,161.00	111,070.24	71.58
Stockholders' Equity				
Capital Stock	150,000.00	150,000.00		
Retained Earnings	133,640.44	106,719.00	26,921.44	25.23
Dividends	−20,000.00	−18,000.00	−2,000.00	11.11
Net Income	69,465.34	44,921.44	24,543.90	54.64
Total Stockholders' Equity	333,105.78	283,640.44	49,465.34	17.44
Total Liabilities & Equity	599,337.02	438,801.44	160,535.58	36.59

In Figure 10.4, notice that the change in the Cash account from the previous year to the current year agrees with the increase shown on the statement of cash flows in Figure 10.8. Notice that the changes in Land, Building, and Store Equipment accounts agree with the amounts on the statement of cash flows.

Comparative Balance Sheet—Vertical Analysis

The vertical analysis of the balance sheet compares the balance sheet at the end of the current and previous years. Each item on the balance sheet for this year and for last year is expressed as a percentage of the **total assets** for the appropriate year. A comparative balance sheet with vertical analysis for Fossen Corporation is shown in Figure 10.5.

FIGURE 10.5

Balance Sheet (Vertical Analysis)

Fossen Corporation
Balance Sheet Vertical Analysis
For Years Ended 12/31/— and 12/31/—

	Current Amount	Current Percent	Previous Amount	Previous Percent
Assets				
Cash	67,534.52	11.27	8,216.44	1.87
Notes Receivable	15,091.00	2.52	15,143.00	3.45
Interest Receivable	335.00	0.06	450.00	0.10
Accounts Receivable	59,650.00	9.95	45,255.00	10.31
Merchandise Inventory	77,933.00	13.00	69,508.00	15.84
Store Supplies	1,520.00	0.25	962.00	0.22
Office Supplies	1,835.50	0.31	414.00	0.09
Prepaid Insurance	3,063.00	0.51	963.00	0.22
Total Current Assets	226,962.02	37.87	140,911.44	32.11

(continued)

Land	94,500.00	15.77	73,000.00	16.64	**FIGURE 10.5**
Building	286,500.00	47.80	212,000.00	48.31	*(Concluded)*
Accum. Depr. Building	−38,479.00	−6.42	−21,479.00	−4.89	
Office Equipment	11,145.00	1.86	13,600.00	3.10	
Accum. Depr. Office Eqpt.	−3,587.00	−0.60	−2,987.00	−0.68	
Store Equipment	31,200.00	5.21	29,700.00	6.77	
Accum. Depr. Store Eqpt.	−8,904.00	−1.49	−5,944.00	−1.35	
Total Plant Assets	372,375.00	62.13	297,890.00	67.89	
Total Assets	599,337.02	100.00	438,801.44	100.00	
Liabilities					
Interest Payable	1,325.00	0.22	650.00	0.15	
Accounts Payable	97,111.00	16.20	19,761.00	4.50	
Salaries Payable	1,454.00	0.24	1,250.00	0.28	
Notes Payable	4,950.00	0.83	10,000.00	2.28	
Current Liabilities	104,840.00	17.49	31,661.00	7.22	
Mortgage Note Payable	161,391.24	26.93	123,500.00	28.14	
Long-Term Liabilities	161,391.24	26.93	123,500.00	28.14	
Total Liabilities	266,231.24	44.42	155,161.00	35.36	
Stockholders' Equity					
Capital Stock	150,000.00	25.03	150,000.00	34.18	
Retained Earnings	133,640.44	22.30	106,719.00	24.32	
Dividends	−20,000.00	−3.34	−18,000.00	−4.10	
Net Income	69,465.34	11.59	44,921.44	10.24	
Total Stockholders' Equity	333,105.78	55.58	283,640.44	64.64	
Total Liabilities & Equity	599,337.02	100.00	438,801.44	100.00	

Ratio Analysis Report

When the ratio analysis report is chosen, the Ratio Analysis dialog box shown in Figure 10.6 will appear. Enter the total number of shares of stock outstanding for the current period (65,000) in the Shares Stock Outstanding text box, enter the market price per share (4.85) in the Price Per Share text box, and click OK. The ratio analysis report is shown in Figure 10.7.

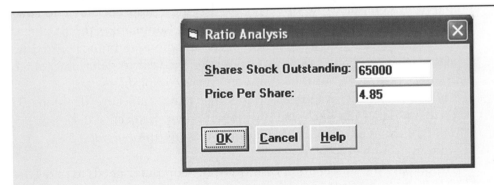

FIGURE 10.6

Ratio Analysis Dialog Box

FIGURE 10.7	**Fossen Corporation** **Ratio Analysis** **For Years Ended 12/31/— and 12/31/—**	
Ratio Analysis Report		

Earnings Performance Analysis
Rate Earned on Average Total Assets	13.38%
Rate Earned on Average Stockholders' Equity	22.53%
Rate Earned on Net Sales	8.40%
Earnings Per Share	1.07
Price-Earnings Ratio	4.53 times

Efficiency Analysis
Accounts Receivable Turnover Ratio	15.76 times
Average Days for Payment	23 days
Merchandise Inventory Turnover Ratio	8.05 times
Average Number of Days Sales in Merch. Inv.	45 days

Short-Term Financial Strength
Working Capital	122,122.02
Current Ratio	2.16 times
Acid-Test Ratio	1.21 times

Long-Term Financial Strength Analysis
Debt Ratio	44.42%
Equity Ratio	55.58%
Equity Per Share	5.12

Statement of Cash Flows

There are two methods of reporting cash flows from operating activities are (1) the direct method, and (2) the indirect method. The **direct method of reporting cash flow** reports the operating cash receipts and payments. The difference between the operating cash receipts and the operating cash payments is reported as the net cash flow from operating activities.

The **indirect method of reporting cash flow** reconciles the net income with the net cash flow from operations. It begins with the net income and removes any item that does not affect cash. If a statement of cash flows is being prepared manually, the indirect method is more efficient because less data are needed to prepare the report. If the statement of cash flows is being prepared by computer, the direct method is more appropriate. The computer analyzes each transaction that affects cash, summarizes the data, and prepares the statement of cash flows. It can be tedious and time consuming to manually analyze all of the transactions for the year to determine which ones affect cash flow, but the computer can accomplish this task in a few seconds. The indirect method requires that many subjective decisions be made about data to be included on the statement. Subjective decisions are difficult for a computer to make. For these reasons, the *Integrated Accounting* 6e software uses the direct method.

To prepare the statement of cash flows, the computer needs to know the ranges of account numbers for long-term assets and liabilities. These data are provided when the business is set up in the Classify Accts. tab in the Setup Accounting System window (this will be covered in Chapter 12).

The statement of cash flows shows the cash receipts and payments grouped by operating activities, investing activities, and financing activities.

The computer places the cash transactions affecting long-term liabilities or capital in the financing activities section. The cash transactions that affect long-term assets are placed in the investing activities section. The computer analyzes the cash transactions and places the totals for the offsetting debits and credits for the Cash account in the appropriate section of the statement of cash flows.

The computer analyzes all of the journal entries for the year. When the computer encounters a transaction involving the Cash account, it analyzes that transaction to determine the effect on cash flow. For example, if the computer encounters a credit to Cash, the computer then analyzes the entries above and below the cash credit to determine the parts of that transaction.

You will encounter one type of transaction that you must record differently than you would in a manual system. This situation arises because part of the transaction should not be used to calculate cash flow, but another part of the transaction does affect cash flow.

For example, assume that Fossen Corporation receives $2,050.00 in cash for the sale of office equipment. The cost of the equipment was $2,455.00 and associated accumulated depreciation is $535.00. Usually, you would record this entry as shown here.

Cash	$2,050.00	
Accum. Depr. Office Eqpt	$535.00	
Office Equipment		$2,455.00
Gain on Sale Office Eqpt		$130.00

If you enter the transaction into the computer in this way, the statement of cash flows will show the $130.00 gain in the operating activities section and the $2,455.00 and $535.00 amounts in the investing activities section. However, the statement should show the $2,050.00 amount in the investing activities section, and the gain should not appear on the statement. Therefore, you can separate the entry as follows: (1) enter the cash receipt portion of the transaction into the computer via the Journal Entries/Cash Receipts window (as shown in the following first journal entry); and (2) enter the remainder of the transaction into the computer via the General Journal window (as shown in the following second journal entry), so that the data will appear in the proper section of the statement of cash flows.

Cash	$2,050.00	
Office Equipment		$2,050.00
Accum. Depr. Office Eqpt	$535.00	
Office Equipment		$405.00
Gain on Sale Office Eqpt		$130.00

Because office equipment is classified as a long-term asset, the computer will place the $2,050.00 cash receipt in the investing activities section of the statement of cash flows. The other entries will not be reflected in the statement because they do not affect cash. When you encounter this entry in the sample problem, it will be illustrated for you in the appropriate journal in this manner.

The computer shows the statement of cash flows in more detail than a manual statement would. For example, rather than summarizing the cash received from customers, the computer shows the amount of cash provided from cash sales and collected from accounts receivable, less the sales discounts. The total of these three amounts is the cash received from customers. A statement of cash flows for Fossen Corporation is shown in Figure 10.8. Notice that the bottom of the report reconciles cash at the beginning and the end of the year.

FIGURE 10.8

Statement of Cash Flows

Fossen Corporation
Statement of Cash Flows
For Year Ended 12/31/—

Cash Flows from Operating Activities		
Notes Receivable	102,552.00	
Accounts Receivable	649,245.00	
Merchandise Inventory	45,045.00	
Sales	64,350.00	
Sales Discounts	−3,595.00	
Cost of Merchandise Sold	−45,045.00	
Interest Income	1,948.00	
Total Cash Received		814,500.00
Merchandise Inventory	−2,450.00	
Store Supplies	2,287.30	
Office Supplies	2,034.90	
Prepaid Insurance	7,250.00	
Accounts Payable	526,780.00	
Notes Payable	5,050.00	
Sales Salaries Expense	63,785.10	
Advertising Expense	11,500.00	
Misc. Selling Expense	1,525.00	
Office Salaries Expense	20,261.00	
Utilities Expense	8,776.72	
Misc. General Expense	415.00	
Interest Expense	5,536.14	
Corporate Income Tax	24,872.00	
Total Cash Paid		677,623.16
Net Cash Flow from Operating Activities		136,876.84
Cash Flows from Investing Activities		
Office Equipment	2,050.00	
Total Cash Received		2,050.00
Land	21,500.00	
Building	74,500.00	
Store Equipment	1,500.00	
Total Cash Paid		97,500.00
Net Cash Flow from Investing Activities		−95,450.00
Cash Flows from Financing Activities		
Mortgage Note Payable	40,000.00	

(continued)

Total Cash Received		40,000.00
Mortgage Note Payable	2,108.76	
Dividends	20,000.00	
Total Cash Paid		22,108.76
Net Cash Flow from Financing Activities		17,891.24
Net Increase in Cash		59,318.08
Cash at Beginning of Year		8,216.44
Cash at End of Year		67,534.52

FIGURE 10.8

(Concluded)

Chapter Summary

- Horizontal analysis compares the ending balance of each account for the current year with the ending balance for the previous year and shows the percentage of change.

- Vertical analysis shows the relationship of the component parts to the total.

- The ratio analysis reports information about the earnings, efficiency, and financial strength of a business.

- The statement of cash flows reports cash receipts and payments and the change in cash for a business.

- The statement of cash flows classifies cash flows into (1) cash flows from operating activities, (2) cash flows from investing activities, and (3) cash flows from financing activities.

- The comparative income statement horizontal and vertical analysis reports compare the income statement for the current year to the income statement for the previous year.

- The comparative balance sheet horizontal and vertical analysis reports compare the balance sheet as of the end of the current year to the balance sheet as of the end of the previous year.

- The ratio analysis report contains four classifications of analysis: (1) earnings performance analysis, (2) efficiency analysis, (3) short-term financial strength, and (4) long-term financial strength.

- The computer uses the direct method (reports the operating cash receipts and the operating cash payments) to generate the statement of cash flows.

- The sale of office equipment, store equipment, and so on should be entered into the computer as follows: (1) Enter the cash receipt portion of the transaction into the cash receipts journal, and (2) enter the depreciation and gain on the sale in the general journal so the data will appear in the proper section of the statement of cash flows.

Sample Problem 10-S

The following transactions for Fossen Corporation occurred during the current year. The transactions are illustrated within the step-by-step instructions. Because this problem does not use the accounts payable and accounts receivable reporting capability of the software, the vendor and customer names need not be entered.

1   Start *Integrated Accounting* 6e.

2   Open the file named IA6 Problem 10-S.

3   Enter your name in the Your Name text box.

4   Use the Save As menu item from the File menu to save the data with a file name of 10-SBC Your Name (where 10-S identifies the problem, and BC represents Before Closing).

5   Change the title of Heating and Lighting Exp. to Utilities Expense in the chart of accounts.

6   Enter the general journal transactions.

Enter the data from the following transaction statements as illustrated in Figure 10.9.

General Journal Transactions

Feb. 10   Received merchandise returned on account from a customer, $6,000.00. The cost of the merchandise returned was $4,200.00. The credit memo applies to Sales Invoice No. 6619.

Aug. 17   Returned merchandise purchased on account; $4,000.00; the debit memo applies to Invoice No. 2718.

Sep. 15   Accepted a 60-day, 11% note on account for $82,500.00; Reference, Note.

Oct. 15   Accepted a 60-day, 11% note on account for $20,000.00; Reference, Note.

Dec. 26   The transaction entered on December 26 records the depreciation and gain on the sale of office equipment as shown in the cash receipts journal.

FIGURE 10.9

General Journal

Date	Refer.	Account	Debit	Credit
02/10/__	6619	4120 Sales Returns & Allow.	6000.00	
		1140 Merchandise Inventory	4200.00	
		1130 Accounts Receivable		6000.00
		5110 Cost of Merchandise Sold		4200.00
08/17/__	2718	2120 Accounts Payable	4000.00	
		1140 Merchandise Inventory		4000.00
09/15/__	Note	1120 Notes Receivable	82500.00	
		1130 Accounts Receivable		82500.00
10/15/__	Note	1120 Notes Receivable	20000.00	
		1130 Accounts Receivable		20000.00
12/26/__	4414	1250 Accum. Depr. Office Eqpt.	535.00	
		1240 Office Equipment		405.00
		7120 Gain on Sale Office Eqpt.		130.00

7   **Enter the purchases journal transactions.**

Enter the data from the following transaction statements as illustrated in figure 10.10.

Purchases Journal Transactions

Jan. 04   Purchased merchandise on account, $60,000.00; Invoice No. 2713.

Feb. 02   Purchased merchandise on account, $50,000.00; Invoice No. 2714.

Mar. 16   Purchased merchandise on account, $56,000.00; Invoice No. 2715.

Apr. 29   Purchased merchandise on account, $35,000.00; Invoice No. 2716.

May 14   Purchased merchandise on account, $60,500.00; Invoice No. 2717.

June 18   Purchased merchandise on account, $46,000.00; Invoice No. 2718.

July 10   Purchased merchandise on account, $57,280.00; Invoice No. 2719.

Aug. 19   Purchased merchandise on account, $37,000.00; Invoice No. 2720.

Sep. 28   Purchased merchandise on account, $47,000.00; Invoice No. 2721.

Oct. 11   Purchased merchandise on account, $53,000.00; Invoice No. 2722.

Nov. 15   Purchased merchandise on account, $62,000.00; Invoice No. 2723.

Dec. 21   Purchased merchandise on account, $44,350.00; Invoice No. 2724.

Date	Refer.	Mrch. Inv. Dr.	A.P. Credit
01/04/--	2713	60000.00	60000.00
02/02/--	2714	50000.00	50000.00
03/16/--	2715	56000.00	56000.00
04/29/--	2716	35000.00	35000.00
05/14/--	2717	60500.00	60500.00
06/18/--	2718	46000.00	46000.00
07/10/--	2719	57280.00	57280.00
08/19/--	2720	37000.00	37000.00
09/28/--	2721	47000.00	47000.00
10/11/--	2722	53000.00	53000.00
11/15/--	2723	62000.00	62000.00
12/21/--	2724	44350.00	44350.00

FIGURE 10.10

Purchases Journal

8   **Enter the cash payments journal transactions.**

Enter the data from the following transaction statements as illustrated in Figure 10.11.

Cash Payments Journal Transactions

Jan. 28   Paid cash on account, $14,000.00; Check No. 8350.

29   Paid cash for store supplies, $307.00; Check No. 8351.

Feb. 16   Paid cash for land, $21,500.00; building, $74,500.00; Check No. 8352.

20   Paid cash for office supplies, $589.90; Check No. 8353.

23   Paid cash for insurance, $2,250.00; Check No. 8354.

Mar. 09   Paid cash on account, $60,000.00; Check No. 8355.

15   Paid cash for store supplies, $1,980.30; Check No. 8356.

22   Paid cash for miscellaneous selling expense, $1,525.00; Check No. 8357.

Apr. 15   Paid cash for office supplies, $1,445.00; Check No. 8358.

May 03   Paid cash for store equipment, $1,500.00; Check No. 8359.

20   Paid cash on account, $106,000.00; Check No. 8360.

June 10   Paid cash on account, covering an invoice amount of $60,500.00; less 2% discount, $1,210.00; Check No. 8361.

20   Paid cash for salaries, $42,423.10; sales salaries, $32,285.10; office salaries, $10,138.00; Check No. 8362.

July 11   Paid cash for advertising, $11,500.00; Check No. 8363.

Aug. 12   Paid cash for mortgage, $6,694.90; principal, $2,108.76; interest, $4,586.14; Check No. 8364.

Oct. 16   Paid cash on account, $171,280.00; Check No. 8365.

Nov. 09   Paid cash dividends, $20,000.00; Check No. 8366.

20   Paid cash for miscellaneous general expense, $415.00; Check No. 8367.

27   Paid cash for electrical bill, $8,776.72; Check No. 8368.

Dec. 10   Paid cash on account, covering an invoice amount of $62,000.00, less 2% discount, $1,240.00; Check No. 8369.

15   Paid cash for income tax, $24,872.00; Check No. 8370.

27   Paid cash for salaries, $41,623.00; sales salaries, $31,500.00; office salaries, $10,123.00; Check No. 8371.

28   Paid cash for insurance premium, $5,000.00; Check No. 8372.

29   Paid cash for note payable, $6,000.00; principal, $5,050.00; interest, $950.00; Check No. 8373.

30   Paid cash on account, $53,000.00; Check No. 8374.

FIGURE 10.11

Cash Payments Journal

Date	Refer.	Acct. No.	Debit	Credit	A.P. Debit	Mrch. Inv. Cr	Cash Credit
01/28/--	8350				14000.00		14000.00
01/29/--	8351	1150	307.00				307.00
02/16/--	8352	1210	21500.00				96000.00
		1220	74500.00				
02/20/--	8353	1160	589.90				589.90
02/23/--	8354	1170	2250.00				2250.00
03/09/--	8355				60000.00		60000.00
03/15/--	8356	1150	1980.30				1980.30
03/22/--	8357	6160	1525.00				1525.00
04/15/--	8358	1160	1445.00				1445.00
05/03/--	8359	1260	1500.00				1500.00
05/20/--	8360				106000.00		106000.00
06/10/--	8361				60500.00	1210.00	59290.00
06/20/--	8362	6110	32285.10				42423.10
		6210	10138.00				
07/11/--	8363	6120	11500.00				11500.00
08/12/--	8364	2210	2108.76				6694.90
		8110	4586.14				
10/16/--	8365				171280.00		171280.00
11/09/--	8366	3130	20000.00				20000.00
11/20/--	8367	6280	415.00				415.00
11/27/--	8368	6220	8776.72				8776.72
12/10/--	8369				62000.00	1240.00	60760.00
12/15/--	8370	9110	24872.00				24872.00
12/27/--	8371	6110	31500.00				41623.00
		6210	10123.00				
12/28/--	8372	1170	5000.00				5000.00
12/29/--	8373	2140	5050.00				6000.00
		8110	950.00				
12/30/--	8374				53000.00		53000.00

9   Enter the sales journal transactions.

Enter the data from the following transaction statements as illustrated in Figure 10.12.

Sales Journal Transactions

Jan. 20   Sold merchandise on account, $87,250.00; Sales Invoice No. 6621. The cost of the merchandise sold was $60,900.00.

Feb. 22   Sold merchandise on account, $55,500.00; Sales Invoice No. 6622. The cost of the merchandise sold was $39,800.00.

Mar. 10   Sold merchandise on account, $46,000.00; Sales Invoice No. 6623. The cost of the merchandise sold was $32,000.00.

Apr. 17   Sold merchandise on account, $64,000.00; Sales Invoice No. 6624. The cost of the merchandise sold was $45,000.00.

May 25   Sold merchandise on account, $77,000.00; Sales Invoice No. 6625. The cost of the merchandise sold was $54,000.00.

June 15   Sold merchandise on account, $60,000.00; Sales Invoice No. 6626. The cost of the merchandise sold was $43,500.00.

July 21   Sold merchandise on account, $28,500.00; Sales Invoice No. 6627. The cost of the merchandise sold was $19,950.00.

Aug. 19   Sold merchandise on account, $81,895.00; Sales Invoice No. 6628. The cost of the merchandise sold was $58,265.00.

Sep. 17   Sold merchandise on account, $92,000.00; Sales Invoice No. 6629. The cost of the merchandise sold was $68,400.00.

Oct. 26   Sold merchandise on account, $64,000.00; Sales Invoice No. 6630. The cost of the merchandise sold was $45,800.00.

Nov. 16   Sold merchandise on account, $53,995.00; Sales Invoice No. 6631. The cost of the merchandise sold was $37,800.00.

Dec. 26   Sold merchandise on account, $62,000.00; Sales Invoice No. 6632. The cost of the merchandise sold was $46,995.00.

FIGURE 10.12

Sales Journal

Date	Refer.	Sales Credit	Cost Mrch Sold Dr.	Mrch. Inv. Cr.	A.R. Debit
01/20/--	6621	87250.00	60900.00	60900.00	87250.00
02/22/--	6622	55500.00	39800.00	39800.00	55500.00
03/10/--	6623	46000.00	32000.00	32000.00	46000.00
04/17/--	6624	64000.00	45000.00	45000.00	64000.00
05/25/--	6625	77000.00	54000.00	54000.00	77000.00
06/15/--	6626	60000.00	43500.00	43500.00	60000.00
07/21/--	6627	28500.00	19950.00	19950.00	28500.00
08/19/--	6628	81895.00	58265.00	58265.00	81895.00
09/17/--	6629	92000.00	68400.00	68400.00	92000.00
10/26/--	6630	64000.00	45800.00	45800.00	64000.00
11/16/--	6631	53995.00	37800.00	37800.00	53995.00
12/26/--	6632	62000.00	46995.00	46995.00	62000.00

10   **Enter the cash receipts journal transactions.**

Enter the data from the following transaction statements as illustrated in Figure 10.13.

Cash Receipts Journal Transactions

Jan. 09   Issued a mortgage note payable for $40,000.00; Reference, Note.

25   Received cash on account covering Sales Invoice No. 6615 for $39,000.00; no discount.

Feb. 08   Received cash on account covering Sales Invoice No. 6621 for $87,250.00; less 2% discount, $1,745.00.

Mar. 13   Received cash on account covering Sales Invoice No. 6622 for $55,500.00; no discount.

Apr. 12   Received cash on account covering Sales Invoice No. 6623 for $46,000.00; no discount.

May 08   Received cash on account covering Sales Invoice No. 6624 for $64,000.00; less 2% discount, $1,280.00.

June 19   Received cash on account covering Sales Invoice No. 6625 for $77,000.00; no discount.

July 28   Received cash on account covering Sales Invoice No. 6626 for $60,000.00; no discount.

Aug. 07   Received cash on account covering Sales Invoice No. 6627 for $28,500.00; less 2% discount, $570.00.

Oct. 19 Received cash on account covering Sales Invoice No. 6629 for $74,000.00; no discount.

Nov. 10 Received cash for a note receivable, $86,000.00; principal, $84,412.00; interest, $1,588.00; Cash Receipt No. 4411.

30 Sold merchandise for cash, $64,350.00; Cash Receipt No. 4412. The cost of the merchandise sold was $45,045.00.

Dec. 09 Received cash on account covering Sales Invoice No. 6631 for $53,995.00; no discount.

12 Received cash for a note receivable, $18,500.00; principal, $18,140.00; interest, $360.00; Cash Receipt No. 4413.

26 Received cash for sale of office equipment, $2,050.00; Cash Receipt No. 4414; cost of equipment was $2,455.00 and associated depreciation is $535.00.

NOTE The cash receipt portion of the transaction has been entered in the cash receipts journal and the remainder of the transaction has been entered in the general journal so the data will appear in the proper section of the statement of cash flows.

28 Received cash on account covering Sales Invoice No. 6630 for $64,000.00; no discount.

FIGURE 10.13

Cash Receipts Journal

Date	Refer.	Acct. No.	Debit	Credit	A.R. Credit	Sales Credit	Sales Disc. Dr.	Cost Mrch Sold Dr.	Mrch. Inv. Cr.	Cash Debit
01/09/--	Note	2210		40000.00						40000.00
01/25/--	6615				39000.00					39000.00
02/08/--	6621				87250.00		1745.00			85505.00
03/13/--	6622				55500.00					55500.00
04/12/--	6623				46000.00					46000.00
05/08/--	6624				64000.00		1280.00			62720.00
06/19/--	6625				77000.00					77000.00
07/28/--	6626				60000.00					60000.00
08/07/--	6627				28500.00		570.00			27930.00
10/19/--	6629				74000.00					74000.00
11/10/--	4411	1120		84412.00						86000.00
		7110		1588.00						
11/30/--	4412					64350.00		45045.00	45045.00	64350.00
12/09/--	6631				53995.00					53995.00
12/12/--	4413	1120		18140.00						18500.00
		7110		360.00						
12/26/--	4414	1240		2050.00						2050.00
12/28/--	6630				64000.00					64000.00

11 Display the chart of accounts.

The chart of accounts is shown in Figure 10.14.

FIGURE 10.14

Chart of Accounts

Fossen Corporation
Chart of Accounts
12/31/—

Assets
1110   Cash
1120   Notes Receivable
1125   Interest Receivable
1130   Accounts Receivable
1140   Merchandise Inventory
1150   Store Supplies
1160   Office Supplies
1170   Prepaid Insurance
1210   Land
1220   Building
1230   Accum. Depr. Building
1240   Office Equipment
1250   Accum. Depr. Office Eqpt.
1260   Store Equipment
1270   Accum. Depr. Store Eqpt.

Liabilities
2110   Interest Payable
2120   Accounts Payable
2130   Salaries Payable
2140   Notes Payable
2210   Mortgage Note Payable

Stockholders' Equity
3110   Capital Stock
3120   Retained Earnings
3130   Dividends
3140   Income Summary

Revenue
4110   Sales
4120   Sales Returns & Allow.
4130   Sales Discounts

Cost
5110   Cost of Merchandise Sold

Expenses
6110   Sales Salaries Expense
6120   Advertising Expense
6130   Depr. Exp. Store Eqpt.
6140   Insurance Expense Selling
6150   Store Supplies Expense
6160   Misc. Selling Expense
6210   Office Salaries Expense
6220   Utilities Expense
6240   Depr. Exp. Building
6250   Depr. Exp. Office Eqpt.
6260   Insurance Expense General
6270   Office Supplies Expense
6280   Misc. General Expense

(continued)

Other Revenue
7110   Interest Income
7120   Gain on Sale Office Eqpt.

Other Expense
8110   Interest Expense

Corporate Income Tax
9110   Corporate Income Tax

FIGURE 10.14

(Concluded)

12   **Display the journal entries.**

The reports are shown in Figure 10.15 (a) through (e), respectively.

FIGURE 10.15(A)

General Journal Report

Fossen Corporation
General Journal
12/31/—

Date	Refer.	Acct.	Title	Debit	Credit
02/10	6619	4120	Sales Returns & Allow.	6,000.00	
02/10	6619	1140	Merchandise Inventory	4,200.00	
02/10	6619	1130	Accounts Receivable		6,000.00
02/10	6619	5110	Cost of Merchandise Sold		4,200.00
08/17	2718	2120	Accounts Payable	4,000.00	
08/17	2718	1140	Merchandise Inventory		4,000.00
09/15	Note	1120	Notes Receivable	82,500.00	
09/15	Note	1130	Accounts Receivable		82,500.00
10/15	Note	1120	Notes Receivable	20,000.00	
10/15	Note	1130	Accounts Receivable		20,000.00
12/26	4414	1250	Accum. Depr. Office Eqpt.	535.00	
12/26	4414	1240	Office Equipment		405.00
12/26	4414	7120	Gain on Sale Office Eqpt.		130.00
			Totals	117,235.00	117,235.00

FIGURE 10.15(B)

Purchases Journal Report

Fossen Corporation
Purchases Journal
12/31/—

Date	Inv. No.	Acct.	Title	Debit	Credit
01/04	2713	1140	Merchandise Inventory	60,000.00	
01/04	2713	2120	Accounts Payable		60,000.00
02/02	2714	1140	Merchandise Inventory	50,000.00	
02/02	2714	2120	Accounts Payable		50,000.00
03/16	2715	1140	Merchandise Inventory	56,000.00	
03/16	2715	2120	Accounts Payable		56,000.00
04/29	2716	1140	Merchandise Inventory	35,000.00	
04/29	2716	2120	Accounts Payable		35,000.00

(continued)

FIGURE 10.15(B)

(Concluded)

				Debit	Credit
05/14	2717	1140	Merchandise Inventory	60,500.00	
05/14	2717	2120	Accounts Payable		60,500.00
06/18	2718	1140	Merchandise Inventory	46,000.00	
06/18	2718	2120	Accounts Payable		46,000.00
07/10	2719	1140	Merchandise Inventory	57,280.00	
07/10	2719	2120	Accounts Payable		57,280.00
08/19	2720	1140	Merchandise Inventory	37,000.00	
08/19	2720	2120	Accounts Payable		37,000.00
09/28	2721	1140	Merchandise Inventory	47,000.00	
09/28	2721	2120	Accounts Payable		47,000.00
10/11	2722	1140	Merchandise Inventory	53,000.00	
10/11	2722	2120	Accounts Payable		53,000.00
11/15	2723	1140	Merchandise Inventory	62,000.00	
11/15	2723	2120	Accounts Payable		62,000.00
12/21	2724	1140	Merchandise Inventory	44,350.00	
12/21	2724	2120	Accounts Payable		44,350.00
			Totals	608,130.00	608,130.00

FIGURE 10.15(C)

Cash Payments Journal Report

Fossen Corporation
Cash Payments Journal
12/31/—

Date	Ck. No.	Acct.	Title	Debit	Credit
01/28	8350	2120	Accounts Payable	14,000.00	
01/28	8350	1110	Cash		14,000.00
01/29	8351	1150	Store Supplies	307.00	
01/29	8351	1110	Cash		307.00
02/16	8352	1210	Land	21,500.00	
02/16	8352	1220	Building	74,500.00	
02/16	8352	1110	Cash		96,000.00
02/20	8353	1160	Office Supplies	589.90	
02/20	8353	1110	Cash		589.90
02/23	8354	1170	Prepaid Insurance	2,250.00	
02/23	8354	1110	Cash		2,250.00
03/09	8355	2120	Accounts Payable	60,000.00	
03/09	8355	1110	Cash		60,000.00
03/15	8356	1150	Store Supplies	1,980.30	
03/15	8356	1110	Cash		1,980.30
03/22	8357	6160	Misc. Selling Expense	1,525.00	
03/22	8357	1110	Cash		1,525.00
04/15	8358	1160	Office Supplies	1,445.00	
04/15	8358	1110	Cash		1,445.00
05/03	8359	1260	Store Equipment	1,500.00	
05/03	8359	1110	Cash		1,500.00

(continued)

05/20	8360	2120	Accounts Payable	106,000.00	
05/20	8360	1110	Cash		106,000.00
06/10	8361	2120	Accounts Payable	60,500.00	
06/10	8361	1110	Cash		59,290.00
06/10	8361	1140	Merchandise Inventory		1,210.00
06/20	8362	6110	Sales Salaries Expense	32,285.10	
06/20	8362	6210	Office Salaries Expense	10,138.00	
06/20	8362	1110	Cash		42,423.10
07/11	8363	6120	Advertising Expense	11,500.00	
07/11	8363	1110	Cash		11,500.00
08/12	8364	2210	Mortgage Note Payable	2,108.76	
08/12	8364	8110	Interest Expense	4,586.14	
08/12	8364	1110	Cash		6,694.90
10/16	8365	2120	Accounts Payable	171,280.00	
10/16	8365	1110	Cash		171,280.00
11/09	8366	3130	Dividends	20,000.00	
11/09	8366	1110	Cash		20,000.00
11/20	8367	6280	Misc. General Expense	415.00	
11/20	8367	1110	Cash		415.00
11/27	8368	6220	Utilities Expense	8,776.72	
11/27	8368	1110	Cash		8,776.72
12/10	8369	2120	Accounts Payable	62,000.00	
12/10	8369	1110	Cash		60,760.00
12/10	8369	1140	Merchandise Inventory		1,240.00
12/15	8370	9110	Corporate Income Tax	24,872.00	
12/15	8370	1110	Cash		24,872.00
12/27	8371	6110	Sales Salaries Expense	31,500.00	
12/27	8371	6210	Office Salaries Expense	10,123.00	
12/27	8371	1110	Cash		41,623.00
12/28	8372	1170	Prepaid Insurance	5,000.00	
12/28	8372	1110	Cash		5,000.00
12/29	8373	2140	Notes Payable	5,050.00	
12/29	8373	8110	Interest Expense	950.00	
12/29	8373	1110	Cash		6,000.00
12/30	8374	2120	Accounts Payable	53,000.00	
12/30	8374	1110	Cash		53,000.00
			Totals	799,681.92	799,681.92

FIGURE 10.15(C)

(Concluded)

Fossen Corporation
Sales Journal
12/31/—

FIGURE 10.15(D)

Sales Journal Report

Date	Inv. No.	Acct.	Title	Debit	Credit
01/20	6621	1130	Accounts Receivable	87,250.00	
01/20	6621	5110	Cost of Merchandise Sold	60,900.00	
01/20	6621	4110	Sales		87,250.00
01/20	6621	1140	Merchandise Inventory		60,900.00

(continued)

FIGURE 10.15(D)

(Concluded)

02/22	6622	1130	Accounts Receivable	55,500.00	
02/22	6622	5110	Cost of Merchandise Sold	39,800.00	
02/22	6622	4110	Sales		55,500.00
02/22	6622	1140	Merchandise Inventory		39,800.00
03/10	6623	1130	Accounts Receivable	46,000.00	
03/10	6623	5110	Cost of Merchandise Sold	32,000.00	
03/10	6623	4110	Sales		46,000.00
03/10	6623	1140	Merchandise Inventory		32,000.00
04/17	6624	1130	Accounts Receivable	64,000.00	
04/17	6624	5110	Cost of Merchandise Sold	45,000.00	
04/17	6624	4110	Sales		64,000.00
04/17	6624	1140	Merchandise Inventory		45,000.00
05/25	6625	1130	Accounts Receivable	77,000.00	
05/25	6625	5110	Cost of Merchandise Sold	54,000.00	
05/25	6625	4110	Sales		77,000.00
05/25	6625	1140	Merchandise Inventory		54,000.00
06/15	6626	1130	Accounts Receivable	60,000.00	
06/15	6626	5110	Cost of Merchandise Sold	43,500.00	
06/15	6626	4110	Sales		60,000.00
06/15	6626	1140	Merchandise Inventory		43,500.00
07/21	6627	1130	Accounts Receivable	28,500.00	
07/21	6627	5110	Cost of Merchandise Sold	19,950.00	
07/21	6627	4110	Sales		28,500.00
07/21	6627	1140	Merchandise Inventory		19,950.00
08/19	6628	1130	Accounts Receivable	81,895.00	
08/19	6628	5110	Cost of Merchandise Sold	58,265.00	
08/19	6628	4110	Sales		81,895.00
08/19	6628	1140	Merchandise Inventory		58,265.00
09/17	6629	1130	Accounts Receivable	92,000.00	
09/17	6629	5110	Cost of Merchandise Sold	68,400.00	
09/17	6629	4110	Sales		92,000.00
09/17	6629	1140	Merchandise Inventory		68,400.00
10/26	6630	1130	Accounts Receivable	64,000.00	
10/26	6630	5110	Cost of Merchandise Sold	45,800.00	
10/26	6630	4110	Sales		64,000.00
10/26	6630	1140	Merchandise Inventory		45,800.00
11/16	6631	1130	Accounts Receivable	53,995.00	
11/16	6631	5110	Cost of Merchandise Sold	37,800.00	
11/16	6631	4110	Sales		53,995.00
11/16	6631	1140	Merchandise Inventory		37,800.00
12/26	6632	1130	Accounts Receivable	62,000.00	
12/26	6632	5110	Cost of Merchandise Sold	46,995.00	
12/26	6632	4110	Sales		62,000.00
12/26	6632	1140	Merchandise Inventory		46,995.00
			Totals	1,324,550.00	1,324,550.00

FIGURE 10.15(E)

Cash Receipts Journal Report

**Fossen Corporation
Cash Receipts Journal
12/31/—**

Date	Refer.	Acct.	Title	Debit	Credit
01/09	Note	1110	Cash	40,000.00	
01/09	Note	2210	Mortgage Note Payable		40,000.00
01/25	6615	1110	Cash	39,000.00	
01/25	6615	1130	Accounts Receivable		39,000.00
02/08	6621	1110	Cash	85,505.00	
02/08	6621	4130	Sales Discounts	1,745.00	
02/08	6621	1130	Accounts Receivable		87,250.00
03/13	6622	1110	Cash	55,500.00	
03/13	6622	1130	Accounts Receivable		55,500.00
04/12	6623	1110	Cash	46,000.00	
04/12	6623	1130	Accounts Receivable		46,000.00
05/08	6624	1110	Cash	62,720.00	
05/08	6624	4130	Sales Discounts	1,280.00	
05/08	6624	1130	Accounts Receivable		64,000.00
06/19	6625	1110	Cash	77,000.00	
06/19	6625	1130	Accounts Receivable		77,000.00
07/28	6626	1110	Cash	60,000.00	
07/28	6626	1130	Accounts Receivable		60,000.00
08/07	6627	1110	Cash	27,930.00	
08/07	6627	4130	Sales Discounts	570.00	
08/07	6627	1130	Accounts Receivable		28,500.00
10/19	6629	1110	Cash	74,000.00	
10/19	6629	1130	Accounts Receivable		74,000.00
11/10	4411	1110	Cash	86,000.00	
11/10	4411	1120	Notes Receivable		84,412.00
11/10	4411	7110	Interest Income		1,588.00
11/30	4412	1110	Cash	64,350.00	
11/30	4412	5110	Cost of Merchandise Sold	45,045.00	
11/30	4412	4110	Sales		64,350.00
11/30	4412	1140	Merchandise Inventory		45,045.00
12/09	6631	1110	Cash	53,995.00	
12/09	6631	1130	Accounts Receivable		53,995.00
12/12	4413	1110	Cash	18,500.00	
12/12	4413	1120	Notes Receivable		18,140.00
12/12	4413	7110	Interest Income		360.00
12/26	4414	1110	Cash	2,050.00	
12/26	4414	1240	Office Equipment		2,050.00
12/28	6630	1110	Cash	64,000.00	
12/28	6630	1130	Accounts Receivable		64,000.00
			Totals	905,190.00	905,190.00

13 **Display the trial balance.**

The trial balance report dated December 31 of the current year is shown in Figure 10.16.

FIGURE 10.16

Trial Balance

Fossen Corporation
Trial Balance
12/31/—

Acct. Number	Account Title	Debit	Credit
1110	Cash	67,534.52	
1120	Notes Receivable	15,091.00	
1130	Accounts Receivable	59,650.00	
1140	Merchandise Inventory	77,933.00	
1150	Store Supplies	3,249.30	
1160	Office Supplies	2,448.90	
1170	Prepaid Insurance	8,213.00	
1210	Land	94,500.00	
1220	Building	286,500.00	
1230	Accum. Depr. Building		21,479.00
1240	Office Equipment	11,145.00	
1250	Accum. Depr. Office Eqpt.		2,452.00
1260	Store Equipment	31,200.00	
1270	Accum. Depr. Store Eqpt.		5,944.00
2120	Accounts Payable		97,111.00
2140	Notes Payable		4,950.00
2210	Mortgage Note Payable		161,391.24
3110	Capital Stock		150,000.00
3120	Retained Earnings		133,640.44
3130	Dividends	20,000.00	
4110	Sales		836,490.00
4120	Sales Returns & Allow.	6,000.00	
4130	Sales Discounts	3,595.00	
5110	Cost of Merchandise Sold	593,255.00	
6110	Sales Salaries Expense	62,945.10	
6120	Advertising Expense	11,500.00	
6160	Misc. Selling Expense	1,525.00	
6210	Office Salaries Expense	19,851.00	
6220	Utilities Expense	8,776.72	
6280	Misc. General Expense	415.00	
7110	Interest Income		1,498.00
7120	Gain on Sale Office Eqpt.		130.00
8110	Interest Expense	4,886.14	
9110	Corporate Income Tax	24,872.00	
	Totals	1,415,085.68	1,415,085.68

End-of-Year Activities

After the yearly transactions have been processed, the adjusting entries must be entered into the computer and displayed. The financial statements may then be displayed. The following adjustment data are for the current year for Fossen Corporation.

Accrued interest income $335.00

Inventory of supplies on December 31:

    Store supplies..$1,520.00

    Office supplies $1,835.50

Insurance expired during the year:

    Selling..$3,350.00

    General...$1,800.00

Depreciation for the year:

    Building..$17,000.00

    Store equipment..$2,960.00

    Office equipment $1,135.00

Salaries accrued on December 31:

    Sales salaries $928.00

    Office salaries...$526.00

Accrued interest expense $1,325.00

1 Enter the adjusting entries in the general journal. Your completed journal should appear as shown in Figure 10.17.

FIGURE 10.17

General Journal (Adjusting Entries)

Date	Refer.	Account	Debit	Credit
12/31/--	Adj.Ent.	1125 Interest Receivable	335.00	
		7110 Interest Income		335.00
12/31/--	Adj.Ent.	6150 Store Supplies Expense	1729.30	
		1150 Store Supplies		1729.30
12/31/--	Adj.Ent.	6270 Office Supplies Expense	613.40	
		1160 Office Supplies		613.40
12/31/--	Adj.Ent.	6140 Insurance Expense Selling	3350.00	
		6260 Insurance Expense General	1800.00	
		1170 Prepaid Insurance		5150.00
12/31/--	Adj.Ent.	6240 Depr. Exp. Building	17000.00	
		1230 Accum. Depr. Building		17000.00
12/31/--	Adj.Ent.	6130 Depr. Exp. Store Eqpt.	2960.00	
		1270 Accum. Depr. Store Eqpt.		2960.00
12/31/--	Adj.Ent.	6250 Depr. Exp. Office Eqpt.	1135.00	
		1250 Accum. Depr. Office Eqpt.		1135.00
12/31/--	Adj.Ent.	6110 Sales Salaries Expense	928.00	
		6210 Office Salaries Expense	526.00	
		2130 Salaries Payable		1454.00
12/31/--	Adj.Ent.	8110 Interest Expense	1325.00	
		2110 Interest Payable		1325.00

2 **Display the adjusting entries.**

Enter Adj.Ent. in the Reference text box (or select Adj.Ent. from the drop-list). The adjusting entries report is shown in Figure 10.18.

FIGURE 10.18

General Journal Report (Adjusting Entries)

Fossen Corporation
General Journal
12/31/—

Date	Refer.	Acct.	Title	Debit	Credit
12/31	Adj.Ent.	1125	Interest Receivable	335.00	
12/31	Adj.Ent.	7110	Interest Income		335.00
12/31	Adj.Ent.	6150	Store Supplies Expense	1,729.30	
12/31	Adj.Ent.	1150	Store Supplies		1,729.30
12/31	Adj.Ent.	6270	Office Supplies Expense	613.40	
12/31	Adj.Ent.	1160	Office Supplies		613.40
12/31	Adj.Ent.	6140	Insurance Expense Selling	3,350.00	
12/31	Adj.Ent.	6260	Insurance Expense General	1,800.00	
12/31	Adj.Ent.	1170	Prepaid Insurance		5,150.00
12/31	Adj.Ent.	6240	Depr. Exp. Building	17,000.00	
12/31	Adj.Ent.	1230	Accum. Depr. Building		17,000.00
12/31	Adj.Ent.	6130	Depr. Exp. Store Eqpt.	2,960.00	
12/31	Adj.Ent.	1270	Accum. Depr. Store Eqpt.		2,960.00
12/31	Adj.Ent.	6250	Depr. Exp. Office Eqpt.	1,135.00	
12/31	Adj.Ent.	1250	Accum. Depr. Office Eqpt.		1,135.00
12/31	Adj.Ent.	6110	Sales Salaries Expense	928.00	
12/31	Adj.Ent.	6210	Office Salaries Expense	526.00	
12/31	Adj.Ent.	2130	Salaries Payable		1,454.00
12/31	Adj.Ent.	8110	Interest Expense	1,325.00	
12/31	Adj.Ent.	2110	Interest Payable		1,325.00
			Totals	31,701.70	31,701.70

3 **Use Check on the toolbar to check your work.**

4 **Display the income statement.**

The income statement is shown in Figure 10.19.

FIGURE 10.19

Income Statement

Fossen Corporation
Income Statement
For Year Ended 12/31/—

Operating Revenue		
Sales	836,490.00	101.16
Sales Returns & Allow.	−6,000.00	−0.73
Sales Discounts	−3,595.00	−0.43
Total Operating Revenue	826,895.00	100.00
Cost		
Cost of Merchandise Sold	593,255.00	71.74
Total Cost	593,255.00	71.74
Gross Profit	233,640.00	28.26
Operating Expenses		
Sales Salaries Expense	63,873.10	7.72
Advertising Expense	11,500.00	1.39
Depr. Exp. Store Eqpt.	2,960.00	0.36
Insurance Expense Selling	3,350.00	0.41
Store Supplies Expense	1,729.30	0.21
Misc. Selling Expense	1,525.00	0.18
Selling Expenses	84,937.40	10.27
Office Salaries Expense	20,377.00	2.46
Utilities Expense	8,776.72	1.06
Depr. Exp. Building	17,000.00	2.06
Depr. Exp. Office Eqpt.	1,135.00	0.14
Insurance Expense General	1,800.00	0.22
Office Supplies Expense	613.40	0.07
Misc. General Expense	415.00	0.05
Administrative Expenses	50,117.12	6.06
Total Operating Expenses	135,054.52	16.33
Net Income from Operations	98,585.48	11.92
Other Revenue		
Interest Income	1,833.00	0.22
Gain on Sale Office Eqpt.	130.00	0.02
Other Expense		
Interest Expense	6,211.14	0.75
Net Income before Income Tax	94,337.34	11.41
Income Tax		
Corporate Income Tax	24,872.00	3.01
Net Income after Income Tax	69,465.34	8.40

5 **Display the retained earnings statement.**

The retained earnings statement is shown in Figure 10.20.

FIGURE 10.20		
Retained Earnings Statement	**Fossen Corporation** **Retained Earnings Statement** **For Year Ended 12/31/—**	
	Retained Earnings (Beg. of Period)	133,640.44
	Dividends	−20,000.00
	Net Income	69,465.34
	Retained Earnings (End of Period)	183,105.78

6 **Display the balance sheet.**

The balance sheet is shown in Figure 10.21.

FIGURE 10.21		
Balance Sheet	**Fossen Corporation** **Balance Sheet** **12/31/—**	
	Assets	
	Cash	67,534.52
	Notes Receivable	15,091.00
	Interest Receivable	335.00
	Accounts Receivable	59,650.00
	Merchandise Inventory	77,933.00
	Store Supplies	1,520.00
	Office Supplies	1,835.50
	Prepaid Insurance	3,063.00
	Total Current Assets	226,962.02
	Land	94,500.00
	Building	286,500.00
	Accum. Depr. Building	−38,479.00
	Office Equipment	11,145.00
	Accum. Depr. Office Eqpt.	−3,587.00
	Store Equipment	31,200.00
	Accum. Depr. Store Eqpt.	−8,904.00
	Total Plant Assets	372,375.00
	Total Assets	599,337.02
	Liabilities	
	Interest Payable	1,325.00
	Accounts Payable	97,111.00
	Salaries Payable	1,454.00
	Notes Payable	4,950.00
	Current Liabilities	104,840.00
	Mortgage Note Payable	161,391.24
	Long-Term Liabilities	161,391.24
	Total Liabilities	266,231.24

(continued)

Stockholders' Equity		
Capital Stock	150,000.00	
Retained Earnings	133,640.44	
Dividends	−20,000.00	
Net Income	69,465.34	
Total Stockholders' Equity		333,105.78
Total Liabilities & Equity		599,337.02

FIGURE 10.21

(Concluded)

7   Display the income statement (horizontal analysis).

The income statement (horizontal analysis) is shown in Figure 10.22.

FIGURE 10.22

Income Statement (Horizontal Analysis)

Fossen Corporation Income Stmt. Horizontal Analysis For Years Ended 12/31/— and 12/31/—				
	Current Period	Previous Period	Change	Percent
Operating Revenue				
Sales	836,490.00	786,150.00	50,340.00	6.40
Sales Returns & Allow.	−6,000.00	−5,645.00	−355.00	6.29
Sales Discounts	−3,595.00	−6,070.94	2,475.94	−40.78
Total Operating Revenue	826,895.00	774,434.06	52,460.94	6.77
Cost				
Cost of Merchandise Sold	593,255.00	577,285.62	15,969.38	2.77
Total Cost	593,255.00	577,285.62	15,969.38	2.77
Gross Profit	233,640.00	197,148.44	36,491.56	18.51
Operating Expenses				
Sales Salaries Expense	63,873.10	66,477.00	−2,603.90	−3.92
Advertising Expense	11,500.00	10,250.00	1,250.00	12.20
Depr. Exp. Store Eqpt.	2,960.00	2,644.00	316.00	11.95
Insurance Expense Selling	3,350.00	2,970.00	380.00	12.79
Store Supplies Expense	1,729.30	2,360.00	−630.70	−26.72
Misc. Selling Expense	1,525.00	704.00	821.00	116.62
Selling Expenses	84,937.40	85,405.00	−467.60	−0.55
Office Salaries Expense	20,377.00	18,605.00	1,772.00	9.52
Utilities Expense	8,776.72	8,956.00	−179.28	−2.00
Depr. Exp. Building	17,000.00	10,845.00	6,155.00	56.75
Depr. Exp. Office Eqpt.	1,135.00	1,425.00	−290.00	−20.35
Insurance Expense General	1,800.00	1,540.00	260.00	16.88
Office Supplies Expense	613.40	601.00	12.40	2.06
Misc. General Expense	415.00	345.00	70.00	20.29
Administrative Expenses	50,117.12	42,317.00	7,800.12	18.43
Total Operating Expenses	135,054.52	127,722.00	7,332.52	5.74
Net Income from Operations	98,585.48	69,426.44	29,159.04	42.00

(continued)

FIGURE 10.22					
(Concluded)	Other Revenue				
	Interest Income	1,833.00	3,470.00	−1,637.00	−47.18
	Gain on Sale Office Eqpt.	130.00	200.00	−70.00	−35.00
	Other Expense				
	Interest Expense	6,211.14	4,650.00	1,561.14	33.57
	Net Income before Income Tax	94,337.34	68,446.44	25,890.90	37.83
	Income Tax				
	Corporate Income Tax	24,872.00	22,655.00	2,217.00	9.79
	Net Income after Income Tax	69,465.34	45,791.44	23,673.90	51.70

8 Display the income statement (vertical analysis).

The income statement (vertical analysis) is shown in Figure 10.23.

FIGURE 10.23

Income Statement (Vertical Analysis)

Fossen Corporation
Income Stmt. Vertical Analysis
For Years Ended 12/31/— and 12/31/—

	Current Amount	Current Percent	Previous Amount	Previous Percent
Operating Revenue				
Sales	836,490.00	101.16	786,150.00	101.51
Sales Returns & Allow.	−6,000.00	−0.73	−5,645.00	−0.73
Sales Discounts	−3,595.00	−0.43	−6,070.94	−0.78
Total Operating Revenue	826,895.00	100.00	774,434.06	100.00
Cost				
Cost of Merchandise Sold	593,255.00	71.74	577,285.62	74.54
Total Cost	593,255.00	71.74	577,285.62	74.54
Gross Profit	233,640.00	28.26	197,148.44	25.46
Operating Expenses				
Sales Salaries Expense	63,873.10	7.72	66,477.00	8.58
Advertising Expense	11,500.00	1.39	10,250.00	1.32
Depr. Exp. Store Eqpt.	2,960.00	0.36	2,644.00	0.34
Insurance Expense Selling	3,350.00	0.41	2,970.00	0.38
Store Supplies Expense	1,729.30	0.21	2,360.00	0.30
Misc. Selling Expense	1,525.00	0.18	704.00	0.09
Selling Expenses	84,937.40	10.27	85,405.00	11.03
Office Salaries Expense	20,377.00	2.46	18,605.00	2.40
Utilities Expense	8,776.72	1.06	8,956.00	1.16
Depr. Exp. Building	17,000.00	2.06	10,845.00	1.40
Depr. Exp. Office Eqpt.	1,135.00	0.14	1,425.00	0.18
Insurance Expense General	1,800.00	0.22	1,540.00	0.20
Office Supplies Expense	613.40	0.07	601.00	0.08
Misc. General Expense	415.00	0.05	345.00	0.04
Administrative Expenses	50,117.12	6.06	42,317.00	5.46
Total Operating Expenses	135,054.52	16.33	127,722.00	16.49
Net Income from Operations	98,585.48	11.92	69,426.44	8.96

(continued)

Other Revenue				
Interest Income	1,833.00	0.22	3,470.00	0.45
Gain on Sale Office Eqpt.	130.00	0.02	200.00	0.03
Other Expense				
Interest Expense	6,211.14	0.75	4,650.00	0.60
Net Income before Income Tax	94,337.34	11.41	68,446.44	8.84
Income Tax				
Corporate Income Tax	24,872.00	3.01	22,655.00	2.93
Net Income after Income Tax	69,465.34	8.40	45,791.44	5.91

FIGURE 10.23

(Concluded)

---

9 **Display the balance sheet (horizontal analysis).**

The balance sheet (horizontal analysis) is shown in Figure 10.24.

Fossen Corporation
Balance Sheet Horizontal Analysis
For Years Ended 12/31/— and 12/31/—

	Current Period	Previous Period	Change	Percent
Assets				
Cash	67,534.52	8,216.44	59,318.08	721.94
Notes Receivable	15,091.00	15,143.00	−52.00	−0.34
Interest Receivable	335.00	450.00	−115.00	−25.56
Accounts Receivable	59,650.00	45,255.00	14,395.00	31.81
Merchandise Inventory	77,933.00	69,508.00	8,425.00	12.12
Store Supplies	1,520.00	962.00	558.00	58.00
Office Supplies	1,835.50	414.00	1,421.50	343.36
Prepaid Insurance	3,063.00	963.00	2,100.00	218.07
Total Current Assets	226,962.02	140,911.44	86,050.58	61.07
Land	94,500.00	73,000.00	21,500.00	29.45
Building	286,500.00	212,000.00	74,500.00	35.14
Accum. Depr. Building	−38,479.00	−21,479.00	−17,000.00	79.15
Office Equipment	11,145.00	13,600.00	−2,455.00	−18.05
Accum. Depr. Office Eqpt.	−3,587.00	−2,987.00	−600.00	20.09
Store Equipment	31,200.00	29,700.00	1,500.00	5.05
Accum. Depr. Store Eqpt.	−8,904.00	−5,944.00	−2,960.00	49.80
Total Plant Assets	372,375.00	297,890.00	74,485.00	25.00
Total Assets	599,337.02	438,801.44	160,535.58	36.59
Liabilities				
Interest Payable	1,325.00	650.00	675.00	103.85
Accounts Payable	97,111.00	19,761.00	77,350.00	391.43
Salaries Payable	1,454.00	1,250.00	204.00	16.32
Notes Payable	4,950.00	10,000.00	−5,050.00	−50.50
Current Liabilities	104,840.00	31,661.00	73,179.00	231.13
Mortgage Note Payable	161,391.24	123,500.00	37,891.24	30.68
Long-Term Liabilities	161,391.24	123,500.00	37,891.24	30.68
Total Liabilities	266,231.24	155,161.00	111,070.24	71.58

(continued)

FIGURE 10.24

*Balance Sheet
(Horizontal Analysis)*

FIGURE 10.24

(Concluded)

Stockholders' Equity				
Capital Stock	150,000.00	150,000.00		
Retained Earnings	133,640.44	106,719.00	26,921.44	25.23
Dividends	−20,000.00	−18,000.00	−2,000.00	11.11
Net Income	69,465.34	44,921.44	24,543.90	54.64
Total Stockholders' Equity	333,105.78	283,640.44	49,465.34	17.44
Total Liabilities & Equity	599,337.02	438,801.44	160,535.58	36.59

10 **Display the balance sheet (vertical analysis).**

The balance sheet (vertical analysis) is shown in Figure 10.25.

FIGURE 10.25

Balance Sheet (Vertical Analysis)

Fossen Corporation
Balance Sheet Vertical Analysis
For Years Ended 12/31/— and 12/31/—

	Current Amount	Current Percent	Previous Amount	Previous Percent
Assets				
Cash	67,534.52	11.27	8,216.44	1.87
Notes Receivable	15,091.00	2.52	15,143.00	3.45
Interest Receivable	335.00	0.06	450.00	0.10
Accounts Receivable	59,650.00	9.95	45,255.00	10.31
Merchandise Inventory	77,933.00	13.00	69,508.00	15.84
Store Supplies	1,520.00	0.25	962.00	0.22
Office Supplies	1,835.50	0.31	414.00	0.09
Prepaid Insurance	3,063.00	0.51	963.00	0.22
Total Current Assets	226,962.02	37.87	140,911.44	32.11
Land	94,500.00	15.77	73,000.00	16.64
Building	286,500.00	47.80	212,000.00	48.31
Accum. Depr. Building	−38,479.00	−6.42	−21,479.00	−4.89
Office Equipment	11,145.00	1.86	13,600.00	3.10
Accum. Depr. Office Eqpt.	−3,587.00	−0.60	−2,987.00	−0.68
Store Equipment	31,200.00	5.21	29,700.00	6.77
Accum. Depr. Store Eqpt.	−8,904.00	−1.49	−5,944.00	−1.35
Total Plant Assets	372,375.00	62.13	297,890.00	67.89
Total Assets	599,337.02	100.00	438,801.44	100.00
Liabilities				
Interest Payable	1,325.00	0.22	650.00	0.15
Accounts Payable	97,111.00	16.20	19,761.00	4.50
Salaries Payable	1,454.00	0.24	1,250.00	0.28
Notes Payable	4,950.00	0.83	10,000.00	2.28
Current Liabilities	104,840.00	17.49	31,661.00	7.22
Mortgage Note Payable	161,391.24	26.93	123,500.00	28.14
Long-Term Liabilities	161,391.24	26.93	123,500.00	28.14
Total Liabilities	266,231.24	44.42	155,161.00	35.36

(continued)

Stockholders' Equity					
Capital Stock	150,000.00	25.03	150,000.00	34.18	
Retained Earnings	133,640.44	22.30	106,719.00	24.32	
Dividends	−20,000.00	−3.34	−18,000.00	−4.10	
Net Income	69,465.34	11.59	44,921.44	10.24	
Total Stockholders' Equity	333,105.78	55.58	2,83,640.44	64.64	
Total Liabilities & Equity	599,337.02	100.00	438,801.44	100.00	

FIGURE 10.25

(Concluded)

11   Display the ratio analysis report.

When the ratio analysis report is chosen, the Ratio Analysis dialog box shown in Figure 10.26 will appear. Enter the total number of shares of stock outstanding for the current period (65,000) in the Shares Stock Outstanding text box and the market price per share (4.85) in the Price Per Share text box. Click OK. The Ratio Analysis report is shown in Figure 10.27.

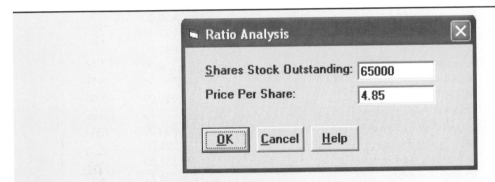

FIGURE 10.26

Ratio Analysis Dialog Box

FIGURE 10.27

Ratio Analysis Report

Fossen Corporation
Ratio Analysis
For Years Ended 12/31/— and 12/31/—

Earnings Performance Analysis	
Rate Earned on Average Total Assets	13.38%
Rate Earned on Average Stockholders' Equity	22.53%
Rate Earned on Net Sales	8.40%
Earnings Per Share	1.07
Price-Earnings Ratio	4.53 times
Efficiency Analysis	
Accounts Receivable Turnover Ratio	15.76 times
Average Days for Payment	23 days
Merchandise Inventory Turnover Ratio	8.05 times
Average Number of Days Sales in Merch. Inv.	45 days
Short-Term Financial Strength	
Working Capital	122,122.02
Current Ratio	2.16 times
Acid-Test Ratio	1.21 times
Long-Term Financial Strength Analysis	
Debt Ratio	44.42%
Equity Ratio	55.58%
Equity Per Share	5.12

12 Display the statement of cash flows.

The statement of cash flows is shown in Figure 10.28.

FIGURE 10.28

Statement of Cash Flows

Fossen Corporation
Statement of Cash Flows
For Year Ended 12/31/—

Cash Flows from Operating Activities		
Notes Receivable	102,552.00	
Accounts Receivable	649,245.00	
Merchandise Inventory	45,045.00	
Sales	64,350.00	
Sales Discounts	−3,595.00	
Cost of Merchandise Sold	−45,045.00	
Interest Income	1,948.00	
Total Cash Received		814,500.00
Merchandise Inventory	−2,450.00	
Store Supplies	2,287.30	
Office Supplies	2,034.90	
Prepaid Insurance	7,250.00	
Accounts Payable	526,780.00	
Notes Payable	5,050.00	
Sales Salaries Expense	63,785.10	
Advertising Expense	11,500.00	
Misc. Selling Expense	1,525.00	
Office Salaries Expense	20,261.00	
Utilities Expense	8,776.72	
Misc. General Expense	415.00	
Interest Expense	5,536.14	
Corporate Income Tax	24,872.00	
Total Cash Paid		677,623.16
Net Cash Flow from Operating Activities		136,876.84
Cash Flows from Investing Activities		
Office Equipment	2,050.00	
Total Cash Received		2,050.00
Land	21,500.00	
Building	74,500.00	
Store Equipment	1,500.00	
Total Cash Paid		97,500.00
Net Cash Flow from Investing Activities		−95,450.00
Cash Flows from Financing Activities		
Mortgage Note Payable	40,000.00	
Total Cash Received		40,000.00
Mortgage Note Payable	2,108.76	
Dividends	20,000.00	
Total Cash Paid		22,108.76

(continued)

Net Cash Flow from Financing Activities	17,891.24	**FIGURE 10.28**
Net Increase in Cash	59,318.08	*(Concluded)*
Cash at Beginning of Year	8,216.44	
Cash at End of Year	67,534.52	

13   Generate an income statement graph.

The income statement graph is shown in Figure 10.29.

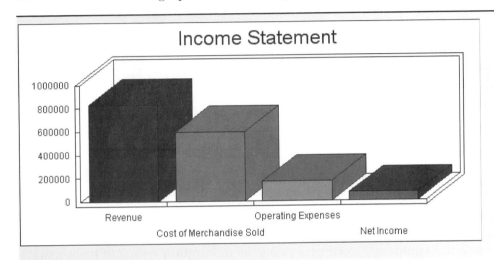

FIGURE 10.29

Income Statement Graph

14   Save your data with a file name of 10-SBC Your Name.

15   Optional spreadsheet integration activity.

The management of Fossen Corporation asked you to use a spreadsheet template to prepare a comparative statement of stockholders' equity with horizontal analysis. This report will enable management to review trends in stockholders' equity.

a. Start your spreadsheet software and load the spreadsheet template file IA6 Spreadsheet 10-S.

b. Refer to the financial analysis reports generated in this problem and complete the heading information in cells A1 and A3.

c. Enter the appropriate data (in the cells containing "Data") from the financial analysis reports you generated in this problem and complete the formulas in row 20 of the spreadsheet. Add Capital Stock (end of period) to Retained Earnings (end of period) in both the current and previous period columns, and copy and paste the existing Amount and Percent column formulas.

d. Print your spreadsheet report. Your completed spreadsheet should appear as shown in Figure 10.30.

e. Save the spreadsheet to your disk with a file name of 10-S Your Name.

FIGURE 10.30

Completed Spreadsheet of Comparative Statement of Stockholders' Equity

Fossen Corporation
Comparative Statement of Stockholders' Equity
For Periods Ended 12/31/— and 12/31/—

	Current Period	Previous Period	Increase/ Amount	Decrease Percent
Capital Stock (Beginning of Period)	$150,000.00	$150,000.00	$0.00	0.00%
Additional Capital Stock Issued	$0.00	$0.00	$0.00	
Capital Stock (End of Period)	$150,000.00	$150,000.00	$0.00	0.00%
Retained Earnings (Beginning of Period)	$133,640.44	$106,719.00	$26,921.44	25.23%
Net Income after Federal Income Tax	$69,465.34	$44,921.44	$24,543.90	54.64%
Total	$203,105.78	$151,640.44	$51,465.34	33.94%
Less Dividends Declared	$20,000.00	$18,000.00	$2,000.00	11.11%
Retained Earnings (End of Period)	$183,105.78	$133,640.44	$49,465.34	37.01%
Stockholders' Equity (End of Period)	$333,105.78	$283,640.44	$49,465.34	17.44%

16 **Optional word processing integration activity.**

Use the company's word processing memorandum template to prepare a memorandum to management containing the comparative statement of stockholders' equity prepared in the spreadsheet.

a. Copy the comparative statement of stockholders' equity (cells A1–E21) from the spreadsheet to the clipboard.

b. Start your word processing application software and load template file IA6 Wordprocessing 10-S (load as a text file).

c. Enter your name in the FROM field and the current date in the DATE field.

d. Position the insertion point at the location indicated and paste the statement. Format the document to match Figure 10.31.

e. Print the completed document.

f. Save the document to your disk or folder with a file name of 10-S Your Name.

MEMORANDUM

TO:	Management
FROM:	Student Name
DATE:	(Today's Date)
SUBJECT:	Comparative Statement of Stockholder's Equity

The following Comparative Statement of Stockholder's Equity with horizontal analysis has been prepared as per your request:

Fossen Corporation
Comparative Statement of Stockholders' Equity
For Periods Ended 12/31/— and 12/31/—

	Current Period	Previous Period	Increase/ Amount	Decrease Percent
Capital Stock (Beginning of Period)	$150,000.00	$150,000.00	$0.00	0.00%
Additional Capital Stock Issued	$0.00	$0.00	$0.00	
Capital Stock (End of Period)	$150,000.00	$150,000.00	$0.00	0.00%
Retained Earnings (Beginning of Period)	$133,640.44	$106,719.00	$26,921.44	25.23%
Net Income after Federal Income Tax	$69,465.34	$44,921.44	$24,543.90	54.64%
Total	$203,105.78	$151,640.44	$51,465.34	33.94%
Less Dividends Declared	$20,000.00	$18,000.00	$2,000.00	11.11%
Retained Earnings (End of Period)	$183,105.78	$133,640.44	$49,465.34	37.01%
Stockholders' Equity (End of Period)	$333,105.78	$283,640.44	$49,465.34	17.44%

17 **Generate and post the closing journal entries.**

Choose Generate Closing Journal Entries from the Options menu and post the closing entries.

18 **Display the computer-generated closing entries.**

Use a reference of Clo.Ent. The closing entries are shown in Figure 10.32.

FIGURE 10.32

Closing Entries

Fossen Corporation
General Journal
12/31/—

Date	Refer.	Acct.	Title	Debit	Credit
12/31	Clo.Ent.	4110	Sales	836,490.00	
12/31	Clo.Ent.	7110	Interest Income	1,833.00	
12/31	Clo.Ent.	7120	Gain on Sale Office Eqpt.	130.00	
12/31	Clo.Ent.	3140	Income Summary		838,453.00
12/31	Clo.Ent.	3140	Income Summary	768,987.66	
12/31	Clo.Ent.	4120	Sales Returns & Allow.		6,000.00
12/31	Clo.Ent.	4130	Sales Discounts		3,595.00
12/31	Clo.Ent.	5110	Cost of Merchandise Sold		593,255.00
12/31	Clo.Ent.	6110	Sales Salaries Expense		63,873.10
12/31	Clo.Ent.	6120	Advertising Expense		11,500.00
12/31	Clo.Ent.	6130	Depr. Exp. Store Eqpt.		2,960.00
12/31	Clo.Ent.	6140	Insurance Expense Selling		3,350.00
12/31	Clo.Ent.	6150	Store Supplies Expense		1,729.30
12/31	Clo.Ent.	6160	Misc. Selling Expense		1,525.00
12/31	Clo.Ent.	6210	Office Salaries Expense		20,377.00
12/31	Clo.Ent.	6220	Utilities Expense		8,776.72
12/31	Clo.Ent.	6240	Depr. Exp. Building		17,000.00
12/31	Clo.Ent.	6250	Depr. Exp. Office Eqpt.		1,135.00
12/31	Clo.Ent.	6260	Insurance Expense General		1,800.00
12/31	Clo.Ent.	6270	Office Supplies Expense		613.40
12/31	Clo.Ent.	6280	Misc. General Expense		415.00
12/31	Clo.Ent.	8110	Interest Expense		6,211.14
12/31	Clo.Ent.	9110	Corporate Income Tax		24,872.00
12/31	Clo.Ent.	3140	Income Summary	69,465.34	
12/31	Clo.Ent.	3120	Retained Earnings		69,465.34
12/31	Clo.Ent.	3120	Retained Earnings	20,000.00	
12/31	Clo.Ent.	3130	Dividends		20,000.00
			Totals	1,696,906.00	1,696,906.00

19 **Display the post-closing trial balance.**

The trial balance is shown in Figure 10.33.

FIGURE 10.33

Post-Closing Trial Balance

	Fossen Corporation Trial Balance 12/31/—		

Acct. Number	Account Title	Debit	Credit
1110	Cash	67,534.52	
1120	Notes Receivable	15,091.00	
1125	Interest Receivable	335.00	
1130	Accounts Receivable	59,650.00	
1140	Merchandise Inventory	77,933.00	
1150	Store Supplies	1,520.00	
1160	Office Supplies	1,835.50	
1170	Prepaid Insurance	3,063.00	
1210	Land	94,500.00	
1220	Building	286,500.00	
1230	Accum. Depr. Building		38,479.00
1240	Office Equipment	11,145.00	
1250	Accum. Depr. Office Eqpt.		3,587.00
1260	Store Equipment	31,200.00	
1270	Accum. Depr. Store Eqpt.		8,904.00
2110	Interest Payable		1,325.00
2120	Accounts Payable		97,111.00
2130	Salaries Payable		1,454.00
2140	Notes Payable		4,950.00
2210	Mortgage Note Payable		161,391.24
3110	Capital Stock		150,000.00
3120	Retained Earnings		183,105.78
	Totals	650,307.02	650,307.02

20 **Save your data with a file name of 10-SAC Your Name (where 10-S identifies the problem, and AC represents After Closing).**

If you have access to the Internet, use your browser to obtain resources (books, articles, etc.) that have been published to help users understand, analyze, or interpret financial statements. *Hint:* Use financial analysis or financial statements as your search string. Report your findings. Be sure to include the sources, including the URLs (Web addresses), of your reported findings.

INTERNET ACTIVITY

21 **Use Check on the toolbar to check your work.**

22 **End the *Integrated Accounting* 6e session.**

Chapter 10 Student Exercises

NAME

I Matching

Directions *For each of the definitions, write the letter of the appropriate term in the space provided.*

a. total operating revenue
b. total assets
c. ratio analysis

d. horizontal analysis
e. statement of cash flows
f. vertical analysis

1.____ A type of analysis that provides a comparison between the ending balance for the current year and the ending balance for the previous year for each item on a statement and shows the percentage of the change.

2.____ A type of analysis that shows the relationship of the component parts to the total.

3.____ The income statement figure on which the percentages are calculated using vertical analysis.

4.____ The balance sheet figure on which the asset percentages are calculated using vertical analysis.

5.____ The statement that reports the receipts and payments of cash and shows the change in the Cash account.

6.____ A report that lists financial information about the earnings, efficiency, and financial strength of a business.

II Questions

Directions *Answer each of the following questions in the space provided.*

1. What are the four major sections of the ratio analysis report? _____

_____

_____

_____

_____

2. What three classifications of cash receipts and payments appear on the statement of cash flows?

_____

_____

_____

3. How does the software use the account number ranges to classify long-term assets and liabilities in the statement of cash flows? _____

_____

_____

_____

4.   Which of the two methods of determining cash flow from operating activities is used by the *Integrated Accounting* 6e software? _____

_____

_____

5.   Why is the method in the previous question used? _____

_____

_____

6.   Do any of the adjusting entries in Sample Problem 10-S affect the statement of cash flows? Why or why not? _____

_____

_____

_____

Problem 10-A

Follow the step-by-step procedures provided to complete this problem for Fossen Corporation. Answer Audit Questions 10-A on pages 451–453, and click Info. on the toolbar for helpful check figures to audit your work as you work through the problem.

1   Start *Integrated Accounting* 6e.

2   Open the file named IA6 Problem 10-A.

3   Enter your name in the Your Name text box.

4   Save the data to your disk with a file name of 10-ABC Your Name (where 10-A identifies the problem, and BC represents Before Closing).

5   Add Gain on Sale Store Eqpt. to the chart of accounts. Assign account number *7130* to Gain on Sale Store Eqpt.

6   Enter the general journal transactions.

General Journal Transactions

Jan. 01   Record reversing entries required by the previous year's adjusting entries. Use the data presented in the sample problem as the basis for your reversing entries. Enter Rev.Ent. in the Reference text box. Reverse the entries for Interest Income, Salaries Expense, and Interest Expense.

Feb. 01   Returned merchandise purchased on account, $7,000.00; the debit memo applies to Invoice No. 2725.

Aug. 16   Accepted a 60-day 10.25% note on account for $50,250.00; Reference, Note.

Dec. 10   Received merchandise returned on account, $9,150.00. The cost of the merchandise returned was $6,400.00. The credit memo applies to Sales Invoice No. 6643.

7   Enter the purchases journal transactions.

Purchases Journal Transactions

Jan. 03   Purchased merchandise on account, $66,950.00; Invoice No. 2725.

Feb. 20   Purchased merchandise on account, $44,500.00; Invoice No. 2726.

Mar. 25   Purchased merchandise on account, $58,000.00; Invoice No. 2727.

Apr. 19   Purchased merchandise on account, $35,000.00; Invoice No. 2728.

May 23   Purchased merchandise on account, $58,500.00; Invoice No. 2729.

June 28   Purchased merchandise on account, $41,000.00; Invoice No. 2730.

July 09   Purchased merchandise on account, $56,890.00; Invoice No. 2731.

Aug. 24   Purchased merchandise on account, $33,000.00; Invoice No. 2732.

Sep. 25   Purchased merchandise on account, $43,500.00; Invoice No. 2733.

Oct. 29   Purchased merchandise on account, $50,250.00; Invoice No. 2734.

Nov. 25 Purchased merchandise on account, $12,750.00; Invoice No. 2735.

Dec. 18 Purchased merchandise on account, $35,000.00; Invoice No. 2736.

8 **Enter the cash payments journal transactions.**

Cash Payments Journal Transactions

Jan. 02 Paid cash on account covering an invoice amount of $44,350.00; less 2% discount, $887.00; Check No. 8375.

Feb. 09 Paid cash on account covering an invoice amount of $47,000.00; Check No. 8376.

15 Paid cash for advertising, $13,750.00; Check No. 8377.

27 Paid cash for miscellaneous general expense, $400.00; Check No. 8378.

Mar. 10 Paid cash on account covering an invoice amount of $59,950.00; Check No. 8379.

20 Paid cash for an insurance premium, $5,250.00; Check No. 8380.

Apr. 08 Paid cash on account covering an invoice amount of $44,500.00; Check No. 8381.

18 Paid cash for office equipment, $3,100.00; Check No. 8382.

May 10 Paid cash on account covering an invoice amount of $58,000.00; Check No. 8383.

June 10 Paid cash on account covering an invoice amount of $35,000.00; Check No. 8384.

15 Paid cash for miscellaneous selling expense, $850.00; Check No. 8385.

26 Paid cash for salaries, $46,905.05; sales salaries, $36,892.60; office salaries, $10,012.45; Check No. 8386.

July 07 Paid cash on account covering an invoice amount of $41,000.00; less 2% discount, $820.00; Check No. 8387.

15 Paid cash on account covering an invoice amount of $58,500.00; Check No. 8388.

21 Paid cash for store supplies, $2,115.32; Check No. 8389.

Aug. 09 Paid cash for mortgage, $14,250.00; principal, $4,290.20; interest, $9,959.80; Check No. 8390.

Sep. 01 Paid cash on account covering an invoice amount of $33,000.00; less 2% discount, $660.00; Check No. 8391.

15 Paid cash for note payable, $14,650.00; principal, $14,260.00; interest, $390.00; Check No. 8392.

Oct. 06 Paid cash on account covering an invoice amount of $43,500.00; less 2% discount, $870.00; Check No. 8393.

20 Paid cash dividends, $20,000.00; Check No. 8394.

28 Paid cash for electrical bill, $8,991.47; Check No. 8395.

Nov. 07 Paid cash on account covering an invoice amount of $50,250.00; less 2% discount, $1,005.00; Check No. 8396.

15 Paid cash for office supplies, $1,173.24; Check No. 8397.

Dec. 09 Paid cash for income tax, $26,800.00; Check No. 8398.

23 Paid cash for salaries, $47,406.50; sales salaries, $37,108.34; office salaries, $10,298.16; Check No. 8399.

9   **Enter the sales journal transactions.**

Sales Journal Transactions

Jan. 04   Sold merchandise on account, $80,000.00; Sales Invoice No. 6633. The cost of the merchandise sold was $55,000.00.

Feb. 13   Sold merchandise on account, $59,150.00; Sales Invoice No. 6634. The cost of the merchandise sold was $40,500.00.

Mar. 11   Sold merchandise on account, $39,000.00; Sales Invoice No. 6635. The cost of the merchandise sold was $27,500.00.

Apr. 25   Sold merchandise on account, $66,000.00; Sales Invoice No. 6636. The cost of the merchandise sold was $45,200.00.

May 28   Sold merchandise on account, $73,750.00; Sales Invoice No. 6637. The cost of the merchandise sold was $50,000.00.

June 25   Sold merchandise on account, $66,000.00; Sales Invoice No. 6638. The cost of the merchandise sold was $45,200.00.

July 27   Sold merchandise on account, $38,575.00; Sales Invoice No. 6639. The cost of the merchandise sold was $26,350.00.

Aug. 27   Sold merchandise on account, $71,000.00; Sales Invoice No. 6640. The cost of the merchandise sold was $49,410.00.

Sep. 29   Sold merchandise on account, $80,000.00; Sales Invoice No. 6641. The cost of the merchandise sold was $55,000.00.

Oct. 31   Sold merchandise on account, $58,225.50; Sales Invoice No. 6642. The cost of the merchandise sold was $40,700.00.

Nov. 30   Sold merchandise on account, $51,000.00; Sales Invoice No. 6643. The cost of the merchandise sold was $35,200.00.

Dec. 21   Sold merchandise on account, $65,000.00; Sales Invoice No. 6644. The cost of the merchandise sold was $44,500.00.

10   **Enter the cash receipts transactions.**

Cash Receipts Transactions

Jan. 06   Received cash on account covering Sales Invoice No. 6632 for $62,000.00; less 2% discount, $1,240.00.

Feb. 15   Received cash on account covering Sales Invoice No. 6633 for $80,000.00; no discount.

20   Received cash on account covering Sales Invoice No. 6634 for $59,150.00; less 2% discount, $1,183.00.

Mar. 11   Sold merchandise for cash, $59,995.00; Cash Receipt No. 4415. The cost of the merchandise sold was $42,000.00.

Apr. 02   Received cash on account covering Sales Invoice No. 6628 for $32,000.00; no discount.

May 10   Received cash on account covering Sales Invoice No. 6635 for $39,000.00; no discount.

June 03   Received cash on account covering Sales Invoice No. 6637 for $73,750.00; less 2% discount, $1,475.00.

July 20   Issued a note payable for cash, $14,500.00; Reference, Note.

Aug. 09	Received cash on account covering Sales Invoice No. 6638 for $66,000.00; less 2% discount, $1,320.00.
Sep. 07	Received cash on account covering Sales Invoice No. 6639 for $38,575.00; less 2% discount, $771.50.
Oct. 10	Received cash for a note receivable, $51,225.00; principal, $50,382.00; interest, $843.00. Cash Receipt No. 4416.
20	Received cash on account covering Sales Invoice No. 6641 for $80,000.00; no discount.
Nov. 10	Received cash on account covering Sales Invoice No. 6642 for $58,225.50; less 2% discount, $1,164.51.
Dec. 15	Sold merchandise for cash, $62,000.00. Cash Receipt No. 4417. The cost of the merchandise sold was $42,500.00.
28	Received cash for sale of store equipment, $3,400.00; Cash Receipt No. 4418. Cost of store equipment was $3,650.00 and associated depreciation is $315.00. Be sure to enter the depreciation and gain on the sale of this store equipment in the general journal.

11   Display the chart of accounts.

12   Display the journal entries and make corrections if necessary.

13   Display the trial balance.

End-of-Year Activities

After the yearly transactions have been processed, the adjusting entries must be entered into the computer and displayed. The financial statements may then be displayed. The following adjustment data are for Fossen Corporation. Use the trial balance report prepared in Step 13 as the basis for preparing the adjusting entries.

Accrued interest income	$307.50
Inventory of supplies on December 31:	
Store supplies	$2,815.00
Office supplies	$1,505.00
Insurance expired during the year:	
Selling	$4,595.00
General	$2,500.00
Depreciation for the year:	
Building	$19,000.00
Store equipment	$3,935.00
Office equipment	$2,020.00
Salaries accrued on December 31:	
Sales salaries	$1,296.00
Office salaries	$602.00
Accrued interest expense	$1,755.00

1 Enter the adjusting entries in the general journal. Enter a reference of Adj.Ent. in the Reference text box.

2 Display the adjusting entries.

3 Use Check on the toolbar to check your work.

4 Display the income statement.

5 Display the retained earnings statement.

6 Display the balance sheet.

7 Display the financial statement analysis reports (income statement horizontal analysis; income statement vertical analysis; balance sheet horizontal analysis; balance sheet vertical analysis; ratio analysis; statement of cash flows). Use 65,000 shares outstanding and $4.85 price per share for the ratio analysis report.

8 Generate a balance sheet graph.

9 Save your data with a file name of 10-ABC Your Name.

10 Optional spreadsheet integration activity.

Prepare a comparative statement of stockholders' equity with horizontal analysis.

a. Start your spreadsheet software and load the spreadsheet template file IA6 Spreadsheet 10-S. (If you completed the optional spreadsheet activity in Sample Problem 10-S, load your completed spreadsheet instead.)

b. Refer to the financial analysis reports generated in this problem and complete the heading information in cells A1 and A3.

c. Enter the appropriate data (in the cells containing "Data") from the financial analysis reports you generated in this problem, and complete the formulas in row 20 of the spreadsheet.

d. Print your spreadsheet report.

e. Save the spreadsheet to your disk with a file name of 10-A Your Name.

11 Optional word processing integration activity.

Prepare a memorandum to management containing the comparative statement of stockholders' equity prepared in the spreadsheet.

a. Copy the comparative statement of stockholders' equity (cells A1–E21) from the spreadsheet to the clipboard.

b. Start your word processing application software and load template file IA6 Wordprocessing 10-S (load as a text file).

c. Enter your name in the FROM field and the current date in the DATE field.

d. Position the insertion point at the location indicated and paste the statement. Format the document as necessary.

e. Print the completed document.

f. Save the document to your disk or folder with a file name of 10-A Your Name.

12 **Generate and post the closing journal entries.**

13 **Display the computer-generated closing entries. Use a reference of Clo.Ent.**

14 **Display the post-closing trial balance.**

15 **Save your data with a file name of 10-AAC Your Name (where 10-A identifies the problem, and AC represents After Closing).**

If you have access to the Internet, use your browser to obtain information about e-mail etiquette (netiquette) or e-mail abuse. *Hint:* Use computer, Internet, etiquette as your search string. Report your findings. Be sure to include the sources, including URLs (Web addresses), of your reported findings.

16 **Use Check on the toolbar to check your work.**

17 **End the *Integrated Accounting* 6e session.**

Audit Questions 10-A

NAME _____

Directions   *Write the answers to the following questions in the space provided.*

1.   What are the total purchases on account for the current year? ——————————

   ——

2.   What are the total debits and total credits shown on the sales journal report?

   Total debits: ————————————————————————————————————

   Total credits: ————————————————————————————————————

3.   What are the total debits and total credits shown on the cash receipts journal report?

   Total debits: ————————————————————————————————————

   Total credits: ————————————————————————————————————

4.   What are the total debits and total credits shown on the general journal report for adjusting entries?

   Total debits: ————————————————————————————————————

   Total credits: ————————————————————————————————————

5.   What are the total sales returns and allowances shown on the income statement after adjusting entries for the current year? ————————————————————————

   ——

6.   What is the net income after income tax for the current year? ——————————————

   ——

7.   What is the amount of cash on the balance sheet after adjusting entries have been entered?

   ——

8.   What is the amount of accounts receivable on the balance sheet after adjusting entries have been entered? ————————————————————————————————

   ——

9.   What is the amount of accounts payable on the balance sheet after adjusting entries have been entered? ——————————————————————————————————————

   ——

10.   What are the total liabilities and equity shown on the balance sheet as of December 31?

   ——

11.   What is the change in net income from operations from the previous year to the current year expressed as a percentage? ————————————————————————————

   ——

12.   What is the change in gross profit from the previous year to the current year expressed in dollars?

   ——

13.   What is the change in operating expenses from the previous year to the current year expressed as a percentage? _____

_____

14.   What are the total operating expenses for the previous year and the current year expressed as dollars?

   Previous year: _____

   Current year: _____

15.   What are the net income after income tax figures for the previous year and the current year expressed in dollars?

   Previous year: _____

   Current year: _____

16.   What is the interest income for the current year shown on the income statement?

_____

17.   What is the change in the amount of the Cash account from the previous year to the current year? Does this amount agree with the change shown on the statement of cash flows?

_____

_____

18.   What is the change in the amount of the Land account? _____

_____

19.   What is the change in the amount of the accumulated depreciation for office equipment?

_____

20.   What is the change in total assets from the previous year to the current year expressed in dollars?

_____

21.   What is the change in total assets from the previous year to the current year expressed as a percentage? _____

_____

22.   What amount in the current year is equal to the capital stock, plus retained earnings, minus the dividends, plus the net income? _____

_____

23.   What is the change in stockholders' equity from the previous year to the current year expressed in dollars? _____

_____

24.   What is the change in stockholders' equity from the previous year to the current year expressed as a percentage? _____

_____

25. What are the accounts receivable for the previous year and the current year expressed as percentages of total assets?

    Previous year: ———————————————————————————————

    Current year: ———————————————————————————————

26. What are the total liabilities for the previous year and the current year expressed as percentages of total liabilities and stockholders' equity?

    Previous year: ———————————————————————————————

    Current year: ———————————————————————————————

27. What is the rate earned on average total assets? ———————————————

    ———————————————————————————————————————

28. What were the earnings per share? ———————————————————

    ———————————————————————————————————————

29. What is the net cash flow from operating activities? ———————————————

    ———————————————————————————————————————

30. What is the total cash received from operating activities? ———————————

    ———————————————————————————————————————

31. What is the total cash paid from financing activities? ———————————

    ———————————————————————————————————————

32. What is the net change in cash for the year? ———————————————

    ———————————————————————————————————————

33. What is the balance of the Cash account at the beginning of the year? ———————

    ———————————————————————————————————————

34. What is the balance of the Cash account at the end of the year? ———————

    ———————————————————————————————————————

35. How much cash was received from interest income on the statement of cash flows?

    ———————————————————————————————————————

Problem 10-B

Follow the step-by-step procedures provided to complete this problem for Fossen Corporation. Answer Audit Questions 10-B on pages 460–462 as you work through the problem.

1 Start *Integrated Accounting* 6e.

2 Open the file named IA6 Problem 10-B.

3 Enter your name in the Your Name text box.

4 Save the data with a file name of 10-BBC Your Name (where 10-B identifies the problem, and BC represents Before Closing).

5 Add Gain on Sale Store Eqpt. to the chart of accounts. Assign account number *7130* to Gain on Sale Store Eqpt.

6 Enter the general journal transactions.

General Journal Transactions

Jan. 01	Reversing entries required by the previous year's adjusting entries. Use the data presented in the sample problem as the basis for your reversing entries. Enter Rev.Ent. in the Reference text box. Reverse the entries for Interest Income, Salaries Expense, and Interest Expense.
Feb. 01	Returned merchandise purchased on account, $7,100.00; the debit memo applies to Invoice No. 2725.
Aug. 16	Accepted a 60-day 9.75% note on account for $52,000.00; Reference, Note.
Dec. 10	Received merchandise returned on account, $9,350.00. The cost of the merchandise returned was $6,675.00. The credit memo applies to Sales Invoice No. 6643.

7 Enter the purchases journal transactions.

Purchases Journal Transactions

Jan. 30	Purchased merchandise on account, $67,000.00; Invoice No. 2725.
Feb. 20	Purchased merchandise on account, $44,795.00; Invoice No. 2726.
Mar. 25	Purchased merchandise on account, $59,000.00; Invoice No. 2727.
Apr. 19	Purchased merchandise on account, $33,110.00; Invoice No. 2728.
May 23	Purchased merchandise on account, $57,835.00; Invoice No. 2729.
June 28	Purchased merchandise on account, $41,960.00; Invoice No. 2730.
July 09	Purchased merchandise on account, $57,075.00; Invoice No. 2731.
Aug. 24	Purchased merchandise on account, $33,420.00; Invoice No. 2732.
Sep. 25	Purchased merchandise on account, $43,996.00; Invoice No. 2733.

Oct. 29   Purchased merchandise on account, $50,000.00; Invoice No. 2734.

Nov. 25   Purchased merchandise on account, $12,000.00; Invoice No. 2735.

Dec. 18   Purchased merchandise on account, $35,500.00; Invoice No. 2736.

8   Enter the cash payments journal transactions.

Cash Payments Journal Transactions

Jan. 02   Paid cash on account covering an invoice amount of $44,350.00; less 2% discount, $887.00; Check No. 8375.

Feb. 09   Paid cash on account covering an invoice amount of $47,000.00; Check No. 8376.

15   Paid cash for advertising, $13,800.00; Check No. 8377.

27   Paid cash for miscellaneous general expense, $450.00; Check No. 8378.

Mar. 10   Paid cash on account covering an invoice amount of $59,900.00; Check No. 8379.

20   Paid cash for an insurance premium, $5,630.00; Check No. 8380.

Apr. 08   Paid cash on account covering an invoice amount of $44,795.00; Check No. 8381.

18   Paid cash for office equipment, $3,000.00; Check No. 8382.

May 10   Paid cash on account covering an invoice amount of $59,000.00; Check No. 8383.

June 10   Paid cash on account covering an invoice amount of $33,110.00; Check No. 8384.

15   Paid cash for miscellaneous selling expense, $905.00; Check No. 8385.

26   Paid cash for salaries, $46,487.36; sales salaries, $37,105.07; office salaries, $9,382.29; Check No. 8386.

July 07   Paid cash on account covering an invoice amount of $41,960.00; less 2% discount, $839.20; Check No. 8387.

15   Paid cash on account covering an invoice amount of $57,835.00; Check No. 8388.

21   Paid cash for store supplies, $2,296.38; Check No. 8389.

Aug. 09   Paid cash for mortgage, $14,150.00; principal, $4,190.63; interest, $9,959.37; Check No. 8390.

Sep. 01   Paid cash on account covering an invoice amount of $33,420.00; less 2% discount, $668.40; Check No. 8391.

15   Paid cash for note payable, $14,935.00; principal, $14,671.11; interest, $263.89; Check No. 8392.

Oct. 06   Paid cash on account covering an invoice amount of $43,996.00; less 2% discount, $879.92; Check No. 8393.

20   Paid cash dividends, $22,000.00; Check No. 8394.

28   Paid cash for electrical bill, $9,013.42; Check No. 8395.

Nov. 07   Paid cash on account covering an invoice amount of $50,000.00; less 2% discount, $1000.00; Check No. 8396.

15   Paid cash for office supplies, $1173.43; Check No. 8397.

Dec. 09   Paid cash for income tax, $27,850.00; Check No. 8398.

23   Paid cash for salaries, $47,624.75; sales salaries, $37,613.27; office salaries, $10,011.48; Check No. 8399.

9   **Enter the sales journal transactions.**

Sales Journal Transactions

Jan. 04   Sold merchandise on account, $79,995.50; Sales Invoice No. 6633. The cost of the merchandise sold was $55,150.00.

Feb. 13   Sold merchandise on account, $59,250.00; Sales Invoice No. 6634. The cost of the merchandise sold was $40,950.00.

Mar. 11   Sold merchandise on account, $41,000.00; Sales Invoice No. 6635. The cost of the merchandise sold was $28,100.00.

Apr. 25   Sold merchandise on account, $65,895.00; Sales Invoice No. 6636. The cost of the merchandise sold was $45,200.00.

May 28   Sold merchandise on account, $73,820.00; Sales Invoice No. 6637. The cost of the merchandise sold was $50,600.00.

June 25   Sold merchandise on account, $66,995.00; Sales Invoice No. 6638. The cost of the merchandise sold was $45,895.00.

July 27   Sold merchandise on account, $37,928.00; Sales Invoice No. 6639. The cost of the merchandise sold was $25,930.00.

Aug. 27   Sold merchandise on account, $72,000.00; Sales Invoice No. 6640. The cost of the merchandise sold was $49,140.00.

Sep. 29   Sold merchandise on account, $79,835.00; Sales Invoice No. 6641. The cost of the merchandise sold was $54,885.00.

Oct. 31   Sold merchandise on account, $60,150.00; Sales Invoice No. 6642. The cost of the merchandise sold was $41,100.00.

Nov. 30   Sold merchandise on account, $52,000.00; Sales Invoice No. 6643. The cost of the merchandise sold was $35,500.00.

Dec. 21   Sold merchandise on account, $69,785.00; Sales Invoice No. 6644. The cost of the merchandise sold was $46,500.00.

10   **Enter the cash receipts transactions.**

Cash Receipts Transactions

Jan. 06   Received cash on account covering Sales Invoice No. 6632 for $62,000.00; less 2% discount, $1,240.00.

Feb. 15   Received cash on account covering Sales Invoice No. 6633 for $79,995.50; no discount.

20   Received cash on account covering Sales Invoice No. 6634 for $59,250.00; less 2% discount, $1,185.00.

Mar. 11   Sold merchandise for cash, $58,000.00; Cash Receipt No. 4415. The cost of the merchandise sold was $40,100.00.

Apr. 02   Received cash on account covering Sales Invoice No. 6628 for $30,250.00; no discount.

May 10   Received cash on account covering Sales Invoice No. 6635 for $41,000.00; no discount.

June 03	Received cash on account covering Sales Invoice No. 6637 for $73,820.00; less 2% discount, $1,476.40.
July 20	Issued a note payable for cash, $15,000.00; Reference, Note.
Aug. 09	Received cash on account covering Sales Invoice No. 6638 for $66,995.00; less 2% discount, $1,339.90.
Sep. 07	Received cash on account covering Sales Invoice No. 6639 for $37,928.00; less 2% discount, $758.56.
Oct. 10	Received cash for a note receivable, $50,840.00; principal, $50,000.00; interest, $840.00. Cash Receipt No. 4416.
20	Received cash on account covering Sales Invoice No. 6641 for $79,835.00; no discount.
Nov. 10	Received cash on account covering Sales Invoice No. 6642 for $60,150.00; less 2% discount, $1,203.00.
Dec. 15	Sold merchandise for cash, $61,950.00. Cash Receipt No. 4417. The cost of the merchandise sold was $42,800.00.
28	Received cash for sale of store equipment, $3,500.00; Cash Receipt No. 4418. Cost of store equipment was $3,700.00 and associated depreciation is $340.00. Be sure to enter the depreciation and gain on the sale of this store equipment in the general journal.

11 **Display the chart of accounts.**

12 **Display the journal entries and make corrections if necessary.**

13 **Display the trial balance.**

End-of-Year Activities

After the yearly transactions have been processed, the adjusting entries must be entered into the computer and displayed. The financial statements may then be displayed. The following adjustment data are for Fossen Corporation. Use the trial balance report prepared in Step 13 as the basis for preparing the adjusting entries.

Accrued interest income	$308.60
Inventory of supplies on December 31:	
Store supplies	$2,845.00
Office supplies	$1,498.00
Insurance expired during the year:	
Selling	$4,625.00
General	$2,540.67
Depreciation for the year:	
Building	$19,025.00
Store equipment	$3,925.65
Office equipment	$2,027.05
Salaries accrued on December 31:	
Sales salaries	$1,289.92
Office salaries	$589.41
Accrued interest expense	$1,760.00

1 Enter the adjusting entries in the general journal. Enter a reference of Adj.Ent. in the Reference text box.

2 Display the adjusting entries.

3 Display the income statement.

4 Display the retained earnings statement.

5 Display the balance sheet.

6 Display the financial statement analysis reports (income statement horizontal analysis; income statement vertical analysis; balance sheet horizontal analysis; balance sheet vertical analysis; ratio analysis; statement of cash flows). Use 65,000 shares outstanding and $4.85 price per share for the ratio analysis report.

7 Generate a balance sheet graph.

8 Save your data with a file name of 10-BBC Your Name.

9 Optional spreadsheet integration activity.

Prepare a comparative statement of stockholders' equity with horizontal analysis.

a. Start your spreadsheet software and load the spreadsheet template file IA6 Spreadsheet 10-S. (If you completed the optional spreadsheet activity in Sample Problem 10-S, load your completed spreadsheet instead.)

b. Refer to the financial analysis reports generated in this problem and complete the heading information in cells A1 and A3.

c. Enter the appropriate data (in the cells containing "Data") from the financial analysis reports you generated in this problem, and complete the formulas in row 20 of the spreadsheet.

d. Print your spreadsheet report.

e. Save the spreadsheet to your disk with a file name of 10-B Your Name.

10 Optional word processing integration activity.

Prepare a memorandum to management containing the comparative statement of stockholders' equity prepared in the spreadsheet.

a. Copy the comparative statement of stockholders' equity (cells A1–E21) from the spreadsheet to the clipboard.

b. Start your word processing application software and load template file IA6 Wordprocessing 10-S (load as a text file).

c. Enter your name in the FROM field and the current date in the DATE field.

d. Position the insertion point at the location indicated and paste the statement. Format the document as necessary.

e. Print the completed document.

f. Save the document to your disk or folder with a file name of 10-B Your Name.

11 **Generate and post the closing journal entries.**

12 **Display the computer generated closing entries. Use a reference of Clo.Ent.**

13 **Display the post-closing trial balance.**

14 **Save your data with a file name of 10-BAC Your Name (where 10-B identifies the problem, and AC represents After Closing).**

If you have access to the Internet, use your browser to research ethical guidelines as related to the use of computers and the Internet. *Hint:* Use computers and Internet ethics as your search string. Be sure to include the sources, including URLs (Web addresses), of items you include in your list.

INTERNET
ACTIVITY

15 **End the *Integrated Accounting* 6e session.**

Audit Questions 10-B

NAME _____

Directions *Write the answers to the following questions in the space provided.*

1. What are the total purchases on account for the current year? _____

    _____

2. What are the total debits and total credits shown on the sales journal report?

    Total debits: _____

    Total credits: _____

3. What are the total debits and total credits shown on the cash receipts journal report?

    Total debits: _____

    Total credits: _____

4. What are the total debits and total credits shown on the general journal report for adjusting entries?

    Total debits: _____

    Total credits: _____

5. What are the total sales discounts shown on the income statement after adjusting entries for the current year? _____

    _____

6. What is the net income after income tax for the current year? _____

    _____

7. What is the amount of cash on the balance sheet after adjusting entries have been entered?

    _____

8. What is the amount of accounts receivable on the balance sheet after adjusting entries have been entered? _____

    _____

9. What is the amount of accounts payable on the balance sheet after adjusting entries have been entered? _____

    _____

10. What is the total stockholders' equity shown on the balance sheet as of December 31?

    _____

11. What is the change in net income from operations from the previous year to the current year expressed as a percentage? _____

    _____

12. What is the change in gross profit from the previous year to the current year expressed in dollars?

    _____

13. What is the change in operating expenses from the previous year to the current year expressed as a percentage? _____

    _____

14. What are the total operating expenses for the previous year and the current year expressed as dollars?

    Previous year: _____

    Current year: _____

15. What are the net income after income tax figures for the previous year and the current year expressed in dollars?

    Previous year: _____

    Current year: _____

16. What is the interest income for the current year shown on the income statement?

    _____

17. What is the change in the amount of the Cash account from the previous year to the current year? Does this amount agree with the change shown on the statement of cash flows?

    _____

    _____

18. What is the change in the amount of the Building account? _____

    _____

19. What is the change in the amount of accumulated depreciation for office equipment?

    _____

20. What is the change in total assets from the previous year to the current year expressed in dollars?

    _____

21. What is the change in total assets from the previous year to the current year expressed as a percentage? _____

    _____

22. What amount in the current year is equal to the capital stock, plus retained earnings, minus the dividends, plus the net income? _____

    _____

23. What is the change in stockholders' equity from the previous year to the current year expressed in dollars? _____

    _____

24. What is the change in stockholders' equity from the previous year to the current year expressed as a percentage? _____

    _____

25. What are the accounts receivable for the previous year and the current year expressed as percentages of total assets?

    Previous year: _____

    Current year: _____

26. What are the total liabilities for the previous year and the current year expressed as percentages of total liabilities and stockholders' equity?

    Previous year: _____

    Current year: _____

27. What is the rate earned on average stockholders' equity?

    _____

28. What is the equity per share? _____

    _____

29. What is the net cash flow from operating activities? _____

    _____

30. What is the total cash received from operating activities? _____

    _____

31. What is the total cash paid from financing activities? _____

    _____

32. What is the net change in cash for the year? _____

    _____

33. What is the balance of the Cash account at the beginning of the year? _____

    _____

34. What is the balance of the Cash account at the end of the year? _____

    _____

35. How much cash was paid for store supplies? _____

    _____

Departmentalized Accounting

Upon completion of this chapter, you will be able to:

- Identify the components and procedures used to process a departmentalized accounting system.

- Maintain departmental accounts.

- Enter departmental transactions.

- Display gross profit statements.

Introduction

In the previous chapters you learned how to complete the accounting cycle for non-departmentalized businesses using a computer. This chapter will identify the differences you will encounter when processing an accounting cycle for a departmentalized business by using examples from a corporation called Lacina Windows & Doors. Lacina Windows & Doors is a merchandising business, organized as a corporation, which uses a periodic inventory system (previous businesses in this text have used perpetual inventory systems). The chart of accounts for this business includes **cost of merchandise accounts** that show the cost or price of the merchandise that is purchased for resale to customers. (Cost of merchandise accounts include purchases, purchases returns and allowances, and purchases discounts.) The **Purchases** account is used to record the merchandise purchased for resale. At the end of this chapter, you will complete a sample problem that will take you through an entire departmentalized accounting cycle.

A **departmentalized accounting system** is used when each of the various departments within the business needs management information. Lacina Windows & Doors is a merchandising business on a monthly accounting cycle. Transactions will be recorded for the month of February, and all accounting activities through the end-of-month processing will be covered. Lacina Windows & Doors uses two departments: Department 1 for windows and Department 2 for doors.

When a departmentalized accounting system is used, the chart of accounts must contain separate **departmental accounts** for each department that requires departmental information. In the *Integrated Accounting* 6e software, **department numbers** are entered in the chart of accounts in a grid cell box separate from the account number. This approach allows the account numbering scheme to be unaffected by departmentalization.

Figure 11.1 shows the chart of accounts for Lacina Windows & Doors. Notice that merchandise accounts, income summary accounts, revenue accounts, and cost accounts exist for each of the two departments.

Lacina Windows & Doors
Chart of Accounts
02/28/—

FIGURE 11.1

*Lacina Windows &
Doors Chart of Accounts*

Assets
1110   Cash
1130   Accounts Receivable
1140   Allow. for Doubt. Accts.
1150   Merch. Inventory—Windows ⟶ Separate merchandise inventory accounts for each of the two departments.
1151   Merch. Inventory—Doors
1160   Office Supplies
1170   Store Supplies
1180   Prepaid Insurance
1510   Office Equipment
1520   Accum. Depr.—Office Eq.
1530   Store Equipment
1540   Accum. Depr.—Store Eq.

Liabilities
2110   Vouchers Payable
2120   Sales Tax Payable
2130   Salaries Payable
2140   Corporate Income Tax Pay.

Stockholders' Equity
3110   Capital Stock
3120   Retained Earnings
3130   Dividends
3140   Income Summary—Windows ⟶ Separate income summary accounts for each of the two departments.
3141   Income Summary—Doors

Revenue
4110   Sales—Windows
4120   Sales Ret. & All.—Windows
4130   Sales Discounts—Windows ⟶ Separate revenue accounts for each of the two departments.
4210   Sales—Doors
4220   Sales Ret. & All.—Doors
4230   Sales Discounts—Doors

Cost
5110   Purchases—Windows
5120   Prch. Ret. & All.—Windows
5130   Purchases Disc.—Windows ⟶ Separate cost accounts for each of the two departments.
5210   Purchases—Doors
5220   Prch. Ret. & All.—Doors
5230   Purchases Disc.—Doors

Expenses
6110   Advertising Expense
6120   Deprec. Exp.—Store Eq.
6130   Sales Salary Expense
6140   Store Supplies Expense
6510   Uncollectible Accts. Exp.
6520   Deprec. Exp.—Office Eq.
6540   Insurance Expense

(continued)

FIGURE 11.1

(Concluded)

6560	Heating & Lighting Exp.
6570	Rent Expense
6580	Admin. Salary Expense
6590	Telephone Expense
6600	Office Supplies Expense

Corporate Income Tax
| 9110 | Corporate Income Tax Exp. |

Departmental Accounting

Departmentalized accounting system data are entered into the computer using the same purchase orders, vouchers, sales invoices, and journals you used in the previous chapters. The only difference is that some of the data entered must be identified as belonging to a specific department. These minor differences are covered in the chart of accounts, purchase orders, vouchers, sales invoices, cash payments journal, and cash receipts journal discussions that follow.

Chart of Accounts

The Account Maintenance/Accounts window is used to maintain the chart of accounts by adding new accounts, changing existing accounts, or deleting accounts. When a departmentalized accounting system is used, the Chart of Accounts window includes an additional grid cell for the department number as illustrated in the partial chart of accounts shown in Figure 11.2.

FIGURE 11.2

Chart of Accounts for a Departmentalized System

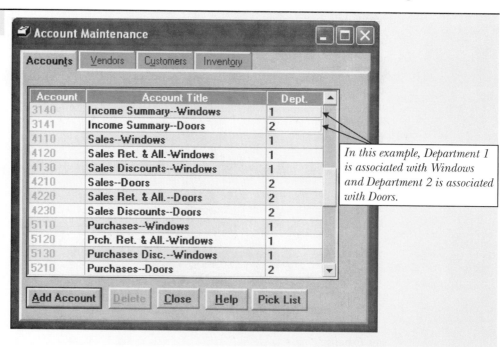

In this example, Department 1 is associated with Windows and Department 2 is associated with Doors.

The procedure for maintaining the chart of account for departmental processing is near identical to that you have already used in previous chapters. The only difference is the existence of the Dept. grid cell.

Purchase Orders

An example of a purchase order involving the purchase of merchandise for two departments is illustrated in Figure 11.3. Notice that the appropriate department's account number must be entered (or selected from the chart of accounts list) into the GL Account grid cell.

Feb. 08   Ordered 14 Picture Window—Double at $625.00 each, and 5 Wood Patio Door—Single at $670.00 each on account from Quade Corporation, terms 2/10, n/30. Purchase Order No. 1145.

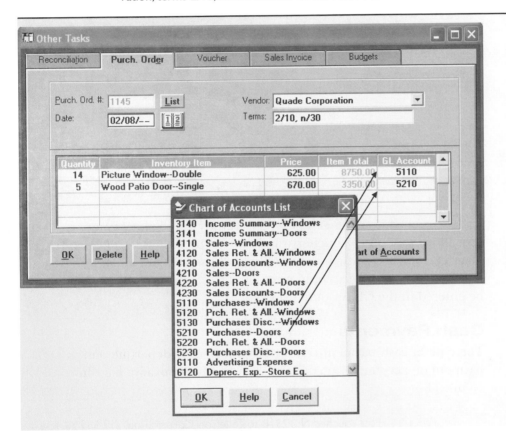

FIGURE 11.3

Example of a Purchase Order Involving Two Departments

Vouchers (and Purchases Returns)

An example of a voucher transaction involving the receipt of merchandise for two departments is illustrated in Figure 11.4. Again, notice that the appropriate department's account number must appear in the GL Account grid cell. The account numbers entered in the corresponding purchase order will be placed in the GL Account grid cells when the purchase order is selected.

Feb. 24   Received 8 Wood Entry Door—Double at $1,695.00 each, and 12 Casement Slider—Single windows at $195.00 each for Purchase Order No. 1144 from Gunderson, Inc., terms 2/10, n/30. Voucher No. 2330.

FIGURE 11.4

Example of a Voucher Transaction Involving Two Departments

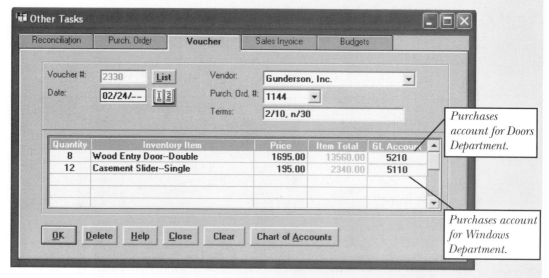

The procedure to enter a purchases return transaction is the same as the procedure to enter a voucher transaction. The only difference is that the quantity returned must be entered as a *negative* value, and the Purchases Return and Allowance account number of the appropriate department must be entered in the GL Account grid cell.

Cash Payments

The type of cash payment transaction affected by departmentalization is a payment on account subject to a cash discount. An example is illustrated in Figure 11.5.

> Feb. 17   Paid Voucher No. 2318 to Tollefson Corporation, $12,589.58, less 2% discount for windows merchandise, $251.79. Check No. 7209.

FIGURE 11.5

Example of a Cash Payment with a Departmental Discount

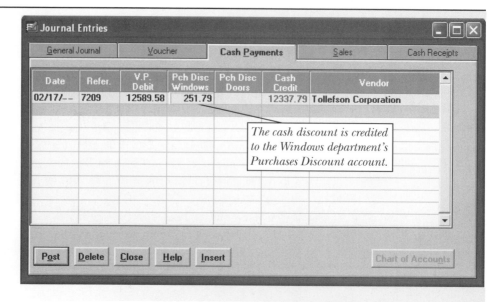

Sales Invoices

An example of a transaction involving the sale of merchandise for two departments is illustrated in Figure 11.6. Notice that the appropriate department's account number must be entered (or selected from the chart of accounts list) into the GL Account grid cell.

Feb. 02   Sold 5 Casement Crank—Double windows at $769.00 each and 1 Therm. Patio Door–Double at $1,995.00 to Helen Murray, terms 30 days, 6% sales tax. Sales Invoice No. 4632.

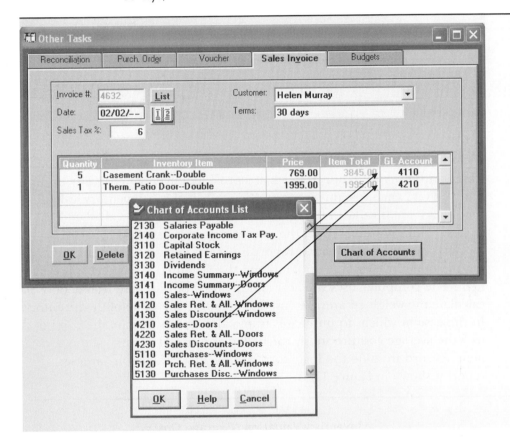

FIGURE 11.6

Example of a Sales Transaction Involving Two Departments

The procedure to enter a sales return transaction is the same as the procedure to enter a sales invoice. The only difference is that the quantity returned must be entered as a *negative* value, and the Sales Return and Allowance account number of the appropriate department must be entered in the GL Account grid cell.

Cash Receipts

When a transaction involving a receipt of cash on account subject to a cash discount is recorded in the cash receipts journal, the cash discount must be entered in the appropriate department's Sales Discounts grid cell. An example is illustrated in Figure 11.7.

Feb. 10   Received cash on account from Rebecca Beyer, covering Sales Invoice No. 4615 for $15,731.39; less 2% discount for windows merchandise, $203.80; less 2% discount for doors merchandise, $110.83.

FIGURE 11.7

*Example of a Cash
Receipt Involving
Departmental Discounts*

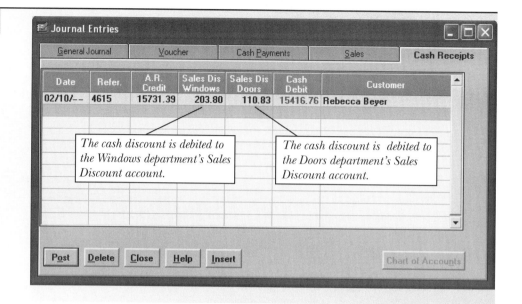

Inventory Valuation Reports

Three inventory valuation reports are provided: average cost, last in, first out (LIFO), and first in, first out (FIFO). All three inventory valuation reports are identical with the exception that the Cost and calculated Value at Cost columns are based on the chosen valuation method.

The **average cost valuation report** lists each item in the inventory showing the quantity currently on hand and the weighted average cost for each item. The computer uses the cost and quantity of purchase transactions to calculate the weighted average cost and compute the value of the inventory. In the case in which no purchases transactions are available, the computer uses the average cost previously calculated and stored in the inventory stock item's record to value the inventory. An inventory valuation (average cost) report is shown in Figure 11.8.

FIGURE 11.8

*Inventory Valuation
(Average Cost) Report*

**Lacina Windows & Doors
Inventory Valuation (Average Cost)
02/28/—**

Stock No.	Description	On Hand	Cost	Value At Cost	Retail Price	Value At Retail
110	Awning Window—Double	53	415.00	21,995.00	850.00	45,050.00
120	Casement Crank—Double	46	380.00	17,480.00	769.00	35,374.00
130	Casement Crank—Single	80	195.00	15,600.00	395.00	31,600.00
140	Casement Slider—Double	53	380.00	20,140.00	769.00	40,757.00
150	Casement Slider—Single	66	195.00	12,870.00	395.00	26,070.00
160	Casement Picture—Bay	97	715.00	69,355.00	1,495.00	145,015.00
170	Picture Window—Double	74	625.00	46,250.00	1,295.00	95,830.00
180	Picture Window—Glider	80	535.00	42,800.00	1,085.00	86,800.00
210	Garage Fire Door	90	200.00	18,000.00	425.00	38,250.00
220	Therm. Patio Door—Double	13	985.00	12,805.00	1,995.00	25,935.00
230	Therm. Patio Door—Single	18	550.00	9,900.00	1,125.00	20,250.00
240	Vinyl Patio Door—Double	26	565.00	14,690.00	1,175.00	30,550.00

(continued)

250	Vinyl Patio Door—Single	36	320.00	11,520.00	645.00	23,220.00
260	Wood Patio Door—Double	5	1,195.00	5,975.00	2,450.00	12,250.00
270	Wood Patio Door—Single	21	670.00	14,070.00	1,345.00	28,245.00
280	Wood Entry Door—Double	13	1,695.00	22,035.00	3,500.00	45,500.00
290	Wood Entry Door—Single	17	895.00	15,215.00	1,895.00	32,215.00
	Total Inventory Value			370,700.00		762,911.00

FIGURE 11.8

(Concluded)

The **LIFO valuation report** is based on the assumption that the last items received into inventory are the first to be sold. Therefore, any items remaining in the inventory are the first items received. The computer calculates LIFO on a perpetual basis according to the order that transactions are entered. The report lists the quantity in inventory for each different cost. The quantity and cost are extended to provide an inventory valuation based on the LIFO valuation method. The inventory valuation (LIFO) report is identical to the average valuation report shown in Figure 11.8 except that the Cost and calculated Value at Cost columns are based on the LIFO method.

The **FIFO valuation report** is based on the assumption that the first items received into inventory are the first sold. Therefore, any items remaining in inventory are the last items received. The report shows the quantity in inventory for each different cost. The quantity and cost are extended to provide an inventory valuation based on the FIFO valuation method. The inventory valuation (FIFO) report is identical to the average valuation report shown in Figure 11.8 except that the Cost and calculated Value at Cost columns are based on the FIFO method.

Gross Profit Statements

The **gross profit statements** show the sales and purchases for each department. The gross profit statements for Lacina Windows & Doors are shown in Figures 11.9 (a) through (c), respectively. The computer generated three statements when this Gross Profit Statements option was selected: one statement for Department 1 (windows), a second statement for Department 2 (doors), and a third statement that consolidated the two departments into one report. Each statement reports monthly and yearly revenue and costs. This provides information about the profitability of each department and the business as a whole.

FIGURE 11.9(A)

Gross Profit Statement—Department 1 (Windows)

Lacina Windows & Doors
Gross Profit Statement Department 1
For Period Ended 02/28/—

	Monthly Amount	Monthly Percent	Yearly Amount	Yearly Percent
Operating Revenue				
Sales—Windows	57,067.00	103.48	122,421.00	103.37
Sales Ret. & All.—Windows	−850.00	−1.54	−1,800.00	−1.52
Sales Discounts—Windows	−1,070.74	−1.94	−2,190.74	−1.85
Total Operating Revenue	55,146.26	100.00	118,430.26	100.00
Cost of Merchandise Sold				
Beginning Inventory	256,560.00	465.24	256,560.00	216.63
Purchases—Windows	17,875.00	32.41	55,685.00	47.02
Prch. Ret. & All.—Windows	−195.00	−0.35	−765.00	−0.65
Purchases Disc.—Windows	−251.79	−0.46	−436.79	−0.37
Merchandise Available for Sale	273,988.21	496.84	311,043.21	262.64
Less Ending Inventory	−246,495.00	−446.98	−246,495.00	−208.14
Cost of Merchandise Sold	27,493.21	49.86	64,548.21	54.50
Gross Profit	27,653.05	50.14	53,882.05	45.50

FIGURE 11.9(B)

Gross Profit Statement—Department 2 (Doors)

Lacina Windows & Doors
Gross Profit Statement Department 2
For Period Ended 02/28/—

	Monthly Amount	Monthly Percent	Yearly Amount	Yearly Percent
Operating Revenue				
Sales—Doors	33,145.00	103.18	63,330.00	103.69
Sales Ret. & All.—Doors	−425.00	−1.32	−1,000.00	−1.64
Sales Discounts—Doors	−595.33	−1.85	−1,253.33	−2.05
Total Operating Revenue	32,124.67	100.00	61,076.67	100.00
Cost of Merchandise Sold				
Beginning Inventory	113,495.00	353.30	113,495.00	185.82
Purchases—Doors	26,815.00	83.47	43,215.00	70.76
Prch. Ret. & All.—Doors	−200.00	−0.62	−435.00	−0.71
Purchases Disc.—Doors	−357.50	−1.11	−472.50	−0.77
Merchandise Available for Sale	139,752.50	435.03	155,802.50	255.09
Less Ending Inventory	−124,210.00	−386.65	−124,210.00	−203.37
Cost of Merchandise Sold	15,542.50	48.38	31,592.50	51.73
Gross Profit	16,582.17	51.62	29,484.17	48.27

FIGURE 11.9(c)

Consolidated Gross Profit Statement

Lacina Windows & Doors
Consolidated Gross Profit Statement
For Period Ended 02/28/—

	Monthly Amount	Monthly Percent	Yearly Amount	Yearly Percent
Operating Revenue				
Sales—Windows	57,067.00	65.39	122,421.00	68.20
Sales Ret. & All.—Windows	−850.00	−0.97	−1,800.00	−1.00
Sales Discounts—Windows	−1,070.74	−1.23	−2,190.74	−1.22
Sales—Doors	33,145.00	37.98	63,330.00	35.28
Sales Ret. & All.—Doors	−425.00	−0.49	−1,000.00	−0.56
Sales Discounts—Doors	−595.33	−0.68	−1,253.33	−0.70
Total Operating Revenue	87,270.93	100.00	179,506.93	100.00
Cost of Merchandise Sold				
Beginning Inventory	370,055.00	424.03	370,055.00	206.15
Purchases—Windows	17,875.00	20.48	55,685.00	31.02
Prch. Ret. & All.—Windows	−195.00	−0.22	−765.00	−0.43
Purchases Disc.—Windows	−251.79	−0.29	−436.79	−0.24
Purchases—Doors	26,815.00	30.73	43,215.00	24.07
Prch. Ret. & All.—Doors	−200.00	−0.23	−435.00	−0.24
Purchases Disc.—Doors	−357.50	−0.41	−472.50	−0.26
Merchandise Available for Sale	413,740.71	474.09	466,845.71	260.07
Less Ending Inventory	−370,705.00	−424.77	−370,705.00	−206.51
Cost of Merchandise Sold	43,035.71	49.31	96,140.71	53.56
Gross Profit	44,235.22	50.69	83,366.22	46.44

Chapter Summary

■ Accounts in the chart of accounts that show the cost or price of merchandise purchased for resale to customers are called cost of merchandise accounts and include the Purchases, Purchases Returns and Allowances, and Purchases Discounts accounts.

■ A departmentalized accounting system is used when management information is needed for each of the various departments within the business.

■ The chart of accounts contains separate accounts for each department that requires departmental information.

■ Department numbers are entered in the chart of accounts in a grid cell separate from the account number so that the numbering scheme is unaffected by departmentalization.

■ Merchandise inventory accounts, income summary accounts, revenue accounts, and cost accounts must exist for each department.

■ Departmentalized accounting transaction data are entered into the computer using the same purchase order, voucher, sales invoice, and journal entries you used in the previous chapters. The only difference is that some of the data entered must be identified as belonging to a specific department.

■ The gross profit statement shows the sales and purchases for each department.

■ A gross profit statement is generated for each department, and an additional statement is generated that consolidates each department's data into one report.

Sample Problem 11-S

This sample problem illustrates the use of a departmentalized accounting system. In this problem, you will process the transactions for the month of February and complete the monthly cycle for Lacina Windows & Doors. The chart of accounts, vendors, customers, and account balances for Lacina Windows & Doors will be the basis for this problem. The monthly transactions and adjusting entries are illustrated within the step-by-step instructions that follow.

1 Start *Integrated Accounting* 6e.

2 Open the file named IA6 Problem 11-S.

3 Enter your name in the Your Name text box.

4 Use the Save As menu item from the File menu to save the data to your disk with a file name of 11-S Your Name.

5 Change the title of Utilities Expense to Heating & Lighting Exp. in the chart of accounts.

6 Delete Market Research Expense from the chart of accounts.

7 Add Quade Corporation to the vendor list.

8 Delete Thomas Nessler from the customer list.

9 Add Bridget Whitney to the customer list.

10 Change the name of the customer Bickell Construction to Bickell Construction Co.

11 Enter the budget data shown here.

Account Title	Budget
Total Revenue	$1,270,000.00
Cost of Merchandise Sold	$825,000.00
Advertising Expense	$7,000.00
Deprec. Exp.—Store Eq.	$4,500.00
Sales Salary Expense	$150,000.00
Store Supplies Expense	$6,500.00
Uncollectible Accts. Exp.	$2,000.00
Deprec. Exp.—Office Eq.	$3,500.00
Insurance Expense	$4,000.00
Heating & Lighting Exp.	$12,000.00

Rent Expense	$34,000.00
Admin. Salary Expense	$50,000.00
Telephone Expense	$12,000.00
Office Supplies Expense	$7,000.00
Corporate Income Tax Exp.	$45,000.00

12 Enter the purchase orders and vouchers transactions.

Click Tasks on the toolbar, then click the Purchase Order and Voucher tabs to enter the following transactions.

Purchase Orders and Vouchers Transactions

Feb. 08 Ordered 14 Picture Window—Double at $625.00 each on account from Quade Corporation, terms 2/10, n/30. Purchase Order No. 1145.

09 Received 25 Casement Picture—Bay windows at $715.00 each for Purchase Order No. 1142 from Neubert Corporation, terms 2/10, n/30. Voucher No. 2327.

12 Ordered 25 Vinyl Patio Door—Double at $565.00 each on account from Lancaster, Inc., terms 2/10, n/30. Purchase Order No. 1146.

20 Received 26 Garage Fire Doors at $200.00 each for Purchase Order No. 1143 from Tollefson Corporation, terms 2/10, n/30. Voucher No. 2329.

22 Ordered 12 Wood Patio Door—Double at $1,195.00 each on account from Lancaster, Inc., terms 2/10, n/30. Purchase Order No. 1147.

24 Received 8 Wood Entry Door—Double at $1,695.00 each, and 9 Wood Entry Door–Single at $895.00 each for Purchase Order No. 1144 from Gunderson, Inc., terms 2/10, n/30. Voucher No. 2330.

26 Returned 1 Garage Fire Door at $200.00 to Tollefson Corporation. Voucher No. R2329. (Be sure to enter the quantity as −1 to indicate a return of one item, and the door department's purchases returns and allowances account number.)

26 Returned 1 Casement Crank—Single window at $195.00 to Neubert Corporation. Voucher No. R2309.

13 Enter the vouchers journal transactions.

Click Journal on the toolbar and use the Voucher tab to enter the following transactions.

Vouchers Journal Transactions

Feb. 01 Record Voucher No. 2325 to Benco Utilities Co., for monthly heating and lighting, $885.15.

01 Record Voucher No. 2326 to Citizens Telephone Co., for monthly telephone bill, $932.61.

15 Record Voucher No. 2328 to Creative Advertising Co., for advertising, $300.00.

26 Record Voucher No. 2331 to reimburse the payroll bank account for monthly salaries: sales salaries, $10,042.00; administrative salaries, $3,953.00; total, $13,995.00.

26   Record Voucher No. 2332 to L & S Properties, Inc., for monthly rent, $2,825.00.

26   Record Voucher No. 2333 to Commissioner of Revenue for sales tax liability, $3,670.00.

14   Enter the cash payments journal transactions.

Click Journal on the toolbar and use the Cash Payments tab to enter the following transactions.

Cash Payments Journal Transactions

Feb. 02   Paid Voucher No. 2325 to Benco Utilities Co., $885.15. Check No. 7205.

05   Paid Voucher No. 2302 to Lancaster, Inc., $5,090.65, no discount. Check No. 7206

09   Paid Voucher No. 2326 to Citizens Telephone Co., $932.61. Check No. 7207.

11   Paid Voucher No. 2304 to Gunderson, Inc., $10,684.43, no discount. Check No. 7208.

17   Paid Voucher No. 2318 to Tollefson Corporation, $12,589.58, less 2% discount for windows merchandise, $251.79. Check No. 7209.

21   Paid Voucher No. 2328 to Creative Advertising Co., $300.00. Check No. 7210.

24   Paid Voucher No. 2327 to Neubert Corporation, $17,875.00, less 2% discount for door merchandise, $357.50. Check No. 7211.

28   Paid Voucher No. 2331 to Payroll Bank Account, $13,995.00. Check No. 7212.

28   Paid Voucher No. 2332 to L & S Properties, Inc., $2,825.00. Check No. 7213.

28   Paid Voucher No. 2333 to Commissioner of Revenue, $3,670.00. Check No. 7214.

15   Enter the sales invoices transactions.

Click Tasks on the toolbar, then click on the Sales Invoice tab to enter the following transactions.

Sales Invoices Transactions

Feb. 02   Sold 5 Casement Crank—Double windows at $769.00 each, and 1 Therm. Patio Door—Double at $1,995.00 to Helen Murray, terms 30 days, 6% sales tax. Sales Invoice No. 4632.

08   Sold 3 Wood Entry Door—Double at $3,500.00, 1 Garage Fire Door at $425.00, 21 Casement Crank—Double windows at $769.00 each, and 1 Wood Patio Door—Double at $2,450.00 to Penkhus Remodeling, Inc., terms 2/10, n/30, no sales tax. Sales Invoice No. 4633.

15   Sold 1 Vinyl Patio Door—Double at $1,175.00, and 7 Casement Slider— Single windows at $395.00 to Bridget Whitney, terms 30 days, 6% sales tax. Sales Invoice No. 4634.

18   Sold 32 Casement Slider—Double windows at $769.00 each, 2 Picture window—Double at $1,295.00, 1 Wood Entry Door—Double at $3,500.00, and 3 Wood Patio Door—Double at $2,450.00 to Quality Contractors, terms 2/10, n/30, no sales tax. Sales Invoice No. 4635.

23   Granted credit to Bickell Construction Co., for 1 Awning Window—Double at $850.00, no sales tax. Sales Return No. R4610. (Note: be sure to enter the quantity as −1 to indicate a return of one item, and the window department's sales returns and allowances account number.)

26   Sold 2 Wood Patio Door—Double at $2,450.00 each, and 2 Garage Fire Doors at $425.00 each, and 18 Casement Slider—Single windows at $395.00 each to Schaefer Builders, terms 2/10, n/30, no sales tax. Sales Invoice No. 4636.

28   Granted credit to Schaefer Builders for 1 Garage Fire Door at $425.00, no sales tax. Sales Return No. R4636.

16   Enter the cash receipts journal transactions.

Click Journal on the toolbar and use the Cash Receipts tab to enter the following transactions.

Cash Receipts Journal Transactions

Feb. 07   Received cash on account from Penkhus Remodeling, Inc., covering Sales Invoice No. 4603 for $3,755.00; no discount.

10   Received cash on account from Rebecca Beyer, covering Sales Invoice No. 4615 for $15,731.39; less 2% discount for windows merchandise, $203.80; less 2% discount for doors merchandise, $110.83.

14   Received cash on account from Helen Murray, covering Sales Invoice No. 4632 for $6,190.40; no discount.

16   Received cash on account from Bickell Construction Co., covering Sales Invoice No. 4605 for $21,117.87; no discount.

18   Received cash on account from Bridget Whitney, covering Sales Invoice No. 4634 for $4,176.40; no discount.

24   Received cash on account from Penkhus Remodeling, Inc. covering Sales Invoice No. 4633 for $29,524.00; less 2% discount for windows merchandise, $322.98; less 2% discount for doors merchandise, $267.50.

26   Received cash on account from Quality Contractors, covering Sales Invoice No. 4635 for $38,048.00; less 2% discount for windows merchandise, $543.96; less 2% discount for doors merchandise, $217.00.

17   Display the chart of accounts, vendor, and customer lists.

The reports are shown in Figures 11.10 (a) through (c), respectively.

FIGURE 11.10(A)

Chart of Accounts

Lacina Windows & Doors
Chart of Accounts
02/28/—

Assets
1110	Cash
1130	Accounts Receivable
1140	Allow. for Doubt. Accts.
1150	Merch. Inventory—Windows
1151	Merch. Inventory—Doors
1160	Office Supplies
1170	Store Supplies
1180	Prepaid Insurance
1510	Office Equipment
1520	Accum. Depr.—Office Eq.
1530	Store Equipment
1540	Accum. Depr.—Store Eq.

Liabilities
2110	Vouchers Payable
2120	Sales Tax Payable
2130	Salaries Payable
2140	Corporate Income Tax Pay.

Stockholders' Equity
3110	Capital Stock
3120	Retained Earnings
3130	Dividends
3140	Income Summary—Windows
3141	Income Summary—Doors

Revenue
4110	Sales—Windows
4120	Sales Ret. & All.—Windows
4130	Sales Discounts—Windows
4210	Sales—Doors
4220	Sales Ret. & All.—Doors
4230	Sales Discounts—Doors

Cost
5110	Purchases—Windows
5120	Prch. Ret. & All.—Windows
5130	Purchases Disc.—Windows
5210	Purchases—Doors
5220	Prch. Ret. & All.—Doors
5230	Purchases Disc.—Doors

Expenses
6110	Advertising Expense
6120	Deprec. Exp.—Store Eq.
6130	Sales Salary Expense
6140	Store Supplies Expense
6510	Uncollectible Accts. Exp.
6520	Deprec. Exp.—Office Eq.
6540	Insurance Expense

(continued)

FIGURE 11.10(A)

(Concluded)

6560	Heating & Lighting Exp.
6570	Rent Expense
6580	Admin. Salary Expense
6590	Telephone Expense
6600	Office Supplies Expense

Corporate Income Tax
9110	Corporate Income Tax Exp.

FIGURE 11.10(B)

Vendor List

Lacina Windows & Doors
Vendor List
02/28/—

Vendor Name
Benco Utilities Co.
Citizens Telephone Co.
Commissioner of Revenue
Creative Advertising Co.
Enders Supply Co.
Gunderson, Inc.
L & S Properties, Inc.
Lancaster, Inc.
Neubert Corporation
Paulson, Inc.
Payroll Bank Account
Quade Corporation
Tollefson Corporation

FIGURE 11.10(C)

Customer List

Lacina Windows & Doors
Customer List
02/28/—

Customer Name
Bickell Construction Co.
Bridget Whitney
George Lentz
Helen Murray
Penkhus Remodeling, Inc.
Phillip Gilbert
Quality Contractors
Rebecca Beyer
Schaefer Builders

18 **Display the purchase order, voucher, and sales invoice registers for the month of February.**

The reports are shown in Figures 11.11 (a) through (c), respectively.

FIGURE 11.11(A)

Purchase Orders Register

Lacina Windows & Doors
Purchase Order Register
02/28/—

P.O. Number	P.O. Date	Vendor Name	P.O. Amount
1145	02/08/—	Quade Corporation	8,750.00
1146	02/12/—	Lancaster, Inc.	14,125.00
1147	02/22/—	Lancaster, Inc.	14,340.00
		Total Amount	37,215.00

FIGURE 11.11(B)

Vouchers Register

Lacina Windows & Doors
Voucher Register
02/28/—

Invoice Number	Invoice Date	Vendor Name	Invoice Amount
2327	02/09/—	Neubert Corporation	17,875.00
2329	02/20/—	Tollefson Corporation	5,200.00
2330	02/24/—	Gunderson, Inc.	21,615.00
R2309	02/26/—	Neubert Corporation	−195.00
R2329	02/26/—	Tollefson Corporation	−200.00
		Total Amount	44,295.00

FIGURE 11.11(C)

Sales Invoice Register

Lacina Windows & Doors
Sales Invoice Register
02/28/—

Invoice Number	Invoice Date	Customer Name	Invoice Amount	Sales Tax
4632	02/02/—	Helen Murray	5,840.00	350.40
4633	02/08/—	Penkhus Remodeling, Inc.	29,524.00	
4634	02/15/—	Bridget Whitney	3,940.00	236.40
4635	02/18/—	Quality Contractors	38,048.00	
4636	02/26/—	Schaefer Builders	12,860.00	
R4610	02/23/—	Bickell Construction Co.	−850.00	
R4636	02/28/—	Schaefer Builders	−425.00	
		Total Amount	88,937.00	586.80

19 **Display the inventory transactions report for the month of February.**

The report is shown in Figure 11.12.

Lacina Windows & Doors
Inventory Transactions
02/28/—

Date	Description	Inv./ P.O.	Quantity Sold	Selling Price	Quan. Ord.	Quan. Recd.	Cost Price
Sales Invoices							
02/02	Casement Crank—Double	4632	5	769.00			
	Therm. Patio Door—Double		1	1,995.00			
02/08	Wood Entry Door—Double	4633	3	3,500.00			
	Garage Fire Door		1	425.00			
	Casement Crank—Double		21	769.00			
	Wood Patio Door—Double		1	2,450.00			
02/15	Vinyl Patio Door—Double	4634	1	1,175.00			
	Casement Slider—Single		7	395.00			
02/18	Casement Slider—Double	4635	32	769.00			
	Picture Window—Double		2	1,295.00			
	Wood Entry Door—Double		1	3,500.00			
	Wood Patio Door—Double		3	2,450.00			
02/26	Wood Patio Door—Double	4636	2	2,450.00			
	Garage Fire Door		2	425.00			
	Casement Slider—Single		18	395.00			
02/23	Awning Window—Double	R4610	−1	850.00			
02/28	Garage Fire Door	R4636	−1	425.00			
Purchase Orders							
02/08	Picture Window—Double	1145			14		
02/12	Vinyl Patio Door—Double	1146			25		
02/22	Wood Patio Door—Double	1147			12		
Vouchers							
02/09	Casement Picture—Bay	2327				25	715.00
02/20	Garage Fire Door	2329				26	200.00
02/24	Wood Entry Door—Double	2330				8	1,695.00
	Wood Entry Door—Single					9	895.00
02/26	Casement Crank—Single	R2309				−1	195.00
02/26	Garage Fire Door	R2329				−1	200.00
	Totals		98		51	66	

20 **Display the average cost inventory valuation report.**

Select Valuation (Average Cost) and click OK. The report appears in Figure 11.13.

FIGURE 11.13

Inventory Valuation (Average Cost) Report

Lacina Windows & Doors
Inventory Valuation (Average Cost)
02/28/—

Stock No.	Description	On Hand	Cost	Value At Cost	Retail Price	Value At Retail
110	Awning Window—Double	53	415.00	21,995.00	850.00	45,050.00
120	Casement Crank—Double	46	380.00	17,480.00	769.00	35,374.00
130	Casement Crank—Single	80	195.00	15,600.00	395.00	31,600.00
140	Casement Slider—Double	53	380.00	20,140.00	769.00	40,757.00
150	Casement Slider—Single	66	195.00	12,870.00	395.00	26,070.00
160	Casement Picture—Bay	97	715.00	69,355.00	1,495.00	145,015.00
170	Picture Window—Double	74	625.00	46,250.00	1,295.00	95,830.00
180	Picture Window—Glider	80	535.00	42,800.00	1,085.00	86,800.00
210	Garage Fire Door	90	200.00	18,000.00	425.00	38,250.00
220	Therm. Patio Door—Double	13	985.00	12,805.00	1,995.00	25,935.00
230	Therm. Patio Door—Single	18	550.00	9,900.00	1,125.00	20,250.00
240	Vinyl Patio Door—Double	26	565.00	14,690.00	1,175.00	30,550.00
250	Vinyl Patio Door—Single	36	320.00	11,520.00	645.00	23,220.00
260	Wood Patio Door—Double	5	1,195.00	5,975.00	2,450.00	12,250.00
270	Wood Patio Door—Single	21	670.00	14,070.00	1,345.00	28,245.00
280	Wood Entry Door—Double	13	1,695.00	22,035.00	3,500.00	45,500.00
290	Wood Entry Door—Single	17	895.00	15,215.00	1,895.00	32,215.00
	Total Inventory Value			370,700.00		762,911.00

21 **Display the general, vouchers, cash payments, sales, and cash receipts journal reports.**

The journal reports are shown in Figure 11.14 (a) through (e), respectively.

FIGURE 11.14(A)

General Journal Report

Lacina Windows & Doors
General Journal
02/28/—

Date	Refer.	Acct.	Title	Debit	Credit
02/23	R4610	4120	Sales Ret. & All.—Windows	850.00	
02/23	R4610	1130	AR/Bickell Construction Co.		850.00
02/26	R2329	2110	VP/Tollefson Corporation	200.00	
02/26	R2329	5220	Prch. Ret. & All.—Doors		200.00
02/26	R2309	2110	VP/Neubert Corporation	195.00	
02/26	R2309	5120	Prch. Ret. & All.—Windows		195.00
02/28	R4636	4220	Sales Ret. & All.—Doors	425.00	
02/28	R4636	1130	AR/Schaefer Builders		425.00
			Totals	1,670.00	1,670.00

FIGURE 11.14(B)

Vouchers Journal Report

Lacina Windows & Doors
Vouchers Journal
02/28/—

Date	Inv. No.	Acct.	Title	Debit	Credit
02/01	2325	6560	Heating & Lighting Exp.	885.15	
02/01	2325	2110	VP/Benco Utilities Co.		885.15
02/01	2326	6590	Telephone Expense	932.61	
02/01	2326	2110	VP/Citizens Telephone Co.		932.61
02/09	2327	5110	Purchases—Windows	17,875.00	
02/09	2327	2110	VP/Neubert Corporation		17,875.00
02/15	2328	6110	Advertising Expense	300.00	
02/15	2328	2110	VP/Creative Advertising Co.		300.00
02/20	2329	5210	Purchases—Doors	5,200.00	
02/20	2329	2110	VP/Tollefson Corporation		5,200.00
02/24	2330	5210	Purchases—Doors	21,615.00	
02/24	2330	2110	VP/Gunderson, Inc.		21,615.00
02/26	2331	6130	Sales Salary Expense	10,042.00	
02/26	2331	6580	Admin. Salary Expense	3,953.00	
02/26	2331	2110	VP/Payroll Bank Account		13,995.00
02/26	2332	6570	Rent Expense	2,825.00	
02/26	2332	2110	VP/L & S Properties, Inc.		2,825.00
02/26	2333	2120	Sales Tax Payable	3,670.00	
02/26	2333	2110	VP/Commissioner of Revenue		3,670.00
			Totals	67,297.76	67,297.76

FIGURE 11.14(C)

Cash Payments Journal Report

Lacina Windows & Doors
Cash Payments Journal
02/28/—

Date	Ck. No.	Acct.	Title	Debit	Credit
02/02	7205	2110	VP/Benco Utilities Co.	885.15	
02/02	7205	1110	Cash		885.15
02/05	7206	2110	VP/Lancaster, Inc.	5,090.65	
02/05	7206	1110	Cash		5,090.65
02/09	7207	2110	VP/Citizens Telephone Co.	932.61	
02/09	7207	1110	Cash		932.61
02/11	7208	2110	VP/Gunderson, Inc.	10,684.43	
02/11	7208	1110	Cash		10,684.43
02/17	7209	2110	VP/Tollefson Corporation	12,589.58	
02/17	7209	1110	Cash		12,337.79
02/17	7209	5130	Purchases Disc.—Windows		251.79
02/21	7210	2110	VP/Creative Advertising Co.	300.00	
02/21	7210	1110	Cash		300.00

(continued)

				Debit	Credit
02/24	7211	2110	VP/Neubert Corporation	17,875.00	
02/24	7211	1110	Cash		17,517.50
02/24	7211	5230	Purchases Disc.—Doors		357.50
02/28	7212	2110	VP/Payroll Bank Account	13,995.00	
02/28	7212	1110	Cash		13,995.00
02/28	7213	2110	VP/L & S Properties, Inc.	2,825.00	
02/28	7213	1110	Cash		2,825.00
02/28	7214	2110	VP/Commissioner of Revenue	3,670.00	
02/28	7214	1110	Cash		3,670.00
			Totals	68,847.42	68,847.42

FIGURE 11.14(C)

(Concluded)

Lacina Windows & Doors
Sales Journal
02/28/—

FIGURE 11.14(D)

Sales Journal Report

Date	Inv. No.	Acct.	Title	Debit	Credit
02/02	4632	1130	AR/Helen Murray	6,190.40	
02/02	4632	4110	Sales—Windows		3,845.00
02/02	4632	4210	Sales—Doors		1,995.00
02/02	4632	2120	Sales Tax Payable		350.40
02/08	4633	1130	AR/Penkhus Remodeling, Inc.	29,524.00	
02/08	4633	4210	Sales—Doors		13,375.00
02/08	4633	4110	Sales—Windows		16,149.00
02/15	4634	1130	AR/Bridget Whitney	4,176.40	
02/15	4634	4210	Sales—Doors		1,175.00
02/15	4634	4110	Sales—Windows		2,765.00
02/15	4634	2120	Sales Tax Payable		236.40
02/18	4635	1130	AR/Quality Contractors	38,048.00	
02/18	4635	4110	Sales—Windows		27,198.00
02/18	4635	4210	Sales—Doors		10,850.00
02/26	4636	1130	AR/Schaefer Builders	12,860.00	
02/26	4636	4210	Sales—Doors		5,750.00
02/26	4636	4110	Sales—Windows		7,110.00
			Totals	90,798.80	90,798.80

Lacina Windows & Doors
Cash Receipts Journal
02/28/—

FIGURE 11.14(E)

Cash Receipts Journal Report

Date	Refer.	Acct.	Title	Debit	Credit
02/07	4603	1110	Cash	3,755.00	
02/07	4603	1130	AR/Penkhus Remodeling, Inc.		3,755.00
02/10	4615	1110	Cash	15,416.76	
02/10	4615	4130	Sales Discounts—Windows	203.80	
02/10	4615	4230	Sales Discounts—Doors	110.83	
02/10	4615	1130	AR/Rebecca Beyer		15,731.39

(continued)

FIGURE 11.14(E)	02/14	4632	1110	Cash	6,190.40	
(Concluded)	02/14	4632	1130	AR/Helen Murray		6,190.40
	02/16	4605	1110	Cash	21,117.87	
	02/16	4605	1130	AR/Bickell Construction Co.		21,117.87
	02/18	4634	1110	Cash	4,176.40	
	02/18	4634	1130	AR/Bridget Whitney		4,176.40
	02/24	4633	1110	Cash	28,933.52	
	02/24	4633	4130	Sales Discounts—Windows	322.98	
	02/24	4633	4230	Sales Discounts—Doors	267.50	
	02/24	4633	1130	AR/Penkhus Remodeling, Inc.		29,524.00
	02/26	4635	1110	Cash	37,287.04	
	02/26	4635	4130	Sales Discounts—Windows	543.96	
	02/26	4635	4230	Sales Discounts—Doors	217.00	
	02/26	4635	1130	AR/Quality Contractors		38,048.00
				Totals	118,543.06	118,543.06

22 Display the trial balance.

The trial balance is shown in Figure 11.15.

FIGURE 11.15

Trial Balance

Lacina Windows & Doors
Trial Balance
02/28/—

Acct. Number	Account Title	Debit	Credit
1110	Cash	117,120.30	
1130	Accounts Receivable	12,526.00	
1140	Allow. for Doubt. Accts.		850.00
1150	Merch. Inventory—Windows	256,560.00	
1151	Merch. Inventory—Doors	113,495.00	
1160	Office Supplies	2,450.00	
1170	Store Supplies	3,000.00	
1180	Prepaid Insurance	920.00	
1510	Office Equipment	20,260.00	
1520	Accum. Depr.—Office Eq.		10,115.00
1530	Store Equipment	23,920.00	
1540	Accum. Depr.—Store Eq.		8,650.00
2110	Vouchers Payable		30,121.09
2120	Sales Tax Payable		586.80
2140	Corporate Income Tax Pay.		4,000.00
3110	Capital Stock		305,000.00
3120	Retained Earnings		155,170.53
4110	Sales—Windows		122,421.00
4120	Sales Ret. & All.—Windows	1,800.00	
4130	Sales Discounts—Windows	2,190.74	
4210	Sales—Doors		63,330.00
4220	Sales Ret. & All.—Doors	1,000.00	

(continued)

4230	Sales Discounts—Doors	1,253.33	
5110	Purchases—Windows	55,685.00	
5120	Prch. Ret. & All.—Windows		765.00
5130	Purchases Disc.—Windows		436.79
5210	Purchases—Doors	43,215.00	
5220	Prch. Ret. & All.—Doors		435.00
5230	Purchases Disc.—Doors		472.50
6110	Advertising Expense	1,100.00	
6120	Deprec. Exp.—Store Eq.	425.00	
6130	Sales Salary Expense	22,542.00	
6140	Store Supplies Expense	680.00	
6510	Uncollectible Accts. Exp.	250.00	
6520	Deprec. Exp.—Office Eq.	325.00	
6540	Insurance Expense	335.00	
6560	Heating & Lighting Exp.	1,775.15	
6570	Rent Expense	5,625.00	
6580	Admin. Salary Expense	7,277.72	
6590	Telephone Expense	1,853.47	
6600	Office Supplies Expense	770.00	
9110	Corporate Income Tax Exp.	4,000.00	
	Totals	702,353.71	702,353.71

FIGURE 11.15

(Concluded)

End-of-Month Activities

After the monthly transactions have been processed, the adjusting entries must be entered and posted. The financial statements may then be displayed. The following adjustment data are for the month of February for Lacina Windows & Doors and the adjusting entries are illustrated within the step-by-step instructions.

Merchandise inventories on February 28:
Windows $246,495.00
Doors $124,210.00
Insurance expired during February......................$410.00
Inventories of supplies on February 28:
Office supplies $1,995.00
Store supplies..$2,500.00
Depreciation for February:
Office Equipment...$315.10
Store equipment...$415.25
Uncollectible accounts expense increase............$200.00
Salaries Payable:
Sales salaries...$3,835.00
Administrative salaries $515.00
Additional income tax owed...............................$3,500.00

1   Enter the adjusting entries. Key Adj.Ent. in the Reference text box.

2   Display the adjusting entries.

The adjusting entries report is shown in Figure 11.16.

FIGURE 11.16

General Journal Report (Adjusting Entries)

Lacina Windows & Doors
General Journal
02/28/—

Date	Refer.	Acct.	Title	Debit	Credit
02/28	Adj.Ent.	3140	Income Summary—Windows	10,065.00	
02/28	Adj.Ent.	1150	Merch. Inventory—Windows		10,065.00
02/28	Adj.Ent.	1151	Merch. Inventory—Doors	10,715.00	
02/28	Adj.Ent.	3141	Income Summary—Doors		10,715.00
02/28	Adj.Ent.	6540	Insurance Expense	410.00	
02/28	Adj.Ent.	1180	Prepaid Insurance		410.00
02/28	Adj.Ent.	6600	Office Supplies Expense	455.00	
02/28	Adj.Ent.	1160	Office Supplies		455.00
02/28	Adj.Ent.	6140	Store Supplies Expense	500.00	
02/28	Adj.Ent.	1170	Store Supplies		500.00
02/28	Adj.Ent.	6520	Deprec. Exp.—Office Eq.	315.10	
02/28	Adj.Ent.	1520	Accum. Depr.—Office Eq.		315.10
02/28	Adj.Ent.	6120	Deprec. Exp.—Store Eq.	415.25	
02/28	Adj.Ent.	1540	Accum. Depr.—Store Eq.		415.25
02/28	Adj.Ent.	6510	Uncollectible Accts. Exp.	200.00	
02/28	Adj.Ent.	1140	Allow. for Doubt. Accts.		200.00
02/28	Adj.Ent.	6130	Sales Salary Expense	3,835.00	
02/28	Adj.Ent.	6580	Admin. Salary Expense	515.00	
02/28	Adj.Ent.	2130	Salaries Payable		4,350.00
02/28	Adj.Ent.	9110	Corporate Income Tax Exp.	3,500.00	
02/28	Adj.Ent.	2140	Corporate Income Tax Pay.		3,500.00
			Totals	30,925.35	30,925.35

3 **Use Check on the toolbar to check your work.**

4 **Display the gross profit statements.**

The gross profit statements reports are shown in Figures 11.17 (a) through (c), respectively.

NOTE When the gross profit statements report is selected, three reports will be generated—one for each department and a consolidated report.

FIGURE 11.17(A)

*Gross Profit Statement—
Department 1 (Windows)*

Lacina Windows & Doors
Gross Profit Statement Department 1
For Period Ended 02/28/—

	Monthly Amount	Monthly Percent	Yearly Amount	Yearly Percent
Operating Revenue				
Sales—Windows	57,067.00	103.48	122,421.00	103.37
Sales Ret. & All.—Windows	−850.00	−1.54	−1,800.00	−1.52
Sales Discounts—Windows	−1,070.74	−1.94	−2,190.74	−1.85
Total Operating Revenue	55,146.26	100.00	118,430.26	100.00
Cost of Merchandise Sold				
Beginning Inventory	256,560.00	465.24	256,560.00	216.63
Purchases—Window	17,875.00	32.41	55,685.00	47.02
Prch. Ret. & All.—Windows	−195.00	−0.35	−765.00	−0.65
Purchases Disc.—Windows	−251.79	−0.46	−436.79	−0.37
Merchandise Available for Sale	273,988.21	496.84	311,043.21	262.64
Less Ending Inventory	−246,495.00	−446.98	−246,495.00	−208.14
Cost of Merchandise Sold	27,493.21	49.86	64,548.21	54.50
Gross Profit	27,653.05	50.14	53,882.05	45.50

FIGURE 11.17(B)

*Gross Profit Statement—
Department 2 (Doors)*

Lacina Windows & Doors
Gross Profit Statement Department 2
For Period Ended 02/28/—

	Monthly Amount	Monthly Percent	Yearly Amount	Yearly Percent
Operating Revenue				
Sales—Doors	33,145.00	103.18	63,330.00	103.69
Sales Ret. & All.—Doors	−425.00	−1.32	−1,000.00	−1.64
Sales Discounts—Doors	−595.33	−1.85	−1,253.33	−2.05
Total Operating Revenue	32,124.67	100.00	61,076.67	100.00
Cost of Merchandise Sold				
Beginning Inventory	113,495.00	353.30	113,495.00	185.82
Purchases—Doors	26,815.00	83.47	43,215.00	70.76
Prch. Ret. & All.—Doors	−200.00	−0.62	−435.00	−0.71
Purchases Disc.—Doors	−357.50	−1.11	−472.50	−0.77
Merchandise Available for Sale	139,752.50	435.03	155,802.50	255.09
Less Ending Inventory	−124,210.00	−386.65	−124,210.00	−203.37
Cost of Merchandise Sold	15,542.50	48.38	31,592.50	51.73
Gross Profit	16,582.17	51.62	29,484.17	48.27

FIGURE 11.17(c)

Consolidated Gross Profit Statement

Lacina Windows & Doors
Consolidated Gross Profit Statement
For Period Ended 02/28/—

	Monthly Amount	Monthly Percent	Yearly Amount	Yearly Percent
Operating Revenue				
Sales—Windows	57,067.00	65.39	122,421.00	68.20
Sales Ret. & All.—Windows	−850.00	−0.97	−1,800.00	−1.00
Sales Discounts—Windows	−1,070.74	−1.23	−2,190.74	−1.22
Sales—Doors	33,145.00	37.98	63,330.00	35.28
Sales Ret. & All.—Doors	−425.00	−0.49	−1,000.00	−0.56
Sales Discounts—Doors	−595.33	−0.68	−1,253.33	−0.70
Total Operating Revenue	87,270.93	100.00	179,506.93	100.00
Cost of Merchandise Sold				
Beginning Inventory	370,055.00	424.03	370,055.00	206.15
Purchases—Windows	17,875.00	20.48	55,685.00	31.02
Prch. Ret. & All.—Windows	−195.00	−0.22	−765.00	−0.43
Purchases Disc.—Windows	−251.79	−0.29	−436.79	−0.24
Purchases—Doors	26,815.00	30.73	43,215.00	24.07
Prch. Ret. & All.—Doors	−200.00	−0.23	−435.00	−0.24
Purchases Disc.—Doors	−357.50	−0.41	−472.50	−0.26
Merchandise Available for Sale	413,740.71	474.09	466,845.71	260.07
Less Ending Inventory	−370,705.00	−424.77	−370,705.00	−206.51
Cost of Merchandise Sold	43,035.71	49.31	96,140.71	53.56
Gross Profit	44,235.22	50.69	83,366.22	46.44

5 **Display the income statement.**

The income statement is shown in Figure 11.18.

FIGURE 11.18

Income Statement

Lacina Windows & Doors
Income Statement
For Period Ended 02/28/—

	Monthly Amount	Monthly Percent	Yearly Amount	Yearly Percent
Operating Revenue				
Sales—Windows	57,067.00	65.39	122,421.00	68.20
Sales Ret. & All.—Windows	−850.00	−0.97	−1,800.00	−1.00
Sales Discounts—Windows	−1,070.74	−1.23	−2,190.74	−1.22
Sales—Doors	33,145.00	37.98	63,330.00	35.28
Sales Ret. & All.—Doors	−425.00	−0.49	−1,000.00	−0.56
Sales Discounts—Doors	−595.33	−0.68	−1,253.33	−0.70
Total Operating Revenue	87,270.93	100.00	179,506.93	100.00
Cost of Merchandise Sold				
Beginning Inventory	370,055.00	424.03	370,055.00	206.15
Purchases—Windows	17,875.00	20.48	55,685.00	31.02

(continued)

					FIGURE 11.18
Prch. Ret. & All.—Windows	−195.00	−0.22	−765.00	−0.43	
Purchases Disc.—Windows	−251.79	−0.29	−436.79	−0.24	*(Concluded)*
Purchases—Doors	26,815.00	30.73	43,215.00	24.07	
Prch. Ret. & All.—Doors	−200.00	−0.23	−435.00	−0.24	
Purchases Disc.—Doors	−357.50	−0.41	−472.50	−0.26	
Merchandise Available for Sale	413,740.71	474.09	466,845.71	260.07	
Less Ending Inventory	−370,705.00	−424.77	−370,705.00	−206.51	
Cost of Merchandise Sold	43,035.71	49.31	96,140.71	53.56	
Gross Profit	44,235.22	50.69	83,366.22	46.44	
Operating Expenses					
Advertising Expense	300.00	0.34	1,100.00	0.61	
Deprec. Exp.—Store Eq.	415.25	0.48	840.25	0.47	
Sales Salary Expense	13,877.00	15.90	26,377.00	14.69	
Store Supplies Expense	500.00	0.57	1,180.00	0.66	
Total Selling Expenses	15,092.25	17.29	29,497.25	16.43	
Uncollectible Accts. Exp.	200.00	0.23	450.00	0.25	
Deprec. Exp.—Office Eq.	315.10	0.36	640.10	0.36	
Insurance Expense	410.00	0.47	745.00	0.42	
Heating & Lighting Exp.	885.15	1.01	1,775.15	0.99	
Rent Expense	2,825.00	3.24	5,625.00	3.13	
Admin. Salary Expense	4,468.00	5.12	7,792.72	4.34	
Telephone Expense	932.61	1.07	1,853.47	1.03	
Office Supplies Expense	455.00	0.52	1,225.00	0.68	
Total Admin. Expenses	10,490.86	12.02	20,106.44	11.20	
Total Operating Expenses	25,583.11	29.31	49,603.69	27.63	
Net Income from Operations	18,652.11	21.37	33,762.53	18.81	
Net Income before Income Tax	18,652.11	21.37	33,762.53	18.81	
Income Tax					
Corporate Income Tax Exp.	3,500.00	4.01	7,500.00	4.18	
Net Income after Income Tax	15,152.11	17.36	26,262.53	14.63	

6 Display the retained earnings statement.

The retained earnings statement is shown in Figure 11.19.

Lacina Windows & Doors **Retained Earnings Statement** **For Period Ended 02/28/—**		FIGURE 11.19
Retained Earnings (Beg. of Period)	155,170.53	*Retained Earnings*
Net Income	26,262.53	*Statement*
Retained Earnings (End of Period)	181,433.06	

Display the balance sheet.

The balance sheet is shown in Figure 11.20.

FIGURE **11.20**	Lacina Windows & Doors	
Balance Sheet	Balance Sheet	
	02/28/—	
Assets		
Cash	117,120.30	
Accounts Receivable	12,526.00	
Allow. for Doubt. Accts.	−1,050.00	
Merch. Inventory—Windows	246,495.00	
Merch. Inventory—Doors	124,210.00	
Office Supplies	1,995.00	
Store Supplies	2,500.00	
Prepaid Insurance	510.00	
Total Current Asset	504,306.30	
Office Equipment	20,260.00	
Accum. Depr.—Office Eq.	−10,430.10	
Store Equipment	23,920.00	
Accum. Depr.—Store Eq.	−9,065.25	
Total Plant Assets	24,684.65	
Total Assets		528,990.95
Liabilities		
Vouchers Payable	30,121.09	
Sales Tax Payable	586.80	
Salaries Payable	4,350.00	
Corporate Income Tax Pay.	7,500.00	
Total Liabilities		42,557.89
Stockholders' Equity		
Capital Stock	305,000.00	
Retained Earnings	155,170.53	
Net Income	26,262.53	
Total Stockholders' Equity		486,433.06
Total Liabilities & Equity		528,990.95

8 **Display the budget report.**

The budget report is shown in Figure 11.21.

Lacina Windows & Doors
Budget Report
For Period Ended 02/28/—

	Budget	Actual	Diff. From Budget	%
Operating Revenue				
Operating Revenue	1,270,000.00	179,506.93	−1,090,493.07	−85.87
Cost of Merchandise Sold	825,000.00	96,140.71	−728,859.29	−88.35
Gross Profit	445,000.00	83,366.22	−361,633.78	−81.27
Operating Expenses				
Advertising Expense	7,000.00	1,100.00	−5,900.00	−84.29
Deprec. Exp.—Store Eq.	4,500.00	840.25	−3,659.75	−81.33
Sales Salary Expense	150,000.00	26,377.00	−123,623.00	−82.42
Store Supplies Expense	6,500.00	1,180.00	−5,320.00	−81.85
Uncollectible Accts. Exp.	2,000.00	450.00	−1,550.00	−77.50
Deprec. Exp.—Office Eq.	3,500.00	640.10	−2,859.90	−81.71
Insurance Expense	4,000.00	745.00	−3,255.00	−81.38
Heating & Lighting Exp.	12,000.00	1,775.15	−10,224.85	−85.21
Rent Expense	34,000.00	5,625.00	−28,375.00	−83.46
Admin. Salary Expense	50,000.00	7,792.72	−42,207.28	−84.41
Telephone Expense	12,000.00	1,853.47	−10,146.53	−84.55
Office Supplies Expense	7,000.00	1,225.00	−5,775.00	−82.50
Total Operating Expenses	292,500.00	49,603.69	−242,896.31	−83.04
Net Income from Operations	152,500.00	33,762.53	−118,737.47	−77.86
Net Income before Income Tax	152,500.00	33,762.53	−118,737.47	−77.86
Income Tax				
Corporate Income Tax Exp.	45,000.00	7,500.00	−37,500.00	−83.33
Net Income after Income Tax	107,500.00	26,262.53	−81,237.47	−75.57

FIGURE 11.21

Budget Report

9 **Generate a most profitable items and an actual versus budget graph.**

The most profitable inventory items and actual versus budget graphs are shown in Figures 11.22 (a) and (b), respectively.

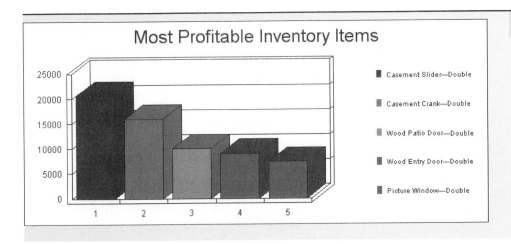

FIGURE 11.22(A)

Income Statement Graph

FIGURE 11.22(B)

Actual versus Budget Graph

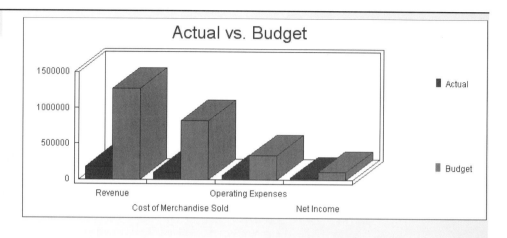

10 **Click Save on the toolbar to save the data file.**

11 **Calculate a loan payment amount using the Loan Planner.**

Lacina Windows & Doors is considering purchasing land and a building. Management has narrowed its loan down to two local banks and has asked you to use the Loan Planner to furnish loan payment information based upon the data provided from each bank.

Choose the Planning Tools menu item from the Extras menu or click on the Tools toolbar. When the Planning Tools window appears, click the Loan Planner tab, enter the bank 1 data and display a loan amortization schedule. Repeat the procedure for bank 2. The loan amortization schedule shown in Figure 11.23 is for bank 1.

Bank 1	Bank 2
Loan amount..........................$250,000.00	Loan amount..........................$250,000.00
Annual interest....................................7.75%	Annual interest....................................7.25%
Number of payments............................360	Number of payments............................180

FIGURE 11.23

Loan Amortization Schedule (Bank 1)

Lacina Windows & Doors
Loan Amortization Schedule
02/28/—

Payment Number	Payment Amount	Principal	Interest	Loan Balance
(Loan Amount)				250,000.00
1	1,791.03	176.45	1,614.58	249,823.55
2	1,791.03	177.59	1,613.44	249,645.96
3	1,791.03	178.73	1,612.30	249,467.23
4	1,791.03	179.89	1,611.14	249,287.34
5	1,791.03	181.05	1,609.98	249,106.29
6	1,791.03	182.22	1,608.81	248,924.07
7	1,791.03	183.40	1,607.63	248,740.67
8	1,791.03	184.58	1,606.45	248,556.09
9	1,791.03	185.77	1,605.26	248,370.32
10	1,791.03	186.97	1,604.06	248,183.35

(continued)

11	1,791.03	188.18	1,602.85	247,995.17
12	1,791.03	189.39	1,601.64	247,805.78
13	1,791.03	190.62	1,600.41	247,615.16
14	1,791.03	191.85	1,599.18	247,423.31
15	1,791.03	193.09	1,597.94	247,230.22

352	1,791.03	1,690.21	100.82	13,921.03
353	1,791.03	1,701.12	89.91	12,219.91
354	1,791.03	1,712.11	78.92	10,507.80
355	1,791.03	1,723.17	67.86	8,784.63
356	1,791.03	1,734.30	56.73	7,050.33
357	1,791.03	1,745.50	45.53	5,304.83
358	1,791.03	1,756.77	34.26	3,548.06
359	1,791.03	1,768.12	22.91	1,779.94
360	1,791.44	1,779.94	11.50	.00

FIGURE 11.23

(Concluded)

12 Optional spreadsheet integration activity.

Complete a spreadsheet template file that provides monthly consolidated gross profit information for Lacina Windows & Doors in a different format than that generated by *Integrated Accounting* 6e.

a. Copy the gross profit statement (all three statements will be copied) to the clipboard in spreadsheet format.

b. Start your spreadsheet software and load the spreadsheet template file: IA6 Spreadsheet 11-S.

c. Select cell A1 as the current cell (if not already selected) and paste the gross profit statements copied to the clipboard in step a into the spreadsheet.

d. Enter the appropriate cell references for Department 1 (Windows) into their corresponding cells in B110–B128.

e. Enter the appropriate cell references for Department 2 (Doors) into their corresponding cells in C110–C128.

f. In cell D110, enter the formula appropriate for your spreadsheet software to sum the two departments. Copy the formula to the appropriate cells in D111–D128.

g. In cell E110, enter the formula appropriate for your spreadsheet software to calculate the component percentage of total operating revenue. Copy the formula to the appropriate cells in E111–E128.

h. Print the completed monthly consolidated gross profit statement. The completed statement is shown in Figure 11.24.

i. Save the template file with a file name of 11-S Your Name.

Lacina Windows & Doors
Consolidated Gross Profit Statement
For Period Ended 02/28/—

	Monthly Windows	Monthly Doors	Monthly Total	Monthly Percent
Operating Revenue				
Sales	$57,067.00	$33,145.00	$90,212.00	103.37%
Sales Ret. & Allow.	($850.00)	($425.00)	($1,275.00)	−1.46%
Sales Discounts	($1,070.74)	($595.33)	($1,666.07)	−1.91%
Total Operating Revenue	$55,146.26	$32,124.67	$87,270.93	100.00%
Cost of Merchandise Sold				
Beginning Inventory	$256,560.00	$113,495.00	$370,055.00	424.03%
Purchases	$17,875.00	$26,815.00	$44,690.00	51.21%
Prch. Ret. & Allow.	($195.00)	($200.00)	($395.00)	−0.45%
Purchases Disc.	($251.79)	($357.50)	($609.29)	−0.70%
Merchandise Available for Sale	$273,988.21	$139,752.50	$413,740.71	474.09%
Less Ending Inventory	($246,495.00)	($124,210.00)	($370,705.00)	−424.77%
Cost of Merchandise Sold	$27,493.21	$15,542.50	$43,035.71	49.31%
Gross Profit	$27,653.05	$16,582.17	$44,235.22	50.69%

13 Optional word processing integration activity.

Use your word processor to enhance the appearance of the monthly spreadsheet consolidated gross profit statement for distribution to the management of Lacina Windows & Doors.

a. Copy the completed gross profit statement from the spreadsheet (cells A101–E129) to the clipboard.

b. Start your word processing application software, create a new document, and paste the report.

c. Format the report to enhance its appearance. An example of the formatted report appears in Figure 11.25.

d. Save the document to your disk or folder with a file name of 11-S Your Name.

e. End your spreadsheet and word processing sessions.

FIGURE **11.25**

Formatted Monthly Consolidated Gross Profit Statement

Lacina Windows & Doors
Consolidated Gross Profit Statement
For Period Ended 02/28/—

	Monthly Windows	Monthly Doors	Monthly Total	Monthly Percent
Operating Revenue				
Sales	$57,067.00	$33,145.00	$90,212.00	103.37%
Sales Ret. & Allow.	($850.00)	($425.00)	($1,275.00)	−1.46%
Sales Discounts	($1,070.74)	($595.33)	($1,666.07)	−1.91%
Total Operating Revenue	$55,146.26	$32,124.67	$87,270.93	100.00%
Cost of Merchandise Sold				
Beginning Inventory	$256,560.00	$113,495.00	$370,055.00	424.03%
Purchases	$17,875.00	$26,815.00	$44,690.00	51.21%
Prch. Ret. & Allow.	($195.00)	($200.00)	($395.00)	−0.45%
Purchases Disc.	($251.79)	($357.50)	($609.29)	−0.70%
Merchandise Available for Sale	$273,988.21	$139,752.50	$413,740.71	474.09%
Less Ending Inventory	($246,495.00)	($124,210.00)	($370,705.00)	−424.77%
Cost of Merchandise Sold	$27,493.21	$15,542.50	$43,035.71	49.31%
Gross Profit	$27,653.05	$16,582.17	$44,235.22	50.69%

If you have access to the Internet, use your browser to find a company's statement of retained earnings. *Hint:* Use retained earnings as your search string. Report your findings. Be sure to include the sources, including the URLs (Web addresses), of your reported findings.

14   End the *Integrated Accounting* **6e session.**

Chapter 11 Student Exercises

NAME

I True/False

Directions   *If the statement is true, write T in the space provided. If the statement is false, write F in the space provided.*

1._____ Accounts in the chart of accounts that show the cost or price of merchandise purchased for resale to customers are called cost of merchandise accounts.

2._____ An account used to record the cost of the merchandise purchased for resale is called the resale account.

3._____ A departmentalized system uses a separate merchandise inventory account for each department.

4._____ A departmentalized system uses a separate accounts payable account for each department.

5._____ A purchases return transaction is entered in the cash payments journal.

6._____ A sales return transaction is entered in the cash receipts journal.

7._____ The appropriate general ledger account number must be keyed for each department when entering purchase order, voucher, and sales invoice transactions.

8._____ When a cash payment on account transaction involves a discount, the discount amount is entered into the appropriate department's purchases discounts account.

9._____ When a cash receipt on account transaction involves a discount, the discount amount is entered into the appropriate department's sales discounts account.

10._____ When the gross profit statements option is chosen, a separate report is generated for each department.

II Questions

Directions   *Answer each of the following questions in the space provided.*

1.   How does the computer determine the value of the inventory based on average cost as shown in the average cost inventory valuation report? _____

_____

_____

_____

2.   What assumption does the computer make when generating the Inventory Valuation (LIFO) report? _____

_____

_____

_____

3.   What assumption does the computer make when generating the Inventory Valuation (FIFO) report?   _____

_____

_____

_____

Problem 11-A

Problem 11-A is a continuation of Sample Problem 11-S. Follow the step-by-step procedures provided to complete this problem for Lacina Windows & Doors for the month of March of the current year. Answer Audit Questions 11-A on pages 507–508, and click Info. on the toolbar for helpful check figures as you work through the problem.

1 Start *Integrated Accounting* 6e.

2 Open the file named IA6 Problem 11-A.

3 Enter your name in the Your Name text box.

4 Save the data to your disk with a file name of 11-A Your Name.

5 Add Chatfield Company to the vendor list.

6 Delete George Lentz from the customer list.

7 Add Eugene Resnick to the customer list.

8 Enter the following general journal transaction.

General Journal Transaction

Mar. 01 Prepare reversing entries required by February adjustments. Use the adjustment data presented in Sample Problem 11-S as the basis for your reversing entries. Enter Rev.Ent. in the Reference text box.

9 Enter the purchase orders and vouchers transactions.

Purchase Orders and Vouchers Transactions

Mar. 02 Ordered 26 Casement Crank—Double windows at $380.00 each on account from Quade Corporation, terms 2/10, n/30. Purchase Order No. 1148.

06 Returned 1 Wood Entry Door—Single at $895.00 to Gunderson, Inc. Voucher No. R2330.

14 Received 14 Picture Window—Double at $625.00 each for Purchase Order No. 1145 from Quade Corporation, terms 2/10, n/30. Voucher No. 2336.

22 Received 5 Wood Patio Door—Double at $1,195.00 each for Purchase Order No. 1147 from Lancaster, Inc., terms 2/10, n/30. Voucher No. 2338.

26 Ordered 24 Casement Slider—Double windows at $380.00 each on account from Paulson, Inc., terms 2/10, n/30. Purchase Order No. 1149.

31 Returned 1 Casement Slider—Single window at $195.00 to Neubert Corporation. Voucher No. R2307.

10   **Enter the vouchers journal transactions.**

Vouchers Journal Transactions

Mar. 01   Record Voucher No. 2334 to Benco Utilities Co., for monthly heating and lighting, $1,037.55.

01   Record Voucher No. 2335 to Citizens Telephone Co., for monthly telephone bill, $897.30.

15   Record Voucher No. 2337 to Creative Advertising Co., for advertising, $325.00.

26   Record Voucher No. 2339 to reimburse the payroll bank account for monthly salaries: sales salaries, $10,301.00; administrative salaries, $4,016.00; total, $14,317.00.

26   Record Voucher No. 2340 to L & S Properties, Inc., for monthly rent, $2,825.00.

31   Record Voucher No. 2341 to Commissioner of Revenue for sales tax liability, $586.80.

11   **Enter the cash payments journal transactions.**

Cash Payments Journal Transactions

Mar. 02   Paid Voucher No. 2334 to Benco Utilities Co., $1,037.55. Check No. 7215.

05   Paid Voucher No. 2335 to Citizens Telephone Co., $897.30. Check No. 7216.

11   Paid Voucher No. 2336 to Quade Corporation, $8,750.00, less 2% discount for window merchandise, $175.50. Check No. 7217.

17   Paid Voucher No. 2329 to Tollefson Corporation, $5,000.00, less 2% discount for door merchandise, $100.00. Check No. 7218.

21   Paid Voucher No. 2337 to Creative Advertising Co., $325.00. Check No. 7219.

24   Paid Voucher No. 2309 to Neubert Corporation, $289.40, no discount. Check No. 7220.

30   Paid Voucher No. 2339 to Payroll Bank Account, $14,317.00. Check No. 7221.

30   Paid Voucher No. 2340 to L & S Properties, Inc., $2,825.00. Check No. 7222.

31   Paid Voucher No. 2341 to Commissioner of Revenue, $586.80. Check No. 7223.

12   **Enter the sales invoices transactions.**

Sales Invoices Transactions

Mar. 02   Sold 17 Casement Slider—Double windows at $769.00 each, and 3 Wood Entry Door—Single at $1,895.00 to Bickell Construction Co., terms 2/10, n/30, no sales tax. Sales Invoice No. 4637.

04   Granted credit to Bickell Construction Co., for 1 Casement Slider—Double window at $769.00, no sales tax. Sales Return No. R4637.

05   Sold 1 Wood Entry Door—Double at $3,500.00, 3 Garage Fire Doors at $425.00, 12 Casement Crank—Double windows at $769.00 each, and 1 Therm. Patio Door—Double at $1,995.00 to Quality Contractors, terms 2/10, n/30, no sales tax. Sales Invoice No. 4638.

09   Granted credit to Quality Contractors for 1 Garage Fire Door at $425.00, no sales tax. Sales Return No. R4638.

15   Sold 1 Wood Patio Door—Double at $2,450.00, and 6 Casement Crank—Single windows at $395.00 to Phillip Gilbert, terms 30 days, 6% sales tax. Sales Invoice No. 4639.

18   Sold 16 Casement Crank—Double windows at $769.00 each, 2 Casement Picture—Bay windows at $1,495.00, 1 Wood Entry Door—Single at $1,895.00, and 3 Vinyl Patio Door—Single at $645.00 to Penkhus Remodeling, Inc., terms 2/10, n/30, no sales tax. Sales Invoice No. 4640.

29   Sold 1 Wood Patio Door—Single at $1,345.00 each, 1 Garage Fire Door at $425.00, and 10 Casement Slider—Single windows at $395.00 each to Eugene Resnick, terms 30 days, 6% sales tax. Sales Invoice No. 4641.

13   Enter the cash receipts journal transactions.

Cash Receipts Journal Transactions

Mar. 03   Received cash on account from Schaefer Builders, covering Sales Invoice No. 4636 for $12,435.00; less 2% discount for windows merchandise, $142.20; less 2% discount for doors merchandise, $106.50.

10   Received cash on account from Bickell Construction, covering Sales Invoice No. 4637 for $17,989.00; less 2% discount for windows merchandise, $241.05; less 2% discount for doors merchandise, $118.73.

14   Received cash on account from Quality Contractors, covering Sales Invoice No. 4638 for $15,573.00; less 2% discount for windows merchandise, $184.56; less 2% discount for doors merchandise, $126.90.

18   Received cash on account from Phillip Gilbert, covering Sales Invoice No. 4639 for $5,109.20; no discount.

28   Received cash on account from Penkhus Remodeling, Inc., covering Sales Invoice No. 4640 for $19,124.00; less 2% discount for windows merchandise, $305.88; less 2% discount for doors merchandise, $76.60.

14   Display the vendor and customer lists.

15   Display the purchase order, voucher, and sales invoice registers for the month of March.

16   Display the inventory transactions report for the month of March.

17   Display the average cost inventory valuation report.

18   Display the general, vouchers, cash payments, sales, and cash receipts journal reports for the month of March.

19   Display the trial balance.

End-of-Month Activities

After the monthly transactions have been processed, the adjusting entries must be entered into the general journal. The financial statements may then be displayed. Use the adjustment data for the month of March for Lacina Windows & Doors and the trial balance report prepared in Step 19 as the basis for preparing the adjusting entries.

Merchandise inventories on March 31:
- Windows $234,450.00
- Doors $119,500.00

Insurance expired during March............................$210.00

Inventories of supplies on March 31:
- Office supplies $1,600.00
- Store supplies...$1,850.00

Depreciation for March:
- Office equipment...$315.10
- Store equipment...$415.25

Uncollectible accounts expense increase............$100.00

Salaries Payable:
- Sales salaries...$3,992.00
- Administrative salaries $579.00

Additional income tax owed.............................$3,500.00

1 Enter the adjusting entries in the general journal. Enter a reference of Adj.Ent. in the Reference text box.

2 Display the adjusting entries.

3 Use Check on the toolbar to check your work.

4 Display the gross profit statements.

5 Display the income statement.

6 Display the retained earnings statement.

7 Display the balance sheet.

8 Display the budget report.

9 Generate a least profitable items and an actual versus budget graph.

10 Click Save on the toolbar to save the data file.

11 Calculate a loan amount using the Loan Planner.

The management of Lacina Windows & Doors believe they can comfortably afford a loan payment of $1,750.00 per month for the purchase of land and a building. They asked you to use the loan planner to find the loan amount given the interest rate and number of payments information provided by two local banks.

 Select the Loan Amount option in the Calculate grouping, and then enter the following loan information:

Bank 1	Bank 2
Annual interest...................................8.00%	Annual interest...................................7.50%
Number of payments...........................360	Number of payments...........................180
Payment amount.......................$1,750.00	Payment amount.......................$1,750.00

12 Optional spreadsheet integration activity.

Prepare a monthly consolidated gross profit statement spreadsheet template file for Lacina Windows & Doors.

a. Copy the gross profit statement (all three statements will be copied) to the clipboard in spreadsheet format.

b. Start your spreadsheet software and load the spreadsheet template file IA6 Spreadsheet 11-S. If you completed the spreadsheet activity in Sample Problem 11-S, load your completed spreadsheet file instead.

c. Select cell A1 as the current cell (if not already selected) and paste the gross profit statements copied to the clipboard in step a into the spreadsheet. If you loaded the spreadsheet template file you completed in Sample Problem 11-S, skip to step h.

d. Enter the appropriate cell references for Department 1 (Windows) into their corresponding cells in B110–B128.

e. Enter the appropriate cell references for Department 2 (Doors) into their corresponding cells in C110–C128.

f. In cell D110, enter the formula appropriate for your spreadsheet software to sum the two departments. Copy the formula to the appropriate cells in D111–D128.

g. In cell E110, enter the formula appropriate for your spreadsheet software to calculate the component percentage of total operating revenue. Copy the formula to the appropriate cells in E111–E128.

h. Print the completed monthly consolidated gross profit statement. Use the spreadsheet report shown in Figure 11.24 as a guide.

i. Save the template file with a file name of 11-A Your Name.

13 Optional word processing integration activity.

Use your word processor to enhance the appearance of the monthly spreadsheet consolidated gross profit statement for distribution to the management of Lacina Windows & Doors.

a. Copy the completed gross profit statement from the spreadsheet (cells A101–E129) to the clipboard.

b. Start your word processing application software, create a new document, and then paste the report.

c. Format the report to enhance its appearance. Use the example shown in Figure 11.25 as a guide.

d. Save the document to your disk or folder with a file name of 11-A Your Name.

e. End your spreadsheet and word processing sessions.

If you have access to the Internet, use your browser to locate a source that explains its procedures for estimating or recording uncollectible accounts. *Hint:* Use uncollectible accounts as your search string. Report your findings. Be sure to include the sources, including the URLs (Web addresses), of your reported findings.

14   End the *Integrated Accounting* 6e session.

Audit Questions 11-A

NAME

Directions   *Write the answers to the following questions in the space provided.*

1. What is the total amount of purchase orders shown on the purchases orders register for the month of March? _____

2. What is the total of the Invoice Amount column shown on the voucher register report for the month of March? _____

3. What is the total of the Invoice Amount column shown on the sales invoice register report for the month of March? _____

4. What is the total number of items sold shown on the inventory transactions report for the month of March? _____

5. What are the totals of the Debit and Credit columns from the general journal report (before adjusting entries) for the month of March?

    Total debits: _____

    Total credits: _____

6. What are the totals of the Debit and Credit columns from the vouchers journal for the month of March?

    Total debits: _____

    Total credits: _____

7. What are the totals of the Debit and Credit columns from the cash payments journal for the month of March?

    Total debits: _____

    Total credits: _____

8. What are the totals of the Debit and Credit columns from the sales journal for the month of March?

    Total debits: _____

    Total credits: _____

9. What are the totals of the Debit and Credit columns from the cash receipts journal for the month of March?

    Total debits: _____

    Total credits: _____

10. What is the total monthly gross profit of each department after adjusting entries are made?

    Department 1: _____

    Department 2: _____

11.   What is the total yearly gross profit shown on the consolidated gross profit statement report after the adjusting entries are made? _____

_____

12.   What is the amount of net income after income tax for the month? _____

_____

13.   What is the amount of retained earnings at the end of the period? _____

_____

14.   What are the total assets shown on the balance sheet? _____

_____

15.   What are the total liabilities shown on the balance sheet? _____

_____

16.   How much over or under budget is gross profit? _____

_____

17.   What is the calculated loan amount for bank 1? _____

_____

18.   What is the calculated loan amount for bank 2? _____

_____

Problem 11-B

Problem 11-B is a continuation of Sample Problem 11-S. Follow the step-by-step procedures provided to complete this problem for Lacina Windows & Doors for the month of March of the current year. Answer Audit Questions 11-B on pages 515–516 as you work through the problem.

1 Start *Integrated Accounting* 6e.

2 Open the file named IA6 Problem 11-B.

3 Enter your name in the Your Name text box.

4 Save the data to your disk with a file name of 11-B Your Name.

5 Add Cornelius Company to the vendor list.

6 Delete George Lentz from the customer list.

7 Add Everett Lindner to the customer list.

8 Enter the following general journal transaction.

General Journal Transaction

Mar. 01   Prepare reversing entries required by February adjustments. Use the adjustment data presented in Sample Problem 11-S as the basis for your reversing entries. Enter Rev.Ent. in the Reference text box.

9 Enter the purchase orders and vouchers transactions.

Purchase Orders and Vouchers Transactions

Mar. 03   Ordered 25 Casement Crank–Double windows at $380.00 each on account from Quade Corporation, terms 2/10, n/30. Purchase Order No. 1148.

05   Returned 1 Wood Entry Door–Single at $895.00 to Gunderson, Inc. Voucher No. R2330.

15   Received 14 Picture Window–Double at $625.00 each for Purchase Order No. 1145 from Quade Corporation, terms 2/10, n/30. Voucher No. 2336.

21   Received 12 Vinyl Patio Door–Double at $565.00 each for purchase Order No. 1146 from Lancaster, Inc., terms 2/10, n/30. Voucher No. 2338.

27   Ordered 25 Casement Slider–Double windows at $380.00 each on account from Paulson, Inc., terms 2/10, n/30. Purchase Order No. 1149.

31   Returned 1 Casement Slider–Single window at $195.00 to Neubert Corporation. Voucher No. R2307.

10   **Enter the vouchers journal transactions.**

Vouchers Journal Transactions

Mar. 01   Record Voucher No. 2334 to Benco Utilities Co., for monthly heating and lighting, $1,098.73.

03   Record Voucher No. 2335 to Citizens Telephone Co., for monthly telephone bill, $919.10.

15   Record Voucher No. 2337 to Creative Advertising Co., for advertising, $335.00.

26   Record Voucher No. 2339 to reimburse the payroll bank account for monthly salaries: sales salaries, $10,170.00; administrative salaries, $4,021.00; total, $14,191.00.

28   Record Voucher No. 2340 to L & S Properties, Inc., for monthly rent, $2,825.00.

31   Record Voucher No. 2341 to Commissioner of Revenue for sales tax liability, $586.80.

11   **Enter the cash payments journal transactions.**

Cash Payments Journal Transactions

Mar. 02   Paid Voucher No. 2334 to Benco Utilities Co., $1,098.73. Check No. 7215.

05   Paid Voucher No. 2335 to Citizens Telephone Co., $919.10. Check No. 7216.

11   Paid Voucher No. 2336 to Quade Corporation, $8,750.00, less 2% discount for window merchandise, $175.50. Check No. 7217.

17   Paid Voucher No. 2329 to Tollefson Corporation, $5,000.00, less 2% discount for door merchandise, $100.00. Check No. 7218.

21   Paid Voucher No. 2337 to Creative Advertising Co., $335.00. Check No. 7219.

24   Paid Voucher No. 2309 to Neubert Corporation, $289.40, no discount. Check No. 7220.

30   Paid Voucher No. 2339 to Payroll Bank Account, $14,191.00. Check No. 7221.

30   Paid Voucher No. 2340 to L & S Properties, Inc., $2,825.00. Check No. 7222.

31   Paid Voucher No. 2341 to Commissioner of Revenue, $586.80. Check No. 7223.

12   **Enter the sales invoices transactions.**

Sales Invoices Transactions

Mar. 02   Sold 20 Casement Slider–Double windows at $769.00 each, and 2 Wood Entry Door–Single at $1,895.00 to Bickell Construction Co., terms 2/10, n/30, no sales tax. Sales Invoice No. 4637.

04   Granted credit to Bickell Construction Co. for 1 Casement Slider–Double window at $769.00, no sales tax. Sales Return No. R4637.

05   Sold 1 Wood Entry Door–Double at $3,500.00, 2 Garage Fire Doors at $425.00, 10 Casement Crank–Double windows at $769.00 each, and 1 Therm. Patio Door–Double at $1,995.00 to Quality Contractors, terms 2/10, n/30, no sales tax. Sales Invoice No. 4638.

09   Granted credit to Quality Contractors for 1 Garage Fire Door at $425.00, no sales tax. Sales Return No. R4638.

15   Sold 1 Wood Patio Door–Double at $2,450.00, and 8 Casement Crank–Single windows at $395.00 to Phillip Gilbert, terms 30 days, 6% sales tax. Sales Invoice No. 4639.

18   Sold 18 Casement Crank–Double windows at $769.00 each, 2 Casement Picture–Bay windows at $1,495.00, 1 Wood Entry Door—Single at $1,895.00, and 3 Vinyl Patio Door–Single at $645.00 to Penkhus Remodeling, Inc., terms 2/10, n/30, no sales tax. Sales Invoice No. 4640.

30   Sold 1 Wood Patio Door–Single at $1,345.00 each, 12 Casement Slider–Single windows at $395.00 each to Everett Lindner, terms 30 days, 6% sales tax. Sales Invoice No. 4641.

13   **Enter the cash receipts journal transactions.**

Cash Receipts Journal Transactions

Mar. 02   Received cash on account from Schaefer Builders, covering Sales Invoice No. 4636 for $12,435.00; less 2% discount for windows merchandise, $142.20; less 2% discount for doors merchandise, $106.50.

09   Received cash on account from Bickell Construction, covering Sales Invoice No. 4637 for $18,401.00; less 2% discount for windows merchandise, $287.06; less 2% discount for doors merchandise, $80.96.

14   Received cash on account from Quality Contractors, covering Sales Invoice No. 4638 for $13,610.00; less 2% discount for windows merchandise, $153.80; less 2% discount for doors merchandise, $118.40.

21   Received cash on account from Phillip Gilbert, covering Sales Invoice No. 4639 for $5,946.60; no discount.

28   Received cash on account from Penkhus Remodeling, Inc., covering Sales Invoice No. 4640 for $20,662.00; less 2% discount for windows merchandise, $336.64; less 2% discount for doors merchandise, $76.60.

14   **Display the vendor and customer lists.**

15   **Display the purchase order, voucher, and sales invoices registers for the month of March.**

16   **Display the inventory transactions report for the month of March.**

17   **Display the average cost inventory valuation report.**

18   **Display the general, vouchers, cash payments, sales, and cash receipts journal reports for the month of March.**

19   **Display the trial balance.**

End-of-Month Activities

After the monthly transactions have been processed, the adjusting entries must be entered into the general journal. The financial statements may then be displayed. Use the adjustment data for the month of March for Lacina Windows & Doors and the trial balance report prepared in Step 19 as the basis for preparing the adjusting entries.

Merchandise inventories on March 31:
Windows $233,585.00
Doors...$121,670.00
Insurance expired during March...........................$215.00
Inventories of supplies on March 31:
Office supplies $1,610.00
Store supplies..$1,865.00
Depreciation for March:
Office equipment..$315.10
Store equipment...$415.25
Uncollectible accounts expense increase...........$100.00
Salaries Payable:
Sales salaries...$4,017.00
Administrative salaries $583.00
Additional income tax owed..............................$3,500.00

1   **Enter the adjusting entries in the general journal. Enter a reference of Adj.Ent. in the Reference text box.**

2   **Display the adjusting entries.**

3   **Display the gross profit statements.**

4   **Display the income statement.**

5   **Display the retained earnings statement.**

6   **Display the balance sheet.**

7   **Display the budget report.**

8   **Generate a top customer sales and an actual versus budget graph.**

9   **Click Save on the toolbar to save the data file.**

10   **Use the Loan Planner to calculate a loan amount given the following information from two different banks:**

Bank 1	Bank 2
Annual interest.................................7.75%	Annual interest.................................7.25%
Number of payments...........................360	Number of payments...........................180
Payment amount.......................$2,000.00	Payment amount.......................$2,000.00

11 Optional spreadsheet integration activity.

Prepare a monthly consolidated gross profit statement spreadsheet template file for Lacina Windows & Doors.

a. Copy the gross profit statement (all three statements will be copied) to the clipboard in spreadsheet format.

b. Start your spreadsheet software and load the spreadsheet template file IA6 Spreadsheet 11-S. If you completed the spreadsheet activity in Sample Problem 11-S or Problem 11-A, load either of these completed spreadsheet files instead.

c. Select cell A1 as the current cell (if not already selected) and paste the gross profit statements copied to the clipboard in step a into the spreadsheet. If you loaded the spreadsheet template file you completed in Sample Problem 11-S or Problem 11-A, skip to step h.

d. Enter the appropriate cell references for Department 1 (Windows) into their corresponding cells in B110–B128.

e. Enter the appropriate cell references for Department 2 (Doors) into their corresponding cells in C110–C128.

f. In cell D110, enter the formula appropriate for your spreadsheet software to sum the two departments. Copy the formula to the appropriate cells in D111–D128.

g. In cell E110, enter the formula appropriate for your spreadsheet software to calculate the component percentage of total operating revenue. Copy the formula to the appropriate cells in E111–E128.

h. Print the completed monthly consolidated gross profit statement. Use the spreadsheet report shown in Figure 11.24 as a guide.

i. Save the template file with a file name of 11-B Your Name.

12 Optional word processing integration activity.

Use your word processor to enhance the appearance of the monthly spreadsheet consolidated gross profit statement for distribution to the management of Lacina Windows & Doors.

a. Copy the completed gross profit statement from the spreadsheet (cells A101–E129) to the clipboard.

b. Start your word processing application software, create a new document, and then paste the report.

c. Format the report to enhance its appearance. Use the example shown in Figure 11.25 as a guide.

d. Save the document to your disk or folder with a file name of 11-B Your Name.

e. End your spreadsheet and word processing sessions.

If you have access to the Internet, use your browser to locate business planning tools that are available via Shareware. *Hint:* Use Shareware as your first search string. When Shareware is found, enter the name of a planning tool (such as savings, loan amortization, retirement, calendars, and planners, etc.) in the business or home/personal categories. Describe the functionality of one of the planning tools you find. Be sure to include the sources and the URLs (Web addresses), of your reported findings.

13 **End the *Integrated Accounting* 6e session.**

Audit Questions 11-B

NAME

Directions   *Write the answers to the following questions in the space provided.*

1.   What is the total amount of purchase orders shown on the purchases orders register for the month of March? _____

2.   What is the total of the Invoice Amount column shown on the voucher register report for the month of March? _____

3.   What is the total of the Invoice Amount column shown on the sales invoice register report for the month of March? _____

4.   What is the total number of items sold shown on the inventory transactions report for the month of March? _____

5.   What are the totals of the Debit and Credit columns from the general journal report (before adjusting entries) for the month of March?

Total debits: _____

Total credits: _____

6.   What are the totals of the Debit and Credit columns from the vouchers journal for the month of March? _____

Total debits: _____

Total credits: _____

7.   What are the totals of the Debit and Credit columns from the cash payments journal for the month of March? _____

Total debits: _____

Total credits: _____

8.   What are the totals of the Debit and Credit columns from the sales journal for the month of March? _____

Total debits: _____

Total credits: _____

9.   What are the totals of the Debit and Credit columns from the cash receipts journal for the month of March? _____

Total debits: _____

Total credits: _____

10.   What is the total monthly gross profit of each department after adjusting entries are made?

Department 1: _____

Department 2: _____

11.   What is the total yearly gross profit shown on the consolidated gross profit statement report after the adjusting entries are made? _____

_____

12.   What is the amount of net income after income tax for the month? _____

_____

13.   What is the amount of retained earnings at the end of the period? _____

_____

14.   What are the total assets shown on the balance sheet? _____

_____

15.   What are the total liabilities shown on the balance sheet? _____

_____

16.   How much over or under budget is gross profit? _____

_____

17.   What is the calculated loan amount for bank 1? _____

_____

18.   What is the calculated loan amount for bank 2? _____

_____

COMPREHENSIVE PROBLEM 3

This comprehensive problem involves completing the accounting cycle for Clark Garage Door Co., for the month of December. Clark Garage Door Co., is a departmentalized business, organized as a corporation, with two departments: residential and commercial. Complete the audit questions located at the end of this problem after finishing the month's work and before closing entries.

1　Start *Integrated Accounting* 6e.

2　Open the file named IA6 Comp Problem 03.

3　Enter your name in the Your Name text box.

4　Enter the purchase orders and vouchers transactions.

Dec. 03　Ordered 14 Premium 9 × 7 Panel residential doors at $265.00 each on account from Schaefer Bros. Mfg., terms 2/10, n/30. Purchase Order No. 1248.

05　Returned 2 Std. 9 × 7 Non Ins. Panel residential doors at $189.00 each, and 1 Pro 16 × 9 Sheet Metal commercial door at $625.00 to Henderson Company. Voucher No. R2396.

15　Received 35 Std. 9 × 7 Ins. Panel residential doors at $225.00 each, and 30 Std. 9 × 7 Non Ins. Panel residential doors at $189.00 each for Purchase Order No. 1245 from Delaney Manufacturing, terms 2/10, n/30. Voucher No. 2436.

22　Received 30 Arrow 16 × 9 Panel Steel commercial doors at $785.00 each for Purchase Order No. 1246 from Spencer Industries., terms 2/10, n/30. Voucher No. 2437.

29　Ordered 11 Kat 16 × 9 Ribbed Steel commercial doors at $995.00 each on account from Spencer Industries, terms 2/10, n/30. Purchase Order No. 1249.

5　Enter the vouchers journal transactions.

Dec. 01　Record Voucher No. 2433 to S & R Utilities Co., for monthly heating and lighting, $342.65.

03　Record Voucher No. 2434 to Central Telephone Co., for monthly telephone bill, $591.63.

14　Record Voucher No. 2435 to Grams Advertising Co., for advertising, $3,250.00.

27　Record Voucher No. 2438 to reimburse the payroll bank account for monthly salaries, $10,487.00.

28　Record Voucher No. 2439 to Moser Rental Agency for monthly rent, $2,450.00.

31　Record Voucher No. 2440 to Commissioner of Revenue for sales tax liability, $224.30.

6　Enter the cash payments journal transactions.

Dec. 02　Paid Voucher No. 2433 to S & R Utilities Co., $342.65. Check No. 6852.

05　Paid Voucher No. 2434 to Central Telephone Co., $591.63. Check No. 6853.

11　Paid Voucher No. 2396 to Henderson Company, $29,884.98, no discount. Check No. 6854.

19　Paid Voucher No. 2436 to Delaney Manufacturing, $13,545.00, less 2% discount for residential merchandise, $270.90. Check No. 6855.

21　Paid Voucher No. 2435 to Grams Advertising Co., $3,250.00. Check No. 6856.

27　Paid Voucher No. 2437 to Spencer Industries, $23,550.00, less 2% discount for commercial merchandise, $471.00. Check No. 6857.

30　Paid Voucher No. 2438 to payroll bank account, $10,487.00. Check No. 6858.

30   Paid Voucher No. 2439 to Moser Rental Agency, $2,450.00. Check No. 6859.

31   Paid Voucher No. 2440 to Commissioner of Revenue, $224.30. Check No. 6860.

7   Enter the sales invoices transactions.

Dec. 02   Sold 8 Premium 16 × 7 Wood residential doors at $1,150.00 each, and 5 Arrow 22 × 10 Panel Steel commercial doors at $2,195.00 to PK Builder Supply Co., terms 2/10, n/30, no sales tax, Sales Invoice No. 5437.

04   Granted credit to Currie Builders, Inc., for 1 returned Std. 16 × 7 Non Ins Panel residential door at $669.00, no sales tax, Sales Return No. R5371.

05   Sold 5 Std. 16 × 7 Non Ins. Panel residential doors at $669.00 each, 7 Pro 22 × 10 Sheet Metal commercial doors at $1,789.00 each, and 2 Kat 16 × 9 Ribbed Steel commercial doors at $1,995.00 each to Preston Construction, terms 2/10, n/30, no sales tax, Sales Invoice No. 5438.

09   Granted credit to Renner Garage Doors for 1 returned Pro 16 × 9 Sheet Metal commercial door at $1,250.00, no sales tax, Sales Return No. R5388.

15   Sold 6 Premium 16 × 7 Panel residential doors at $925.00 each, and 15 Std. 9 × 7 Ins. Panel residential doors at $445.00 each to Schomer Construction, terms 30 days, no sales tax, Sales Invoice No. 5439.

20   Sold 12 Arrow 16 × 9 Panel Steel commercial doors at $1,569.00 each to Atwood Building Center, terms 2/10, n/30, no sales tax, Sales Invoice No. 5440.

30   Sold 5 Premium 16 × 7 Panel residential doors at $925.00 each, 3 Std. 9 × 7 Non Ins. Panel residential doors at $379.00 each, and 12 Std. 16 × 7 Non Ins. Panel residential doors at $669.00 each to Frentz Remodeling Co., terms 30 days, no sales tax, Sales Invoice No. 5441.

8   Enter the cash receipts journal transactions.

Dec. 06   Received cash on account from Currie Builders, Inc., covering Sales Invoice No. 5371 for $26,004.72, no discount.

07   Received cash on account from Atwood Building Center, covering Sales Invoice No. 5368 for $9,202.83, no discount.

09   Received cash on account from Dobson Contractors, Inc., covering Sales Invoice No. 5377 for $13,945.97, no discount.

10   Received cash on account from Owens Building Supplies, covering Sales Invoice No. 5370 for $10,199.82, no discount.

14   Received cash on account from PK Builder Supply Co., covering Sales Invoice No. 5437 for $20,175.00; less 2% discount for residential merchandise, $184.00; less 2% discount for commercial merchandise, $219.50.

21   Received cash on account from Preston Construction, covering Sales Invoice No. 5438 for $19,858.00; less 2% discount for residential merchandise, $317.36, less 2% discount for commercial merchandise, $79.80.

28   Received cash on account from Schomer Construction, covering Sales Invoice No. 5439 for $12,225.00; less 2% discount for residential merchandise, $244.50.

30   Received cash on account from Atwood Building Center, covering Sales Invoice No. 5440 for $18,828.00; less 2% discount for commercial merchandise, $376.56.

9   Display the purchase order, voucher, and sales invoice registers for the month of December.

10   Display the inventory list report.

11 Display the inventory transactions report for the month of December.

12 Display the inventory valuation (average cost) report.

13 Display the general, vouchers, cash payments, sales, and cash receipts journal reports for the month of December.

14 Display the trial balance.

15 Display the schedule of accounts payable.

16 Display the schedule of accounts receivable.

End-of-Month Activities

After the monthly transactions have been processed, the adjusting entries must be entered into the general journal. The financial statements may then be displayed. Use the following adjustment data for the month of December for Clark Garage Door Co., and the trial balance report prepared in Step 14 as the basis for preparing the adjusting entries.

Merchandise inventories on December 31:
    Residential..$158,785.00
    Commercial...$179,860.00
Insurance expired during December..............$155.00
Inventories of supplies on December 31:......$500.00
Depreciation for December:
    Automobiles..$487.62
    Office equipment..$139.25
    Warehouse equipment.......................................$168.92
Uncollectible accounts expense increase......$200.00
Interest receivable...$115.41
Accrued interest expense....................................$174.82
Salaries payable $979.13
Additional income tax owed..........................$1,200.00

1 Enter the adjusting entries in the general journal. Enter a reference of Adj.Ent. in the Reference text box.

2 Display the adjusting entries.

3 Display the gross profit statements.

4 Display the income statement.

5 Display the retained earnings statement.

6 Display the balance sheet.

7 Display the income statement (horizontal analysis).

8   **Display the income statement (vertical analysis).**

9   **Display the balance sheet (horizontal analysis).**

10   **Display the balance sheet (vertical analysis).**

11   **Save your data with a file name of C-3BC Your Name (where C-3 identifies the problem, and BC represents Before Closing).**

12   **Complete the Audit Questions for Comprehensive Problem 3 on pages 513.**

Display reports as necessary to answer the questions.

13   **Generate and post the closing journal entries.**

14   **Display the closing entries.**

15   **Display the post-closing trial balance.**

16   **Save your data with a file name of C-3AC Your Name (where C-3 identifies the problem, and AC represents After Closing).**

17   **End the *Integrated Accounting* 6e session.**

Audit Questions for Comprehensive Problem 3

NAME

Directions   *Write the answers to the following questions in the space provided.*

1.   What is the total amount of purchase orders shown on the purchases order register?   ———

_____

2.   What is the total amount of the Invoice Amount column shown on the voucher register report for the month of December?   _____

_____

3.   What is the total amount of Invoice Amount column shown on the sales invoice register report for the month of December?   _____

_____

4.   What is the total number of items sold shown on the inventory transactions report for the month of December?   _____

_____

5.   What is the total inventory value at cost shown on the inventory valuation (average cost) report?

_____

6.   What are the totals of the Debit and Credit columns from the general journal report (before adjusting entries)?

Total debits: _____

Total credits: _____

7.   What are the totals of the debit and credit columns from the vouchers journal?

Total debits: _____

Total credits: _____

8.   What are the totals of the debit and credit columns from the cash payments journal?

Total debits: _____

Total credits: _____

9.   What are the totals of the debit and credit columns from the sales journal?

Total debits: _____

Total credits: _____

10.   What are the totals of the debit and credit columns from the cash receipts journal?

Total debits: _____

Total credits: _____

11.   What is the total of vouchers payable as of the end of December?   _____

_____

12.   What is the total of accounts receivable as of the end of December?   _____

_____

13.   What is the total gross profit for department 1 for the month?   _____

_____

14.   What is the total gross profit for department 2 for the month?   _____

_____

15.   What is the total amount of gross profit for the month including department 1 and department 2?

_____

16.   What are the total operating expenses for the year?   _____

_____

17.   What is the net income after income tax for the year?   _____

_____

18.   What are the total retained earnings at the end of the period?   _____

_____

19.   What are the total assests shown on the balance sheet?   _____

_____

20.   What are the total liabilities shown on the balance sheet?   _____

_____

21.   What is the change from the previous year to the current year in the total operating revenue
expressed as a percentage?   _____

_____

22.   What are the amounts of gross profit for the previous year and current year?

Previous year: _____

Current year: _____

23.   What are the total amounts of revenue for residential and revenue for commercial for the current year expressed as a percentage of total operating revenue?

Total revenue—residential: _____

Total revenue—commercial: _____

24.   What are the total amounts of operating expenses for the previous year and the current year expressed as percentages of total operating revenue?

Previous year: _____

Current year: _____

25.   What is the change from the previous year to the current year in the amount of the Office Equipment account?   _____

_____

26.   What is the change from the previous year to the current year of the Accumulated Depreciation—Warehouse Equipment account expressed as a percentage?   _____

_____

27. What is the change in total assets from the previous year to the current year expressed in dollars? _____

_____

28. What is the change in total assets from the previous year to the current year expressed as a percentage? _____

_____

29. What is the change in stockholders' equity from the previous year to the current year expressed in dollars? _____

_____

30. What is the change in stockholders' equity from the previous year to the current year expressed as a percentage? _____

_____

31. What are the amounts of accounts receivable for the previous year and the current year expressed as percentages of total assets?

Previous year: _____

Current year: _____

32. What are the amounts of total liabilities for the previous year and the current year expressed as percentages of total liabilities and stockholders' equity?

Previous year: _____

Current year: _____

Accounting System Setup

Upon completion of this chapter, you will be able to:

- Establish company information.

- Establish the chart of accounts, vendors, and customers.

- Establish account classifications, extended classifications, required accounts, and financial statement subtotals.

- Establish account balances through the general journal.

- Use the journal wizard to create special journals.

- Perform fixed assets, payroll, and inventory setup.

- Display and print setup information.

Introduction

In this text, you have loaded opening balance files for preestablished accounting systems. Because these accounting system files were already established, you did not use several of the features designed to tailor the accounting system and enter opening balances data. For example, either a service or a merchandising business can be set up as a sole proprietorship, a partnership, or a corporation. The accounting system can be set up so that the accounting cycle is completed each month or only once per fiscal period. Special journals may be customized and designed specifically to meet the needs of a business. Because many software packages are written to handle a wide variety of business processing tasks, it is unlikely that a business user will utilize all of the capabilities and capacities of a given system.

In this chapter, you will learn how to set up opening balances data for Zallek Corporation, a merchandising business organized as a corporation.

Planning

Before setting up a computerized accounting system, you must carefully plan, design, and gather data. For example, account numbers must be assigned to each account to identify each account as an asset, liability, equity, revenue, or expense account. Account balances must match the totals of related subsidiary ledgers, while assets, liabilities, and equity account balances must be current. Total debit balances must equal total credit balances before entering data into the computer.

System Setup Specifications

The tasks for setting up a computerized accounting system are outlined in this chapter. The order in which they must be performed is detailed in the problems at the end of the chapter. The menu items and windows that were used in previous chapters for accounting system processing will not be covered again in this chapter.

New

The **New command** in the File menu clears any existing data from memory in preparation for setting up a new accounting system. If you have data in memory, you should save it before you choose New. You will be asked to enter your name in the Your Name text box so that the computer can associate your name with the newly created file.

Setup Accounting System

The Setup Accounting System window is used to provide setup **company information** to *Integrated Accounting* 6e. It can be accessed by choosing Setup Accounting System from the Data menu or clicking on Setup on the toolbar. The six tabs in this window are used to tailor the accounting system to the needs of the business being established.

Company Information

The Setup Accounting System window with the Company Info. tab illustrating setup data for Zallek Corporation is shown in Figure 12.1. The purpose and function of each text box, check box, and option button in the Company Info. tab is described in Table 12.1.

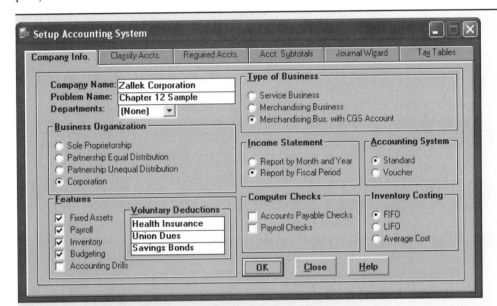

FIGURE 12.1

Company Information

Option	Description	
Company Name	The name of the company is displayed and printed as part of the heading for each report.	**TABLE 12.1** *Company Information Text Boxes and Option Settings*
Problem Name	The problem name is printed at the top of the report along with the student name. The problem name also appears in the upper right corner of the *Integrated Accounting* 6e application window as a reminder of the problem currently in computer memory.	
Departments	This drop-down list allows you to select from three options: None, 2, or 3.	
Business Organization	The business organization option is used by the software during financial statement preparation and period-end closing.	
Features	A check box is provided for each type of accounting system to be included during setup. Appropriate windows, reports, data entry tabs, and so on are automatically activated based on the features selected. For example, when the Payroll check box is selected, an Employees tab appears in the Account Maintenance	

(continued)

TABLE 12.1 *(Concluded)*		window to permit employee maintenance. A Payroll tab appears in the Tasks window to permit entry of payroll transactions, and a Payroll Reports option appears in the Reports window that enables the user to display and print various payroll reports. When the Payroll feature is checked, a Voluntary Deductions group box will appear permitting the user to enter the names of up to three different voluntary deductions that are to be withheld from the employees' pay.
	Type of Business	The type of business option is used by the software to determine the format of the income statement. If the Merchandising Business option is chosen, the income statement contains a Cost of Goods Sold section where the cost of goods sold is determined based on beginning inventory, purchases, and ending inventory and requires an inventory adjusting entry. If the Merchandising Business with CGS option is chosen, the income statement expects that there will be a Cost of Goods Sold account instead of a Purchases account. In this case, it simply uses the Cost of Goods Sold account. In addition, the sales invoice entry will generate a journal entry that not only records the sale at retail, but also debits Cost of Merchandise Sold and credits Merchandise Inventory at cost based on the inventory costing method selected (LIFO, FIFO, or average). The journal entry generated by a purchase invoice will debit the Merchandise Inventory account rather than the Purchases account.
	Income Statement	If this option is set to Month & Year, the income statement will include a column for the current month and another column for the current year. Also included for each column is a percentage, indicating the percent of each amount in relation to total operating revenue. If this option is set to Fiscal Period, only the amount column and percent of total operating revenue is included on the income statement representing the current fiscal period.
	Accounting System	This option allows you to specify whether or not a voucher system is being used.
	Computer Checks	If the Accounts Payable Checks option is set on, accounts payable checks will be created each time a cash payment that involves a vendor is entered into the computer. If the Payroll Checks option is set on, paychecks will be created each time an employee's payroll transaction is entered.
	Inventory Costing	This option allows you to specify the method of inventory valuation to be used by the computer during processing of a perpetual inventory system. The inventory costing option will appear only if both the Inventory feature and the Merchandising Business with CGS account options have been selected.

When the Company Info. tab is active, enter the company name, problem name, and click on the Departments drop-down list to select the number of departments (if any). Select the appropriate business organization and click on each Features check box to indicate the accounting system setup data to be included in setup. If the Payroll feature is selected, the Voluntary Deductions group box will appear. Enter the names of up to three different voluntary deductions that are to be withheld from the employee's pay. Next, select the appropriate type of business, income statement, and accounting system. Click on the appropriate Computer Checks box to indicate whether the computer is to generate payable or payroll checks. If neither of the check boxes is checked, the computer assumes that checks are written manually. Finally, if both the Inventory and the Merchandising Business with CGS (Cost of Goods Sold) Account features have been selected, select the method of inventory valuation to be used by the computer during processing.

Classify Accounts

The **classify accounts** feature allows you to classify the accounts based on account number ranges. The example shown in Figure 12.2 contains the account number ranges for Zallek Corporation. To perform financial statement analysis, the computer needs to know the range of account numbers for long-term assets and long-term liabilities. These data are provided in the Extended Classification section of the window.

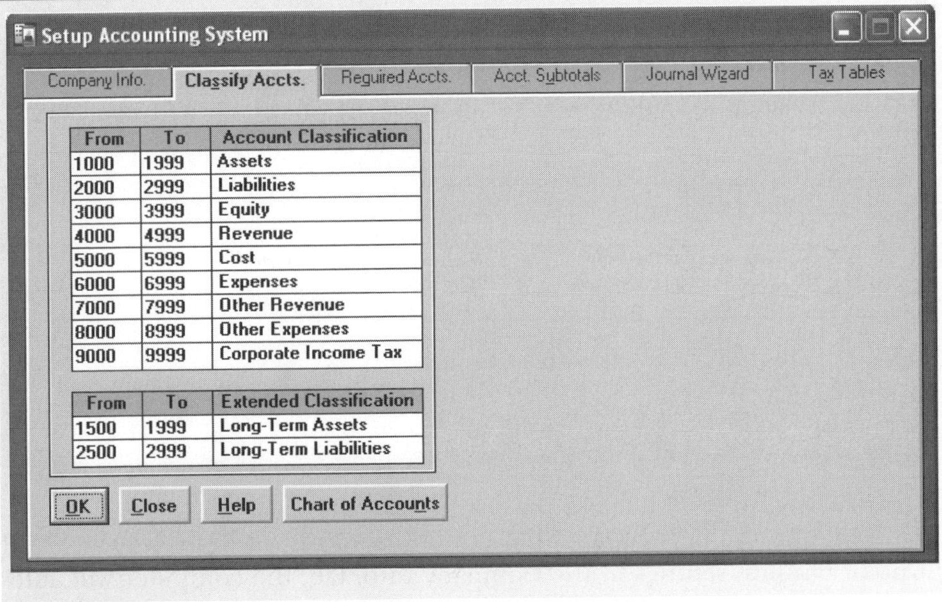

FIGURE 12.2

Classify Accounts

The account classifications shown in Figure 12.2 are also the default classifications used by the *Integrated Accounting* system. Unless the account classification numbering scheme is different, it will not be necessary to change the account ranges. If they must be changed, do *not* enter the actual range of account numbers: Enter the *potential* range. For example, if your chart of accounts currently has five assets ranging from account number 1110 to 1150, you should not specify the actual range, 1110 to 1150. Specify the potential range, such as 1000 to 1999, so that asset accounts added later will be included in the assets classification automatically. If your chart of accounts does not include a certain classification, enter the anticipated account number range for that classification. For example, if your chart of accounts does not include Other Expenses, include a range of account numbers that are to be reserved for Other Expenses in case they are added to the chart of accounts at a later date.

To enter account classifications, click the Classify Accts. tab. If the account classifications are different from those shown, enter the account number range for each of the classes of accounts. You may click Chart of Accounts to select an account from the Chart of Accounts List window.

Required Accounts

Because you have a great deal of flexibility in assigning account numbers and titles, you must provide the computer with specific **required accounts**—that is, the account numbers that you have assigned to certain key accounts. The computer needs this information to prepare financial statements, carry out integration among the systems (i.e., payroll, purchase order, sales order processing), and to complete period-end closing tasks. The Required Accounts tab showing a partial list of required accounts for Zallek Corporation is illustrated in Figure 12.3.

FIGURE 12.3

Required Accounts

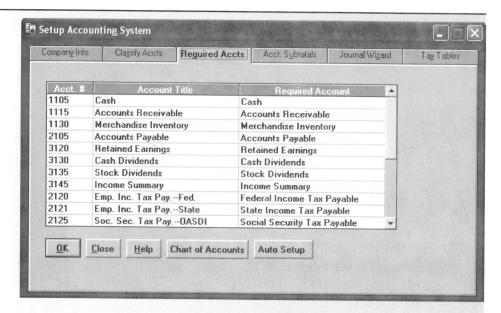

Based on the departmentalization, business organization, features, and type of business settings in the Company Info. tab, the computer will automatically determine and list the accounts it requires. For example, if the type of business is a service business, no merchandise inventory accounts are required. For a departmental merchandising business, Merchandise Inventory and Income Summary accounts are required for each department. For a sole proprietorship and a partnership, capital accounts are listed. For a corporation, a stock dividends account is required. If the corporation does not have stock dividends, enter the account number for the cash dividends account number.

To specify the required accounts, click the Required Accts. tab., then click Auto Setup. The computer will search the newly entered chart of accounts and attempt to match the required accounts to the account titles. All matching accounts are displayed. Enter the account number for each of the unmatched accounts. You may click Chart of Accounts to select an account from the Chart of Accounts List window.

Account Subtotals

The purpose of the **account subtotals** feature is to allow you to specify where subtotals are to be printed on the financial statements. For example, you may wish to tailor the balance sheet so that a subtotal prints after current assets and another after fixed assets. To set up subtotals, enter the account number range of the accounts to be included in the subtotal and the title to be printed on the subtotal line. The account number ranges need not reference actual accounts. Instead, the potential range should be entered so that it will not be necessary to modify the account number range as accounts are added to the chart of accounts. The account subtotals for Zallek Corporation are shown in Figure 12.4.

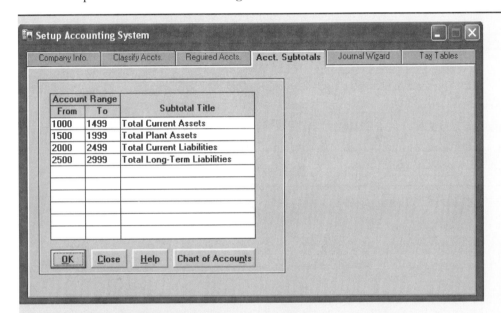

FIGURE 12.4

Account Subtotals

Journal Wizard

The **journal wizard**, shown in Figure 12.5, can be used to create special general, purchases, cash payments, sales, and cash receipts journals. Using special journals simplifies the process of entering transaction data into the computer. Basic default journals are automatically provided when a new business is established. The journal wizard may be used to expand these default journals to better meet the needs of the business being established. New journals will be saved to disk along with your data and will be used when entering future transaction data. The journal wizard may also be used with a previously established company data file to create special journals to more efficiently handle data entry activities. The following procedures and examples create a special cash payments journal.

FIGURE 12.5

Journal Wizard

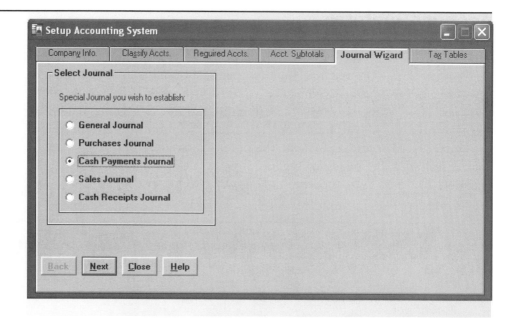

Click the Journal Wizard tab and select the journal to be created (Cash Payments Journal). Click Next to continue. The dialog window shown in Figure 12.6 will appear.

FIGURE 12.6

Establish Offsetting Account Information

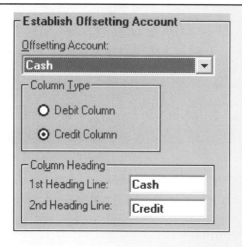

Click the drop-down text box to select the offsetting account (Cash), then click on either the Debit or Credit Column. (The offsetting Cash account will be credited). Enter a one- to two-line heading to identify the offsetting account column on the journal (Cash Credit). Click Next to continue. The dialog window shown in Figure 12.7 will appear.

FIGURE 12.7

General Debit and Credit Column Dialog Box

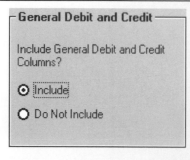

Click on Include or Do Not Include to indicate whether general debit and credit columns should be used in the journal (select Include). Click Next to continue. The dialog box shown in Figure 12.8 will appear.

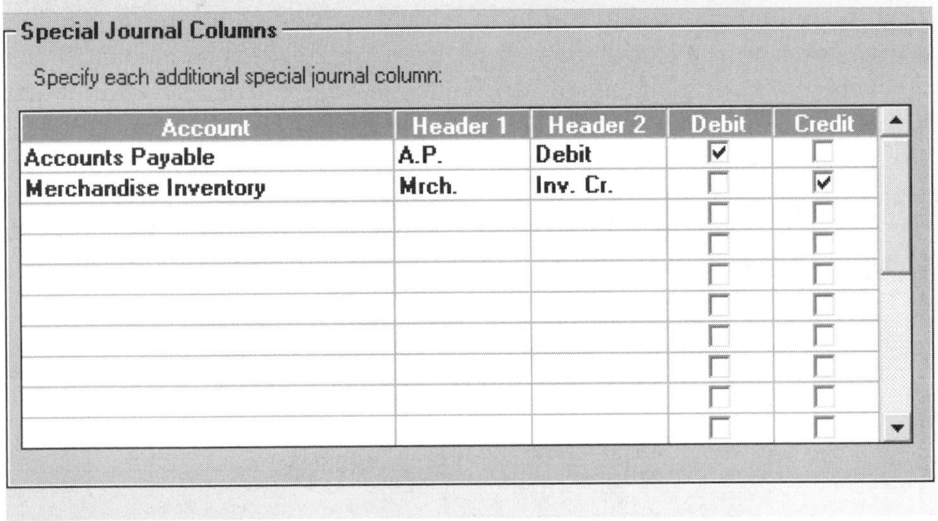

FIGURE 12.8

Special Journal Columns

Special Journal Columns

Specify each additional special journal column:

Account	Header 1	Header 2	Debit	Credit
Accounts Payable	A.P.	Debit	☑	☐
Merchandise Inventory	Mrch.	Inv. Cr.	☐	☑
			☐	☐
			☐	☐
			☐	☐
			☐	☐
			☐	☐
			☐	☐
			☐	☐

Use the account drop-down list to select the account to be included on the journal, enter the first and second header to identify the account column on the journal, and click on the Debit or Credit check box to indicate whether the account is to be treated as a debit or credit amount. Repeat this procedure for each column to be added to the journal and click Finish.

Click the appropriate tab in the Journal Entries window and verify that the newly created journal is correct (see Figure 12.9).

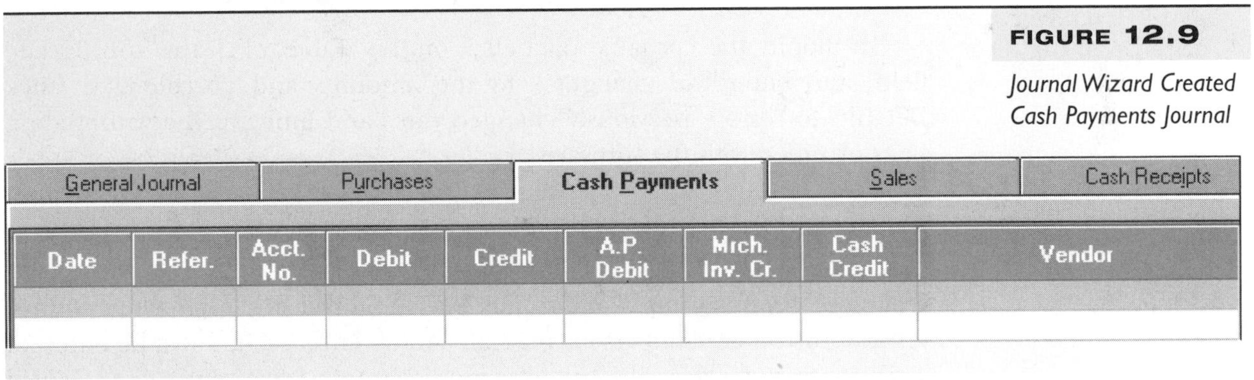

FIGURE 12.9

Journal Wizard Created Cash Payments Journal

| General Journal | | Purchases | | **Cash Payments** | | Sales | | Cash Receipts |

Date	Refer.	Acct. No.	Debit	Credit	A.P. Debit	Mrch. Inv. Cr.	Cash Credit	Vendor

The Date and Refer. columns will also be included as the left-most columns on the journal. A Vendor or Customer column will also be automatically added as the right-most column to journals with amount columns associated with accounts payable or accounts receivable, if the computer detects that corresponding vendor and customer files have been established.

Tax Tables

The **Tax Tables** dialog box contains three sections. The Federal Tax Brackets section contains the federal withholding rates. You may update these rates by referring to IRS Circular E (Employer's Tax Guide), Table 7 (Annual Payroll). The State Tax Brackets section contains the state withholding rates used by the software for the problems in this textbook. Like the federal rates, the state rates may be updated by referring to your state's employer's tax guide. The Rates and Limits section contains the various tax rates, upper limits, and allowance amounts required by the software to calculate employee and employer payroll taxes. The new rates will be saved to disk along with your data and will be used to compute withholding rates for future payrolls.

It is recommended that you *not* change these rates (unless instructed to do so) when working with payroll problems in this text-workbook. If the brackets, rates, or percentages are changed, the calculated withholding amounts will no longer match the solutions provided to your instructor. The Tax Table tab is shown in Figure 12.10.

FIGURE 12.10

Tax Table

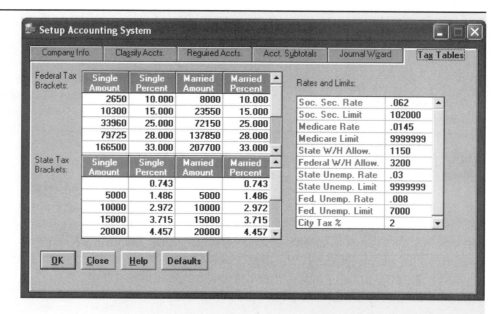

To modify the tax table data click on Tax Table, click the appropriate field, and enter the change(s) to the amounts and percentages. Click Defaults to restore previously changed rates and limits to the withholding rates provided with the software.

System Setup Data

Once the company information has been entered, the chart of accounts, vendor, customer, fixed assets, payroll, and inventory data must be entered. This process was described in previous chapters. New setup features will now be discussed.

Accounts Pick List

As an alternative to entering the chart of accounts entries, you can click **Pick List**, located below the Chart of Accounts in the Accounts window, to select accounts from a master chart of accounts list. You should use the Chart of Accounts window to enter accounts that do not appear in the pick list or to change the account titles as desired. The accounts pick list is shown in Figure 12.11.

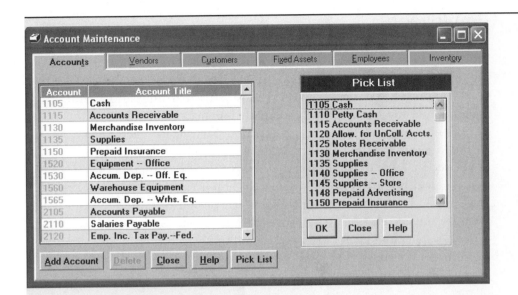

FIGURE 12.11

Chart of Accounts with Pick List

Click Accts. on the toolbar, click the Accounts tab, and then click Pick List. Select an account from the accounts Pick List column and click OK. The selected account will be placed in the Chart of Accounts Maintenance list. Click Add Account (or press the Enter key) to add the selected account to the chart of accounts. The selected account will be added to the chart of accounts in account number sequence and will appear in the chart of accounts column. To remove an account from the chart of accounts, simply select the desired account and click Delete.

Opening Balances

General ledger opening balance data are entered into the computer via the general journal you used when entering general journal entries in previous chapters. Each opening balance is posted as a separate general journal entry. Likewise, each customer account balance must be entered as a separate entry.

If the accounting system setup does not include inventory, the total of the balances for all the customers will be the balance of the Accounts Receivable general ledger account. Also, each vendor account balance must be entered as a separate entry. Again, the total of the balances for all the vendors will be the balance of the Accounts Payable general ledger account.

As opening balance data are entered, the debit and credit totals will not be equal, however, you should post each transaction anyway. By entering BALANCE in the reference grid cells, the computer will know that the entry is an opening balance and will therefore not display the error message warning you that the entry is not in balance. After all data have been entered, you should verify the accuracy of your input by making sure that the debit and credit totals shown on the trial balance are equal.

Fixed Assets

Each of the fixed assets must be entered into the computer. If you need more information on adding fixed assets, refer to Chapter 7.

Employees

Each of the employees must be entered into the computer. If you need more information on adding employees, refer to Chapter 8. If the accounting system is being established at a time other than the beginning of a new year, you must establish the quarterly and yearly earnings and withholdings for each employee. Quarterly and yearly balances are established by either of two methods: (1) by running simulated payrolls for each pay period up to the desired date, or (2) by entering one payroll transaction for each employee for each quarter that represents the sum of that employee's earnings and withholdings for the quarter. In either case, the payroll is date sensitive so be sure to use the appropriate pay-period or end-of-quarter dates. Because the accounting system for Zallek Corporation is being established on February 1, and each employee is paid once each month, one simulated payroll can be run for the month of January to bring the quarterly and yearly balances up-to-date.

Inventory

Two tasks are required to set up an inventory system: (1) data for each stock item must be entered, and (2) purchase order, purchase invoice, and sales invoice historical data must be entered. The procedure to enter stock items was described in Chapter 5. After the company's stock items have been entered, the historical data may be entered.

When purchase orders, and the voucher (purchase invoices) historical data are entered, the computer will perform system integration as explained in Chapter 5. Therefore, the accounts payable, merchandise inventory, and vendor account balances will be updated automatically. Likewise, when the sales invoices historical data is entered, the computer will perform system integration as explained in Chapter 6. Therefore, the accounts receivable, revenue, merchandise inventory, cost, and customer account balances will be updated automatically.

Chapter Summary

- Before setting up a computerized accounting system, you must carefully plan, design, and gather data.

- The New command in the File menu clears any existing data from memory in preparation for setting up a new accounting system.

- The Setup Accounting System window is used to provide setup information to the *Integrated Accounting* software.

- A Features check box is provided on the Company Info. tab for each accounting system to be included during setup (fixed assets, inventory, payroll, budgeting). Appropriate windows, reports, data entry tabs, and so on are automatically activated based on the features selected.

- Selecting the Income Statement Report by Month and Year option under the Company info. tab will cause generated Income Statement reports to include a column for the current month and another column for the current year. Also included for each dollar amount column will be a percentage column, indicating the percent of each dollar amount in relation to total operating revenue. If the Report by Fiscal Period option is selected, only one dollar amount column and corresponding percentages for the fiscal period will be included on the statements.

■ When the Accounts Payable Checks option is set to on, accounts payable checks will be created each time a cash payment involving a vendor is entered into the computer. If the Payroll Checks option is set to on, paychecks will be created each time an employee's payroll transaction is entered.

■ Classify Accounts allows you to classify the accounts based on account number ranges.

■ Required accounts are needed by the computer to prepare financial statements, carry out integration among the systems (i.e., payroll, sales order processing), and to complete period-end closing tasks.

■ The Acct. Subtotals tab may be used to specify where subtotals are to be included on the financial statements.

■ The journal wizard can be used to create special general, purchases, cash payments, sales, and cash receipts journals to improve the efficiency of entering transaction data into the computer.

■ The federal tax brackets, state tax brackets, rates, and limits in the tax tables are required by the software to calculate employee and employer payroll taxes.

■ When establishing accounts, clicking on the Pick List button will cause a master chart of accounts to be displayed from which accounts may be selected and customized.

■ If *BALANCE* is entered in the general journal reference grid cells, the computer will know that the entry is an opening balance and will therefore not display the error message warning you that the entry is not in balance.

■ If payroll is being established at a time other than the beginning of a new year, you must establish the quarterly and yearly earnings and withholdings for each employee by either of two methods: (1) by running simulated payrolls for each pay period up to the desired date, or (2) by entering one payroll transaction for each employee for each quarter that represents the sum of that employee's earnings and withholdings for the quarter.

■ Two tasks are required to setup an inventory system: (1) enter the data for each stock item, and (2) enter purchase order, voucher (purchase invoice), and sales invoice historical data.

Sample Problem 12-S

In this problem, you will setup a complete accounting system. You will complete the processing necessary to setup the accounting, fixed assets, payroll, inventory, and budget data for Zallek Corporation as of February 1 of the current year. To complete the tutorial problem, follow the step-by-step instructions provided.

1   **Start *Integrated Accounting* 6e.**

2   **Use the New command to erase data in memory and prepare the computer for setup.**

Choose New from the File menu.

3   **Enter your name in the Your Name text box.**

4   **Enter information into the data fields and set the check boxes and option buttons in the Setup Accounting Systems' Company Info. tab window as follows:**

Click Setup on the toolbar, then select the Company Info. tab.

Company Name	Zallek Corporation
Problem Name	Chapter 12 Sample
Departments	None
Business Organization	Corporation
Features	Fixed Assets
	Payroll
	Health Insurance
	Union Dues
	Savings Bonds
	Inventory
	Budgeting
Type of Business	Merchandising Bus. with CGS Account
Income Statement	Report by Fiscal Period
Accounting System	Standard
Computer Checks	None
Inventory Costing	FIFO

5   **Turn the transaction summary feature off if necessary.**

Click transactions summary in the Help menu to toggle the feature off (a check mark indicates the feature is on, the absence of a check mark indicates the feature is off).

6   **Enter the chart of accounts.**

Click Accts. on the Toolbar. When the Accounts Maintenance window appears, click the Accounts tab and click Pick List. When the Pick List window appears, select the desired account and click OK to place the selected account in the Chart of Accounts window (or simply double-click on the desired account). Click Add Account to add the account to the chart of accounts.

Note that several of the account titles chosen from the pick list should be changed to match Zallek Corporation's chart of accounts.

As an alternative, enter each of the accounts. The completed chart of accounts is shown in Figure 12.12.

Account	Account Title
1105	Cash
1115	Accounts Receivable
1130	Merchandise Inventory
1135	Supplies
1150	Prepaid Insurance
1520	Equipment -- Office
1530	Accum. Dep. -- Off. Eq.
1560	Warehouse Equipment
1565	Accum. Dep. -- Wrhs. Eq.
2105	Accounts Payable
2110	Salaries Payable
2120	Emp. Inc. Tax Pay.--Fed.
2121	Emp. Inc. Tax Pay.--State
2122	Emp. Inc. Tax Pay.--City
2125	Soc. Sec. Tax Pay.--OASDI
2126	Medicare Tax Payable
2130	Sales Tax Payable
2135	Unemp. Tax Pay. -- Fed.
2140	Unemp. Tax Pay. -- State
2150	Health Ins. Prem. Pay.
2160	Union Dues Payable
2170	Savings Bonds Payable
3105	Capital Stock
3120	Retained Earnings
3130	Cash Dividends
3135	Stock Dividends
3145	Income Summary
4105	Sales
4110	Sales Discount
4115	Sales Ret. and Allow.
5110	Cost of Merchandise Sold
6105	Advertising Expense
6120	Depr. Exp. -- Off. Eq.
6125	Depr. Exp. -- Wrhs. Eq.
6150	Insurance Expense
6155	Miscellaneous Expense
6170	Payroll Taxes Expense
6180	Rent Expense
6195	Salary Exp.--Office
6197	Salary Exp.--Wrhs.
6200	Supplies Expense
7110	Interest Income
8105	Interest Expense
9105	Corporate Income Tax

FIGURE 12.12

Chart of Accounts

7 Enter the vendors.

Click on Vendors in the Accounts Maintenance window and enter each of the vendors as shown in Figure 12.13.

FIGURE 12.13

Vendors

Vendor Name
Browne Insurance Agency
Elbert Manufacturing
Engle Power Tools
Fossen Industries, Inc.
Landrum Tool Supply
Payroll Bank Account
Southwest Utilities
Tilton Advertising
Wellington Tool Corp.
Wingert Office Supplies

8 Enter the customers.

Click on Customers in the Accounts Maintenance window and enter each of the customers shown in Figure 12.14.

FIGURE 12.14

Customers

Customer Name
Beyer Rental Agency
C & S Industrial Tools
Dotson Tool & Die Co.
Millard Power Tools
Sandstrom Hardware
Wetzel Tools, Inc.
Willmont Industries

9 Verify account classification and extended account classification data. (The software will automatically determine account classifications.)

Click Setup on the toolbar and choose Classify Accts. tab. Verify the appropriate account number ranges as shown in Figure 12.15.

FIGURE **12.15**

Account Classification

From	To	Account Classification
1000	1999	Assets
2000	2999	Liabilities
3000	3999	Equity
4000	4999	Revenue
5000	5999	Cost
6000	6999	Expenses
7000	7999	Other Revenue
8000	8999	Other Expenses
9000	9999	Corporate Income Tax

From	To	Extended Classification
1500	1999	Long-Term Assets
2500	2999	Long-Term Liabilities

10 **Enter the following required account data.**

Click on Required Accts. Click Auto Setup to cause the computer to try and match as many required accounts to the account titles in the chart of accounts as possible. Complete the unmatched required accounts by entering the appropriate account numbers or using the Chart of Accounts list box to select the desired accounts. The completed required accounts are shown in Figure 12.16.

FIGURE **12.16**

Required Accounts

Acct. #	Account Title	Required Account
1105	Cash	Cash
1115	Accounts Receivable	Accounts Receivable
1130	Merchandise Inventory	Merchandise Inventory
2105	Accounts Payable	Accounts Payable
3120	Retained Earnings	Retained Earnings
3130	Cash Dividends	Cash Dividends
3135	Stock Dividends	Stock Dividends
3145	Income Summary	Income Summary
2120	Emp. Inc. Tax Pay.--Fed.	Federal Income Tax Payable
2121	Emp. Inc. Tax Pay.--State	State Income Tax Payable
2125	Soc. Sec. Tax Pay.--OASDI	Social Security Tax Payable
2126	Medicare Tax Payable	Medicare Tax Payable
2150	Health Ins. Prem. Pay.	Health Insurance Payable
2160	Union Dues Payable	Union Dues Payable
2170	Savings Bonds Payable	Savings Bonds Payable
6170	Payroll Taxes Expense	Payroll Tax Expense
2140	Unemp. Tax Pay. -- State	Unemployment Tax Payable--State
2135	Unemp. Tax Pay. -- Fed.	Unemployment Tax Payable--Feder
2110	Salaries Payable	Salaries Payable
2122	Emp. Inc. Tax Pay.--City	City Income Tax Payable

11 Enter the account subtotals.

Click on Acct. Subtotals and enter the appropriate account number ranges and subtotal titles as shown in Figure 12.17.

FIGURE 12.17

Account Subtotals

Account Range		Subtotal Title
From	To	
1000	1499	Total Current Assets
1500	1999	Total Plant Assets
2000	2499	Total Current Liabilities
2500	2999	Total Long-Term Liabilities

12 Enter the general ledger opening balances.

Click Journal on the toolbar, click the General Journal tab, and enter the data from the general journal shown in Figure 12.18.

FIGURE 12.18

General Ledger Opening Balances

Date	Refer.	Account	Debit	Credit
02/01/__	BALANCE	1105 Cash	23543.47	
02/01/__	BALANCE	1135 Supplies	1950.00	
02/01/__	BALANCE	1150 Prepaid Insurance	1345.00	
02/01/__	BALANCE	1520 Equipment -- Office	13640.00	
02/01/__	BALANCE	1530 Accum. Dep. -- Off. Eq.		2897.65
02/01/__	BALANCE	1560 Warehouse Equipment	29495.00	
02/01/__	BALANCE	1565 Accum. Dep. -- Wrhs. Eq.		5917.36
02/01/__	BALANCE	3105 Capital Stock		45500.00
02/01/__	BALANCE	3120 Retained Earnings		15658.46

13 Enter budget amounts.

Click Tasks on the toolbar, click the Budgets tab and enter the budget amounts shown in Figure 12.19.

FIGURE 12.19

Budget Amounts

Account Title	Budget
Total Revenue	175000.00
Cost of Merchandise Sold	132000.00
Advertising Expense	6000.00
Depr. Exp. -- Off. Eq.	3600.00
Depr. Exp. -- Wrhs. Eq.	4550.00
Insurance Expense	8550.00
Miscellaneous Expense	2250.00
Payroll Taxes Expense	25000.00
Rent Expense	36000.00
Salary Exp.--Office	46000.00
Salary Exp.--Wrhs.	34500.00
Supplies Expense	4500.00
Interest Income	2400.00
Interest Expense	6500.00
Corporate Income Tax	45000.00

14 Display a chart of accounts, vendor list, and customer list.

Click Reports on the toolbar. Select and display the chart of accounts, vendor list, and customer list (set the Run Date to February 1 of the current year). Examine each report in Figure 12.20 and verify that the data you entered is correct.

Zallek Corporation
Chart of Accounts
02/01/—

FIGURE 12.20

Chart of Accounts, Vendor List, and Customer List

Assets
1105 Cash
1115 Accounts Receivable
1130 Merchandise Inventory
1135 Supplies
1150 Prepaid Insurance
1520 Equipment—Office
1530 Accum. Dep.—Off. Eq.
1560 Warehouse Equipment
1565 Accum. Dep.—Wrhs. Eq.

Liabilities
2105 Accounts Payable
2110 Salaries Payable
2120 Emp. Inc. Tax Pay.—Fed.
2121 Emp. Inc. Tax Pay.—State
2122 Emp. Inc. Tax Pay.—City
2125 Soc. Sec. Tax Pay.—OASDI
2126 Medicare Tax Payable
2130 Sales Tax Payable
2135 Unemp. Tax Pay.—Fed.
2140 Unemp. Tax Pay.—State
2150 Health Ins. Prem. Pay.
2160 Union Dues Payable
2170 Savings Bonds Payable

Stockholders' Equity
3105 Capital Stock
3120 Retained Earnings
3130 Cash Dividends
3135 Stock Dividends
3145 Income Summary

Revenue
4105 Sales
4110 Sales Discount
4115 Sales Ret. and Allow.

Cost
5110 Cost of Merchandise Sold

Expenses
6105 Advertising Expense
6120 Depr. Exp.—Off. Eq.
6125 Depr. Exp.—Wrhs. Eq.

(continued)

FIGURE 12.20

(Concluded)

6150	Insurance Expense
6155	Miscellaneous Expense
6170	Payroll Taxes Expense
6180	Rent Expense
6195	Salary Exp.—Office
6197	Salary Exp.—Wrhs.
6200	Supplies Expense

Other Revenue
7110	Interest Income

Other Expense
8105	Interest Expense

Corporate Income Tax
9105	Corporate Income Tax

**Zallek Corporation
Vendor List
02/01/—**

Vendor Name
Browne Insurance Agency
Elbert Manufacturing
Engle Power Tools
Fossen Industries, Inc.
Landrum Tool Supply
Payroll Bank Account
Southwest Utilities
Tilton Advertising
Wellington Tool Corp.
Wingert Office Supplies

**Zallek Corporation
Customer List
02/01/—**

Customer Name
Beyer Rental Agency
C & S Industrial Tools
Dotson Tool & Die Co.
Millard Power Tools
Sandstrom Hardware
Wetzel Tools, Inc.
Willmont Industries

15 **Save the setup data to your disk with a file name of 12-S Your Name.**

16 **Enter the data to set up the Fixed Assets.**

Click Accts. on the toolbar. Choose the Fixed Assets tab and enter the fixed asset data shown in Figure 12.21.

Asset numbers 100 through 199 are assigned to office equipment, and asset numbers 200 through 299 are assigned to warehouse equipment.

FIGURE 12.21

Fixed Assets

No.	Asset Name	Date Acquired	Use. Life	Original Cost	Salvage Value	Accum Depr.	Depr. Exp.	Depr. Meth.
110	Facsimile Machine	06/30/06	5	365.00	50.00	1530	6120	SL
120	File Cabinet	11/30/07	7	625.00	75.00	1530	6120	MACRS
130	Copy Machine	08/31/07	5	2650.00	250.00	1530	6120	SL
140	Telephone System	05/31/06	5	10000.00	500.00	1530	6120	DDB
210	Delivery Van	10/01/06	10	8750.00	300.00	1565	6125	DDB
220	Computer System	07/12/07	5	2995.00	200.00	1565	6125	SL
230	Shelving	01/01/08	10	17750.00	1250.00	1565	6125	SYD

17   **Display a fixed assets list report.**

The report is shown in Figure 12.22.

FIGURE 12.22

Fixed Assets Report

Zallek Corporation
Fixed Assets List
02/01/—

Asset	Date Acquired	Depr. Method	Useful Life	Original Cost	Salvage Value	Depr. Accts
110 Facsimile Machine	06/30/06	SL	5	365.00	50.00	1530 6120
120 File Cabinet	11/30/07	MACRS	7	625.00	75.00	1530 6120
130 Copy Machine	08/31/07	SL	5	2,650.00	250.00	1530 6120
140 Telephone System	05/31/06	DDB	5	10,000.00	500.00	1530 6120
210 Delivery Van	10/01/06	DDB	10	8,750.00	300.00	1565 6125
220 Computer System	07/12/07	SL	5	2,995.00	200.00	1565 6125
230 Shelving	01/01/08	SYD	10	17,750.00	1,250.00	1565 6125
Total Fixed Assets				43,135.00		

18   **Save the data.**

19   **Verify that the city tax rate is set to 2.0% in the payroll tax tables.**

Click Setup on the toolbar. Choose Tax Tables and enter 2 in the City Tax % text box if necessary. Click OK. The completed tax table is shown in Figure 12.23.

FIGURE 12.23

Tax Tables

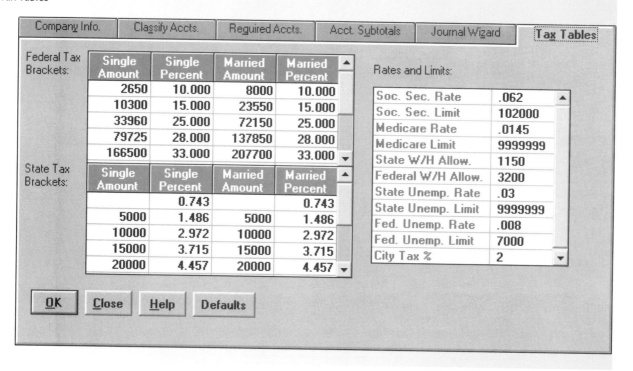

20 **Enter the employee data.**

Click Accts. on the toolbar. Choose the Employees and enter the employee data shown on in Figure 12.24.

FIGURE 12.24

Employees

No.	Employee Name	Address	City, State, Zip	Social Sec. No.
110	Bickett, John	1967 Sutter Ave.	Omaha, NE 68503-5010	567-94-8271
120	Mendez, Bella	4950 Fieldstone Dr.	Omaha, NE 68507-6318	426-17-9947
130	Powers, Dawn	85 Lakota Ct.	Omaha, NE 68519-9436	698-45-2314
140	Tischer, Scott	6280 Kenyon Rd.	Omaha, NE 68511-8705	445-13-1593

With. Allow.	Number Pay Per.	G.L. No.	Salary Amount	Hourly Rate	Marital Status
3	12	6195	4550.00		Married ▼
1	12	6195	4725.00		Single ▼
3	12	6197		14.25	Married ▼
1	12	6197		14.25	Single ▼

21 **Enter and process the January payroll transactions. Withhold all three voluntary deductions this pay period (health insurance, union dues, and savings bonds).**

Click Tasks on the toolbar. Choose Payroll and enter the January payroll transaction data shown in Figure 12.25 (have the computer calculate the withholding taxes). Be sure to use 01/31/— as the payroll date and start check numbering with Check No. 4360.

FIGURE 12.25

January Payroll Transactions

Date	Employee Name	Check No.	Salary	Reg. Hours	O.T. 1 1/2	O.T. Double	SUTA Tax	FIT
01/31/--	Bickett, John	4360	4550.00					397.71
01/31/--	Mendez, Bella	4361	4725.00					766.58
01/31/--	Powers, Dawn	4362		176.00	2.50			109.48
01/31/--	Tischer, Scott	4363		176.00				271.20

SIT	CIT	Soc. Sec. (OASDI)	Medicare (HI)	Health Insurance	Union Dues	Savings Bonds	Net Pay
159.76	91.00	282.10	65.98	125.00		200.00	3228.45
178.83	94.50	292.95	68.51	85.00		100.00	3138.63
64.22	51.23	158.81	37.14	125.00	10.00	50.00	1955.56
70.38	50.16	155.50	36.37	85.00	10.00	75.00	1754.39

22 **Generate and post the journal entry for the current payroll.**

Choose Current Payroll Journal Entry from the Options menu. Click Yes when asked if you want to generate the journal entry. When the entry appears in the Current Payroll Journal Entries dialog box, click Post. The journal entry will reappear, posted, in the general journal.

23 **Generate and post the employer's payroll taxes journal entry.**

With the General Journal window still displayed, choose Employer's Payroll Taxes from the Options menu. Click Yes when asked if you want to generate the journal entry. When the entries appear in the Payroll Taxes Journal Entries dialog box, click Post. The journal entries will reappear, posted, in the general journal.

24 **Display the employee list.**

The report is shown in Figure 12.26.

FIGURE **12.26**

Employee List

Zallek Corporation
Employee List
02/01/—

Emp. No.	Employee Name/Address	Soc. Sec./ Mar. Stat.	# Pay Periods	G.L. Acct.	Salary/ Rate
110	Bickett, John 1967 Sutter Ave. Omaha, NE 68503-5010	567-94-8271 Married W/H 3	12	6195	4,550.00
120	Mendez, Bella 4950 Fieldstone Dr. Omaha, NE 68507-6318	426-17-9947 Single W/H 1	12	6195	4,725.00
130	Powers, Dawn 85 Lakota Ct. Omaha, NE 68519-9436	698-45-2314 Married W/H 3	12	6197	14.25
140	Tischer, Scott 6280 Kenyon Rd. Omaha, NE 68511-8705	445-13-1593 Single W/H 1	12	6197	14.25

25 **Display the payroll report.**

The payroll report is shown in Figure 12.27.

FIGURE **12.27**

Payroll Report

Zallek Corporation
Payroll Report
02/01/—

		Current	Quarterly	Yearly
110-Bickett, John	Gross Pay	4,550.00	4,550.00	4,550.00
6195-Salary	FIT	397.71	397.71	397.71
Married Acct. 6195	SIT	159.76	159.76	159.76
W/H 3 567-94-8271	Soc. Sec.—OASDI	282.10	282.10	282.10
Pay Periods 12	Medicare—HI	65.98	65.98	65.98
Salary 4,550.00	CIT	91.00	91.00	91.00
Hourly Rate	Health Insurance	125.00	125.00	125.00
Reg. Hours	Union Dues			
O.T. Hours	Savings Bonds	200.00	200.00	200.00
Check Number 4360	Employee SUTA			
Check Date 01/31/08	Net Pay	3,228.45	3,228.45	3,228.45
120-Mendez, Bella	Gross Pay	4,725.00	4,725.00	4,725.00
6195-Salary	FIT	766.58	766.58	766.58
Single Acct. 6195	SIT	178.83	178.83	178.83
W/H 1 426-17-9947	Soc. Sec.—OASDI	292.95	292.95	292.95
Pay Periods 12	Medicare—HI	68.51	68.51	68.51
Salary 4,725.00	CIT	94.50	94.50	94.50
Hourly Rate	Health Insurance	85.00	85.00	85.00
Reg. Hours	Union Dues			
O.T. Hours	Savings Bonds	100.00	100.00	100.00
Check Number 4361	Employee SUTA			
Check Date 01/31/08	Net Pay	3,138.63	3,138.63	3,138.63

(continued)

130-Powers, Dawn	Gross Pay	2,561.44	2,561.44	2,561.44	**FIGURE 12.27**
6197-Salary	FIT	109.48	109.48	109.48	*(Concluded)*
Married Acct. 6197	SIT	64.22	64.22	64.22	
W/H 3 698-45-2314	Soc. Sec.—OASDI	158.81	158.81	158.81	
Pay Periods 12	Medicare—HI	37.14	37.14	37.14	
Salary	CIT	51.23	51.23	51.23	
Hourly Rate 14.25	Health Insurance	125.00	125.00	125.00	
Reg. Hours 176.00	Union Dues	10.00	10.00	10.00	
O.T. Hours 2.50	Savings Bonds	50.00	50.00	50.00	
Check Number 4362	Employee SUTA				
Check Date 01/31/08	Net Pay	1,955.56	1,955.56	1,955.56	
140-Tischer, Scott	Gross Pay	2,508.00	2,508.00	2,508.00	
6197-Salary	FIT	271.20	271.20	271.20	
Single Acct. 6197	SIT	70.38	70.38	70.38	
W/H 1 445-13-1593	Soc. Sec.—OASDI	155.50	155.50	155.50	
Pay Periods 12	Medicare—HI	36.37	36.37	36.37	
Salary	CIT	50.16	50.16	50.16	
Hourly Rate 14.25	Health Insurance	85.00	85.00	85.00	
Reg. Hours 176.00	Union Dues	10.00	10.00	10.00	
O.T. Hours	Savings Bonds	75.00	75.00	75.00	
Check Number 4363	Employee SUTA				
Check Date 01/31/08	Net Pay	1,754.39	1,754.39	1,754.39	
Payroll Summary	Gross Pay	14,344.44	14,344.44	14,344.44	
	FIT	1,544.97	1,544.97	1,544.97	
	SIT	473.19	473.19	473.19	
	Soc. Sec.—OASDI	889.36	889.36	889.36	
	Medicare—HI	208.00	208.00	208.00	
	CIT	286.89	286.89	286.89	
	Health Insurance	420.00	420.00	420.00	
	Union Dues	20.00	20.00	20.00	
	Savings Bonds	425.00	425.00	425.00	
	Employee SUTA				
	Net Pay	10,077.03	10,077.03	10,077.03	

26   **Save the data.**

27   **Enter the inventory stock item data.**

Click Accts. on the toolbar. Choose the Inventory tab and enter the inventory stock items shown in Figure 12.28.

FIGURE **12.28**

Inventory Stock Items

Stock No.	Description	Unit Meas.	Reorder Point	Retail Price
110	Air Hammer	EA	6	895.00
120	Band Saw	EA	10	39.95
130	Circular Saw	EA	12	45.95
140	Cordless Drill	EA	12	49.95
150	Industrial Stapler	EA	15	41.25
160	Electric Drill	EA	12	45.95
170	Nail Gun	EA	6	69.95
180	Power Band Saw	EA	5	499.00
190	Table Saw	EA	5	729.99

28 Enter the purchase order historical data.

Click Tasks on the toolbar. Choose Purchase Order and enter the following data.

PO#	Date	Vendor	Terms	Qty	Inventory Item	Price
371	02/01	Elbert Manufacturing	30 days	20	Air Hammer	$524.00
372	02/01	Landrum Tool Supply	30 days	40	Band Saw	$22.25
				50	Circular Saw	$27.00
				65	Cordless Drill	$28.50
373	02/01	Fossen Industries	30 days	36	Industrial Stapler	$25.00
				35	Electric Drill	$27.00
374	02/01	Wellington Tool Corp.	30 days	25	Nail Gun	$41.00
375	02/01	Engle Power Tools	30 days	16	Power Band Saw	$290.00
				22	Table Saw	$426.00

29 Enter the purchase invoice historical data.

Choose the Purchase Invoice tab and enter the following data.

PI#	Date	Vendor	PO #	Terms	Qty	Inventory Item	Price
517	02/01	Elbert Manufacturing	371	30 days	6	Air Hammer	$524.00
					12	Air Hammer	$535.00
518	02/01	Landrum Tool Supply	372	30 days	40	Band Saw	$22.25
					25	Circular Saw	$27.00
					25	Circular Saw	$25.00
					30	Cordless Drill	$28.50
					30	Cordless Drill	$29.95
519	02/01	Fossen Industries	373	30 days	36	Industrial Stapler	$25.00
					35	Electric Drill	$27.00
520	02/01	Wellington Tool Corp.	374	30 days	12	Nail Gun	$41.00
					10	Nail Gun	$39.50
521	02/01	Engle Power Tools	375	30 days	8	Power Band Saw	$290.00
					8	Power Band Saw	$295.00
					10	Table Saw	$439.00
					12	Table Saw	$426.00

30 **Enter the sales invoice historical data.**

Choose the Sales Invoice tab and enter the following data.

 WARNING The inventory valuation (Merchandise Inventory account balance) may be affected by the order in which transactions are entered. Therefore, making corrections or changing the sequence in which transactions are entered may affect the first in, first out (FIFO) method of valuation used in this problem. If you must make a correction to opening balances historical data, it is a good idea to delete all subsequent entries related to the inventory first and then reenter each occurrence in the order presented.

Inv#	Date	Tax	Customer	Terms	Qty	Inventory Item	Price
847	02/01	6%	Beyer Rental Agency	30 days	5	Air Hammer	$895.00
					6	Cordless Drill	$49.95
					4	Industrial Stapler	$41.25
					8	Nail Gun	$69.95
848	02/01	6%	C & S Industrial Tools	30 days	2	Air Hammer	$895.00
					15	Industrial Stapler	$41.25
					4	Nail Gun	$69.95
					8	Table Saw	$729.99
849	02/01	6%	Dotson Tool & Die Co.	30 days	4	Band Saw	$39.95
					10	Circular Saw	$45.95
					8	Cordless Drill	$49.95
850	02/01	6%	Millard Power Tools	30 days	6	Air Hammer	$895.00
					4	Nail Gun	$69.95
					7	Power Band Saw	$499.00
					8	Table Saw	$729.99
851	02/01	6%	Sandstrom Hardware	30 days	12	Band Saw	$39.95
					15	Circular Saw	$45.95
					18	Cordless Drill	$49.95
					9	Electric Drill	$45.95
852	02/01	6%	Wetzel Tools, Inc.	30 days	5	Band Saw	$39.95
					8	Circular Saw	$45.95
					6	Cordless Drill	$49.95
					12	Electric Drill	$45.95
853	02/01	6%	Willmont Industries	30 days	3	Air Hammer	$895.00
					5	Electric Drill	$45.95
					7	Power Band Saw	$499.00

31 **Display the inventory list report.**

The report appears in Figure 12.29.

FIGURE **12.29**

Inventory List Report

Zallek Corporation
Inventory List
02/01/—

Stock No.	Description	Unit Meas.	On Hand	On Order	Reorder Point	Last Cost	Retail Price
110	Air Hammer	EA	2	2	6	535.00	895.00
120	Band Saw	EA	19	0	10	22.25	39.95
130	Circular Saw	EA	17	0	12	25.00	45.95
140	Cordless Drill	EA	22	5	12	29.95	49.95
150	Industrial Stapler	EA	17	0	15	25.00	41.25
160	Electric Drill	EA	9	0	12	27.00	45.95
170	Nail Gun	EA	6	3	6	39.50	69.95
180	Power Band Saw	EA	2	0	5	295.00	499.00
190	Table Saw	EA	6	0	5	426.00	729.99

32 **Display the inventory transactions report.**

The report appears in Figure 12.30.

FIGURE **12.30**

Inventory Transactions Report

Zallek Corporation
Inventory Transactions
02/01/—

Date	Description	Inv./P.O.	Quantity Sold	Selling Price	Quan. Ord.	Quan. Recd.	Cost Price
Sales Invoices							
02/01	Air Hammer	847	5	895.00			
	Cordless Drill		6	49.95			
	Industrial Stapler		4	41.25			
	Nail Gun		8	69.95			
02/01	Air Hammer	848	2	895.00			
	Industrial Stapler		15	41.25			
	Nail Gun		4	69.95			
	Table Saw		8	729.99			
02/01	Band Saw	849	4	39.95			
	Circular Saw		10	45.95			
	Cordless Drill		8	49.95			
02/01	Air Hammer	850	6	895.00			
	Nail Gun		4	69.95			
	Power Band Saw		7	499.00			
	Table Saw		8	729.99			
02/01	Band Saw	851	12	39.95			
	Circular Saw		15	45.95			
	Cordless Drill		18	49.95			
	Electric Drill		9	45.95			
02/01	Band Saw	852	5	39.95			
	Circular Saw		8	45.95			
	Cordless Drill		6	49.95			
	Electric Drill		12	45.95			

(continued)

FIGURE 12.30

(Concluded)

02/01	Air Hammer	853	3	895.00			
	Electric Drill		5	45.95			
	Power Band Saw		7	499.00			

Purchase Orders

02/01	Air Hammer	371			20		
02/01	Band Saw	372			40		
	Circular Saw				50		
	Cordless Drill				65		
02/01	Industrial Stapler	373			36		
	Electric Drill				35		
02/01	Nail Gun	374			25		
02/01	Power Band Saw	375			16		
	Table Saw				22		

Purchase Invoices

02/01	Air Hammer	517				6	524.00
	Air Hammer					12	535.00
02/01	Band Saw	518				40	22.25
	Circular Saw					25	27.00
	Circular Saw					25	25.00
	Cordless Drill					30	28.50
	Cordless Drill					30	29.95
02/01	Industrial Stapler	519				36	25.00
	Electric Drill					35	27.00
02/01	Nail Gun	520				12	41.00
	Nail Gun					10	39.50
02/01	Power Band Saw	521				8	290.00
	Power Band Saw					8	295.00
	Table Saw					10	439.00
	Table Saw					12	426.00
	Totals		199		309	299	

33 **Save your data.**

34 **Display a trial balance, schedule of accounts payable, and schedule of accounts receivable.**

The reports are shown in Figure 12.31. Check the debit and credit totals of the trial balance report to make sure they equal. If the trial balance is out of balance, or the accounts receivable and accounts payable account balances are not correct, it can be assumed that a keying error has been made, and that corrections are necessary.

FIGURE 12.31

Trial Balance, Schedule of Accounts Payable, and Schedule of Accounts Receivable

Zallek Corporation
Trial Balance
02/01/—

Acct. Number	Account Title	Debit	Credit
1105	Cash	23,543.47	
1115	Accounts Receivable	42,757.11	
1130	Merchandise Inventory	6,627.65	
1135	Supplies	1,950.00	
1150	Prepaid Insurance	1,345.00	
1520	Equipment—Office	13,640.00	
1530	Accum. Dep.—Off. Eq.		2,897.65
1560	Warehouse Equipment	29,495.00	
1565	Accum. Dep.—Wrhs. Eq.		5,917.36
2105	Accounts Payable		30,421.50
2110	Salaries Payable		10,077.03
2120	Emp. Inc. Tax Pay.—Fed.		1,544.97
2121	Emp. Inc. Tax Pay.—State		473.19
2122	Emp. Inc. Tax Pay.—City		286.89
2125	Soc. Sec. Tax Pay.—OASDI		1,778.72
2126	Medicare Tax Payable		415.99
2130	Sales Tax Payable		2,420.22
2135	Unemp. Tax Pay.—Fed.		114.76
2140	Unemp. Tax Pay.—State		430.33
2150	Health Ins. Prem. Pay.		420.00
2160	Union Dues Payable		20.00
2170	Savings Bonds Payable		425.00
3105	Capital Stock		45,500.00
3120	Retained Earnings		15,658.46
4105	Sales		40,336.89
5110	Cost of Merchandise Sold	23,793.85	
6170	Payroll Taxes Expense	1,642.44	
6195	Salary Exp.—Office	9,275.00	
6197	Salary Exp.—Wrhs.	5,069.44	
	Totals	159,138.96	159,138.96

Zallek Corporation
Schedule of Accounts Payable
02/01/—

Name	Balance
Elbert Manufacturing	9,564.00
Engle Power Tools	14,182.00
Fossen Industries, Inc.	1,845.00
Landrum Tool Supply	3,943.50
Wellington Tool Corp.	887.00
Total	30,421.50

(continued)

FIGURE **12.31**

(Concluded)

Zallek Corporation
Schedule of Accounts Receivable
02/01/—

Name	Balance
Beyer Rental Agency	5,829.26
C & S Industrial Tools	9,040.18
Dotson Tool & Die Co.	1,080.03
Millard Power Tools	15,881.68
Sandstrom Hardware	2,630.18
Wetzel Tools, Inc.	1,503.56
Willmont Industries	6,792.22
Total	42,757.11

35   Create a special combination journal.

Zallek Corporation wants to use a combination journal to enter all their transactions into the computer. (Some companies that do not have a large volume of transactions prefer to journalize all transactions in a single journal called a combination or multi-column journal). Click Setup on the toolbar. Click Journal Wizard and select the General Journal option. Click Next and create a Sales Credit column, a Cash Debit column, and a Cash Credit column. The completed journal with the additional columns is shown in Figure 12.32. Select the General Journal from the Journal Entries window to verify that your new combination journal is correct. Notice that the opening balance data have been automatically placed in the appropriate columns.

FIGURE **12.32**

Journal Wizard Created Combination Column Journal

Date	Refer.	Account	Debit	Credit	Sales Credit	Cash Debit	Cash Credit	Vendor/Customer
02/01/--	BALANCE					23543.47		
02/01/--	BALANCE	1135 Supplies	1950.00					
02/01/--	BALANCE	1150 Prepaid Insurance	1345.00					
02/01/--	BALANCE	1520 Equipment -- Office	13640.00					
02/01/--	BALANCE	1530 Accum. Dep. -- Off. Eq.		2897.65				
02/01/--	BALANCE	1560 Warehouse Equipment	29495.00					
02/01/--	BALANCE	1565 Accum. Dep. -- Wrhs. Eq.		5917.36				
02/01/--	BALANCE	3105 Capital Stock		45500.00				
02/01/--	BALANCE	3120 Retained Earnings		15658.46				

36 **Save your data.**

If you have access to the Internet, use your browser to find information about the history, usage, or coding of the Universal Product Code (UPC). *Hint:* Use Universal Product Code as your search string. Report your findings. Be sure to include the sources, including URLs (Web addresses), of your reported findings.

37 **End the *Integrated Accounting* 6e session.**

Chapter 12 Student Exercises

NAME

I True/False

Directions   *If the statement is true, write T in the space provided. If the statement is false, write F in the space provided.*

1.____   The New menu command clears any existing data from memory in preparation for setting up a new system.

2.____   *Integrated Accounting* supports 12 departments.

3.____   *Integrated Accounting* allows for accounts payable and payroll checks to be prepared manually or by computer.

4.____   *Integrated Accounting* allows for a monthly or yearly accounting cycle.

5.____   Classify accounts is used to specify the account numbers needed to generate the payroll journal entries.

6.____   The required accounts need not be specified during setup.

7.____   If payroll records are being established at a time other than the beginning of a new year, quarterly and yearly earnings and withholdings must be created for each employee.

8.____   *Integrated Accounting* allows accounts to be added to the chart of accounts by selecting them from a master list of accounts.

9.____   The general, purchases, cash payments, sales, and cash receipts journals included in the software cannot be changed.

10.____   Tax brackets, rates, and limits provided by the software cannot be changed.

II Questions

Directions   *Answer each of the following questions in the space provided.*

1.   The Income Statement option under the Company Info. Tab allows two settings. List the two settings and explain the difference between them. _____

_____

_____

2.   How are the data collected on the Required Accounts window used? _____

_____

_____

3.   What is the purpose of the Account Subtotals tab? _____

_____

_____

4.   What is the purpose of the Classify Accounts tab? _____

5.   What are the two methods that can be used to create quarterly and yearly historical data for payroll setup? _____

6.   What is the purpose of the journal wizard? _____

7.   What is the purpose of the Tax Tables tab in the Setup Accounting System window?

Problem 12-A

In this problem, you will set up the accounting, fixed assets, payroll, inventory, and budgeting data for Minter Irrigation Co. Minter Irrigation Co., is a merchandising business organized as a sole proprietorship, is not departmentalized, prepares checks manually, generates the income statement by fiscal period, uses a perpetual inventory system (merchandising business with CGS account), uses the FIFO method to value its inventory, and uses a standard accounting system. The trial balance, schedule of accounts payable, schedule of accounts receivable, budget amounts, fixed assets, employees, and inventory data required to setup the opening balances as of January 1 of the current year are provided as follows:

General Ledger Account Titles and Balances

Account Number	Account Title	Debit	Credit
Assets			
1105	Cash	$11,875.00	
1115	Accounts Receivable		
1120	Allow. for Uncoll. Accts.		
1130	Merchandise Inventory		
1140	Supplies—Office	$2,425.00	
1145	Supplies—Wrhs.	$1,895.00	
1150	Prepaid Insurance	$3,200.00	
1520	Equipment—Office	$7,155.00	
1530	Accum. Dep.—Off. Eq.		$1,650.50
1560	Warehouse Equipment	$18,075.00	
1565	Accum. Dep.—Wrhs. Eq.		$4,536.80
Liabilities			
2105	Accounts Payable		
2110	Salaries Payable		
2120	Emp. Fed. Inc. Tax Pay.		
2121	Emp. State Inc. Tax Pay.		
2122	Emp. City Inc. Tax Pay.		
2125	Soc. Sec. Tax Pay.—OASDI		
2126	Medicare Tax Payable—HI		
2130	Sales Tax Payable		
2135	Unemp. Tax Pay.—Fed.		
2140	Unemp. Tax Pay.—State		
2150	Health Ins. Prem. Pay.		
2160	Dental Ins. Prem. Pay.		
2170	Credit Union Deduct. Pay.		
Owner's Equity			
3110	Robert Minter, Capital		$38,437.70
3120	Robert Minter, Drawing		
3135	Income Summary		
Revenue			
4105	Sales		
4110	Sales Discount		
4115	Sales Ret. and Allow.		
Cost			
5110	Cost of Merchandise Sold		

Expenses

6105		Advertising Expense
6130		Depr. Exp.—Off. Eq.
6140		Depr. Exp.—Wrhs. Eq.
6150		Insurance Expense
6155		Miscellaneous Expense
6170		Payroll Taxes Expense
6180		Rent Expense
6195		Salary Exp.—Office
6197		Salary Exp.—Wrhs.
6215		Telephone Expense
6225		Utilities Expense

Vendors

Alpha Irrigation Co.
C-Tech Manufacturing Inc.
Deco Electronics
Reed Irrigation Systems

Customers

Cardinal Sprinkler Inc.
Delta Irrigation
Green Landscape Co.
Maxx's Lawn Care
Rain Cloud Sprinkler Co.
Webb Lawn Sprinklers

Budget Amounts

Account Title	Budget Amount
Total Revenue	$620,000.00
Cost of Merchandise Sold	$420,000.00
Advertising Expense	$2,500.00
Depr. Exp.—Off. Eq.	$725.00
Depr. Exp.—Wrhs. Eq.	$2,100.00
Insurance Expense	$5,250.00
Miscellaneous Expense	$1,000.00
Payroll Tax Expense	$15,000.00
Rent Expense	$25,000.00
Salary Exp.—Office	$50,000.00
Salary Exp.—Wrhs.	$45,000.00
Telephone Expense	$5,000.00
Utilities Expense	$7,250.00

Fixed Assets

Asset No.	Asset Name	Date Acquired	Useful Life	Original Cost	Salvage Value	Accum. Deprec.	Deprec. Exp.	Deprec. Method*
Office Equipment								
110	Copy Machine	03/21/06	6	$3,000.00	$220.00	1530	6130	SL
120	Facsimile Machine	01/28/07	5	$875.00	$75.00	1530	6130	SL
130	File Cabinet	04/20/07	10	$760.00	$50.00	1530	6130	SL
140	Computer System	02/24/07	5	$2,500.00	$250.00	1530	6130	MACRS
Warehouse Equipment								
210	Fork Lift	08/31/07	8	$4,000.00	$450.00	1565	6140	DDB
220	Shelving	09/30/07	10	$4,200.00	$400.00	1565	6140	DDB
230	Conveyor Belt	02/20/07	10	$9,895.00	$750.00	1565	6140	SYD

*DDB, double-declining balance method; MACRS, modified accelerated cost recovery system; SL, straight-line method; SYD, sum-of-the-years-digits.

Employees

No.	Name Address, City/State	SS No.	W/H Allow.	No. Pay Periods	G.L. Acct.	Salary/ Rate	Mar. Stat.
210	Abler, Lillian 4521 Monroe St. Abilene, TX 79605-2100	435-24-5449	3	26	6195	$2,450.00	Mar.
220	Boswell, Paul 1873 Campbell Ave. Abilene, TX 79601-5816	767-33-8092	1	26	6197	$2,200.00	Single
230	Linton, Thomas 109 Whiperwill Dr. Abilene, TX 79601-5337	587-45-4204	1	26	6197	$12.95	Single
240	Monson, Shirley 745 Stuart Ln. Abilene, TX 79605-5450	495-30-9083	2	26	6195	$12.75	Mar.

 NOTE Because the payroll system is being established on the first day of a new calendar year, it is not necessary to establish current, quarter-to-date, or year-to-date opening balances data.

Inventory

Stock Items

Stock No.	Description	Unit of Measure	Reorder Point	Retail Price
1010	Reed Deluxe Heads	EA	30	$185.00
1020	Alpha S-10 Heads	EA	50	$60.00
1030	C-Tech Spr. Heads	EA	30	$124.00
1040	Reed Strip Spray	EA	50	$76.00
3010	Deco 32-S Control	EA	25	$400.00
3020	C-Tech Control System	EA	18	$230.00
3030	Deco Control Box	EA	30	$185.00

Inventory Historical Data

Purchase Orders

PO#	Date	Vendor	Terms	Qty	Inventory Item	Price
235	01/01	Reed Irrigation Systems	30 days	100	Reed Deluxe Heads	$100.00
236	01/01	Alpha Irrigation Co.	30 days	250	Alpha S-10 Heads	$39.00
237	01/01	C-Tech Manufacturing Inc.	30 days	200	C-Tech Spr. Heads	$81.25
238	01/01	Reed Irrigation Systems	30 days	225	Reed Strip Spray	$49.00
239	01/01	Deco Electronics	30 days	80	Deco 32-S Control	$228.00
240	01/01	C-Tech Manufacturing Inc.	30 days	60	C-Tech Control System	$135.00
241	01/01	Deco Electronics	30 days	100	Deco Control Box	$110.00

Purchase Invoices

PI#	Date	Vendor	PO #	Terms	Qty	Inventory Item	Price
421	01/01	Reed Irrigation Systems	235	30 days	45	Reed Deluxe Heads	$100.00
					45	Reed Deluxe Heads	$110.00
422	01/01	Alpha Irrigation Co.	236	30 days	250	Alpha S-10 Heads	$39.00
423	01/01	C-Tech Manufacturing Inc.	237	30 days	100	C-Tech Spr. Heads	$81.25
					100	C-Tech Spr. Heads	$80.00

424	01/01	Reed Irrigation Systems	238	30 days	225	Reed Strip Spray	$49.00
425	01/01	Deco Electronics	239	30 days	35	Deco 32-S Control	$228.00
					45	Deco 32-S Control	$237.00
426	01/01	C-Tech Manufacturing Inc.	240	30 days	60	C-Tech Control System	$135.00
427	01/01	Deco Electronics	241	30 days	100	Deco Control Box	$110.00

Sales Invoices

Inv#	Date	Tax	Customer	Terms	Qty	Inventory Item	Price
762	01/01	6%	Maxx's Lawn Care	30 days	60	Reed Deluxe Heads	$185.00
763	01/01	6%	Delta Irrigation	30 days	167	Alpha S-10 Heads	$60.00
764	01/01	6%	Cardinal Sprinkler Inc.	30 days	146	C-Tech Spr. Heads	$124.00
765	01/01	6%	Rain Cloud Sprinkler Co.	30 days	164	Reed Strip Spray	$76.00
766	01/01	6%	Green Landscape Co.	30 days	53	Deco 32-S Control	$400.00
767	01/01	6%	Webb Lawn Sprinklers	30 days	29	C-Tech Control System	$230.00
768	01/01	6%	Cardinal Sprinkler Inc.	30 days	65	Deco Control Box	$185.00

Complete the following steps and answer Audit Questions 12-A on pages 557–558 as you work through the problem.

1 Start *Integrated Accounting* 6e.

2 Use the New command from the File menu to prepare the computer for setup.

3 Enter your name in the Your Name text box.

4 Enter information into the data fields and set the check boxes and option buttons in Setup Accounting System.

5 Enter the chart of accounts data.

6 Enter the vendors.

7 Enter the customers.

8 Verify account classification and extended account classification number ranges.

9 Complete the required accounts.

10 Enter the account subtotals data (account number ranges) to provide the following subtotals:

Total Current Assets

Total Fixed Assets

Total Current Liabilities

Total Long-Term Liabilities

11   Enter the opening balances from the trial balance shown at the beginning of this problem.

12   Enter budget amounts.

13   Display a chart of accounts, vendor list, and customer list.

14   Save your data with a file name of 12-A Your Name.

15   Enter the fixed assets.

16   Display the fixed assets list report.

17   Save the data to your disk.

18   Enter the employee data.

19   Display the employee list.

20   Enter a 1.5% city tax rate in the payroll tax tables.

21   Save the data to your disk.

22   Enter the inventory stock items.

23   Enter the purchase order historical data.

24   Enter the purchase invoice historical data.

25   Enter the sales invoice historical data.

26   Display an inventory list report.

27   Display an inventory transaction report.

28   Display a trial balance, schedule of accounts payable, and schedule of accounts receivable.

29   **Create a special cash payments journal.**

Expand the current cash payments journal to include a Mrch. Inv. Cr. column for entering purchases discounts. Use the Cash Payments Journal option of the journal wizard to create the expanded journal.

30   **Save your data to disk.**

If you have access to the Internet, use your browser to find information about a current business acquisition. *Hint:* Use business acquisition as your search string. Report your findings. Be sure to include the sources, including URLs (Web addresses), of your reported findings.

31 **End the *Integrated Accounting* 6e session.**

Audit Questions 12-A

NAME _____

Directions   *Write the answers to the following questions in the space provided.*

Fixed Assets

1.   What is the salvage value of Asset Number 120 (Facsimile Machine)?   _____

_____

2.   What date was Asset Number 230 (Conveyor Belt) acquired?   _____

_____

3.   What is the total original cost of all assets?   _____

_____

Payroll

4.   What is the salary amount for Paul Boswell?   _____

_____

5.   What is Shirley Monson's hourly pay rate?   _____

_____

6.   What is Thomas Linton's address?   _____

_____

Inventory

7.   What is the last cost of C-Tech Spr. Heads?   _____

_____

8.   What is the total number of items sold?   _____

_____

9.   What is the total number of items ordered?   _____

_____

10.   What is the total number of items received?   _____

_____

Accounting

11.   What is the total of the Credit column on the trial balance?   _____

_____

12. What is the balance in the Accounts Receivable account on the trial balance?

_____

13. What is the balance in the Accounts Payable account on the trial balance? _____

_____

14. What is the amount owed to C-Tech Manufacturing Inc.? _____

_____

15. What is the total owed to all vendors? _____

_____

16. What is the amount due from Rain Cloud Sprinkler Co.? _____

_____

17. What is the amount due from all customers? _____

_____

18. List the column headings on the new Cash Payments Journal. _____

_____

Problem 12-B

In this problem, you will perform the accounting system setup for Pristine Cleaning Service, a cleaning service owned and operated by Laurie Pristine. Pristine Cleaning Service is a service business that is organized as a sole proprietorship, is nondepartmentalized, prepares checks manually, generates the income statement by fiscal period, and uses a standard accounting system. The trial balance, schedule of accounts payable, and schedule of accounts receivable for Pristine Cleaning Service as of February 1 of the current year are provided as follows:

General Ledger Account Titles and Balances

Account Number	Account Title	Debit	Credit
Current Assets			
1105	Cash	$2,395.00	
1115	Accounts Receivable	$6,500.00	
1125	Notes Receivable	$1,200.00	
1135	Supplies	$500.00	
1150	Prepaid Insurance	$350.00	
Fixed Assets			
1500	Equipment—Cleaning	$2,300.00	
1510	Accum. Dep.—Cln. Eq.		$672.10
1520	Equipment—Office	$5,200.00	
1530	Accum. Dep.—Off. Eq.		$1,705.40
Current Liabilities			
2105	Accounts Payable		$1,200.00
2130	Sales Tax Payable		
Long-Term Liabilities			
2505	Notes Payable		$4,500.00
Capital			
3110	Laurie Pristine, Capital		$10,367.50
3120	Laurie Pristine, Drawing		
3130	Income Summary		
Revenue			
4105	Sales		
4110	Sales Discount		
Expenses			
6105	Advertising Expense		
6120	Depr. Exp.—Cln. Eq.		
6130	Depr. Exp.—Off. Eq.		
6145	Insurance Expense		
6190	Telephone Expense		
6200	Utilities Expense		
6210	Vehicle Expense		
Other Revenue			
7110	Interest Income		
Other Expense			
8105	Interest Expense		

Schedule of Accounts Payable

Name	Balance
Brooks Hardware	$270.80
Gaffer Cleaning Supply	$269.05
Morton Office Products	$153.41
Snell Advertising, Inc.	$506.74
Total	$1,200.00

Schedule of Accounts Receivable

Name	Balance
Berg Retirement Center	$500.00
Gary Owens	$87.50
Holman Corporation	$1,975.00
Ruth Parker	$137.50
Taber & Associates	$3,800.00
Total	$6,500.00

Complete the following steps and answer Audit Questions 12-B on page 562 as you work through the problem.

1 Start *Integrated Accounting* 6e.

2 Use the New command from the File menu to prepare the computer for setup.

3 Enter your name in the Your Name text box.

4 Enter information into the data fields and set the check boxes and option buttons in Setup Accounting System.

5 Enter the chart of accounts data.

6 Enter the vendors.

7 Enter the customers.

8 Verify account classification and extended account classification account number ranges.

9 Verify the required accounts data.

10 Enter the following account subtotals:

Total Current Assets

Total Fixed Assets

Total Current Liabilities

Total Long-Term Liabilities

11 Enter the opening balances from the trial balance, schedule of accounts payable, and schedule of accounts receivable (shown at the beginning of this problem) into the general journal.

HINT Because this accounting system does not involve an inventory, the vendor and customer account balances shown in the schedules of accounts payable and accounts receivable must be entered with the rest of the opening balances in the general journal to establish the accounts receivable and accounts payable account balances. Figure 12.33 shows how the customer balances are entered (the same procedure is required to enter the vendor balances).

FIGURE 12.33

Customer Account Balances Entered into the General Journal

Date	Refer.	Account	Debit	Credit	Vendor/Customer
02/01/--	BALANCE	1115 Accounts Receivable	500.00		Berg Retirement Center
02/01/--	BALANCE	1115 Accounts Receivable	87.50		Gary Owens
02/01/--	BALANCE	1115 Accounts Receivable	1975.00		Holman Corporation
02/01/--	BALANCE	1115 Accounts Receivable	137.50		Ruth Parker
02/01/--	BALANCE	1115 Accounts Receivable	3800.00		Taber & Associates

12 Display a chart of accounts, vendor list, and customer list. (Be sure to set the run date to February 1, of the current year.)

13 Display a trial balance, schedule of accounts payable, and schedule of accounts receivable.

14 Display a balance sheet.

15 Create a special cash receipts journal.

Expand the current cash receipts journal to include sales, sales tax payable, and sales discounts. Use the Cash Receipts Journal option of the journal wizard to create the expanded journal.

16 Save your data with a file name of 12-B Your Name.

If you have access to the Internet, use your browser to find information about a current merger of two or more companies. *Hint:* Use business merger as your search string. Report your findings. Be sure to include the sources, including URLs (Web addresses), of your reported findings.

INTERNET ACTIVITY

17 End your *Integrated Accounting* 6e session.

Audit Questions 12-B

NAME

Directions *Write the answers to the following questions in the space provided.*

1. What is the total of the Credit column on the trial balance? _____

   _____

2. What is the balance in the accounts receivable account on the trial balance? _____

   _____

3. What is the balance in the accounts payable account on the trial balance?

   _____

   _____

4. What is the amount owed to Snell Advertising, Inc.? _____

   _____

5. What is the total owed to all vendors? _____

   _____

6. What is the amount due from Holman Corporation? _____

   _____

7. What is the amount due from all customers? _____

   _____

8. From the balance sheet, what are the total current assets? _____

   _____

9. From the balance sheet, what are the total fixed assets? _____

   _____

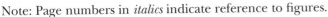

Index

Note: Page numbers in *italics* indicate reference to figures.

A

Accelerated cost recovery
  system (ACRS), 289–90
Access keys, *6*
Accountant, role of, 2, 26
Account classification
  in account number, 20
  identifying, 33
  statement of cash flows and,
  410–13
Accounting
  definition of, 2, 26
  double entry, 21–22
Accounting clerks, role of, 2, 27
Accounting cycle
  of bank reconciliation,
  43–94
  introduction to, 44, 60
  of a merchandising business,
  95–142
  of service business, 43–94
Accounting equation
  formula for, 18, *22*
  report, *20*, 32
  transactions and, 18, *18*
Accounting organizations web
  search, 34
Accounting period, 44
Accounting principles, effects
  of basic, 18
Accounting services web search, 86
Accounting software, Integrated
  application window, *5*
  data storage in, 3
  flexibility of, 3
  functions of, 7, 27
  installation of, 4, 25–26
  memory requirements for, 4
  operating procedure in, 5–6
  types of information in, *24*
  user interface in, 3
  working procedure in, 4
Accounting software web
  search, 92

Accounting system, explore
  to display cash account
  activity, 33
  to display current balance, 33
  location of, 23
  purpose of, 23
  window, *24*
Accounting system setup
  account subtotals, 531, *531*
  budget amounts, 542
  classify accounts, 529–30, *529*
  combination journals, *555*
  company information,
  527–29, *527*
  employees, 536
  fixed assets, 535
  historical data, 536
  introduction to, 518
  inventory, 536
  journal wizard, *531–33*, *532*
  opening balances, 535
  pick list, 534–35
  planning, 518
  required accounts, 530, *530*
  tax tables, 533–34
  vendor setup, 540, *540*
  voucher system, 144
Accounting system window, 527
Accounts maintenance. *See*
  Accounting system setup
  adding new accounts, 44
  changing account titles, *45*
  chart of, 44–45
  deleting inactive accounts, 44
Accounts payable ledger
  Hagan Appliances, *223*
  report, 102
  Tanner Wholesale Co, *125*
Accounts payable. *See* Purchase
  order system
Accounts receivable ledger
  Palmer Vacuum Center,
  263–64
  report, 102
  Tanner Wholesale Co, *125*

Accounts receivable. *See* Sales
  order processing
Accounts tab, functions of, 61
Account subtotals, 531, *531*
Account title, changing, *45*
Acquisition, business, 564
ACRS. *See* Accelerated cost
  recovery system (ACRS)
Actual versus budget graph, *166*
Adj.Ent. reference column, 48
Adjusted bank balance, 18, *59*
Adjusting entries
  analyzed by worksheet, 49
  definition of, 48, 61
  trial balance before, 49
Advertising, 99
Amortization of a
  bond issue, 389
Analysis, bases for, 394
Annual contribution, in college
  planner, 17
Appropriation for plant
  expansion, 373
Appropriation to purchase treasury
  stock, 372
Asset disposition, 288
Assets, 18
Audit checks, 23
Auto setup, of required
  accounts, 541
Average cost method, in inventory
  valuation, 250

B

Backup file, 12, 209, 249
Balance sheet
  account detail on, 54
  definition of, 54
  Fossen Corporation, *407–9,*
  430–31, 433–35
  Hubbell Building Supplies, *164*
  Lacina Windows & Doors, *492*
  Mellen Corporation, *376–77*
  Morgan Consulting, 55